In Step with
Middle School and Junior High Students
... Because It's the *Only* Program
Written Just for Them!

ALL NEW!

TEEN LIVING

Prentice Hall

TEACHER'S RESOURCE BOOK

TEEN LIVING
Annotated Teacher's Edition
Prentice Hall

It speaks to your students as no other program can...to their reading abilities, their needs, their interests.

Involving chapter openers use a case study approach, drawing students into the chapter through a realistic *conversational vignette.*

Students' reading is guided through...
- pre-reading objectives
- manageable sections
- end-of-section reviews
- clear page design

A comfortable writing style puts students at ease and on track.

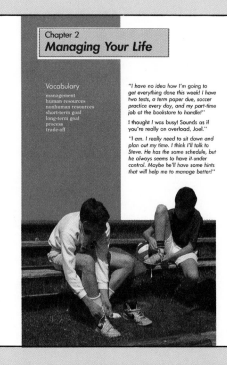

Chapter 2
Managing Your Life

Vocabulary
management
human resources
nonhuman resources
short-term goal
long-term goal
process
trade-off

"I have no idea how I'm going to get everything done this week! I have two tests, a term paper due, soccer practice every day, and my part-time job at the bookstore to handle!"

I thought I was busy! Sounds as if you're really on overload, Joel."

"I am. I really need to sit down and plan out my time. I think I'll talk to Steve. He has the same schedule, but he always seems to have it under control. Maybe he'll have some hints that will help me to manage better!"

REINFORCEMENT: Ask students to make a list of five things in their lives that need personal management. Possibilities include doing homework, being responsible for tasks at home, buying clothes, and taking care of a younger sibling.

Section 2.1
What Is Management?

As you read, think about:
- the different resources you use to manage your life. (p. 25)
- how the six steps of the management process help make any project easier. (p. 27)

Managing better is important to everyone, from a fast food restaurant owner to a rock star or the president of the United States. All of these are managers. They plan ahead, they organize, they use their talents to do their jobs to the best of their abilities. You do not have to have a job to be a manager. Most people use the skills of a manager every day. You use management skills to get to school on time, to buy clothes, to get a good grade on a test. As an adult you will be responsible for managing your life. Learning about the management process will help you in all areas of your life.

What Management Means

Management is the method you use to organize and control something. Managing your life in a responsible way is a large part of becoming a mature person. Your resources, goals, and values all affect how you manage your life. These factors influence all of your management decisions.

PHOTO: Ask students what resources they think that they get manage.

Any talent takes time and effort to develop. What talents do you have?

Resources

Your *resources* are the things in your life that help you live successfully and meet the goals you set for yourself.

Resources can be either human or nonhuman. **Human resources** include your knowledge, skills, and abilities. They also include the people around you, friends, teammates, teachers, employers, neighbors, and, of course, family members. Your health, feelings, and attitudes are also human resources.

Nonhuman resources include money, time, food, clothing, and resources in your community, such as parks, schools, and libraries.

DISCUSS: Why are things like family, health, and feelings considered human resources? What role do these resources play in your life?

Chapter 2/*Managing Your Life*   25

A teacher is an important human resource. Do you take advantage of opportunities for help?

more intensively, you will finish sooner and have more time for leisure activities.

If there are some areas you find more difficult than others, write answers to questions about those sections without checking the text or your notes. You may find it helpful to get a member of your family to ask you key questions.

Set Study Goals

Set short-term goals, then reward yourself with a short break. For example, tell yourself that you will take a 10-minute break as soon as you finish two more math problems or answer two more science questions. When you reach your goal, walk around or do a few stretching exercises. Eat an apple. You will feel refreshed when you go back to work.

Think Positively

Give yourself as much chance to enjoy the subject you are studying as you can. Think how proud you will be if you do well. Focus on parts of the subject that apply to your own life. If, for example, you would like to start your own business eventually, think how helpful math skills will be in keeping business records.

Don't be afraid to do well. It may seem unlikely, but many people are afraid to succeed. They are frightened of the responsibility that comes with success. You probably hear expressions of this negative attitude all the time.

"I've *never* been any good at math," Joanna says.

"Science has always been way over my head!" Carl declares.

Don't let yourself fall into this negative way of thinking. Dare to be the best you can be.

For Review
1. List five ways to make the most of your class time so that you can improve how you learn.
2. Describe the steps you should follow to take good notes.
3. Name five important study skills.

See page T34 for teaching suggestions.

Learning to Manage
Finding the Time

Look back at the conversation on page 24. Joel is trying to figure out how to manage time for all of his responsibilities and activities. Now read how he tries to improve his time management. Then answer the questions that follow.

Joel saw Steve at his locker the next afternoon as they were both getting ready for soccer practice.

"How's it going?" Steve asked.

"Not so well," Joel replied. "Steve, how do you manage to get everything done?"

"Let's talk after practice, OK?"

As they walked home, Steve explained his method of managing to Joel. He said that he blocked out each month on a large calendar. He filled in dates of tests and when papers were due ahead of time. He also blocked out hours taken up with soccer practice and games. Then he filled in the hours spent at his part-time job. He slotted in leisure time and social activities he knew were coming up.

"Sounds like Steve-the-Robot-Man!" Joel said, half-jokingly.

Steve laughed. "It doesn't always work out as planned. Things often happen to change the schedule, but at least I have a basic plan mapped out for each month."

"What about work, Steve? I've really been thinking about quitting even though I need the money."

"Well, Joel, I asked to cut back to one afternoon a week at the restaurant until soccer ends. The trade-off is less money for more time, but I didn't have to quit."

"That's a good idea, Steve. I'm going to talk to my boss tomorrow. Something has to be cut back. It can't be my grades, or I'm in big trouble—with my parents, my teachers, and the soccer coach! I even thought about quitting the team, but I really enjoy it."

"I hope you don't do that, Joel. We need you. Of course . . . if you quit, then I might get to play goalie."

Joel laughed when he saw the sly look on his friend's face.

"No way, Steve! I'm going home right now to map out a plan to manage my time. I plan to keep my position—in the classroom *and* on the field!"

Questions
1. What advice would you have given to Joel? Explain your reasons.
2. Do you think Joel's time management plan will work? Why or why not?
3. Think about any problems you have had managing your time. How have you tried to solve them? Have you been successful? Why or why not?

A culminating activity, *Learning to Manage,* brings the chapter to closure by applying chapter concepts to a real-life situation.

To aid vocabulary development, vocabulary words are...
- previewed
- set in bold type and defined
- spelled phonetically
- reviewed at chapter end

...and *all* form the end-of-book **glossary.**

40   Unit 1/*About You*

Sample pages are reduced. Actual size: 8" x 10."

The balance of skills and concepts reflects the laboratory orientation of your course.

a project. If you do, chances are you will have to rip out stitching or cut a new piece of fabric. Take the time to arrange your work space and to gather your materials. You will learn how to plan a project properly later in this chapter.

Schedule Your Time

Schedule your sewing project. Estimate the time it will take to complete it and how much of the work you can do in class. Revise your schedule as you go along. Allow extra time for steps you will need help with. You may need your teacher's help when attaching a collar, sleeves, or a zipper. You will need a friend's help to measure hems.

Mark Personal Equipment

Label all your personal equipment with your name to avoid mixups. The night before a class, check that you have all the materials you need. Keep your materials together in a box or sewing basket, and store it in a safe place.

For Review

1. Name three important safety rules you should follow when using a sewing machine.
2. Name two ways you can cooperate with the other students in your sewing laboratory.
3. Name two ways that you can organize yourself to make your sewing project more efficient.

To save time, buy all your notions when you buy your fabric.

Section 18.2
Choosing Your Project, Pattern, and Fabric

As you read, think about:

■ the importance of choosing a sewing project that is suitable for you.
■ how to choose and read a pattern envelope.
■ how to take your measurements.
■ how to select the correct fabric and notions for your sewing project.

Knowing how to sew can be helpful to you in many ways. If you can make a vest or tote bag, you can choose just the fabric,

Hands-on projects encourage self-reliance and time management skills.

Photo and art captions become teaching tools. Students learn from visual as well as verbal content. Additional annotations appear in your Teacher's Edition.

End-of-section reviews check recall of content.

Did You Know? features present interesting and useful sidelights related to the chapter content.

How Much Time Do You Have?

Your schedule is an important consideration in meal planning. If you have a paper route before school, the time you can spend preparing breakfast or making lunch is limited. Sports or other after-school activities can make your supper preparations rushed. If someone helps, your job will be easier. Read recipes carefully to see how much time they require, including time to cook or chill a food. Also add time needed for chopping or mixing. If these things take too long, you may need to select a different recipe.

After you have considered your daily schedule, block out the time you have to prepare meals. Remember to plan time to make breakfast, even if you're rushed in

Sometimes you have to do two things at once to make time for breakfast.

Did You Know?

Forty guests will consume approximately

■ 2 gallons of soup
■ 2 quarts of gravy or sauce
■ Lemonade made from 2 dozen lemons, 2 pounds of sugar, and 2 gallons of water
■ 1 peck (8 quarts) of potatoes
■ 20 pounds of chicken or turkey, dressed
■ 2 gallons of ice cream

the morning. If you are responsible for planning a family meal, think about ways to save time. For example, you could use spare time in the afternoon to make a casserole ahead of time and freeze it. Baked chicken pieces can be prepared in advance and refrigerated. Having the ingredients on hand for quick last-minute dishes, such as stir-fried vegetables, is another good planning idea.

If you have time-saving kitchen equipment, learn how to use it. Chapter 14 has information about using specific kitchen equipment.

Plan Appealing Meals

How a meal looks may be more important than you realize. Variety in color, shape, and texture improves a meal's chances of success. Look at the menu below and think about how to make it look more appealing.

Fish
Mashed Potatoes   Creamed Cauliflower
Roll   Butter
Vanilla Pudding
Milk

Although the foods are nutritious, they are all soft, similar in color and shape, and fairly bland. The next menu looks a lot more interesting.

Fish
Baked Potato   Broccoli
Cornbread   Butter
Fresh Fruit Cup
Milk

To plan meals that are varied and appetizing, keep these guidelines in mind.

• Vary the flavors in a meal. If you make sweet and sour meatballs and carrots glazed with sugar and butter, the overall taste could be a bit *too* sweet. Crisp green beans would be a better choice of vegetable. Spaghetti with tomato sauce is a good combination because the spicy tomato taste blends well with the bland spaghetti.
• Use foods of different colors. Breaded chicken, carrots, and sweet potatoes are similar in color. If you substitute green peas and french fried potatoes, your meal will be more appealing to the eye.
• Include different textures to add interest to a meal. A crisp salad with crunchy cucumbers and celery contrasts well with a soft food like sweet potatoes.
• Serve foods of different shapes. Hamburger patties, boiled potatoes, and

What attention to variety and nutrition do you see here?

peas are all round. If you substitute carrots cut lengthwise for one of the vegetables, your meal will look much more interesting.

Consider Food Costs

If you are doing the family food shopping, first look carefully at exactly how much money you have to spend. Your family may budget food by the week or by the month. Then plan ahead to stay within your budget. Look for specials on canned and frozen foods that you can store for future use. If meat is on sale, you might buy more than you need and freeze some of it. You can save money *and* time by creating your own convenience foods. Suppose that

TEEN LIVING
Prentice Hall

High-interest features in each chapter add even *more* practical insights to your course.

Careers features lead students to think about the range of career choices available to them.

Technology features remind students that change is ever-present and influential in their daily lives.

Health and Safety features underscore the role that health and safety play in your students' lives.

Leadership and Citizenship features show students how they can make a contribution to their community.

Careers

Parenting as a Career

Entertainer, supervisor, protector of the weak, role model for the young, care giver to the sick, counselor to the troubled, teacher, coach, one-on-one listener, group leader—which of these careers would you like to have? If you become a parent, you will have them all—and others, too. What's more, you will practice these varied careers day in and day out.

Parenting is often taken for granted, but it is very [...] commitment [...] no prizes. It [...] wards but [...] sacrifices, s[...] They range [...] comfort a c[...] ond job to [...] a career th[...] you've beg[...] on love. Pa[...] love and se[...] to, and pro[...] baby. The [...] guage mar[...]

be to teach a child to behave in an acceptable way. Discipline should be carried out calmly but with firmness. It should be consistent. If a specific behavior is sometimes punished and sometimes not, the child will be confused. Children must understand the reason they are being disciplined.

Physical Needs

Correct diet, clothing, and enough sleep and exercise are more important during

Technology

Home Efficiency

Imagine what it would be like if both your parents were professional efficiency experts—and you had 11 brothers and sisters! *Cheaper by the Dozen* tells the true story of just such a family. The Gilbraths managed their home with the same techniques they used to increase factory production.

[...]

Set Your Goal

Setting your goal means deciding what you want to accomplish. In this case, your goal is to improve the condition of your room. Specifically, decide what changes you want to make. You need to find a new bedspread and wash the curtains. You plan to build some wall shelves to hold books, records, and other items. You also plan to paint the walls.

[Analy]ze Your Resources

[An]alyze what resources you already [ha]d those you will need to make the [...] you want. You can get ideas for [...]ing your room in books and maga[...] the library. You need people to [...]u paint and move furniture. You [...]money for supplies like paint and [...] You may also need money to buy [...]bedspread or curtains.

[Make] a Plan and Assign [Resou]rces

[The ne]xt step is to plan the project and [...]resources. Friends and family [...]s agree to help you paint. Your [...]roblem, therefore, is money. You [...]ly what you have saved from your [...]e and babysitting. When you fig[...] the costs, you find you cannot [...]o buy everything on your list.

[Make] Adjustments

[...]st now revise your plans and find [...]resources. Your sister says she will [...]u make a bedspread, so you will

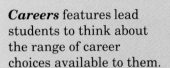

Health and Safety

Childproofing Your Home

Little children find ways to hurt themselves that bigger people would not think of. One way to prevent these accidents is to get down on your hands and knees. Look at your home from a toddler's viewpoint. What looks interesting? That electrical outlet? Maybe a finger would fit into it. . . .

Your toddler's-eye tour will reveal many potential hazards. Adapt them using these childproofing guidelines.

- Cover all unused electrical outlets. Repair frayed cords and appliances that could cause shocks. Keep cords out of reach, and put away appliances when not in use.
- Use safety gates at the top and bottom of stairs and near other danger zones, such as food preparation areas. Install guards on dangerous doors and windows. Put childproof locks on cabinets containing matches, medicine, vitamins, cleaning supplies, and cosmetics. Use child-resistant caps on all medicine.
- Remove unstable furniture and tie kitchen chairs down so that they can't be used to climb up to the stove. Always turn pot handles away from

- Keep matches away from children. Make sure matches are cold and wet before throwing them away.
- Use screens in front of fireplaces, and keep them closed while the fireplace is being used.
- Do not let papers or trash accumulate.

Poisons

Things you use every day can be deadly to small children. Soap, shampoo, paint, and household cleaning products can all be poisonous if swallowed. Medicine can also be dangerous if too much is taken. A home with small children should be childproofed against such dangers. Particularly in the bathroom and kitchen, items should be stored on high shelves or in locked cabinets. Also make sure children do not put houseplants in their mouths, as some leaves and berries are poisonous.

If a poisoning accident does occur, call immediately for assistance. Keep the telephone numbers of poison control centers and of your local hospital emergency room by the telephone. Be prepared to give information about what and how much was swallowed and the victim's approximate age and weight.

Electricity

Electric shocks are usually caused by [...] with electrical cords and outlets [...] correct use of appliances. Follow [...]elines.

[...]ords and make sure they are in [...]air.

[...] wires away from water. Do not [...]ords using wet hands.

Leadership and Citizenship

Volunteering

What's a great way to make new friends, learn new skills, explore career possibilities, help others, and feel really good about yourself? For many teens, the answer is volunteering in a health-related field. Check with your school, United Way, religious and community organizations, and health care institutions.

- You can help out in a hospital by delivering meals, running errands, or visiting with the patients.
- You can also help residents in a nursing home read, answer mail, or get around outdoors. You can join in games, such as checkers, or be the friend who cares enough to visit regularly and chat.
- Many homebound elderly or disabled people live alone. Teens can be "telephone buddies" who regularly check on their well-being or home visitors who help out while paying a friendly visit. Escorts assist with medical appointments, shopping, or outings.
- Many organizations provide recreation for disabled children and adults. You can volunteer to help with children's crafts or swimming lessons. You can even enjoy your favorite sport while helping a disabled person play it with you. What could you volunteer to do in your community?

includes asking your doctor the right questions to get the most from medical checkups. Learning how to keep your own health records is important, too.

Regular Health Care

It is important for you and your family to choose a health care facility that meets your needs. Health care facilities include doctors' offices, clinics, health maintenance organizations (HMOs), and hospitals. Be sure to choose a health facility before an emergency occurs. Make sure that the health professionals there are aware of any health problems you have. The facility you pick should have on record your complete medical history. This includes important data such as your blood type and a history of childhood diseases and allergies.

Preventive Medicine

Even if you are feeling perfectly healthy, regular checkups can pinpoint medical problems at an early stage and prevent them from becoming more serious. Besides regular physical examinations, you should have your teeth and your eyes checked regularly. In addition, you know from experience the way your mind and body work. If you notice a change or have any unusual pains, make an appointment for an examination.

Choosing Health Care

The kind of health care you and your family choose will depend on a number of factors, particularly the kind of health

All features end with a question that involves students in the material and transforms the reading into a teaching/learning activity.

To help you integrate these features into the lessons, your Teacher's Edition includes discussion questions and suggested answers.

Chapter Reviews lead students of all abilities to mastery through a variety of practice and applications.

A *Summary* reviews briefly the chapter content.

Vocabulary exercises give students practice using new words correctly.

Questions check recall of facts...basic comprehension ...application and analysis.

Skill Activities reinforce students' decision-making, human relations, communications, critical thinking, and laboratory skills...reinforce basic academic skills.
All are clearly labeled.

Chapter 2 Review

Summary

Everyone is a manager. By using human and nonhuman resources and the six steps of the management process, you will be more successful as a manager. These six steps are:
1. Set a goal.
2. Analyze your resources.
3. Make a plan and assign resources.
4. Make adjustments.
5. Carry out the plan.
6. Evaluate the results.
   Learning to manage time effectively is important. Having a plan for organizing and using your time helps you to do this.
   Good study skills help you to make the best use of class time and to be more successful in preparing for and taking tests. Learning to take notes accurately and in outline form will help you both in and out of the classroom.

Vocabulary

Complete each of the following sentences with the correct word from the vocabulary list below.

process   human resources
management   short-term goal
nonhuman   long-term goal
resources   trade-off

1. Knowledge, skills, abilities, and the people around you can be called _____.

2. Something you want to accomplish in the near future is called a _____.
3. A series of thoughts and actions that lead to a particular result is called a _____.
4. Giving up one thing in order to gain by another is called a _____.
5. The method you use to organize and control something is called _____.
6. Things such as time and money that can be used to reach a goal are called _____.
7. Things you want to accomplish in the distant future are called _____.

Questions

1. What resources do you manage in order to get to school on time? How effective do you think your management of these resources is? Use the steps in the management process to answer.
2. Are your health, feelings, and attitudes human or nonhuman resources? Explain your answer.
3. What is the purpose of keeping a monthly calendar?
4. Name two activities that you could do at the same time on a school day.
5. If you are having trouble solving a homework problem, what can you do to refresh your mind?

6. Why is it important to plan your leisure time as well as your work time? Explain your answer.
7. Why should you listen carefully during class?
8. Why is it a good idea to take part in class discussions?
9. When taking class notes, should you write down everything that is said or only some of what is said? Explain your answer.
10. Is it a good idea to borrow someone else's notes if you have missed a class? Why or why not?

Skill Activities

1. Critical Thinking Using the six steps in the management process to help you, plan and give a class party. The guest of honor will be the student with the next closest birthday. On the blackboard, list all the necessary preparation for the event under each step in the management process. Following the party, evaluate your management skills. How did the management process help you to organize the details for the party and ensure its success?

2. Communication Ask one student to tell a story and instruct the rest of the class to listen carefully. Each student will then take turns retelling the story. Was the last story the same as the original? Do they resemble each other? What does this activity tell us about our listening skills?

3. Laboratory Bring to class a list of all your activities for the next month. Be sure to include all appointments, after-school commitments, school games, and so on. Using construction paper, create a calendar clearly listing these events. Bring the calendar home and display it on your refrigerator. At the end of the month, evaluate whether this was helpful in organizing your time and energy. Bring your calendar back to class and share what you have found out about the way you manage your time.

4. Human Relations Friends sometimes help each other improve their study skills so that they can learn more and do better in school. With a classmate, act out a situation in which one friend coaches another to improve study skills. If you play the part of the coach, be sure to make as many suggestions as you can remember. Give examples of what you mean so that your suggestions are clear. If you play the friend getting advice, make sure you describe your problems and the kind of help you need. When you have finished, reverse roles and go over the activity again. Share your experience with the class.

42

43

To help you meet individual needs, your Teacher's Edition categorizes both Skill Activities and Questions by level of difficulty.

FULL TEACHING SUPPORT
In the Annotated Teacher's Edition...

Every student page of the **Annotated Teacher's Edition** offers at least one note or activity for...
- background
- discussion
- reteaching
- enrichment
- photos and art

The Teacher's Guide of the **Annotated Teacher's Edition** presents...
- a scope and sequence
- a formal statement of objectives
- chapter-by-chapter teaching suggestions
- answers to review material in the student book
- and *two ribbon bookmarks* so you can hold your place in both sections simultaneously

PHOTO: Ask students to discuss the kinds of interests and accomplishments that their grandparents are especially interested in seeing, showing, or hearing about.

Do you have something to share with older family members?

usually shoulders all the family's financial obligations as well as being responsible for running the household and caring for the children. If you are part of a single-parent family, you can help by understanding all of the stresses your parent faces. Do your share of the household chores and be available to supervise younger siblings.

Did You Know?

■ One out of six (about six million) children in the United States between the ages of six and sixteen lives in a single-parent family.

Older Family Members

There are probably a number of older members in your extended family. In addition to grandparents, you may have older aunts and uncles. Some of them may live busy, independent lives. Others may have problems such as loss of hearing, failing eyesight, and memory loss. They may live with you, nearby, or far away. They may live alone or with others.

Older people have a lot to give: love, experience, time, and skills. Include them in your life. They need respect, acceptance, and affection just as all of us do.

You can learn a lot about the past by having older people tell you about their early growing-up experiences. These may be very different from your own.

ENRICHMENT: Have students interview an older family member or neighbor about a political event that took place before the students or even their parents were born.

REINFORCEMENT: In class, have students write a letter to a grandparent or other older relative or friend who lives far away.

106 Unit 2/Relationships

---

actual jobs in the classified section of the newspaper. The class should discuss the interviews in detail once they are completed.
4. You might suggest that students consult the *Occupational Outlook Handbook* and other appropriate reference materials in the library to gather information about educational requirements and salaries.

Chapter 8

Managing Your Money

Chapter Organization

Section 8.1   *Money as a Resource (student book page 167)*
  Sources of Income
  Making Money Choices

Section 8.2   *A Spending Plan (student book page 171)*
  Look at Your Spending
  Your Spending Plan

Section 8.3   *Money Management Services (student book page 175)*
  Banking
  Other Forms of Money Management
  What Is Credit?

Chapter Vocabulary

barter   (p. 167)
budget   (p. 171)
fixed expenses   (p. 171)
flexible expenses   (p. 172)
deposit   (p. 176)
balance   (p. 176)

interest   (p. 177)
principal   (p. 178)
compounded   (p. 178)
endorse   (p. 179)
invest   (p. 180)
stockholders   (p. 181)
credit   (p. 181)

Chapter Objectives

After reading this chapter, students should be able to:
1. Explain the importance of using money wisely. (8.1)
2. Describe the various sources of money. (8.1)
3. Explain how to set priorities when managing money. (8.1)
4. Explain how to organize a spending plan. (8.2)
5. Explain how to estimate a budget according to expenditures and income. (8.2)
6. Explain how to follow and adjust a budget. (8.2)
7. Describe the different kinds of checking and savings accounts available in banks. (8.3)
8. Describe the various ways of investing money. (8.3)
9. Explain the meaning and purpose of credit. (8.3)

Program Resources

Student text pages 166–187
Teacher's Resource Book
  Skill/Development Worksheet 8
  Laboratory/Application Worksheet 8
  Reinforcement Worksheet 8
  Enrichment Worksheet 8
  Transparency Master 8
  Information Master 8
  Chapter 8 Test

Teaching Suggestions

The dots represent skill levels required to answer each question or complete each activity:
• requires recall and comprehension
•• requires application and analysis
••• requires synthesis and evaluation

Into the Chapter

••• **Developing a Financial Plan** Ask the class how they would reach their financial goal. Arrangements can be made for a class to go on an all-day outing to a local amusement park. However, to do so, the class must raise $300 over the next four months. Divide the students into small groups and have each group develop a plan for raising the money. Have groups share their ideas.

Other Activities

•• 1. **Applying Information on Money Management** Divide the class into two teams. Have each team develop a set of questions about money management. Questions should cover such areas as differentiating between needs and wants and flexible and fixed expenses, as well as questions about budgeting monetary resources and expenses. Have teams alternate asking questions.
• 2. **Comprehending Information on Bank Accounts** Have pairs of students role-play the following situation: A bank officer explains to a prospective customer various kinds of accounts the bank offers. The customer should help guide the discussion by asking specific questions. Then have partners reverse roles and role-play the bank officer explaining how to open a savings and a checking account.

••• 3. **Researching and Organizing Information on Money Management Systems** Have the class prepare a pamphlet that provides information on the various kinds of money management systems mentioned in the text. Divide students into groups and assign one of the following categories to each group: savings accounts, certificates of deposit, stocks, bonds, and mutual funds. Groups should research the way their assigned system works and prepare a written report to be included in the pamphlet.

Learning to Manage (p. 185)

Concepts

■ items that are wanted are not always needed
■ students can earn money to buy part or all of an item they want
■ if an item is important enough to have, it is important enough to save for
■ one should buy goods and services that are wanted with the money that is left after paying for those that are needed

Discussion Questions

1. Why might "Everyone has one" not be a good reason for buying something?
2. What can students do to earn money?
3. Why didn't Billy's parents fix the washing machine instead of buying a new car battery?
4. Why did Billy decide that repairing the washing machine was more important than buying the new cowboy boots he wanted?
5. When is it a good time to buy something that is wanted but not needed?

Answers to Discussion Questions

Answers will vary but will probably include the following ideas.

In the Teacher's Resource Book...

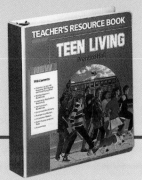

TEACHER'S RESOURCE BOOK
TEEN LIVING
Prentice Hall

Worksheets for...
- Skill Development
- Laboratory/Application
- Reinforcement
- Enrichment

Name _____ **Skill Development Worksheet 10**

The Shopping Spree

Chapter 10

You will be going back to school next month and have decided to take $150.00 from your summer earnings to buy back-to-school clothes. You begin by making up a budget for your purchases. Mark the number of each of the following items that you want to purchase. Then total up the costs and make sure that your total is less than $150.00.

Item 1: ____ stone-washed jeans at $19.95 per pair.   Cost:_____.

Item 2: ____ pair leather sneakers at $29.00 per pair.   Cost:_____.

Item 3: ____ pair white socks at $1.99 per pair.   Cost:_____.

Item 4: ____ white cotton sweatshirt at $15.00 apiece.   Cost:_____.

Item 5: ____ woolen sweater at $35.00 apiece.   Cost:_____.

Item 6: ____ denim jacket at $21.00 apiece.   Cost:_____.

Total:

Suppose that y...
more than you...
on this new in...

Item 1: ____
Item 2: ____
Item 3: ____
Item 4: ____
Item 5: ____
Item 6: ____

© Prentice Hall, I...

Name _____ **Laboratory/Application Worksheet 15**

Changing a Recipe

Chapter 15

Read the recipe below and answer each question as it pertains to increasing or decreasing the recipe.

Baking Powder Biscuits (makes about 16)

2 cups sifted all-purpose flour   1/4 cup shortening

Name _____ **Reinforcement Worksheet 14**

Communication Building Blocks

Chapter 14

Match each word below to the block with the correct definition.

a. sender   d. sign language   g. verbal communications
b. message   e. Braille   h. body language
c. feedback   f. receiver

Sending messages with words	The information that is sent
Raised dots on special paper form letters and words	The response or answer that the receiver gives
Sending messages through expressions, gestures, and the way you stand	The person who gets the message
A series of hand gestures that represent words	The person who directs or sends the message

© Prentice Hall, Inc.   Teacher's Resource Book, Teen Living R1

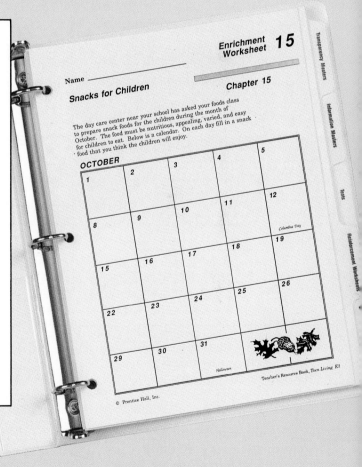

Name _____ **Enrichment Worksheet 15**

Snacks for Children

Chapter 15

The day care center near your school has asked your foods class to prepare snack foods for the children during the month of October. The food must be nutritious, appealing, varied, and easy for children to eat. Below is a calendar. On each day fill in a snack food that you think the children will enjoy.

OCTOBER

1	2	3	4	5
8	9	10	11	12
15	16	17	18	19 Columbus Day
22	23	24	25	26
29	30	31 Halloween		

© Prentice Hall, Inc.   Teacher's Resource Book, Teen Living E1

Transparency Masters
Information Masters
Tests
Reinforcement Worksheets

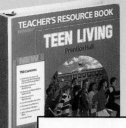

Tailor-made to help you manage your course...to help your students manage their lives.

Name _____   Information **17**
Master

Natural Fibers in the Clothes You Wear

Chapter 17

Transparency **5**
Master

The Family Life Cycle

Chapter 5

2 years   2.5 years

10 - 15 ± years

3.5 years

Name _____   Chapter **1**
Test

Chapter 1 Test

I. Match the following terms with the definitions given below. Write the letter of the correct term on the line next to the term's definition

Terms

a. impulse   e. goals   i. personality
b. peers   f. values   j. adolescence
c. ethics   g. environment   k. self-concept
d. stereotype   h. heredity

Definitions

Answers
_____ 1. ideas or beliefs that are important to a person
_____ 2. the early teenage years
_____ 3. members of one's own age group
_____ 4. the total of characteristics passed on from parents
_____ 5. an expectation of what a person is like
_____ 6. the total of all of a person's physical and emotional characteristics
_____ 7. a sudden choice influenced by the mood of the moment
_____ 8. a person's total surroundings
_____ 9. moral standards based on a person's beliefs about what is good and bad, right and wrong
_____ 10. the things that a person hopes to accomplish in life

II. On the line before each question, write the letter of the best answer.

_____ 11. Which of the following does NOT affect one's self-concept?
a. values   c. new experiences
b. basic human needs   d. goals

_____ 12. A ___ person makes decisions and acts independently.
a. confused   c. content
b. mature   d. sincere

_____ 13. Which of the following stands in the way of broadening your understanding of people?
a. environment   c. standards
b. ethics   d. stereotyping

© Prentice Hall, Inc.   Teacher's Resource Book, *Teen Living* T1

- **Information Masters** for student handout
- **Transparency Masters** for you
- **Chapter and Unit Tests**

And ...
- **Program Overview**
- **Skill Development Chart**
- **Scope and Sequence of Skills**
- **Answer Keys** for worksheets and tests

TEEN LIVING

For more information, please write:

PRENTICE HALL
Simon and Schuster Secondary Group
Prentice Hall School Division
Englewood Cliffs, NJ 07632

Or call TOLL FREE:
1-800-848-9500

Printed in USA
© by Prentice Hall
Englewood Cliffs, NJ
All rights reserved.
139–02271-6

ANNOTATED TEACHER'S EDITION
TEEN LIVING

Prentice Hall
Needham, Massachusetts
Englewood Cliffs, New Jersey

CREDITS

Project Editor: Carol Domblewski
Contributing Writer: Barbara Smith
Production/Manufacturing Coordinator:
  Roger Powers
Copy/Production Editor:
  Deborah Fogel
Design Director:
  L. Christopher Valente
Design Coordinator: Richard Dalton
Development Contributions:
  TextMasters
Design Production:
  Susan Gerould/PERSPECTIVES
Book Design: The Brownstone
  Group, Inc.
Cover Design: Martucci Studio

REVIEWER CONSULTANTS

Mary Blankonship
Bass Middle School
Nashville, TN

Debra Boswell
Daniels Middle School
Raleigh, NC

Wanda Christner
Peru Junior High School
Peru, IN

Raye Anne Crittenden
Monnig Middle School
Fort Worth, TX

Renee Fishman
Dumont Public Schools
Dumont, NJ

Sheryl Gilmore
Palm Spring Junior High
Hialeah, FL

Diana Krug
Peru Junior High
Peru, IN

Lynn Jorgenson
Carpenter Middle School
Plano, TX

Betty Ladymon
Atwell Middle School
Dallas, TX

Marlene Lovato
Coronado High School
Gallina, NM

Melanie McGuire
Fannin Middle School
Amarillo, TX

Elouise B. Merke
Miami Springs Middle School
Miami Springs, FL

Geraldine Mrozowski
Detroit Public Schools
Detroit, MI

Lynne Novogroski
Wellesley Public Schools
Wellesley, MA

Joan C. Parham
Hulcy Middle School
Dallas, TX

Iva Price
Stockard Middle School
Dallas, TX

Maria Reza
School-Based Health Programs
Reseda, CA

Ruth Ann Schultz
Cazenovia Public Schools
Cazenovia, NY

Elizabeth Starewicz
Wilbur Wright Middle School
Munster, IN

Teresa M. Stone
Bethel Junior High
Spanaway, WA

Julia Tingle
East Milbrook Middle School
Raleigh, NC

Sandra Wilson
Dunbar Middle School
Fort Worth, TX

 A Simon & Schuster Company

Annotated Teacher's Edition

CONTENTS

Unit 1 *About You*

Unit 2 *Relationships*

Introduction

The Nature of Home Economics Instruction

Exploratory Home Economics is a course about life. It is the one subject in which students learn how to set goals, make decisions, manage money, create nutritious meals, and make smart clothing choices. It is the one subject that introduces students to the very special issues that revolve around the family, marriage, parenthood, and the developing child. It is the one subject that helps students grow into adult roles as productive and responsible members of society by teaching them about career choices and about the dual role of homemaker/wage-earner. There is no other subject so centrally focused on the affairs and concerns of everyday life and the choices, self-concepts, and needs and wants of those who live it.

Because Home Economics is a course about living life, it is relevant to every student, whatever his or her future might hold. In what other course will students set goals having to do with their entire lives and not just with one aspect of these lives? In what other course will students think about their futures in terms of the big picture and not just in terms of one part of their development? In what other course will students be challenged to consider their personal resources and how best to manage them? In what other course will they even be led to the realization of what their many resources are? In what other course will students discuss pressing personal issues such as dating and relationships with friends, siblings, and family members?

Because Home Economics deals with the entire life cycle and touches on every aspect along the way, it is a course that is relevant to all students, whatever their ability levels or goals. The Home Economics umbrella is a large one, with something for everyone. Some students will love the excursions into shopping and personal finance. Others will find themselves challenged and rewarded in the foods or clothing lab. All students will be broadened by their introduction to family, marriage, parenting, and child development issues, and all will learn far more than they knew before about the world of careers.

Home Economics Across the Curriculum

Besides being so fundamental to day-to-day living as well as fundamental to long-term goals and decisions, a course in Home Economics helps students practice and improve other academic skills. Recently, many educators have been concerned about learning across the curriculum. In particular, there has been a cry for the integration of basic skills in all content areas. Such integration is not new to the Home Economics teacher. Home Economics has steadfastly remained a subject for which learning across the curriculum and integration are both naturals. The following pages provide some guidelines for introducing these kinds of cross-curricular activities to your exploratory Home Economics course.

Basic Skills and the Home Economics Classroom

Reading Skills

Reading is one content area integrated into the study of Home Economics. Some of this reading is of the textbook, which is the kind of practice that students get in other courses. But students in Home Economics read a great variety of materials; perhaps they read more varying sorts of materials in this course than they do in most others. Each of these reading tasks hones slightly different skills. For example, students learn to read recipes; these must be read carefully and with absolute accuracy. Students also learn to read patterns. These require the same careful attention to detail, as well as skill in interpreting and following graphic instructions. Students also learn how to read some of the specialized forms of communication that they encounter in the marketplace: unit pricing, hang tags, warranties, and other similar sources of information about purchases. Practice in such a variety of reading tasks makes Home Economics a course in real-life reading skills.

Teen Living is a highly readable and manageable text. Nonetheless, students will benefit from help with reading techniques. This guidance might take two forms: instruction in appropriate reading styles for various activities, and instruction in the SQ3R study method.

Reading Style. Many students read all material in the same way. However, the ability to read at different rates for different purposes is essential to reading proficiency. The sections, or individual lessons, in *Teen Living* contain new material that must be read slowly, carefully, and systematically (see the discussion of SQ3R, below). How fast a student reads this depends on his or her background and knowledge, as well as on the difficulty of the material itself.

In addition to developing the ability to read at a rate most conducive to comprehension, students should become familiar with two faster reading techniques—skimming and scanning. Skimming is used to get a general impression of content by hitting high points at a high viewing speed. Thus a student skimming a chapter might glance at the headings, at boldfaced or highlighted words, and at the first and last sentences of paragraphs. Scanning is a method of finding a single piece of information—a specific term, number, detail, or answer—by looking through the material quickly. Thus a student might scan a section to find a key word from a Chapter Review question. When the key word is found, the student would then slow down and read carefully to determine whether the passage answers the question.

SQ3R. A reading and study system known as SQ3R (Survey, Question, Read, Recite, and Review) is a very effective method for learning new concepts. Share with your students the following explanation of the SQ3R method:

SQ3R

The first step is to **survey** the chapter. Read the section titles and the items listed under the heading "As You Read."

Next, make a list of **questions** to be answered during the reading. These can be based on the chapter and section titles, the For Review questions, and the photographs and art. These questions will give a purpose to your reading and can also be used as a quiz after reading.

Then **read** the chapter to find answers to those questions. Reading with a purpose is a powerful aid to comprehension. Making a set of notes is also useful.

After reading the chapter, **recite** the answers to your questions. Try to answer them from memory, using your own words.

Finally, **review** the chapter to check your answers. Then, write out answers to any questions that your teacher assigns.

Readability. Careful attention was given to readability in the development of *Teen Living*. Several standard readability formulas (including Dale-Chall, Harris Jacobson, and Fry) were used to ensure that junior-high/middle-school students of average ability would be able to read the text without difficulty. In addition, the writers, editors, and designers of the text addressed a number of other factors affecting readability, including *format, lesson design and organization, concept density, conceptual difficulty,* and *repetition and reinforcement of key ideas.* Each chapter of *Teen Living* is divided into sections, and each section focuses on just one or two important concepts. The chapters and sections follow a logical sequence, and important terms and concepts are highlighted. Prereading questions are provided at the beginning of each section to guide the students' reading. These questions, along with the Summary in the Chapter Review, constitute an overview of the chapter content.

Study Skills

In addition to teaching your students the SQ3R method, you may wish to review basic study skills. These include note-taking, recording assignments, using the library, and test-taking.

Note-taking. Explain to your students that taking notes in complete sentences is quite difficult, for demonstrations and class discussions usually proceed rapidly, and there rarely is time enough to write every idea out in finished form. Instead, students should take notes using a rough outline form, with abbreviations for commonly occurring words. Students should begin each note-taking session by writing the date in the upper left-hand corner of a sheet of paper, preferably a sheet in a notebook or folder reserved for Home Economics. Then, main ideas should be written in short phrases, and subordinate ideas should be placed beneath these main ideas and marked by dashes. The *Teacher's Resource Book* provides practice in study skills.

Recording Assignments. Encourage your students to use a separate page in their notebooks or folders to record assignments. Stress the importance of taking down all essential information, including the date of the assignment, the assignment itself, the materials needed, and the date due.

Library Research. For some assignments, such as researching food in other cultures, you may wish to have your students do library work. To prepare the students for such an assignment, take them on a tour of your school library and point out the reference section and the sections containing materials related to Home Economics. Explain how to use the card catalog and such major reference works as almanacs and the *Readers' Guide to Periodical Literature.*

Test-taking. Before giving your students quizzes or examinations, it is a good idea to review basic test-taking skills. You may wish to share with them "Taking Tests," the Information Master for Chapter 2.

Writing Skills

Writing skills are important for a number of reasons. First, success in many courses depends to some extent on writing ability. Second, writing is essential to success in many jobs and everyday activities. Third, writing can be a tool for thought. By putting their ideas down in writing, students can refine these ideas, can clarify their thinking, and can make important discoveries about themselves and their worlds.

Writing is a part of each Home Economics course. As in every course, there are questions to answer and reports to write. Additionally, there is often practice in letter writing, such as in the letter of complaint about a product or service. Frequently, there is also practice in writing in chart form, an effective and necessary means of communication in our information-centered world.

One of the first things to emphasize to students is your expectations about their writing. When students answer questions, they should use complete sentences. They should also proofread their work for correct spelling, grammar, and mechanics. When they write paragraph-length pieces, as they will for some of the reinforcement and enrichment activities, they should remember that a paragraph has a main idea that is fully developed in supporting sentences. If your students write longer papers or reports, they should remember that their ideas must be organized to support and develop a main point, or thesis.

Whenever you assign paragraphs or longer pieces of writing, it is a good idea to spend some time talking to your students about the writing process and how it applies to the specific assignment. You may wish to share with your students the Information Masters on the Process of Writing in the *Teacher's Resource Book*.

Suggested Writing Activities. There are many types of writing activities that are appropriate for Home Economics students. The following are a few suggestions:

1. Lab reports detailing the nature and purpose of a project, the materials used, the steps taken to complete it, the results observed, and the conclusions drawn

2. Journal entries (including a running log of summaries of material learned from the text and in class, and discussions of its application to situations in the students' everyday lives)

3. Dialogues illustrating common situations in interpersonal relationships (including dialogues between friends, family members, and employers and employees)

4. Advertising copy illustrating various kinds of common consumer traps

5. Recipes or a class cookbook

6. Instructions for carrying out household activities such as maintenance or cleaning

7. Reviews of fashion or food

Mathematics Skills

Many areas of Home Economics require the application of mathematical concepts. For example, in order to learn about personal finance, Home Economics students are often asked to practice keeping a checkbook or preparing a household budget. To do these things, students must add, subtract, and sometimes multiply and divide. These basic operations are also used in the foods laboratory to convert the amounts of ingredients given in recipes to amounts appropriate for the number of people to be served. Mathematics is also involved in a number of areas of consumer studies, as when students calculate costs-per-serving or compare unit prices. To understand what credit costs the consumer, students may go on to more complex operations such as calculating actual costs based on compounding of interest.

The editors and writers of *Teen Living* have been careful to avoid introducing in the text any mathematical concepts beyond the level of simple arithmetic. Those sections of the text that employ mathematical concepts can be understood by anyone who understands measurement, estimation, and basic arithmetic.

Introducing Mathematics Activities. Whenever you introduce an activity that will require mathematics, it is probably a good idea to spend some time reviewing the operations involved. For example, when introducing the concept of unit prices, you might begin by writing the following problem on the board:

Pete wants to buy some spray cleaner. A pint of brand A costs $2.95. A quart of brand B costs $6.80. Which is the better buy?

Write on the board the steps in solving the problem, as follows:

1. Convert all amounts to a single type (in this case, ounces).

1 pint of Brand A = 16 ounces
1 quart of Brand B = 32 ounces

2. Divide the cost of each product by its amount.

Brand A: $2.95 ÷ 16 = $0.18
Brand B: $6.80 ÷ 32 = $0.21

3. Compare the resulting costs per unit to see which is less expensive.

Brand A = 18 cents per ounce
Brand B = 21 cents per ounce

After showing your students more problems, give them some to solve on their own, and walk around helping them as needed.

Suggested Mathematics Activities. The following are examples of mathematics activities that you may wish to have your students do in conjunction with *Teen Living:*

1. Calculating costs of generic vs name brand medicines
2. Reading a thermometer
3. Planning the budget for a family event (a vacation, a birthday party, etc.)
4. Calculating costs of prenatal services
5. Calculating costs of rearing a child
6. Preparing formula for infants
7. Predicting short-term and long-term income and expenses
8. Figuring the dollar value of employment benefits
9. Preparing a household budget
10. Determining the costs of credit
11. Preparing payments of bills
12. Determining amount of change due
13. Comparing costs of products
14. Calculating savings from coupons, discounts, and sales
15. Comparing costs of renting and buying
16. Making floor plans to scale
17. Comparing nutrients/calories in various foods
18. Estimating nutrients and calories in meals
19. Calculating unit prices
20. Preparing a food budget

21. Planning meals within the food budget
22. Adding costs of groceries
23. Using scales for measurement
24. Calculating needed amounts of ingredients based on recipes and on number of persons to be served
25. Measuring liquid and dry ingredients
26. Raising or lowering yield of recipes by calculating increase or decrease in ingredients
27. Determining time required to prepare a given dish or meal
28. Using a candy or meat thermometer
29. Making metric conversions
30. Comparing costs of eating at home and eating at restaurants
31. Dividing a bill in a restaurant
32. Making a personal clothing budget
33. Calculating costs related to clothing purchases, including cleaning costs and costs of accessories
34. Figuring costs for a clothing construction project, including materials and time
35. Comparing costs of purchased and constructed garments

Content from Across the Curriculum

The conceptual framework of Home Economics includes and intersects with curricula of many other disciplines.

Science and Home Economics

The following are some of the many science-related Home Economics activities that you can introduce to your classes.

1. Psychology of Personality and Development. In conjunction with Unit 1, which deals with personal development and interpersonal relations, you may want your students to explore the following psychology topics:

a. Maslow's Hierarchy of Human Needs. Ask a student from your class to do some research on Maslow's hierarchy by consulting encyclopedia articles and introductory psychology textbooks. Have the student prepare an oral report to present to the class.

b. Kohlberg's Stages of Moral Development. Again, ask a student to do some research on this topic by consulting encyclopedias and introductory psychology texts. Have the student present an oral report to the class.

c. Behavior Modification. Introduce your students to the basic concepts of stimulus, response, and reinforcement. Then have your students use this behavioral model to explain how a bad habit might be broken.

d. Theories of Personality. Find an introductory psychology text that contains a simplified account of the major personality theories. One such text is Prentice Hall's *Psychology: Exploring Behavior*. Divide your students into groups, and have each group study one personality theory and report on it to the class.

2. Psychology of Problem Solving and Decision Making. Read the chapters on problem solving and decision making in Lindsay and Norman's *Human Information Processing* (New York: Academic Press, 1973). Share with your students simplified models of their problem-solving and decision-making strategies.

3. Computer Science and Personal Financial Planning. If your school provides computers for instructional purposes, and if you have access to software developed for the planning and tracking of personal finances, demonstrate this software to your students. Better yet, have a local computer software vendor come to your class to give a demonstration.

4. Chemistry and Food Science. Show a videotape of the *Nova* television program entitled "The Making of a Junk Food" to your class when you are presenting the chapter on nutrition. Videotapes of *Nova* programs can be obtained by calling 1(800)621-2131.

If there is a foods testing laboratory or a foods manufacturer in your community, invite a research chemist from this organization to speak to your class about his or her job.

5. Nutritional Biology. Divide your class into groups and give each group one of the following topics to explore:

a. Calories and weight gain

b. The responsibilities of the Food and Drug Administration

c. Facts and fallacies about vitamins

d. The digestive process

e. Recommended Daily Allowances

f. Facts and fallacies about dieting

g. Proper nutrition and the prevention of heart disease

h. Proper nutrition and the prevention of colon cancer

i. Proper nutrition and the prevention of birth defects

Have each group prepare a presentation on its assigned topic.

6. Engineering and the Clothing and Textiles Industries. If there is a clothing or textiles factory in your area, have a student interview a manager from this factory to learn about the role of the industrial engineer in the manufacture of textiles or clothing. Have the student present an oral report to the class.

Social Studies and Home Economics

The following are some joint social studies and Home Economics activities that you may wish to introduce to your classes.

1. Sociology and the Life Cycle. When your class is studying the family life cycle, have one student do some research on Erik Erikson's Stages of Human Development and give a report.

2. Ethnographic Studies and Foods. In connection with your foods unit, have your students identify ten ethnic groups in the United States or around the globe and then prepare a dish from the cuisine of each of these groups.

3. Economics, Career Planning, and Personal Finance. Invite a colleague from social studies to visit your class to discuss the following topics from economics:

    a. Interest rates
    b. Supply, demand, pricing, and inflation
    c. Opportunity costs
    d. Consumer debt
    e. Transfer payments
    f. Unemployment

Emphasize the relation of each topic to career planning and resource management.

4. World History and Fashion. Divide your class into groups and assign each group a specific time and place in world history. Have each group research the clothing worn by people in its time and place, and ask each group to present findings to the class. Presentations should include visual materials, such as drawings of the articles of clothing discussed. You may wish to take this activity a step further and actually have students design and construct articles of clothing that might have been worn in each time and place.

5. American History and Careers. Invite a career counselor or a colleague from your school's social studies department to visit your class to discuss changes in the American work force. This person might divide the history of careers in America into three phases: the Agrarian Age, in which most jobs were related to farming; the Industrial Age, in which most jobs were related to smokestack industries; and the Information Age, in which most jobs are service or information related.

Language Arts and Home Economics

The following are some joint language arts and Home Economics activities that you may wish to introduce in your classes:

1. Clothing and Theatre Arts. If your school has a theatre department or a drama club, you may wish to enroll some of your students as costume designers for school productions. Discuss this possibility with the theatre teacher or director.

2. Speech and Personal Relations. Invite a speech teacher from your school to visit your class to discuss the following topics related to Chapter 4 of *Teen Living:*

    a. The communications model (sender, receiver, message, and feedback)
    b. Verbal elements of communication
    c. Nonverbal elements of communication
    d. Participating in a discussion
    e. Effective interpersonal communication
    f. Conflict management and speech

Art and Home Economics

The following are some joint art and Home Economics activities that you may wish to introduce to your classes:

1. Color and Clothing. In connection with Chapter 17, "Your Clothes," invite a colleague from the art department to visit your class to discuss the color wheel and such aspects of color as hue, value, intensity, tints, shades, and color schemes.

2. Interior Design. Consider engaging a colleague from the art department to work with you to prepare and teach a brief unit on interior design.

3. The Aesthetic Appeal of Foods. Divide your class into groups, and have each group prepare a meal and meal service plan to be evaluated for its visual appeal by top students from art classes in your school.

Accommodating the Exceptional Student

In the past, children with severe physical, mental, or emotional disabilities were segregated from their nondisabled peers. Some attended special schools. Far too many grew up with less than adequate schooling.

Federal Law PL 94–142 completely changes this situation. Today students with disabilities must be integrated into the school community. The disabling condition or conditions must be identified, analyzed, and evaluated, and a suitable educational plan must be devised for the student. Such plans may call for partial integration into the school community, with some instruction taking place in special education classes, or total integration, with selected special services, such as speech therapy.

In all cases, a fundamental goal is the integration of the child who is disabled into the mainstream of the school community, and ultimately into the mainstream of society. The plans should reflect agreement among student, parents, and school authorities on suitable learning activities.

It is the responsibility of the Home Economics teacher, indeed, of all teachers, to participate in the development of the educational plan of each disabled student in a class. Then, whatever is needed to facilitate learning must be developed and put into place.

Types of Disabilities

Different types of disabilities turn up in the classroom. Poor sight, blindness, mechanical impairments of the arms, legs, and spine, and other health problems are *physical impairments.*

Emotional disturbance is any condition involving the emotions, such as a tendency to unprovoked outbursts of anger, that interferes with normal functioning.

Conditions that interfere with a student's ability to use language are called *communicative disabilities.* These include deafness, hearing loss, speech problems, and certain specific learning disabilities—dysfunction in one or more of the psychological processes involved in either using or understanding language.

Disorders such as dyslexia, developmental aphasia, perceptual problems, and minimal brain damage are called *specific learning disabilities.*

Finally, intellectual functioning slower than the range of function considered normal is referred to as *mild mental retardation.*

Reaching Disabled Students

Students with disabilities, like other classroom children, continually interact with their environment while learning about it and developing skills. However, a considerable body of research has established that certain disabled children can be hindered in their growth when classroom instruction is based primarily on reading, listening, and writing. Meaningful instruction of these children must meet their special needs. These needs depend upon the nature of their disabilities and their experiential background. Usually, what is required are appropriate experiences focused on student participation before, during, and after presentation of concepts.

Participatory experiences provide the background necessary for disabled students to structure, interpret, and assimilate concepts. The experiences affect the time for processing ideas, the form of sensory input, and the quality of interpretive discussion. For example, visually impaired students benefit greatly by being allowed to manipulate lesson objects and materials before and during the time of instruction. This provides a background of physical characteristics that the teacher can use to great advantage. Students with no visual disabilities can readily obtain the same background by viewing the objects as the lesson begins. Of course, the foods and clothing units in an exploratory Home Economics course lend themselves quite readily to such experiential treatment. The real challenge is to develop comparable experiential activities for lessons of a purely academic nature. Thus, when presenting lessons on communication and relationships, individualized role-playing activities might be preferable to discussion of communication theory.

While it is often possible to motivate students with disabilities to memorize the terms and definitions needed to answer textbook review questions, this is often nothing more than a rote task that does not require understanding.

A teaching strategy consistent with the account of the disabled student given above is as follows: First, students should be permitted to solve simple, open-ended problems by means of manipulative activities. Working out skills activities, handling materials and equipment used for demonstrations, and carrying out any other activities specially designed with students' disabilities and abilities in mind will meet this need. For some students, laboratory activities will be suitable. Second, students should read the text, or have the text paraphrased for them, as needed, and then interact directly with the teacher. As the concepts being taught are discussed in class, reference should be made to the concrete activities previously carried out to help students to assimilate and integrate the desired content. Third, students should be given simple convergent problems that call for the use of concepts covered. A useful technique, when feasible, is to modify "For Review" questions so that each answer can take the form of an action rather than the form of a written statement. Finally, if needed, appropriate remedial learning activities can be devised and administered.

Reaching the Gifted Student

Far too often the gifted student is neglected on the grounds that bright children need little attention or guidance in order to achieve at a satisfactory level. Nevertheless, left to his or her own resources and required to master only the content and skills presented to the average learner, the gifted child often tunes out and experiences anger and frustration. Such students, who also have very special needs, very quickly master whatever is taught and thus are bored by the lack of mental stimulation inherent in plodding through learning activities that fail to challenge them. Some gifted students therefore rebel and develop behavior problems.

Challenge your gifted students by setting for them the following types of tasks:

1. reading sophisticated supplementary materials

2. researching in greater depth the concepts treated in the textbook

3. explaining concepts or providing demonstrations to other students

4. assuming more freedom and responsibility with regard to the exercises, activities, and projects that they undertake

5. becoming active in community organizations whose work bears on some aspect of Home Economics

Safety in the Foods and Clothing Laboratories

Before beginning your foods and clothing units, copy and distribute the following handouts from the opening section of the *Teen Living Teacher's Resource Book:*

1. Safety in the Foods Laboratory
2. Foods Laboratory Safety Agreement
3. Safety in the Clothing Laboratory
4. Clothing Laboratory Safety Agreement

The first and third of these handouts explain in detail the procedures that students must follow in order to conduct laboratory activities safely. The second and fourth of these handouts are contracts for your students to sign. The contracts are simply agreements to abide by the safety rules presented in the other handouts.

It is probably a good idea to spend some time going over each handout with your classes. You may wish to demonstrate potential dangers and emergency procedures as you discuss the handouts with your students.

Using Teen Living

Teen Living is an exploratory Home Economics program written especially for junior-high/middle-school students. A complete introduction to the world of Home Economics, *Teen Living* includes

▪ Student book
  500 pages, 5 units, 20 chapters *for the student,* abundantly illustrated with photos and charts
▪ Annotated Teacher's Edition
  656 pages, 144 of which are only for the teacher
  Also included in the Annotated Teacher's Edition is the complete student book. The pages of the student book have been annotated especially for the teacher with the kind of information needed on the spot. These annotations include cross-references, page references for answers, information for discussion, suggestions for reteaching, activities, situations for role-playing, and facts to give you ongoing support.
▪ Teacher's Resource Book
  416 pages of worksheets, transparency and information masters, as well as tests

The Student Book

Units at a Glance

Unit I   *About You (student book pages 1–69)*
This unit explores self-concept, managing resources, and wellness.

Unit II   *Relationships (student book pages 70–143)*
This unit focuses on communication and relationships, the family, and child development and parenting.

Unit III   *Resource Management (student book pages 144–247)*
This unit examines important choices relating to money, part-time jobs, shopping, careers, and housing.

Unit IV   *Foods and Nutrition (student book pages 248–383)*
This unit introduces students to a broad range of food and health issues, including meal planning, kitchen skills, food preparation, and meals and manners.

Unit V   *Clothing and Textiles (student book pages 384–475)*
This unit begins with the students' own clothing choices and then moves rapidly on to the basics of sewing.

Chapters at a Glance

Every chapter includes the following:

Vocabulary List

A list of boldfaced terms that are defined in the chapter. Each word in the vocabulary list reappears in the Chapter Review as well as in the glossary.

Sections

For teaching and reading ease, each chapter is divided into highly manageable sections. Each could be considered a separate lesson for those concepts you want to emphasize. Sections have been created to provide a choice in the amount of content you treat at one time; in no way are these prescriptive markers or barriers to using the chapter as a whole.

As You Read

A list of the key concepts covered within each section focuses students' reading.

Learning to Manage Features

These features present real-life dilemmas that your students face. Each begins with a dialogue that introduces the problem as well as the chapter content. The feature ends, and the dilemma is resolved, at the conclusion of each chapter. Questions are included to stimulate discussion and active participation and to reinforce the concepts involved.

Theme Features

Four themes are echoed throughout the book: *leadership and citizenship, health and safety, careers,* and *technology.* In every chapter, there is a single-focus teaching capsule devoted to broadening your students' understanding of one of these themes. Chapter-by-chapter, the theme features are as follows:

Chapter 1 Positive Peer Pressure (Leadership and Citizenship)

Chapter 2 Home Efficiency (Technology)

Chapter 3 Volunteering (Leadership and Citizenship)

Chapter 4 Interpreters for the Deaf (Careers)

Chapter 5 Help for Children of Alcoholics (Health and Safety)

Chapter 6 Parenting as a Career (Careers)

Chapter 7 Home Economics Teacher (Careers)

Chapter 8 The Balancing Act (Health and Safety)

Chapter 9 Corporate Citizenship (Leadership and Citizenship)

Chapter 10 From Cash Box to Computer (Technology)

Chapter 11 Childproofing Your Home (Health and Safety)

Chapter 12 The Food and Drug Administration (Health and Safety)

Chapter 13 Super-Marketing (Technology)

Chapter 14 Kitchens Are Our Business (Careers)

Chapter 15 Food From Space Lands Safely (Technology)

Chapter 16 Serving the Elderly (Leadership and Citizenship)

Chapter 17 Jacquard Loom (Technology)

Chapter 18 Secondhand Business Is First Rate (Careers)

Chapter 19 Danger! Children at Work (Health and Safety)

Chapter 20 "Constructing" a Difference (Leadership and Citizenship)

Did You Know? Features

These features include interesting "trivia" and tantalizing bits of information that pique your students' interest. Everything is here, from statistics on the changing family to the history of buttons. These features appear in every chapter in positions where they can most effectively complement, extend, or enliven the content.

For Review Questions

Questions that probe students' recall and understanding of the main points appear at the end of every section. Such questions serve as intermediary checks on the students' understanding of their reading and provide an opportunity for self-evaluation or teacher assistance before the end of the chapter.

Chapter Review

Every chapter closes with a two-page chapter review. This includes a chapter summary and a fill-in-the-blank activity using the vocabulary words in the chapter. This is followed by review questions (at a range of ability levels) that probe your students' mastery of the chapter as a whole as well as its central concepts. Every chapter review also includes activities that focus on communication, critical thinking, resource management, decision making, application/laboratory, and human relations skills.

Additional Support

Glossary (pages 481–486)

Every vocabulary word is contained in an easy-to-use glossary.

Appendix of Charts (pages 477–480)

Three charts appear in the index: The Daily Food Guide, a guide to the types and number of servings of foods that should be eaten daily by various age groups; the U.S. RDA, the government's recommended dietary allowances; and a chart listing calories, fat, and protein in common foods.

Index (pages 487–498)

Annotated Teacher's Edition

The Annotated Teacher's Edition contains

- The complete student book
- Its own Table of Contents
- Introduction (pages 1–9)
  This essay addresses reinforcing basic skills; teaching Home Economics across the school curriculum; as well as ways of understanding the special needs of students from varying populations. It also addresses safety in the foods and clothing labs.
- Scope and Sequence Chart (pages 17–21)
  Each unit is covered in a full-page chart. Content strands are resource management, individual development, relationships, family and social responsibilities, preparation for adulthood, consumer skills and money management, health and safety, and careers.
- Skills Chart (pages 22–26)
  A full-page chart is devoted to each unit. Highlighted skills are decision making and problem solving, critical thinking, communication, management application, human relations, laboratory, mathematics, and leadership and citizenship. Page numbers, accompanied by brief explanatory text, are provided.
- Lesson Plans (pages 27–138)
  There is a fully developed lesson plan for every chapter. Every lesson plan lists the chapter's vocabulary; it also provides an outline of the chapter, showing at a glance the division into sections. A complete list of objectives and a list of program resources follow. Activities and teaching suggestions for getting into the chapter, as well as activities to sustain interest as you progress through the chapter, with indications of level of difficulty, are given. There are discussion questions (and answers) for teaching the theme feature as well as the Learning to Manage feature. Complete answers to all the For Review questions contained in the chapter, as well as Chapter Review questions, follow. Finally, an extended discussion of ways of responding to skill activities is provided.
- Fully annotated student text
  The Annotations
  The annotations are contained right on the pupil book pages. Their purpose is to refer you quickly to related information; to alert you to key concepts to stress; to provide you with ideas for restatement, reinforcement, enrichment, role playing, homework assignments, and evaluation; and to add interesting facts to those already presented.

Teaching Annotations

Purpose

Reteaching

Refocus attention on the key points in the chapter. Make sure students of all abilities know what the main points are.

Examples

Running, jogging, and playing basketball or tennis are all examples of exercises that cause the body to perspire. Perspiration causes a loss of body water, which must then be replaced. What foods and beverages will replace water loss? (student book page 261) **This annotation complements both the photo and the text on page 261 and reteaches the body's need for water.**

Stress that when your students cut out a pattern, they must keep the fabric flat on the table. If they put their hands underneath the cloth or lift it in any way, they risk inaccurate cutting. (student book page 450) **This annotation appears beneath a discussion of layout, cutting, and pinning and reteaches the need for good cutting technique.**

Reinforcement

Make an abstract concept more concrete and understandable by creating an easy activity or group task. Restate, emphasize, and stress central ideas.

Have students mount pictures of food onto a bulletin or felt board. Use the pictures to demonstrate the difference between colorful, appealing meals and bland, unappealing meals. (student book page 281) **This annotation suggests an activity that will show students what the text tells them about meal planning.**

Review the procedure for exiting the school when the fire alarm rings. Remind students that talking is not allowed during a fire drill. Explain why. (Student book page 63) **This annotation reinforces abundant concern for safety throughout the text and, in particular, the discussion of fire safety.**

Enrichment

Present an activity or assignment that demonstrates a concept while challenging or more fully engaging your students. Provide opportunities for role-playing.

Make a chart comparing babysitting with other part-time jobs. Consider pay, flexibility, and levels of responsibility and reward. (student book page 136) **This annotation causes students to use higher-order thinking skills to analyze the rewards and drawbacks of babysitting.**

Assign each student a color. Have students cut ten one-inch squares of the color. Have them put them in a row from dark to light to observe their increasing intensity. (student book page 229) **This annotation helps students to take an abstract concept like *intensity* and make it concrete. In this way, their understanding of the use of color in home furnishings is enriched.**

Discuss

Raise issues; present problems to solve in large and small groups; stimulate thinking beyond the page. Invite students to bring insights from their own lives to bear on the content you present.

What is the difference between having a strong self-concept and being conceited? (student book page 6) **This annotation takes the discussion of self-concept and adds a real dimension of limits and boundaries to it. It helps students explore healthy outlets for their egos versus those that can be damaging to themselves or others.**

What goods or services would you buy to make yourself feel special, make yourself feel older, make yourself feel athletic? What does buying these products say about you? (student book page 208) **This annotation is a springboard from the text's discussion of influences on buying to the students' own experiences with and feelings about products they have purchased.**

Note

Introduce interesting related facts, word histories, and quotations that increase your students' knowledge, their cultural literacy, and their sense of wonder. Be able to refer easily to related information in the text.

Some words related to fabrics and weaves are named for their places of origin. For example, *madras* is named after Madras, India; *denim* is named after Nîmes, France, since it comes *de* (from) Nîmes; and *worsted* is named after Worthstede, England. (student book page 400) **This annotation introduces word histories to add colorful background information to the text's discussion of fabrics.**

Fish that are low in fat and high in protein are tuna, halibut, cod, flounder, haddock, ocean perch, and carp. Fish that are slightly higher in fat are salmon, mackerel, herring, and lake trout. (student book page 297) **This annotation enhances the discussion of buying fish by introducing additional information related to nutrition.**

Photo & Art

Some students respond more to pictures than to words. Tap the visual modality by fully probing the photo's or the art's careful relationship to the text.

How does the body language here communicate this family's positive relationship? (student book page 76) **This annotation takes a concept introduced earlier—nonverbal communication—and causes students to reapply it to analyze attitudes of pride and satisfaction about a family's home. It also causes students to focus on, rather than regard as decoration, the carefully selected photos in the text.**

Point out the work triangle. Explain why the triangle is the ideal shape for a kitchen work area. Coach students to provide reasons why short sides of a work triangle are desirable. (student book page 307) **This annotation helps you to use the artwork as a teaching resource and causes students to analyze an illustration of an efficient kitchen.**

Teacher's Resource Book

The *Teacher's Resource Book* is a binder containing 416 pages and nine categories of resources, all conveniently arranged by content and purpose and easily pulled out and reproduced for class use. The *Teacher's Resource Book* provides worksheets and blackline masters for each chapter in the student text. You may not use them all, but you have variety and choice for flexible teaching. Specifically, it contains the following types of support and enrichment:

■ An Overview and a Scope and Sequence, Skill Development, and Pacing Chart

The Overview explains in detail how to use the material in the *Teacher's Resource Book*. The charts show the scope and sequence of both content and skills instruction in the student text.

■ Skill Development Worksheets

The Skill Development Worksheets provide concentrated work on home economics, reading, writing, and math skills.

■ Laboratory/Application Worksheets

The Laboratory/Application worksheets provide active experience in foods and clothing.

■ Reinforcement Worksheets

The Reinforcement Worksheets can be used for remedial purposes or to reinforce skills learned earlier.

■ Enrichment Worksheets

The Enrichment Worksheets provide interesting applications beyond those pursued elsewhere in the program and are especially appropriate for gifted Home Economics students, ones who need additional challenges.

■ Transparency Masters

The Transparency Masters can be made into overheads and used to enliven your classroom discussions and presentations.

■ Information Masters

The Information Masters, developed to be used as class handouts, provide important information related to chapter concepts. Some, like the Information Master on the Heimlich Maneuver, repeat in $8\frac{1}{2} \times 11$ format charts shown in the text; others, like the list of storage guidelines, supplement the material in the text.

■ Chapter and Unit Tests

Both objective and essay test items are provided. These tests are keyed to the chapters and units in the student edition.

■ Answer Keys

Answer Keys are provided for all materials in the *Teacher's Resource Book*.

Unit 1

Resource Management

25 human and nonhuman resources; **26** setting goals; **27–29, 33–34** management process; **38, 41** managing time; **37** taking class notes; **45** wellness; **45–46** stress; **52–53** depression; **54–55** health care; **56** health records; **62** managing own life; **63–66** meeting emergencies; **67** getting in shape

Individual Development

3 self-concept; **4, 7–9, 18** personality and physical characteristics; **6** heredity and environment; **10** adjusting to physical growth; **14** exploring options; **14, 18–19, 26** standards and values; **15, 16** peer pressure; **16–20** making decisions; **21** seeking advice; **34** planning leisure time; **36–37** speaking up in class; **40** thinking positively; **45** wellness; **46** fitness; **47–48** hygiene and grooming; **49–51** emotions; **58** dangers of alcohol; **60–61** dangers of smoking; **62** saying "No!" to drugs

Relationships

3 how family and friends see you; **7** changing behavior; **11–12** family roles; **12–13** avoiding stereotypes; **21** new in school; **29** asking for help; **47** personal hygiene; **51** friendship as stress reliever; **52** sharing feelings; **59** helping alcoholic

Family and Social Responsibilities

12 understanding family roles; **13** dealing with conflict; **19** personal decisions and family; **54** volunteer work; **55** family health care; **58** danger of social drinking; **59** helping alcoholic in family; **60** respect for nonsmokers

Preparation for Adulthood

10, 51–52 adjusting to change; **13** becoming mature; **16–20** making decisions; **54–56** keeping health records; **57–62** avoiding substance abuse; **63–66** coping with emergencies

Consumer Skills & Money Management

28 analyzing money resources; **55** paying for health care

Health and Safety

45 wellness; **45** diet; **46** fitness; **47–48** hygiene and grooming; **48–49** dental care; **49** rest and relaxation; **49** physical and mental health; **50–51** stress; **52–53** depression; **53–56** medical care; **57** substance abuse; **58–60** alcohol; **60–61** smoking; **61** prescription drugs; **62** illegal drugs; **63–66** emergencies and first aid; **67** getting in shape

Careers

7 goals in career planning; **17** career decisions; **54** volunteer work in health; **55** public health services

SCOPE AND SEQUENCE

Unit 2

Resource Management

85 resolving conflicts with friends; **95** resolving differences; **117** helping older relative; **135–141** babysitting

Individual Development

73 communication; **75** paying attention to others; **75** appropriate dress; **76** discussing when disagreeing; **79** relating to family; **83–84** peer pressure; **88** growing at own rate; **91** belonging to a group; **91** group leadership; **93** respecting others; **99, 102** becoming independent; **111** coping with family illness; **114–115** seeking help

Relationships

72–73 confiding in friends; **74** nonverbal communication; **75** listening; **76** avoiding prejudice; **77–78** relating to others; **79–82** relating to family; **82–86** friendships; **87** group activities; **87–89** boy-girl relationships; **89–90** future relationships; **95** resolving differences; **108** marriage

Family and Social Responsibilities

75 listening attentively; **77–82** relating to family; **82–86** friendships; **90** your community; **92** good citizenship; **93** respecting others; **98, 106–107, 110, 117** relating to older relative; **99–102** family and society; **102–107** family roles; **107–110** family life cycle; **110–116** family crises; **120, 135–140** babysitting

Preparation for Adulthood

73 communication; **75–76** listening and responding; **76** mature listening; **78** forming relationships; **89–90** future relationships; **94** Future Homemakers of America; **127–135** parenting; **135–141** babysitting

Consumer Skills and Money Management

102 family economy; **102, 128** cost of raising a child

Health and Safety

112 help for children of alcoholics; **121–122** prenatal care; **130–133, 136–141** caring for children; **132** safety chart

Careers

80 interpreters for the deaf; **94** Future Homemakers of America; **105** parents and other care givers; **130** parenting

Unit 3

Resource Management

149 skills and aptitudes; **153–154** career; **157** time; **158** goals and jobs; **166–169, 185** managing money; **168–169** priorities; **176–180** banking; **180–181** investing; **181–184** credit; **193** consumer rights; **205–206** shopping plan; **212–214** buying guidelines; **227–230** design elements; **231–232, 237, 245** organizing space; **239–240** home maintenance

Individual Development

147 work as fulfillment; **150** entry-level jobs; **159–160** self-image; **151, 160, 162** career; **167–168** earning money; **174** budget; **183–184** credit; **209–210** peer approval; **223** home and self-expression; **234–235** personal space

Relationships

148 community; **149** work with children; **162** co-workers; **185** family responsibilities; **209–210** influence on buying; **223–224** family home; **234** inviting friends home; **235–236** sharing space

Family and Social Responsibilities

152, 157 careers and family; **167** community; **185** money and family; **192** volunteer work; **193–194** consumer responsibilities; **223, 234** home and family; **235, 236, 245** sharing space; **236** personal space; **238** cooperation

Preparation for Adulthood

149–155 careers; **157** family and career; **159–160** job interview; **172** expenses; **172, 174** budget; **176** banking; **181–184** credit; **189** free enterprise; **212, 219** successful shopping; **215–218** quality products; **223–226** housing; **234** living space; **237–240** home maintenance

Consumer Skills and Money Management

152, 157 education; **158** employment; **167–168** managing money; **169, 171–175** spending; **176–180** banking; **181–184** credit; **189–191** free enterprise; **191–192** entrepreneurship and teens; **195** contracts; **198** Better Business Bureau; **204, 205–206** comparison shopping; **208–209** ads; **210–212** sales; **214–215** impulse buying

Health and Safety

160 job safety ; **172** health care; **193** consumer right to safety; **194, 195** safe products; **223, 233, 237, 241–244** home safety; **241–242** fire; **242** poison; **242** childproofing

Careers

146, 147, 158–159 career search; **149, 154** skills and aptitudes; **150–151** kinds of jobs; **152–153** career trends; **155–157** training; **162–163** careers in home economics; **162** schooling; **167** part-time jobs; **192** teen entrepreneur

SCOPE AND SEQUENCE

Unit 4

Resource Management

255 combining foods; **263–264** Daily Food Guide; **264–265** Dietary Guidelines; **266–267** calories; **278, 285, 286, 301** food shopping; **279–282** meal choices; **292–300** high quality food; **304** kitchen efficiency; **305–308, 325** organizing kitchen; **311** kitchen storage; **314–316** kitchen tools; **329** cooking supplies; **329–331** work plan; **319, 321, 331–334, 355** recipes; **335–350** principles of cookery; **364–365** packing lunch; **369** preparing food

Individual Development

267–268 ideal weight; **273–274** eating disorders; **279** nutrition needs; **280** scheduling; **309** hygiene; **361** importance of breakfast; **370** helping elderly; **376** table manners

Relationships

252–253, 269 eating with friends; **278–301** family shopping; **329** cooking for others; **357** cooking with friends; **376** table manners; **379–380** restaurant behavior

Family and Social Responsibilities

252, 279 family food customs; **270** family, friends, and diet; **272** eating and lifestyle; **313** giving first aid; **368–369** family dinner; **370** serving the elderly; **370–373** serving food; **376** table manners; **379–380** restaurant behavior

Preparation for Adulthood

263 importance of good diet when young; **278, 283, 284–290** food shopping; **281** meal planning; **281–282** food budget; **308–313** kitchen safety; **331–334** using recipes; **335–350** principles of cookery; **369** dinner for one

Consumer Skills and Money Management

281–282, 293–294 food costs; **284** food shopping; **286** coupons; **286** comparison shopping; **290** shopping tips; **319** ingredients; **329** grocery list; **364** packing lunch; **369** buying food for one; **380** restaurant paying and tipping

Health and Safety

251, 254–261 nutrition; **262–263** poor eating habits; **262–265** daily food needs; **264–265** Dietary Guidelines; **265–267** calories; **267–270** weight control; **268** exercise; **270–271** fad diets; **273–274** eating disorders; **274** athletes and eating; **275, 366-367** healthful snacks; **279** nutrition needs; **283** cleanliness in food stores; **287** food labels; **288** U.S. RDA; **289–290** additives; **290–291** storing food; **294, 296, 298** food inspection; **308, 311–313** kitchen safety

Careers

318 managing test kitchen; **370** serving the elderly

Unit 5

Resource Management

386, 390, 413 clothing choices; **391** applying elements of design to clothing; **395–396** clothing inventory; **399** sewing; **407–412** clothing care and storage; **418–419** organization; **419** scheduling time; **426–428** choosing fabric; **429** sewing management; **432–444** sewing equipment; **437** using instruction manual; **441–442** care of sewing machine; **444–447, 455** fabric preparation; **447–451** using pattern; **459–463** hand sewing; **463–472** machine construction

Individual Development

386–389 clothing choices; **388** clothing and image; **392–394** choosing colors; **394–395** choosing textures/patterns; **395–400** planning wardrobe; **418–419** organization; **420** choosing a project; **464** helping the needy; **473** fixing up clothing

Relationships

387–388 community clothing customs; **418** working with others; **458, 473** getting advice on sewing

Family and Social Responsibilities

387 clothing customs

Preparation for Adulthood

386, 413 clothing choices; **387** proper dress; **389–390** fashion; **395–400** planning wardrobe; **407–412** clothing care and storage; **417** sewing safely; **420** operating consignment shop; **426–427** care labeling; **427** shopping for quality; **459–473** learning to sew

Consumer Skills and Money Management

389–398 reasonably priced clothing; **396** repairing clothing; **396** a buying plan; **397–398** clothes shopping; **399–400** consignment and outlet stores; **402** expense of natural fibers; **410** expense of dry cleaning; **412** clothing storage; **420** budget and project; **426–428** choosing fabric; **443** cost of serger; **472** recycling clothing; **473** thrifty shopping

Health and Safety

388 clothing as protection; **406** flame-retardant finishes; **409** using iron safely; **417–418** safety in sewing laboratory; **435, 459** using thimble; **436** child labor; **450** scissors safety

Careers

404 textile and computer industries; **420** running consignment shop; **464** preparation for careers in home economics

SKILLS

Decision Making and Problem Solving

7, 51 goals; **11–12, 14** priorities; **13** accepting responsibility; **15** peer pressure; **16–17** making choices; **18–19** values; **19–20** model for decision making; **23** family, responsible decisions, daily roles; **23** avoiding stereotyping; **32** scheduling; **42** management process; **42** human/nonhuman resources; **42** class discussion; **53** seeking help for depression; **54** choosing family health care; **57–58** substance abuse; **58, 69** alcohol; **60–61** smoking; **62** drugs; **63–66** emergencies

Critical Thinking

4 self; **23** emotional needs; **23** independence; **23** role-playing conflicts; **27, 43** management process; **29** evaluating results; **37** focusing on main idea; **43** planning leisure time; **52** analyzing personal problems; **54** preventive medicine; **58** recognizing drinking problems; **69** reducing stress; **69** drugs

Communication

9 asking for help; **35–36** listening in class; **36–37** speaking up in class; **43** testing listening skills; **52** sharing feelings; **54** talking to elderly and disabled; **56** asking the doctor questions; **59** asking for help for alcoholism; **62** seeking drug counseling; **63–64** making emergency phone calls

Management Application

21, 25 learning to manage life; **24** setting priorities; **26** setting goals; **27–29, 33–34** steps in the management process; **30–31, 35, 41** managing time; **38–40** developing study skills; **50–51** managing stress; **56** keeping health records; **59** finding help for alcoholism; **67** getting in shape

Human Relations

2 making friends; **3** knowing self; **5** working with others; **7** basic needs and values; **9, 52** helping others; **10–11** new people; **12** family roles; **13** dealing with conflict; **15** standards and respect; **16** positive peer pressure; **19** independence and family; **23** helping family or community member

Laboratory

23 display about self; **69** emergency card for telephone

Mathematics

5 helping with math homework; **17** math skills and careers; **40** thinking positively about math; **60** smoking statistics

Leadership and Citizenship

5–6, 9 community; **13–14, 20** being responsible; **14–15, 19, 26** standards; **16** peer pressure; **28–29, 40** setting goals; **37** joining in class discussion; **52, 54** volunteer work; **62** saying "No!" to drugs; **63–66** meeting emergencies

Unit 2

Decision Making and Problem Solving	**76** communication problems; **78, 97, 105** compromises; **80–81** family problems; **83–84** peer pressure; **84–86** friendship problems; **88–89** dating decisions; **96** reading body language; **97** friends and clique; **107** consulting older family members; **111** dealing with illness and death in family; **114** help in crises; **118** time at home; **119** sibling problems; **119** explaining death; **119** family stress help; **124, 128–135** parents caring for children; **135–136** deciding to babysit; **137–138** safety while babysitting; **138–143** decisions with children
Critical Thinking	**75–76** attentive listening; **79** flexibility; **85** resolving conflicts; **118** buying a home; **119** family crisis; **119** critiquing TV with family; **136** planning to babysit; **142** language and child development; **143** toddler frustrations; **143** stimulating baby's mental needs
Communication	**73–74** model; **74** verbal and nonverbal; **75** listening; **76, 95** solving problems; **77** strategies; **78** understanding others; **80** interpreting for deaf; **87** boy-girl relationships; **89** ending a relationship; **96** audience; **97** body language; **102–105** relating to siblings; **105** with parents; **107** with older family members; **110–111** crisis; **113** dealing with divorce; **116** support groups for addicts; **133–134** children and language
Management Application	**76** communication strategies; **78** keeping communication channels open; **82** adjusting to family changes; **95** resolving conflict; **105** relating to siblings; **107, 117** being responsive to older relatives; **110–116** managing family crises
Human Relations	**72–73, 77–78, 82–86** relating to friends; **78, 93** respecting others; **79–82, 97** community help; **97** writing to friend; **102–107** family; **85** conflicts; **86** new friends; **87–90** dating; **89–90** marriage; **110–116** family crises; **127–134** parenting
Laboratory	**97** creating an ad; **119** preparing recipe for senior citizens; **143** making playdough for preschooler; **143** observing children
Mathematics	**101** figures about families
Leadership and Citizenship	**91** group leadership; **92–94** good citizenship; **94** Future Homemakers of America; **103** role of eldest sibling; **114** seeking help for family; **128–134** parental responsibilities

SKILLS

Unit 3

Decision Making and Problem Solving	**147, 151–152** choosing a career; **164** career decisions; **167–168** money choices; **169–170** goals; **176–180** bank services; **187** expenses and income; **187** spending plan; **191** community problems; **198–200** agencies and consumer; **202** needs and wants; **220** status symbols; **220** sales and bargains
Critical Thinking	**149** careers **152** trade-offs; **168** evaluating decisions; **187, 206** purchases; **191–192, 203** entrepreneur; **193–194** consumer rights and responsibilities; **211–212** sales and bargains; **217** consumer protection; **220–221** advertising; **234** use of space
Communication	**159** contacts and jobs; **159** letters of application; **160** thank-you notes; **162** co-workers; **165** interviewing; **167** advertising class projects; **194, 203** consumer complaints; **195** contracts; **196** verbal complaints; **196–198, 203** letters of complaint; **208–209** advertising; **209–210** consulting friends and family
Management Application	**153, 158–159** career research; **154–155** job experience; **155** co-op programs; **160, 162** management skills on job; **166–167, 185** money management; **168–170** goals; **171–174** spending plan; **180–181** investing; **181–184** credit; **191, 219** use of resources; **231, 234** organizing space; **239–244** home maintenance; **240** energy conservation
Human Relations	**147–149** careers in social services; **155** volunteer work; **157** career and family; **167** friends; **189** free enterprise and human potential; **204, 219** family shopping; **209–210** influences on shopping; **223** home and emotional needs; **235–236, 238, 245** sharing space and responsibilities at home
Laboratory	**165** skills for home economics job; **187** making "Job Wanted" poster; **203** setting up mock business; **221** comparison shopping; **221** researching products; **247** making something for room
Mathematics	**148–149, 153, 156** careers in math, computers, accounting; **169–170, 173–174** budgeting; **180** balancing checking account; **180–181** investing; **210** computerized cash register
Leadership and Citizenship	**148** community; **149–153** career choices; **155** volunteer work; **157** career and family; **160, 162** behavior at work; **167** neighborhood chores; **189–191** free enterprise; **191–192** entrepreneurship; **192** corporate citizenship

Unit 4

Decision Making and Problem Solving

251–254, 262–265 choosing foods; **269** good eating habits; **276** hunger and appetite; **277** fat in diet; **277** energy needs; **277** exercise; **277** carbohydrates and protein; **292–300** buying quality food; **303** labels and ingredients; **305–308, 325** organizing kitchen; **309–311** preventing food spoilage; **326** personal hygiene; **328, 345, 349** baking problems; **340–341** retaining nutrients; **366** combining foods

Critical Thinking

251–252, 269 eating habits; **255, 263** combining foods; **265–266** how the body uses food; **266–267** calories; **270** fad diets; **273–274** eating disorders; **277** vitamins; **277** emotions and eating; **303** coupons; **312–313** acting in emergencies; **321** what ingredients do; **325** organizing kitchen; **327** safety checklist; **368** Daily Food Guide

Communication

277 discussing food and nutrition; **318** managing test kitchen; **329** working together; **360** planning dinner party; **368–369** family dinner; **378–380** restaurant behavior

Management Application

253–254, 281–282 cost of food; **267–268, 269–270** weight control; **279** Daily Food Guide; **280–281** meal planning; **290** storing foods; **292–300** buying quality food; **301** shopping management; **311–313** preventing kitchen accidents; **318** managing a kitchen; **329–331** a work plan

Human Relations

279, 368–369 family meals; **304, 325** helping in kitchen; **318** managing test kitchen; **329** working together; **376** table manners; **379–380** restaurant behavior

Laboratory

277 Daily Food Guide; **301** meal planning; **301** listing prices; **315, 324, 327** mixing and measuring; **320–321, 323, 327** recipes; **357** making cake; **357** planning bake sale; **359** preparing vegetables; **359, 381** menus

Mathematics

265–267 counting calories; **286** coupons; **287** unit pricing; **288–289** food labels; **310–311** temperatures; **315** measuring tools; **322–324** measurement; **334** increasing/decreasing recipes; **380** restaurant tipping

Leadership and Citizenship

274 helping those with eating disorders; **278, 301** food shopping for family; **313** helping in emergencies; **357** cooperating with group; **370** serving the elderly

SKILLS

Unit 1

About You

Chapter 1

Looking at You

Chapter Organization

Chapter Vocabulary

self-concept (p. 3)
adolescence (p. 3)
personality (p. 4)
heredity (p. 6)
environment (p. 6)
values (p. 7)
goals (p. 7)
stereotype (p. 12)
standards (p. 14)
ethics (p. 14)
peers (p. 15)
impulse (p. 17)

Chapter Objectives

After reading this chapter, students should be able to:

1. Explain what individual characteristics make up their personality. (1.1)
2. Explain how their self-concept is shaped by their values and goals. (1.1)
3. Explain what they can do to build a strong self-concept. (1.1)
4. Explain the kinds of changes they experience as adolescents. (1.2)
5. Explain the roles they play in life. (1.2)
6. Describe the important characteristics of a mature person. (1.2)
7. Explain how their standards of behavior help to develop character and strengthen self-concept. (1.2)
8. Describe the various ways to reach a decision. (1.3)
9. Describe the factors that influence their own decisions. (1.3)

10. Explain the importance of knowing and following the steps in the decision-making process. (1.3)

Program Resources

Student text pages 2–23
Teacher's Resource Book
    Skill/Development Worksheet 1
    Laboratory/Application Worksheet 1
    Reinforcement Worksheet 1
    Enrichment Worksheet 1
    Transparency Master 1
    Information Master 1
    Chapter 1 Test

Teaching Suggestions

The dots represent skill levels required to answer each question or complete each activity:
  •requires recall and comprehension
  ••requires application and analysis
  •••requires synthesis and evaluation

Into the Chapter

•Creating a Word-and-Picture Album

Ask students to put together picture albums of themselves from infancy to the present. They can use family photos, school pictures, drawings, or a combination of these. Above each picture, have them write short captions, ranging in length from one word to two or three sentences, that characterize their personalities at that age. Have them compare the various photos in their albums to see if they maintained the same personality traits at different stages of development. Then ask volunteers to read the captions in their albums, and have the group discuss whether their personality traits at earlier stages of development match traits of their personalities at the present time.

Other Activities

••• 1. **Categorizing Personality Traits** Ask students to choose a public figure they admire, such as a politician, a famous musician, or an athlete. Have them make a list of the personality traits that helped to make that person a success. Then have students choose one important trait and write a paragraph describing a situation in which that trait was used to advantage.

• 2. **Building a Positive Self-concept** Have students find a short story or article about a teenager who overcomes a social, emotional, or physical handicap to achieve a personal goal. Have them summarize their selections for the class and then discuss the way that building a positive self-concept helped the teen to succeed.

••• 3. **Overcoming Prejudice** Have students briefly discuss why some adults stereotype all teenagers as loud, self-centered, aggressive people, and have students think of ways teens can help overcome this prejudice. Then divide the class into small groups and have each group present a skit in which teens behave in a way that changes an adult's stereotypical picture of teens.

•• 4. **Coping with Peer Pressure** Ask students to think of ways to solve the following problem: Kate meets a new friend whom she likes very much. However, her friend wants her to go with him to beer-drinking parties that Kate does not want to go to. Discuss whether Kate can find a way to maintain the friendship without lowering her own standards of behavior.

••• 5. **Decision Making** Have the class think of three or four specific situations in which a teen must make a difficult decision. List each one on the board. Then have each student choose one situation and write a solution to the problem, using the six steps in the decision-making process.

Learning to Manage (p. 21)

Concepts

■ the desire of adolescents to be accepted
■ the difficulty of change
■ determining personal skills and strengths
■ strategies for making new friends

Discussion Questions

1. Why does it feel so important to many teens to fit in when beginning at a new school?
2. What can you do to help overcome feelings of insecurity in a new environment?
3. What positive actions can a teen take to make himself or herself noticed?
4. Picture yourself at a lunch table with a group of students you have just met. What would you talk about? How would you act?
5. What actions could you take to make a newcomer at your school feel welcome?

Answers to Preceding Questions

Answers will vary but will probably include the following ideas.
1. They feel lonely and miss their old school and former friends; they are unsure that they will fit into their new school and community.
2. You can focus on your special abilities and talents and find ways to share them with others; you can get involved in activities you enjoy; and you can get help from others including family and friends.
3. To receive positive notice a teen can be friendly, join in activities that he or she can do well, get help from others in meeting new friends, participate in a wide variety of en-

deavors, learn to speak up, and express interest in others.
4. Choose a subject that you think most of them are interested in, listen carefully to what others say, ask questions, be enthusiastic without dominating the conversation.
5. Introduce yourself, be friendly and show your interest in the newcomer, introduce him or her to other students, and include the newcomer in a social event or other activity.

Answers to Questions (p. 21)

Answers will vary but will probably include the following ideas.
1. Personal characteristics that would help people make new friends include being friendly, being active in joining new groups, and having a positive self-concept.
2. Specific organizations can be found through the school counselor, community centers, religious organizations, and the yellow pages section of the telephone book.
3. Answers will include a variety of changes in family life, moves to a new community, peer relationships, and situations at school or at a part-time job.

Leadership and Citizenship

Positive Peer Pressure (page 16)

Peer pressure is always a serious issue for adolescents. We, as adults, cannot protect teens from the strong social pressures exerted by their peers, but we can help them develop attitudes and skills that will make it easier for them to cope with these pressures.

A goal of this chapter and its theme feature is to help students learn these concepts and skills: self-understanding, building a strong self-concept, developing positive roles and responsibilities, and learning to make deliberate, thoughtful decisions. There are also positive ways that teens can make appropriate choices even when these choices are unpopular with their peers, and teens can provide positive role models for their peers and for younger children.

Discussion Questions

1. Why do you think peer pressure is so difficult to deal with?
2. What can you do to resist negative peer pressure?
3. Why is it important to make your own decisions, rather than always going along with what your friends decide?
4. What can you do to provide a positive role model for younger students at your school?

Answers to Preceding Questions

Answers will vary but will probably include the following ideas.

1. All of us want to feel we belong; being part of a group makes us feel secure.
2. You can set your own goals and make your own decisions based on what is best for you. You can develop a strong self-concept and accept responsibility for your own actions.
3. What is right for someone else may not be right for you. Practicing positive decision-making skills builds self-esteem.
4. You can be sure your own attitudes and actions are positive, and you can then meet with younger students to demonstrate positive ways they can deal with problems such as smoking, drugs, and alcohol. You can join a group of teens that works with younger students, or you can work on a one-to-one basis to help a sibling or younger friend to learn to resist negative peer pressures.

Answers to For Review

Knowing Yourself (p. 9)

1. The various characteristics that form personality are physical, emotional, mental, social, and moral.

2. Environment can affect personality by changing hereditary characteristics. For example, exercise and diet can strengthen muscles that were weak through heredity.
3. Understanding needs, values, and goals helps in forming a strong self-concept.
4. To form a strong self-concept, it is important to use the following steps: 1) think positively about yourself; 2) accept personality traits that cannot be changed; 3) focus on abilities and talents; 4) learn from actions; 5) accept praise; 6) be active; 7) ask help when necessary; 8) work to change behavior that interferes with self-concept and relationships with others.

Growing and Changing (p. 15)

1. Teenagers experience a rapidly changing world and the need to adjust to new experiences, new people, and personal physical growth.
2. In order to establish which roles are most important and in what order various tasks should be done, it is absolutely essential to set priorities.
3. A mature person accepts responsibility, understands personal strengths and weaknesses, has a strong self-concept, makes decisions, acts independently, and loves and trusts family and friends.
4. What a person stands for is related to character and self-concept by the way he or she acts when called upon to live up to personal standards and feelings of self-worth.

Making Smart Decisions (p. 20)

1. A decision may be reached in the following ways: 1) avoid the problem by letting things happen as they will; 2) follow the example or advice of others; 3) follow impulse; 4) act through habit; 5) base a decision on fear or self-consciousness.

2. The following factors influence decision making: 1) perceptions; for example, the friends you choose can be based on your personal interests and your self-concept; 2) money and time; for example, choosing swimming over skiing because ski equipment is expensive and getting to the slopes takes time, whereas swimming in the community pool is free, and getting to the pool takes only a few minutes; 3) personal values; for example, resisting the temptation to copy a friend's report because your values tell you that it is ethically wrong to do so; 4) outside influences; for example, dressing in a certain way in order to wear almost exactly the same items and to have the same sense of fashion as peers; 5) the law; for example, following school rules for the sake of safety.

3. The six steps toward making a successful decision are 1) identify the problem; 2) consider choices; 3) gather information; 4) examine information and weigh outcomes of various choices; 5) make the decision; 6) evaluate the decision.

Chapter 1 Review

Vocabulary Answers (p. 22)

1. self-concept
2. adolescent
3. personality
4. heredity
5. environment
6. Values
7. goals
8. stereotype
9. ethics
10. peers
11. impulse

Chapter Questions (p. 23)

1. Family members live with you every day and know you very well. Teachers do not spend nearly as much time with you as family members do. They know only that part of your personality that surfaces in class.

2. During adolescence, emotions change rapidly, and moods often shift from one extreme to another. Feelings are easily hurt, and anger often surfaces quickly. An interest in the opposite sex commonly produces confusing feelings.

3. Teens can work with other young people in projects that serve others and that are run by local religious organizations. They might participate in a local cleanup day or help to raise funds for a cause in which they believe. Students might also cite projects such as a child care program that operates during religious services or a visiting program that allows teens to spend some time with the residents of a local nursing home.

4. Weak muscles can be strengthened through exercise and a healthy diet.

5. Answers will depend upon the perceived needs of individual students. Many students will probably mention the need to feel wanted by family and friends and the need to have one's ideas and feelings accepted and approved by others. Students should be able to explain why the need identified is important to them.

6. Many students will probably mention that they moved at one time or another and had to adjust to a new neighborhood and new friends. Many students might also mention a family change—unemployment, death, or a divorce—that forced them to adjust to new circumstances or new people. Students should be able to describe the adjustments that they had to make.

7. During adolescence, teens gradually take on responsibility for their actions.

They are moving toward maturity. A mature person has the ability to make decisions and act independently.

8. Students might mention the roles of son or daughter, brother or sister in the home, student and member of a team at school, and employee in the outside world. Students may also mention various other roles, such as church member, babysitter, and trusted friend.

9. Learning to avoid stereotyping allows a person to broaden his or her understanding of people. People are accepted more easily and their personalities understood over time. They are not prejudged.

10. No one can be totally independent. Everyone needs to share things with family and friends in an environment of trust, acceptance, respect, and love.

11. A person should have a strong moral character because a strong moral character demonstrates to the self and to others that the individual respects the rights of others and stands by his or her moral code.

12. Students are likely to name various signs, such as the willingness to make decisions, the willingness to be responsible for one's actions, the willingness to be judged for acting responsibly, and the ability to judge one's own strengths and weaknesses.

13. A practical method that can be used to set time priorities is to divide one's time between school, home chores, and leisure time. It is useful to make a schedule to be sure that too much time is not devoted to one type of an activity at the expense of others.

14. Your family is so emotionally involved in the decisions that you make because they care about you deeply and want to be sure that you make decisions that are in your best interests.

15. If you make a bad decision, it is important to note where you went wrong. This information will allow you to approach a similar problem in a new way the next time.

Skill Activities

1. Students who role-play each conflict should be given time to prepare at least the broad outline of what they intend to say. The more time you give for careful preparation, the more likely your students will be to surface fundamental issues in their role-playing. Guided preparation, accompanied by some feedback from you, can enhance most role-playing activities. Be sure that students review the decision-making model before they begin. You might want students to identify recent conflicts that they have had for additional role-playing opportunities.

2. Remind students that creativity is necessary to construct a display that accurately represents an individual's self-assessment. This is especially true of the section that expresses personality. You might want to ask students to find at least five pictures that represent aspects of personality. If students experience difficulty getting started on this section, you might point out that pictures of animals can be used to express personality traits. Pictures of people expressing various emotions are also suitable. Ask students not to place their names on their displays. Displays could then be circulated, and students could guess who constructed each display.

3. You might want to establish a set number of coupons to be prepared. Ten would be a manageable number. You might also want students to focus on a particular group in the community that really needs help, such as the elderly. Before students prepare cards, you might want to conduct a class discussion of the kinds of services that the elderly could use in your community.

Chapter 2

Managing Your Life

Chapter Organization

Chapter Vocabulary

management (p. 25)
human resources (p. 25)
nonhuman resources (p. 25)
short-term goal (p. 26)
long-term goal (p. 26)
process (p. 27)
trade-off (p. 29)

Chapter Objectives

After reading this chapter, students should be able to:

1. Explain the resources they can use in life management. (2.1)
2. Explain how the six steps of the management process help make projects easier. (2.1)
3. Explain how time is a very important resource. (2.2)
4. Explain how the management process helps in organizing time. (2.2)
5. Describe how the management process helps in planning activities and leisure. (2.2)
6. Explain the importance of using class time well. (2.3)
7. Describe how to take good class notes. (2.3)
8. Explain how study skills help them to learn more effectively. (2.3)

Program Resources

Student text pages 24–43
Teacher's Resource Book
Skill/Development Worksheet 2
Laboratory/Application Worksheet 2
Reinforcement Worksheet 2
Enrichment Worksheet 2
Transparency Master 2
Information Master 2
Chapter 2 Test

Teaching Suggestions

The dots represent skill levels required to answer each question or complete each activity:
•requires recall and comprehension
••requires application and analysis
•••requires synthesis and evaluation

Into the Chapter

••**Managing a Day of Leisure** Ask students to imagine that a research company is surveying how teens like to spend their leisure time. They will pay each teenager in the study one hundred dollars plus all expenses if she or he will spend

12 continuous hours on a minimum of five activities plus the time necessary to get to and from the various activities and time for at least two meals. There is no limit on the amount that can be spent. Have students plan their 12-hour day of leisure and then compare the activities they chose and the amount of time they would devote to each.

Other Activities

•• 1. **Studying Time Management** Have students interview busy adults about the way they organize their time on a typical work day. Have each student make a chart labeled with the kind of work the person interviewed does. The chart should show how much time is spent on the job, at meals, sleeping, doing household chores, and participating in leisure activities. Have students compare and discuss their charts, noting that people spend their time differently, depending on the work they do and on their lifestyle.

••• 2. **Managing Study Time** Discuss the importance of scheduling a time for doing homework when there are no interruptions from phone calls. Point out that friends often resent being told they must call back when they are eager to talk, and brainstorm ways to resolve this problem. Then have students work in pairs to role-play situations in which they schedule times for homework and times for phone calls and then explain this to friends.

• 3. **Recognizing the Importance of Note-taking** Have students perform an experiment to demonstrate the importance of taking notes when listening to detailed information that they want to retain. Prepare two similar sets of complicated directions for one thing, such as a complex recipe. First have the students try to retain the directions you read to them without writing anything down. Have them recall what they remember and write it on the board. Then have them take notes while listening to the second set of directions. Have them compare their notes with the sketchy notes on the board.

••• 4. **Demonstrating How the Management Process Works** Have the class name four or five famous people in history that they are all familiar with. Tell them they are going to write a class story about one of them, and have them vote on the one they wish to write about. Have them identify the goal that person achieved and research the resources he or she needed to achieve the goal. After they have researched details of how their subject adjusted and carried out the plan for reaching the goal, have the class dictate a story based on the six steps in the management process.

Learning to Manage (p. 41)

Concepts

■ planning the effective use of time
■ using strategies for organizing time

Discussion Questions

1. Steve told Joel that he would explain how to manage after soccer practice and not before. What does that tell you about Steve and his ability to manage time?
2. When marking a calendar with scheduled events, why is it a good idea to mark the amount of time each takes?
3. Would Steve's method of management be as useful during the summer months as it is during the school months?
4. Is it better to schedule large chunks of time for homework, half-hour periods each day, or a combination of these? Give reasons for your answer.

5. Describe a trade-off that Joel might make in his schedule to allow time for both work and soccer, besides the one Steve used.

Answers to Preceding Questions

Answers will vary but will probably include the following ideas.

1. Steve is an organized person. He wants to be at soccer practice on time. He knows that the best time to explain his system to Joel is while the two of them are walking home.
2. If events are marked with the hours they are scheduled, it is easier to know how much time can be allotted to other activities.
3. Steve's method of management would be just as useful during the summer months. It would allow him to schedule work time and leisure time efficiently.
4. Uninterrupted periods of two hours or more are important when sustained work on a paper or test is necessary, but shorter periods of time can also be useful.
5. Joel might be able to schedule work at a time when he is not at soccer; he might take time off during soccer season and make it up later.

Answers to Questions (p. 41)

Answers will vary but will probably include the following ideas.

1. Joel should apply the management process to meet his goal of managing his time better. He should follow Steve's suggestion for scheduling his time on a calendar and making trade-offs to fit all important items into his schedule.
2. Joel's time management plan will probably work if he is realistic about the plan that he creates and if he is serious about his commitment to it.
3. If students have difficulty with this question, have them focus on a common time management problem such as writing a long paper or completing a major science or social studies project.

Technology

Home Efficiency (page 28)

The time management process can be used to increase efficiency in any endeavor, including home chores and personal care. The report on the way the Gilbreths—a pair of efficiency experts—organized their home and their family of twelve children provides some important concepts in time management. These include the importance of time and motion study techniques to discover the most efficient way to perform simple home chores. The concept of saving time by accomplishing two tasks at the same time is also introduced.

Discussion Questions

1. What kind of home chore lends itself to dovetailing with another activity? Give three examples.
2. Name three ways to prepare a work space to make your study time more efficient.
3. Why is it important to plan an entire project before you begin?

Answers to Preceding Questions

Answers will vary but will probably include the following ideas.

1. A chore that is performed somewhat mechanically can be dovetailed with an activity that takes mental effort but does not require use of the hands. Examples are ironing, sewing, and washing that can be combined with listening to the weather report, giving someone information, and reviewing material mentally.
2. Before beginning to study, adjust the lighting, sharpen pencils, and collect paper, books, and other materials.
3. Planning a project in advance allows you to schedule time, collect needed materials, and gather necessary information so that you are not repeatedly interrupted once you begin working on the project.

Answers to For Review

What Is Management? (p. 29)

1. Some resources that can be used in life management are *human,* such as knowledge, skills, friends, relatives, neighbors, and personal health, feelings, and attitudes. Other resources are *nonhuman,* such as money, time, food, clothing, and community resources.
2. The following is a brief description of the management process: 1) Set your goal, that is, decide what needs to be accomplished. 2) Analyze resources. Check the resources at hand, look through sources to get ideas, line up helpers, and get supplies. 3) Make a plan and assign resources. Decide what is to be done, ask for helpers, decide how to finance the project. 4) Make adjustments. Revise the plan according to the money and help that is actually available. 5) Carry out the plan. Do what has been planned. 6) Evaluate the results. When the project is finished, review the plan. Find out what parts of the plan worked and search for remedies for parts that did not work.

Managing Time (p. 34)

1. Time is an important resource because it is limited. Within given amounts of time there are chores, studies, and leisure activities. Time needs to be budgeted so that people can lead productive and balanced lives.
2. Using the management process helps to organize time on a major project by providing a method for scheduling sufficient time for each part of the project. This avoids rushing to finish and prevents stress.
3. Planning leisure time makes social life more interesting and fun. If leisure is planned, no time is lost worrying about unfinished work.

Managing for Learning (p. 40)

1. Five ways to make the most of class time and improve learning include 1) be prepared; 2) develop listening skills; 3) learn what the teacher expects; 4) speak up in class; 5) take good class notes; 6) use an outline; 7) focus on main ideas; 8) review your notes.
2. Three ways to take good class notes are 1) use an outline; 2) focus on main ideas; 3) review notes after class.
3. Five important study skills are 1) organize study time; 2) find a good place to work; 3) organize study materials; 4) learn to concentrate; 5) think positively.

Chapter 2 Review

Vocabulary Answers (p. 42)

1. human resources
2. short-term goal
3. process
4. trade-off
5. management
6. standards
7. nonhuman resources
8. long-term goals

Chapter Questions (p. 42)

1. The goal is getting to school on time. Resources include an alarm clock set to allow enough time for breakfast and other preparation. The next step would be to make a plan and assign resources. This is likely to include laying out clothing the night before. The fourth step is to make adjustments in the plan. It might not be possible to leave enough time for bathing along with everything else, so that activity might be moved to the night before. The fifth step would be to carry out the plan.

The final step would be to evaluate the plan, noting that part of it that worked and those parts of it that were unsatisfactory. Most students would probably agree that they haven't really been managing the resources needed to get to school on time very well.

2. Health, feelings, and attitudes are human resources. They are characteristics of human beings that help them to live successfully.

3. The purpose of keeping a monthly calendar is to allow you to schedule important events during a month so that your time can be more intelligently managed.

4. A person could put notes for a class speech in order while reciting a memorized passage at the same time. Students might suggest other examples. Make sure that both activities can actually be carried out at the same time.

5. If a student is having trouble solving a homework problem, he or she can take a short break to refresh the mind.

6. Planning leisure time as well as work time is important because it can make social life more interesting and more enjoyable.

7. Listening carefully in class is important because it will save time later when homework must be done. Listening carefully will also make test taking less stressful.

8. It is a good idea to take part in class discussions because taking part will give the teacher a chance to know you as a participating member of the class.

9. When taking class notes, it is important to write down only part of what is said. Notes should be taken in outline form. Ideas should be noted in only a few words. Details should be briefly listed under an appropriate heading. If you try to write down everything, you will lose track of what is being said. The idea is to write down the most important things that are said in class, the things that the teacher emphasizes.

10. It is not a good idea to borrow someone's notes if you have missed a class. Everyone takes notes differently, and you may not be able to follow another person's outline. Try to get the information you missed from the teacher.

Skill Activities

1. You might want to assign one student to the task of recording all of the preparation steps that will be necessary in order to give a successful party. The student assigned could list steps 2, 3, and 4 on the board. As students analyze resources, plan and assign them, and make adjustments, appropriate notes could be made under each step. The final plan could then be recorded and studied during the evaluation.

2. Before you begin this activity, you might want to ask students to think of a story that they want to tell in class. The story should take at least three or four minutes to tell. It should be about a series of events. It could be a summary of a recent television drama or of a movie. After a bit of planning time, you might want to ask for volunteers, or you might want to choose someone to tell a story. If possible, record the story so that the original version can be compared with the last telling. At the end of this activity, you will probably want to make the point that listening is indeed a very difficult skill. People often listen selectively and bring their own experiences to what they hear. Since the chances are very good that the last story will differ markedly from the first story, you might want to repeat this activity after urging students to listen more closely and more carefully.

3. You might want to remind students that an appropriate calendar cannot be hurriedly assembled. In order to construct an accurate

one, students should find out what school activities are planned over the next month. They should also consult with parents to discover what family activities are planned. Such important things as dental appointments should not be overlooked. Friends should also be consulted to determine what social activities have been scheduled. You might want to make the point that monthly calendars can help to manage time only if they are consulted regularly after they are first constructed. It is a good idea to check the calendar once a week so that changes that occur can be noted.

4. You might want to vary this activity somewhat by asking students to identify a subject that they find most difficult to study for. Best subjects can also be identified. Students who need help with particular subjects could then be matched with students who do well in those subjects. The coaches could then identify study skills that they employ to do well in the particular subject.

Chapter 3

Wellness

Chapter Organization

Section 3.1 *Everyday Health (student book page 45)*
What Is Wellness?
Making Healthy Choices
Hygiene and Grooming
Dental Care
Rest and Relaxation

Section 3.2 *Mental Health (student book page 49)*
Developing a Healthy Personality
Dealing with Stress
Emotional Ups and Downs
Depression

Section 3.3 *Managing Health Decisions (student book page 53)*
Regular Health Care
Keeping Health Records

Section 3.4 *Learning About Substance Abuse (student book page 57)*
Substance Abuse
Alcohol
Tobacco
Drugs

Section 3.5 *Emergencies and First Aid (student book page 63)*
Meeting Emergencies

Chapter Vocabulary

wellness (p. 45)
nutrition (p. 45)
hygiene (p. 47)
stress (p. 50)
depression (p. 52)
substance abuse (p. 57)
addiction (p. 57)
alcoholism (p. 58)
drug (p. 61)

Chapter Objectives

After reading this chapter, students should be able to:

1. Explain how diet and exercise contribute to good health. (3.1)
2. Explain the important role of hygiene and grooming. (3.1)
3. Explain how proper dental care contributes to health and appearance. (3.1)

4. Explain the important roles that both rest and relaxation play in maintaining mental and physical health. (3.1)
5. Describe how people's emotional states affect their health. (3.2)
6. Explain ways to deal with stress and sudden mood shifts. (3.2)
7. Explain ways to deal with periods of depression. (3.2)
8. Explain how to stay healthy through regular health care. (3.3)
9. Describe how to ask doctors the right questions to get the most from medical checkups. (3.3)
10. Explain the importance of keeping accurate health records. (3.3)
11. Explain how alcohol can endanger physical and mental health. (3.4)
12. Explain how tobacco can endanger physical and mental health. (3.4)
13. Explain the importance of rules for taking prescription and nonprescription legal drugs. (3.4)
14. Explain how illegal drugs endanger physical and mental health. (3.4)
15. Explain how to react in emergency situations. (3.5)
16. Explain how to help an accident victim until medical help arrives. (3.5)

Program Resources

Student text pages 44–69
Teacher's Resource Book
    Skill/Development Worksheet 3
    Laboratory/Application Worksheet 3
    Reinforcement Worksheet 3
    Enrichment Worksheet 3
    Transparency Master 3
    Information Master 3
    Chapter 3 Test

Teaching Suggestions

The dots represent skill levels required to answer each question or complete each activity:
  •requires recall and comprehension
  ••requires application and analysis
•••requires synthesis and evaluation

Into the Chapter

•**Making Wellness Posters** Have students design a series of posters on various categories of wellness including maintaining a healthy body, good mental health, a balanced diet, a sound hygiene program, a regular exercise program, and regular medical and dental checkups. Assign pairs of students one of the categories. Have them label their posters with the category they are illustrating. Students can draw, paint, or use magazine illustrations for their posters. Display the posters in the classroom.

Other Activities

•• 1. **Researching Fitness Exercises** Divide the class into four groups. Have each group research specific exercises in each of the four main exercise categories: muscular, aerobic, flexibility, and coordination. Have the groups demonstrate the exercises they have found.

• 2. **Recalling Factors in Maintaining Dental Health** Ask students to compose a chart that lists all the important factors that go into maintaining healthy teeth and gums. Remind them to include information on procedures for brushing and flossing teeth regularly, having regular dental checkups, and following safety measures to protect teeth from injury during active sports. The charts should be as specific as possible and may be illustrated.

3. **Maintaining a Schedule That Promotes Wellness** Have students plan a schedule that includes wellness activities. They should plan time for at least a half hour of exercise each day, eight hours of sleep, time to relax over healthy, enjoyable meals, and leisure time to reduce stress. Ask them to include scheduled health activities on the monthly calendar of time management that they developed in Chapter 2.

4. **Recognizing Causes of Mental Stress** Have pairs of students role-play a session between a doctor and a patient who is seeking the cause of recent mental stress. Both the doctor and the patient should carefully examine and discuss the patient's daily habits. Then both should suggest various possible causes.

5. **Avoiding Traffic Accidents** Remind students that one of the major causes of teen injuries and death is traffic accidents. Ask students what they would do when they find that the person who is to take them home from a party is drinking, taking drugs, behaving in a reckless way, or may not be able to drive safely for any reason. List their answers on the board. Then ask each student to write a brief story about the way a teen copes with this situation. Have volunteers share their stories with the class.

Learning to Manage (p. 67)

Concepts

▪ strategies for improving physical fitness
▪ the importance of establishing a regular program of exercise
▪ a high-protein, low-sugar diet increases energy supply
▪ adolescents need a minimum of eight hours sleep a night

Discussion Questions

1. How do you think Rachel's poor physical condition affects her school work? personal attitudes? general appearance?
2. Why does Peg do stretching exercises before she begins to run?
3. Why should junk foods be kept to a minimum in the diet?
4. What happens to your body when you don't get enough sleep?
5. Maintaining a program for good physical fitness is not always easy to do. What suggestions could you make for helping people stick to their physical fitness programs?

Answers to Preceding Questions

Answers will vary but will probably include the following ideas.

1. Physical conditioning affects many aspects of a person's life. Given Rachel's poor physical conditioning and her diet, she probably does not have as much energy for school and other activities as she could have. Being in good physical shape also affects a person's sense of self-esteem. When you know you are in good shape, it helps give you a feeling of self-confidence. It also affects your appearance. It generally improves such things as your posture, the way you walk, and the feeling you give off as a person.
2. Peg limbers up her muscles before submitting them to the stress of running.
3. Junk foods are full of empty calories that do not provide the balance of nutrients the body needs.
4. When you do not get enough sleep, you have very little energy, you may have a headache, and your eyes may be red and irritated.
5. If you plan a training program and write it down, it will remind you to follow the plan you have worked out. By making a schedule you will be sure to allow time to carry out

your program. It also helps some people to maintain their fitness program if they find others who want to join their routine. Finally, find some way to reward yourself for a job well done.

Answers to Questions (p. 67)

Answers will vary but will probably include the following ideas.

1. Peg's plan involves a regular exercise program, a balanced diet, and eight hours of sleep each night.
2. Rachel will use both human and nonhuman resources. She will use the suggestions and companionship of Peg and also of her teammates. She will use the nonhuman resources of time and food to carry out her fitness program and to reach her goal of being in shape.
3. Answers will evaluate individuals' ratings on exercise, diet, sufficient sleep, personal hygiene, and mental health as well as regular medical and dental checkups and avoidance of substance abuse.

Leadership and Citizenship

Volunteering (p. 54)

Teens are often not aware of the acute need in their community for volunteers. In a culture that so often emphasizes self-centered goals and competitive behavior, it is important that the concept of public service be instilled in the formative years. Volunteer work relieves the self-absorption that is characteristic of teens.

You may wish to have a class committee compile a list of local health-related agencies that welcome teen volunteers and post their findings in the classroom.

Discussion Questions

1. How can volunteer work in health-related fields help you explore career possibilities?

2. How should you dress when you volunteer in a hospital or nursing home?
3. Why is personal hygiene especially important when you visit hospital patients?
4. When you work with the ill, the elderly, or with children, how does your own mental attitude affect their response to you?

Answers to Preceding Questions

Answers will vary but will probably include the following ideas.

1. You can find out if you would enjoy working with children, the elderly, or the handicapped; you can talk to professionals in the health field in which you volunteer, you can get firsthand information about the kinds of jobs available in the field.
2. You should dress in comfortable but conservative, neat clothes.
3. Sick people are especially susceptible to diseases that can be transmitted by unwashed hands.
4. They will be cheered up if you are friendly, interested in them, and a good listener. If you are impatient, inattentive, or make them feel inferior, your visit will not be helpful.

Answers to For Review

Everyday Health (p. 49)

1. A balanced diet is the most important part of an active life because the right food in the right amounts provides fuel for daily energy needs.
2. Two kinds of exercises are aerobic exercises, which build up the heart and lungs, and flexibility exercises, which increase the ability to bend, stretch, and twist easily.
3. Five important hygiene and grooming tips are 1) eat a balanced diet for healthy skin; 2) cleanse skin thoroughly to help cure acne; 3)

use sunscreening agents when spending any length of time in the sun; 4) shampoo hair regularly; 5) keep fingernails clean and trimmed.
4. Sugars and starches in the diet will cause plaque to build up.
5. Sleep is necessary for physical and mental health. Lack of sleep can cause nervousness. Lack of sleep generally will also result in irritability.

Mental Health (p. 53)

1. It is important to understand one's own emotions in order to be able to express them in positive ways.
2. Three ways to relieve stress are exercise, relaxation, and setting attainable goals.
3. The best way to help a seriously depressed friend is to give emotional support and to encourage him or her to get help from a trained professional who can deal with depression.

Managing Health Decisions (p. 56)

1. Two major factors that contribute to good health are following a wellness program and getting the right medical care.
2. A family should have health insurance so that it will not have to pay high medical costs itself.
3. Immunization, which is usually given by injection, prevents specific diseases, such as the flu, tuberculosis, or tetanus.
4. To prepare for a visit to the doctor, it is a good idea to make a list of symptoms first. Then reflect on what you have done about them yourself.
5. It is important to keep copies of family health records at all times. This should be done in case the family changes health facilities or in case the records have been misplaced or are hard to obtain.

Substance Abuse (p. 63)

1. Alcohol abuse can cause serious problems, including loss of employment, extreme illness, and the breakdown of family and other relationships.
2. Nonsmokers who breathe the smoke from smokers' cigarettes are at risk for lung and heart disease.
3. Three of the rules to follow regarding medication prescribed by a doctor or sold over the counter are 1) read and follow directions carefully; 2) never take a drug prescribed for someone else; and 3) be sure to tell your doctor if you are taking more than one kind of medicine.
4. The following are examples of some of the extreme changes that take place in the bodies of those who take illegal drugs: smoking marijuana regularly causes greater lung damage than tobacco does; heroin causes heart and lung damage, skin abscesses, a general breakdown of the entire body, and resistance to disease.

Emergencies and First Aid (p. 66)

1. In case of a fire in the home: 1) leave the house immediately; 2) call the fire department from a firebox or a neighbor's home; 3) if there is smoke, crawl on the floor toward an exit; 4) if doors are hot, find another way out.
2. A home first-aid kit should include sterile gauze or cotton and 3 percent hydrogen peroxide.
3. The Heimlich Maneuver is a way of helping a person who is choking. It can be used on anybody over the age of one.
4. Minor burns on a small area can be cooled with ice wrapped in sterile cloth. Cotton or other material that will stick to the burn should not be used.

Chapter 3 Review

Vocabulary Answers (p. 68)

1. Depression
2. drug
3. Addiction
4. hygiene
5. Stress
6. alcoholism
7. substance abuse
8. wellness
9. Nutrition

Chapter Questions (p. 68)

1. The five parts of a long-term wellness program are a healthy diet, sufficient exercise, good hygiene and grooming, proper dental care, and rest and relaxation.

2. A regular exercise program can greatly improve the way a person looks and feels. A regular exercise program also helps to control appetite and body weight by burning excess calories. It develops muscles, too, allowing a person to stand straighter and move more gracefully. Regular exercise also strengthens bones and tones muscles as well as strengthening the heart and lungs. Finally, people who exercise regularly are more relaxed, sleep better, and have more energy.

3. A daily bath or shower can make the skin healthier by removing bacteria that can cause skin problems and unpleasant odors. A balanced diet that includes a lot of green, leafy vegetables and a minimum of sweets and fatty foods can also make the skin healthier. Avoiding too much exposure to the rays of the sun also promotes healthy skin by guarding against premature aging and skin cancer.

4. Before going out in the sun for any length of time, a person should apply a sun-blocking or sunscreening agent in the appropriate strength.

5. A balanced diet helps to ensure healthy teeth and gums. An improper diet causes plaque buildup that can cause gum disease. Sugar and starch promote tooth decay.

6. It is important for you to understand your own emotions because only through understanding them can you learn to control them. Learning to cope with emotional upsets can improve total wellness.

7. A certain amount of stress is good for you because it makes you feel alive and prepares you to meet new challenges. Tension builds up and is then released in positive action.

8. Stress can be caused by tension that builds up when you face an important challenge. Mental stress is caused by a situation that continually makes you tense and anxious. Stress is also caused by physical factors, such as hunger, continual noise, and lack of fresh air, sleep, and exercise.

9. Applying the management process to your life can help reduce stress because it permits you to identify clear goals that you are capable of meeting. It allows you to concentrate on these goals and to stop worrying about things that are outside your control.

10. If you have a disagreement with a friend, it is a good idea to identify ways of resolving the misunderstanding. Be willing to talk over the disagreement. Take a positive approach to resolving the disagreement.

11. It is essential for a person to obtain professional help when that person is seriously depressed for a number of days. When depression lasts this long, a person needs the support of a mental health professional.

12. It is dangerous to use alcohol as a subsititute for facing problems. Although drinking might bring temporary relief, it is never a

solution to loneliness, boredom, or depression.

13. Support organizations include Alcoholics Anonymous (AA), Al-Anon, and Alateen.

14. Three dangerous substances in cigarettes are carbon monoxide, nicotine, and tar.

15. Drugs can destroy relationships, can ruin one's life, and can lead to crime.

Skill Activities

1. Write suggestions and possible ways to handle them on the board. The most typical situations can be acted out. Emphasize the important role that peer pressure plays in most of these situations.

2. You might want to assign students to specific health topics. In addition to requesting booklets on these topics, students could do some additional research.

3. As a variation you might want to ask students to identify types of exercises that they prefer. Students who enjoy similar types of exercises could then be matched to develop a program that both would enjoy.

4. If your community does not have a 911 number for emergencies, make sure that students list the appropriate number for the police and fire departments. Also, be sure that students know the agency that provides ambulance service in your community as well as the phone number to call.

Unit 2

Relationships

Chapter 4

Relating to Others

Chapter Organization

Chapter Vocabulary

communication (p. 73)
sender (p. 73)
message (p. 73)
receiver (p. 73)
feedback (p. 73)
verbal communication (p. 74)
nonverbal communication (p. 74)
body language (p. 74)
prejudice (p. 76)
parliamentary procedure (p. 92)

Chapter Objectives

After reading this chapter, students should be able to:

1. Explain how knowledge of the communication process can help in daily life. (4.1)
2. Explain how to use verbal and nonverbal communication. (4.1)
3. Explain how the ability to express oneself clearly and listen can help in getting along with people. (4.1)
4. Explain how happiness and success depend on how a person relates to others. (4.2)
5. Explain the importance of family. (4.2)
6. Explain how having a wide variety of friendships can enrich life. (4.2)
7. Explain how to build good relationships. (4.2)
8. Explain how to make the change from friendship to a romantic relationships. (4.3)
9. Explain how realistic attitudes toward boy-girl relationships can help avoid dating disappointments. (4.3)
10. Explain how experiences as an adolescent can help in future relationships. (4.3)
11. Explain how to develop relationships within a group. (4.4)
12. Describe ways to become a leader. (4.4)
13. Explain how to improve a community through good citizenship. (4.4)

Program Resources

Student text pages 72–97
Teacher's Resource Book
    Skill/Development Worksheet 4
    Laboratory/Application Worksheet 4
    Reinforcement Worksheet 4
    Enrichment Worksheet 4
    Transparency Master 4
    Information Master 4
    Chapter 4 Test

Teaching Suggestions

The dots represent skill levels required to answer each question or complete each activity:
• requires recall and comprehension
•• requires application and analysis
••• requires synthesis and evaluation

Into the Chapter
•• Finding New Ways to Communicate
Tell students that we communicate with one another in many ways: we speak, we sing, and we express how we feel by our facial expressions and by the way we move our bodies. Yet, there are times when we cannot communicate verbally. Have volunteers role-play the following situation. One person arrives at an airport in a foreign country. He or she does not speak the language, and there is no one who can translate. A friendly person comes to help the stranger. How does he or she communicate his or her need to find an inexpensive hotel and a taxi to get there? You may wish to extend the activity to other situations in which people convey ideas without speaking.

Other Activities

• **1. Giving Verbal Instructions** The outcome of this activity will probably surprise students. Divide the class into pairs. Provide each pair with a piece of string. Partners should sit back-to-back. Then have one partner give step-by-step instructions on how to tie a bow using the string. He or she should not watch the other partner as the instructions are carried out. Discuss the important role nonverbal communication can play in relaying directions.

2. **Communicating Emotions** Have volunteers pantomime the following emotions and have the class guess which is being expressed: excitement, fear, anger, sadness, boredom, and confusion.

3. **Understanding the Meaning of Empathy** Have students check the dictionary for definitions of *empathy* and *sympathy*. Have them discuss the difference and give three examples of each.

4. **Resolving a Problem with a Friend** Ask students to think of typical arguments that arise between two teenagers who are close friends. Discuss ways that the teenagers could apply the management process to help solve their misunderstanding. Then have students write a brief story about how a pair of teenagers resolve a conflict by following the steps of the management process.

Learning to Manage (p. 95)

Concepts

▪ strong emotions can block communication
▪ careful listening promotes communication
▪ placing blame blocks communication
▪ empathy promotes good communication

Discussion Questions

1. Why is it difficult to understand what a person is saying when one is angry?
2. How does being a good listener help solve misunderstandings with a friend?
3. Why is it a good idea to avoid placing blame for misunderstandings?
4. Why is a feeling of empathy so important in close human relationships?
5. What should Sue say to her brother about his having forgotten to give her Joni's phone message?

Answers to Preceding Questions

Answers will vary but will probably include the following ideas:
1. When you are angry, you are concentrating on your anger and shut off what is being said.
2. By listening carefully to a friend's point of view and reasons for behaving in a certain way, you can understand your friend's position.
3. Placing blame causes more anger or hurt feelings without solving the problem.
4. If you can identify with a person and understand what he or she is feeling, you overcome misunderstandings that arise from not getting the message the person was sending.
5. She might explain to her brother how disappointed she was to miss Joni's party, and then ask him if he would write down phone messages in the future.

Answers to Questions (p. 95)

Answers will vary but will probably include the following ideas.
1. It might be best to wait until Sue cooled down and then drop her a note telling her about the value of her friendship.
2. Students will probably say they solved a problem with a friend by apologizing, compromising, explaining, or forgetting about the problem and going on from there.

Careers

Interpreters for the Deaf (page 80)

A career as a sign-language interpreter is based on communication skills; it requires ability in both receiving and sending messages. Have students discuss other skills as well as personality traits that are important in this career. Then point out that a number of careers require the ability to interpret. For example, teachers must translate complicated information into language their students can understand, and lawyers must interpret the law to their clients.

Discussion Questions

1. Why is flexibility necessary in a career of signing for the deaf?
2. What personality traits are important in a career interpreting for the deaf?
3. Describe in what way the communication skill of interpreting is used in three separate careers.

Answers to Preceding Questions

Answers will vary but will probably include the following ideas.

1. You need to be able to adjust to many different kinds of people and to be able to switch from one subject to another.
2. You need to be sensitive to others' feelings, have a strong self-concept, and be able to "think on your feet."
3. Translators work in international business and government; scientists interpret results of experiments in written reports; police interpret what happened at the scene of an accident or a crime.

Answers to For Review

Communication (p. 77)

1. The four elements of communication are sender, message, receiver, and feedback.
2. Sign language is a type of communication because it allows people to communicate through hand gestures. Braille is a form of communication because it is a method by which blind people can read.

3. People should show they are paying attention by responding with positive feedback, by asking questions, by being sensitive to feelings that are being expressed, and by attentive facial expressions and posture.
4. Students may name any three of the following: show respect for others; state your ideas and opinions calmly and clearly; listen carefully to what the other person is saying; ask questions if you don't understand; avoid unfocused criticism; accept responsibility for your own actions and opinions; and work toward a goal of mutual enjoyment, understanding, and trust.

Relationships (p. 86)

1. A strong self-concept enables people to relate well to others and to feel confident.
2. Two basic skills that can help maintain good family relationships are talking with family members and listening to them.
3. To gain the respect of parents, work with them to develop rules. Then follow the rules.
4. Four important elements of a true friendship are mutual understanding, respect, empathy, and good communication.
5. A good example of positive peer pressure is a person's urging his or her friend to work with young children at a community center.

Dating (p. 90)

1. Group dating gives people time to be friends and overcome feelings of shyness.
2. Relationships must be based on reality; otherwise there is bound to be disappointment.
3. Experiences gained during adolescence teach that changing relationships are part of growing and learning.

Community (p. 94)

1. A new person in a neighborhood might join extracurricular clubs, neighborhood clubs, or groups doing volunteer work.

2. Some of the qualities of a good leader are the ability to meet group goals, to involve everyone, to keep order at meetings, and to see that each person has a chance to speak and vote.
3. Some of the rewards of good citizenship are increased maturity and the reinforcement of self-respect.

Chapter 4 Review

Vocabulary Answers (p. 96)

1. communication
2. Parliamentary procedure
3. Verbal communication
4. body language
5. Feedback
6. Nonverbal communication
7. message
8. prejudice
9. sender
10. receiver

Chapter Questions (p. 96)

1. Five types of verbal communication are oral, written, sign language, braille, and vocal communication.
2. A close friend can know that you are sad simply by looking at your slow walk, drooping posture, or sad expression. A close friend can recognize that you are happy by looking at your facial expression. Students should be encouraged to offer additional examples of how body language expresses a friend's feelings or emotions.
3. The relationship between your audience and the way you communicate is one of assessing the proper form of communication for a particular audience. If your audience is a friend, you will probably communicate informally. You will communicate more formally with an acquaintance or a stranger. Watching for feedback from an audience lets a person know whether or not the communication was understood.
4. A person who dresses too casually for a job interview runs the risk of communicating lack of seriousness. Casual clothing is appropriate for relaxing with close friends. It is not appropriate for a formal situation.
5. When you have a disagreement with someone, you must be willing to compromise.
6. Empathy means the willingness to put one's self in another person's place in order to understand and share what that other person is feeling.
7. It is important to compromise in order to resolve a disagreement with a close friend or relative because compromise can preserve the relationship. Compromise means that each person who disagrees accepts some of the issues raised by the other. In this way they can find common ground that is agreeable to both.
8. Three events that cause change in existing family relationships are the arrival of a baby, the arrival of a new step-parent and his or her children, and the absence of a parent in order to take a full-time job outside the home after being in the home for many years.
9. If friends constantly compete with each other, the friendship that they have is no longer comfortable and relaxed. The feelings of security and understanding that are the benefits of friendship might vanish. Friends should encourage each other to do as well as possible. They should not try to outdo each other.
10. A group of friends is made up of people who enjoy each other's company and get along very well together. Entry into the group is open to others with similar interests. A *clique,* on the other hand, is a narrow, exclusive group. People in a clique make themselves feel important by looking down on those who are outside the group.
11. Students should point out that shared interests are more important in a date then physical appearance. They may point

out that physical appearance is a surface quality. It will not take the place of shared thoughts and similar attitudes.

12. Over 90 percent of Americans marry.

13. A *community* is an area in which a person lives. It includes the home, the neighborhood, the school, and the religious organization to which the person belongs. It may include cultural or ethnic groups. Ultimately, a community extends to an entire town or city, state, country, and finally to every part of the world.

14. The role of a leader during a meeting is to keep order and to see to it that the meeting covers all the items that need to be discussed. The leader must see to it that each person who participates has an opportunity to speak and to vote.

15. Courtesy can be shown to others in public places by not blocking doors or exits and by remaining well behaved and quiet so as not to disturb others. Students should be able to suggest various additional activities, such as holding doors open for others and not blocking the views of those who are watching a play or sporting event.

Skill Activities

1. Once various groups have been identified, you might want to focus attention upon each. If it becomes clear that no one in the class has enough information about the group's purpose, a student can be assigned to gather additional information. For organizations whose purposes are understood, individual students might be asked to identify skills that they possess that would be useful to the group.

2. With sufficient preparation time, students should be able to use nonverbal communication to act out each of these terms. Students might be asked to identify other terms that could be acted out in a similar way. Students

might experiment with the following idioms: *run with the ball, get one's act together, egg on one's face, go down the tube,* and *off the wall.*

3. Students should complete this activity with their own families and report results to the class. Perhaps the class can vote on which family project was truly unique for spending the $5,000 prize.

4. You might want to vary this activity somewhat by asking students to write a letter to thank someone for a recent act of kindness or courtesy. You might want to discuss with students beforehand the human relations value of acknowledging a kindness in writing.

5. Students might illustrate their advertisements with pictures from magazines and newspapers. Consider allowing students to use the format of a "Wanted" poster to list the qualities that a friend should have.

Chapter 5

The Family

Chapter Organization

Chapter Vocabulary

family (p. 99)
siblings (p. 99)
nuclear family (p. 99)
extended family (p. 100)
blended family (p. 100)
rural (p. 100)
urban (p. 100)
mobile (p. 101)
economy (p. 102)
inflation (p. 102)
socialized (p. 108)
custody (p. 113)

Chapter Objectives

After reading this chapter, students should be able to:

1. Explain the different kinds of families that make up our society. (5.1)
2. Describe the trends in our society that affect families. (5.1)
3. Explain how an adolescent's role within the family changes. (5.2)
4. Explain how to promote understanding among family members. (5.2)
5. Describe the kinds of changes and stages families go through. (5.3)
6. Explain how parents' lives change when their children have grown. (5.3)
7. Describe how problems are part of family life. (5.4)
8. Explain how to cope with major family crises. (5.4)

Program Resources

Student text pages 98–119
Teacher's Resource Book
   Skill/Development Worksheet 5
   Laboratory/Application Worksheet 5
   Reinforcement Worksheet 5
   Enrichment Worksheet 5
   Transparency Master 5
   Information Master 5
   Chapter 5 Test

Teaching Suggestions

The dots represent skill levels required to answer each question or complete each activity:
 •requires recall and comprehension
 ••requires application and analysis
 •••requires synthesis and evaluation

Into the Chapter

••**Recognizing the Diversity in Families**
Have students make a group collage showing a wide variety of families. First, have the class brainstorm a list of different kinds of families. Write the list on the board. It might include families living in different environments —inner-city, rural, and suburban, single-parent families, childless families, and families with many children. Have students collect magazine and newspaper pictures of different kinds of families and form them into a large collage on butcher paper or poster board. Have students label each picture. Display the collage in the classroom.

Other Activities

••• 1. **Identifying Types of Families** List the following family structures on the board: 1) single-parent, 2) childless, 3) only-child, 4) nuclear family with siblings, 5) blended family with children from both parents' former marriages, and 6) family household that includes a grandparent. Divide the class into six groups and assign one family structure to each group. Have each group compose a list of the advantages of the kind of family they have been assigned. Have the lists presented to the class for discussion and comparison.

•• 2. **Resolving Family Conflicts** Have students name common conflicts that occur between teens and their families. The list might include conflicts over chores, keeping teen's room clean, teen's choice of friends, noise, telephone calls, and teen's showing disrespect for parents. Divide the class into small groups. Ask each group to choose one item to develop into a skit. The skit should present the family conflict and then show how it was resolved. Have the audience discuss whether they agree with the resolution presented in the skit.

• 3. **Finding Examples in Literature** Ask students to find short stories or novels that revolve around a family. Have them use their school library or other public library. Ask them to write a description of the kind of family depicted in a particular story and give an example of the way the family members related to one another. Have volunteers read their summaries to the class and discuss their feelings about the interactions of the family members.

•• 4. **Applying the Management Process** Have each student choose a problem that a teen may face in family life. Have him or her use the management process to help resolve the problem.

••• 5. **Coping with Family Crises** Have students discuss ways to cope with the various family crises discussed in the text, such as divorce, death, or family violence. Then have pairs of students select a family crisis on which to base the following role-play: A teenager talks to a younger sibling to help him or her deal with a family crisis. Have the audience discuss the suggestions expressed in the role-play and add others.

Learning to Manage (p. 117)

Concepts

▪ Meeting needs of an elderly member of the family

▪ Importance of empathy when relating to an elderly family member

▪ Using cooperative problem-solving within a family

Discussion Questions

1. Mark's grandfather was happy to discuss his boredom with Mark, but he might not have wished to do so. Give three reasons why an older person might not want to talk about his or her loneliness with a younger family member.

2. During their conference, Mark's family arranged to have grandfather share their chores. Give three suggestions of ways they might help him find leisure activities and new friends outside the family to help overcome his isolation and boredom.

3. Why might it be unwise of Mark to have asked his grandfather to cook tomorrow's dinner?

4. Suppose that in answer to Mark's question "How's it going?" his grandfather had said he was upset because Mark's loud music made him nervous. What could Mark do to

reestablish a friendly relationship with his grandfather?

5. All of the suggestions made to Mark's grandfather were ways he could help other members of the family. Name two ways Mark could offer to help his grandfather.

Answers to Preceding Questions

Answers will vary but will probably include the following ideas:

1. An older family member may not want to burden the teenager with problems, may be afraid of being misunderstood, or may be embarrassed to talk about private feelings.
2. The family might help him contact community projects for the elderly, introduce him to members of their religious congregation, or give a party to introduce him to friends and neighbors.
3. Mark should check with his mother and other members of the family before arranging for his grandfather to cook dinner or help with shopping.
4. He could apologize and explain he had not realized his music bothered his grandfather. They could cooperate in working out a schedule that included some quiet times and some times when Mark could play his music.
5. Mark could offer to share some leisure time with his grandfather, watching a game on television or walking around the neighborhood. He could do chores for his grandfather such as running errands or bringing books from the library.

Answers to Questions (p. 117)

Answers will vary but will probably include the following ideas.

1. As a result of retiring and growing older, his or her life slows down, and without work, there may be empty hours to fill. Body processes also slow down and there may be

physical problems such as reduced eyesight and hearing loss.
2. A teen could provide companionship and help with errands and chores.
3. Lists of activities and facilities for the elderly can be collected from the yellow pages of the phone book, from public and private social agencies, and from government offices concerned with elderly affairs.

Health and Safety

Children of Alcoholics (p. 112)

The subject of alcoholic parents should be approached with great care since there may be students in the classroom who have alcoholics in their families. They may not wish people outside the family to know about their situation. Great caution should be used so that their privacy is not invaded. Discussion should be kept on a general level, and students should not be required to personalize discussion or written work that is handed in to the teacher. If you sense embarrassment, shift the discussion to a related topic.

Discussion of the problem can be very helpful in making children of alcoholics aware that other teenagers are involved in similar problems and that personal help is available.

Discussion Questions

1. If a friend confided in you that his or her parent was drinking heavily and asked what could be done, what would you suggest?
2. Why do you think children of alcoholics suffer from guilt feelings?
3. Alateen and other self-help groups have proved very effective in helping teenaged children of alcoholics face the problem of an alcoholic parent and in helping them cope with the problem. Why do you think these groups are so successful?

Answers to Preceding Questions

Answers will vary but will probably include the following ideas.

1. Students would do well to suggest that it is not the fault of their friend, but it is very painful for him or her to cope with the problem. Therefore, outside help may be indicated. In addition, students could offer to help their friend find help from an adult trained in working with families of alcoholics. Students might also refer him or her to Al-Anon.
2. Children are so emotionally attached to parents that they feel responsible for a parent's problems or failings. The alcoholic parent may have blamed the child for causing his or her problem with alcohol.
3. Self-help groups such as Alateen are composed of teenagers, all of whom share the same problem, so individuals overcome their embarrassment and sense of guilt. They are also not afraid to express their feelings and tell about their personal problems because they trust that other members will guard their right to privacy and not pass on information about them outside the group.

Answers to For Review

Family and Society (p. 102)

1. A nuclear family consists of a husband and wife and their children, natural or adopted. A blended family consists of families that were once separate but are now combined. Blended families occur when people with children marry and bring their children together into a new family.
2. Inflation lessens a family's buying power, with great rises in the cost of housing, food, clothing, and medical care.

Family and You (p. 107)

1. A child is completely dependent on its parents, whereas an adolescent takes on more and more responsibilities. Parents begin to depend on adolescents for certain things. Attitudes towards brothers and sisters may also change in the adolescent years.
2. Regular meetings help a family to clarify misunderstandings, divide household chores, and support each other.
3. One of the ways to demonstrate caring about older family members is to spend time with them, talking to them and listening to them.

Family Life Cycle (p. 110)

1. The series of changes a family goes through is called the family life cycle.
2. Most often, the family life cycle begins with marriage, continues through childbearing and raising preschoolers, school-age children, and teenagers. Next, the family launches the children into further schooling or jobs. When the children are grown and move away from their parents' home, the parents focus again on their own interests and each other.

Family Crises (p. 116)

1. Families whose members talk over their problems, support and encourage each other, and function well as a group can best cope with a major crisis.
2. Children often feel guilty when parents separate because they imagine that they are to blame for the separation. Parents need to reassure their children that this is not the case.
3. A person who is suffering extreme stress, who has low self-esteem, or who was abused as a child is apt to use violence as a means of solving family conflicts.

Chapter 5 Review

Vocabulary Answers (p. 118)

1. socialized
2. rural
3. mobile
4. family
5. economy
6. custody
7. blended family
8. urban
9. extended family
10. nuclear family
11. siblings
12. Inflation

Chapter Questions (p. 118)

1. Three kinds of families are nuclear, extended, and blended.
2. A rural society is one in which people live on farms. An urban society is one in which most of the population is clustered in and around big cities.
3. In what was basically a rural society, most families actually worked where they lived. These families were self-sufficient. They grew and raised their own food and made their own clothes. All activity was centered at the home. Today, few people work at home. They buy their food at supermarkets and purchase most of their clothes.
4. It is difficult for many extended families to get together today because the society is very mobile. People move frequently and often take jobs far from where they were born. Members of extended families often live at great distances from each other.
5. Inflation might affect a family's decision to buy a new home because during a period of inflation prices rise quickly and lessen a family's buying power. Housing prices in particular rise so quickly that many families cannot afford to buy a home.
6. The eldest child in a family is usually capable and responsible because he or she often helps to care for younger siblings and participates more fully in family decisions.
7. The middle child in a family almost always has parents who are more relaxed than they were with their firstborn child. The middle child often gets to try things earlier than the elder child did. Also, middle children frequently have the pleasant experience of sharing their skills and knowledge with younger children. Students should have little difficulty identifying a fictional middle child who enjoys one or more of the advantages identified.
8. It can be difficult to have an elder sibling who has special skills in music or athletics because people might expect a younger child to have those same skills.
9. You can work toward improving relations with siblings by talking things over with them when disagreements arise. Participating in regular family meetings is a good way to clarify misunderstandings, divide up household chores, and support one another.
10. The role of a single parent is especially difficult because he or she bears total responsibility for the children and must make important decisions alone. Also, a single parent must frequently bear all of the family's financial burdens while running the household and caring for the children.
11. You can show that you care about older family members by giving some of your time to them. You can also run errands for older people who have difficulty getting around. You can also help with some of the more demanding household and yard chores. You can also share a hobby with an older family member and keep him or her informed about your activities. Older relatives who live at greater distances from you would welcome occasional cards and letters.
12. The family life cycle begins with marriage and continues through child-bearing to

raisingpreschoolers,school-agechildren,and teenagers. Then the family launches the children into further schooling or jobs. Finally, the children are grown and move away from the home of their parents. When this occurs, the parents focus again on their own interests and each other.

13. It is important for adolescents to communicate well with their families because when families experience a crisis of some kind, the ability to communicate becomes absolutely necessary. The family must meet together to express their concerns and to offer each other support.

14. You can help out during a family crisis by talking over problems with other family members and by offering encouragement and support to the other family members.

15. You should explain the death of a family member to the children in that family in a very gentle and simple way that they can understand. It is also important to be truthful and straightforward.

Skill Activities

1. You might want to ask students to report the results of the discussion that followed the show to the rest of the class. You might also want students to discuss the approach that such shows take to the family, paying particular attention to how realistic such shows are.

2. Students should report their findings in class. You might want to assign students to talk to specific older age groups. It would be interesting to get the views of older people who lived their teenage years in the 1930s, 1940s, 1950s, and 1960s. Students could discuss and compare the responses of the various groups. It would be particularly interesting to compare the five things that each group thinks are most different about teenage life today.

3. You might consider making this a whole-class activity. Specific students could be assigned to prepare the meal. Others could handle other arrangements, such as setting up a time for the meal and handling the transportation of class members. Students should discuss their experiences after the event.

4. You might want students to gather information about all of the groups in your community that offer family support services. The specific responsibilities of each group could be explained in some detail, resulting in a comprehensive "Family Stress Directory."

Chapter 6

Child Development & Parenting

Chapter Organization

Chapter Vocabulary

prenatal stage (p. 121)
embryo (p. 121)
fetus (p. 121)
developmental tasks (p. 123)
pattern (p. 123)
physical development (p. 123)
mental development (p. 123)
social development (p. 123)
reflexes (p. 124)
discipline (p. 129)
immunization (p. 131)

Chapter Objectives

After reading this chapter, students should be able to:

1. Explain the importance of proper diet and medical care for a pregnant woman. (6.1)
2. Describe how children develop mentally and socially, as well as physically. (6.1)
3. Describe the rapid growth that occurs during the first year of life. (6.1)
4. Explain the important roles and responsibilities of parents. (6.2)
5. Describe the emotional, physical, and mental needs of children. (6.2)
6. Describe the steps involved in being a successful babysitter. (6.3)
7. Explain the basic needs of children who are cared for by a babysitter. (6.3)
8. Explain how to deal with different kinds of children when babysitting. (6.3)

Program Resources

Student text pages 120–143
Teacher's Resource Book
    Skill/Development Worksheet 6
    Laboratory/Application Worksheet 6
    Reinforcement Worksheet 6
    Enrichment Worksheet 6
    Transparency Master 6
    Information Master 6
    Chapter 6 Test

Teaching Suggestions

The dots represent skill levels required to answer each question or complete each activity:
 •requires recall and comprehension
 ••requires application and analysis
•••requires synthesis and evaluation

Into the Chapter

•**Building Awareness of Stages of Child Development Through Playthings** Collect eight or ten toys, story books, and simple games that are appropriate for three stages of early childhood development: infant, toddler, and preschooler. Divide the class into small groups and assign one item to each group. Have each group identify the age at which the item will be most appreciated and whether or not it is safe for that age group. Ask each group to identify ways their item promotes the physical, mental, or emotional development of a child. Have the groups present their findings.

Other Activities

•• 1. **Researching and Applying Facts on Childhood Development** Have students make an Early Childhood chart. In a column on the left, list the six stages of development: 1) prenatal; 2) birth to three months; 3) three to nine months; 4) nine months to a year; 5) toddlers (one to three years); and 6) preschoolers (three to five years). The following categories should be listed horizontally across the top of the chart: 1) physical; 2) mental; 3) emotional; and 4) social. Horizontal and vertical lines should be drawn to form a box for each stage/category. Assign each box to a group of students who will gather facts about their assignment, compile them, and list them in the appropriate box. Have students use the chart to study and compare various stages of development.

2. Evaluating Parenting Have each student compile a two-column list of the satisfactions and the sacrifices of parenting. Have them compare and discuss their lists. Then have them write a brief essay on whether they plan to have children when they are adults.

3. Practicing Communication and Child Guidance Skills Have the class discuss ways to deal with aggressive young children for whom they are babysitting. Then have pairs of students role-play how a teen should deal with a child who intentionally misbehaves or refuses to obey. One of each pair should play the babysitter and the other partner the part of the child.

Learning to Manage (p. 141)

Concepts

- the interests of young children change quickly
- children respond well to activities that interest them
- babysitters should learn which activities interest children at different ages
- many interesting projects can be made from materials found around the home

Discussion Questions

1. Why may children be unhappy today doing activities that they and their babysitter enjoyed a few months ago?
2. What are the advantages of taking part in the favorite activities of the children for whom one babysits?
3. Why would three children in the same family each want to do something different?
4. What will Mike and Bobby probably do together the next time Mike babysits?
5. How can a babysitter who does not know what a youngster likes to do find out what interests that child?

Answers to Preceding Questions

1. They may have matured physically or mentally during that time and therefore find the activity less challenging.
2. Children who are engaged in a pleasurable activity are interested and happy. The day is, therefore, fun for both child and babysitter.
3. Each child is a different age, a different level of maturity. Each has different interests.
4. They will probably do something Mike learned in FHA: make hand puppets, play with play dough, or make a spaceship.
5. The babysitter can ask the parents or the child what the child likes to do.

Answers to Questions (p. 141)

Answers will vary but will probably include the following ideas.

1. Get information from friends who have young brothers or sisters or who babysit. Ask questions of parents. Take courses in child care. Join youth groups such as Future Homemakers of America or 4-H. Read articles and books about child care.
2. (1) **Play time.** Help child get used to absence of parents. Have child show his or her toys and games. Play for a while with the child until he or she feels at ease.
   (2) **Learning time.** Teach the child something new about birds, flowers, leaves, houses, workers, etc.
   (3) **Activity time.** Take the child for a walk. Identify objects previously discussed.
   (4) **Singing time.** Sing favorite songs with the child. Have the child act out a song or clap its rhythm.
   (5) **Lunch time.** Serve something nutritious that the child likes to eat.
   (6) **Story time.** Read the child a story about birds, flowers, etc. Make it a calm and soothing period.
   (7) **Nap time.** Have the child take a nap.
   (8) **Outdoor fun time.** Play on the swings and slides at the playground.

(9) **Indoor fun time.** Tell jokes or riddles; play "Simon Says" or simple board games.

(10) **TV time.** Watch television with the child. (Make sure it is a program of the parents' choice.) Follow that with quiet time before the parents' arrival.

(11) **Parents' time.** Greet the parents. Relay any messages. Let the child tell them the day's activities. Praise the child for his or her accomplishments.

Careers

Parenting as a Career (page 130)

Parenting is rarely looked upon as a career, or a profession, or a calling. Because of the obvious importance of parenting, however, it is most appropriate to consider it as a career that demands great skill, plenty of knowledge, careful and constant attention, and, perhaps most of all, devotion.

Students are very familiar with the importance of careers in people's lives. They have been told for many years that their careers will occupy their lives and provide them with challenges and rewards. This theme feature is designed to emphasize the importance of parenting by viewing it as a career. Throughout the chapter this importance is continually made clear by demonstrating the indispensable role of the parent. This feature draws greater attention to that role by clearly identifying the many skills that are needed to succeed as a parent. Few careers actually demand so many varied skills.

A discussion of "Parenting as a Career" can help students appreciate the challenging and demanding role of parenting.

Discussion Questions

1. People prepare for most careers by completing a training program of some kind. How can people prepare for the career of parenting?
2. People usually retire at the end of their careers. Do parents ever retire?
3. People who have a career are paid for their work with money. How are parents paid?

Answers to Preceding Questions

Answers will vary but will probably include the following ideas.

1. People can prepare themselves for the career of parenting in a class such as Home Economics, where they can learn about the stages of development in children and the responsibilities of parents. Another way that they can prepare themselves is by closely observing their own parents. A third way that they can prepare is by gradually accepting some of the parents' responsibilities by guiding and caring for younger brothers and sisters.
2. Although certain responsibilities of parents come to an end at some point, no one ever really retires from parenting. No matter how old the children become, parents continue to express love and affection and give guidance and advice.
3. While parents are not paid a salary for their careers, they are paid in satisfaction at all stages of development, including when their children become mature and productive members of society. They are also paid in satisfaction when their children become parents themselves.

Answers to For Review

Stages of Development (p. 127)

1. Three of the important guidelines for a healthy pregnancy are 1) eat a balanced diet; 2) maintain the correct weight gain; and 3) follow a moderate exercise program.
2. Two developmental tasks of an infant are sitting up and standing.
3. During the first year of life, most babies

learn to move around by themselves; they usually triple their birth weight; and their mental and social development advances very rapidly.

Parenting (p. 135)

1. The three major responsibilities of parents are meeting the physical, mental, and emotional needs of their children.
2. A child's self-concept is built on awareness of the acceptance and love offered by his or her family.
3. The three basic physical needs of a child are correct diet, clothing, and enough sleep and exercise.

Babysitting (p. 140)

1. Three of the points to establish before accepting a babysitting job are parental permission to take the job, what the duties will be, and how much the job pays.
2. The major responsibilities of a babysitter are being sure that the children are safe and that their basic needs are met.
3. It is best to respond to an aggressive child by remaining calm and firm, then distracting the child with a game or an activity.

Chapter 6 Review

Vocabulary Answers (p. 142)

1. reflexes
2. pattern
3. prenatal stage
4. Immunization
5. Physical development
6. Discipline
7. mental development
8. embryo
9. Social development
10. Developmental tasks
11. fetus

Chapter Questions (p. 142)

1. A nutritionally balanced diet is important because a developing fetus gets all its nutrients from what the mother eats.
2. A pregnant woman's smoking is extremely harmful to the fetus. Tobacco contains nicotine and carbon monoxide, which are carried to the baby through the bloodstream.
3. Young children learn developmental tasks by watching other people. They pattern, or model, their behavior on what they observe others doing. They also figure things out for themselves by experimenting.
4. Language is important to a child's development because mental development involves the ability to understand language. Most human thoughts are formed in words.
5. Newborn babies cry to express the fact that they are experiencing a problem of some kind. They may be hungry, hot, cold, tired, or in pain. The newborn may also simply be wet, and uncomfortable as a result.
6. Many students will probably say that the most frustrating thing about being a toddler is the desire to be independent along with the inability to accomplish the desired task. Students may mention other frustrations, such as a toddler's desire to speak before being able to form sentences. Students should be able to offer an explanation for any answer. Many students will probably say that the most frustrating thing about taking care of toddlers is their constant desire to explore and their getting into trouble when they do so.
7. Preschoolers ask so many questions because their mental development is advancing rapidly. At the same time, their language ability is increasing greatly.
8. It is extremely important to read stories to

preschoolers because the reading teaches them the joys of reading and prepares them to read themselves. Reading to children assists their mental development and encourages them to use their imaginations.

9. Most students will probably say that the greatest emotional need of a child is the need for affection, love, and acceptance. These students will probably point out that the child's greatest emotional need is the same as an adolescent's greatest emotional need. People of all ages need affection, love, and acceptance. Other answers are acceptable provided that they are explained.

10. Proper diet is important to babies and young children because what they eat in their first few years will significantly affect their health for the rest of their lives. Children grow so fast that an improper diet for even a short period of time can prevent bones, muscles, and vital organs from developing correctly. Insufficient nutrients can also affect a child's mental development.

11. Three household items that can be dangerous to children are cleaning materials, medicines, and cosmetics. All of these items should be stored in a place where children cannot reach them.

12. Many students will probably say that the most important way to stimulate a child's mental development is to provide the child with a variety of things to experience, such as safe toys in various interesting shapes and colors. These items provide a variety of experiences for a young child. Other answers will be acceptable provided that they are explained.

13. If the telephone rings while you are taking care of a small child, you should see that the child is safe before answering it. If you are watching a small, active child, you should take the child with you when you answer the telephone.

14. You should comfort a child who is crying because his or her parents have gone out by

drawing the child's attention to something of interest. You might, for example, draw a funny picture and ask the child to guess what you are drawing.

15. Children aged between three and six are rather coordinated and are very imaginative as well. Therefore, activities such as throwing and catching a large ball, games such as "Follow the Leader" and "London Bridge," and activities that involve dancing, singing, and skipping would be most appropriate. This age group also enjoys drawing, painting, and working with clay. Imaginative activities such as role-playing, dressing up, and storytelling would also be enjoyable. These children also enjoy playing with toy cars and trucks and with dolls and puppets. Students might propose other activities.

Skill Activities

1. Students might experiment with forming the dough into various shapes. They may then report to the class on the shapes that were most appealing to children.

2. Before students begin to list activities, you might want them to explain what kinds of activities would be most appropriate for the age group. As activities are listed, students who have had experience using them with the age group might comment on their effectiveness. As a class project, you might want to consider having students compile a "Babysitter's Survival Guide." The guide might list and explain various activities that have been successfully used with various age groups.

3. Consider asking students to bring their Babysitter Information Sheets to class. The class as a whole could then study the individual sheets and develop a single comprehensive sheet that could be used by any student who accepts babysitting jobs. The finished sheet could be presented to parents to be completed before they leave the house. The

sheet would then contain the vital and essential information that every babysitter should have.

4. You might want to assign students to observe specific age groups at play. The class discussion could center on the activities that all groups seemed to enjoy and the activities that appealed to only one age group.

Unit 3

Resource Management

Chapter 7

Careers

Chapter Organization

Chapter Vocabulary

Chapter Objectives

After reading this chapter, students should be able to:

1. Explain why people need and want to work. (7.1)
2. Describe ways to select the right career. (7.1)
3. Explain how to get information about various fields of work. (7.1)
4. Explain what steps they can take now to plan a future career. (7.2)
5. Describe the kind of training and education their future career requires. (7.2)
6. Explain the careful planning needed for

balancing a career with family responsibilities. (7.2)

7. Explain how to find out where there are job openings in their fields of interest. (7.3)
8. Describe the steps involved in applying for a job. (7.3)
9. Explain how to make the right start in a new job. (7.3)

Program Resources

Student text pages 146–165
Teacher's Resource Book
    Skill/Development Worksheet 7
    Laboratory/Application Worksheet 7
    Reinforcement Worksheet 7
    Enrichment Worksheet 7
    Transparency Master 7
    Information Master 7
    Chapter 7 Test

Teaching Suggestions

The dots represent skill levels required to answer each question or complete each activity:
•requires recall and comprehension
••requires application and analysis
•••requires synthesis and evaluation

Into the Chapter

•Creating "A World of Careers" Collage Have students make a collage using magazine illustrations of people working at a variety of jobs. Suggest that they include pictures of unusual careers—circus performer, marine biologist, or deep-sea diver, for example—as well as more ordinary jobs such as police officer or salesperson. When the collage is complete, discuss some of the reasons for choosing the pictured careers.

Other Activities

•• **1. Categorizing Career Choices** Have students brainstorm a list of as many careers as they can think of and write them on the board. Next have students form the list of careers into a series of job clusters. Select eight or nine job clusters and form a group of students to work on each cluster. Have the groups research the skills, training, and education needed to get an entry level job and find out what the chances are for advancement in various jobs within the cluster. Have each group report its findings to the class.

••• **2. Writing a Story** Have students write a one-page story about an elderly person who looks back over a long career. Ask the person to describe the kind of work he or she did and tell about early failures and successes. Some students may choose to focus on one particular episode in their character's job history while others may enjoy creating an entire history, perhaps also providing the visual aid of a timeline.

•• **3. Researching a Career** Have each student make an in-depth study of a career that particularly interests her or him. Have students consider the skills, aptitudes, and personality traits that are needed in the field they have chosen. They should research the availability of jobs in the field and the training and education required. They should also consider the restrictions of the career they are considering, such as long hours, few chances for advancement, physical hazards of the work, and geographic limitations. Have students present a brief report of their findings, either orally or in writing.

Learning to Manage (p. 163)

Concepts

■ people are a good source of information about their jobs

■ chefs, nutritionists, interior decorators, child care workers, and others can supply information about Home Economics jobs

■ speakers who know what questions a group would like answered, give the most useful information

■ many people are eager to share information about their work

■ each person's job is probably of interest to at least one student

Discussion Questions

1. Why is career information obtained from people sometimes better than that obtained from books?
2. Why would students who are not yet ready to join the work force be interested in career information?
3. Why would Mrs. Lopez accept as speakers volunteers who do not have Home Economics jobs?
4. Why do you think Mr. Parks canceled regular classes on "Career Day"?
5. What positive changes did "Career Day" make in the school and in the lives of its students?

Answers to Preceding Questions

Answers will vary but will probably include the following ideas.

1. People can answer specific questions about their jobs. They are experts in their own field, and their information may be more up-to-date than that in a book.
2. Students can get a better idea of the jobs they would like to have in the future and know what they can do now to prepare for those jobs.
3. Some students may be interested in careers outside the Home Economics field.
4. He felt that the career information to be gained was more important than the regular class work.
5. Students who learn about a job that interests them have a better idea of how to prepare for that career. Future students will see the videotape and learn about those careers. The school will hold a "Career Day" each year.

Answers to Questions (p. 163)

Answers will vary but will probably include the following ideas.

1. Although students may list a wide variety of careers, individuals should be able to explain why certain personal traits and abilities would be an asset in their chosen field. They should also be able to offer evidence to support the contention that they possess those characteristics.
2. Students might want to know why the speaker likes or dislikes the job. They will be interested in preparation needed for the job, duties required, and pay and fringe benefits. They may want to know how one goes about finding a job in that field and where they can find other information about that career.

Careers

Home Economics Teacher (page 150)

Few students actually understand what a career involves. Most have only a general notion of the talents and responsibilities of those who work. By concentrating on the Home Economics teacher, this theme feature singles out one type of work that requires broad knowledge and numerous skills and aptitudes.

A discussion of the training and talents of the Home Economics Teacher will provide students with some idea of job requirements and abilities.

Discussion Questions

1. Why would a Home Economics teacher have to be someone with a variety of interests?
2. What is the major difference between teaching a course in Family Life and supervising the activities in a food or clothing lab?
3. Communication plays a major role in the Home Economics teacher's job. What role does communication paly in most jobs?

Answers to Preceding Questions

Answers will vary but will probably include the following ideas.

1. A Home Economics teacher would have to be someone with a variety of interests because the field of Home Econimics draws on a wide variety of other subjects, such as chemistry, sociology, psychology, and economics.
2. In a course such as Family Life, the teacher's main responsibility would be to present and explain the subject matter. In lab courses, the teacher would have to demonstrate various techniques and closely supervise students as they practiced those techniques.
3. Communication is an important skill in virtually every job. Workers must be able to communicate throughout the day with supervisors, fellow workers, and customers.

Answers to For Review

Work Decisions (p. 153)

1. Three reasons for working besides making money are to be useful and active, to gain personal satisfaction, and to give life focus and dignity.
2. It is possible to narrow career choices by investigating careers related to personal aptitudes.
3. Two government publications that describe fields with the most jobs available are the *Occupational Outlook Quarterly* and the *Occupational Outlook Handbook*.

Career Preparation (p. 157)

1. Three advantages of doing part-time work after school or in the summer are 1) getting job experience in a future career; 2) discovering skills and aptitudes; and 3) learning to work well with others. (Other possible answers: learning how to organize time, earning spending money.)
2. To become an elementary school teacher, it is necessary to have a college degree and to have studied child development and methods of teaching reading, math, and other basic subjects.
3. One of the trade-offs that working parents make is to find adequate and affordable child care so that they can give attention both to their children and their work.

Getting the Job (p. 162)

1. Four good sources of job information are 1) newspaper ads; 2) employment agencies; 3) personal contacts; and 4) canvassing.
2. When going on a job interview it is important to dress formally—boys in jacket and tie and girls in a businesslike dress or suit.
3. Three ways to work toward succeeding at a job are to 1) be prompt and reliable; 2) be willing to accept increasing responsibilities; 3) get along with fellow employees without socializing on company time. (Other possible answers: dress correctly, follow safety rules and job procedures, work to live up to employers' expectations, aim for carrying out work with less supervision.)

Chapter 7 Review

Vocabulary Answers (p. 164)

1. reference
2. Aptitudes
3. Fringe benefits
4. job cluster
5. Entry level
6. apprenticeship
7. professions

Chapter Questions (p. 164)

1. Some people would prefer to work in the arts even though many of the jobs pay very little. These are people who are very creative and who want to spend their lives painting, writing, acting, or performing music.
2. When you are deciding on a career, you should take into consideration your own interests, your skills, and your aptitudes.
3. The value in taking an entry level position is that it can provide the experience and training that is needed to advance to a higher level. Also, an entry level position will provide an opportunity to see at first hand if a particular field of work is of interest.
4. Six jobs that are often referred to as professions are physician, accountant, dentist, university professor, lawyer, and veterinarian. In general, a job may be considered a profession if a specialized college degree is required in order to get the job.
5. A part-time job selling clothing would be a good one for a person interested in a career in the fashion industry.
6. A debating team would be helpful for students who have an interest in a political career. The students would gain experience speaking in front of an audience and in supporting a position. The Future Farmers of America would be an appropriate club for students interested in farming. The club's activities would offer hands-on experience and acquaint students with issues important to farmers.
7. Permission to use someone's name as a reference should always be obtained beforehand. Obtain permission by writing or calling the person.
8. If a potential employer asks you about yourself during a job interview, your answer should focus on skills and experiences that show that you would make a valuable employee. An interviewer is always interested in how you can do the job that is available.
9. After the interview is over, the applicant should promptly write a note thanking the employer for the opportunity to interview.
10. Three kinds of jobs in the Home Economics field are teacher, product specialist, and nutritionist. Students may identify any of the careers listed on the chart on page 161.

Skill Activities

1. You might want students to examine the classified pages in the local newspapers for part-time jobs that interest them and that they believe they could get and do. The skills and talents that students have that would be essential for such jobs could then be listed below the want ads.
2. You might wish to assign students to interview people in a number of different jobs so that there is little or no duplication. Each student could then report on the interview in class. The class would therefore obtain information on a wide range of jobs.
3. Be sure students identify jobs that they could actually get. You might want to identify

actual jobs in the classified section of the newspaper. The class should discuss the interviews in detail once they are completed.

4. You might suggest that students consult the *Occupational Outlook Handbook* and other appropriate reference materials in the library to gather information about educational requirements and salaries.

Chapter 8

Managing Your Money

Chapter Organization

Chapter Vocabulary

barter (p. 167)
budget (p. 171)
fixed expenses (p. 171)
flexible expenses (p. 172)
deposit (p. 176)
balance (p. 176)
interest (p. 177)
principal (p. 178)
compounded (p. 178)
endorse (p. 179)
invest (p. 180)
stockholders (p. 181)
credit (p. 181)

Chapter Objectives

After reading this chapter, students should be able to:

1. Explain the importance of using money wisely. (8.1)
2. Describe the various sources of money. (8.1)
3. Explain how to set priorities when managing money. (8.1)
4. Explain how to organize a spending plan. (8.2)
5. Explain how to estimate a budget according to expenditures and income. (8.2)
6. Explain how to follow and adjust a budget. (8.2)
7. Describe the different kinds of checking and savings accounts available in banks. (8.3)
8. Describe the various ways of investing money. (8.3)
9. Explain the meaning and purpose of credit. (8.3)

Program Resources

Student text pages 166–187
Teacher's Resource Book
    Skill/Development Worksheet 8
    Laboratory/Application Worksheet 8
    Reinforcement Worksheet 8
    Enrichment Worksheet 8
    Transparency Master 8
    Information Master 8
    Chapter 8 Test

Teaching Suggestions

The dots represent skill levels required to answer each question or complete each activity:
- •requires recall and comprehension
- ••requires application and analysis
- •••requires synthesis and evaluation

Into the Chapter

•••**Developing a Financial Plan** Ask the class how they would reach the following goal. Arrangements can be made for a class to go on an all-day outing to a local amusement park. However, to do so, the class must raise $300 over the next four months. Divide the students into small groups and have each group develop a plan for raising the money. Have groups share their ideas.

Other Activities

•• 1. **Applying Information on Money Management** Divide the class into two teams. Have each team develop a set of questions about money management. Questions should cover such areas as differentiating between needs and wants and flexible and fixed expenses, as well as questions about budgeting monetary resources and expenses. Have teams alternate asking questions.

• 2. **Comprehending Information on Bank Accounts** Have pairs of students role-play the following situation: A bank officer explains to a prospective customer various kinds of accounts the bank offers. The customer should help guide the discussion by asking specific questions. Then have partners reverse roles and role-play the bank officer explaining how to open a savings and a checking account.

••• 3. **Researching and Organizing Information on Money Management Systems** Have the class prepare a pamphlet that provides information on the various kinds of money management systems mentioned in the text. Divide students into groups and assign one of the following categories to each group: savings accounts, certificates of deposit, stocks, bonds, and mutual funds. Groups should research the way their assigned system works and prepare a written report to be included in the pamphlet.

Learning to Manage (p. 185)

Concepts

- items that are wanted are not always needed
- students can earn money to buy part or all of an item they want
- if an item is important enough to have, it is important enough to save for
- one should buy goods and services that are wanted with the money that is left after paying for those that are needed

Discussion Questions

1. Why might "Everyone has one" not be a good reason for buying something?
2. What can students do to earn money?
3. Why didn't Billy's parents fix the washing machine instead of buying a new car battery?
4. Why did Billy decide that repairing the washing machine was more important than buying the new cowboy boots he wanted?
5. When is it a good time to buy something that is wanted but not needed?

Answers to Discussion Questions

Answers will vary but will probably include the following ideas.

1. Even though "everyone has one," it might not be good for an individual because it is too expensive, wasteful, or unhealthful.
2. Students can babysit, run errands for the neighbors, deliver newspapers or advertising fliers, do yard work, help neighbors paint or clean their houses, build and sell objects, wash cars, and so forth.
3. They probably felt the car was needed more than the washing machine. The car may be used to transport children to school, to pick up groceries, and to get Billy's father to job interviews.
4. The washing machine may be used almost every day to keep the family's clothes clean. Without the washing machine, Billy's mother has to spend money at the laundromat. Billy can use his old boots until the family's financial situation changes for the better.
5. Determine how much money is available and what needs to be spent. Buy the wanted item with money that remains after all needs are met.

Answers to Questions (p. 185)

Answers will vary but will probably include the following ideas.
1. Billy's parents probably have to pay rent, buy food and clothes, pay taxes and insurance, pay for utilities such as their gas, electricity, and telephone. They may have medical and/or dental expenses and bills for items previously purchased on credit.
2. Setting financial priorities now helps a person distinguish between goods and services that are essential and those that are merely desirable.

Health and Safety

The Balancing Act (p. 172)

Most students have probably thought very little about how much it costs to operate the household in which they live. This theme feature attempts to get students to think about these costs by focusing on how a typical family spends the money that it earns. The feature serves to demonstrate to students why it is important to learn to manage one's money. Intelligent money-managing skills will ultimately result in the ability to cope with a household budget such as the one presented here.

Discussion Questions

1. Which of the monthly expenses of American families are basically fixed expenses?
2. Which expenses of the American family might have to be sacrificed to pay for fixed expenses?
3. How can you cooperate with your family in controlling the family budget?

Answers to Preceding Questions

Answers will vary but will probably include the following ideas.
1. Except for savings and investments and vacations and recreation, all of the expenses on the list are basically fixed expenses. In some instances, transportation, health care, clothing, education, and child care might be slightly flexible but not significantly so.
2. Savings and investments and vacations and recreation might have to be sacrificed completely to pay for fixed expenses.
3. Students can help control the family budget in several ways. They can help with the food budget by avoiding waste and expensive snack foods. They can take proper care of themselves so that medical and dental costs can be kept under control. They can take good care of their clothing to keep clothing expenses to a minimum, and they can help with home maintenance expenses by turning off unneeded lights and by keeping thermostats at reasonable levels.

Answers to For Review

Money as a Resource (p. 171)

1. Six steps to use to help manage money wisely are 1) identify the problem; 2) consider choices; 3) gather information; 4) consider the outcome of each choice; 5) make a decision; 6) evaluate the decision.
2. Most teenagers get money from an allowance and from part-time jobs.
3. Needs consist of items that are essential, such as bus fare to and from school if school is at a great distance. Wants consist of items and events that are not essential, such as going to a movie.

A Spending Plan (p. 175)

1. It is important to have a clear spending plan in order to know how much money is available, how much money is needed, and to avoid uncertainty about meeting expenses.
2. Two important headings to use when estimating a budget are *income* and *expenses*.
3. Two important advantages of following a budget are a sense of satisfaction regarding effective money management and having money saved that can be used for emergency spending.

Money Management (p. 184)

1. Five advantages of a checking account are the ability to 1) deposit income and keep it safe until needed; 2) cash checks; 3) pay bills by mail; 4) avoid the risk of carrying large amounts of money; 5) have written proof that a bill has been paid. (Other possible answers: you can stop payment on a lost or stolen check, or you can keep track of spending.)
2. The seven steps to take in writing a check are 1) be sure the check is numbered; 2) write the date in the space provided; 3) write the payee's name on the line after the words, "Pay to the order of"; 4) write the amount in numbers in the space beside the dollar sign; 5) write the amount in words below the name of the payee, starting at the beginning of the line so that no one can add a word to change the amount; 6) note the purpose of the check in the memo section if there is one; 7) sign your name.
3. Mutual funds are collections of various stocks and bonds owned by one company.
4. Three advantages of buying on credit are that it 1) eliminates having to carry large amounts of cash; 2) aids in taking advantage of sales and discounts; 3) helps in building good credit references. Three disadvantages of buying on credit are that it 1) can lead to overspending; 2) can involve paying at inconvenient times; 3) can mean financial losses if payments cannot be met. (Other possible answers: advantages: provides records of expenses, provides funds for financial emergencies; disadvantage: it costs money.)

Chapter 8 Review
Vocabulary Answers (p. 186)

1. balance
2. Fixed expenses
3. compounded
4. credit
5. barter
6. invest
7. deposit
8. principal
9. flexible expenses
10. interest
11. stockholders
12. budget
13. endorse

Chapter Questions (p. 187)

1. It is important to set priorities in managing money because only by setting priorities can money be managed well. Priorities must be set in order to manage money according to a plan.

2. Building toward a long-term financial goal by saving money regularly will enable you to have something that you could otherwise not afford. It will also prove that you are a mature, responsible person.

3. The first step in budgeting your money is to keep a record of all your expenses. This is done by noting how much you spend for everything you buy, no matter how small the amount.

4. It is essential to keep your expenses lower than your income. This will allow you to save some money for long-range goals. It will also allow you to have money available for unexpected miscellaneous expenses.

5. Most students will probably say that it is never wise to borrow money from friends. A surprisingly large debt can be accumulated in a very short period of time. Also, the borrower may not be able to repay when the friend needs the money, and the friendship could be damaged. Some students might say that money can be borrowed from friends in real emergencies when the borrower is sure that the money can be rapidly repaid. The acceptance of an answer should be based upon the soundness of the explanation.

6. Most people have checking accounts because money can be deposited and kept safe until needed. Checks can usually be cashed rather easily. Also, checks make it possible to pay bills by mail. In addition, being able to pay by check avoids the need to carry about large sums of money. Finally, checks provide written proof that bills are paid, and the monthly statement makes it possible to keep track of spending.

7. A NOW account is a checking account that pays interest provided that a minimum balance is maintained in the account.

8. Because interest rates that are paid vary from one institution to another, it is a good idea to shop around for a bank when opening a savings account. In this way, the highest rate of interest, as well as the most convenient terms, can be found.

9. It is important for you to be certain that the money you put into a bank is insured by the federal government so that if the bank gets into financial difficulty, your money will be returned to you.

10. The purpose of filling out a signature card is to permit the bank to be sure that your signature on a check or a withdrawal slip is genuine.

11. A check is cleared when the bank receives the money from the account that it was drawn on.

12. Companies offer stock for sale to the public in order to raise money that they use to operate.

13. Buying something on credit sometimes costs more than paying cash because unless the bill is paid quickly, interest must be paid on the money that is borrowed or on the unpaid portion of the money borrowed.

14. A charge account is an account that allows someone to make purchases now and pay for them later.

15. To obtain credit, a person must be at least 18 years old, have a permanent address, and be working full time. A person must also have a checking or savings account in good order and a good credit history or credit rating.

Skill Activities

1. You might want to conduct a class discussion before students work on written plans for the $100. The wisdom of coming up with a balanced plan for the money—one that allocates at least some percentage to savings—can be discussed. Written plans can be presented later in class, and the wisest or the unique ones identified.

2. Students can be assigned to collect this information from several banks by visiting or calling them. The various accounts can then be analyzed and compared. The ones with the most beneficial and favorable terms can be identified.

3. To prepare students for this activity, you might want to select an item and then discuss in class how a plan for its purchase can be assembled. You will probably want to point out to students that only items that can realistically be purchased should be chosen. To demonstrate how unrealistic certain items actually are, you might want to choose an item, such as an expensive sports car or a completely new sound system for a car or home. Show students exactly and graphically how much the item would cost and how long it would take to purchase it using resources that are available to students.

4. Remind students that they should identify talents that they have that they do not feel are directly marketable. For example, point out that a person who is well organized and who keeps personal possessions in an orderly manner does indeed possess a sought-after skill. Ask students to identify other basic skills acquired through everyday living that employers would regard as valuable for their employees.

Chapter 9

You Are a Consumer

Chapter Organization

Chapter Vocabulary

consumer (p. 189)
free enterprise (p. 189)
competition (p. 190)
supply (p. 190)
demand (p. 191)
entrepreneurship (p. 191)
warranty (p. 194)
contract (p. 195)

Chapter Objectives

After reading this chapter, students should be able to:
1. Describe how the wants and needs of consumers are met. (9.1)

2. Explain the features of the free enterprise system. (9.1)

3. Explain how the free enterprise system enables Americans to be entrepreneurs. (9.1)

4. List the characteristics of an entrepreneur. (9.1)

5. Describe how teens can be entrepreneurs. (9.1)

6. Identify reasons why it is important to learn about the rights of a consumer. (9.2)

7. List the various rights that a consumer has. (9.2)

8. Explain the importance of exercising one's responsibilities as a consumer. (9.2)

9. Describe the importance of warranties and contracts for goods and services. (9.2)

10. Identify various laws that protect your rights and interests as a consumer. (9.2)

11. Explain how to exercise one's rights as a consumer. (9.2)

Program Resources

Student text pages 188–203
Teacher's Resource Book
    Skill/Development Worksheet 9
    Laboratory/Application Worksheet 9
    Reinforcement Worksheet 9
    Enrichment Worksheet 9
    Transparency Master 9
    Information Master 9
    Chapter 9 Test

Teaching Suggestions

The dots represent skill levels required to answer each question or complete each activity:
  •requires recall and comprehension
  ••requires application and analysis
  •••requires synthesis and evaluation

Into the Chapter

•••**Discovering Reasons Why Consumers Select a Product** Have the class collect a number of empty hand lotion containers and the price of each and arrange them on a display table. Have students vote for the hand lotion they like best and write the reasons for their choices. On an index card beside each brand, note the number of votes a product received and the reasons it was chosen. Among other reasons, students may choose a brand because they like an ad for it, because they like the shape or size of the container, because it is cheap, because someone they know uses and likes it, or because it is so expensive that they decide "it must be good." Discuss how difficult it is to judge the actual merit of cosmetics such as hand lotion. Then ask students how they might find out the true merit of a product and whether or not it is priced fairly.

Other Activities

••• 1. **Becoming an Entrepreneur** Brainstorm ideas for starting an after-school neighborhood business. Then have students, working individually or in small groups, form a specific plan for organizing a business venture. Ask them to use the management process in making their plans. They must decide how to raise money to pay for materials to make a product, or ways to buy a product they wish to sell. They should set a schedule of work hours, set prices, and decide how to advertise and distribute their product. Or, if it is a service they are offering, they must decide the best way to identify and reach customers. Have students present their plans to the class for further suggestions.

•• 2. **Planning a Verbal Complaint** Have students write a response to the following letter from a close friend. "I am terribly upset. I bought an expensive sweater. The first time I washed it, it shrank. I followed the washing directions on the label exactly. Mom says I should take the sweater back to the store, but as you know, I'm shy, and I don't know what to say. Tell me what I can do to convince the store they should replace the sweater. Please give me some tips."

•• 3. **Deciding Where to Get Help** Describe the following problem to the class: An airline lost Marlene's new sleeping bag on her trip home from camp. She filed a formal complaint and sent a copy of the sales slip for the sleeping bag, but the airline refuses to answer her letters and telephone calls. Have students write a brief report on what steps she could take to get help from resources in her community.

Learning to Manage (p. 201)

Concepts

▇ be aware of the returns policy of the store in which you buy a product
▇ warranties differ greatly
▇ read the "fine print" in a warranty before purchasing an item
▇ it pays to buy a reliable product

Discussion Questions

1. Why was Pete unable to return the radio to the store he bought it from?
2. If Pete had returned the broken radio to the store a week after he bought it, would the store have given him a new radio? Why?
3. Will the company that manufactured Pete's radio replace it? Why?
4. Why is Pete unhappy about sending his broken radio to the repair department listed in the warranty?

5. Why should you read the warranty carefully before deciding to buy the product?

Answers to Discussion Questions

Answers will vary but will probably include the following ideas.
1. The store does not accept returns after 30 days. Pete bought the radio about 42 days before he attempted to return it.
2. No, the store would not have given him a new radio because the warranty does not cover repairs on parts other than the plastic casing. The store cannot afford to give him a new radio because it cannot exchange the broken radio for a new one.
3. No, because the broken part was not covered in the warranty.
4. Even though the radio will be repaired, Pete will have to pay the costs of shipping and repairs. He has no idea how much the repairs will cost. He will be without his radio from six to eight weeks, while it is being repaired.
5. The warranty gives some idea of the quality of the product as well as an indication of the expense involved if something goes wrong with it. The consumer might decide to buy another product, even if more expensive, rather than a poorly warrantied product.

Answers to Questions (p. 201)

Answers will vary but will probably include the following ideas.
1. If I were Pete, I would write a letter of complaint to the company, sending a copy of my warranty and sales slip. I would explain that, even though the repairs are not covered by the warranty, I would expect a product from that company to last longer than six weeks. I would tell the company that I found their warranty misleading, and I would ask it to replace or repair the radio free of charge.
2. Pete's first error was neglecting to read the warranty carefully. His second error was

buying the radio.

3. Students should compare warranties for period covered, parts and/or labor guaranteed, proof of purchase required, procedure for sending product to the factory or repair department, and the consumer's cost of shipping and repairs.

Leadership and Citizenship

Corporate Citizenship (p. 192)

This theme feature offers two examples of what American businesses have done to make life better for their employees and to make a valuable contribution to people in need. The examples will be useful in making the point that businesses are not heartless and distant enterprises that are interested only in making a profit. This feature helps to demonstrate that business is not the "enemy" in a free enterprise system, even though it may sometimes be viewed in such a way in the producer/consumer relationship. Businesses supply goods and services that people need and want. As the examples illustrate, they often supply services that improve people's lives in other ways.

A discussion of "Corporate Citizenship" can be a vehicle for identifying and appreciating the productive things that businesses often do.

Discussion Questions

1. Can you identify other large companies that contribute to society by acting as good corporate citizens?
2. How do businesses in your community contribute to good causes?
3. What benefits come to companies that contribute to good causes?

Answers to Preceding Questions

Answers will vary but will probably include the following ideas.

1. Almost all large companies contribute to a variety of charitable organizations. Several large companies sponsor national scholarship programs. Large companies also match their employee's contributions to various charitable organizations.
2. A variety of businesses in all communities support numerous local activities from youth programs to local arts groups. In some communities, certain business leaders are well known for their support of local programs of all kinds.
3. Companies that make contributions are able to deduct the costs from the taxes that they must pay. As in the first example, companies can attract good employees by their activities. As in the second example, some companies receive good publicity from their charitable activities.

Answers to For Review

Free Enterprise (p. 192)

1. *Goods* are material products, such as food, clothing, appliances, and automobiles. *Services* are actions performed for money on a consumer's behalf.
2. A successful entrepreneur is a person who has a creative imagination, is aware of people's needs and wants, has a willingness to take risks, is ready to accept responsibility, is willing to work hard, and is able to use resources skillfully.
3. Experience as a teen entrepreneur can be valuable by allowing a young person to choose a business that is of interest, to set working hours that do not interfere with school, to learn about setting rates of pay, to explore long-term career goals, and to hire unemployed friends as the business grows.

Consumers (p. 200)

1. Four basic rights in the consumer "Bill of Rights" are the right to safety, the right to choose, the right to be informed, and the right to be heard.
2. Responsibilities that go with consumer rights include the following: 1) use products safely; 2) think about your choices; 3) gather accurate information; 4) make complaints when necessary; 5) know all of your consumer rights.
3. Three laws that protect the consumer are the Care Labeling Act (which requires manufacturers to attach permanent care labels to every garment), the Consumer Product Safety Act (which established the Consumer Product Safety Commission, a federal agency that conducts safety tests and sometimes issues recalls), and the Truth-in-Advertising Act (which requires that the manufacturer be able to prove what is claimed about a product and that products are sold at advertised prices).
4. The first part of a well-written complaint letter provides personal information. In addition to the writer's name, and address, a telephone number is useful so that the company representative can respond by calling. The second part is the salutation, which should always include the actual name of the person to whom one is writing. The third part describes the facts of purchase, including the name of the product or service, the style or model number, the date of purchase, and the price paid. The fourth part presents the reason for the complaint in the form of a brief and polite statement. The fifth and final part proposes the consumer's solution to the problem and suggests a reasonable time for the manufacturer to resolve it.

Chapter 9 Review

Vocabulary Answers (p. 202)

1. Competition
2. consumer
3. entrepreneurship
4. Supply
5. warranty
6. Demand
7. contract
8. free enterprise

Chapter Questions (p. 202)

1. Two characteristics of the free enterprise system are the freedom to start a business and make a profit and the freedom to choose what products and services to buy. (Other answers: freedom to choose where to shop, to own private property, to choose your own career)
2. *Goods* are material products, such as food, clothing, appliances, and automobiles. *Services* are actions performed for money on a customer's behalf.
3. The three steps in the system of meeting wants and needs are *production*—making goods and providing services; *distribution*—getting goods and services to people; and *consumption*—selecting, buying, and using goods and services.
4. In a free enterprise system, government involvement must be carefully controlled because people must have the freedom to carry out economic activities. If government interfered with any of these basic freedoms, it would control the system.
5. Consumers benefit from competition between businesses that try to outdo each other in producing products that more

people want in order to produce greater profits. Consumers gain higher quality goods and services as well as greater freedom of choice.

6. According to the principle of supply and demand, the choices that consumers make help to determine what businesses produce. The amount and kinds of goods and services that are available to consumers is the supply. What consumers want is the demand. Consumer demand directly determines what is supplied.

7. Here are some reasons that could support each characteristic.
   - *A creative imagination* This is a very important quality of an entrepreneur. A person who is creative will be able to identify consumer needs that less imaginative people might overlook.
   - *An awareness of people's needs and wants* This skill is very important. The successful entrepreneur must be able to tell what people need and want even if consumers themselves are not always aware of their needs and wants.
   - *A willingness to take a risk* This ability is basic to all successful entrepreneurs. People who do not possess this willingness will simply not be entrepreneurs because all successful entrepreneurs must take risks.
   - *A willingness to accept responsibility* Entrepreneurs must be willing to accept responsibility for their own decisions. This is the price that must be paid by those who believe their own ideas are sound and worthwhile.
   - *A willingness to work hard* All entrepreneurs must work hard and often very hard. Success almost always depends upon the entrepreneur's single-minded dedication to his or her beliefs.
   - *An ability to use resources skillfully* The entrepreneur must be able to determine the skills and talents that are available to make the organization successful and must be able to use those abilities to the fullest. A successful entrepreneur must get the best out of himself or herself as well as others.

8. Four basic consumer rights are the right to safety, the right to choose, the right to be informed, and the right to be heard. (Other answers: the right to have their complaints heard and acted upon and the right to consumer education)

9. Concerning the safety of a product, consumers are responsible for familiarizing themselves with all the instructions that come with a product and that must be understood so that the product might be used safely. If the product turns out to be defective, consumers have the additional responsibility of informing the store where the product was purchased and the product's manufacturer as well. If the defect is serious, the consumer has the additional responsibility of notifying the appropriate governmental agency.

10. A consumer must complain about a product that does not meet safety standards. The manufacturer may not be aware that the product does not meet the standards. More important, other consumers might not be aware of the hazards associated with the product. Consumers who complain can help prevent injuries to others.

11. Before signing a written contract, be sure to read and understand all of its terms.

12. The Truth-in-Advertising Act is designed to prevent sellers from making false or misleading claims for a product or service. The act requires sellers to be able to prove that a product or service will do what the seller claims. It also prohibits sellers from charging a higher price than is advertised.

13. In making an effective verbal complaint about a product, consumers should follow these steps:
    - Locate the sales slip, warranty, and contract that applies to the product, and return to the store without delay.

- If the product purchased was damaged or defective, check to see if the warranty covers damaged or defective products.
- Note what is wrong with the product or the service and decide how you would like the seller to resolve the problem.

14. It is important to address a letter of complaint to the person in charge because that person alone can give you the satisfaction you deserve. Letters addressed generally ("To Whom It May Concern") stand a good chance of getting lost or overlooked. Also, the person who goes to the trouble of finding out the name of the person in charge has already shown that he or she cares enough about the complaint to find out the name of the person to be contacted.

15. The Better Business Bureau is a nonprofit organization sponsored by local business in all parts of the country. Since 1916 it has protected consumer interests by actively promoting honest business practices. The Better Business Bureau will assist consumers in resolving complaints against business organizations.

Skill Activities

1. Be sure to set aside a considerable amount of time for identifying an appropriate product. Help students identify a product that could actually be made in class. The product should be one that other students may want to buy. Consider having students work in small groups to identify appropriate products. Each group could identify one product. Then the class as a whole could choose the product for which there seems to be the greatest need. Students should then estimate approximate costs. Be sure to impress upon them that costs go beyond raw materials. An estimate of labor costs should then be made. An overhead cost for such items as rent, heat, and electricity should also be made. Profit cannot be figured until all of these costs are known. Point out that profits can be distributed to the owners of the business, or they can be retained by the business to provide for growth or expansion. Before students develop an advertising campaign for the product, have them identify the places where advertising is likely to be seen by the potential purchasers of the product.

2. Students have probably had experience with a product that had to be assembled. As often happens, a part is missing or the directions are completely confusing. Since the frustration in this kind of a situation is so intense and memorable, you might want students who have experienced it to focus on this kind of situation in their letters.

3. Before students begin their research, you might want to introduce them to the kinds of information that *Consumer Reports* provides. Point out that a particular consumer might be interested in one kind of information rather than another. A potential purchaser of an automobile who is interested in performance will be mainly interested in the information that has something to do with the information on the engine's power and speed. An economy-minded purchaser is likely to be more interested in information about fuel consumption and frequency of repair. You might want to go through a typical report in class.

4. Before students are asked to role-play, you will probably want to give both the plaintiff and the defendant the opportunity to prepare the broad outlines of the case. You might want to have the defendant and the plaintiff switch roles at the end of a presentation. To add variety and to provide as many students as possible with the opportunity to role-play, you might want to ask students to develop additional scenarios. Students might be asked to identify their own based upon their personal experiences with consumer complaints.

Chapter 10

Skillful Shopping

Chapter Organization

Chapter Vocabulary

comparison shopping   (p. 205)
emotional appeals   (p. 208)
status symbols   (p. 209)
impulse buyer   (p. 215)

Chapter Objectives

After reading this chapter, students should be able to:

1. Assemble a shopping plan. (10.1)
2. Describe how to obtain information about products and services before making a purchase. (10.1)
3. Choose the best place to shop. (10.1)
4. Identify various ways in which advertising, family and peer pressure, and sales affect shopping decisions. (10.1)
5. Make suitable adjustments to a shopping plan. (10.2)
6. Describe how to shop for quality merchandise. (10.2)
7. Explain the importance of knowing store policies regarding returns and exchanges. (10.2)

Program Resources

Student text pages 204–221
Teacher's Resource Book
    Skill/Development Worksheet 10
    Laboratory/Application Worksheet 10
    Reinforcement Worksheet 10
    Enrichment Worksheet 10
    Transparency Master 10
    Information Master 10
    Chapter 10 Test

Teaching Suggestions

The dots represent skill levels required to answer each question or complete each activity:
 •requires recall and comprehension
 ••requires application and analysis
•••requires synthesis and evaluation

Into the Chapter

•**Using the Yellow Pages** Demonstrate how to use the yellow pages of the local telephone book efficiently. Give several examples of different categories of stores where a specific product might be found such as *Department Stores, Pharmacies, Markets,* and *Hardware—Retail.* Collect five or six directories of yellow pages and distribute one to each of five or six groups. Then play the following game: Name a product that is sold in a variety of stores. Have each group list

T78

as many categories as they can of stores that might sell the product. They must write the exact wording given in the yellow pages. Limit search time to a few minutes. Repeat the process several times, and, after the class confirms categories are correct, name the winning group.

Other Activities

•• 1. **Applying the Shopping Plan** Discuss why it is necessary to adjust the shopping plan when shopping for another person. Then have each student make a shopping plan for the purchase of a birthday gift for a friend. Remind them that they will need to consider the tastes and interests of the recipient. Ask students to list actual items that would appeal to their friend and tell the outcome of the shopping tour.

••• 2. **Evaluating Ads** Have each of several groups design a bulletin board that demonstrates ways that advertisements attract consumers. Have each group collect magazine ads that use a variety of methods such as sex appeal, fear appeal, rational appeal, humorous appeal, emotional appeal, and reinforcing status symbols. Each ad in the displays should be described in a caption.

••• 3. **Evaluating Consumer Behavior** Have the class compile a list of "Shopping *Do*s and *Don't*s." You may wish to have each student compile a preliminary list before completing the final one.

Learning to Manage (p. 219)

Concepts

■ smart shoppers do comparison shopping before making a purchase
■ consumers can research the value of products in objective publications such as *Consumer Reports*

■ the least expensive product may end up costing the most
■ "sale" prices differ widely from store to store
■ unwanted features on some products result in excessive cost
■ some warranties are better than others
■ some service is better, and usually more costly, than others
■ a service contract on a new product may not be necessary

Discussion Questions

1. Why is it usually not a good idea to buy a product as soon as you realize you need or want it?
2. Is it always a good idea to buy the product that is most highly rated in *Consumer Reports?* Why?
3. Is it always a good idea to buy the least expensive product you can find? Why?
4. Why is it sometimes a good idea to pay cash for a product rather than buying it on the installment plan?
5. Why are some service contracts more valuable than others?

Answers to Preceding Questions

Answers will vary but will probably include the following ideas.
1. By buying before comparing brands, warranties, prices, and service, the consumer runs the risk of acquiring inferior merchandise at an inflated price.
2. No, because although the product may rate high in comparison to similar items, it may include a number of features the consumer does not need or want and, therefore, cost more than necessary.
3. No, because the merchandise may be damaged or discontinued. The manufacturer and/or the store may not stand behind

the product. The item may be poorly made or insufficiently warrantied.

4. Interest charges on the unpaid balance of consumer loans can be very high, thus causing the real price of a product to be much higher than its advertised price.

5. Service contracts that offer better repair value than are warrantied by the manufacturer are more valuable to the consumer than are those that duplicate the manufacturer's offer.

Answers to Questions (p. 219)

Answers will vary but will probably include the following ideas.

1. They might have bought it if the *store* were going out of business, as long as the manufacturer's warranty was valid and repair service was not dependent on the store's existence. They should probably not buy it if the *manufacturer* is going out of business, for the warranty would be worthless.

2. Students may suggest home appliances such as refrigerators, washing machines, dish washers, or entertainment centers, as well as homes, cars, boats, and other big-ticket items. Their plan for comparison shopping should include reading objective reports, advertising, manufacturer's sales literature, and possibly consumer comments. It should also include comparison of warranties, store-by-store prices and services, and credit charges.

Technology

Cash Box to Computer (p. 210)

This theme feature allows students to get some idea of the complex nature of shopping from the store's point of view. Intelligent shopping demands considerable knowledge and a well thought-out plan on the consumer's part. To make it all possible, the store owner needs complex machinery to deal with modern shopping. Machinery that records sales, reads pricing codes, checks credit status, and adjusts inventory is essential to the modern retailer.

A discussion of "Cash Box to Computer" will give students a glimpse of modern shopping from the retailer's standpoint.

Discussion Questions

1. If all purchases were made with cash, would computerized record keeping be necessary?
2. How do computerized cash registers save shoppers valuable time?
3. How do computerized cash registers permit store owners to lower prices?

Answers to Preceding Questions

Answers will vary but will probably include the following ideas.

1. If all purchases were made with cash, store owners would simply have to keep track of the amounts of purchases. Credit cards make complex machinery necessary because the balances in customer's accounts must be known at the time that purchases are made.
2. Computerized cash registers save shoppers valuable time because they check a variety of necessary records very quickly.
3. Computerized cash registers save store owners money by making fewer employees necessary. If the machines did not exist, more people would be needed to do record keeping by hand. The lower labor costs that the machinery makes possible can be passed along to consumers in the form of lower prices.

Answers to For Review

Planning Purchases (p. 212)

1. The first step in a shopping plan is to define needs. The second step is to consider alter-

natives that might be available. The third step is to decide what specific features the item must have. The fourth step is review the budget that is available. The fifth step is to do comparison shopping to determine what other products might be available. The sixth and final step is to gather all information to organize the final shopping trip.

2. In deciding where to shop, a consumer should consider the convenience of a seller's location, the quality of the merchandise that the seller carries, the selection of merchandise that the seller offers, the reputation of the seller, and the methods of payment that the seller accepts.

3. Two other factors that influence buying decisions are peer pressure and family.

Shopping Wisely (p. 218)

1. When using a shopping plan, a consumer can be flexible by adjusting the plan if it is discovered that some element of it must be changed. When the plan was first constructed, for example, the consumer might have established a certain budget. But as the plan was followed, the consumer might have found that certain extra features of a product were essential. Becoming convinced of this, the consumer demonstrates flexibility by adjusting the original budget upward.

2. When judging the quality of a product, the seven factors that should be considered are safety, performance, durability, convenience, consumer protection (warranty terms), the manufacturer's reputation, and the care and maintenance that the product requires.

3. The most important step in returning or exchanging a purchase is to understand policies and procedures that a particular store follows in accepting returns and exchanges. These procedures are usually set forth on signs in the store. If they aren't, the consumer can ask a member of the store's staff.

Chapter 10 Review

Vocabulary Answers (p. 220)

1. status symbols
2. Comparison shopping
3. emotional appeals
4. impulse buyer

Chapter Questions (p. 220)

1. The six steps in a shopping plan are to define needs, consider alternatives, identify requirements, review budget, gather information, and organize the shopping trip.

2. There are many reasons why it is not always practical to buy the least expensive item. The least expensive item may lack features that a consumer needs. The least expensive item may also be less durable than a more expensive item, and it might not perform as well as a more costly item. Also, it might often require more frequent and expensive maintenance. The consumer's main task is to locate the highest quality item that he or she can afford. Since quality is the most important consideration, it is often best to pay more rather than less.

3. Companies spend so much money on advertising because their profits depend upon their ability to make consumers aware of their products and to convince consumers to buy their products.

4. Many television ads make rational appeals to consumers. An ad for a breakfast cereal, for example, may attempt to persuade consumers to buy the product by concentrating on the nourishment that the product provides. An ad for an automobile might attempt to persuade consumers by supplying information on the car's economical performance.

5. In the advertising technique called *endorsement,* a famous person promotes a product or service and suggests that consumers try it.

In the advertising technique called *testimonial,* an ordinary person promotes a product or service and suggests that consumers try it.

6. Advertising helps consumers in many ways. It advises consumers that certain products and services are currently available. It also introduces consumers to new products that have just become available. In addition, advertising provides useful information about special sales and discounts and rebate programs. Advertising can mislead consumers by persuading them to buy products and services that they don't really need. However, consumers who understand advertising techniques should be able to use advertising as a source of product information.

7. Many examples of status symbols in today's society can be identified. One commonly encountered status symbol is the expensive foreign automobile, which is often used to demonstrate social and financial position. Another status symbol is the second or vacation home, which can be used to express social and financial success. Other status symbols are designer clothes, expensive jewelry, specialized video equipment, cameras, and works of art.

8. Sales are not always sources of bargains. A bargain is a service or product that is purchased at a low price *and* satisfies one of the consumer's needs. A product purchased at a low price is not really a bargain if it is not useful or easily usable. Nor is a product a bargain if higher priced accessories must be purchased to make it usable. Genuine bargains can be found at certain kinds of sales. But these items must always meet and satisfy a consumer's need. To determine whether a consumer has located a real bargain, the answer should be "yes" to each of the following questions: Is the product needed? Is the product in usable condition? Is the sale price less than the regular price at other stores? Would the product be purchased even if it were not on sale?

9. Department stores, discount stores, specialty stores, and factory outlets are four types of stores. Students may list any of the related advantages and disadvantages from the chart on page 207.

10. A high price does not always indicate a better quality product.

Skill Activities

1. In completing this activity, students must be sure to identify a brand of sneakers that can be found in the three places mentioned. Consider substituting another product if comparative information cannot be obtained from the three sources identified here. Make sure that students understand that the main purpose of the activity is to provide them with practice in gathering information from various sources and then comparing that information. Impress upon students that the items to be compared must be identical. In guiding students to determine the best value, make sure that they understand the cost of such factors as time and distance. A product that costs two dollars more at a department store a mile away might be a better value than a lower-priced product at a discount store thirty miles away. A higher price might represent a better value even if a consumer must wait three weeks for the product to be delivered from a mail-order source.

2. If students select ads from television, they should describe the ads clearly in class before identifying the techniques used and explaining their degree of persuasiveness. Ads taken from magazines should be brought to class and displayed. It would be well to permit class discussion of the persuasiveness of each ad presented because people disagree about how effective ads are. You might want to assign particular techniques to particular students. To guarantee that all ad-

vertising techniques are illustrated, you might want to bring additional examples to class.

3. Explain to students that most adults have had the consumer experiences listed here. Have students present and compare the results of their information gathering in class. Give students who wish to report differing results or personal shopping experiences time to do so. As the presentations take place, try to identify the most common sources of dissatisfaction. Try also to identify the ways in which various kinds of stores handled consumer complaints.

4. You might want to allow students to work on this activity in small groups. Each group should begin with a brainstorming session during which the product to be advertised is identified. You might consider having each group develop an ad for the same type of product. You might also consider assigning a type of product to each group. After a product is identified or assigned, be sure that students have sufficient time to plan the ad before it is developed. Once the ad is planned, individual members may work on individual parts—attention-getting headlines, copy, artwork—or they may work together to complete the ad.

5. You might ask students to report back to the class after they implement their shopping plans. Their reports can focus on how helpful their shopping plans were. They could also report on whatever changes or revisions they made to their plans as they implemented them.

6. Make sure that students understand they will have to read and study the entire article that accompanies the test results in order to understand exactly how the products were tested and rated. In instances where numerous products are tested and rated, you might allow students to report on the most highly rated, the least highly rated, and, say, three others in between.

Chapter 11

Housing and Home Furnishings

Chapter Organization

T83

Chapter Vocabulary

mortgage (p. 226)
condominium (p. 226)
co-op (p. 226)
design (p. 227)
value (p. 229)
intensity (p. 229)
monochromatic (p. 229)
analogous (p. 229)
complementary (p. 230)
split-complementary (p. 230)
triadic (p. 230)
proportion (p. 231)

Chapter Objectives

After reading this chapter, students should be able to:

1. Explain how a home provides shelter and satisfies emotional needs. (11.1)
2. Explain how the kind of home people choose is influenced by economics, values, and availability. (11.1)
3. Describe the advantages and disadvantages of renting and buying housing. (11.1)
4. Explain how design elements and principles can be used to decorate a home. (11.2)
5. Describe the best way to organize the space in a home. (11.2)
6. Describe how to improve the use of personal space. (11.3)
7. Explain how to add a personal decorating touch. (11.3)
8. Explain how to maintain personal space that is shared. (11.3)
9. Describe how to care for a home by keeping it clean and organized. (11.4)
10. Explain how family cooperation helps to make home care easier. (11.4)
11. Explain how to conserve energy at home. (11.4)
12. Explain how to prevent accidents at home. (11.5)
13. Describe how to keep a home secure. (11.5)

Program Resources

Student text pages 222–247
Teacher's Resource Book
    Skill/Development Worksheet 11
    Laboratory/Application Worksheet 11
    Reinforcement Worksheet 11
    Enrichment Worksheet 11
    Transparency Master 11
    Information Master 11
    Chapter 11 Test

Teaching Suggestions

The dots represent skill levels required to answer each question or complete each activity:
•requires recall and comprehension
••requires application and analysis
•••requires synthesis and evaluation

Into the Chapter

•••Recognizing the Diversity of Housing

Brainstorm the many different kinds of housing that exist today, have existed in the past, and may exist in the future. Have students compile for display in the classroom an illustrated list of types of housing. They should present as wide a selection as possible, including such examples as housing in outer space, ancient cave dwellings, castles, and palaces, as well as temporary housing—field huts, for example. Discuss how different kinds of housing meet different needs.

Other Activities

••• 1. **Designing a Room** Divide the class into small groups. Have each group design a room of its choice. Ask them to provide an illustrated report as if they were design consultants or interior decorators. Have them present a floor plan, a description of furnishings, and samples of the color scheme, fabrics, and lighting they propose to use. Have groups present their plans to the class for discussion.

•• **2. Analyzing Housing Conditions** Have students find a short story or incident in a novel that addresses the way living quarters affect an individual or a family, either positively or negatively. Have students summarize their selections and discuss with the class the relationship of the story's characters to the place where they lived.

••• **3. Explaining Safety Measures to Children** Divide the class into pairs. Have each pair take turns role-playing the following discussions between a teen and a younger sibling or other young child: 1) Teenager teaches a six-year-old what to do if there is a fire at home; and 2) Teenager talks to an eight-year-old about safety hazards in the home, how to prevent them, and what to do in an emergency. Emphasize the importance of presenting information in a way that does not cause anxiety or "put ideas in the head" of the young child about experimenting with dangerous activities.

Learning to Manage (p. 245)

Concepts

▇ two or more children often have to share a room

▇ careful planning can create adequate space and privacy in a shared room

▇ magazines and books are good sources of decorating ideas

▇ chores as well as time for privacy can be scheduled

▇ trading chores is often a good way to get everything accomplished painlessly

Discussion Questions

1. Why didn't Anna's mother remodel the house to give both Anna and Judy their own room?
2. How did the two girls solve the space problem?
3. How did the two girls solve the privacy problem?
4. How can two people with different personalities share duties without annoying each other?
5. What are the advantages and disadvantages of living with a "neatnik"?

Answers to Preceding Questions

Answers will vary but will probably include the following ideas.

1. The house may be too small to set aside an additional bedroom. Anna's mother and husband-to-be may have to live on a limited budget that does not permit remodeling expenses.
2. They solved the space problem by adding a second bar in the closet, keeping bulky clothing in storage boxes under their beds, and measuring and planning where to place Judy's furniture.
3. They solved the privacy problem by making a folding screen to serve as a room divider and checking their schedules for a time when each girl could be alone in the room.
4. They can make out a schedule for carrying out those duties and agree to stick to it. Each person can agree to do more than his or her share of certain chores in return for equal consideration by his or her partner.
5. "Neatniks" keep their surroundings neat and clean; their living quarters always look well organized. But they are often demanding and fussy; those who live with them often find it difficult to live in relaxed clutter.

Answers to Questions (p. 245)

Answers will vary but will probably include the following ideas.

1. They could work out a schedule that gives each girl the room for a certain amount of time every second day. Or they could agree to be alone in the room each day for half that amount of time.
2. Judy and Anna's plan for sharing their room seems realistic and workable because they have foreseen and planned to solve the problems of space, privacy, and maintenance.
3. Move the desk away from the window to avoid temptation to look outside instead of doing homework. Gain more space in the closet by putting shoes into a bag hung on the inside of the closet door, discarding or storing under the bed garments that do not fit or are seldom worn. Build storage shelves from orange crates or bricks and boards for books, models, and other possessions.

Health and Safety

Childproofing Your Home (page 242)

This theme feature emphasizes that a home must be made safe for *all* its occupants. The special needs of children might easily be overlooked. When small children are part of a family, it is the responsibility of the older family members to evaluate the home's potential hazards to the children. Items that are not at all dangerous for most people can be great threats to the safety of children, who find just about anything worthy of investigation.

A discussion of "Childproofing Your Home" can make students aware of their responsibility to assist in making the home safe for younger brothers and sisters.

Discussion Questions

1. What special threat does the kitchen range pose to a toddler?
2. How could a common household item, such as a pair of scissors, be dangerous in the hands of a small child?
3. How might the presence of a small child in the home create dangers for adults?

Answers to Preceding Questions

Answers will vary but will probably include the following ideas.

1. The kitchen range has knobs that a child would like to turn and buttons that a child would like to push. The flame of gas burners is hard to resist. The red glow of electric burners is also very attractive to a child.
2. A small child could easily be cut or even stabbed by a pair of scissors. Scissors could also injure others.
3. The presence of a small child creates special dangers for adults because small children commonly leave their playthings lying about. Older people can easily trip over toys left in hallways and on stairways.

Answers to For Review

Housing Decisions (p. 226)

1. Two important needs that a home fulfills are the physical need for shelter and the emotional need for security.
2. The location of a new home is important because of the necessity of being conveniently close to schools, child care centers, and parents' places of work.
3. Types of housing include single-family homes, townhouses, duplexes, multiplexes, mobile homes, condominiums, and co-ops.

Making a House a Home (p. 233)

1. The four elements of design are lines, colors, textures, and patterns.

2. Three important principles of design that can be used in decorating a home are scale, balance, and harmony. (Other possible answers: proportion, emphasis.)
3. A floor plan makes it possible to plan efficient use of space; therefore, it saves time and frustration.

Your Own Space (p. 236)

1. One way to improve the use of personal space is to make a floor plan. (Other possible answers: painters might set up an easel near a window, music lovers might put a radio on a bedside table.)
2. Accessories such as pictures, pillows, plants, and lamps can make a room personal. Displays such as photos, pennants, shells, and rocks can also make a room unique.
3. In order to share a room and still have personal space, divide the room in half using bunk beds, a bookcase, shelves, roll-up blinds, or folding screens.

Home Care (p. 240)

1. Three storage ideas for keeping clutter under control are 1) store clothes not being used in empty suitcases; 2) store flat items or shoes in cardboard suit boxes under beds; 3) put a small shelf above a bed for a clock or magazines. (Other possible answers: put away items after using them; keep items where they are used; store items used often where they can be reached easily; put a hook on the bathroom door for shower caps and robes; use foam egg cartons or plastic containers in a desk or chest drawers for pins or coins.)
2. A cleaning schedule helps a family to plan when jobs will be done as well as who will do them.
3. Four ways to conserve energy in the home are 1) take shorter showers; 2) turn off lights and appliances when they are not needed; 3) do not overload the clothes dryer; 4) defrost the refrigerator regularly. (Other possible answers: do not leave refrigerator door open; use fluorescent bulbs; use warm or cold settings on the washing machine; do not use clothes dryer if line drying will do as well; use the dishwasher only for a full load.)

Home Safety (p. 244)

1. Three ways to prevent home falls are 1) wipe up spills right away; 2) use step stools to reach items on high shelves; 3) arrange furniture so that it does not interfere with traffic paths. (Other possible answers: use nonskid mats and rugs; make sure carpets are firmly tacked down; keep stairways clear, well lit, and in good repair.)
2. Three guidelines for preventing fires are 1) keep the area around the stove clean and free of grease; 2) make sure no one smokes in bed; 3) use screens in front of fireplaces. (Other possible answers: keep items such as potholders and paper towels away from the stove; keep electric cords in good repair; keep matches away from children; do not allow papers or trash to accumulate.)
3. Two ways of preventing electric shocks in the home are 1) inspect cords and make sure they are in good repair; 2) keep wires away from water, and do not plug in cords with wet hands. (Other possible answers: cover outlets that young children might be able to reach; do not use a hair dryer or telephone in the bathtub or when standing on a wet spot on the floor.)
4. When receiving a "wrong number" phone call, do not give information to the caller. Ask what number was called, and politely tell the caller it is the wrong number.

Chapter 11 Review

Vocabulary Answers (p. 246)

1. Condominium
2. value
3. monochromatic
4. split-complementary
5. Intensity
6. mortgage
7. analogous
8. complementary
9. co-op
10. triadic
11. Proportion
12. design

Chapter Questions (p. 247)

1. A person who has a mortgage repays the loan in monthly installments that include interest charges.
2. A condominium is an individual unit, within a building, that is owned by one or more individuals. People who belong to a co-op differ from condominium owners in that they do not own the unit that they are living in. Instead they are joint owners of the entire building.
3. Furniture with curved shapes gives a room a softer feeling than it would have if the furniture were angularly shaped. Combining both curved and angularly shaped furniture in a room creates a feeling of informality.
4. You can make a small room seem larger by painting the walls a light color.
5. An object is out of scale when it is considerably larger or smaller than the object it is placed next to or is too large or small relative to the setting in which it is placed.
6. To create a room that has informal balance, arrange the furniture unevenly around the center. Informal balance differs from formal balance in that the furniture on each side of the center is not the same size or type.
7. One of the best ways to personalize a room is to use accessories and displays that reflect your own taste.
8. Insulation is used to conserve energy and to keep the house at a comfortable temperature. Weatherstripping is one method of home insulation, using fiber, metal, or plastic strips around doors and windows. Other ways to insulate include putting insulation materials inside walls and ceilings; installing storm windows or plastic sheets over windows; and using window shades or drapes.
9. The three most common causes are grease fires, faulty wiring, and cigarettes.
10. The first thing you should do to make your home secure is install good locks.

Skill Activities

1. Before students make a cleaning schedule for the Home Economics room and assigned tasks, discuss with them exactly what cleaning has to be done. The tasks to be accomplished will almost always be more numerous and involved than students believe they will be. The same is true of the home maintenance chores. A parent would have to identify the specific tasks to accomplish.
2. Before students begin this activity, reinforce the basic need for personal space. The visitor will need not only a place for clothing and other belongings but also a place within the room that is reserved for him or her alone. This will almost always be a chair and a table or desk.
3. Suggest to students that the wall hanging, banner or pillow might also illustrate some aspect of the family's history or background. Students may discover various graphic ways to illustrate a family's ethnic background.

Unit 4

Foods and Nutrition

Chapter 12

Food and Health

Chapter Organization

Chapter Vocabulary

nutrients (p. 251)
essential amino acids (p. 254)
fat-soluble vitamins (p. 256)
saturated fats (p. 256)
unsaturated fats (p. 256)
cholesterol (p. 256)
water-soluble vitamins (p. 259)
calorie (p. 266)
basal metabolism (p. 267)
anorexia nervosa (p. 273)
bulimia (p. 274)

Chapter Objectives

After reading this chapter, students should be able to:
1. Explain how both body and mind need food. (12.1)

2. Explain how culture, religion, and family influence what they eat. (12.1)
3. Explain how the availability of food affects its cost. (12.1)
4. Explain why the body needs the essential nutrients. (12.2)
5. Describe sources of proteins, carbohydrates, fats, vitamins, minerals, and water. (12.2)
6. Explain how following the Daily Food Guide can help them have a balanced diet. (12.3)
7. Explain how following dietary guidelines can help them to be healthy. (12.3)
8. Explain how good eating and exercise habits can result in an ideal weight. (12.4)
9. Explain why fad diets are unhealthy. (12.4)
10. Explain why eating disorders are serious illnesses. (12.4)

Program Resources

Student text pages 250–277
Teacher's Resource Book
    Skill/Development Worksheet 12
    Laboratory/Application Worksheet 12
    Reinforcement Worksheet 12
    Enrichment Worksheet 12
    Transparency Master 12
    Information Master 12
    Chapter 12 Test

Teaching Suggestions

The dots represent skill levels required to answer each question or complete each activity:

•requires recall and comprehension
••requires application and analysis
•••requires synthesis and evaluation

Into the Chapter

•••**Interpreting People's Reactions to Food** Collect five or six pictures showing people participating in a variety of meals or snacks. The pictures should be as diverse as possible, showing different settings, different menus, and a variety of people of different ages. For example, they might include a happy family picnic, a family arguing over dinner, or even astronauts eating a meal under the weightless conditions of outer space. Assign one picture to each of five or six groups. Have each group prepare and present a skit about their picture, making up dialogue that reveals what is going on among the people, whether the menu is a healthy one, and whether the people are enjoying the food. Have the class discuss why the people in each skit responded to the meal as they did.

Other Activities

••• 1. **Planning a Healthy Meal** Have students consider the following situation: You are babysitting a six-year-old and must prepare dinner for yourself and the child. You are to get the ingredients at the corner grocery. You cannot spend more than $7, and you are not to buy anything that has to be cooked. The meal should be well-balanced. Have students write a one-page paper describing the meal they planned.

••• 2. **Finding Motivations for Eating Well** Have students brainstorm a list of excuses people give for postponing a diet to lose weight. Ask students to distinguish legitimate reasons from those that are not. Then ask students to compile a list of ways they might motivate themselves to begin a healthy diet and stay with it.

3. Improving the Diet Distribute copies of a recent cafeteria menu or other typical school luncheon menu. Ask students to substitute two dishes for two on the menu. The substitutions should be nutritionally healthy and should balance with the other foods.

Learning to Manage (p. 275)

Concepts

▪ healthy snacks are easy to make
▪ healthy snacks can provide energy
▪ adolescents can eat higher-calorie snacks than adults without fear of gaining weight
▪ popcorn, cheese, fruit, cream, spaghetti sauce, meat, peanut butter, and crackers can be used to make healthy snacks
▪ healthy snacks can be delicious

Discussion Questions

1. Why do you think students in Mr. Torres's class thought that "healthy" tasted boring?
2. If raw vegetables are considered healthy foods, why didn't Mr. Torres serve carrots and celery to the class?
3. Give two or three examples of an unhealthy snack.
4. Give two or three examples of a healthy snack.
5. Which of the healthy snacks made in Mr. Torres's class would you like to eat? Why?

Answers to Preceding Questions

Answers will vary but will probably include the following ideas.
1. Because those students were not in the habit of eating healthy snacks, they did not know what pleasant tastes they were missing.
2. Although carrots and celery are healthy foods, Mr. Torres realized that adolescents can eat higher-calorie, and more appealing, snacks without gaining weight.
3. Candy, sugary soft drinks, cookies, potato chips, ice cream, cake, and pie are examples of unhealthy snacks. They should be eaten only occasionally.
4. Raw fruits and vegetables, lean meat, poultry, fish, whole-grain cereals, and nuts are examples of healthy snacks.
5. Most students will probably like one or more of the snacks described in the text; some may like them all. Students should identify their favorite ingredient(s) in each snack.

Answers to Questions (p. 275)

Answers will vary but will probably include the following ideas.
1. Because tastes differ, students may name a wide variety of snacks; encourage them to think of snacks other than those described in the text. They should list every ingredient in the snack and, referring to student book pages 263–264 if necessary, name the food group each belongs to.
2. Many recipes may be suggested. Encourage students to keep the Dietary Guidelines (student book page 265) in mind while creating and collecting their recipes.
3. Most students will probably have at least modified their snack choices because of what they have learned. Encourage those who have not to try some of the new class recipes.

Health and Safety

The Food and Drug Administration (page 262)

One of the goals of this chapter has been to increase student awareness about good nutrition and the need for maintaining a healthy diet. In today's world, however, it takes more than knowing what to eat to insure a healthy diet. Because we rely heavily on an abundance of canned, frozen, and other prepackaged food products, people are not always sure of exactly what it is they are eating.

Discussion of "The Food and Drug Administration" can help students focus on how to insure the purity, safety, and nutritional value of the foods they buy.

Discussion Questions

1. Federal law requires that all packaged foods be clearly labeled with a list of ingredients. What other information would you like the FDA to require manufacturers to list on the labels of all canned and packaged foods?
2. If you were an inspector for the FDA, what combination of announced and surprise inspections would you want to make at food packaging plants? Why? .
3. Many fresh vegetables are sold at produce stands that are not easily regulated by the FDA. What questions might you ask these independent sellers to help insure the healthfulness of the food you want to buy?

Answers to Preceding Questions

Answers will vary but will probably include the following ideas.
1. Other information consumers might find useful could be the calories per serving, the Recommended Daily Allowance of nutrients per serving, and the packaging date.
2. Planned and surprise inspections can help insure both the cleanliness and safety of food packaging plants. Planned visits can make it clear to businesses exactly what is expected of them. Suitably forewarned, the food packager has ample opportunity to ask any question he or she might have and to bring his or her plant up to standards. Surprise inspec-

tions help insure that food packaging plants do not slip below the minimum standards in between planned inspections.
3. You might ask the following: Where was it grown? When was it picked? What kind of pesticides, if any, were used? Was anything done to the vegetables to make them look more attractive for sale?

Answers to For Review

Why We Eat What We Eat (p. 254)

1. The most important reason for eating is to supply the body with essential nutrients.
2. Three factors that influence food choices are family food customs, the foods friends eat, and religious customs. (Other possible answers: advertising, availability.)
3. Food that is available locally may be expensive if it is out of season in the local area and must be transported.

Nutrition and You (p. 261)

1. Most animal foods—meat, fish, poultry, eggs, and dairy products—contain essential amino acids. These foods are called *complete* proteins. Plant foods—cereals, nuts, and some vegetables—may contain some but not all the essential amino acids. These foods are called *incomplete proteins.*
2. The body needs carbohydrates because they are the major source of energy, and without the proper amount of carbohydrates, the body cannot use other nutrients properly.
3. Answers include proteins—meat; carbohydrates—rice; fats—egg yolks; vitamin C—oranges; minerals—peas; and water—fruit.

Daily Food Guide (p. 265)

1. The Daily Food Guide is important because it helps in planning a balanced diet for each day.

2. The six dietary guidelines that can help people get the nutrients they need are 1) eat a variety of foods; 2) maintain ideal weight; 3) avoid too much fat, saturated fat, and cholesterol; 4) eat foods with adequate starch and fiber; 5) avoid too much sugar; 6) avoid too much sodium.

Calories and Weight (p. 274)

1. The factors that influence a person's ideal weight are height, build, and overall health.
2. Diet pills can cause high blood pressure, shakiness, rapid heartbeat, kidney failure, and sometimes drug abuse. Fasting can cause depression or even sudden death.
3. Eating disorders are illnesses caused when people take extreme measures to lose weight. One such disorder is *anorexia nervosa*, caused by an obsession with thinness. Its victims cannot stop dieting, and actually starve themselves, resulting in serious illness or death. Victims of *bulimia*, another eating disorder, eat compulsively, then induce vomiting or take laxatives to rid the body of food. The result can be serious illness or death.

Chapter 12 Review

Vocabulary Answers (p. 276)

1. Nutrients
2. anorexia nervosa
3. essential amino acids
4. fat-soluble vitamins
5. Saturated fats
6. Unsaturated fats
7. cholesterol
8. water-soluble vitamins
9. calorie
10. basal metabolism
11. bulimia

Chapter Questions (p. 276)

1. Hunger is a feeling you get when your body needs food. Appetite is different from hunger in that it stems from a psychological need rather than a physical need of the body.
2. The functions of protein are to promote physical growth and to build and repair body tissue.
3. Meat, fish, poultry, eggs, and dairy products are complete protein foods.
4. Four sources of dietary fiber are fruits with their peel, whole-grain breads, cereals, and vegetables.
5. Although your body needs only a small amount of fat, you should not avoid all fat in your diet. Some fat is needed to carry into the body certain vitamins. These vitamins, called fat-soluble vitamins, are transported by fat rather than water. Fats also promote normal growth and healthy skin.
6. It is not necessary to take vitamin pills. A person can obtain whatever vitamins his or her body needs through proper diet.
7. Vitamin C helps the body form collagen.
8. Calcium and phosphorous are two minerals necessary for building healthy bones and teeth.
9. The five food groups are milk-cheese, meat-poultry-fish-bean, fruits-vegetables, bread-cereal, and fats-sweets.
10. At least four daily servings of fruits and vegetables are recommended.
11. Age, height, and body type affect how many calories your body burns in the course of a day's activities. For example, growing children and teenagers need more energy than older people. The rate at which a person is growing also affects number of calories needed. People with more muscle than fat need more calories than those with more fat than muscle.

12. There are many benefits you can derive from regular exercise. It can help you lose weight, firm up the body, keep the heart healthy, lift the spirits, and make you generally feel good.

13. The Dietary Guidelines for Americans are (1) eat a variety of foods; (2) maintain your ideal weight; (3) avoid too much fat, saturated fat, and cholesterol; (4) eat foods with enough starch and fiber; (5) avoid too much sugar; and (6) avoid too much sodium.

14. A person trying to gain weight should not eat large amounts of fatty foods. Though a high fat diet can help one gain weight, there are many health risks associated with eating large amounts of fats.

15. The result of a diet low in carbohydrates and high in protein can be headaches, a feeling of weakness, and heart or kidney disease.

Skill Activities

1. You might want students also to prepare a diet for a person who is slightly underweight. Students may also attempt to assign calorie counts to the various diets. This information is readily available from a variety of sources.
2. You might consider having students assemble their own emotionally related eating experiences before they brainstorm together. Virtually everyone will have had experiences where eating was clearly and closely related to an emotional state.
3. Each student's eating profile can shed considerable light upon that individual's diet. Each student can use the information that is gathered to analyze his or her personal eating pattern. You will probably want to urge students to use this information to develop plans that are more in line with amounts recommended in the Daily Food Guide.

4. Students might also include situations where someone is being urged not to eat a particular food or foods. Where young children are involved, situations that focus upon attempting to get them to try new foods are common.

Chapter 13

Meal Planning

Chapter Organization

Chapter Vocabulary

generic brands   (p. 286)
unit price   (p. 287)
convenience foods   (p. 287)
U.S. Recommended Daily Allowances (U.S. RDA)   (p. 288)
open dating   (p. 289)
additive   (p. 289)
pasteurized   (p. 292)
homogenized   (p. 292)

Chapter Objectives

After reading this chapter, students should be able to:

1. Describe their nutritional needs. (13.1)
2. Explain the relationship between a person's schedule and the time needed for meal planning. (13.1)
3. Plan appealing meals on a budget. (13.1)
4. Describe the various kinds of food stores. (13.2)
5. Explain the importance of smart shopping. (13.2)
6. Describe what food labels tell you. (13.2)
7. Describe how to store various kinds of food. (13.2)
8. Identify the various kinds of food products. (13.3)
9. List ways to determine the freshness of foods when shopping. (13.3)
10. Explain how to shop for high quality food. (13.3)

Program Resources

Student text pages 278–303
Teacher's Resource Book
    Skill/Development Worksheet 13
    Laboratory/Application Worksheet 13
    Reinforcement Worksheet 13
    Enrichment Worksheet 13
    Transparency Master 13
    Information Master 13
    Chapter 13 Test

Teaching Suggestions

The dots represent skill levels required to answer each question or complete each activity:
 •requires recall and comprehension
 ••requires application and analysis
 •••requires synthesis and evaluation

Into the Chapter

•**Estimating Food Costs** To prepare for the activity, collect a number of supermarket ads from the Sunday paper. Divide the class into three groups, and have each group plan an appealing, well-balanced, and inexpensive picnic for a family of four. After they have decided on a menu, they should list all the ingredients they will need. Have them list the price of each item, using the newspaper ads to estimate prices. Have each group present their menu and priced shopping list to the class. After discussion, ask the students to vote for the best plan in terms of taste, appeal, health, and cost.

Other Activities

••• 1. **Planning a Series of Meals** Ask students to plan for the following situation: You and three friends are going on an overnight camping trip. You will leave Friday afternoon and return Saturday after lunch. Plan three meals—Friday's dinner, and Saturday's breakfast and lunch. Students should design well-balanced menus consisting of foods that do not spoil easily and are easy to prepare on an outdoor camp oven.

2. **Estimating Food Quantities** Tell students to suppose they are going to a buffet dinner and have agreed to bring a fruit salad for thirty people. Have them plan the kinds of fruit and the quantity of each kind that they would need for the salad.

3. **Including Cheese in Meals** Have students brainstorm ways to include cheese in breakfast, lunch, and dinner menus. From a group of cookbooks collected in the classroom, have each student find a recipe that would be appropriate for each meal. Then have them build a well-balanced, low-cholesterol menu around the cheese recipes they have chosen for the three meals.

Learning to Manage (p. 301)

Concepts

- food prices are usually less in supermarkets than in small grocery stores
- coupons can help you reduce the cost of groceries
- store brands usually cost less than name brands
- to reduce impulse buying, avoid shopping when hungry
- promptly freeze or otherwise properly store meat, fish, and vegetables

Discussion Questions

1. How do you think Karen felt when she learned that all she had to do while her parents were away was shop and put the food away? Why?
2. Why was the money that Karen's mother had left for groceries running low by the end of the week?
3. What could Karen and Jane have done to avoid wasting the fish?
4. Why did the girls have to eat hamburger three nights in a row? How could they have avoided that boring diet?
5. What, where, and how do you think Karen will buy the food for the next two nights? Why?

Answers to Preceding Questions

Answers will vary but will probably include the following ideas.

1. She was probably relieved because she thought buying and storing food was easy.
2. The money was running low because (1) Karen shopped in a small grocery store instead of a supermarket, (2) forgot to use coupons to help pay for the groceries, (3) had to buy name brands rather than store brands, and (4) bought snack items not on her list because she was hungry when she shopped.
3. They could have eaten the fish the first night, while it was fresh. They didn't do that because they had not planned their meals carefully.
4. They had to eat hamburger three nights in a row to keep it, like the fish, from spoiling. If they had planned their meals better, they could have divided the hamburger into three parts and frozen it for later use.
5. Karen will probably shop, after she has eaten, in the supermarket. She will use coupons to help keep prices in line. She will have to buy inexpensive items such as eggs and pasta because her supply of money is low.

Answers to Questions

Answers will vary but will probably include the following ideas.

1. Karen (1) wasted money by shopping at a more expensive store, not using coupons, buying name brands, and buying unnecessary items; (2) wasted food by not using the fish while it was fresh; and (3) neglected to freeze part of the hamburger because she and Jane had not planned their meals carefully.

2. The meals students plan will probably vary widely. Be sure each student lists all ingredients, excluding staples, and estimates the cost of each. Ask students to write a brief report about their meal results, including any problems they may have had. Leftovers can be refrigerated, frozen, or used in another dish such as a casserole.

3. Students who do not shop for groceries on a regular basis may greatly over- or underestimate prices. Have them discuss the accuracy of their estimates. Students may want to bring supermarket ads from local newspapers or shoppers to class to find "Buys of the Week."

Technology

Super-Marketing (page 284)

This theme feature takes a look at the supermarket, the principal type of food store in this country today. The feature provides students with a brief history of its development and offers an insight into some of the marketing concepts that such stores employ. Students who are not familiar with shopping practices before the 1930s will probably find it hard to believe that smaller stores which emphasized personalized service were once the rule rather than the exception.

A discussion of "Super-Marketing" will provide students with an overview of what has become an American institution.

Discussion Questions

1. Why is one-stop shopping almost absolutely necessary in modern American society?
2. Why can supermarkets offer lower prices than the smaller, specialty food stores?
3. What kinds of products are displayed near supermarket check-out counters? What is the connection between these products and impulse buying?

Answers to Preceding Questions

Answers will vary but will probably include the following ideas.

1. In modern American society, few people have the time available to visit three or four stores in order to complete the week's shopping for essentials. With the limited time available, they rely upon the kind of store that stocks all needed merchandise under one roof. Also, many women who once handled most of the shopping are increasingly part of the workforce today.

2. Supermarkets can buy in great quantity because of their size. This allows them to pay the lowest prices available because they can buy in bulk. In addition, because they are basically self-service stores, their labor costs are far lower than stores that feature personalized service.

3. Various magazines as well as candy items are generally kept near supermarket check-out counters. People page through the magazines while waiting in line, find something that interests them, and decide to buy the magazine. Young children, who are often bored while waiting in line with their parents, see the candy items and often persuade their parents to buy them.

Answers to For Review

Meal Choices (p. 282)

1. Food may be seasoned with spices other than salt for someone who is on a low-sodium diet.
2. Time can be saved in preparing meals by making a casserole in one's spare time and then freezing it for later use. Pieces of baked chicken could be prepared in advance and then refrigerated. Quick, last-minute dishes could also be prepared.

3. It is important to serve foods of different colors at a meal because the different colors make the foods more appealing to the eye.

Food Shopping (p. 292)

1. Supermarkets, food warehouses, convenience stores, farmers' markets, produce stands, co-ops, and specialty stores are seven different kinds of food stores.
2. The purpose of planning ahead for food shopping is to save money. A shopper who checks ads for sales, decides what to serve during the following week, and then carefully prepares a list to avoid buying a lot of extras, can save as much as 20 cents on each dollar spent.
3. By law, every food label must contain the name of product, the name and address of the company that manufactures, distributes, or packs the product; a description of the product; a list of ingredients in order of quantity, beginning with the largest amount and including flavorings, preservatives, and artificial coloring; and nutritional information that indicates how much of a nutrient has been added.
4. Meat should be tightly wrapped for storage in paper, foil, or plastic. It may also be stored in an airtight plastic container.

High Quality Food (p. 300)

1. Skim milk has most of the fat removed and contains 0.5 percent or less of fat. Nonfat dry milk is a powdered form of milk that is prepared by removing most of the water and fat from liquid milk.
2. Three ways to tell if beef is tender are if there is marbling, or deposits of fat, scattered throughout; if the piece of meat was located on the animal in places where muscles receive very little exercise; and if the meat is from the rib, T-bone, or wedge bone.

3. Three clues to quality when buying poultry are meaty breasts and legs, well-distributed fat, and skin that has few blemishes or pinfeathers.

Chapter 13 Review

Vocabulary Answers (p. 302)

1. U.S. Recommended Daily Allowances
2. generic brands
3. pasteurized
4. additive
5. unit price
6. open dating
7. convenience foods
8. homogenized

Chapter Questions (p. 302)

1. When one says that various textures add interest to a meal, one means that certain textures contrast well with others. The crispness of a fresh salad, for example, goes well with the softness of a dish such as mashed potatoes.
2. It would be best to do the family food shopping in a supermarket rather than a convenience store. For one thing, the supermarket would have a broader selection of items. But most important, the prices at a supermarket would be noticeably lower than the prices at a convenience store.
3. Supermarkets normally carry thousands of items and provide such services as bagging and customized meat cutting. Food warehouses, on the other hand, are "no frills" stores that usually provide fewer services. Customers generally have to supply their own containers and fill them themselves. Also, food warehouses frequently have a rather limited selection of products or may only stock certain items in very large amounts.

4. Produce in a farmer's market is usually fresher than the same product in a supermarket because it comes directly from the farmers who sell it. It is less expensive for the same reason. The farmers grow, pick, deliver, and sell the product themselves and do not have to pay others to perform any of these services.

5. Shoppers should use coupons to purchase items that are truly needed and not to purchase items simply because a coupon is available.

6. The cereal contains the largest amount of corn, the ingredient that is listed first. Federal law requires that the ingredient that is present in the largest amount be listed first.

7. The *sell by* date that is found on foods that lose their freshness fast gives the last date on which the store should sell the item. The date does allow for some storage time at home, however.

8. It is important to know the *expiration date* on labels of baby food because the date is the last date on which the food can be safely used.

9. Sodium nitrate is used to prevent the growth of harmful bacteria in processed meats. Sodium nitrate can produce chemicals that cause cancer. Students who agree that sodium nitrate is dangerous will cite the fact that it can indeed produce cancer-causing chemicals. Those who agree that sodium nitrate is not dangerous are likely to make the point that it has been used for years without causing cancer that can easily be attributed to its use. They may also point out that tests that establish that a substance can produce cancer are carried out on laboratory animals that are exposed to large doses of the substances. These tests are not conducted on humans.

10. Fish and meat both spoil quickly.

11. It is dangerous to shop for food while hungry because hunger can cause impulse buying. Hunger also makes purchasing junk food more likely.

12. Beef is tender if there is *marbling,* or deposits of fat, scattered throughout, if the piece comes from muscles on the animal that receive little exercise, and if the piece is from the rib, T-bone, or wedge bone.

13. "Meatless" meat looks very much like actual meat, but is made from textured soy products. The protein that remains after the oil is removed from the soybeans is formed into a fiber that is used in products that resemble meat. Its nutritional value is close to the nutritional value of real meat.

14. A fillet of fish is a boneless piece of a fish's side cut away from the backbone.

15. The kind of rice found in most grocery stores is white rice. It is enriched to replace the nutrients lost in its processing. Brown rice has more nutrients than white rice. It has a chewy texture and nutlike flavor, and it takes longer to cook.

Skill Activities

1. Before students begin work on this activity, tell them to keep careful track of the costs associated with each type of pizza. Remind them that each of the three types to be prepared should be the same. A frozen pizza should not be compared with a homemade sausage pizza. As the food is prepared, someone in the group should be appointed to keep track of preparation time. You might want to consider having students who have nothing to do with the preparation judge such characteristics as appearance and taste. To accomplish this efficiently, the lab partners might devise a rating sheet which could be filled out by each evaluator. After the pizzas are prepared and evaluated, each lab group should meet to discuss the results of the experi-

ment. All factors to be evaluated should be compared and conclusions drawn.

2. Point out to students before they begin work on this assignment that part of the task involves the naming of the new cereal. Students should devise a name that will appeal to potential buyers. You might want to limit this activity to a cereal that has obvious nutritional value. The goal of the assignment would then be to invent a cereal that would be both appealing and nutritional. Students who are artistically inclined could design the entire package as well as the label.
3. Remind students to keep such characteristics as color, shape, texture, and flavor in mind as they plan their menu. Students should be asked to come up with a menu that is both nourishing and appealing. You might want to limit the activity to meals that are economical, meals that can easily be purchased by students for, perhaps, $1.50. It might be possible to arrange with the cafeteria manager to prepare and serve the meals that are the most nourishing and appealing.
4. You might consider expanding this activity to include as many of the various types of stores identified in this chapter as can be conveniently found in your area.

Chapter 14

Basic Kitchen Skills

Chapter Organization

Section 14.1 *The Organized Kitchen (student book page 305)*
Today's Kitchen

Section 14.2 *Safety First (student book page 308)*
Keeping Everything Clean
Keeping Food Safe
Safety in the Kitchen
In Case of Emergency

Section 14.3 *Kitchen Tools and Equipment (student book page 314)*
Kitchen Tools
Cleaning Tools
Pots and Pans
Small Appliances

Section 14.4 *Using Recipes (student book page 319)*
Choosing a Recipe
Components of Recipes
Formats of Recipes
What Ingredients Do

Section 14.5 *Measuring (student book page 322)*
Systems of Measurements
Abbreviations
Measuring Dry Ingredients
Measuring Liquids
Measuring Shortening

Chapter Vocabulary

sanitation (p. 308)
bacteria (p. 308)
toxins (p. 308)
hygiene (p. 309)
bakeware (p. 317)
cookware (p. 317)
recipe (p. 319)

Chapter Objectives

After reading this chapter, students should be able to:

1. Describe how a kitchen is divided into various work areas. (14.1)
2. Identify the tools, equipment, and space that

each area needs. (14.1)

3. Describe why sanitation is important in the kitchen. (14.2)
4. Identify ways to protect foods from spoilage. (14.2)
5. Explain how to maintain a safe kitchen and how to handle kitchen emergencies. (14.2)
6. Name the basic kitchen tools that are required for cooking and baking. (14.3)
7. Explain the difference between cookware and bakeware. (14.3)
8. Describe how to select different kinds of small appliances. (14.3)
9. Demonstrate how to evaluate and how to select a recipe. (14.4)
10. Identify what a clear recipe should include. (14.4)
11. Describe the four different forms of recipes. (14.4)
12. Demonstrate how standard and metric systems of measurements are used in recipes. (14.5)
13. Describe ways to measure dry ingredients, liquid ingredients, and shortening accurately. (14.5)

Program Resources

Student text pages 304–327
Teacher's Resource Book
 Skill/Development Worksheet 14
 Laboratory/Application Worksheet 14
 Reinforcement Worksheet 14
 Enrichment Worksheet 14
 Transparency Master 14
 Information Master 14
 Chapter 14 Test

Teaching Suggestions

The dots represent skill levels required to answer each question or complete each activity:

•requires recall and comprehension
••requires application and analysis
•••requires synthesis and evaluation

Into the Chapter

•**Inspecting the Foods Lab** Take students on a tour of the foods lab. Identify each piece of large and small equipment and show them where smaller equipment is stored. Assign each student a unit and give them a diagram of the unit. Have them open each drawer and identify the equipment therein.

Other Activities

•• 1. **Planning Kitchen Storage** Give each student a copy of the following list of kitchen items: bug spray, oven cleaner, scouring pads, dishwashing detergent, ammonia, a product for unplugging drains, poultry shears, cooking spoons, and kitchen knives. Ask them to note where they would store each one and their reasons for doing so. Discuss how their storage plan would be altered if there were young children in the household.

 • 2. **Identifying Words** Read the following words to students, allowing time for them to write each one as it is read: sanitation, hygiene, salmonella poisoning, botulism, toxins. Then have them define each one in their own words. Have them check the spelling and definitions themselves or exchange papers to check answers.

••• 3. **Writing a Recipe** Have students discuss what ingredients go into pizza topping. Then have each student write his or her recipe for a favorite topping. Remind them to list all ingredients and proportions and then to give careful step-by-step directions.

Learning to Manage (p. 325)

Concepts

- kitchens can often be reorganized to improve their efficiency
- storing bakeware near the stove saves steps
- silverware and dishes should be stored near the sink, where they are washed
- dish towels and paper towels should be hung near the sink
- spices should be stored away from heat and moisture and where they are easy to find
- pots, pans, and cooking utensils that are used often should be handy and easy to locate

Discussion Questions

1. Why do parents sometimes fail to organize their kitchens well?
2. Do you think Dan was previously aware of the organization of the kitchen in his house? What caused his interest in that subject?
3. What changes in the organization of the kitchen did Dan suggest to save steps?
4. Should spices be stored in a rack between the stove and the sink? Why?
5. How should frequently used cooking utensils be stored or displayed? Why?

Answers to Discussion Questions

Answers will vary but will probably include the following ideas.
1. Parents are often too close to the problem to recognize it. They usually work each day in the kitchen without giving much thought to its efficiency.
2. No, Dan was probably not aware of the organization of his kitchen. It was his Home Economics assignment that called his attention to that subject.
3. He suggested storing the bakeware nearer to the stove and storing dishes, silverware, and towels nearer to the sink.
4. No, spices should be stored away from both the stove and the sink because they are adversely affected by heat and moisture.
5. Cooking utensils that are used frequently should be kept near the stove or preparation area where they will be needed. Storing or displaying them where they will be easy to find will save much time that is usually wasted while searching for them among other, less frequently used utensils.

Answers to Questions (p. 325)

Answers will vary but will probably include the following ideas.
1. Students should consider the placement of small appliances such as toasters and mixers as well as large appliances such as stoves and refrigerators. They should also consider traffic patterns between storage, preparation, cooking, and dining areas and answer the following questions. Can appliances or kitchen areas be rearranged to save steps? Are foods stored safely and conveniently? Are frequently used cooking utensils easy to find?
2. Students will probably find many changes, such as relocating pots and dishes, that can be made without cost. They should realize that built-in appliances are more difficult and costly to move than are free-standing appliances. Many kitchen shortcomings, such as limited space and poor placement of major appliances, may have to be "lived with" on a limited budget. Those factors should be taken into consideration when evaluating the suitability of a house.

Careers

Kitchens Are Our Business (page 318)

This theme feature introduces the business home economist, the person who manages the test kitchens that all large food products companies maintain. The recipes that these test kitchens develop often exert great appeal on potential buyers. The recipe that is printed on a box or can label or that is presented in a product ad frequently persuades consumers to buy the product. The store demonstrations that these business home economists conduct frequently achieve the same purpose.

A discussion of "Kitchens Are Our Business" will make students aware of the promotional steps that food producers take to gain acceptance for their products.

Discussion Questions

1. Why do food producers frequently offer free recipe booklets that feature one or more of their products?
2. How does the offering of a toll-free number that consumers can use to talk to someone on the test kitchen staff benefit the company that produces the food?
3. Why do so many of the recipes that test kitchens prepare emphasize ease of preparation?

Answers to Preceding Questions

Answers will vary but will probably include the following ideas.

1. Free recipe booklets are potentially even more beneficial to the food producer than individual recipes that often appear on boxes and can labels. The producer hopes that the consumer will try many of the recipes included in the booklet, thereby requiring additional purchases of the product.
2. The food producer benefits because the consumer feels that there is a very close association between the consumer and the producer. The consumer believes that the producer is supportive of the product to the point that a person is available for guidance and to answer questions.
3. The food producer knows that there are many demands upon the time of modern

consumers. Few people have the time to get involved in time-consuming preparations.

Answers to For Review

The Organized Kitchen (p. 308)

1. The five major work areas found in most kitchens are the range area, the refrigerator area, the preparation area, the sink/cleanup area, and the eating area.
2. The range area will usually have a gas or an electric range and, perhaps, a microwave oven. Pots, pans, and potholders, as well as often used utensils, such as spoons and spatulas, will be kept nearby.
3. Ingredients that are used frequently, such as flour and pasta, should be kept near the preparation area. Bowls and other commonly used utensils and small appliances should also be kept nearby.

Safety First (p. 313)

1. Before handling food, people should wash their hands with soap and hot water. During the food preparation process, they should wash their hands again after sneezing or coughing, playing with a pet, going to the toilet, or touching their face or hair. Those who have open cuts on their hands should wear plastic gloves.
2. To guard against food poisoning from hot and cold foods, a good rule to observe is to be sure that hot foods are hot and cold foods cold before serving them. Hot foods should be served above a temperature of 140°F (60°C). Cold foods should be served at a temperature of about 40°F (5°C).
3. Fires and burns may be prevented in the kitchen by keeping pans from being knocked off a range by turning their handles toward the back of the stove; avoiding being burned by steam by lifting lids away from the user;

using dry pot holders to lift utensils because wet pot holders can cause steam burns; never using dish towels or paper towels near the stove because they can catch fire; and by using baking soda, salt, or a fire extinguisher (but never water) if grease catches fire.

Kitchen Tools and Equipment (p. 319)

1. The six basic types of kitchen tools are tools for cutting, tools for stirring and moving, tools for measuring, tools for separating and mixing, tools for baking, and general tools, such as can openers, cleaning brushes, and scouring pads.
2. Cookware consists of the pots and pans that are used on top of the range. Bakeware consists of the dishes and pans that are used in the oven.
3. A food processor chops, slices, grates, grinds, shreds, and mixes.

Using Recipes (p. 321)

1. Someone who sees a new recipe that he or she wants to try should ask these two questions: Will it appeal to family and guests as well as to me? Are the needed ingredients available; and if they must be purchased, are their costs within my budget?
2. Six components of a clearly written recipe are the list of ingredients that will be used, the amount of each ingredient that will be needed, step-by-step preparation instructions, the type and size of pans and dishes that will be used, the cooking times and temperature as well as any other instructions, and the number of servings that the recipe will produce.
3. The four standard formats for writing recipes are the *standard format,* in which the ingredients and amounts are listed first, followed by the directions in a numbered list or paragraph; the *descriptive format,* in which

the ingredients are listed in one column, the amounts in a second column, and the directions in a third column; the *action format,* in which step-by-step directions are presented with the ingredients and amounts right below each direction; and the *narrative format,* in which ingredients, amounts, and directions are included in a paragraph.

Measuring (p. 324)

1. The two systems of measurement in use in the world today are the standard system and the metric system.
2. Two methods for measuring dry ingredients accurately are filling a measuring cup or spoon with the correct amount and then using the straight edge of a spatula to level off the ingredient and filling a measuring spoon to overflowing and then leveling it off.

Chapter 14 Review

Vocabulary Answers (p. 326)

sanitation, bacteria, toxins, hygiene, cookware, bakeware, recipe

Chapter Questions (p. 326)

1. Pots and pans should be stored in the range area, for that is the area where they are used.
2. Many toxins are poisonous. A person who eats foods containing toxins can become quite ill and may even die.
3. It is important to practice personal hygiene when handling food because personal hygiene is necessary for sanitation. Sanitation keeps an environment clean and as free from bacteria as possible.
4. A cook should never use the same spoon for tasting and stirring. Using the same spoon

for tasting and stirring spreads germs and bacteria.

5. Food poisoning results from food spoilage. Spoilage occurs when the bacteria growing in the food make it unfit and unsafe for eating.

6. *Trichinosis* is caused by tiny worms that grow in pork. It is a serious illness that can be avoided only by cooking the pork thoroughly to an internal temperature of at least 170° F (75° C).

7. A person can tell that canned foods are spoiled by noting cans that are leaking or bulging. Such cans should never be bought and their contents should never be eaten. Canned foods that do not look right or smell right should also be thrown out.

8. The best way to disconnect an electric appliance is to grasp the plug and pull it out of the wall. It is never a good idea to jerk the cord instead.

9. If grease catches fire, baking soda or salt should be put on the flames. If the fire is in a pot, a lid should be put on the pot. If the fire is in the oven, the oven door should be closed. A fire extinguisher can be used if the fire is very small.

10. All cookware or bakeware can be cleaned in detergent and hot water. The following cautions apply to specific materials. Aluminum should be cleaned by hand and never put in a dishwasher. Cast-iron cookware should never be scoured nor should glassware, enamel vessels, or cookware and bakeware with nonstick finishes. Ceramic glassware and stainless steel items may be scoured if needed.

11. Students should explain why they believe the appliance they select is most useful. Students who select toasters might explain that the appliances do a job very conveniently that could only be done otherwise by using an entire oven. Students who choose toaster ovens might point out that they are particularly useful for preparing single or small portions. Students who choose blenders might note that the appliances do a job that might otherwise take a very long time. Students who select food processors might point out that the machines simplify and shorten tasks that can be very difficult and time-consuming. Students who choose electric frying pans might note that the appliances eliminate messy splashings and maintain absolutely even temperatures.

12. The answer will, of course, depend upon individual preferences. Ease of use should be the reason that is offered to explain why a particular format is a favorite. Most students will probably prefer the standard format, for most people find it to be the easiest to use and follow.

13. It is important to follow a recipe carefully so that it will come out properly. To adjust the ingredients, you might need an equivalent measures chart.

14. Flour is used in baked foods because its solid nature provides the basic structure of these foods.

15. It is important to know metric measurements because the metric system is increasingly being used. As this occurs, metric measuring equipment is coming into wider use.

Skill Activities

1. Have students review the sample recipes on page 320 before attempting this activity. Also, you might want them to examine the recipes available in their own homes to locate examples of the various kinds of formats. You might want to have students work with the favorite family recipe that they brought to class for Activity 4.

2. The sifted flour will weigh less than the unsifted flour. The unsifted flour has

greater bulk and therefore more weight. Students should be able to explain that using unsifted flour could easily affect a recipe that called for sifted flour because more flour than necessary would be used. This would be a good time to reemphasize the important point that recipes must be carefully followed if appropriate results are desired.

3. Be sure that students have an opportunity to examine photographs of kitchen plans before they begin this activity. You might want to have students begin by drawing the floor plan of the kitchen with which they are most familiar. The plan they will develop here would therefore be an improvement on the plan they are currently used to. Remind students that the kitchens they design should be as efficient as possible. This means that everything should be arranged in such a way that everything is as convenient as possible for the persons who use it. You might consider challenging students to design a kitchen that uses a small amount of space, the kind of kitchen that is commonly found in contemporary apartments.

4. Consider having each student explain the recipe brought to class. Students can point out why the recipe is particularly worthwhile. Have students explain such features as the dish's tastefulness, its appearance, its ease of preparation, its budget-sparing features, and its nutritional value. Have students discuss and then decide how they might structure the class recipe booklet. It could be randomly structured, or it could be organized by types of dishes, by preparation time, by nutritional standards, or in accordance with some other plan.

5. You might want to begin by having students note the kinds of storage, cleanliness, and cooking procedures that should be followed.

With this list in hand, they may then conveniently evaluate the specific procedures followed in their own kitchens or in the school kitchen. You can broaden this activity by having students consider other safety problems, such as the electrical problems that might be posed by too many appliances and too few electrical outlets. Have them also consider the availability of fire suppression equipment in the kitchen.

Chapter 15

Food Preparation

Chapter Organization

Section 15.4 *Convection and Microwave Cooking (student book page 351)*
Convection Ovens
Microwave Ovens
Principles of Microwave Cookery

Chapter Vocabulary

work plan (p. 329)
curdling (p. 336)
emulsion (p. 337)
microwaves (p. 351)

Chapter Objectives

After reading this chapter, students should be able to:
1. Explain the importance of having a plan for working in the kitchen. (15.1)
2. Describe how to prepare work plans for school and home. (15.1)
3. Explain how knowing cooking terms can help develop cooking skills. (15.2)
4. Identify the principles involved in making changes to a recipe. (15.2)
5. Explain how different foods react when they are combined in recipes. (15.3)
6. Describe the different cooking techniques used to prepare food. (15.3)
7. Explain the difference between dry-heat and moist-heat cooking methods. (15.3)
8. Explain the difference between convection ovens and microwave ovens. (15.4)
9. Identify the principles and uses of cooking in a microwave oven. (15.4)
10. Explain the importance of the proper care and use of microwave ovens. (15.4)

Program Resources

Student text pages 328–359
Teacher's Resource Book
Skill/Development Worksheet 15
Laboratory/Application Worksheet 15
Reinforcement Worksheet 15
Enrichment Worksheet 15
Transparency Master 15
Information Master 15
Chapter 15 Test

Teaching Suggestions

The dots represent skill levels required to answer each question or complete each activity:
•requires recall and comprehension
••requires application and analysis
•••requires synthesis and evaluation

Into the Chapter

••**Writing Directions in Correct Sequence** Distribute a sheet of directions for preparing scrambled eggs in which the steps are out of order. Ask students to unscramble the scrambled-eggs recipe by listing the directions in correct sequence. They should also list the ingredients and the equipment needed.

Other Activities
•• 1. **Analyzing and Applying Information** Have pairs of students role-play a TV interview with a famous chef. They should prepare for their interviews by making a list of questions and answers about food preparation from the text.
••• 2. **Using Chapter Vocabulary** Have small groups of students create crossword puzzles, using words taken from the chapter that relate to food preparation. Have the

completed crosswords reproduced and distributed to the class.

- **3. Identifying Categories of Bread** Distribute a list of various kinds of breads, sequenced in random order. Have students divide the list into three separate lists: 1) *Quick (Baking-powder) Breads,* such as corn muffins and cranberry loaf bread; 2) *Yeast Breads,* such as dinner rolls and whole wheat sandwich breads; and 3) *Unleavened Breads,* such as pita bread and tortillas.
- **4. Preparing Snacks for Special Occasions** Have students prepare small party sandwiches and/or baked goods for a faculty meeting, teachers' in-service workshop, or for parents' night.

Learning to Manage (p. 357)

Concepts

- ingredients must be measured exactly
- the pan used in baking a cake must be the size specified in the recipe
- bakers must use the exact ingredients called for in a recipe
- oven temperature is critical
- although baking time is important, cakes should be tested for doneness

Discussion Questions

1. Why did Joanne probably think that baking a cake would be easy?
2. What two mistakes will cause the batter of a cake to overflow the pan it is baked in?
3. Give one reason why a cake might not rise.
4. Why might a cake sink in the middle?
5. Why might a cook deliberately change a recipe?

Answers to Preceding Questions

Answers will vary but will probably include the following ideas.

1. She had probably never baked a cake before, and since most of the cakes she had seen had turned out well, she assumed it was easy to bake one.
2. Cake batter will overflow the pan if too much baking powder is added or if the pan is too small.
3. A cake will not rise if little or no baking powder has been used.
4. A cake might sink in the middle after it cools if it is not thoroughly cooked. It should be tested for doneness before being removed from the oven.
5. A cook might deliberately change a recipe if he or she has to or wants to substitute one or more ingredients. A cook might double or halve the recipe when cooking for a larger or smaller group of people than can be served by the original recipe.

Answers to Questions (p. 357)

Answers will vary but will probably include the following ideas.

1. Before students bake their cakes, the teacher may wish to review the recipes they have chosen to be sure they understand each measurement and term. Students should compute the cost of each ingredient used, since that information will be needed in Exercise 2.
2. Students can use the cost of each ingredient used in Exercise 1 as a guide when estimating costs for the bake sale. Students should total the cost of ingredients used in Exercise 1 when setting a price for that cake. Remind them that the 10 percent profit takes only the cost of ingredients into account; it does not include the cost of energy or labor. Nor does it include overhead. What would a professional baker, who would include those costs, have to charge for the same cake to make a profit?

Technology

Food from Space Lands Safely (p. 340)

This theme feature describes some of the things that NASA has done to make it possible for astronauts in space to eat nutritious, easy-to-prepare foods. In addition to serving the needs of the space program, these technologies have resulted in consumer products that have benefited various groups. These products demonstrate recent advances in food preparation techniques and provide some solutions to the age-old problems of food deterioration and food preservation. It is now possible to carry nutritious food about easily and to serve it quickly with a minimum of effort.

A discussion of "Food from Space Lands Safely" will help students to understand some of the benefits of modern food technology.

Discussion Questions

1. Why would freeze-dried foods and retort-pouch foods be particularly appealing to those on a backpacking trip?
2. Why would these foods be particularly interesting to Civil Defense officials who are in charge of planning for disasters?
3. Under normal circumstances, would these foods ever replace conventional foods prepared in standard ways?

Answers to Preceding Questions

Answers will vary but will probably include the following ideas.
1. Backpackers go out of their way to be sure they do not have to carry bulky items that are heavy. Freeze-dried foods and retort-pouch foods take up very little space and are lightweight and easy to carry.
2. Civil Defense officials would be interested in these foods because they could very easily be stored in shelters that are designed to accommodate people in times of disasters.
3. These foods are nutritious and tasty. However, under normal circumstances they would never replace conventional foods prepared in the normal way. Part of the appeal of food comes from its appearance and its texture. People would not want to sacrifice those characteristics.

Answers to For Review

In the Kitchen (p. 331)

1. A work plan for the kitchen should list the jobs to be done, the steps to follow, and the time required for each task.
2. One advantage of working in a group when preparing a meal is that several jobs can be done at the same time.

Using a Recipe (p. 334)

1. A person who uses a recipe will find preparation terms, cutting terms, and mixing terms.
2. It is sometimes necessary to change a recipe because more or fewer people than were expected have to be fed.

Cookery Principles (p. 350)

1. Milk, cheese, eggs, fats, and sugars are often called for in recipes.
2. Tender foods are cooked by the dry-heat method. The heat is direct and no water or liquid is added to the pan. Less tender foods are cooked by the moist-heat method. The foods are cooked in water or some other liquid.
3. Three examples of cooking meat or poultry with moist heat are by *braising* it, cooking it in a small amount of water in a covered

pan; by *simmering* large pieces covered with liquid; and by *stewing* smaller cuts covered with liquid.

4. Four ways of cooking fresh vegetables are by boiling, steaming, baking, and stir-frying.

Microwave Cooking (p. 356)

1. A conventional oven merely provides heat at a preset temperature and often cooks food unevenly. In a convection oven, fans circulate the heat at high speeds, allowing the heated air to hit the food from all sides and cook it more evenly and quickly.

2. Waves of energy called microwaves hit the food from all sides in a microwave oven. This causes the molecules in the food to rub against each other, producing friction. The friction creates the heat that cooks the food.

3. Metal cookware cannot be used in a microwave oven because the metal reflects the microwaves and prevents them from reaching and cooking the food.

4. Two advantages of microwave ovens are that they save energy and are easy to clean. Two disadvantages of microwave ovens are that not all foods can be cooked in less time and some food tastes better when cooked in a conventional oven.

Chapter 15 Review

Vocabulary Answers (p. 358)

1. emulsion
2. work plan
3. Microwaves
4. Curdling

Chapter Questions (p. 358)

1. The purpose of a work plan in food preparation is to list the jobs that have to be done, the steps to follow to get them done, and to indicate the time that will be required to complete each task.

2. A recipe for two people can be adapted to feed four by doubling it. If a recipe is doubled, a larger pan will be needed and more cooking time will be necessary.

3. An egg that is roasted in its shell in an oven might explode because the yolk cooks faster than the white due to its high fat content.

4. Fruits and vegetables should be prepared in their skins as often as possible because many of the vital nutrients are in their peels or skins.

5. When cut fruit is exposed to the air, it loses the vitamins that it contains, especially Vitamin C.

6. Steaming is a good way to prepare vegetables because the vegetables are not actually immersed in water. When vegetables are immersed in water, some of the nutrients seep out and are lost.

7. An emulsion is a combination of oil and another liquid, beaten so that the ingredients do not separate. Egg yolks are the emulsifying agent in mayonnaise.

8. Sirloin steak is a cut of meat that does not need much cooking time. The same is true of other steaks that are lean. Meat with a lot of connective tissue needs much longer cooking time.

9. When meat is broiled, it is cooked above or below a direct source of heat. The fat from the meat drips into the heat source or into the bottom of the broiling pan. When meat is fried, it is cooked in fat that is added to the pan and in its own fat as well.

10. Pork should always be cooked to the point that it is well done.

11. Fish requires a short cooking time because it has very little connective tissue.

12. Rice should not be rinsed either before or after cooking. Water tends to rinse away

some of the nutrients that are in rice.

13. Brown sugar is granulated sugar with molasses added for color and flavor. Both light and dark brown sugar are available. The dark variety has the stronger flavor.
14. A glass container can be used in a microwave oven because glass transfers the microwaves to the food that is being cooked.
15. Food cooked in a microwave oven should be stirred or rearranged so that the heat is distributed evenly.

Skill Activities

1. You might want to point out to students that chicken is a very popular dish because it is nutritious, low in calories, and relatively inexpensive. Therefore, there are literally hundreds of recipes available in numerous sources. Many cookbooks, for example, are devoted exclusively to chicken. Also, chicken can be cooked in a wide variety of ways and is therefore within the capability level of virtually everyone. In many sources of chicken recipes, students will find menus for chicken dinners. They may wish to choose one of these. You might ask students to estimate the cost per serving for the meal they choose. This may be compared with the cost per serving for a meal that uses a more expensive entrée, such as lamb or beef.
2. You might want students to develop an actual poster that will be displayed next to a microwave oven at home. It should be the kind of poster that would attract younger brothers and sisters to read it. Students can make their posters more appealing and effective by adding appropriate art work.
3. Suggest that students record their observations in writing. Written observations can be compared in class among those students who have chosen to experiment with the same vegetable.
4. Suggest to students that they consider visiting a local hospital or nursing home. Those who prepare the menus in these institutions are very familiar with the needs of those who are on the special diets identified.

Chapter 16

Meals and Manners

Chapter Organization

Section 16.1	*Breakfast (student book page 361)* *Quick Breakfast Ideas*
Section 16.2	*Lunch and Snacks (student book page 364)* *Packing a Good Lunch* *Lunch Recipes* *Snacks*
Section 16.3	*Dinner (student book page 367)* *A Nutritious Dinner* *Dinner for One*
Section 16.4	*Table Settings and Etiquette (student book page 370)* *Serving Food* *Setting the Table* *Table Manners* *Dining Out*

Chapter Vocabulary

etiquette (p. 370)
cover (p. 373)
reservation (p. 378)
entrée (p. 379)

table d'hôte   (p. 379)
prix fixe   (p. 379)
à la carte   (p. 379)

Chapter Objectives

After reading this chapter, students should be able to:
1. Explain the importance of a healthy breakfast. (16.1)
2. Identify a variety of foods that can make up a good breakfast. (16.1)
3. Describe how to make some good breakfast foods. (16.1)
4. Pack a healthy lunch. (16.2)
5. Plan a special lunch. (16.2)
6. Identify a variety of nutritious snacks. (16.2)
7. Explain the importance of eating a healthy dinner. (16.3)
8. List different ways in which meals can be served. (16.4)
9. Describe the correct way to set a table. (16.4)
10. Explain the value of using table manners at home and elsewhere. (16.4)
11. Explain the importance of knowing and observing the rules of restaurant etiquette. (16.4)

Program Resources

Student text pages 360–383
Teacher's Resource Book
    Skill/Development Worksheet 16
    Laboratory/Application Worksheet 16
    Reinforcement Worksheet 16
    Enrichment Worksheet 16
    Transparency Master 16
    Information Master 16
    Chapter 16 Test

Teaching Suggestions

The dots represent skill levels required to answer each question or complete each activity:
• requires recall and comprehension
•• requires application and analysis
••• requires synthesis and evaluation

Into the Chapter

•• **Planning and Presenting a Classroom Breakfast Party** Have students plan and prepare a healthy, simple classroom breakfast. Have them plan the menu, the shopping list, and how the food will be served. Divide the class into groups to perform various tasks: shopping, cooking, setting up a buffet table, decorating, serving, and cleaning up. You may wish to have students prepare a formal invitation to the principal, counselor, or other school administrative personnel.

Other Activities

•• 1. **Preparing a Cookbook** Have each student write a recipe for his or her favorite sandwich. Combine the recipes into an attractive classroom cookbook titled "Super Sandwiches," designed by students and illustrated with some black-and-white drawings. Reproduce copies for all the students in the class.

•• 2. **Demonstrating Good Manners** Bring a tea service to class. Have students research in books of etiquette to find the way to serve a formal tea. Then have them set a table for a formal tea. Have small groups take turns role-playing the pouring and serving of the tea, asking guests to choose lemon, cream, or sugar, and making polite party conversation with the guests.

••• **3. Planning a Salad Luncheon** Have the class brainstorm ideas for creating a luncheon built around a main-course salad. Have students suggest ideas for healthy, appealing salads that include protein as well as green and yellow vegetables. Have them offer suggestions for table settings and decorations. Then have each student write his or her plans for a salad luncheon. Have them describe the salad and name the other foods they plan to serve. Have them describe the dishes, tablecloth and napkins, and decorations they would like to have. They may wish to look for decorating ideas in magazines about cooking, entertaining, and table decoration.

Learning to Manage (p. 381)

Concepts

- large dinner parties require careful planning
- duties involved in giving a dinner party include meal planning, shopping, cooking, table setting, decorating, and cleaning up
- some dishes can be cooked and frozen before the dinner
- decorations can be created for little or no cost
- flowers and candles add an air of formality to a table setting

Discussion Questions

1. Why did the class give a dinner party for Mrs. White? Why didn't they ask her what she would like to eat?
2. Do you think Mrs. White would be a good judge of the way the dinner was planned, cooked, and served? Why?
3. Why do you think the class divided itself into committees?
4. What decisions do you think went into planning the meal?

5. Which tasks could be completed before the day of the dinner party? Which tasks had to be completed on the day of the party?

Answers to Preceding Questions

Answers will vary but will probably include the following ideas.

1. The class gave a dinner party for Mrs. White because they liked her and she was retiring. They didn't ask what she would like to eat because the party was to be a surprise.
2. Yes, Mrs. White would be a good judge because she was an excellent Home Economics teacher.
3. The class probably divided itself into committees to make sure that no detail was overlooked. Working in committees also prevented a few students from having to do all the work and spread out the chores so that each person could have the satisfaction of contributing to the effort.
4. Students probably had to determine which foods were favorites of Mrs. White, which foods would be enjoyed by the teachers, and which foods would cause no problems for diners who had allergies or were on special diets. The food could cost no more than the money students had. It also had to be prepared beforehand and easy to serve.
5. Meal planning, shopping, cooking, and some decorating could be done before the day of the dinner party. Decorating that might be seen by Mrs. White before the dinner (thereby spoiling the surprise), table setting, serving, and cleanup would have to be done on the day of the dinner.

Answers to Questions (p. 381)

Answers will vary but will probably include the following ideas.

1. In planning the party, students will want to consider the ages, food preferences, and dietary needs of the guests. They will also

want to take into consideration the cost of various ingredients and the ease of preparing, cooking, and serving various dishes. They will need to determine the reason for giving the dinner party to decide whether it should be formal or informal, theme oriented, decorated in a certain manner, and so forth.

2. Students should be sure to include a napkin and all dishes, flatware, and glasses in their drawing. The centerpiece may be purchased or created at home; it should be appropriate for the age or ages and interests of the guests and the reason for or theme of the dinner party.

Leadership and Citizenship

Serving the Elderly (p. 370)

Most adolescents consider the problems of the elderly to be remote. Aging is more an eagerly anticipated matter of "growing up" than "growing old." This theme feature helps students focus on the fact that they are currently in only one phase of a total life cycle. It also helps them understand how their nutritional needs and eating habits will evolve over the years.

A discussion of "Serving the Elderly" can raise student consciousness about the need for community services as well as the opportunity for them to volunteer their help to the elderly.

Discussion Questions

1. In addition to three meals a day, what other types of prepared foods might you want to deliver to elderly people who have a difficult time preparing foods for themselves?
2. Why do you think "companionship at mealtimes is almost as important as the meals themselves" for many elderly people?
3. What would you do if you were delivering meals to an elderly person and noticed that previous meals were going uneaten?

Answers to Preceding Questions

Answers will vary but will probably include the following ideas.

1. Elderly persons who have a difficult time preparing meals for themselves would probably appreciate the delivery of nutritious snacks. Preparing healthy snacks can feel as troublesome as preparing a meal when you are not in good health. It would also be helpful to make sure these elderly persons had a supply of frozen meals on hand in the event there was some interruption in delivery services. These meals require little effort on the part of the elderly person or someone who might be able to give them assistance.
2. Companionship at mealtimes is important to many elderly people because it helps them feel connected to the outside world. It also reassures them that someone cares about them and their well-being.
3. If you noticed that meals were going uneaten, it would be wise to inquire as to the nature of the problem. Some people, both elderly and young, are hesitant to complain about a service for fear they might be misunderstood. Find out if the person's unwillingness to eat is a matter of taste, a dietary problem that is health-related, or perhaps a sign of an emotional problem.

Answers to For Review

Breakfast (p. 363)

1. Breakfast is an important meal because the body needs nourishment after a night's sleep. Breakfast provides the body with the fuel it needs to perform during the day.
2. The traditional American breadfast includes foods such as juice, cereal, toast, and some form of eggs.

3. Waffles, pancakes, muffins, tortillas, biscuits, loaf breads, coffee cakes, and muffins are all types of quick breads.
4. Measure and sift the dry ingredients in a bowl. Mix liquid ingredients in a separate bowl. Pour liquid ingredients into dry ingredients. Stir until moistened. Spoon batter into greased muffin tins or loaf pan to two-thirds full. Bake according to recipe.

Lunch and Snacks (p. 367)

1. Some foods, such as meat, milk, and eggs, spoil quickly at room temperature. This is why it is important to keep hot foods hot and cold foods cold when packing a lunch.
2. Keep lettuce crisp by packing it in a plastic bag or a plastic container with a lid.
3. The following snacks are nutritious and easily prepared: fresh fruit, fresh vegetables, nuts, popcorn, fruit juice, milk, salad, and peanut butter sandwiches.

Dinner (p. 369)

1. A well-planned dinner should include foods from the four food groups that will supply needed proteins, vitamins, and minerals.
2. Health professionals often recommend a light dinner for those people who eat late in the evening. This gives the body enough time to burn the calories before sleep.
3. Here are some useful tips for those people who prepare dinners for one. Save time and avoid waste by buying frozen vegetables. Cook only what you need and save the remainder for later use. Buy only small amounts of fresh fruits and vegetables to ensure freshness. Buy large packages of poultry and meat and freeze the unused portions in individual packages for later use. Label the packages with the name of the food and the date it was bought.

Table Settings and Etiquette (p. 380)

1. *Head-of-the-table service* is usually used at formal or special occasions. Plates and serving dishes are placed near the person sitting at the head of the table. This person serves the food and passes it to others. Sometimes a second person serves the vegetables or salad. Foods like bread and butter are passed around the table.
2. The dinner knife is placed to the right of the plate with the cutting edge next to the plate. The butter knife is placed across the butter plate or vertically along the right side of the butter plate.
3. When a meal ends, place your napkin to the left of your plate, thank the cook, and ask to be excused if you wish to leave the table.
4. The purpose of a tip is to show appreciation for good service. It has nothing to do with the quality of the food that was served.

Chapter 16 Review

Vocabulary Answers (p. 382)

1. reservation
2. *prix fixe; table d'hôte*
3. *à la carte*
4. *entrée*
5. cover
6. etiquette

Chapter Questions (p. 382)

1. The traditional American breakfast consists of foods such as juice, toast, cereal, and eggs. Any food, however, can be a breakfast food as long as it doesn't have too many sweets and constitutes a balanced meal.
2. When using the muffin method, overmixed batter can cause a tough product.

3. To keep a packed lunch cool, add a frozen item or a container of refreezable gel to the lunch.
4. Bananas, cheese, and avocados are examples of rich foods that provide nutritious snacks.
5. Many machine snacks, such as soft drinks and candy, are sugary and lack nutritional value.
6. Meat, poultry, fish, cheese, or egg dishes are suitable main dish foods.
7. An appetizer is a light food served before the main part of the meal.
8. Dinner can be an important time for families to relax together and talk about the day's events.
9. Easy-to-eat foods are the most appropriate types of food to serve at a buffet.
10. When the salad is eaten before the main course, the salad fork is placed on the outside.
11. The following centerpieces are suitable for decorating a table: fresh fruit in a basket, fresh vegetables or gourds in a basket, an arrangement of candles, a lone large candle surrounded by greenery, or a craft object.
12. The following are acceptable answers:
   • Taking the time to be well groomed and arrive on time tells your hosts that you appreciate their dinner invitation.
   • Wait until the meal is announced before sitting down at the dinner table.
   • Use your napkin frequently during dinner. It shows you are concerned about your appearance and its effect on others.
   • Sit appropriately at the dinner table. This makes it easier for those around you to eat in comfort without being cramped or jostled.
   • Chew with your mouth closed and do not talk with food in your mouth. This shows respect and consideration for others.
   • Make pleasant conversation. Do not dominate the conversation or pursue a topic that does not interest anyone.

   • Help maintain a smooth flow of food around the table by passing the serving dishes in one direction.
13. Three major categories of restaurants are fast-food, informal, and formal.
14. Make a restaurant reservation by calling on the telephone and giving your name, the date and time you wish to eat, and the number of people who will be eating.
15. If you have a complaint about the food at a restaurant, explain what is wrong to your waiter or waitress in a polite manner.

Skill Activities

1. First, discuss and review balanced diets. To develop interest in this activity, have students imagine they are opening a fast-food breakfast restaurant. Students can develop a menu of at least ten items. Each item should be easily prepared and nutritious. Students might also work together to create appealing names for each item.
2. You might want students to compare the actual menu from a fast-food restaurant with the menu they developed. Students may be surprised at the nutritional content of menu items from the restaurant. Discuss ways to increase their nutritional value.
3. Students should work in groups of five to prepare each skit. One member of the group can be chosen as the waiter or waitress and the other four can be the diners. As each group plans their skit, they should act confused. Then repeat each skit to show more assured behavior.
4. You might want to have students attempt this activity before studying the correct placement shown on pages 374–375 to determine how many students need help. As a student sets a place or demonstrates a procedure, other students can comment and suggest changes. Students can use their artistic abilities when creating a centerpiece.

Unit 5

Clothing and Textiles

Chapter 17

Your Clothes

Laundry
Dry Cleaning
Routine Care
Storage

Chapter Organization

Chapter Vocabulary

style   (p. 389)
fashion   (p. 389)
classic   (p. 389)
fads   (p. 389)
factory surplus   (p. 400)
natural fibers   (p. 400)
manufactured fibers   (p. 402)
blends   (p. 402)

Chapter Objectives

After reading this chapter, students should be able to:

1. List the functions of clothing. (17.1)
2. Explain how clothes affect the impression people make on others. (17.1)
3. Explain how fashion trends and peers influence clothing choices. (17.1)
4. Identify the main elements of clothing design. (17.2)
5. Take a clothing inventory. (17.3)
6. List ways to save money when clothes shopping. (17.3)
7. Describe fibers used in fabrics. (17.4)
8. Explain how fabrics are made. (17.4)
9. Describe proper laundering. (17.5)
10. Explain how to keep clothes in good condition. (17.5)

Program Resources

Student text pages 386–415
Teacher's Resource Book
    Skill/Development Worksheet 17
    Laboratory/Application Worksheet 17
    Reinforcement Worksheet 17
    Enrichment Worksheet 17
    Transparency Master 17
    Information Master 17
    Chapter 17 Test

Teaching Suggestions

The dots represent skill levels required to answer each question or complete each activity:
  •requires recall and comprehension
  ••requires application and analysis
  •••requires synthesis and evaluation

Into the Chapter

•**Selecting Appropriate Clothing** Ask students to imagine that they are buying an outfit for a specific occasion. The can choose any occasion they wish from a dance to a camping trip. They have an unlimited budget. Have each student name the occasion and write a detailed description of the outfit he or she would choose.

Other Activities

•• 1. **Researching Fashion History** Divide the class into three groups. Have each group research what fashions were worn in the 1950s, 1960s, or 1970s. They should research both women's and men's fashions for their assigned era. Ask them to find at least one fashion from their era that has come back into style. Have each group present a summary of their research to the class for discussion.

••• 2. **Organizing Fashion Information** Have students brainstorm a set of questions they might ask a fashion designer about today's clothing styles, for both women and men. Have them include questions about the way fabrics are cut, textures and colors of clothing that are currently popular, and how accessories can be coordinated with clothing. Have each student choose one question to answer in depth, using current fashion magazines as a resource. Ask students to share and discuss their answers.

••• 3. **Designing a Sweater** Give each student a duplicated copy of a drawing of the outline of a crewneck sweater. Have students, using paints, colored pencils, or colored pens, design a sweater by coloring and decorating the drawing. Have them add a brief description of the fabric used and other details that are difficult to illustrate. Have them name the kinds of activities for which their "designer" sweater is appropriate.

Learning to Manage (p. 413)

Concepts

▪ extreme styles quickly date clothing
▪ clothes that are "in" this year may be "out" next year
▪ clothing with designer labels is usually more expensive than less-well-known brands
▪ the quality of expensive clothing may be no better than that of inexpensive clothing
▪ solid colors blend well with clothing of various colors
▪ classic styles will be in vogue for years

■ inexpensive fad items can complement and update basic outfits

Discussion Questions

1. What kind of clothing does Ann like to wear?
2. How has Marie's taste in clothing changed?
3. Give at least two reasons why you think Marie's taste in clothing has changed.
4. Should one ever buy an expensive classic outfit when on a limited budget? Why?
5. Do you always have to choose between "boring" and "crazy," "in" fashions? Explain.

Answers to Preceding Questions

Answers will vary but will probably include the following ideas.

1. Ann likes to wear clothing that is bright, in style, popular, and exciting.
2. Marie used to like the kind of clothing that Ann now likes, but lately she has been buying more traditional, classic clothes that can be worn with a wide variety of clothing and accessories.
3. Marie has matured enough to realize that clothing value is more important than clothing fads. Since she is buying all of her own clothes, she wants to get the most for her money. She is also thinking of the impression she will make on prospective employers, and probably her fellow workers.
4. Yes, the expense of a classic outfit can be justified by the many outfits it will create when combined with other clothing, the length of time it will be serviceable, and the gains it may bring by creating a favorable impression in the community or workforce.
5. No, basic outfits can be rendered less "boring" and more modern by combining them with inexpensive, trendy accessories.

Answers to Questions (p. 413)

Answers will vary but will probably include the following ideas.

1. Marie is buying clothing that is suitable for the world of work. She avoids wasting money on expensive fads, concentrating instead on items that are long lasting and versatile. She indulges herself only in inexpensive "crazy" accessories that are popular today but may be out of style tomorrow.
2. Ann is probably learning about wise clothing decisions as she shops with Marie. Although her tastes are not the same as Marie's, she seems to trust her sister's judgment and advice. As she becomes more and more responsible for the cost of her own clothes, she will probably adopt many of the standards that Marie now uses when purchasing her clothing.
3. Many students will place undue importance on wearing clothing that is "in," since they are so sensitive at this age to peer acceptance. Students should be shown their options without any implication, and corresponding guilt, that their answers are "wrong."

Technology

Jacquard Loom (p. 404)

Technology has made an enormous impact on the clothes we wear. This chapter has carefully pointed out to students that technology has made a vast array of manufactured fibers available to the clothing industry that were once unheard of. This theme feature expands that awareness to include the sophisticated technology that goes into creating the beautiful designs that can be seen in tapestry, brocade, and damask fabrics. Students should understand, however, that not all fabric patterns are created in this manner. It will interest students to learn the long history of the Jacquard loom.

Discussion of "Jacquard Loom" will teach students about the opposition that a new invention may encounter. It will also provide an excellent example of how technological advances in one industry are often picked up and adapted for use in an entirely different industry.

Discussion Questions

1. Would you call Joseph-Marie Jacquard one of the founders of the computer industry? Explain your answer.
2. What purpose does the hole-punched card serve in the Jacquard loom? What changes does the loom need to undergo to change the pattern it produces?
3. If the Jacquard loom were introduced today, do you think the weavers would protest its introduction as the French weavers did during the 1800s? Why?

Answers to Preceding Questions

Answers will vary but will probably include the following ideas.

1. Joseph-Marie could be called one of the founders of the computer industry because the hole-punched cards he created to direct the operation of his loom became the basic method of feeding information into computers. (The idea of using punched cards to code information was picked up by Charles Babbage for use in his calculating machine, the forerunner of the digital computer.)
2. The hole-punched cards tell the loom which needles to use and when to use them. Basically, all that needs to be done to change the pattern that the loom is producing is to change the hole-punched cards that give the loom its operating instructions.
3. Weavers opposed the introduction of the Jacquard loom because they did not want to lose their jobs. This is a natural reaction to loss of income and an uncertain future. Although today's workers may be more accustomed to technological changes, it is quite likely they would have the same reaction as the French weavers. Consider, for example, the reactions of contemporary workers to the introduction of robotics to factory assembly lines. The workers' opposition to the loom might have been less if they were participating in programs that retrained them for work elsewhere.

Answers to For Review

Clothing Choices (p. 390)

1. Modesty, protection, and image are the three main functions of clothing.
2. Clothing can affect your image in the following ways: 1) by helping you to create a sense of individuality; 2) identifying you with a special group; and 3) suggesting your association with a particular status level.
3. The appeal of short-lived clothing fads is one of the primary reasons fashions change from year to year. Many people enjoy change and thus encourage clothing fads through their buying habits. The fashion industry promotes frequent changes in style because it wants people to keep buying new clothes. Finally, fashions also change from year to year because of changes in technology. In today's world, clothes can be produced more quickly and less expensively than ever before.

Design Elements (p. 395)

1. The four elements of clothing design are lines, colors, textures, and patterns.
2. Horizontal lines make a person appear shorter and heavier.
3. Small to average size people generally look best in patterns with a small design.

Planning Your Wardrobe (p. 400)

1. During a clothing inventory, it would be useful to sort your wardrobe into the following three categories: clothes you like and wear; clothes you like but which need repair; and clothes you have outgrown or don't like.
2. The following guidelines can help you work out

a successful clothes buying plan: 1) make a list; 2) buy versatile clothes; 3) make sure some of your larger purchases are classic items and limit fad purchases to smaller things; 4) look for sales and comparison shop; 5) decide, beforehand, how much you can afford to spend, and stay within your budget.

3. There are many ways to save money on clothing. Sales are a good place to start. Sewing your own clothes is another money-saving idea. If you don't have the time, skill, or a sewing machine to make your own clothes, you can trade or share clothes with a relative or friend. Another way to save money on clothing is to shop at consignment or outlet stores. Consignment stores sell used clothing. Outlet stores sell clothes at reduced prices.

Fibers and Fabrics (p. 406)

1. The three main types of fibers used in making fabrics are natural fibers, manufactured fibers, and blends of natural and manufactured fibers.
2. Weaving, knitting, and bonding are the three most common ways of making fabrics.
3. A variety of finishes can be used to improve the fabrics you wear. Durable press, permanent press, and wash-and-wear finishes condition fabrics so that they require little or no ironing. Waterproof and water-repellent finishes help fabrics shed or resist water. Other finishes keep fabrics from easily burning, reduce static cling, and help keep dirt from settling on fabrics.

Clothing Care and Storage (p. 412)

1. Care labels provide important information on how to launder a garment properly.
2. Remember the following steps when using a washer and a dryer: 1) sort clothes according to their temperature and washing cycle

needs; 2) check pockets to make sure they are empty; 3) check for stains that need pretreatment; 4) choose the correct water temperature; 5) do not overload the washer; 6) use the proper amount of detergent; 7) mix bleach in washer water before adding clothes; 8) dry clothes at the correct temperature; 9) when clothes are finished drying, remove them immediately from the dryer; 10) clean the lint filter in the dryer.

3. Routine care of your wardrobe is not difficult if you remember the following points. Make sure to open all fasteners and zippers when taking off or putting on clothes. Air clothes outside the closet. Hang clothes straight, with buttons and zippers closed. Do not throw wet clothes in a pile. Make simple repairs and remove spots as soon as possible.

Chapter 17 Review

Vocabulary Answers (p. 414)

1. style
2. classic
3. factory surplus
4. natural fibers
5. fashion
6. blends
7. fads
8. manufactured fibers

Chapter Questions (p. 414)

1. Formal wear is usually considered proper attire for a wedding. The unwritten dress code would label a guest who appeared in casual clothing as inappropriately dressed.
2. During hot weather, light colored clothing is preferable. Since light colors reflect the sun's rays away from the body, light colors help keep the body cool.

3. By adding unusual accessories, such as an eye-catching belt or scarf, it is possible to dress with a spark of individuality.

4. Designer clothes and certain expensive name brand items of clothing are considered, by many, as "status clothes." Status clothes are often more expensive than similar nondesigner clothes and are likely to go out of style quickly.

5. Students may answer this question in many ways. However, based on the information supplied in the text, a typical answer might explain that a good wardrobe usually consists primarily of classic clothes with a sprinkling of fad items. Most fad items have limited use. Classically styled clothes are more versatile. Not only can they be worn for more than one type of occasion, but they are also easy to mix and match. The ability to use the same clothes in different combinations creates the impression that your wardrobe is larger than it may actually be.

6. Clothes with vertical lines make you appear taller and thinner than you may be.

7. Wear a long jacket to make your legs look shorter.

8. Give yourself a color analysis to determine what colors look best on you. All you need is a mirror and a good light. Hold up colors to your face to see which are most flattering. Try out different values and intensities.

9. Students may suggest a variety of different outfits with complementary color schemes. In order to be complementary, the colors they suggest must be direct opposites on the color wheel. See page 393.

10. A small person might choose a fabric with a fuzzy or shiny texture in order to make himself or herself appear larger.

11. Look for the following signs of quality in the clothing you buy: stitching that is straight and even; thread that is close to the same color as the fabric; seams that do not pucker or ravel; even hems with stitches that do not show through; closings that do not pucker or wrinkle; zippers that function smoothly; securely sewn hooks and eyes; buttonholes that have extra stitching at the ends; facings that lie flat; and matched seams.

12. Different return policies include giving a refund; allowing exchange only; or no returns or exchanges at all.

13. Fabrics made out of fibers such as cotton and linen are comfortable to wear during warm weather because they absorb moisture. Synthetics, such as nylon, do not absorb moisture and are uncomfortable in warm weather.

14. In weaving, the yarn that runs crosswise is the "warp."

15. Although clothes that require dry cleaning are not usually considered a practical purchase, especially if they are light colored, there are special occasions and special fabrics (like some wools and silks) for which you may choose the expense of the upkeep.

Skill Activities

1. You will probably want to break up the class into groups of four or five for this brainstorming activity. So that the factors identified can be shared later, ask each group to appoint a secretary who will record in writing the factors that each group identifies. In addition to factors that relate to clothing, each group will probably identify factors that relate to hygiene and nutrition. Also, each group will probably cite such psychological factors as inner satisfaction and a positive attitude. Make the point that personal appearance relates to a number of factors.

2. Urge students to devote some time to planning before they begin to write their paragraphs. They can begin the planning by determining what it is about themselves that they wish to communicate by the clothing

they choose. What they wish to communicate through their clothing should be expressed in a sentence like the following: "My choice of clothing suggests that I am a very casual and informal person." Before students write the paragraph, they should take the time to list specific examples of clothing choices that support the statement. If you collect the paragraphs and read some of them in class, others could guess the names of the writers, based on their statements.

3. In order to get an appropriate distribution, you might want to assign specific popular brand names to particular students and make this activity into a class study. Students could develop rating charts for the various garments. Using the information on these charts, various comparisons could be made among the examples studied. Students could come to conclusions about such characteristics as level of workmanship and durability. You might also want students to gather information on the costs of the various garments. Using all of the information collected, students could come to a conclusion about which garment is the "Best Buy." Debate over this issue might prove quite enlightening, for it would help to clarify the assignment and individual differences in garment selection.

4. You might want students to report to the class on the results of this activity. You might wish to impress upon them that the laundering of clothing is a little more involved than merely gathering up a pile and tossing it into the washing machine. Of course, simply tossing clothing into a machine can lead to disastrous results.

5. You might want students to work as a group to determine who looks best in which colors. Students might also want to make their own lists of colors that they should avoid under any circumstances. Students can then share their lists with group members and discuss their lists as well.

Chapter 18

Getting Ready to Sew

Chapter Organization

Chapter Vocabulary

pattern (p. 421)
notions (p. 425)
colorfastness (p. 427)

Chapter Objectives

After reading this chapter, students should be able to:

1. Explain the importance of following safety rules in the sewing laboratory. (18.1)
2. Describe how to work smoothly and productively by cooperating with others in the class. (18.1)
3. Explain how to plan time and how to organize materials for successful sewing projects. (18.1)

4. Explain the importance of choosing a suitable sewing project. (18.2)
5. Describe how to choose and read a pattern envelope. (18.2)
6. Describe how to take measurements. (18.2)
7. Explain how to select the correct fabric and notions for a sewing project. (18.2)

Program Resources

Student text pages 416–431
Teacher's Resource Book
    Skill/Development Worksheet 18
    Laboratory/Application Worksheet 18
    Reinforcement Worksheet 18
    Enrichment Worksheet 18
    Transparency Master 18
    Information Master 18
    Chapter 18 Test

Teaching Suggestions

The dots represent skill levels required to answer each question or complete each activity:
 •requires recall and comprehension
 ••requires application and analysis
 •••requires synthesis and evaluation

Into the Chapter

•**Inspecting the Sewing Lab** Familiarize students with the sewing lab by giving them a tour of the room. Explain where supplies, equipment, and student projects will be stored. Demonstrate the condition in which sewing machines should be stored at the end of each class. Assign students equipment boxes to be labeled by name and class.

Other Activities

••• 1. **Experimenting with Fabrics** Collect a number of small samples of materials that vary in weight and thickness. You might, for example, include samples of gingham, duck, organdy, poplin, and heavy denim. Ask students to experiment sewing various fabrics on their machines to find which are difficult and which are easy to work with. Have students make a bulletin board displaying fabrics of different kinds, labeling them, and noting reasons why each is easy or difficult to use.

•• 2. **Checking Colorfastness** Have each student provide a small sample of a fabric to test for colorfastness. Have them use the following procedure: Place a 2″ × 2″ piece of muslin over the eraser end of a pencil. Then rub the muslin over a small area of the fabric. Observe how much color comes off on the muslin. Have students compare and discuss their observations on their tests.

• 3. **Identifying Information** After each student has procured a pattern, ask each one to find and circle the following information on the pattern envelope: 1) the number of pattern pieces, 2) description of the garment to be made, 3) suggested fabrics to use, 4) fabric chart, 5) body measurement chart, and 6) notions.

Learning to Manage (p. 429)

Concepts
    some fabric is harder than others to cut and sew
    ruffles and bows are difficult for beginners

- permanent press material is easy to care for
- students should have a person experienced in sewing check their layout and pinning before they cut out their pattern pieces
- some material is more suitable for formal, evening wear than for everyday use

Discussion Questions

1. What were the advantages and disadvantages of the fabric that Chris chose?
2. How did the girls' patterns differ?
3. Why was Pam's material a good choice?
4. Which skirt do you think will be more serviceable? Why?
5. What lesson or lessons do you think each girl will learn from this project?

Answers to Preceding Questions

Answers will vary but will probably include the following ideas.

1. The fabric that Chris chose was dressy, delicate, and pretty. However, it was expensive, too formal for its intended use, and difficult to cut and to sew.
2. The pattern that Chris chose included ruffles and bows and, therefore, had many parts. Pam's pattern was simpler than Chris's; thus, it was easier to lay out and pin.
3. Pam's material was a good choice because it was less expensive and easier to work with than Chris's and did not require pressing.
4. Pam's skirt was more serviceable than Chris's because it needed no ironing and could be converted from a semiformal long skirt to an everyday short skirt.
5. Chris will probably learn to listen to good advice, to choose her fabric more carefully, and to select a simpler pattern. Both girls will probably learn to begin a project more cautiously and to have their layout and pinning checked by their teacher.

Answers to Questions (p. 429)

Answers will vary but will probably include the following ideas.

1. The sewing project that beginning students choose should meet the following requirements: something that is usable, fun to make, simple, able to be completed fairly quickly, and relatively inexpensive. Steps listed should take the beginner from fabric selection to finished product.
2. Pam chose a simple pattern that had no ruffles and bows. She chose a fabric that was reasonably priced, easy to care for, and easy to cut and sew. Her fabric was suitable for everyday as well as more formal wear.

Careers (p. 420)

Secondhand Business Is First Rate (page 420)

This theme feature introduces students to consignment stores that concentrate on selling secondhand clothing. At a time when the cost of clothing has skyrocketed, such stores fill a real need by allowing consumers to get as much clothing as possible for every dollar spent. These stores also fill a need for sellers. They permit people who no longer want certain clothing articles to turn them into cash. Without consignment stores, such articles of clothing would probably continue to take up space in closets and drawers.

A discussion of "Secondhand Business Is First Rate" will give students an understanding of the important role that consignment stores play in clothing retailing.

Discussion Questions

1. Why might people want to sell clothing in consignment stores?
2. What are some of the reasons that

people might want to buy clothing in consignment stores?

3. If you were to open a consignment store, what kind of clothing would you feature?

Answers to Preceding Questions

Answers will vary but will probably include the following ideas.

1. Some people will want to sell clothing in a consignment store because those who have worn the clothing have outgrown it, because they have grown tired of it, or because they simply never liked it.

2. Some people will want to buy clothing in a consignment store because they have very small clothing budgets and must stretch them as far as possible.

3. The answer will depend upon the area where the store will be located. If many young families with children live in the area, the store owner would be wise to feature children's clothing. If many young, socially active people live in the area, the owner will probably want to feature current fashions.

Answers to For Review

In the Sewing Laboratory (p. 419)

1. When using a sewing machine, a person should sew at an even speed and pay very close attention to what is being sewn. A person should also be very careful to be sure that fingers do not get near the needle. Also, electric cords should be placed as close to the outlet as possible and should never run along spaces where people could fall over them. Finally, extension cords should never be used.

2. A student can cooperate with other students in a sewing laboratory by being willing to wait patiently for a chance to use the sewing machines and the ironing boards and to get the help of the teacher. A student should also allow time for delays. In addition, a student should help clean up by making sure that the sewing machine is down or covered, by returning borrowed equipment, by making sure all equipment is turned off, and by seeing that the floor and other surfaces are free of scraps.

3. To make a sewing project more efficient, work at a steady pace; take the time to arrange the work space and to gather all needed materials; and schedule the sewing project. Finally, label all personal equipment; check before a class to see that all needed equipment is available; and keep all materials together in a box or basket.

Your Project (p. 428)

1. When deciding upon a sewing project, these four guidelines should be kept in mind: 1) the student should choose something that will be enjoyable to make and that will actually be used; 2) the student with little sewing experience should choose a simple project. A student with more advanced skills should choose something more challenging; 3) a student should allow sufficient time to avoid feeling rushed and to permit the correction of mistakes; 4) a student should establish a budget based on the amount of money available and then stay within that budget.

2. The following kinds of information can be found on the back of a pattern envelope: back views of the garment; a description of the garment that tells more about style and details; suggestions for fabrics that will work well with the pattern, along with a list of fabrics that should not be used; a chart showing how much fabric will be needed; a chart showing body measurements and sizes; and a list of notions that will be needed to complete the garment.

3. The fabric must be appropriate for what is being made. The results will not be good, for example, if a sheer fabric is chosen when a sturdy one is needed or if a sturdy fabric is chosen when a sheer one is needed.

Chapter 18 Review

Vocabulary Answers (p. 430)

1. pattern
2. Notions
3. colorfastness

Chapter Questions (p. 430)

1. It is important not to use an extension cord because the extension cord creates a hazard that people can trip over.
2. The iron should be turned off and left in a resting position so that the iron cannot fall over and burn something.
3. While waiting to use a sewing machine in the sewing laboratory, a student can be studying directions for the next step.
4. Consider the following: time needed to complete it, including the time for work done in class; the schedule should be revised as work progresses; and extra time should be left for steps that will require the help of others.
5. Label each piece of equipment with the name of the owner.
6. A pattern catalog can be consulted to get ideas for a sewing project.
7. When preparing to make a garment, it is important to take each measurement twice because accuracy is absolutely necessary or the garment will not fit properly.
8. If the pattern measurements are not exactly the same as the measurements of the person who will wear the garment, a pattern size that comes closest to the wearer's measurements should be bought.
9. The pattern envelope can help a person choose a fabric for the garment being made because it suggests fabrics that work well with the pattern, and it also lists fabrics that should not be used.
10. When selecting a fabric, consider fibers, weight, weave, and design.
11. A pattern can limit the choice of fabrics because of the nature of the garment that the pattern will produce. If the pattern is for a loose-fitting garment for example, the fabric would have to be one that is soft and flowing.
12. A chart on the pattern envelope advises the user about the amount of fabric to purchase.
13. Silk would not be a good choice of fabric for a shirt because it is an expensive and delicate fabric.
14. The three guidelines to follow regarding quality and cost when shopping for a fabric are: Check for imperfections such as snags, spots, and faded colors. Do the wrinkle test by gathering the fabric and crinkling it to determine whether or not the fabric will crease. Do the stretch test to determine whether or not the fabric returns to its original shape after being stretched.
15. If a zipper cannot be found that exactly matches the color of the fabric being used, purchase one that is slightly darker.

Skill Activities

1. Review project considerations and caution students about the need to select a pattern within their capability. Be sure that students understand the importance of fabric choice in the project. The fabric must be appropriate for the garment's purpose. To be sure that students understand the critical role that affordability plays, you might want them to

establish a budget for their project. As they assemble the shopping list of supplies, they can carefully estimate the cost of each item on the list.

2. Before the bulletin board categories are established, you might want to poll the class to identify project ideas that would be of interest to its members. If you wish to do so, make a master list of these projects on the chalkboard. Students who identify particular interests could be assigned to collect pictures that fall within those interest categories.

3. You might want to ask students to collect a set number of fabrics. Each student could present each fabric in class, along with an explanation of its advantages for a particular project. After students have listened to each presentation, urge them to ask questions of the presenter and to supply additional information that a presenter might have overlooked. Some students may be much more knowledgeable about fabrics than others, and the whole class can benefit from these students' comments.

4. You may wish to ask two students to go through this exercise before others in the class attempt it. Make sure that the information on page 422 is followed exactly so that accurate measurements are obtained. Remind students to add a bit to the measurements so that an ease allowance is obtained and the measurements are adjusted for it.

5. Before students begin to work on their project, you might want to conduct a discussion of the areas in your own particular laboratory where safety problems exist. Have students identify each potential danger and then discuss the rules that should be developed for each threat. You might also spend some time discussing the characteristics of effective posters. Lead students to understand that an effective poster is one which commands the attention of those who work in an area.

Chapter 19

Equipment and Preparation

Chapter Organization

Chapter Vocabulary

tension (p. 441)
serger (p. 443)
selvages (p. 445)
fabric grain (p. 445)
true bias (p. 445)
on-grain (p. 445)
pattern guide sheet (p. 447)
cutting layout (p. 449)

Chapter Objectives

After reading this chapter, students should be able to:

1. Explain the importance of having the proper small equipment for sewing. (19.1)
2. Explain the importance of the proper use and

care of the sewing machine. (19.1)

3. Describe how serger sewing can help a person sew well and save time. (19.1)
4. Describe how to prepare fabric for sewing. (19.2)
5. Describe how to lay out a pattern and cut the fabric properly. (19.2)
6. Explain how to mark fabric properly. (19.2)

Program Resources

Student text pages 432–457
Teacher's Resource Book
    Skill/Development Worksheet 19
    Laboratory/Application Worksheet 19
    Reinforcement Worksheet 19
    Enrichment Worksheet 19
    Transparency Master 19
    Information Master 19
    Chapter 19 Test

Teaching Suggestions

The dots represent skill levels required to answer each question or complete each activity:
  •requires recall and comprehension
  ••requires application and analysis
  •••requires synthesis and evaluation

Into the Chapter

•**Learning by Example** Teach students correct procedures by making a garment along with them. Use the same pattern and fabric that they use. Demonstrate each difficult step, such as showing how to fold the cloth for the layout, how to select appropriate pattern pieces, following the cutting layout on the guidesheet, and marking and pinning the fabric. Encourage students to ask questions during the demonstration. Have them practice steps on fabric scraps before working with their garments.

Other Activities

• **1. Identifying Parts of a Sewing Machine** Distribute a diagram of a sewing machine with important parts numbered. As you point out and explain the function of each part, have students find that part on their assigned machines. After all parts have been identified, have students go back and label each numbered part on the diagram.

•• **2. Practicing Sewing Seams** Demonstrate how to sew a seam and trim it with pinking shears. Review estimating procedures. Next show students how to estimate the amount of fabric they can safely cut away. Then have students practice making seams with fabric scraps before they work on their garments.

•• **3. Practicing Pressing Procedures** Demonstrate how to press using a sleeve board, a tailor's ham, a steam roll, and a point presser. Demonstrate how a tailored jacket requires all four pressing tools during construction. Allow each student time to practice, with proper supervision, with each.

Learning to Manage (p. 455)

Concepts

■ before starting to sew, one should gather all the necessary equipment
■ scissors and straight pins are needed to tack down and cut out pattern pieces
■ marking tools are needed to show on fabric the location of items such as tucks, pockets, and trim
■ before fabric is sewn, it should be prepared by preshrinking and straightening

Discussion Questions

1. What equipment did Tony and Harry use when laying out and cutting their pattern pieces?
2. What equipment did Tony and Harry forget to use when laying out and cutting pattern pieces?
3. What equipment used for many sewing projects was not needed by Tony and Harry? Why?
4. What things did the two boys do right before they sewed their projects?
5. Why were they pleased with their projects after sewing but displeased with them later?

Answers to Preceding Questions

Answers will vary but will probably include the following ideas.

1. Tony and Harry used straight pins and scissors when laying out and cutting their pattern pieces.
2. Tony and Harry forgot to use a tracing wheel and carbon paper to mark on their fabric the location of tucks, pockets, and trim.
3. Although many projects require measuring tools, Tony and Harry did not need them because neither of their projects needed to be a certain size.
4. The boys took the following steps:
   a. They gathered all their equipment before beginning to lay out their patterns.
   b. They reviewed Harry's notes before they cut the fabric to be sure they had not forgotten a step.
   c. They frequently checked their work against the cutting layout and checked each other's layouts to be sure they were correct.
   d. They carefully cut out the pieces and marked the fabric (the next day).
5. The projects looked good at first but shrank badly after they were laundered because the boys had forgotten to prepare the fabric.

Answers to Questions (p. 455)

Answers will vary but will probably include the following ideas.

1. Both boys forgot to preshrink and straighten their fabric.
2. Students should tell how to prepare the fabric and should list the equipment as well as the steps needed in laying out a pattern.

Health and Safety

Danger: Children at Work! (p. 436)

As students go through this chapter they will gain a fuller knowledge of the craftsmanship that goes into sewing a well-made garment. For some, it will be their first attempt at adult work. This theme feature gives students a startling look at what was once considered an acceptable work day for a child.

Discussion of "Danger: Children at Work!" will quickly raise the issue of safety in the sewing lab. Though students do not face the same dangers as the mill children did, they can project what might happen if young children were at work in the room.

Discussion Questions

1. How do you think the long work day, lack of rest periods, and general environment of the textile mills affected the mill children's health?
2. Compare the typical work week of the children who worked in the textile mills with the average worker in the United States today.
3. Many students attend school while maintaining part-time jobs. What advantages and disadvantages are there in holding a job and attending school at the same time?

Answers to Preceding Questions

Answers will vary but will probably include the following ideas.

1. The health of the mill children was more than likely seriously affected by their working conditions. Not only did the long work days make them more prone to have a serious accident, but it is also likely that the dirty, poorly ventilated mills made the children more susceptible to other types of disease.
2. Mill children toiled through a 66-hour work week. They worked 11 hours a day, 6 days a week. They were given no rest breaks during their long day, and only 30 minutes for lunch. If they were late, they lost a day's work. Today, the average work week is somewhere between 35 and 40 hours. People work 5 days a week, 8 hours a day. In most cases they have at least two rest breaks per day, plus a lunch break that may be 30 minutes or an hour. An occasional late arrival rarely leads to dismissal, nor does the worker lose a whole day's work. Additionally, workers in the United States today typically have other benefits that the mill children could only have dreamed about—disability pay, health insurance, vacations, and retirement programs.
3. By having a part-time job, a student can gain valuable experience in the work world, learn to manage money, and meet a variety of new people. The major disadvantage of a part-time job is that it may distract a student from schoolwork and close off extracurricular activities that the student may not have the opportunity to participate in elsewhere.

Answers to For Review

Equipment for Sewing (p. 444)

1. The four types of measuring equipment that a person who sews can use are a sewing gauge, a yardstick or meter stick, a tape measure, and a skirt marker.
2. Six guidelines to follow when using a sewing machine are 1) raise the take-up lever and needle to the highest point before beginning to sew so that the thread does not pull out of the needle; 2) make sure that the upper thread and the bobbin thread are pulled back behind the presser foot so they will not get tangled in the bobbin case; 3) place the fabric under the presser foot, with the bulk of it to the left of the machine; 4) place the point of the needle on the stitching line; 5) by turning the handwheel, lower the needle onto the fabric. Then lower the presser foot and use the knee or foot control to stitch at a slow, even speed; 6) turn the handwheel to raise the take-up lever and needle to the highest position. To avoid bending the needle, the fabric should not be pulled toward the person sewing. Slide the fabric toward the back of the machine and clip the threads.
3. A serger can do the following things that a conventional sewing machine cannot do: 1) A serger can trim the seam allowance before it is stitched. 2) A serger uses loopers instead of bobbins. 3) A serger can use more than one spool of thread at a time. There are two-, three-, and four-spool sergers. 4) Some sergers can sew a chainstitch instead of a straight lockstitch, the basic stitch in conventional sewing. The chainstitch is a two-thread stitch that is a little bulkier than a lockstitch. 5) A serger can feed two layers of fabric smoothly. As long as they start out matched, stripes can be matched without basting. 6) Unless the fabric is thick, the presser foot does not have to be lifted when sewing begins. This is so because the feed dogs on a serger are longer.

Preparing Fabric (p. 454)

1. The first basic step in preparing fabric for sewing is to preshrink it. Hand-washable fabric should be soaked in hot water for

30 minutes. Fabric that is not hand-washable must be dry-cleaned. The second basic step is to lay out the fabric and cut it properly, being careful to mark the location of details such as buttonholes and trim.

2. One purpose of the markings on pattern pieces is to mark the *grain line,* a heavy solid line with arrows at both ends. The second purpose is to mark the *cutting line,* a heavy line that outlines the pattern pieces. There might be a scissors symbol printed on the line to indicate the correct direction for cutting. The third purpose is to mark the *stitching line,* a broken line inside the cutting line.

3. General information and layouts for cutting are found on the front side of the pattern guide sheet.

4. Four kinds of marking methods that can be used are the tracing wheel and carbon paper, tailor's chalk and pins, tailor's tacks, and basting.

Chapter 19 Review

Vocabulary Answers (p. 456)

1. pattern guide sheet
2. Tension
3. True bias
4. cutting layout
5. selvage
6. On-grain
7. fabric grain
8. serger

Chapter Questions (p. 456)

1. Small areas, such as seams or hems, should be measured with a *sewing gauge.*
2. Scissors are used to trim fabric and to clip threads. The rings on the handles for inserting the fingers are usually small and of equal size. Shears are used to cut fabric. They have a small ring for the thumb and a larger ring for the other four fingers. They are available for both left-handed and right-handed people.

3. A *tailor's ham* is useful for pressing curved seams and darts.

4. A good way to practice stitching curves and turning corners is to draw curved lines on a piece of paper and then to practice stitching along the lines until one feels confident that it can be done smoothly.

5. To put off cleaning and oiling a sewing machine for several months would serve no purpose under any circumstances. A sewing machine must be cleaned regularly if it is to work properly. A sewing machine must also be oiled occasionally in accordance with the instructions given in the owner's manual.

6. Common problems include a broken needle or thread or skipped stitches.

7. Stitches are made on a serger by means of a knitting process. Each stitch is knitted over a metal prong called a *stitch finger.* The machine uses from two to four spools of thread at a time to stitch.

8. Three advantages of using a serger are 1) a serger is at least twice as fast as a conventional machine; 2) a serger can stitch, trim, and finish off seams all at the same time; 3) a serger will sew straight, curved, or cornered seams, and the fabric does not have to be pinned or basted.

9. A device called a looper replaces the bobbin on a serger.

10. It is necessary to prepare fabric before stitching it so that the finished product will not shrink or change shape.

11. The first step in preparing fabric is to preshrink it. The second step is to find the lengthwise grain, which runs in the same direction as the fabric. This must be identified because most garments are cut with their lengthwise grain running up and down to

increase their strength and durability. The third step is to straighten the grain so that the finished product will hold its shape.

12. The edges of loosely woven fabric can be straightened by pulling a thread. The selvage is clipped. A crosswise yarn is then grasped and pulled. The other hand is used to push the fabric back gently. The yarn that is pulled out will leave a mark that can be cut along. If the yarn breaks midway, it should be cut up to the broken point. The end of the broken yarn should then be located and pulled again.

13. A garment should be a little larger than the body measurements of the wearer to provide *ease* allowance that enables the wearer to move around easily in the clothing.

14. Shaded pieces of a pattern should be placed on the fabric with the printed side down.

15. The best marking method for lightweight and washable fabrics is to use a tracing wheel and carbon paper.

Skill Activities

1. Impress upon students that these difficult manuevers can be mastered only with practice. You might want to consider having students engage in this activity for 15 to 20 minutes each day. Make sure that students number their sketches as they use them. This will allow them to chart and notice their progress. Be sure to see to it that students do not use sketches that are far too complicated for success to be possible. You might want to provide an appropriate sketch for students to use, especially at the beginning stages of the practice.

2. To find out which students need help with this activity, you might want to prepare and then photocopy an unmarked diagram of a machine or copy a clear photograph of a machine. After students have an opportunity to study the diagram on page 438, you could distribute the unlabeled diagrams or photographs and ask students to label the parts. Students who do well with the labeling could be matched with students who need help. These same diagrams or photographs could be redistributed at the end of the laboratory work and used as a test.

3. Before students examine a garment of their own, you might want to bring a garment to class and go through the process of examining it. Such a demonstration will establish a procedure for students to use as they complete the activity.

Chapter 20

Construction Techniques

Chapter Organization

Chapter Vocabulary

basting (p. 460)
easing (p. 461)
gathering (p. 461)
unit construction (p. 463)
assembly-line method (p. 463)
dart (p. 465)
seam (p. 465)
pinking (p. 467)
facing (p. 468)
interfacing (p. 469)

Chapter Objectives

After reading this chapter, students should be able to:
1. Thread a needle properly. (20.1)
2. Describe how to do temporary hand sewing. (20.1)
3. Explain how to do permanent hand sewing. (20.1)
4. Describe how to construct a garment using various sewing machine stitches. (20.2)
5. Explain how to finish seams, and sew facings, fasteners, and hems. (20.2)
6. List different ways to recycle clothing. (20.2)

Program Resources

Student text pages 458–475
Teacher's Resource Book
    Skill/Development Worksheet 20
    Laboratory/Application Worksheet 20
    Reinforcement Worksheet 20
    Enrichment Worksheet 20
    Transparency Master 20
    Information Master 20
    Chapter 20 Test

Teaching Suggestions

The dots represent skill levels required to answer each question or complete each activity:
 •requires recall and comprehension
 ••requires application and analysis
•••requires synthesis and evaluation

Into the Chapter

••**Practicing Sewing Stitches** Draw a variety of lines on a piece of paper—straight, curved, and zigzagged. Add a circle. Reproduce the paper and give each student several copies. Then have students practice stitching along the lines and around the circle without thread in their machines. Demonstrate how to pivot on curves. Suggest that students go slowly and use the hand wheel rather than the foot or knee pedal until they have become adept at stitching. They can then practice faster stitching using the foot or knee pedal.

Other Activities

•• 1. **Practicing Hand Sewing** Have students practice sewing by hand, using the overcast, backstitch, and slip stitch on fabric scraps. Then have them apply an appliqué to a jacket or shirt.
••• 2. **Experimenting with Interfacing Techniques** Collect fabric scraps of different weights and a selection of various types of interfacing. Ask students to experiment with these materials to determine which interfacing is appropriate for each type of fabric. Have them make a bulletin board showing samples of different interfacing and explaining their findings about each example.
•• 3. **Sewing Snaps and Hooks and Eyes** Demonstrate how to sew snaps and hooks and eyes. Have students practice these skills using fabric scraps.

Learning to Manage (p. 473)

Concepts

- inexpensive clothing can sometimes be improved through alteration
- clothing is a good buy if it is made well and fits well
- clothing can be given a new look by adding or removing trimming such as lace

Discussion Questions

1. Why couldn't Pat make a dress for the spring dance?
2. What solution did Kim propose?
3. What steps did Pat have to go through to create her own "designer original"?
4. What percent of the cost of the original dress do you think Pat saved through creative thinking and hand sewing?

Answers to Preceding Questions

Answers will vary but will probably include the following ideas.

1. Pat had neither the time nor a sewing machine.
2. Kim suggested that Pat buy a dress that was plainer than the dress Pat liked but was the same basic style. She thought Pat could find lace in the thrift shop to trim the dress.
3. To create her own "designer original," Pat had to (1) convince her mother of the soundness of the plan, (2) buy the plain dress in Juno's, (3) buy lace-trimmed dresses in the thrift shop, (4) remove and have the lace cleaned, and (5) baste and sew the lace onto the plain dress.
4. Pat probably saved from 25 to 40 percent of the cost of the original dress. Although the plain dress cost only 50 percent as much as the original dress, Pat had the expenses of buying the secondhand dresses and cleaning the lace. That saving gain does not take into account materials and labor.

Answers to Questions (p. 473)

Answers will vary but will probably include the following ideas.

1. Students should list the clothing they could alter and explain what changes they would make to it. Students should consider casual, everyday, and formal wear.
2. It would pay to have a garment professionally altered as long as the cost of alteration did not approach the price of a new garment.
3. Students may mention agencies such as Goodwill Industries, Salvation Army, American Red Cross, and relief organizations, as well as religious and fraternal groups.

Leadership and Citizenship

"Constructing" a Difference (page 464)

This theme feature explains how clothing-related talents have been used by Future Homemakers of America chapters to enrich the lives of needy people. Students should understand that the need for clothing is a basic human need. Clothing construction skills and clothing maintenance skills can be used to provide this basic human need to those who cannot afford appropriate clothing and to those who are not physically able to provide clothing maintenance services for themselves.

A discussion of "'Constructing' a Difference" can show students that clothing skills are much in demand and can be used to improve the lives of people.

Discussion Questions

1. Who in your community could benefit from clothing construction and clothing maintenance skills?

2. How could you identify additional needy people who could benefit from clothing construction and clothing maintenance skills?
3. What sort of clothing-related services could you and your classmates provide to a needy group in your area?

Answers to Preceding Questions

Answers will vary but will probably include the following ideas.

1. Every community has needy individuals and families who could benefit from clothing construction and clothing maintenance services. Depending upon the community, several institutions, such as homeless centers, nursing homes, schools for the handicapped, hospitals, and prisons could all use such skills.
2. Every community's social service agencies are aware of people who could use both clothing construction and clothing maintenance skills. In addition, churches and other religious institutions also know of individuals and groups who need such skills.
3. Those class members who are adept at sewing could provide clothing construction skills. Others who are less adept could perform many maintenance skills. Other assistance could also be offered in the area of general administration, including organizing clothing drives and keeping track of items donated.

Answers to For Review

Hand Sewing (p. 463)

1. A needle threaded with more than two feet of thread is likely to get tangled while you are sewing.
2. Follow these four steps when basting by hand:
   * Sew from right to left if you are right-handed or from left to right if you are left-handed.

   * Sew along the top of the fabric using a running stitch. Sew even stitches about ¼ inch long. Use a longer stitch, however, if you are using a heavy fabric.
   * Save time by sewing several stitches before pulling the thread through.
   * Remove the basting stitches after the fabrics are permanently sewn together.
3. Easing and gathering are both temporary hand sewing techniques that are used when joining two pieces of material that differ in length. Easing is used when one piece of fabric is slightly larger than the other. It is typically used for waistbands and set-in-sleeves. Gathering is used when soft folds of materials are needed to make puffed sleeves, ruffles, and full, unpleated curtains.
4. The strongest kind of hand-sewn stitch is the backstitch.

Machine Construction (p. 472)

1. Unit construction and the assembly line method are two methods for assembling a garment. During unit construction, you complete each section separately and then sew them together. In the assembly-line method, you work on many pieces or sections of the garment at the same time. One type of work is completed on each piece of the garment. For example, if there is hemming that needs to be done, all the hemming is done at one time. When that task is finished, you do another type of work on each piece of the garment. The assembly-line method requires more planning than unit construction, but experienced sewers find it efficient.
2. The purpose of directional sewing is to help prevent the fabric from stretching.
3. The three types of facings are shaped facing, extended facing, and bias facing.
4. Jeans that are worn at the knees can be recycled into shorts. Simply cut and hem the legs to the appropriate length.

Chapter 20 Review

Vocabulary Answers (p. 474)

1. Easing
2. basting
3. unit construction
4. Interfacing
5. assembly-line method
6. Gathering
7. pinking
8. Facing
9. seam
10. dart

Chapter Questions (p. 474)

1. Not all sizes and types of needles are appropriate for every kind of sewing. A ball point needle should be used for knitted fabrics and a regular needle should be used for most other fabrics.
2. Three kinds of temporary hand sewing techniques include basting, easing, and gathering.
3. The purpose of the slip stitch is to attach a folded edge to another piece of fabric. It is used for hems, linings, and patch pockets.
4. A backstitch is used to make or mend seams, to sew in zippers, and to fasten thread ends. It is also used in places that are hard for the machine to reach. It is the strongest of all hand-sewn stitches.
5. If you were to use the unit construction method to make a shirt, you would divide the shirt into three sections—the front, the back, and the sleeves. Each section would be completed separately and then sewn together.
6. The purpose of directional stitching is to help prevent the fabric from stretching.
7. The purpose of stay stitching is to prevent the fabric's edges from stretching.
8. The three places where darts are needed are at the neck, at the waistline, and under the sleeves.
9. You will rarely save time by waiting until you are finished sewing to fit a garment. Invariably, it is more efficient to make minor adjustments as you go along rather than to risk having to make major adjustments, which are very time consuming, after the garment is completed.
10. Pinking shears are scissors that cut in a zigzag pattern. They are used on firmly woven fabrics that do not ravel much.
11. Bias facing is a strip of fabric cut on the bias. It is stitched to a raw garment edge and then turned inside.
12. Unlike other interfacing, fusible interfacing does not have to be stitched on. It has adhesive on one side. When the adhesive is pressed, fusible interfacing becomes attached to the fabric by the heat of the iron.
13. Buttonholes are made by machine. The sewing machine may have a special buttonhole attachment. If it does not, a zigzag stitch is used to make the buttonhole.
14. Here are some simple alterations that can make an old garment usable: change the hemline, sleeves, or neckline, cut off the legs of worn pants and make them into shorts, add or change buttons, and dye the garment another color.
15. Fashion magazines are a good place to look for ideas on how to alter an old outfit so as to give it a new, more contemporary look. They are especially helpful in representing a wide range of color combinations.

Skill Activities

1. Before students select a project, caution them to be sure it is a project that is possible given the student's current level of skill. This can be determined as the pattern guide sheet

is read and the sewing procedures listed. As students note each procedure, they should evaluate their own experience with it, noting those procedures which might require additional practice. Urge students to develop a realistic time schedule for their project. They should identify a desired completion date and then work backward from it. Upon completion, have students review the project and identify any sewing procedures with which they experienced particular difficulty. You may want to go over the most commonly cited trouble spots with the entire class.

2. With a minimum of research, students should be able to identify two or three local agencies that accept clothing. Be sure that students understand that these agencies are looking for usable clothing and not for clothing that is beyond repair. You might want students to conduct a used clothing drive within the class or school. Students might prepare a letter to parents that explains the purpose of the drive and then identifies the condition of the clothing that is sought. Virtually every household includes clothing that is no longer usable by those who live there. Most agencies that collect used clothing are willing to make arrangements to pick up large amounts of clothing collected in such a drive. Your class or your school may want to establish clothing drives on a regular basis. It might be helpful to invite a representative from one of the clothing-collecting agencies to speak to the class on how the organization uses donated material, and on its other activities as well. Such an ongoing program will discourage wastefulness and encourage an interest among students in helping the community.

3. Before this activity begins, you might want a student to report to the class on the wide variety of quilts that can be made. Encourage the students to bring in photographs of quilts especially notable for the imaginativeness of their design or theme. Make sure, however, that the design chosen is suitable to skill level of the class. Students might decide to plan and make a quilt, the design of which is somehow connected with the school or community. After an appropriate quilt is planned and made, students might consider auctioning it to raise additional funds for the sewing laboratory.

Resources

Atlas, Stephen L. *Single Parenting: A Practical Resource Guide*. Englewood Cliffs, NJ: Prentice Hall, 1981.

Bell, Ruth, et al. *Changing Bodies, Changing Lives: A Book for Teens on Sex and Relationships*. New York: Random House, 1981.

Berg, Barbara J. *The Crisis of the Working Mother: Resolving the Conflict Between Family and Work*. New York: Summit Books, 1986.

Better Homes and Gardens Editors. *Better Homes and Gardens Crafts to Decorate Your Home*. Des Moines, IA: Better Homes and Gardens, 1986.

Bigner, Jerry J. *Parent-Child Relations: An Introduction to Parenting*. 2nd Edition. New York: Macmillan Publishing Company, 1985.

Bohannan, Paul. *All the Happy Families: Exploring the Varieties of Family Life*. New York: McGraw-Hill, 1985.

Booher, Dianna Daniels. *Love: First Aid for the Heartaches and Trials of Young Love*. New York: Julian Messner, 1985.

Boston Children's Hospital Staff. *Parent's Guide to Nutrition*. Reading, MA: Addison-Wesley, 1986.

Brazelton, T. Berry. *To Listen to a Child: Understanding the Normal Problems of Growing Up*. Reading, MA: Addison-Wesley, 1984.

Briggs, Dorothy C. *Celebrating Yourself: Enhancing Your Own Self-Esteem*. Garden City, NY: Doubleday, 1986.

Brooks, Jane B. *The Process of Parenting*. 2nd Edition. Palo Alto, Calif.: Mayfield Publishing Company, 1987.

Career Opportunities in the Hotel and Restaurant Industries. Washington: U.S. Department of Labor/Government Printing Office, 1982.

Carroll, David. *Living With Dying: A Loving Guide for Family and Close Friends*. New York: McGraw-Hill, 1985.

Cho, Emily, et al. *It's You: Looking Terrific Whatever Your Type*. New York: Villard Books, 1986.

Clamp, Betty, et al. *Problem-Solving Exercises for Basic Nutrition*. Scottsdale, AZ: Gorsuch Scarisbrick, 1986.

Davis, Marian L. *Visual Design in Dress*. 2nd Edition. Englewood Cliffs, NJ: Prentice Hall, 1987.

Einon, Dorothy. *Play with a Purpose: Learning Games for Children Six Weeks to Ten Years*. New York: Random House, 1985.

Ewy, Donna and Roger. *Teen Pregnancy: The Challenges We Faced, The Choices We Made*. Boulder, CO: Pruet Pub. Co., 1984.

Fayerweather Street School. *The Kids' Book About Death and Dying, by and for Kids*. Boston: Little, Brown & Company, 1985.

Feinbloom, Richard I., and Forman, Betty Yetta. *Pregnancy, Birth and The Early Months: A Complete Guide*. Reading, MA: Addison-Wesley, 1985.

Frings, Gini. *Fashion: From Concept to Consumer*. 2nd Edition. Englewood Cliffs, NJ: Prentice Hall, 1987.

Goodman, Richard M. *Planning for a Healthy Baby: A Guide to Genetic and Environmental*

Risks. New York: Oxford University Press, 1986.

Joan, Polly. *Preventing Teen Suicide: The Living Alternative Handbook.* New York: Human Sciences Press, 1986.

Kefgen, Mary, and Touchie-Specht, Phyllis. *Individuality in Clothing Selection and Personal Appearance: A Guide for the Consumer.* New York: Macmillan and Company, 1986.

Keshet, Jamie. *Love and Power in the Stepfamily: A Practical Guide.* New York: McGraw-Hill, 1986.

Knox, David. *Choices and Relationships: An Introduction to Marriage and the Family.* St. Paul, MN: West Publishing Company, 1985.

Landau, Elaine. *Why Are They Starving Themselves? Understanding Anorexia Nervosa and Bulimia* (Teen Survival Library). New York: Messner, 1983.

Lansky, Vicki. *Practical Parenting Tips.* New York: Bantam Books, 1985.

Leach, Penelope. *The Child Care Encyclopedia.* New York: Alfred A. Knopf, 1984.

Leavenworth, Carol, et al. *Family Living.* Needham, Massachusetts: Prentice Hall, 1988.

Lee, Essie, and Wortman, Richard. *Down Is Not Out: Teenagers and Depression.* New York: Julian Messner, 1986.

Lubic, Ruth Watson, and Hawes, Gene R. *Childbearing: A Book of Choices.* New York: McGraw-Hill, 1987.

Mayesky, Mary, and Neuman, Donald. *Creative Activities for Young Children.* 3rd Edition. Albany, N.Y.: Delmar Publishers, 1985.

Medved, Eva. *Food: Preparation and Theory.* Englewood Cliffs, NJ: Prentice Hall, 1986.

Medved, Eva. *The World of Food.* Needham, Massachusetts: Prentice Hall, 1988.

Neifert, Marianne. *Dr. Mom.* New York: G. P. Putnam's Sons, 1986.

Pruett, Kyle D. *The Nurturing Father.* New York: Warner Books, 1987.

Roberts, Nancy. *Breaking All the Rules: Feeling Good and Looking Great No Matter What Your Size.* New York: Viking, 1985.

Robinson, Catherine. *The Clothing Care Handbook: How to Clean, Iron, Mend, Update, Store, and Maintain Your Wardrobe.* New York: Fawcett Columbine, 1985.

Ryerson, Eric. *When Your Parent Drinks Too Much: A Book for Teenagers.* New York: Facts on File, 1985.

Schulz, David, and Rodgers, Stanley F. *Marriage, the Family, and Personal Fulfillment.* 3rd Edition. Englewood Cliffs, NJ: Prentice Hall, 1985.

Scott, Lucy, and Angwin, Meredith Joan. *Time Out for Motherhood: A Guide for Today's Working Woman to the Financial, Emotional, and Career Aspects of Having a Baby.* Los Angeles, CA: Jeremy P. Tarcher, Inc., 1986.

Silverstein, Alvin and Virginia. *AIDS: Deadly Threat.* Hillside, NJ: Enslow Publishers, Inc., 1986.

Sokolov, Raymond. *How to Cook: An Easy and Imaginative Guide for the Beginner.* New York: William Morrow, 1986.

Vanderhoff, Margil. *Clothing: Concepts and Construction.* Needham, Massachusetts: Prentice Hall, 1988.

Wallach, Janet. *Looks That Work: How to Match Your Wardrobe to Your Professional Profile and Create the Image That's Right For You.* New York: Viking, 1986.

Weisberger, Eleanor. *When Your Child Needs You.* Bethesda, MD: Adler & Adler, 1987.

Worth, Cecilia. *New Parenthood: The First Six Weeks.* New York: McGraw-Hill, 1985.

Zinner, Stephen H. *STDs: Sexually Transmitted Diseases.* New York: Summit Books, 1985.

TEEN LIVING

TEEN LIVING

Prentice Hall
Needham, Massachusetts
Englewood Cliffs, New Jersey

CREDITS

Project Editor: Susan Judge
Editor: Peg Sawyer
Contributing Writers:
    Text Contributions: Lucy Floyd
                    Candice Roman
                    Suzanne Stark
    Theme Features: Lynn Robbins
    Learning to Manage Features:
      Susan Judge
    Skills Activities:
      Linda LaFrance Garvey
      Janet Harrington
      Lynne Novogroski
Production/Manufacturing Coordinator:
    Roger Powers
Copy/Production Editor:
    Deborah Fogel
Design Director:
    L. Christopher Valente
Design Coordinator: Richard Dalton
Development Contributions:
    TextMasters
Design Production:
    Susan Gerould/Perspectives
Book Design: The Brownstone
    Group, Inc.
Cover Design: Martucci Studio
Photo Research:
    Laurel Anderson/Photosynthesis

FIRST EDITION

© 1989 by Prentice-Hall, Inc. All rights reserved. No part of this book may be reproduced in any form or by any means without permission in writing from the publisher. Printed in the United States of America.

ISBN: 0-13-512468-9

10 9 8 7 6 5 4 3 2 1 97 96 95 94 93 92 91 90 89 88

REVIEWER CONSULTANTS

Mary Blankonship
Bass Middle School
Nashville, TN

Debra Boswell
Daniels Middle School
Raleigh, NC

Wanda Christner
Peru Junior High School
Peru, IN

Raye Anne Crittenden
Monnig Middle School
Fort Worth, TX

Renee Fishman
Dumont Public Schools
Dumont, NJ

Sheryl Gilmore
Palm Spring Junior High
Hialeah, FL

Diana Krug
Peru Junior High
Peru, IN

Lynn Jorgenson
Carpenter Middle School
Plano, TX

Betty Ladymon
Atwell Middle School
Dallas, TX

Marlene Lovato
Coronado High School
Gallina, NM

Melanie McGuire
Fannin Middle School
Amarillo, TX

Elouise B. Merke
Miami Springs Middle School
Miami Springs, FL

Geraldine Mrozowski
Detroit Public Schools
Detroit, MI

Lynne Novogroski
Wellesley Public Schools
Wellesley, MA

Joan C. Parham
Hulcy Middle School
Dallas, TX

Iva Price
Stockard Middle School
Dallas, TX

Maria Reza
School-Based Health Programs
Reseda, CA

Ruth Ann Schultz
Cazenovia Public Schools
Cazenovia, NY

Elizabeth Starewicz
Wilbur Wright Middle School
Munster, IN

Teresa M. Stone
Bethel Junior High
Spanaway, WA

Julia Tingle
East Milbrook Middle School
Raleigh, NC

Sandra Wilson
Dunbar Middle School
Fort Worth, TX

 A Simon & Schuster Company

CONTENTS

vi

SUPER
TEEN
CLEAN

Unit 4: **Foods and Nutrition**   **249**

THEME FEATURES

Unit 1

About You

Chapter 1
Looking at You

Vocabulary

The dialogue below introduces "Fitting In," the Learning to Manage feature in this chapter. The case study is continued and the situation discussed further on page 21. See page T29 for teaching suggestions.

"Kate, it's great to hear from you! How are you doing?"

"Hi, Jen. Well, the new house is great, but I'm not so sure about school. It's much bigger than Westvale, and I haven't made any friends yet."

"Give yourself time, Kate. It's only been a few weeks."

"I know, but it's not easy. I don't feel as if I belong here. Maybe I'm doing something wrong. . . . I want to fit in, but how do I do that?"

"Don't be so hard on yourself, Kate. When everyone gets to know you, you'll have lots of friends!"

Section 1.1
Knowing Yourself

As you read, think about:

- what individual characteristics make up your personality. (p. 4)
- how your self-concept is shaped by your values and goals. (p. 7)
- what you can do to build a strong self-concept. (p. 8)

How have your friendships changed since you left elementary school?

Kate is finding it hard to answer the question, "Who am I?" It is not an easy question to answer, especially at this stage of your life, but it's worth the effort. It is important to appreciate all the things that make you the special person you are. You can then manage your life in a happy, fulfilling way. This section will help you to get to know yourself as you continue to grow and change.

Who You Are

There is nobody in the world like you, and nobody knows you as well as you know yourself. Your **self-concept,** the way you see yourself, affects the way you relate to the people and the world around you. You need to understand who you are in order to manage your life in the way you want. And as you change and grow, you need to be aware of what's happening to you. Self-awareness is not only picturing the way you look, it also means understanding your changing attitudes and emotions.

Everyone's personality changes at different stages of life, but there are more rapid changes during **adolescence,** the early teenage years. As you leave childhood behind, you begin to focus more attention on yourself. Sometimes all this self-evaluation may make you self-conscious or embarrassed. At other times you may become so centered on deciding who you are that you fail to respond to other people.

On a printed form you identify yourself by listing simple facts: your name, your address, the address of your school. These facts represent only a small part of the total picture of who you are. If five people are asked to describe what you are like, each description will be different from the others. Members of your family will describe you in one way; your teachers may present a different picture. Your friends might each give yet another view. You may be shy and quiet with some friends and talkative with others. You may argue a lot with your family but seldom speak up for yourself at school.

Furthermore, your relationships with other people change as you and they change. They feel different about you at different times.

NOTE: The most famous person to advise people to know themselves was the Greek philosopher Socrates, who believed that wrong actions occurred when people failed to examine their own reasons and motives fully.

ENRICHMENT: Ask students to write two descriptions of themselves: one as a member of their family sees them and one as their best friends see them.

Individual differences make our world exciting and interesting. What is there about you that makes you unique?

How you feel about yourself also varies. Your moods and attitudes can change from one day to the next. When you are at home alone on a rainy afternoon, you may feel lonely. On another, similar afternoon you might be delighted to spend some time by yourself, enjoying one of your favorite records.

Finding Out Who You Are

One way to understand yourself better is to study the various characteristics, or traits, that make up your total self. The total of all your characteristics, physical and emotional, forms your **personality.** Your personality is unique—no other person has the same personality as you.

People judge you by your personality. It reflects your feelings, your attitudes, and your behavior. It grows and changes throughout your life.

Physical Characteristics Your physical characteristics represent the way your body looks and the way it works. What color are your eyes and hair? Are you tall and thin, or of average height and weight? Are you left-handed or right-handed? You may be proud of some of your physical characteristics. Other traits may make you feel self-conscious.

During adolescence, great changes take place in your body as you grow from a child into an adult. Your height and weight change rapidly. In the early teenage years, girls grow faster than boys. Boys' voices drop to a lower tone and may crack embarrassingly in mid-sentence. At first, these changes may make you feel awkward, but you will get used to them.

Emotional Characteristics The way you behave toward other people largely depends on your emotions. In turn, your emotions partly result from physical characteristics such as your general health and energy level.

During adolescence your emotions change rapidly, and your moods often shift from one extreme to the other. One day you could feel happy and sure of yourself. The next day you feel miserable and self-conscious. You may find that your feelings are easily hurt and that you get angry quickly. You may find you have a new interest in the opposite sex and are not sure how to deal with these new feelings. It is some comfort to know that *many* teenagers have these problems, although they may not admit it.

Mental Characteristics Your mind is different from anybody else's. You may have a wonderful memory but find it hard to express your opinions. You may be good at math but have trouble in social studies. Maybe solving your friends' problems or planning strategies in football is your strong point. Perhaps your special interest is music or painting. As you grow, your intellectual, or mental, interests probably will change. When your emotions are changing so fast, it is sometimes hard to keep your mind focused on schoolwork or other mental activities. You need

to find ways to focus your mind. You should also try to understand both your weaknesses and your special talents.

Social and Moral Characteristics As you grow toward adulthood, you strengthen your own special beliefs and attitudes about both spiritual, or religious, values and the values of your community. Volunteering with other young people can help you to serve others. Or you may want to join in a community cleanup day. Helping to raise funds for a cause you believe in can be satisfying and fun as well. Reinforcing your spiritual values and getting involved in your community are ways

How does this activity reflect social and moral values?

ENRICHMENT: Brainstorm with your class to list as many emotions and moods as they can think of. Then, on their own papers, students should put these in order of how frequently they experience each.

DISCUSS: People often react to other people they meet on the basis of their physical characteristics. Why do they do this? Are there advantages to this? What are the disadvantages?

What physical characteristics do these girls share with their father?

you can put your beliefs and values to work.

Heredity and Environment

There are two major factors that strongly affect your personality. Your **heredity** (huh–*RED*–i–tee) is the total characteristics passed on from your parents. You inherit your basic physical characteristics, such as your coloring and your body type, from your parents, who inherited them from *their* parents. Some of the emotional and mental characteristics you have are also inherited.

Your **environment** consists of your surroundings, including the people around

you. Your family, your friends, your school, your neighborhood, your religion, and all your experiences starting from birth make up your environment. Your environment often changes hereditary characteristics, and you can often make some changes yourself. For example, you may inherit weak muscles. Through exercise and a healthy diet you can make your muscles stronger.

Your heredity and your environment act together to make you the unique person you are.

Did You Know?

Identical twins inherit exactly the same genes. Those who have been separated as babies and brought up in different families are especially interesting to researchers. Their development provides clues as to which traits are inherited and which are the result of upbringing. One pair of twins, reunited after 38 years, discovered they had chosen similar careers, had given their children similar names, and enjoyed similar hobbies. They also drove the same model car in the same color! Just as interesting are the pianist and her twin. Separated at birth, only one showed an interest and talent for music—a trait we usually think of as inborn.

Your Self-Concept

Your self-concept is the overall view you hold of yourself. It begins to develop at birth and continues to grow and change with each new experience. By the time you reach adolescence, you can judge your personality much more clearly than you could in childhood. Now it is most important to form a strong self-concept by understanding your basic needs, your values, and your goals.

First you need to become aware of the basic needs that you share with all other human beings.

Basic Human Needs

Everyone shares the same basic physical and emotional needs. Physical needs include food, clothing, shelter, rest, activity, and protection from harm. Emotional needs include love, respect, companionship, and spiritual satisfaction.

The way you go about meeting all of these needs depends on your own unique personality.

Values

One thing that makes you different from everyone else is your set of **values,** or ideas and beliefs that are important to you. Maintaining friendships and family ties, following religious teachings, and performing community service are examples of values in action.

As you grow into adulthood, you begin to think more about your values, based on the teachings of your family, religion, community, and your own experiences.

Goals

Your self-concept is affected by your **goals,** those things that you hope to accomplish in life. Setting goals and working toward their achievement can help you to build a positive self-concept. Becoming a better soccer player or preparing for a specific career are examples of goals you may have. You will read more in Chapter 2 about how they affect your decisions.

Which basic human needs are these boys meeting?

Your Total Personality

Physical

Mental

Social

Spiritual

Emotional

Each personality has many parts. What would your puzzle look like?

Building a Strong Self-Concept

You need to feel good about yourself in order to get along with others and to have a happy, fulfilling life. Use the following suggestions to build a strong self-concept.

- Think positively about yourself, but be honest in recognizing both your strengths and your weaknesses. Try to turn weaknesses into strengths. For example, if you think of yourself as too quiet, change your judgment to thinking of yourself as a good listener.

- Accept the things in your personality that you cannot change. Work on building a positive view of the parts that you *can* improve.

- Focus on your special abilities and talents. These can include anything from your organizing ability or your athletic skills to your sense of humor and your friendliness.

- Learn from everything you do. Concentrate on your successes. When you do make a mistake, ask yourself what you can do to avoid repeating it.

- When someone praises you, accept the praise. Sometimes it is hard to accept compliments. As you strengthen your self-concept, it will become easier for you to believe positive statements about

DISCUSS: What is the difference between having a strong self-concept and being conceited?

ENRICHMENT: Have students list five things in their own lives that they think they can influence by positive thinking.

yourself. You will then be able to develop the part of you that was praised.

- Be active. Get involved in activities that interest you. Help others with their problems. Develop friendships with people who have a positive attitude toward themselves and the world around them.
- Don't be afraid to ask others for help in coping with your problems and building self-confidence. Friends, family members, and school, church, or community counselors can be helpful.
- Think seriously about making changes in your behavior if it interferes with your self-concept and your relationships with others. Avoid bad habits such as biting your nails, being late, or not looking at people when you talk to them. Don't try to correct everything at once. Work on one habit at a time.

Remember that everyone has some disabilities and limitations. If you stress the positive parts of your personality, you can respect the unique person you are. By doing this, you will be able to build a stronger self-concept.

Changes can make you nervous.

For Review

1. List the various characteristics that form your personality.
2. How does your environment affect your personality?
3. How do your needs, values, and goals affect your self-concept?
4. What steps should you follow to build a strong self-concept?

Section 1.2
Growing and Changing

As you read, think about:

- what kinds of changes you are experiencing as an adolescent. (p. 10)
- the roles you play in your life. (p. 11)
- the important characteristics of a mature person. (p. 13)
- how standards develop your character and self-respect. (p. 14)

A lot of changes are taking place in your life these days—changes in the way you

DISCUSS: Think of ways to overcome bad habits. Consider using small groups, each discussing one bad habit and developing a list of ways to overcome it.

RETEACHING: Emphasize that accepting who you are has a positive effect not only on you but on how others view you.

Chapter 1/*Looking At You*   **9**

look, the way you feel, and the way you see yourself. You are probably being given more freedom and more responsibility. You may choose your own clothes and hairstyle. You begin to focus more on long-range plans and to think about what you will be doing as an adult.

This section will help you understand the great changes that are going on in your life. It will also provide some tips on how you can deal successfully with your new freedom and responsibilities.

A Time of Change

You will be changing and developing all through your life. However, in your teen-age years you are changing faster than you ever will again.

The world you live in is also changing rapidly. When your parents were your age, there were no personal computers. A generation before that, only a few people owned television sets. No one can predict what equally dramatic changes will be taking place when you become an adult.

Adjusting to New Experiences

Throughout your life you are adjusting to growth and change. As a child you faced the first day of school away from familiar faces at home. You learned to play with other children, to share toys and games. You learned about school rules and what you were expected to do in school. You made other major adjustments in your life. Maybe your family moved to a new neighborhood and you became the new kid on the block. Maybe you went away to camp. In these sorts of situations, you had

What changes take place between the ages of seven and fifteen?

ART: Can students locate records of their early physical growth? Have them chart changes that occurred during babyhood (or for any period they can track down). Students may enjoy comparing their own charts with those of their classmates.

Everyone grows at a different rate. There is no exactly right or wrong time for changes to take place.

to adjust to new people and to a new environment.

In adolescence, the way you adjust to new situations changes. In your childhood, older people made all your decisions for you and were totally responsible for your well-being. Now, in your teenage years, your parents are still responsible for you, but they are probably letting you make more and more decisions on your own. The new freedom you have is fun, but you have to work harder at planning and running your own life.

Adjusting to Physical Growth and Change

One of the challenges you face as an adolescent is the adjustment to the physical changes that are taking place. Chances are, your friend's rate of physical change is different from yours. This is perfectly normal. Everyone has a unique timetable of physical growth. Generally, girls develop more rapidly than boys. Some boys do not experience a growth spurt until the age of 15 or 16. Of course, there are exceptions to all of these general rules.

Roles in Your Life

As you grow up you will find that you are playing various *roles*. Within your family you are a daughter or a son and perhaps a sister or a brother. At school you are a student and perhaps a member of a team or a club. At a job you are an employee. Juggling all these roles can be difficult. You might find, for instance, that your boss at a part-time job needs you to work

RETEACHING: Stress that physical changes occur at different rates. No one should be embarrassed by changes that happen more rapidly or slowly to one person than to another.

ENRICHMENT: Have students examine differences in daily routines. They could compare the daily routines of five older students, some of whom will have after-school activities or jobs.

extra hours at the same time as your basketball practice. In situations like this, you have to set *priorities*. You must decide which role is more important. Then you need to explain the situation to the person who is inconvenienced by your decision.

Other people in your life play several roles, too. It is important to understand that they also have to juggle their roles. Your mother has other roles besides being a parent. If she has a job, her role as worker may require her to be away from home at a time when you want to be with her. This can be upsetting, but accepting the fact that she, like you, has to set priorities shows that you are growing up.

Understanding people's roles in life helps you to know what kind of behavior to expect from others and from yourself in specific situations.

Stereotypes

Knowing what to expect from someone in a particular role helps the world run smoothly. However, it is important to remember that everyone is an individual.

A **stereotype** is an expectation of what a person is like. It is an oversimplified view. You might think of a police officer as a person in a uniform who chases law-breakers. You might not think of him or her as an individual who may be a father or a mother.

You may run up against stereotyping that affects your own life. Suppose you are a boy who is interested in writing poetry. Your friends laugh at you when you join a writers' group. They say poetry is only for girls. If you are a girl who loves garden-ing, you'll be angry if you are turned down

In order to play several roles, this mother and daughter must work out a plan together.

DISCUSS: Ask students to describe what the following people look like: a carpenter, a homemaker, a stockbroker, a secretary, and a computer engineer. What stereotypes emerge? Discuss how such stereotypes can be damaging.

NOTE: The word *stereotype* comes to us from printing. A stereotype was a solid metal plate that could be used repeatedly. It never changed.

for a job doing yard work because someone thinks "girls should not do jobs like that." Learning to avoid stereotyping will allow you to broaden your understanding of people.

Growing Up

"I'm sick of everybody telling me what to do," you complain. All day long, people have been ordering you around. Your elder brother, your neighbor, your mother, your teacher, and your coach. Even the dog demanded you refill his water dish by banging it around. Some of them were only trying to help you or teach you; some were depending on you to help them.

Becoming a Mature Person

Adolescence is the stage in your life when you gradually take on responsibility for your decisions and actions. You are moving toward the time when you will be an independent adult. You will earn your living as well as support the needs and wants of the people around you. A mature person is one who accepts this responsibility. Maturity and responsibility go hand in hand.

Understanding your strengths and weaknesses is another sign of maturity. A mature person has a strong self-concept.

A mature person makes decisions and acts independently. However, no one should be totally independent. We all need to share our lives with family and friends in an environment of trust, acceptance, respect, and love.

PHOTO: Discuss effective ways for teens to initiate serious communication with their parents. Consider time of day, tone of voice, location, and body language.

What advice would you give to this father and son?

Dealing with Conflict

A mature attitude is particularly helpful when you have a disagreement with a parent. For example, suppose your mother asks you to take care of your little brother so that she can go shopping. You have already promised to visit a friend's house to work on a special project that is due tomorrow.

Instead of getting upset, try to work out a solution to the problem with your mother. You might arrange to have your friend work with you at your house while you keep an eye on your brother. Perhaps your mother is willing to do her shopping the following day, when you are free.

You can express your maturity in other conflicts as well. Be willing to listen to what the other person has to say. Explain your side of the question calmly. Sometimes it is wise to allow each side to calm down before discussing the problem. Work together to set priorities and to find a solution.

REINFORCEMENT: Have students describe one responsibility that they have assumed at home recently that shows that they are growing up. Some students may prefer to do this as a private activity.

ENRICHMENT: Ask students to think about a recent argument that took place at home. Ask them to list things that they might have done to avoid the argument or to resolve the conflict in a more mature way.

Do you have any projects that are your very own?

Exploring the Options

Adolescence is a time of discovery. It is a time when you test different ways of viewing yourself. You experiment with new clothes and hairstyles. You look for new interests for leisure time. You may form a rock band with some friends, or join a sports team, or do some volunteer work. Perhaps you try several different kinds of part-time jobs. You may do yard work or work after school in a supermarket. You may help in a family business on Saturdays. You explore special skills and talents that help you in your schoolwork. You also begin to think about possible future careers that suit your goals and your interests.

As you explore a variety of options in your social, school, and working life, you will find your self-concept becomes stronger. The broader your experience,

the more self-confident you will become. You will also find you are better prepared for all of the responsibilities that come with maturity.

What Do You Stand For?

Who you are is much more than the combination of your physical, mental, and emotional characteristics. Who you are also depends on your **standards,** the guidelines you set based on the values you believe in. As you grow and change, you develop your own standards of behavior, influenced by your family, your friends, your religion, and your community. Every day you make decisions based on different kinds of standards. For example, you clean your room according to your standards of neatness and organization. There are also moral standards, called **ethics,** which are based on your beliefs about what is good and bad, right and wrong. Someone might risk losing a school election rather than behave unethically by making campaign promises that were impossible to keep.

Standing Up for What Is Right

You probably agree that striving for moral standards such as honesty, dependability, trust, and regard for the rights and feelings of others is important. The difficult part comes when you are called on to carry out those standards. Suppose you find a wallet filled with money. Nobody sees you pick it up. You could use that money to buy something you want very much. If you have the moral courage to return the wallet to its rightful owner, you show that you are a person of strong

These students are raising money for a cause. In what other ways can teens play a positive role in their communities?

moral character. You demonstrate to yourself and others that you respect the rights of others and stand by your own moral code.

Learning to take responsibility for your behavior requires courage and maturity. One of the most difficult situations you can face is having to stand up for your own moral values when other people are trying to force you to go against those values.

Peer Pressure Teenagers are particularly pressured by their **peers,** people of their own age group, to join in undesirable behavior. It is never easy to resist this peer pressure.

You may be urged by a classmate to cheat on a test. You know that this behavior is wrong, but you don't want to be rejected by your classmate. Now is the time to test your character. Say no. You are responsible for your own behavior.

In the long run, people will respect you for standing up for what you believe is right. Not everyone will agree with your moral standards, but in time you will find friends who share your standards of behavior. Most of all, you will strengthen your own self-respect.

See page T30 for answers.

For Review

1. Describe several kinds of changes or new experiences you will have as a teenager.
2. Why must priorities be established when you play various roles?
3. What are some characteristics of a mature person?
4. How is what you stand for related to your character and your self-concept?

Leadership and Citizenship

Positive Peer Pressure

Peer pressure—everyone knows it can be hard to deal with. But peer pressure can also mean kids helping kids. It includes teenagers sharing knowledge with others their own age or acting as positive role models for younger kids.

• A kids-to-kids program in Richardson, Texas, focuses on the dangers of cigarette smoking. Fifth-grade classes are visited by STARS (Students Teaching About the Risks of Smoking). These high-school volunteers are trained in information about smoking and health and also in decision-making skills. They help the fifth graders to decide against smoking.

• CAN (Cooperative Adventures in Nutrition) teams high schoolers with kindergartners in Greenville, North Carolina. Home economics students teach nutrition, cooking, and other kitchen skills to the younger kids. There is great enthusiasm and achievement on the part of both age groups.

• Peer leadership is also an important part of drug and alcohol education in Newton, Massachusetts. To become peer leaders, high-school volunteers learn about drugs and alcohol and about community services. They are also trained in role-playing activities. Finally, they show by example that it's OK to say *no* to drugs and alcohol.

Can you think of examples of positive peer pressure in your area?

Section 1.3

Making Smart Decisions

As you read, think about:

■ the various ways in which a decision is reached. (p. 17)

■ the factors that have an influence on your decisions. (p. 18)

■ the importance of knowing and following steps in the decision-making process. (p. 19)

The ability to make good decisions depends on using information you have gained from making similar decisions in the past. It involves careful planning, too. Being able to make thoughtful decisions is one of the major signs of maturity.

This section concerns different kinds of decisions and provides a model that you can apply to your own decision making.

Making Choices

You make decisions throughout your life. Even as a baby you made choices, though they were simple ones such as deciding whether to take one more mouthful of cereal. As you grew, you made more and more decisions: which game to play, what sweater to wear, whether or not to share a secret with a friend.

In your teenage years, you are called upon to make increasingly important and long-term decisions. As you grow toward adulthood and gain greater independence,

ENRICHMENT: Present the following situation: There is a math test tomorrow; however, your math teacher went home sick at noon. You need to get a good grade, but you have to work after school, and your favorite movie is on television tonight. What do you do? What does your decision say about your values?

you also become more responsible for these decisions.

A *decision* is the act of choosing among different possibilities and reaching a solution. Many decisions are simply a matter of choosing between two *objects*. For example, in order to lose a few pounds, you opt for a dessert of fresh fruit instead of ice cream. It is usually more difficult to choose between two *actions*. Should you go to the library to get books for your history paper or should you clean your messy room? This choice is less obvious. Your decision will depend on other details, such as when your history paper is due and just how messy your room is.

Reaching a Decision

There are various ways in which a decision is reached.

- You can avoid the problem altogether by letting things happen without making any choices yourself. This is all right when the outcome has little effect on you. In most cases, however, it is better for you if you have some control over the outcome.
- You can make a decision based on the example or advice of other people. Considering the advice of an expert is helpful. However, you should consider how your own needs and wants will be affected. Your math teacher can help you get information on careers related to your math skills, but only you can decide if you are interested in working toward a specific career. If you want to be an actor, studying the path chosen by a famous actor can influence your deci-

sion, but your final choice should depend on your personal needs and ability.

- Sometimes your decisions are based on **impulse**—a sudden choice influenced by your mood of the moment. You buy a yellow scarf because the color attracts your eye. When you get home, you find it does not go with any of your other clothes.
- Some decisions are based on habit. For example, you may eat the same breakfast every morning. As you change and grow, it is a good idea to check your habits. Perhaps the time has come to make some new choices.
- Your decisions are sometimes based on fear or self-consciousness. You would like to start a new activity or set a new goal, but you are afraid of looking silly. You want to learn to ice-skate, but you think people will laugh at you. Nobody becomes an expert overnight. It is exciting to set a new goal and work toward it step-by-step. Remember that the first step is usually the hardest.

Would you get a job, try out for a play, or enter a contest?

How can acting as a family member make you feel good about yourself?

equipment is too expensive and the pool in your community is free.

One of the hardest short-term decisions is one you make everyday—how to spend your time. Dividing your time among school, chores, and leisure requires that you set priorities. It is a good idea to make a schedule each week to be sure you don't spend too much time on one part of your life. You will read more about time management in Chapter 2.

Personal Values

As you read earlier in this chapter, values are the strong ideas and beliefs that guide a person's behavior. Your values, then,

Influences on Decisions

Your *perceptions* (per–*SEP*–shuns)—the way you see and understand things —affect the way you make decisions. Your self-concept also influences the choices you make. For example, the kinds of friends you choose depends on how they relate to your interests and on how you see yourself. If you like team sports, your friends probably share your interest. If you think of yourself as shy, you may choose friends who are outgoing and who keep the conversation moving. Or, you may feel more comfortable with quiet friends like yourself.

Money and Time

Your decisions are also influenced by how much money you have for an activity and how much you want to spend on a particular project. You may decide to focus on swimming rather than skiing because ski

Did You Know?

Your brain is divided into two halves, and each half controls very different abilities. The movement of your left arm and leg is controlled by the right half, or right brain. The left brain is the center of verbal and logical abilities. It counts and makes step-by-step plans. When you say, "Be reasonable," you are appealing to a person's left brain. The right brain is imaginative and creative. It lets you dream and draw. When you suddenly "get the picture" or follow a "hunch," you are using your right brain. Scientists have found that one side of the brain is usually dominant.

affect your decisions. You may be tempted to copy your friend's history report, but you refuse because it is ethically wrong. Because you value your relationship with your grandfather, you laugh at his jokes, even if you have heard them before.

Outside Influences

Other people usually affect and are affected by your decisions.

The ideas and attitudes of your peers have a great influence on the choices you make. The way you dress and where you go, your opinions, and the way you use your time are often closely related to what your friends believe in and how they behave. It can be hard to balance your own goals and those of your peers. It is important to stand up for your own values, so that you can meet the important goals you have set for yourself.

Probably the people who are most affected by your decisions are the members of your family. Their decisions also have a great effect on your life. Because they care about you so deeply, your family are more emotionally involved in your decisions than other people. It is important to respect their interest in you. In adolescence, when you are learning to be independent and responsible, you need to work especially hard at maintaining a warm relationship with your family.

It's the Law

Finally, there are some situations in which decisions are not under your control. Everyone must obey the law. Therefore,

Why might this boy have decided to help his neighbor?

it is important to follow school rules and parents' rules for everybody's safety and well-being. Laws and rules are made to protect everyone.

A Model for Decision Making

Every successful decision follows the series of steps given in the model below. When you have an important decision to make, using this model will help you to reach your decision calmly and in an orderly way.

1. *Identify the problem.* For example, you have to provide a costume for your part in the school play.

DISCUSS: What do you think is the most common thing that high school students do as a result of peer pressure? what about junior high and middle school students? elementary school students?

DISCUSS: Can you think of any laws that affect your life and decisions? (If your students have any difficulty, begin with the law that requires them to come to school.)

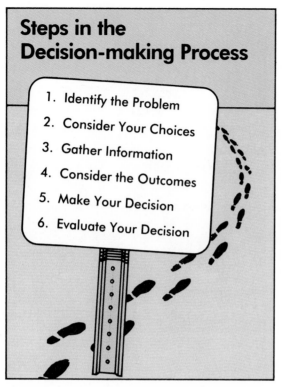

Steps in the Decision-making Process

1. Identify the Problem
2. Consider Your Choices
3. Gather Information
4. Consider the Outcomes
5. Make Your Decision
6. Evaluate Your Decision

How do the decisions that you make today affect your future?

2. *Consider your choices.* You can buy the costume, rent it, or make it yourself.
3. *Gather information.* You find out how much it will cost to buy or rent the costume and how much the materials will cost if you make the costume yourself instead.
4. *Examine the information and weigh the outcomes of the various choices.* You find it costs too much to buy or rent the costume. If you make the costume, you may not have it ready for the dress rehearsal. You have now narrowed your choices.
5. *Make your decision.* You decide to make your costume. Now you need to carry out your decision. How can you

finish it on time? Your friend agrees to help you make it. Your dad offers to drive you to the shopping center to help you find the materials you need. You make a schedule to be sure you and your friend can find the time to work together on the costume.

6. *Evaluate your decision.* Did you make the right choice? Yes, your costume was finished on time and it looked great, although you had to pin the shirt together because time ran out.

It is important to *evaluate,* or judge, the outcome of a decision. Note the mistakes you made, so that you can avoid them next time. If you made the wrong decision, note where you went wrong, then forget about it. Another time, you can approach the problem in a new way.

Taking Responsibility

Whatever the outcome of your decision, take the responsibility for what you decided. Every thoughtful choice you make makes future decisions easier.

Accepting the responsibility for your decisions shows that you are becoming a mature person.

See page T30 for answers.

For Review

1. Describe the various ways in which a decision is reached.
2. List the factors that influence decision making. Give examples.
3. What are the six steps toward making a successful decision?

ENRICHMENT: Ask students to apply the six decision-making steps to the following situation. You need extra spending money. The local newspaper offers you a job every day from 3:00 to 6:00 P.M. Your soccer coach informs you that you made the team and must practice every day from 3:00 to 5:30.

20   Unit 1/*About You*

REINFORCEMENT: Have students write a one-paragraph evaluation of a decision that they made recently.

See page T29 for teaching suggestions.

Learning To Manage

Fitting In

Look back at the telephone conversation on page 2. Kate was feeling lonely in her new school. Now read what she did to try to manage her situation. Then answer the questions that follow.

Kate was determined to get to know people at her new school. She knew that it wasn't going to happen without effort on her part. She went to work on a plan.

First she thought about her strongest interests and talents—music and creative writing and her personal strengths. Her friends always said she was a good listener and that she cheered everyone up with her great sense of humor. Well, it was time to put these things to work!

She decided to open up and talk to her parents about her problem. Her mother suggested that she join a club at school where she could get to know a small group of people who shared an interest with her. Her dad asked her if she wanted to think about joining the youth group at their new church. She decided to look into both of these ideas.

At school, her English teacher told her that people were needed to write for the school newspaper and that there would be a meeting that Wednesday afternoon. Another positive step!

She decided to unpack her clarinet and start practicing again. Band tryouts were coming up soon. She didn't know if she was good enough to win a place in the band. Competition would be stiff here, but she would give it her best shot.

As she struggled with her locker combination that day, Kate muttered, "It's a good thing there's nobody in here counting on me to let them out." Beside her, a girl she recognized from her chemistry class laughed.

"You're new here, aren't you?" she asked.

"I sure am—and wishing I wasn't," Kate replied.

"I know how you feel. I moved here last year. Come on. Have lunch with me and my friends."

"That sounds great. I'm on my way!" Kate smiled. Maybe she *was* on her way after all.

Questions

1. If you moved away, what personal characteristics would help you to make new friends?
2. In your community, what organizations can a newcomer join?
3. Think about a situation in your life that was created by change of some kind. Do you think that you dealt with it well? Why or why not?

See pages T 31-32 for answers and suggestions.

Chapter 1 Review

Summary

Adolescence is the stage in your life when you leave childhood and grow toward becoming a mature adult. It is a time of rapid growth and change. Great changes take place in the way you look, the way you feel, and the way you act. It is a time when you begin to discover who you are and what you stand for.

It is important that you develop a strong self-concept during your teenage years. Learn to recognize and accept the needs, wants, and values that form the unique person you are. Focus on the positive parts of your personality. Use your strengths to help maintain your positive self-concept.

As you become a mature person, your social and spiritual values also develop. You become increasingly responsible for your own actions. You also learn to respect and support the needs, wants, and values of the people around you.

Vocabulary

Complete each of the following sentences with the correct word from the vocabulary list below.

peers (p. 15)
self-concept (p. 3)
goals (p. 7)
values (p. 7)
personality (p. 4)
stereotype (p. 12)

standards (p. 3)
adolescence (p. 14)
impulse (p. 17)
heredity (p. 6)
ethics (p. 14)
environment (p. 6)

1. The way you view yourself, called your _____, affects the way you relate to others and the world.
2. After childhood, _____, or the early teenage years, brings many rapid changes in you, and in your relationships with other people.
3. Your _____ is the total of your physical and emotional characteristics. It is unique.
4. The total of all the characteristics passed on to you from your parents is your _____.
5. Your surroundings, including all the people around you such as your family and friends, are a part of your _____.
6. _____ are the ideas and beliefs that are important to you.
7. The things that you hope to accomplish in life are called _____.
8. An expectation of what a person is like, in oversimplified terms, is a _____.
9. The guidelines you set based on the values you believe in are your _____.
10. Moral standards, or _____, are based on your beliefs about what is good and bad, right and wrong.
11. People of your own age are called your _____.
12. When you make a sudden choice based on your mood of the moment, you are making a decision on _____.

Questions

- •• 1. Why do family members describe you differently than your teachers do?
- • 2. Name some of the emotional characteristics of adolescents.
- • 3. Describe some activities teens can engage in as an outlet for their social and spiritual beliefs and values.
- • 4. Can someone with weak muscles develop stronger ones?
- ••• 5. What, in your opinion, are the two most important basic emotional needs? Explain your answer.
- •• 6. How does your responsibility for decision making change during adolescence?
- •• 7. Name two different roles that you play in your everyday life.
- •• 8. Name two experiences that you had in your childhood that involved an adjustment to change.
- •• 9. What is the value of learning to avoid stereotyping?
- ••• 10. Should a person be totally independent? Explain your answer.
- •• 11. Why should a person have a strong moral character?
- • 12. Name one major sign of maturity.
- • 13. Describe a practical method you can use to set priorities regarding how you spend your time.
- • 14. Why is your family so emotionally involved in the decisions you make?
- • 15. What are your alternatives if you make a bad decision?

The dots represent skill levels required to answer each question or complete each activity:
- • requires recall and comprehension
- •• requires application and analysis
- ••• requires synthesis and evaluation

Skill Activities

Many more activities are contained in the annotations within this chapter.

 1. Decision Making Follow the decision-making model as you use role play to resolve these conflicts for the class. **a.** Two brothers and a sister are arguing about the division of family chores; **b.** A daughter is trying to convince her parents to let her attend her first school dance; **c.** Two students are disputing the lab cleanup rules with their teacher.

 2. Laboratory Design an art display that tells about yourself. First take a piece of paper and divide it into three sections. On the first section, create a display that describes your personality. On the second section, show your favorite color. On the last section, make an illustration of your favorite activities. You can use pictures from magazines or newspapers. At the end of class, the art displays can be put together to form a classroom "quilt."

3. Human Relations List five ways you can help a family or community member. Examples include preparing a meal, walking the dog for a week, washing the dishes, doing the laundry, or cleaning chores. On 3″ x 5″ cards, create a book with coupons for the completion of these jobs and give this gift of your time and talent to your favorite family or community friend.

Chapter 2
Managing Your Life

Vocabulary

The dialogue below introduces "Finding the Time," the Learning to Manage feature in this chapter. The case study is continued and the situation discussed further on page 41. See page T34 for teaching suggestions.

"I have no idea how I'm going to get everything done this week! I have two tests, a term paper due, soccer practice every day, and my part-time job at the bookstore to handle!"

I thought *I* was busy! Sounds as if you're really on overload, Joel."

"I am. I really need to sit down and plan out my time. I think I'll talk to Steve. He has the same schedule, but he always seems to have it under control. Maybe he'll have some hints that will help me to manage better!"

Section 2.1
What Is Management?

As you read, think about:

■ the different resources you use to manage your life. (p. 25)

■ how the six steps of the management process help to make any project easier. (p. 27)

Managing better is important to everyone, from a fast food restaurant owner to a rock star or the president of the United States. All of these are managers. They plan ahead, they organize, they use their talents to do their jobs to the best of their abilities. You do not have to have a job to be a manager. Most people use the skills of a manager every day. You use management skills to get to school on time, to buy clothes, to get a good grade on a test. As an adult you will be responsible for managing your life. Learning about the management process will help you in all areas of your life.

What Management Means

Management is the method you use to organize and control something. Managing your life in a responsible way is a large part of becoming a mature person. Your resources, goals, and values all affect how you manage your life. These factors influence all of your management decisions.

Any talent takes time and effort to develop. What talents do you have?

Resources

Your *resources* are the things in your life that help you live successfully and meet the goals you set for yourself.

Resources can be either human or nonhuman. **Human resources** include your knowledge, skills, and abilities. They also include the people around you, friends, teammates, teachers, employers, neighbors, and, of course, family members. Your health, feelings, and attitudes are also human resources.

Nonhuman resources include money, time, food, clothing, and resources in your community, such as parks, schools, and libraries.

Goals

As you read in Chapter 1, a goal is an end point that you work to achieve. In order to manage your life effectively, you need to set both short-term and long-term goals. A **short-term goal** is one that you want to meet in the near future. Getting a good grade on a test or scoring over 10 points in the basketball game are examples of short-term goals. A **long-term goal** is one you want to accomplish in the more distant future. Traveling to Europe or becoming a professional singer are examples of long-term goals. By planning a series of connected short-term goals, you progress, step-by-step, toward a major goal in your life. Setting a *series* of goals gives meaning and focus to your life.

Values and Standards

You read about values in Chapter 1. As you recall, *values* are the ideas or beliefs you form about what is important and

What do you want to accomplish? Take time to set your goals carefully.

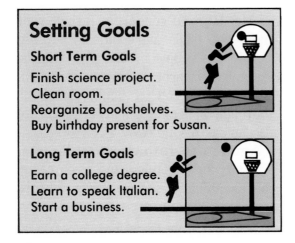

Setting Goals

Short Term Goals

Finish science project.
Clean room.
Reorganize bookshelves.
Buy birthday present for Susan.

Long Term Goals

Earn a college degree.
Learn to speak Italian.
Start a business.

ENRICHMENT: Ask students to list five short-term goals that could be accomplished in one week. Then have students rank the goals according to how easily they might be met within one week. Finally, ask whether all the goals are realistic for the time frame.

desirable in your life. Values, including your feelings about friendship, honesty, and religion, affect the goals you set and the standards by which you live and manage your life.

Your *standards,* the guidelines you use to measure your values and goals, determine your day-to-day behavior and your approach toward the future. Sometimes it may seem easier to drift along without worrying about a specific goal. However, by setting high standards and then striving to meet those standards, you bring excitement to your life. You also earn respect from the people around you and increase your self-respect.

RETEACHING: Emphasize that when setting goals, students must know what their goal is and their reasons for wanting to achieve it. They should avoid setting impractical or impossible goals.

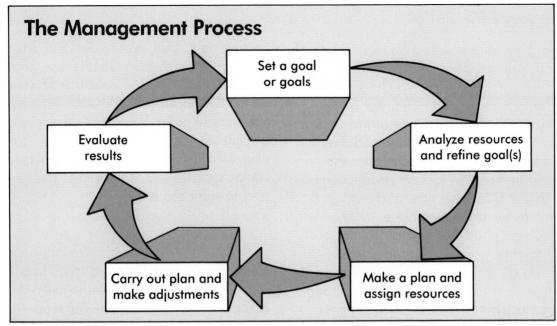

The Management Process

Set a goal or goals

Analyze resources and refine goal(s)

Make a plan and assign resources

Carry out plan and make adjustments

Evaluate results

Sometimes a goal can seem impossible. Using a process can turn a big task into a series of smaller, easier steps.

Process

A **process** is a series of thoughts and actions that lead to a particular result. You use many processes all day long in simple tasks such as tying your shoes and in complex ones such as planning for a life-long career. Both simple and complex processes can be carried out more effectively if you follow the six steps of the management process.

Steps in the Management Process

You have just cleaned up your room and find it still looks messy. What's wrong with it? You glance around. The curtains are stained, the walls are a drab shade of beige, and the bedspread looks as if it had been pulled out of a muddy pond (its colors ran together when you washed it). There are piles of books, records, tapes, and sports equipment on every surface, including the bed, the desk, and the floor. The time has come for some major changes. There is so much to do. Where should you begin?

Following these six steps of the management process will make any project easier for you.

1. Set your goal.
2. Analyze your resources.
3. Make a plan and assign resources.
4. Make adjustments.
5. Carry out the plan.
6. Evaluate the results.

Now let's apply the steps to solve the problem you have in your room.

Technology

Home Efficiency

Imagine what it would be like if both your parents were professional efficiency experts—and you had 11 brothers and sisters! *Cheaper by the Dozen* tells the true story of just such a family. The Gilbreths managed their home with the same techniques they used to increase factory production.

Frank Gilbreth's time and motion studies were famous in the 1920s. He photographed and timed the motions of factory workers. Then he broke down all their actions into small units, such as *searching* for a tool and then *finding* it. Finally, he redesigned machinery and work procedures to eliminate all wasted human motion. His work led to foot levers for garbage cans, improved typewriter design, and more efficient assembly-line techniques.

Gilbreth also practiced what he preached. He used two shaving brushes because that took 17 seconds off his shaving time. But when he tried shaving with two razors, he lost more time bandaging his cuts than he saved using two hands, so he gave it up!

The children were well managed, too. Gilbreth put record players in the bathroom and taught the children to bathe in exactly the time it took one French lesson to play. While there was little wasted motion, there were often hilarious results in the well-dusted, well-bathed, and French-speaking Gilbreth household.

How could you be more efficient?

Set Your Goal

Setting your goal means deciding what you want to accomplish. In this case, your goal is to improve the condition of your room. Specifically, decide what changes you want to make. You need to find a new bedspread and wash the curtains. You plan to build some wall shelves to hold books, records, and other items. You also plan to paint the walls.

Analyze Your Resources

Now analyze what resources you already have and those you will need to make the changes you want. You can get ideas for decorating your room in books and magazines at the library. You need people to help you paint and move furniture. You need money for supplies like paint and lumber. You may also need money to buy a new bedspread or curtains.

Make a Plan and Assign Resources

The next step is to plan the project and assign resources. Friends and family members agree to help you paint. Your main problem, therefore, is money. You have only what you have saved from your allowance and babysitting. When you figure out the costs, you find you cannot afford to buy everything on your list.

Make Adjustments

You must now revise your plans and find other resources. Your sister says she will help you make a bedspread, so you will

DISCUSS: Talk about trade-offs. Ask students to think of a situation in which they had to give something up in order to gain something else. What were the trade-offs?

only have to pay for the material you will use for it.

Your father offers you some paint left over from a painting job he did. Unfortunately, you had planned to paint your room yellow, and this paint is pale green. You decide on a **trade-off.** A trade-off means giving up one thing in order to gain another. In this case, you decide to accept green walls in order to buy the paint rollers you could not otherwise afford. You decide to make another trade-off concerning your brother's offer to give you lumber he has on hand. He can only help you move the wood on Saturday, so you will have to miss the football game. You decide to take advantage of this opportunity to work toward your goal at the cost of giving up an activity you enjoy.

Carry Out the Plan

At last you are ready to proceed with your plan. Your friends help paint, and you and your brother put up the shelves. You wash the curtains, and, together with your sister, you make a bright bedspread.

Evaluate Results

Now that you have completed the project, evaluate the results to see if the management process worked. If you made mistakes, note them so that you can learn not to repeat them. For example, being careful how you wash the bedspread will prevent it from being ruined like the first one. In improving the condition of your room, careful planning was most important. Finding family members and friends

PHOTO: Ask students what trade-offs they would be willing to make for the sake of an important improvement to their room.

What steps of the management process has this girl completed?

to help you made the difference between failure and success.

This example shows how satisfying it can be to take control of a problem and follow the necessary steps to solve it. It is also good to know that you can make big changes with only a few resources. In this case, too, it was important to know how to ask for help from others.

See page T36 for answers.
For Review
1. What are some resources that you use to manage your life?
2. Describe the six steps of the management process.

REINFORCEMENT: Brainstorm with your class to generate specific questions to ask when evaluating a project. Possibilities include, "Did you spend more money (or time) than you had planned?" "What was the most enjoyable part?"

DISCUSS: Have students think about a recent conflict or problem they had to solve. What is generally better—solving a problem alone or asking for help?

Section 2.2

Managing Time

As you read, think about:

■ how time is one of your most important resources. (p. 30)

■ how the management process helps you to organize your time. (p. 33)

■ how the management process helps you to plan individual activities.

(p. 32)

"Oh, I would *love* to go running with you on Saturday," you say to your new friend, "but I don't have the time." You then list all the things you have to do over the weekend. Your friend does not seem convinced. You hope you haven't ruined the beginning of a great friendship.

Most people find it difficult to fit all their activities into the limited time they

What could you do to make better use of your time?

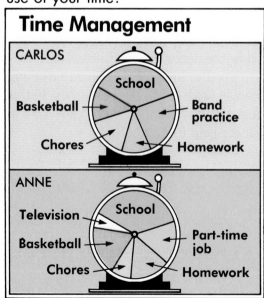

Time Management

have. However, learning to manage time correctly can make life both less stressful and more fun.

This section will give you some helpful tips on how to organize your time so that you can complete your schoolwork, chores, and other projects. In addition, you will still have time to enjoy yourself.

Only 24 Hours

Time is one of your most important resources. How you use it affects your whole life.

Within the span of 24 hours you must find time to eat, sleep, work, and play. The six or seven hours you spend at school are set. Add to that chunk of time the seven or eight hours of sleep you need every night to maintain your physical and emotional health. Then add two hours to eat in an unhurried, relaxed atmosphere. Without even counting part-time work hours, that leaves you only about eight hours a day on weekdays for all of your other activities.

This remaining time is divided among many different things. You need time for chores at home and time for schoolwork. You need time for sports, hobbies, and other leisure activities. The hours you spend with family and friends are also important. So are the quiet hours you spend alone just collecting your thoughts and taking time to relax.

Looking at all these demands on your time, you can see how essential it is for you to manage this important resource effectively. In order to do all the things you need and want to do, you must schedule your time.

Did You Know?

Most of the days of the week get their names from ancient Norse (Scandinavian) mythology. Sunday and Monday (Moon's day) were sacred to the sun and moon respectively. Tuesday was named for Tiu, the Norse god of war; Wednesday for Woden, the chief god; Thursday for Thor, the god of thunder; and Friday for Freya, the goddess of love. Saturday is the only one named for a Roman god, Saturn, god of agriculture.

A Monthly Calendar

Keep a monthly calendar on which you jot down all meetings, due dates for school assignments, invitations, and other scheduled events. Also estimate the hours each of these activities will take. For example, in the square for March 10, you might write, "Basketball practice, 3:00–5:00."

Next fill in activities that do not have set times, such as an hour for fitness exercises. Keep the calendar up to date throughout the month. Be sure you don't schedule two events at the same time.

A Daily Schedule

Make a daily list of "Things to Do." Set *priorities,* that is, list your goals and tasks for that day in order of importance. Mark

the most pressing item number 1, and less important items 2, 3, and so on.

Now make a rough schedule for the day. First take the number 1 item and write down when you plan to take care of it. Then fill in the others, accounting for each hour of the day from the time you get out of school until you go to bed. If you run out of time, you will have to save less important activities for another day. Save the schedule so that you can cross out the items you have completed. At the end of the week you may be surprised to find how much you have accomplished.

Dovetail Activities

Some activities can be *dovetailed,* or overlapped. For example, you can complete some homework while you are doing the laundry. Practicing your speech while doing the dishes allows you to complete both tasks at the same time. There are

Could a daily schedule help you organize your day?

DISCUSS: Talk about the importance of a monthly calendar to a teacher, a businessperson, or a parent working at home. Ask students to speculate on what types of things these people might write in their calendars.

NOTE: There is no solar or lunar reason why a day must have twenty-four hours consisting of sixty minutes. A day could just as easily be divided into ten hours, as the French did just after the revolution. The hours would just be much longer.

A "to do" list is a handy organizer and reminder.

many other ways to dovetail activities. You can make a salad and set the table while the roast is "cooking itself" in the oven. You can have that talk with your sister while you clean up the basement together. Some tasks do *not* lend themselves to dovetailing. Doing homework while watching television is too distracting. Eating your breakfast, braiding your sister's hair, and packing your lunch at the same time stretches your resources too much.

Planning Individual Activities

As well as scheduling different activities, you need to manage your time for a particular activity. Here, too, careful plan-

ning will help you get the most out of your time.

Suppose you have an English paper due on Friday. First figure out, or estimate, about how many hours you will need to do the whole paper. You think it will take five hours in all. Get out your monthly calendar and see when you can squeeze in five hours between now and Friday. If possible, schedule more time early in the week so that you won't feel rushed as the deadline nears. You might even be able to schedule your time so that you can give yourself a "reward" of some free time late in the week.

Did You Know?

In order to manage their activities, human beings have always had an interest in knowing "what time it is." The oldest method of telling time was measuring the sun's shadow as the day progressed. Sundials measured time that way 4,000 years ago. Next came timepieces that showed how long it took for a substance, such as sand or water, to move from one container to another. Hourglasses and water clocks are examples of this type. The first mechanical clocks appeared in the late 1200s, but they didn't have hands or faces. Instead, they told time by ringing a bell.

Avoid Interruptions

When you are working on a difficult task, it is important to concentrate. Avoid interruptions that break your train of thought. Even a brief telephone call in the middle of your scheduled time for homework can make it hard to settle down again. On the other hand, if you are stuck on a problem, it is worth the time to take a short break to stretch and relax. Your mind will return to your work refreshed.

Reward Yourself

Immediately following the end of a large or difficult task, reward yourself. Take at least a short period of time to relax and enjoy yourself. Go for a run with the dog or a bike ride with a friend.

Use the Management Process

To organize your time for a major project, use the steps of the management process you learned about earlier in this chapter.

1. *Set your goal.* As sports reporter for the school newspaper, you have to fill space in the next issue; you decide to interview the new football coach. Your deadline is two weeks away.
2. *Analyze time resources.* First set the time of the interview, since that depends on the coach's schedule. Mark the appointment on your calendar. Then plan the rest of the time you need around the interview.
3. *Assign your time resources.* Make sure you have several hours to prepare your questions before the interview. After-

wards, you will need to schedule enough time to write the article.

4. *Carry out the plan.* This step may seem obvious, but people often make plans and never get around to the actual *doing.* Put your plan into action.
5. *Make adjustments.* As you approach your deadline, you may find you need more time than you estimated. This means you will have to juggle the rest of your schedule to find those extra hours. You might have to change the date of a trip to the movies or get up extra early one or two mornings.
6. *Evaluate results.* When the project is finished, look back on the way you

Everyone needs time for exercise and companionship.

PHOTO: Ask students how these two people are managing their time efficiently.

What outdoor activities do you enjoy when you have time to fill?

managed your time. Learn by your mistakes. You may realize that in future interviews you should ask fewer (or more) questions within the scheduled time. If necessary, you could ask for another appointment to follow up on the first interview. Your experience will also help you better estimate the total time you need to prepare questions and write the article.

Planning Leisure Time

Managing your leisure time well can make your social life more interesting and more fun. Set priorities. If your schedule is tight and you want to attend a football game on Saturday, plan your time carefully. Don't waste hours on the telephone on Friday when you should be doing your math homework. Cut the conversation short so that you can finish your math. Then you can enjoy the game without worrying about making up study hours you have lost.

Avoiding Empty Hours

The pressure of a busy schedule can cause stress. On the other hand, finding yourself with a lot of time to kill can be hard, too. If you find your schedule includes a number of empty hours, plan an activity in advance to fill those hours. You might plan a trip to a museum with a friend or even go by yourself. You could organize a special outing with your family. If you regularly have free time, you could arrange to do some volunteer work at the local community center.

Planning for your leisure hours will help you find time for projects you enjoy and prevent you from getting bogged down in periods of boredom and loneliness. Finding activities you enjoy also helps you learn more about yourself.

See page T36 for answers.

For Review

1. List reasons why time is one of your most important resources.
2. How does the management process help you to organize your time on a major project?
3. Why is it important to plan your leisure time?

Section 2.3
Managing for Learning

As you read, think about:

■ the importance of making good use of class time. (p. 35)

■ how to take good notes in class. (p. 37)

■ how study skills help you learn more effectively. (p. 38)

During adolescence, half of your waking hours are spent in school or doing schoolwork. That is a significant amount of your time. To use those hours most effectively, you have to develop your study skills. This section will help you to make the most of the time you spend in class. You will also learn new ways to organize your schoolwork so that you can improve your grades, yet spend fewer hours doing your homework.

Make the Most of Class Time

The first step in improving your learning skills is to make the most of the time you spend in class. As an added bonus, using class time effectively means you will spend fewer hours on homework. You will know exactly what your homework assignment is. Since you will have paid attention to class discussion, you will already know a good deal about the subject you are working on.

Computers are time-savers for many people.

Be Prepared

It's very boring to listen to people discussing something you don't understand, but you won't have this problem if you do your homework before you come to class. Before class starts, review what you know about the subject to be discussed. Think about what questions you would like to ask your teacher.

Develop Your Listening Skills

Researchers have found that one of the tasks people find most difficult is learning to listen. They have also found that listening is one of the basic learning skills.

Listening carefully to your teacher's questions and instructions is important. Paying attention to class discussion will save you time and stress when you do your homework and later take the test.

It takes training to keep your mind on what is being said, even in a conversation. It is much more difficult to hear instructions correctly. You may find that while the teacher is giving directions for the assignment, your mind wanders. Your thoughts turn to basketball practice or how to strike up a conversation with that interesting new classmate sitting behind you. Those thoughts are important in their own time and place, but not right now. Focus on what the teacher is saying. Write down assignments, dates when papers are due, and other information.

During class discussion, listen to what other people are saying. Students sometimes are so intent on remembering what they themselves want to say that they don't listen to anybody else. They then lose track of the discussion.

Learn What Your Teacher Expects

Listen carefully to the teacher's questions and summary of the discussion. These give you clues about what he or she expects you to do. Each teacher has a slightly different approach. Learn to understand your particular teacher.

Don't Be Afraid to Speak Up

If you don't understand the teacher's instructions or the class discussion, speak up. Wait until the person speaking finishes,

Good listeners ask the right questions, add the right comments, and present a positive attitude.

REINFORCEMENT: Tell students that you will collect their notes on today's class. Then evaluate the notes for how well students have listened.

PHOTO: Ask: How can good listeners show that they are listening without ever saying a word?

Don't be afraid to speak up. Discussions are best when many people add their ideas.

and then ask your question. If you are confused, others probably are, too. They may be even shyer about speaking up in class than you are.

Join in class discussions. This will help the teacher to get to know you. However, don't just speak for the sake of it. Teachers judge you on your performance in class as well as on your homework and tests. Remember that speaking skills, like listening skills, improve with practice.

Take Good Class Notes

"I took six pages of notes, but I couldn't remember a thing!" Have you ever had a similar experience? The notes you take during class can make all the difference in your schoolwork. Learning some simple note-taking skills will help you recall what the teacher said and what main points were covered in class.

RETEACHING: Emphasize that a good listener is a popular individual. Discuss how this applies to an employee, a student, an athlete, a politician, and a counselor.

Use an Outline Take class notes in outline form. Jot down ideas in a few words. Briefly list details about each idea under that heading. If you try to write full sentences, you will lose track of what is being said. Do not include words like *a* and *the*. You can also leave out many verbs. Instead of writing, "The capital of Texas is Austin," write the word *"Texas"*, and underneath it write the words, *"Capital, Austin."* You can also shorten words by inventing your own personal method of abbreviation.

Focus on Main Ideas You cannot possibly write down everything that is said. Note only the main ideas, with a few details listed below them. Put a star beside the ideas that the teacher emphasizes. Whenever you hear, "This is important," or something like, "Now, here is the clue to the whole question," star or underline that point.

DISCUSS: Should taking notes be mandatory in every class? What are the advantages and disadvantages of note-taking during class?

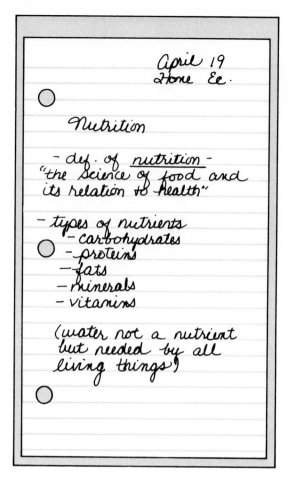

April 19
Home Ec.

○

Nutrition

- def. of nutrition -
"the Science of food and its relation to Health"

- types of nutrients
   - carbohydrates
   - proteins
   - fats
   - minerals
   - vitamins

(water not a nutrient but needed by all living things)

○

Taking notes in outline form helps you see the main ideas.

Review Your Notes After class, review your notes as soon as possible. Rewriting your notes in a more organized form will help you remember all that was said.

If you have to miss a class, find out what you missed as soon as possible. Try to get the information from the teacher rather than another student's notes. Everyone takes notes differently, and you may find that you are not able to follow another person's outline.

Develop Study Skills

A *skill* is the ability to do something well. You can learn study skills in the same way as you learn other skills, such as riding a bicycle or playing the piano. First you learn what to do; then you practice until you do it with ease. You can learn more in less time if you develop the study skills suggested below.

Organize Your Study Time

Apply the system of time management you learned earlier in this chapter to organize the time you spend on schoolwork. Divide your study time among the assignments you have in various subjects. Estimate how much work you have in each subject and how much time each assignment will require. Mark these hours on your monthly calendar and on your daily schedule. Remember to allow enough time for doing research and required reading. Allow extra time for reviewing the day before a test.

Everyone has a particular style of studying. You may find you study best when you have a long period of time to work, for example.

> ### Did You Know?
>
> Studying in a large room with many sources of light is better for your eyes than a small room with a single bright light.

Find a Good Place to Work

Find a quiet, well-lit place to study. It should be a place where you will not be interrupted by other people or by the telephone. It should be away from the television set and the radio. You may need to make special arrangements with other family members to make the right space available. If you find it is too noisy at home, try working at the library.

Be sure your work place has enough light and air. Lack of fresh air will make you sleepy.

Organize Your Study Materials

Organize everything you need before you begin an assignment. You will be surprised how much time you save if you first collect the necessary materials. Make sure you have reference books you need, sharp pencils, pen, paper, typewriter, or other equipment before you sit down to work. Have a pocket dictionary and atlas on hand. These reference books will be helpful for most assignments.

Plan the stages of your work to fit your schedule. Doing this will help to make the most efficient use of your time. For example, if you need an encyclopedia and other reference books for a particular paper, schedule time at the library before you begin writing. It is usually better to do the hardest things first and get them out of the way.

Learn to Concentrate

When your mind wanders, you lose time. When you are interrupted, you waste time getting back to work. Avoid telephone calls during your study time. Concentrate on what you are studying. With practice, you will discover that your concentration skills improve. By being able to work

Avoid interruptions when you study. First, find a quiet place. Then organize everything you will need.

PHOTOS: Ask: Which of these two places would you rather study in? Where would you accomplish more?

NOTE: A person organizing study materials during the Middle Ages would have had no pencils to sharpen, no dictionary, and certainly no typewriter! The pen would probably have been a quill and the paper parchment.

A teacher is an important human resource. Do you take advantage of opportunities for help?

more intensively, you will finish sooner and have more time for leisure activities.

If there are some areas you find more difficult than others, write answers to questions about those sections without checking the text or your notes. You may find it helpful to get a member of your family to ask you key questions.

Set Study Goals

Set short-term goals, then reward yourself with a short break. For example, tell yourself that you will take a 10-minute

break as soon as you finish two more math problems or answer two more science questions. When you reach your goal, walk around or do a few stretching exercises. Eat an apple. You will feel refreshed when you go back to work.

Think Positively

Give yourself as much chance to enjoy the subject you are studying as you can. Think how proud you will be if you do well. Focus on parts of the subject that apply to your own life. If, for example, you would like to start your own business eventually, think how helpful math skills will be in keeping business records.

Don't be afraid to do well. It may seem unlikely, but many people are afraid to succeed. They are frightened of the responsibility that comes with success. You probably hear expressions of this negative attitude all the time.

"I've *never* been any good at math," Joanna says.

"Science has always been way over my head!" Carl declares.

Don't let yourself fall into this negative way of thinking. Dare to be the best you can be.

See page T36 for answers.
For Review

1. List five ways to make the most of your class time so that you can improve how you learn.
2. Describe the steps you should follow to take good notes.
3. Name five important study skills.

REINFORCEMENT: Review time management strategies by asking for examples of things that students can do at night to prepare for the following morning.

ENRICHMENT: Some people say "time is money." Have students write a paragraph explaining how this does or does not relate to managing their resources.

40   Unit 1/*About You*

Learning to Manage

Finding the Time

Look back at the conversation on page 24. Joel is trying to figure out how to manage time for all of his responsibilities and activities. Now read how he tries to improve his time management. Then answer the questions that follow.

Joel saw Steve at his locker the next afternoon as they were both getting ready for soccer practice.

"How's it going?" Steve asked.

"Not so well," Joel replied. "Steve, how do you manage to get everything done?"

"Let's talk after practice, OK?"

As they walked home, Steve explained his method of managing to Joel. He said that he blocked out each month on a large calendar. He filled in dates of tests and when papers were due ahead of time. He also blocked out hours taken up with soccer practice and games. Then he filled in the hours spent at his part-time job. He slotted in leisure time and social activities he knew were coming up.

"Sounds like Steve-the-Robot-Man!" Joel said, half-jokingly.

Steve laughed. "It doesn't always work out as planned. Things often happen to change the schedule, but at least I have a basic plan mapped out for each month."

"What about work, Steve? I've really been thinking about quitting even though I need the money."

"Well, Joel, I asked to cut back to one afternoon a week at the restaurant until soccer ends. The trade-off is less money for more time, but I didn't have to quit."

"That's a good idea, Steve. I'm going to talk to my boss tomorrow. Something has to be cut back. It can't be my grades, or I'm in big trouble—with my parents, my teachers, and the soccer coach! I even thought about quitting the team, but I really enjoy it."

"I hope you don't do that, Joel. We need you. Of course . . . if you quit, then *I* might get to play goalie."

Joel laughed when he saw the sly look on his friend's face.

"No way, Steve! I'm going home right now to map out a plan to manage my time. I plan to keep my position—in the classroom *and* on the field!"

Questions

1. What advice would you have given to Joel? Explain your reasons.
2. Do you think Joel's time management plan will work? Why or why not?
3. Think about any problems you have had managing your time. How have you tried to solve them? Have you been successful? Why or why not?

Chapter 2 Review

Summary

Everyone is a manager. By using human and nonhuman resources and the six steps of the management process, you will be more successful as a manager. These six steps are:

1. Set a goal.
2. Analyze your resources.
3. Make a plan and assign resources.
4. Make adjustments.
5. Carry out the plan.
6. Evaluate the results.

Learning to manage time effectively is important. Having a plan for organizing and using your time helps you to do this.

Good study skills help you to make the best use of class time and to be more successful in preparing for and taking tests. Learning to take notes accurately and in outline form will help you both in and out of the classroom.

Vocabulary

Complete each of the following sentences with the correct word from the vocabulary list below.

process (p. 27)   human resources (p. 25)

(p. 25) management   short-term goal (p. 26)

nonhuman   long-term goal (p. 26)

(p. 25) resources   trade-off (p. 29)

1. Knowledge, skills, abilities, and the people around you can be called _____.

2. Something you want to accomplish in the near future is called a _____.

3. A series of thoughts and actions that lead to a particular result is called a _____.

4. Giving up one thing in order to gain by another is called a _____.

5. The method you use to organize and control something is called _____.

6. Things such as time and money that can be used to reach a goal are called _____.

7. Things you want to accomplish in the distant future are called _____.

Questions

1. What resources do you manage in order to get to school on time? How effective do you think your management of these resources is? Use the steps in the management process to answer.

2. Are your health, feelings, and attitudes human or nonhuman resources? Explain your answer.

3. What is the purpose of keeping a monthly calendar?

4. Name two activities that you could do at the same time on a school day.

5. If you are having trouble solving a homework problem, what can you do to refresh your mind?

The dots represent skill levels required to answer each question or complete each activity:
- • requires recall and comprehension
- • • requires application and analysis
- • • • requires synthesis and evaluation

42

6. Why is it important to plan your leisure time as well as your work time? Explain your answer.

7. Why should you listen carefully during class?

8. Why is it a good idea to take part in class discussions?

9. When taking class notes, should you write down everything that is said or only some of what is said? Explain your answer.

10. Is it a good idea to borrow someone else's notes if you have missed a class? Why or why not?

Skill Activities

Many more activities are contained in the annotations within this chapter.

1. **Critical Thinking** Using the six steps in the management process to help you, plan and give a class party. The guest of honor will be the student with the next closest birthday. On the blackboard, list all the necessary preparation for the event under each step in the management process. Following the party, evaluate your management skills. How did the management process help you to organize the details for the party and ensure its success?

2. **Communication** Ask one student to tell a story and instruct the rest of the class to listen carefully. Each student will then listen carefully. Each student will then take turns retelling the story. Was the last story the same as the original? Do they resemble each other? What does this activity tell us about our listening skills?

3. **Laboratory** Bring to class a list of all your activities for the next month. Be sure to include all appointments, after-school commitments, school games, and so on. Using construction paper, create a calendar clearly listing these events. Bring the calendar home and display it on your refrigerator. At the end of the month, evaluate whether this was helpful in organizing your time and energy. Bring your calendar back to class and share what you have found out about the way you manage your time.

4. **Human Relations** Friends sometimes help each other improve their study skills so that they can learn more and do better in school. With a classmate, act out a situation in which one friend coaches another to improve study skills. If you play the part of the coach, be sure to make as many suggestions as you can remember. Give examples of what you mean so that your suggestions are clear. If you play the friend getting advice, make sure you describe your problems and the kind of help you need. When you have finished, reverse roles and go over the activity again. Share your experience with the class.

Chapter 3
Wellness

Vocabulary

The dialogue below introduces "Getting in Shape," the Learning to Manage feature in this chapter. The case study is continued and the situation discussed further on page 67. See page T40 for teaching suggestions.

"I don't know if I can do this, Peg. I want to make the team, but these practice sessions are too much! I hurt all over and I'm so tired I can barely get my homework done before I fall asleep. Why don't you look tired?"

"Well . . . I've been trying to get in shape since the summer. I run every day, and I've really been watching my diet. It's made a difference. You can get there, too, Rachel."

"Thanks, but right now I'll be lucky to get to Mom's car! Call me tonight and tell me what I need to do to get in shape. I plan to play basketball and feel good doing it!"

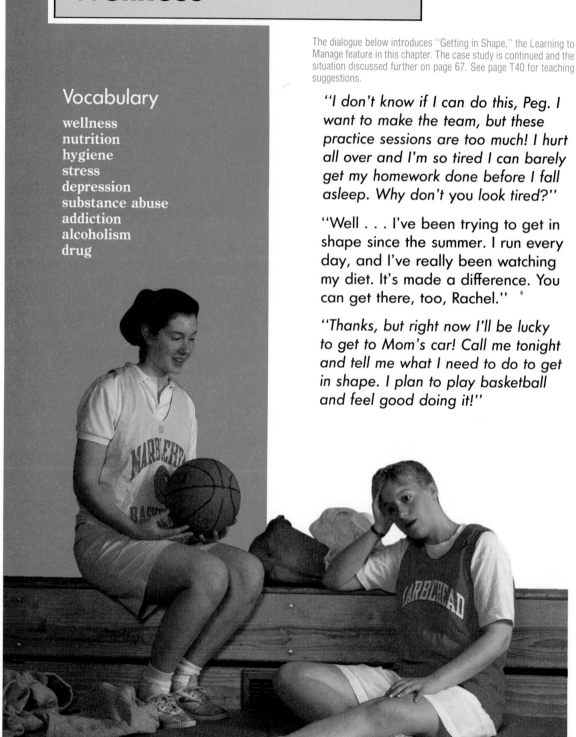

Section 3.1
Everyday Health

As you read, think about:

- how a healthy diet and sufficient exercise contribute to your good health. (p. 45)
- the important role hygiene and grooming play in your life. (p. 47)
- how proper dental care contributes to your health and appearance. (p. 48)
- the importance of rest and relaxation for your mental and physical health. (p. 49)

As Peg is finding out, having energy and feeling well affect everything you do. Good health is the most important resource you can have. When you are not well, you cannot use other important resources, like time and money, very effectively. When you are well, you have the strength to face problems that may arise. You also have the energy to enjoy each day of your life to the fullest. Because of this, it is important to understand how to take care of your health.

What Is Wellness?

Wellness is the state of physical, mental, social, and spiritual health or well-being. It is a way of life that is based on healthy attitudes and actions. It is far more than not being sick. Being well means that you take responsibility for developing healthy habits so that you can make the most of your life. Being well also means that you learn what you need to know in order to make healthy choices.

DISCUSS: A healthy body is the first step toward a healthy mind.

PHOTO: Ask students to comment on what they do to get regular exercise.

How does this photograph say "wellness" to you?

Making Healthy Choices

Healthy eating habits, regular exercise, and good hygiene will all help you to maintain wellness. So will sufficient rest and time for relaxation. In addition, it is important that you always follow correct safety procedures.

A Healthy Diet

The old saying is correct: You *are* what you eat. What you eat and how much you eat help to determine your health, strength, and energy levels.

Nutrition is the science of food and its relation to health. You will learn more about nutrition, including the specific foods your body needs, in Chapter 12. As

REINFORCEMENT: With your class, brainstorm a list of ways to begin each day in a healthy manner.

What makes swimming a healthy exercise choice?

you think about total wellness, remember that it is important to put a healthy, balanced diet first. Without the right food fuels, you won't have the energy you need for your active life.

Fitness and Exercise

A fitness program that includes regular exercise can greatly improve the way you look as well as the way you feel. Regular exercise helps you control your appetite and body weight. Exercise burns excess calories. It develops your muscles so that you stand straighter and move more gracefully. It helps strengthen your bones as well as toning your muscles so that you can lift objects more easily. It strengthens your heart and lungs, too. People who exercise regularly are more relaxed, sleep better, and have more energy.

The best exercise program includes the following types.
- Muscular fitness exercise to build both strength and endurance
- Aerobic exercise to build up your heart and lungs
- Flexibility exercise to increase your ability to bend, stretch, and twist easily and gracefully
- Coordination exercise to improve your ability to coordinate, or match movements of different parts of your body

Your Exercise Program An effective exercise program should include half-hour sessions of steady exercise at least three times a week. Some experts believe it is even better if you exercise regularly every day for a minimum of 20 to 30 minutes.

Begin each exercise period with at least five minutes of stretching exercise. After a period of steady exercise, slow down and then end with more stretching. Consult your doctor to be sure your exercise program is right for you.

Hygiene and Grooming

Personal hygiene plays an important role in how you feel and the impression you make on other people. **Hygiene** includes the care or grooming of your skin, hair, and nails.

Skin Care

A daily bath or shower removes bacteria that can cause skin problems and unpleasant odors. Choose personal care products such as soaps, lotions, and deodorants that fit your special needs. The best are not necessarily the most expensive.

Generally, your skin will be healthier if you eat a balanced diet. Include a lot of green, leafy vegetables and a minimum of sweets and fatty foods.

Acne Many adolescents suffer from skin problems, including the skin disease *acne*. To help cure acne, you must be particularly careful to clean your skin thoroughly in the morning and before you go to bed.

Did You Know?

Your skin is the largest organ in your body. It weighs about eight pounds, and if you laid it out flat, it would measure almost two square yards.

RETEACHING: Emphasize: Pay attention to how you look! Remember that others look at your hair, your skin, your nails, and your clothing.

PHOTO: Do your students have advice to give others on good products that are not necessarily expensive?

Do you use skin care products that are both safe and right for you?

There are a number of medicated soaps and lotions on the market that are made for troubled skin. If you have severe acne or other persistent skin problems, you should get medical advice.

Skin and the Sun Skin specialists now know that the sun's light rays can be harmful. Too much exposure to these rays over a period of time can cause premature aging of the skin and even skin cancer. Sun-blocking or sunscreening agents are now available in varying strengths. When you know you are going to be out in the sun for any length of time, use one of them. Remember that what people may refer to as a "healthy tan" is really *not* healthy for your skin.

Hair Care

Clean, healthy hair forms an important part of your appearance. Wash your hair regularly with a shampoo chosen for your particular kind of hair—normal, oily, or

NOTE: The outer layer of skin is called the *epidermis*, and the second layer is called the *dermis*.

dry. You may want to add a rinse or conditioner. If you tend to have *dandruff*, a scaly scalp, use a dandruff shampoo. Avoid borrowing other people's brushes, combs, and headgear. They can carry disease and head lice.

Nail Care

Keeping your nails clean and trim not only improves your appearance but can prevent infection. Clean your fingernails with a brush, and remove dirt from underneath the nails. Keep nails even. Trim fingernails with clippers or scissors and shape

How do you feel when your hair looks its best?

NOTE: The B Vitamins are helpful in maintaining healthy skin and good eyesight.

them with an emery board. Fingernails should be slightly rounded; toenails should be clipped straight across so that they do not become ingrown. The *cuticle,* the skin that grows over the bottom of the nails, should be pushed back with a towel.

Eye and Ear Care

Keep your eyes protected from too much sunlight. Wear protective goggles for sports or special jobs that can cause eye injury. Do not touch your eyes with dirty hands. If you use eye makeup, be sure that it doesn't irritate your eyes.

Clean your ears of dirt and wax with a clean cloth. Never put a sharp object in your ear; doing so could seriously damage your hearing.

Dental Care

Your happy, healthy smile is an important part of your appearance. A balanced diet helps to keep your teeth and gums in good shape. You should visit a dentist twice a year for a professional cleaning and to

REINFORCEMENT: Ask students to use the school library to research the following health-related careers: manicurist, optician, audiologist, and dermatologist.

have your teeth checked. Some people need braces to straighten teeth.

Careful cleaning several times a day prevents tooth decay. *Plaque* (plak) is a sticky film that continually forms on the teeth. If you don't remove it, the bacteria in plaque will attack the enamel of your teeth and cause cavities. Plaque buildup can also lead to gum diseases, called periodontal (*PEHR*-ee-oh-*DANN*–tuhl) disease. You should use dental floss to remove plaque between the teeth in addition to brushing the teeth. Brush at least twice a day—after every meal, if possible. Floss once a day, preferably at the end of the day. Eating sugars and starches, including sugary soft drinks, builds up plaque. If you wear braces, it is especially important that you clean plaque and food particles from under the braces.

If you play contact sports, such as football and hockey, protect your teeth with a mouthguard.

Rest and Relaxation

In order to be healthy, both mentally and physically, most of you need at least seven or eight hours' sleep every night. Lack of sleep can make you nervous and irritable. Plan your schedule to include enough regular hours of sleep as well as some time for relaxing during the day.

If you suffer from insomnia, that is, difficulty in falling asleep, you may be overtired or tense. When you find you cannot sleep, a warm bath may relax you. A drink of warm milk may also help you to fall asleep. Long-term sleep problems should be discussed with a doctor.

RETEACHING: Correct flossing and brushing is essential to maintaining healthy gums.

See page T41 for answers.
For Review
1. Why is a balanced diet the most important part of an active life?
2. Name two kinds of exercises and tell how they help your body.
3. List five important hygiene and grooming tips.
4. What foods cause plaque buildup?
5. Why is it important for you to get enough sleep each night?

Section 3.2
Mental Health

As you read, think about:
■ how your emotions affect your health. (p. 50)
■ ways to deal with stress and sudden mood shifts. (p. 50)
■ ways to deal with extended periods of depression. (p. 52)

Mental and physical health are closely related. You may be in a bad mood because you have a headache. Then again you may have a headache because you are in a bad mood. Learning to control your emotions and to cope with emotional upsets can improve your total wellness. Knowing more about the sources of stress will make it easier for you to deal with stressful situations. Also, knowing ways to relieve stress will help you to manage it better. Understanding the emotional ups and downs of adolescence can help you to control them.

RETEACHING: Stress that there is no advantage to hiding problems or mistakes. Progress and maturity begin when people can accept their own true feelings and be honest with themselves.

Don't keep your worries inside. Talk to a friend. Give someone a chance to help you.

Developing a Healthy Personality

Mentally healthy people feel good about themselves. We all have times of self-doubt and sadness. Learning to think positively about yourself, especially during difficult times, demonstrates that you are developing a mature, healthy mental attitude.

Understanding your own emotions can help you express them in positive ways. If you accept your own feelings, you are less likely to blame others. Life is more satisfying when you don't hide from your problems. Try to acknowledge them so that you can go about solving them. You should know what you want in life, but don't take yourself too seriously. You need to be able to laugh at yourself.

Dealing with Stress

The body's response to a physical or mental demand is called **stress.** A certain amount of stress is good for you. It makes you feel alive and ready to meet a new challenge. Your tension builds up and is then released in positive action. You feel stress as you walk onto the court before beginning a game of tennis. The game starts, and your tension is released.

Mental stress occurs when a situation has made you tense or anxious. This type of stress causes problems when it lasts for a long period, or when it is sharp and

REINFORCEMENT: With your class, brainstorm a list of physical exercises that your students can do to relieve stress.

REINFORCEMENT: Explain the difference between negative and constructive criticism. Write on the board: "Suzie, stand up straight! Your posture is terrible!" Ask students to rewrite the statement as a constructive criticism.

50   Unit 1/*About You*

unpleasant. Extended emotional stress can make you physically ill.

Stress Management

It is important to recognize the causes of stress and to learn how to deal with them. You can feel as much stress from boredom as you feel from tension and anxiety. Physical factors sometimes cause mental stress. Lack of sleep, too little or too much exercise, hunger, sustained noise, and lack of fresh air can all cause stress.

When your life is full of stress, stop and think how you can relieve your feelings of tension. Take a deep breath, and force yourself to relax. If possible, get away from the stressful situation, if only for a short time. Do some stretching exercises. Take a walk in the fresh air. Relax with a good friend.

Apply the management process to all parts of your life to reduce the level of stress in your life. Set clear goals that you are capable of meeting. Concentrate on these goals. Train yourself not to worry about things that are outside your control.

Emotional Ups and Downs

Have you noticed that your moods change more rapidly than they did in your childhood years? You may feel on top of the world one minute and down in the dumps the next. Your feelings are easily hurt. Sometimes you feel like bursting into tears for no reason. At other times, you can't stop giggling.

These extreme ups and downs occur partly because you are now changing and

Sharing laughter or doing something silly with a friend is a great way to release tension.

DISCUSS: "Laughter is the best medicine" is an old phrase. When is this true for you, and when is it false?

PHOTO: Be sure to mention that laughter that releases stress comes from laughing with people, not at them.

It is normal to feel sad and alone from time to time.

adjusting to new situations as you become an adult. You find you are more sensitive to criticism; at the same time, you are becoming more critical of others. All this can cause stress and quick changes of mood.

When you find yourself in a bad mood, face the mood and work to change it. Don't just sit around feeling sorry for yourself. Take action. Share your feelings with a friend or family member who can give you support. Talking about problems does help.

Strenuous exercise is a good way to relieve tension and cheer yourself up. Volunteering to help others is another great way to help you forget about your problems.

Depression

We all experience times when we feel unhappy and cut off from other people. **Depression** is the state of feeling sad, anxious, and alone. When you are depressed you feel tired and find it difficult to concentrate.

Dealing with Depression

A depressed mood develops from various causes. Sometimes you feel depressed because it seems that nobody understands you. Maybe you had an argument with a good friend. Perhaps your teacher did not give you the grade you expected on a paper or a test. Worse yet, all these things occurred on the same day.

Taking Action First, tackle your problems one at a time. If you are having difficulties at home, see if you can arrange to talk with your family at a quiet time. Take a positive approach to this meeting. Think of ways to resolve misunderstandings with friends. Be willing to talk over a disagreement. If you really believe a teacher undervalues your work, make an appointment to discuss your feelings. Don't just go off and sulk. You may be able to solve the problem by dealing with it in a direct and timely way. It certainly is worth the effort.

Sometimes, however, you find yourself in a situation you cannot control. The feeling of being unable to resolve a problem is called *frustration*. When you are frustrated, you experience a combination of anger and disappointment. This feeling is perfectly normal. In most cases like this, you simply have to accept your frustration, get past the situation, and then forget it. Tell yourself, "Things like this happen to everybody."

Serious Depression

Even the most mature and healthy people become depressed for short periods of time. They learn to accept these moods and to overcome them as soon as possible. Other people, however, experience feelings of depression for a long time and cannot shake off the unhappy mood. This long-term depression can cause serious problems. Sleeplessness, lack of energy, headaches, a change in appetite, and a feeling of loneliness and hopelessness may occur.

If you become seriously depressed for a number of days, you *must* get help. A seriously depressed person needs more than the support of other people. Friendliness from peers and affection from family are important. Even more important, however, is getting help from a professional person trained to deal with depression. You can begin by talking to your school nurse, guidance counselor, or a member of the clergy. If necessary, these people can put you in touch with a mental health professional who can help.

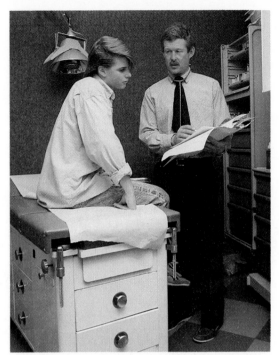

When friends and family can't help, sometimes other people can.

See page T42 for answers.
For Review
1. Why is it important to understand your own emotions?
2. Name three ways to relieve stress in your life.
3. How could you help a seriously depressed friend?

Section 3.3
Managing Health Decisions

As you read, think about:
■ how you can stay healthy through regular health care. (p. 54)
■ ways to ask your doctor the right questions so that you get the most from your medical checkups. (p. 56)
■ the importance of keeping accurate health records. (p. 56)

You can do a great deal toward keeping yourself healthy. In addition to following a wellness program, you can remain healthy by getting the right medical care. This

NOTE: The root "psych" comes from the Greek for "spirit" or "life." The root "ology" means "the study of." Psychology is the study of mental processes and behavior.

REINFORCEMENT: Have students name the individuals in your school and community who are trained to deal with adolescent depression.

Leadership and Citizenship

Volunteering

What's a great way to make new friends, learn new skills, explore career possibilities, help others, and feel really good about yourself? For many teens, the answer is volunteering in a health-related field. Check with your school, United Way, religious and community organizations, and health care institutions.

- You can help out in a hospital by delivering meals, running errands, or visiting with the patients.
- You can also help residents in a nursing home read, answer mail, or get around outdoors. You can join in games, such as checkers, or be the friend who cares enough to visit regularly and chat.
- Many homebound elderly or disabled people live alone. Teens can be "telephone buddies" who regularly check on their well-being or home visitors who help out while paying a friendly visit. Escorts assist with medical appointments, shopping, or outings.
- Many organizations provide recreation for disabled children and adults. You can volunteer to help with children's crafts or swimming lessons. You can even enjoy your favorite sport while helping a disabled person play it with you. What could you volunteer to do in your community?

includes asking your doctor the right questions to get the most from medical checkups. Learning how to keep your own health records is important, too.

Regular Health Care

It is important for you and your family to choose a health care facility that meets your needs. Health care facilities include doctors' offices, clinics, health maintenance organizations (HMOs), and hospitals. Be sure to choose a health facility before an emergency occurs. Make sure that the health professionals there are aware of any health problems you have. The facility you pick should have on record your complete medical history. This includes important data such as your blood type and a history of childhood diseases and allergies.

Preventive Medicine

Even if you are feeling perfectly healthy, regular checkups can pinpoint medical problems at an early stage and prevent them from becoming more serious. Besides regular physical examinations, you should have your teeth and your eyes checked regularly. In addition, you know from experience the way your mind and body work. If you notice a change or have any unusual pains, make an appointment for an examination.

Choosing Health Care

The kind of health care you and your family choose will depend on a number of factors, particularly the kind of health

RETEACHING: Students could begin to develop their own wellness program by writing a list of questions on personal hygiene, eating habits, and exercise to ask their doctor at their next visit.

insurance your family has. Health insurance protects people from having to pay high medical costs themselves. Some people receive insurance for themselves and their families from the companies they work for. Others pay for their own insurance. Medicaid, provided by state and local governments, helps to pay medical bills for low-income families.

Public Health Services

Most schools employ a nurse who provides general health counseling and takes care of minor injuries or illnesses that occur at school. Your school may also have a social worker or psychologist to counsel students on matters of mental health. Such counselors can be very helpful in discussing any questions you have in this area. If necessary, they can refer you for further help.

City, county, state, and federal health departments all provide health information and other services for little or no cost. They often provide *immunization* (im-yah-nigh-*ZAY*-shun) against specific diseases, such as flu, tuberculosis, or tetanus. Immunization, which is usually given by injection, prevents you from getting a disease. Government departments also publish information about how to keep healthy and prevent disease. Free clinics and screening programs to detect diseases may be available in your area.

Do you ask questions when you visit your school nurse?

NOTE: The first school nurses were assigned to schools in New York City in 1902. At the same time, the first health instruction in schools began.

REINFORCEMENT: Invite the school nurse to class to explain the type of general health care administered at your school.

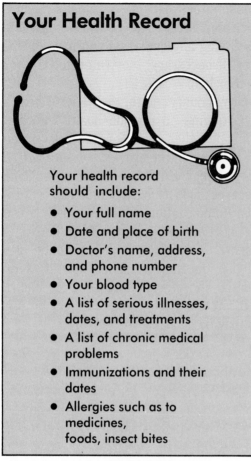

Your Health Record

Your health record should include:

- Your full name
- Date and place of birth
- Doctor's name, address, and phone number
- Your blood type
- A list of serious illnesses, dates, and treatments
- A list of chronic medical problems
- Immunizations and their dates
- Allergies such as to medicines, foods, insect bites

Where is your medical record? Can you find it at a moment's notice?

Visiting Your Doctor

Many people are afraid of doctors and are nervous during a visit to the doctor's office. As a result, they may end up leaving without the information and advice they came to get.

Before you go to see a doctor, prepare for your visit by making a list of your symptoms. Jot down what you have done about them yourself.

Be absolutely sure you understand what the doctor tells you. Do not hesitate to ask the doctor to repeat information. Take notes, especially about any treatment or medicines the doctor prescribes. Ask about what side effects these may have. For example, a side effect of some immunizations is that you may run a slight fever.

Once you are sure you understand the doctor's advice, follow it carefully and take any medicine exactly as prescribed.

Keeping Health Records

It is most important that your doctor's office have a full and up-to-date record of your medical history and that of your family. If you change medical facilities, be sure your records are transferred. You and your family should also keep your own health records. You will then have important information available if other medical records are misplaced or hard to obtain on short notice. Keep all records together in a safe place. The chart on this page shows you all the basic information you should keep on record.

See page T42 for answers.

For Review

1. What two major factors contribute to good health?
2. Why should a family have health insurance?
3. What is immunization?
4. How can you prepare for a visit to the doctor?
5. Why is it important to keep copies of your family's health records?

NOTE: The word *doctor* comes from the Latin for "teacher." How is a doctor also a teacher?

REINFORCEMENT: Discuss with students places where records are sometimes kept—behind a clock, in a drawer with clothing, in a pile of miscellaneous papers—instead of the places where documents should be kept—file cabinets, metal boxes, special drawers for important papers.

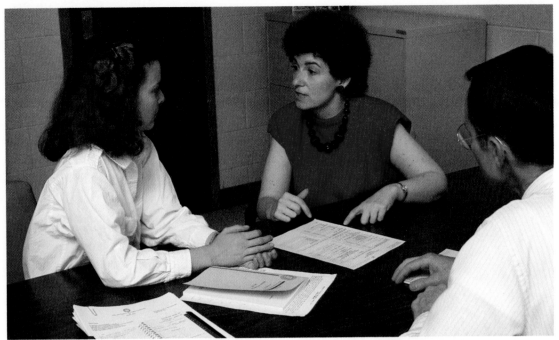

Be informed. Find people who have written information, and ask them questions about alcohol, drugs, and tobacco.

Section 3.4

Learning About Substance Abuse

As you read, think about:

■ how alcohol can endanger your physical and mental health. (p. 58)

■ why rules for taking both prescription and nonprescription legal drugs are extremely important. (p. 61)

■ how illegal drugs can endanger your physical and mental health. (p. 62)

In our country, as in many others, large numbers of people use and misuse alcohol, tobacco, and other drugs. Many physical and mental health problems have been found to be directly related to the use of these substances. You need to understand just how alcohol, drugs, and tobacco affect your health. Once you know the effects of these substances, you can make informed decisions about using them.

Substance Abuse

The misuse of anything to the point of endangering your health can be termed **substance abuse.** The most common forms of substance abuse involve tobacco and drugs, including alcohol. In many cases, substance abuse leads to addiction. **Addiction** occurs when the body develops either a physical or a psychological dependence (or both) on a substance.

DISCUSS: What well-known celebrities have stepped forward to tell their stories about drug or alcohol addiction? What effect has this had on the public?

Alcohol is a *toxic* (*TAHK*-sik), that is, poisonous substance. A large amount of alcohol can cause coma and death. Long-term use causes brain disorders, liver disease, and other life-threatening illnesses. Pregnant women who drink even small amounts of alcohol risk the health of their unborn children.

Who Drinks?

Not everyone drinks. Approximately one-third of American adults have chosen not to drink at all. Many people enjoy neither the taste of alcohol nor the way they feel after using this drug. There are many other individual reasons, including religious ones, for choosing not to consume alcohol.

Those who drink may do so with family or friends at social gatherings. They may feel that drinking relaxes them, makes them more sociable, and helps them forget their problems. Unfortunately, drinking often becomes a substitute for facing problems. Even though alcohol may bring temporary relief, it is far from being a solution for loneliness, boredom, or depression. Using alcohol for reasons such as these is dangerous and often leads to more and heavier drinking. Generally speaking, if people can't have a good time without alcohol, they have a drinking problem.

Alcoholism

The disease caused by an addiction to alcohol is called **alcoholism.** The alcoholic's dependency on alcohol is both

Do you know anyone to give this message to? Do you care enough to send it?

Alcohol

Alcohol is a drug. Misusing it causes serious problems, including extreme illness and the breakdown of family and other relationships. Over half of all automobile accidents in the United States are caused by alcohol. Alcohol affects the brain, the muscles, and the ability to stand and walk. It causes loss of memory and emotional control, blurry vision, and slurred speech.

ENRICHMENT: Assign a one-page paper requiring research on the dangers of alcohol during pregnancy.

NOTE: 18 million Americans have a serious drinking problem. Stress that alcohol claims over 10,000 lives each year.

physical and psychological. Anyone who drinks risks becoming an alcoholic; heavy drinking increases this risk. Researchers think, however, that there may be inherited tendencies toward alcoholism within families. Living in an environment where alcohol is abused also tends to encourage the same behavior in children.

Resources for Help

If anyone you live with or care about has a problem with alcohol, it also affects you. Action must be taken to help solve the problem. However, the alcoholic must first want to help himself or herself before others can help. If the alcoholic is willing, professional help can be found at local community health centers, clinics, and family service agencies. Check the yellow pages of your telephone directory under the heading "Alcoholism Information and Treatment Centers" if you need to find an outside resource in your area.

Three specific organizations that are valuable resources for dealing with alcoholism are Alcoholics Anonymous (AA), Al-Anon, and Alateen. The last two are separate groups that have grown out of Alcoholics Anonymous. There are no membership fees or dues for any of these organizations. They are supported by

Don't think that you are the only one who may need to ask a question about alcohol abuse. It's a common problem.

REINFORCEMENT: Bring a local newspaper to class to show the schedule of weekly AA, Al-Anon, and Alateen meetings.

PHOTO: Ask students to list five things that they think this woman is saying about alcoholism.

voluntary contributions. To locate those closest to you, look in your local telephone directory under Alcoholics Anonymous or Al-Anon.

Tobacco

Tobacco is dangerous in all forms: snuff, chewing tobacco, cigarettes, pipes, and cigars. There is no such thing as a safe cigarette, pipe, or cigar. Similarly, no form of snuff or chewing tobacco is safe. Those who pretend otherwise are simply endangering their own lives.

Why Is Smoking Harmful?

Every year medical researchers find more evidence of how dangerous tobacco use is. Smoking is the leading cause of preventable death in the United States, killing more than 360,000 Americans each year. Cigarettes contain three deadly substances: carbon monoxide, nicotine, and tar. *Carbon monoxide* (mah-*NOCK*-side) replaces oxygen in the blood, results in shortness of breath, and makes the heart beat faster. *Nicotine* (*NICK*-ah-teen) is a poison that attacks the nerves. Tobacco

tars contain cancer-causing substances that build up in the lungs. Smoking affects the stomach, other parts of the digestive tract, and the lungs, heart, and nerves.

According to the Surgeon General, tobacco products, are addicting. The processes that cause tobacco addiction are like those that cause addiction to heroin. Even casual experimentation with tobacco can lead to addiction in later life.

Dangers to Nonsmokers

Nonsmokers who breathe other people's smoke regularly are also at risk for lung and heart disease. To avoid this danger, choose to sit in the nonsmoking sections of public places such as restaurants. Avoid closed rooms where people are smoking. Recent surveys have shown that smokers are becoming more aware that they must respect nonsmokers' wishes. If someone's smoke is bothering you, ask the offender politely either not to smoke or to move somewhere else.

Trying to Quit

People who smoke find it difficult to stop. Smoking, like drugs and alcohol, is addictive. Most communities and health centers have classes for people to learn to quit smoking. The U.S. Public Health Service provides information on the harmful effects of tobacco and ways to avoid the dangerous habit of smoking.

Once a person stops smoking, the body begins to reverse much of the damage that smoking was causing. Feeling healthier and being healthier are the two best reasons to stop smoking.

> ### Did You Know?
>
> Tobacco slows the flow of blood to the skin and thus limits the skin's supply of oxygen and nutrients. This lack can cause premature wrinkling—another good reason to avoid smoking!

NOTE: The Surgeon General warns that cigarette smoking causes lung cancer, heart disease, and may complicate pregnancy.

REINFORCEMENT: Have students collect cigarette ads to see if the same warning appears on each. Ask students if the warning helps prevent them or anyone they know from smoking. If not, what does, or what would?

PHOTO: Ask students to find out the laws in your community that protect nonsmokers. Should there be others?

What rights do nonsmokers have? Why do laws protect them?

Be Smart—Don't Start

If you have never smoked, don't start. Even if you feel a lot of peer pressure to begin smoking, do not give in. Understanding all of the negative physical effects of smoking should help you realize that smart people just don't smoke.

Drugs

Any nonfood substance that alters the mind or the body in some way when it is taken is called a **drug.** It is helpful when learning about drugs to separate them into two categories: legal and illegal drugs.

NOTE: Caffeine is found in coffee, cola, tea, and chocolate.

Legal Drugs

There are many substances that you may not have realized were drugs. Other legal drugs include all of the nonprescription *over-the-counter drugs* that contain chemicals for treating medical problems. In this category are cough syrups, mild pain relievers, and hundreds of other products.

Prescription drugs are the other category of legal drugs. These are controlled more strictly than over-the-counter drugs because they are stronger and more dangerous if abused. A doctor must prescribe them to a particular patient for a specific medical reason.

Use care in taking prescription or over-the-counter medicines. Read and follow

RETEACHING: Stress that prescription drugs can be harmful as well as helpful.

Although some drugs may be common and familiar to you, you still must be careful about using them.

the directions carefully. Never take a drug prescribed for someone else. Make sure your doctor knows if you are taking more than one kind of medicine. Sometimes, two taken together can be very harmful.

Illegal Drugs

Drugs that are considered so dangerous that the law forbids selling or possessing them are *illegal drugs.* Marijuana, heroin, cocaine, and *crack,* the most addictive form of cocaine, are a few of the many illegal drugs.

These drugs are very dangerous. They may cause severe illness and even death, because they cause extreme changes in the body. Smoking marijuana causes even greater lung damage than smoking tobacco. Heroin causes heart and lung damage, skin abscesses, a general breakdown of the entire body, and a lowering of resistance to disease. A heavy dose can bring on convulsions and death. Cocaine and crack are both extremely addictive. They

cause anxiety and heart attacks, mental breakdown, convulsions, and death. These are just a few of the dangerous drugs that are sold illegally. An additional risk is that the drug capsules or needles may be dirty and carry life-threatening diseases.

Saying "No!" to Drugs

Drugs can wreck your relationships with others and ruin every part of your life. Anyone who tells you otherwise is wrong. Once drug users becomes addicts, they have a desperate need. They will even commit violent crimes in order to pay for their habit.

Being responsible for your own health includes saying "No!" to drugs. Don't let peer pressure affect your own good judgment. Take control of your life; don't let drugs control you. You can get information and advice about drugs from your school nurse, your school counselor, or your local public health department.

Did You Know?

Medicines can turn into poisons. Slow chemical changes can make once-effective medications useless or dangerous. Store all drugs in their original containers and check their expiration dates. When medicines are no longer "good," be sure to flush them down the toilet.

RETEACHING: Emphasize the fact that both legal and illegal drugs are subject to abuse and can be addictive.

DISCUSS: What has the media done to stress the importance of saying "No!" to drugs and alcohol?

62   Unit 1/*About You*

See page T42 for answers.

For Review

1. What are the consequences of alcohol abuse?
2. How are nonsmokers affected by smoke from the cigarettes of others?
3. Name at least three simple rules you should follow regarding medication prescribed by a doctor or sold over the counter.
4. Name several extreme changes that take place in the bodies of those who take illegal drugs.

Section 3.5

Emergencies and First Aid

As you read, think about:

- how to react in emergency situations. (p. 63)
- how to help an accident victim until medical help arrives. (p. 64)

You can help prevent accidents by following safety rules. No matter how careful you are, however, emergency situations can occur. Knowing how to react in an emergency can save your life and the lives of others. Accidents and emergencies occur at home and away from home.

Meeting Emergencies

The way you respond to an emergency can make the difference between a minor accident and a serious injury. You might even save a life if you can respond quickly and correctly.

If you see someone on the street in trouble, do not assume that someone else has called the police. Dial 911 or your local police number. Report exactly where the accident or other trouble occurred. In any emergency it is vital to get professional help—medical personnel, police, or firefighters—as soon as possible.

In Case of Fire

If a fire starts, do not panic. Do not risk your life trying to save your possessions. If the fire is *very* small—burning toast, for example—you may be able to put it out yourself. In case of a more serious fire, everyone should leave the house immediately. Call the fire department from a firebox or a neighbor's home. If there is smoke, crawl on the floor toward an exit. There is more oxygen near the floor. Feel a door before going through it. If it is hot, find another way out.

If your clothing or hair should catch fire, practice the "Stop, Drop, and Roll" method advised by fire experts. Stop where you are, drop to the floor or ground, and roll over to extinguish the flames. Do not panic and run; this will cause the flames to spread.

Poisoning

Children are the most common victims of poisoning. If you are there when a poisoning occurs, call a Poison Control Center, a hospital emergency room, or a physician without delay. Keep emergency numbers

REINFORCEMENT: Review the procedure for exiting the school building when the fire alarm rings. Remind students that talking is not allowed during a fire drill. Explain why.

NOTE: Pulling a fire alarm when there is no fire is against the law. Have students find out the penalty for pulling a fire alarm in your community.

by the telephone. You will find the number of your local Poison Control Center in the telephone book. Many procedures related to poisoning have changed, so it is important to get the most accurate information from the Poison Control Center. Provide as much information about the poisoning as you can: the name of the poison, the victim's age, and whether the victim is conscious. Follow instructions carefully while you wait for medical aid.

Bleeding

Keep a well-stocked first-aid kit in your home. It should include sterile gauze or cotton and 3 percent hydrogen peroxide. Minor cuts and scrapes should be thoroughly cleaned with the peroxide and gauze. If a cut is gaping open, use surgical tape to hold the edges together. A deep cut will need to be stitched together. When in doubt, get medical help.

A puncture wound, caused by stepping on a nail, for example, requires immediate medical attention, as it is easily infected.

Does anyone you know wear a medic alert bracelet? What does it say?

Have a tetanus booster shot unless you have had one within the past ten years.

A cut that spurts blood indicates that an artery has been cut. Rapid blood loss can be very dangerous. Apply pressure to the wound. If bleeding continues, apply pressure above the wound, toward the heart. Get medical help quickly.

Choking

If a person chokes and cannot breathe, immediate action is necessary. Use the **Heimlich Maneuver** to dislodge the object that is causing the choking. This procedure can be used on anyone over the age of one.

1. Stand behind the victim.
2. Wrap your arms around the victim's waist.
3. Make a fist with one hand. Place your fist thumbside against the stomach just above the navel and well below the ribs.
4. Place your other hand over the fist.
5. Press your fist with a quick inward and upward thrust into the victim's abdomen.
6. Repeat if necessary. The object should be forced out of the throat.

If you are alone and begin to choke, press your abdomen against a chair.

Burns

Serious burns need immediate attention from skilled medical personnel. If clothing is soaked with hot fat or boiling water, remove it. Cut it away if necessary, but do

First-Aid for Choking

1

- **ASK: Are you choking?**
- If victim cannot breathe, cough, or speak…

2

- **Give the Heimlich Maneuver.**
- Stand behind the victim.
- Wrap your arms around the victim's waist.
- Make a fist with one hand. PLACE your FIST (thumbside) against the victim's stomach in the midline just ABOVE THE NAVEL AND WELL BELOW THE RIB MARGIN.
- Grasp your fist with your other hand.
- PRESS INTO STOMACH WITH A QUICK UPWARD THRUST.

3

- **Repeat thrust if necessary.**

- **If a victim has become unconscious:**

4
- Sweep the mouth.

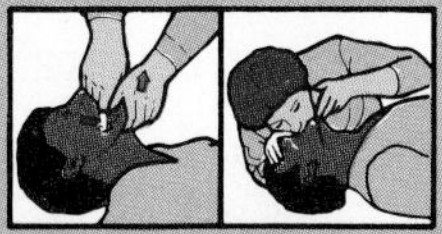

5
- Attempt rescue breathing.

6
- Give 6–10 abdominal thrusts.
- Repeat Steps 4, 5, and 6 as necessary

Everyone should learn how to perform the steps above for choking and how to give rescue breathing and CPR. Call your local American Red Cross chapter for information on these and other first aid techniques.
Caution: The Heimlich Maneuver (abdominal thrust) may cause injury. Do not *practice* on people.

American Red Cross

LOCAL EMERGENCY TELEPHONE NUMBER: _____

Courtesy of the American Red Cross

Are you ready for an emergency? Should everyone be responsible for knowing how to help?

ART: Have students name two places at home and two places at school where they think this chart should be placed.

ENRICHMENT: Present each student with a hypothetical emergency such as poisoning, an injury, or a fire. Bring an old telephone to class for use when having students rehearse making an emergency call reporting the accident.

PHOTO: Have students write a paragraph describing how they would want bystanders to act if they had to be taken to the hospital in an ambulance.

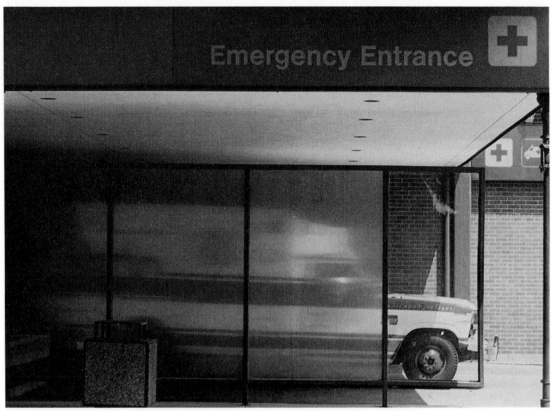

People are often curious when they see an ambulance. What problems can such curiosity cause?

not try to remove cloth that is stuck to the burn. Never apply creams or other ointment to burns. Minor burns on a small area can be cooled with ice wrapped in sterile cloth. Do not use cotton or other material that will stick to the burn. Chemical burns should be flooded with cool, running water for at least 10 minutes.

Eye Treatment

If chemicals have gotten into the eye, get medical help at once. Flood the inner corner of the eye with clean water for five minutes. If an object in the eye does not wash out, take the victim to a doctor. Do not rub the eye, as this can cause the object to scratch the eyeball.

See page T42 for answers.

For Review

1. Describe the emergency procedures you would follow in case of a fire in your home.
2. What should be included in a home first-aid kit?
3. How can you help a person who is choking?
4. How should you treat minor burns?

REINFORCEMENT: Explain that a burn should be immersed in cold water immediately. Tell what this does for a burn.

Learning to Manage
Getting In Shape

Look back at the conversation between Peg and Rachel on page 44. Rachel is feeling the strain of not being in top physical shape. Now read about Rachel's plan to improve her condition. Then answer the questions that follow.

That evening Peg and Rachel talked on the telephone.

"How are all those weary muscles?" Peg asked jokingly.

"Very funny. They're all here and complaining loudly."

"Well, Rachel, you're putting your body through a lot all at once. If you had done it a little more gradually, it wouldn't be so bad. Why don't you try running a short distance with me tomorrow? I stretch first, run a little, then cool down, and it's really helped build up my endurance for all that running up and down the court."

"Well, OK—*if* I have the energy."

"What are you eating?"

"Well, I sleep right up to the last minute, so I skip breakfast; and if I don't like what they're serving in the caf, I eat a bag of chips and an ice cream sandwich. Then I usually have a can of soda and a candy bar before practice. When I come home, though, I eat a pretty good dinner."

"Rachel, you're lucky you have enough energy to tie your sneakers! I'm not kidding. Give your body a break. Do you think the Celtics and the Lakers eat SNACKO bars and drink ZING cola? You need more protein and less sugar. Don't you remember what you learned in Home Ec class? Take it out of the book and *use* it!"

"All right, coach. I'll work on the diet."

"How much sleep are you getting?"

"Well, I've been half asleep all day since basketball practice started a week ago. But if you mean at night, I usually take a nap and then I stay up to watch the JIMMY CLARSEN show. He's really funny. Last night he—"

"Rachel, you're crazy. You need at least eight hours' sleep. No wonder you're feeling so worn out. Meet me tomorrow in the cafeteria and I'll give you a copy of my training plan. I actually wrote one out for myself. It's worked for me and I know it will work for you, too. What do you say?"

"Thanks, Peg, you're a real friend. Besides, I can't let you be the *only* star forward on the Northdale team!"

Questions

1. Explain how Peg's plan involves total health management.
2. What resources will Rachel have to use to reach her goal?
3. How would you rate yourself as a manager of your own health? Explain.

Chapter 3 Review

Summary

To use all your resources to the fullest, you need to build on the basic resource of good health. A healthy diet, exercise, proper hygiene, and rest and relaxation play an important role in your daily wellness program. Emotions also affect your health. Stress, mood shifts, and brief periods of depression are part of every teenager's life. Everyone must learn to deal with them. Knowing when to seek medical care and how to make the most of it is another important part of managing wellness.

Drugs can be positive healing substances when used properly. They can destroy lives if abused. Being responsible for your own health includes making mature choices and saying "No!" to drugs.

Knowing how to prevent accidents at home and learning what to do in case of medical emergencies are important health and safety measures.

Vocabulary

Complete each of the following sentences with the correct word from the vocabulary list below.

addiction (p. 57) nutrition (p. 45)
wellness (p. 45) drug (p. 61)
stress (p. 50) hygiene (p. 47)
alcoholism (p. 58) depression (p. 52)
substance abuse (p. 57)

1. _____ is the state of feeling sad, anxious, and alone.
2. Any nonfood substance that alters the mind or the body in some way when it is taken is called a _____.
3. _____ occurs when the body develops a physical or psychological dependence (or both) on a substance.
4. The care or grooming of your skin, hair, and nails is called _____.
5. _____ is your body's response to a physical or mental demand.
6. The disease that is caused by an addiction to alcohol is called _____.
7. The misuse of anything to the point of endangering your health is called _____.
8. The state of physical, mental, social, and spiritual health is _____.
9. _____ is the science of food and its relation to health.

Questions

• 1. What are the five parts of a long-term wellness program?
• 2. Name some important benefits of a regular exercise program.
•• 3. What can you do to help make your skin healthier?
• 4. What should you do before going out in the sun for any length of time?
• 5. What effect does a balanced diet have on your teeth and gums?

The dots represent skill levels required to answer each question or complete each activity:
• requires recall and comprehension
•• requires application and analysis
••• requires synthesis and evaluation

68

6. Why is it important for you to understand your own emotions?

7. Why is a certain amount of stress good for you?

8. Name at least three causes of stress.

9. How can applying the management process to your life reduce stress?

10. What should you do if you have a disagreement with a friend?

11. When is it essential for a depressed person to get professional help?

12. Is it dangerous for a person to use alcohol as a substitute for facing problems? Explain your answer.

13. Name two support groups for alcoholics and their families.

14. Name three dangerous substances contained in cigarettes.

15. Give three good reasons for saying "No!" to drugs.

Skill Activities

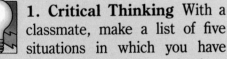

Many more activities are contained in the annotations within this chapter.

 1. Critical Thinking With a classmate, make a list of five situations in which you have found it difficult to say no. For example, a boy in school you like offers you a cigarette. Or, friends invite you for pizza after a movie when you have promised your parents you will come right home. Share the list you have compiled with the rest of the class and brainstorm possible ways to handle these problems. Act out the situations for the class, using the solutions your classmates suggested. Analyze whether the solutions were effective.

 2. Communication Write a letter to the Consumer Information Center, Pueblo, Colorado 81009, and request their Free Publications Catalog. When you receive your catalog, send for free booklets on health topics that interest you. Use the materials you receive to create an informative classroom poster.

 3. Human Relations Plan a fitness program for yourself and a friend. Analyze the kinds of exercise you both enjoy. Try to include stretching, aerobic, coordination, and endurance exercises. Schedule three half-hour sessions a week with your friend. Have fun!

4. Laboratory Make up an emergency number card to tape to your home telephone. Be sure to include the following telephone numbers:

Parents' work numbers
Doctor
Hospital
Fire Department
Police Department
Poison Control Center

Add other numbers that are important to your family.

Unit 2

Relationships

Chapter 4
Relating to Others

Vocabulary

The dialogue below introduces "Getting the Message," the Learning to Manage feature in this chapter. The case study is continued and the situation discussed further on page 95. See page T46 for teaching suggestions.

"Well, we aren't best friends anymore, Joni! You totally left me out of that pajama party Saturday night. And Judy told me what you said about me behind my back!"

"Sue, I didn't say anything bad about you. And I *did* call to ask you over, but—"

"Sure, sure. Some friend you are. You always leave me out; then you expect me to be there when you need me."

"Sue, why won't you listen to me? If you'd just sit down and talk to me about it . . ."

Section 4.1
Good Communication

As you read, think about:

■ how knowing the elements of the communication process can help you in daily life. (p. 73)

■ how to use verbal and nonverbal communication. (p. 74)

■ how your ability to express yourself clearly and listen to others helps you to get along better with people. (p. 75)

Joni and Sue are both talking and listening. We all talk and listen every day. How well people get along, however, depends largely on how well they use talking and listening to communicate.

To sharpen your communication skills, you need to learn about how communication works. You also need to learn about the types of communication that people use. Good communication skills will help you in every area of your life—now and in the future.

What Is Communication?

Communication is the exchange of information between two or more people. This process takes place when people send and receive messages. It involves the exchange of thoughts, opinions, and feelings.

Clear communication helps to build strong friendships.

A Communication Model

Communication consists of four parts.

1. The **sender** is the person who directs, or sends, the message. For example, you, the sender, want to spend the afternoon with a friend, so you telephone her.
2. The **message** is the information that is sent. In this case, the message is that you are asking your friend to come to your house to listen to some new records.
3. The **receiver** is the person who gets the message. In this case, the receiver is your friend.
4. The **feedback** is the response or answer the receiver gives. Your friend may accept your invitation or may refuse it because she is busy. Either way, her answer is the feedback.

RETEACHING: Stress that to communicate effectively, it helps to be quick to listen and not so quick to speak.

REINFORCEMENT: Do an exercise in listening. Whisper a simple message to a student in the front row and have that student whisper the message to the next person and so on until the message reaches the last student. Have that person repeat the message aloud to see how much it has changed.

Signing is now common at public events. What is the advantage to this speaker of having his message signed?

If any of the four elements is lacking, the communication is blocked. If you do not give your message clearly, the receiver will not understand it. If the receiver does not listen carefully, the feedback will be incomplete or incorrect.

Types of Communication

The two major types of communication are verbal and nonverbal.

Verbal communication is the use of words to express ideas or emotions. Verbal communication can be *oral,* that is, spoken; or it can be written. People speak and write in hundreds of different languages. One special method of verbal communication is *sign language.* This involves a series of hand gestures that represent words. *Signing* is one way deaf people communicate.

ENRICHMENT: Some hearing children have learned sign language from a deaf actor on *Sesame Street,* a children's educational television program. See if some of your students know sign language, and, if so, have them demonstrate it in class.

Braille is another form of verbal communication. In this system, raised dots on special paper form letters and words. By running their fingers over these raised dots, blind people are able to read.

Vocal communications send oral messages without using words. They usually send information about feelings or emotions. Cries, moans, sighs, and laughter are examples of vocal communication.

Nonverbal communication means sending messages not with sounds but through **body language.** Your facial expressions, hand and arm gestures, and the way you stand and move all convey your feelings and attitudes. Sometimes these nonverbal messages are actually clearer than verbal ones. A close friend knows when you are sad just by looking at your slow walk, your drooping posture, or your sad expression.

REINFORCEMENT: Have students take turns using body language to communicate anger, frustration, joy, and shyness.

Communication Skills

It takes practice to develop good communication skills. How you speak or write depends a great deal on your audience. You use a different style speaking to a friend than when giving a formal speech in class. The letter to your favorite cousin will be unlike the one you write applying for a job. It will be different not just in what you say but in how you say it.

You also have to check to see that you are getting your message across by listening to feedback. Ask the receiver questions to be sure that you are understood.

Make sure you adjust your tone of voice to suit both the particular message and the receiver. The quiet, warm voice you use when chatting with a friend is different from the carefully-measured, louder voice you use to address a group.

You also need to be aware of the message you send through nonverbal communication. If you look at the person you are talking to, you will hold that person's attention. No matter how interesting your message, you will not communicate it effectively if you stare at the floor while you talk.

The way you dress also communicates something. Casual clothes help you relax when you are with close friends. The same clothes will send the wrong message in a formal situation such as applying for a job.

Listening Skills

Communication can't take place unless the receiver understands the message that is being sent. Learning to listen well

NOTE: Seminars in nonverbal communication are now offered to people in business so that they may better understand what they are communicating to others and learn to "read" others' body language.

involves much more than simply hearing what is said. To build good relationships with your family and your friends, you must listen closely when someone is talking. Put other ideas out of your head. Think about *their* reasons for what they are saying. Studying their nonverbal as well as their verbal messages will help you interpret what they are saying.

A good listener *responds* to what is being communicated with both words and actions. Give positive feedback. Ask questions if you don't understand something. Be sensitive to the feelings being expressed. Show by your facial expression and your posture that you are really paying attention.

Try not to interrupt or jump to conclusions, that is, decide what people are saying before they have finished talking. This takes practice. It also takes practice not to be a *defensive listener*. Defensive

Do you think you are as careful about feedback as you are about receiving messages?

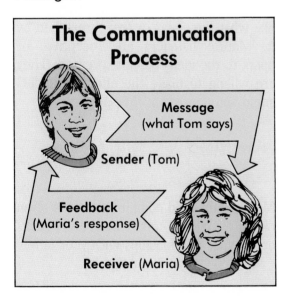

The Communication Process

Message (what Tom says)

Sender (Tom)

Feedback (Maria's response)

Receiver (Maria)

ART: Ask students to give examples of good telephone messages and good feedback.

What does the eye contact tell you about this speaker and listener?

listeners stop listening when they don't like what they hear or feel threatened by it. Mature listeners are receptive, or open, to the ideas being expressed. They are willing to make the effort to understand and appreciate the speaker.

Solving Communication Problems

Maintaining good communication is often difficult. When communication breaks down, your relationships with your family and friends can suffer. Following are some suggestions for solving communication problems.

Avoid Communication Blocks

Strong emotions can interfere with communication. The right time to discuss a problem is not when you are angry. Wait until you are calm and can approach a conversation with an open mind.

When you have a disagreement with someone, avoid accusing or blaming that person. State your own side of the question honestly but in a nonthreatening way.

Avoid general, negative criticism. For example, rather than just saying, "It's all your fault!" try to express specifically what is bothering you. Then say, "Let's see what we can do to solve the problem."

Avoid Prejudice

To keep communication channels open, you have to build a basis of understanding and trust. It is important to learn to respect the rights and opinions of others, even when you disagree with them.

Respecting people who are different from you is a sign of maturity. **Prejudice** is prejudging people unfairly and without knowing the facts about them.

Stereotyping is one form of prejudice. As you read in Chapter 1, a *stereotype* is an oversimplified view of a group of people. "All teenagers are lazy" is a false statement based on a stereotype. To build good communication, avoid stereotyping and other prejudiced opinions.

RETEACHING: First impressions count. Explain how a teacher might react to different postures of students in a classroom.

ENRICHMENT: Have two students role-play a job situation in which an employee has to admit a very costly error to a boss.

76   Unit 2/*Relationships*

Communication Strategies

You can improve your communication skills by following the steps below

1. Show respect for others.
2. State your ideas and opinions calmly and clearly. Use a soft, friendly tone.
3. Listen carefully to what the other person is saying. Interpret nonverbal messages as well as verbal. Be sensitive to the emotions as well as the ideas that are being expressed.
4. Ask questions if you don't understand.
5. Avoid unfocused criticism and seek cooperation in solving problems. Remember that there is nothing to be gained by criticizing things the other person cannot change, such as past actions or family background.
6. Accept responsibility for your own actions and opinions.
7. Work toward a goal of mutual enjoyment, understanding, and trust.

See page T47 for answers.

For Review

1. What are the four elements of communication?
2. Why are sign language and braille considered types of communication?
3. When a friend is talking to you, how can you show that you are paying attention?
4. Name at least three important communication strategies you might follow in order to improve your communication skills.

REINFORCEMENT: Practice good listening skills with your students by reading a paragraph from this chapter and having them feed back to you what they have heard. This is also a way to evaluate a student's comprehension.

Section 4.2
Strong Relationships

As you read, think about:

- how your happiness and success depend on the way you relate to other people. (p. 77)
- the special importance of family relationships. (p. 79)
- how developing a wide variety of friendships can enrich your life. (p. 82)
- ways to build good relationships. (p. 82)

A great deal of our happiness and success in life depends on the way we relate to other people. Everyone needs the understanding, support, and affection that come from good relationships with friends and family members. Because of this, it is important to learn what goes into making and improving good relationships with friends, parents, and other members of your family.

Relating to Others

You have many different kinds of relationships. You have a very slight relationship with people you see often but do not know, such as the mail carrier or the clerk at a neighborhood store. You form a casual acquaintance with others, such as classmates. You may know many classmates who are not close friends. Then you have important relationships that are closer and deeper. These are the relationships you have with your family and your best friends.

RETEACHING: Stress that a happy, well-adjusted person doesn't need to look for flaws in other people. Changing a negative outlook into a positive one helps one person see another person's good qualities.

Family time is important. Do you make an effort to participate?

Important Factors

Because family and friends are so important, the way you relate to them demands great care and attention.

What factors form the basis of a good relationship?

Empathy To understand another person, you must try to put yourself in that person's place. You need to share what he or she is feeling. This kind of identification is called *empathy*. Empathy is an important factor in a relationship. When you have a misunderstanding with a friend or family member, stop for a minute. Think why the other person may be reacting in a certain way. This is not always easy, but it will help you to understand the other point of view.

Good Communication You need to keep communication channels open to maintain a good relationship. You need to be able to explain your own ideas and

attitudes and to listen with an open mind to those held by the other person.

Self-Concept You must have a strong self-concept to form sound relationships with others. Understanding yourself and feeling good about yourself enables you to relate well to other people. It also means you can feel confident about the way they see you.

Responsibility In any relationship, you need to take responsibility for your own actions and attitudes. Blaming others for your own shortcomings can destroy a relationship.

Compromise A good relationship requires unselfishness and generosity. You must be willing to face problems together when they arise. Sharing bad times as well as good times deepens a relationship.

In a close relationship, disagreements occur from time to time. To maintain the relationship, you must be willing to *compromise*. This means that in a disagreement each person accepts some of the issues raised by the other. In this way they can find common ground agreeable to both sides.

Respect and Trust All relationships, whether between friends, family members, teachers, or employers, should be based on respect and trust. To achieve this, you must learn to communicate your own reliability and accept the sincerity of the other person. This requires a mature attitude.

Flexibility As you grow and change, your relationships develop and change, too. This means you need *flexibility,* the ability to adjust to new directions in relationships, and to form new relationships. Many people have trouble adjusting to change. It takes attention and work to recognize and deal with new situations in a relationship.

Family Relationships

The first and most lasting relationship you have is with your family. In childhood you were dependent on your family for your survival and general well-being. In adolescence, your relationship with your family changes. You take on increasing responsibility, not only for yourself but also for your relationship with your parents and other family members.

You and Your Parents

The teenage years are a difficult time for family relationships. It is often difficult for both teenagers and their parents to adjust to their changing roles. Misunderstandings may occur between parents and teenagers as young people move toward more independence. Teenagers may often feel that their parents do not understand them. Parents may set goals for their children which differ from the teenagers' own goals. Parents are still responsible for their teenagers' safety and success. They want their children to have the benefit of their experience.

Having friends feels good. Friends can help you pass the time pleasantly, they can help you learn about your world, and they can introduce you to new friends and activities.

Interpreters for the Deaf

You have probably seen sign-language interpreters for the deaf at work. They are often employed by speakers whose audience may contain some deaf "listeners," or to "sign" television news as broadcasters say it aloud. Interpreting for the deaf (by sign language or orally for those who rely on lipreading) works two ways. It helps the deaf person to understand and to be understood. Interpreters can link the hearing impaired with the hearing world.

Interpreters for the deaf work "from birth to death." In the delivery room, they help a deaf mother communicate with her doctor. At funerals, they interpret the service for deaf mourners. They are also important at medical appointments, in legal transactions, and in schools.

Interpreters must be more than just skilled signers. For certification, the Registry of Interpreters for the Deaf also requires a Code of Ethics. Interpreters must transmit both the spirit and content of a message. They may not take sides or offer personal opinions, and they must keep information confidential. Training for this career is offered at some colleges, but a degree is not necessary.

The lives of the deaf are, of course, as full and varied as other people's. Interpreters, therefore, can make many varied contributions.

Are there any places in your community that teach signing?

Solving Family Problems

When conflicts between you and your parents arise, it is helpful to remember that similar problems come up in every family. The very fact that your family cares deeply about you makes these conflicts more intense.

To maintain a good relationship with your family, use the basic skills you would use to improve any important relationship. Keep communication channels open. Set up regular times when family members can talk.

Remember to use the important skill of *listening*. Pay attention to the other side of an argument, even when you disagree. State your own opinions calmly and fully. Don't just announce, "You'll never understand me!" Accept that your parents love you and want to understand you even when you do not see eye to eye. It is often more difficult to use empathy with family than with friends, but it is worth the effort. Take the time to figure out why a family member is reacting to you in a certain way. That way you may have fewer hurt feelings.

Remember the importance of compromise. If you share a room with a brother or sister, you need to sit down together to discuss problems such as scheduling friends' visits, study time, and listening to different music.

Household chores are often a cause of conflict. Again, communication and compromise are important. Making up a schedule that lists all chores can be very helpful.

Special attention should be paid to establishing rules about your social life.

REINFORCEMENT: On a sheet of paper, have students list three ways in which they can make good relationships with their best friend, their parents, and their siblings even better.

Your family probably sets rules for you. You may be expected home at a certain time, for example. Even when disagreements about rules occur, it is important to build a feeling of trust between you and your parents. Tell your family about your friends and your activities. Introduce some of your friends to your parents. Show your willingness to work with your parents to develop a fair set of rules and then to follow them. If your parents respect your judgment and trust you, they will be more willing to grant you increasing freedom. If you agree to be home by a certain hour, be sure you are. Treat it as a contract based on mutual respect.

People often take their families for granted. We sometimes put more effort into relationships with people far less important to us than our family. Take

PHOTO: Ask: How could these sisters use this time together to their best advantage?

Do you put enough effort into your relationships at home?

responsibility for your actions and work to build trust and respect with the other members of your family. Show them how much you value them.

New Family Relationships

As families grow and change, new members may be added. For example, a new baby may arrive, or a stepparent and his or her children may come to live with you. Other major changes may occur. After

Did You Know?

How many times have you heard a parent say, "Listen to me! If you don't, you'll be sorry someday!" Complaints about children not listening to their parents go back at least 4,000 years. Here is a translation from *The Instructions of Ptahhotep,* an Egyptian book on good manners from about 2000 B.C.: "Heed . . . How worthy it is when a son hearkens to his father. How many misfortunes befall him who hearkens not." Sound familiar?

DISCUSS: Should parents be upset when a child arrives home late and has neglected to call or notify them of the delay? Have students discuss the problem from the parents' point of view.

Do you take the time to let your parents and friends meet?

many years at home, your mother may take a full-time job outside the home.

Such changes are sometimes very difficult and demand a great deal of flexibility and strength on your part.

Often the hardest part is accepting the fact that the situation has changed and that you cannot control it. Be patient with yourself as you adjust to any major changes. Many people find it difficult to learn to live with a new stepparent. Even positive change can be hard. It is natural to be a little jealous of a new baby or a stepsister or stepbrother. As in all relationships, the most important thing is to keep communicating. Share your feelings and ideas with the whole family, including new members.

DISCUSS: Ask students to use compromise to resolve the following conflict. You are invited to spend the night at a friend's house. Your mother informs you that you can't because she needs you at home to babysit for your younger brother.

Sometimes, in spite of family conferences and other efforts to adjust to changing situations at home, there is continued stress. In this case, you and your family should talk to someone who can help you cope with your problems. Time with a community counselor, school psychologist, or member of the clergy can help to defuse family crises.

Friendships

We all need friends to share our joys and help us face our problems. Our friends accept us for who we are. They respect us and believe in us, and we in turn appreciate and trust them. We feel affection for one another.

Friends do not have to be your own age. You can find friends in any age group. Perhaps an elderly neighbor shares a special interest with you. You may form a friendship with a young child whom you

Could you add another band of color to this rainbow?

Friendship

EMPATHY
COMMUNICATION
SELF-CONCEPT
RESPONSIBILITY
RESPECT AND TRUST
COMPROMISE
FLEXIBILITY

ART: Have students write a paragraph about a time when trusting a friend made a big difference. This could be a private exploration. If you will collect the paragraph, say so.

82   Unit 2/*Relationships*

A friend doesn't have to be exactly the same age as you.

helped learn to ride a bike or roller-skate. Developing a wide variety of friendships adds richness to your life.

Responsibilities of Friendship

To maintain a true friendship you need to take responsibility for the relationship. You need mutual understanding, respect, and empathy as well as good communication. The factors that go into a good relationship, described earlier in this chapter, apply to friendships, too. Friends need to feel safe and secure with each other. They usually have similar likes and dislikes and share common interests. You may share an interest in a particular sport with a friend, as well as the same taste in music. However, even more important than similar interests is the bond of trust and affection that eventually forms between good friends.

Peer Pressure

Friends have a strong influence on one another. Almost everyone needs to be accepted, to feel part of a group. Consequently, having friends means you are subject to *peer pressure*, which can be both positive and negative. When a friend urges you to work with young children at your local community center, that is positive peer pressure. When another friend urges you to play instead of studying, that is negative peer pressure.

Belonging to a group can make you feel popular and proud. Is there a group you want to join?

Negative peer pressure can keep you from achieving goals that are important to you. It can lead you away from what you really believe in. It can affect your personal ethical standards and moral code. It may be hard, but you must resist negative peer pressure if you want to follow your own best interests. Developing a strong self-concept will help you do this. If you respect your own personal values, you will find the courage to stand up for what you believe in.

Popularity

Popularity is very important to most teenagers. Having a number of people look up to you and respect you is always reassur-

ing. It reinforces a positive self-concept. It fulfills the basic need to be accepted by others. Most people want to be popular —to be recognized by their friends and classmates as a person everyone likes.

Unfortunately, there are pitfalls in seeking popularity. People sometimes do things they don't want to or don't approve of in order to be popular with a group. Before you join in an activity, think how it affects your long-term goals. If you find yourself in a group that often does things you don't like, you should consider finding new friends.

Problems in Friendships

Problems arise in any friendship. If a friendship is to be a lasting one, you need to face the problems that interfere with your relationship.

Competition You live in a competitive world. You compete in sports, in school, and in looking for a part-time or summer job. Competition causes stress. The stress that pushes you to do your best in a test, competition, or sporting event is good for you. Too much stress, as you learned in Chapter 3, can harm your health and your mental attitude. You do not need to compete in all phases of your life. No one is first in everything.

In a friendship, competition can prove harmful. One of the pleasures of friendship is the feeling of security and understanding a close friend gives you. If you are constantly competing with each other, the friendship is no longer comfortable and relaxed. Learn to know your own strengths and weaknesses and to appreciate those of your friend. In a mature relationship, friends encourage each other to do as well as possible.

Jealousy and Envy Jealousy and envy can also destroy a friendship. We all occasionally envy others when they have something or do something we wish we could have or do. Sometimes it requires maturity to accept other people's good luck and honestly feel happy for them. Overcoming feelings of envy or jealousy will make you a happier, less anxious person. If your friend has more stylish clothing than you do, you may find it difficult to feel warm toward your friend. Instead of wasting your energy feeling jealous, think of positive things in your life that you are happy about.

Cliques There is a difference between a group of friends and a clique. A *clique* is a narrow, exclusive group. People in a clique make themselves feel important by looking down on people outside their group. They enlarge their own importance by their prejudices against people outside the clique. Do not be lured by this immature attitude. A mature friendship does not prevent you from forming warm relationships with people outside your group. A happy, active person may have many separate friendships.

Resolving Conflicts

When conflict arises in a friendship, follow these steps to resolve the problem. First, identify the problem. Then consider all the possible courses of action and decide on the best solution. Apply the decision-

making process you learned in Chapter 2. Working together to resolve conflicts can bring friends closer together. Sometimes, however, you may find that your own feelings and attitudes change as you grow and change. Old friendships may grow stronger, while others fade away. You may also find that as your life changes, so do the feelings and attitudes of your friends. Friends may develop standards you do not agree with, or consider unhealthy and dangerous. If this happens, you will want to seek new and sounder friendships.

How do you feel when your friend has something you wish you had?

ENRICHMENT: Write the word *clique* vertically on the blackboard. Using each letter in the word, have students name words associated with the word *clique*. (Examples: *closeness, crowd, exclusion*)

PHOTO: Remind students that jealousy is a negative but normal feeling.

PHOTO: Discuss the kind of self-discipline that is sometimes required to be a member of a group like a marching band. How might developing this self-discipline help students in later life?

Do you want to make new friends? Think about joining a club, a musical group, or a volunteer group. Having things in common helps friendships grow.

Making New Friends

Finding new friends can be difficult. It takes time to become part of a new group. Do not be discouraged if you make friends slowly. Apply what you have learned in this chapter on building relationships to form new friendships. Join groups that share your interests. Show new acquaintances that you are interested in them. Ask questions about their hobbies and other activities. Volunteer for committees at school and in extracurricular activities. Be open to the ideas and feelings of a wide variety of people. This will help you to make a wide circle of friends.

DISCUSS: A new girl moves into the neighborhood, and you see her the next day at school. She seems nice and you would like to get to know her. What do you do?

See page T47 for answers.

For Review

1. How does a strong self-concept affect your relationships with other people?
2. Name two of the basic skills you should use to maintain a good relationship with your family.
3. What can you do to gain your parents' respect for your judgment?
4. Name four important elements of true friendship.
5. Give an example of positive peer pressure.

ENRICHMENT: Have students research the clubs and extracurricular activities that exist in your school. Have them present two good reasons for joining each.

Section 4.3
Dating

As you read, think about:

■ how to make the change from friendship to a romantic relationship. (p. 87)

■ how realistic attitudes toward boy-girl relationships can help avoid dating disappointments. (p. 88)

■ how your experiences as an adolescent can be helpful to you in future relationships. (p. 89)

In adolescence you begin to relate to the opposite sex in a different way. In this section you will find out how to make the transition from friendships to romantic relationships. You will also learn about the difference between realistic attitudes toward boy-girl relationships and idealized expectations that can cause disappointment. Dating experience in adolescence will help you make sound decisions about long-range commitments and marriage when you become an adult.

Group Activities

In childhood you had playmates of both sexes, but you viewed all your friends, boys and girls, alike. Now, in adolescence, your feelings are changing. You may find the opposite sex both frightening and appealing in a new way.

The first step in forming close boy-girl relationships is usually group dating. You join a group of boys and girls who go together to sporting events, concerts,

PHOTO: Ask students what they think is a good activity for a first date.

A date doesn't have to be fancy to be fun.

dances, or other social activities. As time goes on, you and someone of the opposite sex may be especially attracted to each other. Then you begin to go out together as a couple. You still join in group activities, but you especially enjoy spending time together by yourselves.

Boy-Girl Relationships

Boy-girl relationships are a kind of friendship. However, they have the added factor of physical attraction and strong feelings of affection. Any new situation can be frightening, and dating is no exception. It takes time to feel comfortable in a new relationship. Almost everyone feels awkward at the beginning of a romantic relationship. Your partner on a date very likely feels as shy and unsure as you do.

DISCUSS: All your students probably know some fairy tales such as "Cinderella" and "Sleeping Beauty" in which the romance is very unreal. Have students talk about such fairy tales and what effect they might have on how people think about male-female relationships.

REINFORCEMENT: Divide the class in half. Have the students in one group write anonymous Dear Abby letters asking for advice on a dating issue. Have the other half answer the letters.

Chapter 4/*Relating to Others*   **87**

It's comfortable to become a friend to someone before you decide to go out on a date together.

It is important for you to view the people you date as *friends*. To reinforce the relationship, use the same rules you learned in the previous section for maintaining strong friendships.

Taking Your Time

Some of your friends may begin to date before you do. Don't worry. People develop at different rates, and there is plenty of time. It is better to go too slowly than to jump into romantic relationships before you are ready. If your friends are more popular with the opposite sex than you are, be confident that your time will come. Until then, plan activities that you enjoy with both boys and girls.

It is important to base a relationship on reality. Too often, people have an unrealistic, idealized view of romance. Boys may imagine a relationship with the most beautiful, charming, and understanding girl of their dreams. Some girls dream of meeting "Prince Charming." It is a great mistake to fall in love with an image, whether it is a rock star or your class president. Look beyond the stereotype to the real people you know. Don't place too much emphasis on physical appearance. Try to date someone who shares your interests and can relate to your whole personality. You will have more fun than you will with a person you choose solely

NOTE: *Prince Charming* is a name and expression that comes to us from "Cinderella." The phrase *prince charming* is used to refer to a man who meets all the stereotypically romantic expectations (bravery, chivalry, gallantry, etc.).

on the basis of appearance and physical attraction. Mutual respect, shared thoughts, and similar attitudes are also a vital part of a worthwhile romantic relationship. In a good relationship you should be able to express your true feelings without fear of losing love and respect.

Responsible Behavior

In a romantic relationship, as in all close relationships, you share responsibility for maintaining each person's ethical and moral standards. It takes courage, but it is important that you resist peer pressure if it conflicts with what you believe in. Something that you know is wrong is still wrong no matter how many other people may be doing it.

Ending a Relationship

Adolescence is a time of growth and change. We all learn to some extent from trial and error. When a relationship does not work out, it causes pain for both of the people involved. However, in time each person should be able to realize that changing relationships are part of growing and learning. It is unrealistic to believe that true love happens only once. If, after all your efforts, you break up with someone you have cared about, you must eventually accept the fact. Your experience will help you adjust to a future important relationship later on in your life.

Future Relationships

When you become an adult, you will most probably marry; over 90 percent of Americans do. Many people believe marriage

Is marriage in your future? It is for most people.

provides a sense of security and a closeness that no other situation can give. It
also may offer the reward of raising children in a stable environment.

Marriage, however, is a serious responsibility that should not be taken on lightly.
It is a partnership that must be based on
understanding, compromise, and sensitiv-
ity. It involves the willingness to work
hard to make the relationship work. Communication is another important ingredient in a successful marriage. A good
marriage requires maturity on the part of
both partners.

Not everyone marries. Many people
today choose to remain single. These
people value their independence and have
the opportunity to pursue their own individual goals. Dating does not necessarily
lead to marriage. At any rate, at this stage
it is too early in your life to make such
serious decisions. Now is the time to
develop happy and rewarding relationships which grow and change as you learn
and mature. The experience you gain
during adolescence will help you to find
and maintain a long-term relationship in
the future.

See page T47 for answers.

For Review

1. How is group dating a good way to
   develop boy-girl relationships?
2. Why is it important to base a boy-
   girl relationship on reality?
3. How can the experience you gain
   during adolescence help you in future relationships?

DISCUSS: Time is relative. Question your students on how long
they think a long-term relationship is.

You and Your Community

As you read, think about:

◼ how to develop relationships within a
group. (p. 91)

◼ ways to become a leader. (p. 91)

◼ how you can make your community a
better place through good citizenship.
(p. 92)

In addition to your relationships with
friends and family, you also play a role in
your community. In this chapter you will
learn about relationships within a group.
You will find out what it takes to be a
leader and a good citizen. In addition, you
will learn what you can do to help to make
your community a better place in which to
live.

What Is Community?

Your *community* is the area in which you
live. It includes your home, your neighborhood, your school, and the church,
synagogue, or other religious organization
to which you belong. It may include your
cultural or ethnic group. Perhaps you are
part of a community with special ties to a
foreign country. Your community also extends to your town or city, county, state,
country, and finally to every part of the
world around you.

The same basic rules apply to your
relationship with your community as to
your other relationships. They are: good

A parade is one way for a community to express what it values.

communication, mutual respect, responsibility and accountability.

Being a Group Member

One of your roles in a community is that of group member. You belong to many groups: student groups, work groups, clubs, sports teams. The success of any of these groups depends on how much effort and cooperation each member provides.

Moving to a New Community

The best way to make friends and feel comfortable in a new community is to get involved in community groups. You might join an extracurricular activity at school or a neighborhood club. Check your library for notices of local events and lists of neighborhood activities. You can also meet new friends by getting involved in volunteer work.

Group Leadership Skills

A *leader* is someone who has influence over a group. You can learn the skills that make a good leader. The goal of a leader is to meet group goals and to involve everyone in the group. The leader of a meeting must keep order and see that all the items and issues are discussed.

A leader must see that each person has the opportunity to speak as well as to vote.

Parliamentary procedure is a set of rules for keeping order during meetings. Its history dates back as far as the eleventh century. Today it is followed in the British Parliament and in both houses of the United States Congress. It can help you lead your group in a systematic, efficient way. The rules of parliamentary procedure are listed in a book called *Robert's Rules of Order.*

Good Citizenship

Good citizens take responsibility for their relationship with their community. They respect the property they share with the other people of that community. In a well-run community the parks and streets are free of graffiti and litter. You can contribute toward making your community a more pleasant place. Don't litter. Volunteer for cleanup activities. Help educate others about their part in making your neighborhood a safe, enjoyable place.

Is there a group you could join to help clean up your community? Cleaning up is one way to show that you care.

PHOTO: Ask: What kind of cleanup is needed at your school? What club or group could do it?

ENRICHMENT: As a homework assignment, have your students attend a local school committee, civic group, or student government meeting to observe parliamentary procedure.

ART: Does your school offer leadership or citizenship awards? If not, could the Home Economics department sponsor one?

Good Citizenship

This Good Citizenship Award
is presented to
Juan Angelo
by
Central Junior High School
for his display of these
outstanding qualities
- *Attendance*
- *Generosity*
- *Courtesy*
- *School Spirit*
- *Thoughtfulness*
- *Leadership*

Who would be proud of you if you won an award like this one?

Respecting Others

A good citizen respects the rights of others. Courtesy and cooperation pay off in the long run. Immature teenagers often act thoughtlessly in regard to others. They may be noisy and rude in public places. They sometimes use words or language that offends others. It takes maturity to respect the rights of people outside your peer group. Step aside for a handicapped person on the street. Remember not to block the doors of a bus or subway where people have trouble making their way through a crowd. These are courtesies that show others you are a kind and responsible person; they also reinforce your self-respect.

REINFORCEMENT: Plan a class meeting to discuss a topic appropriate to your school or community. Assign a chairperson and someone to take the minutes of the meeting. Act as a neutral party, but assist discussion whenever necessary.

Sometimes it is hard to behave as you know you should when you are part of a crowd. Try to avoid becoming involved in a situation where immature teenagers become loud and unruly.

Showing courtesy and respect toward parents, teachers, and other adults can make the difference between conflict and cooperation. The adults in charge of community affairs—government leaders, police officers, and firefighters—are there to help the community. They keep things running smoothly and protect you in situations you yourself cannot control. They have years of training and experience. However, to do their jobs effectively, they need your cooperation.

Playing a role in a mock city or state government can give you a chance to learn more about leadership and citizenship.

DISCUSS: Have students identify two individuals whom they feel are exemplary citizens and give their reasons. Then have students list ways in which they themselves can become better citizens.

Future Homemakers of America is citizenship in action.

Future Homemakers of America

One example of citizenship in action is Future Homemakers of America. Involvement in Future Homemakers of America offers members the opportunity to expand their leadership potential and develop *skills for life*—planning, goal setting, problem solving, decision making and interpersonal communication—necessary in the world of work and the home.

Goal The goal of Future Homemakers of America is

to help youth assume active roles in society through home economics education in the areas of personal growth, family life, vocational preparation and community involvement.

Purposes An organization's purposes define its reason for being. Future Homemakers of America, both as a national organization and as individual chapters, works toward fulfilling eight purposes.

- To provide opportunities for self-development and preparation for family and community living and for employment
- To strengthen the function of the family as the basic unit of society
- To encourage democracy through cooperative action in the home and community
- To encourage individual and group involvement in helping achieve world-wide fellowship
- To institute programs promoting greater understanding between youth and adults
- To provide opportunities for decision making and for assuming responsibility
- To become aware of the multiple roles of men and women in today's society
- To develop interest in home economics, home economics careers, and related occupations

These national goals will be shared by your local chapter. As a member you can take part in and help shape the activities undertaken by your chapter to meet these goals.

See page T47 for answers.

For Review

1. If you were new in a neighborhood, what groups might you join to make friends and become involved in the community?
2. Name some of the important qualities of a good leader.
3. What are some of the rewards of good citizenship?

ENRICHMENT: Have students select two of the purposes of FHA listed above. Ask them to name one activity for each that a local FHA club could plan to achieve those purposes. For example, the club could hold a Family Activity Day to promote families' spending time together.

Learning to Manage

Getting the Message

Look back at the conversation between Sue and Joni on page 72. Mr. Flavin, their home economics teacher, has overheard them. Now read how they all try to manage the situation. Then answer the questions that follow.

"Hi, Mr. Flavin, I didn't see you there. I got so mad at Sue I'm afraid I was yelling, too. She's so stubborn!"

"You were both so emotional that I don't think any real messages were getting through, Joni. Remember when we talked about that problem in class? Why don't you give it a try? Set a time to talk; really *listen* to each other; don't blame, accuse, or make general statements; apologize if you should; and look for ways to communicate better."

Joni called Sue after school. The first time, Sue hung up on her. She tried again.

"Haven't you cooled off yet, Sue? Let's get together after supper. Can I come over?"

"Sure, but I may not be here."

"I'll take the chance," Joni replied.

When Joni arrived, Sue led her up to her room and plunked herself down on her desk chair.

"Make it fast. I have a lot of homework to do—and *you* must have a lot of back-stabbing phone calls to make."

"Sue, you go first. Tell me what's bugging you and I'll listen. Then it's my turn and *you* listen."

Sue told Joni how left out she had felt when she found out about the party. She also told Joni what Judy had said. "Judy said that you said you couldn't count on me. That's all I have to say."

"OK, it's my turn. First of all, I called here and left a message with your brother about the party, which we decided to have at the last minute. You didn't call me back so I tried here again when the other girls got to my house, but by then you were out at the movies. Secondly, Judy always misunderstands what people say. When she asked why you weren't there, I joked that you probably had 'more important plans.' Actually, *I* was feeling hurt that *you* hadn't called *me* back."

"Oh, Joni. I'm sorry. That little brother of mine! He *never*—"

Joni laughed. "Listen to yourself, Sue. You're blaming again. *Talk* to him about it when you cool down!"

Questions

1. If you were in Joni's position, and Sue refused to talk to you, what do you think you would do?
2. Describe a communication problem you have had with a friend. How did you solve it?

Chapter 4 Review

Summary

How well people get along together is greatly influenced by their ability to communicate. Good communication involves learning to express yourself clearly and being able to interpret what others communicate, both verbally and nonverbally.

We all depend on other people to help us maintain a happy, fulfilling life. To establish good relationships takes attention and effort. A good relationship requires effective communication, a strong self-concept, empathy for others, and a willingness to compromise when conflicts occur. It also involves mutual respect and trust.

These factors apply to romantic relationships as well as to other friendships and relations with family members. Your relationships with members of a group and with your community are also important. Learning to be a good citizen is a major part of becoming a mature, responsible person.

Vocabulary

Complete each of the following sentences with the correct word from the vocabulary list below.

body language (p. 74)
verbal communication (p. 74)
nonverbal communication (p. 74)
parliamentary procedure (p. 92)
communication (p. 73)

receiver (p. 73)
sender (p. 73)
feedback (p. 73)
message (p. 73)
prejudice (p. 76)

1. The exchange of information between two or more people by the process of sending and receiving messages is called _____.
2. _____ is a set of rules for keeping order during meetings.
3. _____ is the use of words to express ideas or emotions.
4. Facial expressions and body movements that convey feelings and attitudes are called _____.
5. _____ is the response or answer the receiver gives.
6. _____ is sending messages without words or sounds.
7. Information that is sent is called the _____.
8. Prejudging people unfairly without knowing the facts about them is called _____.
9. The person who directs or sends a message to someone else is called the _____.
10. The _____ is the person who gets a message.

Questions

• 1. Name five types of verbal communication.

•• 2. Give some examples of how a close friend's body language tells you how he or she feels.

••• 3. What is the relationship between your audience and the way you communicate?

The dots represent skill levels required to answer each question or complete each activity:
• requires recall and comprehension
•• requires application and analysis
••• requires synthesis and evaluation

96

4. What does a person communicate by dressing too casually when applying for a job?

5. What should you do when you have a disagreement with someone?

6. What is the meaning of the word *empathy*?

7. Why is it important to compromise in order to resolve a disagreement with a close friend or relative?

8. Name three events that cause change in existing family relationships.

9. What is likely to happen to a friendship if friends constantly compete with each other?

10. What is the difference between a group of friends and a *clique*?

11. Which do you consider to be more important in a date: physical appearance or shared interests? Explain your answer.

12. What percent of Americans marry?

13. What is a *community*?

14. What is the role of a leader during a meeting?

15. Name two ways you can show courtesy to others in public places.

Skill Activities.

Many more activities are contained in the annotations within this chapter.

1. Human Relations In a class discussion, brainstorm a list of groups teens can join for sports, community leadership, music and religious activities. Then make a list of groups that welcome teen volunteers, for example, nursing homes, hospitals, and community centers. Which organizations do you already belong to, or wish to belong to? Investigate an organization that you might like to join and share your information with the class.

2. Communication The list below includes some everyday terms for feelings that are also expressions of body activities. See if you can act out some of them!

two-faced	twist your arm
get in your hair	big mouth
pain in the neck	no backbone
brokenhearted	get out of hand
stiff upper lip	catch your eye

3. Decision Making Pretend that your family has won a $5,000 cash prize. Use the decision-making process to work out as a family how the money should be spent.

4. Human Relations Write a letter in class to a person who has been a special friend to you. Explain in your letter why this person is so important to you. Mention the special things he or she has done for you.

5. Laboratory Create an advertisement for "a friend." Make sure you include all the qualities you feel it is important for a friend to have.

Chapter 5
The Family

Vocabulary

The dialogue below introduces "Keeping Active," the Learning to Manage feature in this chapter. The case study is continued and the situation discussed further on page 117. See page T51 for teaching suggestions.

"Mom, Grandpa doesn't seem happy since he came to stay. In fact, he's been sort of grouchy."

"Well, Mark, he's trying to adjust to us. After forty years of marriage, he's also missing Gram a lot. He needs rest and time alone."

"Maybe he's bored, too, Mom."

"You may be right, Mark. You two have always had a close relationship. Why don't you spend some time together and try to get him to tell you how he feels? Dad, Tina, and I will do the same. We want him to know he's an important member of our family."

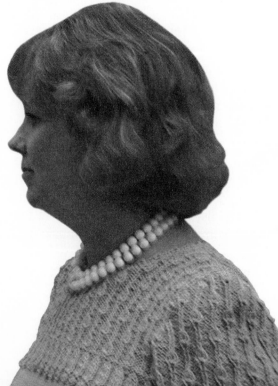

Section 5.1

The Family and Society

As you read, think about:

■ the different kinds of families that make up our society. (p. 99)

■ the trends in our society that affect families. (p. 100)

What is a family? The answer seems obvious, but when you consider all the different kinds of families you know, the answer is not easy. Families can vary in size from two people to dozens of people. Some families live together; others live far apart. Today's families are changing. How would you define yours?

What Is a Family?

A **family** is a group of people who are related by blood or by marriage. The people in the group can range in age from newborn to very elderly. The adult members take responsibility for the physical and emotional needs of the children in the group. They may also care for other adult members who cannot look after themselves. Family members also give one another mutual help and affection.

Your family supplied your food, clothing, and shelter during your early years, when you were dependent upon them for your well-being. They taught you to walk, talk, and get along with other people. They provided a secure environment and gave you the attention and affection all

Doing things as a family gets the work done quickly. Cooperation and sharing help.

humans need. You also learned important moral and ethical values from your family.

Now you most likely are becoming less dependent on your parents for your physical and emotional needs. You are growing increasingly responsible for your own decisions and actions. You are also able to share in family decisions as well as helping with household chores and caring for younger **siblings** (brothers and sisters).

How Are Family Structures Different?

There are many different kinds of families Some special terms are often used to describe family types.

The **nuclear** (*NOO*–klee–er) **family** consists of a husband and wife and their children. The children may be adopted or may be born to that family.

Many children grow up with only one parent.

The **extended family** includes the nuclear family plus other relatives —grandparents, uncles, aunts, cousins, and grandchildren.

The **blended family** consists of families that were once separate but are now combined. Blended families include stepmothers, stepfathers, and stepchildren. This kind of family is formed when people with children marry and bring their children into the newly-created family.

A single-parent family is a household consisting of one or more children but only one parent.

A husband and wife form a family even though they have no children.

Trends in Our Society That Affect Families

Family life has changed a great deal in the past 50 years. Families have fewer children than they used to have. Some couples today decide not to have any children.

There are many more families in which both parents have full-time jobs. There are more divorces now than there were in the past. More people decide to marry later in life or to remain single.

Historical Changes

One hundred years ago, our society was a **rural** one, in which most people lived on farms. Now we live in an **urban** society, in which most of the population is clustered around big cities. This change has greatly affected the lifestyle of the typical American family.

Farm families of the past formed their own closely-knit community of a number of generations living and working together. They were almost totally self-sufficient, growing and raising their own food, making their own clothes, and building their own shelters. Often, many children of several closely-related nuclear families lived under one roof along with their grandparents, aunts, and uncles.

Today's nuclear families are usually smaller and often live farther away from their extended families. Far fewer people work at home. People today are therefore more closely tied to others in their community than they were in the past. We spend less time at home, both at work and at play, than our grandparents did. We buy our food at the supermarket and purchase most of our clothes. We live in cities and suburbs, closer to our neighbors than to our families.

Did You Know?

The family is alive and well in America, but it is changing. For example:

- In the 1950s, the average number of children in a family was 3.3; today it's 1.8.
- In the 1950s, 33 percent of married women between the ages of 20 and 24 had no children; today the figure is 41 percent.
- In the 1940s, teenage girls completed an average of 10.3 years of school; today the average is 12.9 years.

Our Mobile Society

In the past it was not unusual for one family to live for several generations in the same house. Extended families also lived close together in the same community. When people did move, they often did so as a family.

DISCUSS: Ask students where their extended families are. What do students miss when a grandparent lives in another country or very far away? Do they think they might someday live far away from their own children or grandchildren?

Mobile (*MO*–buhl) means fluid or moving. We live in a mobile society. Since 1965, Americans have begun to move much more frequently. People travel more and find jobs far away from where they grew up. Many companies transfer employees and their families from one part of the country to another. You probably have grandparents, uncles, aunts, and cousins who live far away from you. It is difficult to get together with many members of your extended family for this reason. For many families this means that they can usually come together only for very special occasions.

Changing Family Patterns

In today's society there are many divorced couples. One or both of the pair may then remarry. Children of divorced parents may move with one parent to a new community. Some children may spend time separately with both parents, each of whom lives in a different city. This requires great flexibility on the part of the children, who have to adjust to both a new environment and a new family pattern.

Blended families require flexibility, too. When a parent remarries, the spouse's children may become part of the newly-formed family group. It can be difficult to adjust to a stepparent and to stepsisters and stepbrothers. People who do not know each other well are suddenly living together as members of a family. As blended families become more common, psychologists and family counselors are learning more about the problems that they can cause. They are also finding ways to make the adjustment easier.

REINFORCEMENT: Have students develop a list of things that a blended family would need to adjust to. In what areas of family life do blended families need to be flexible?

ART: Ask students to estimate their families' cost of "raising" them just for this week.

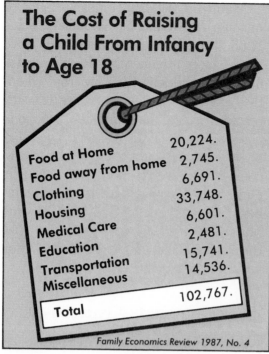

The Cost of Raising a Child From Infancy to Age 18

Food at Home	20,224.
Food away from home	2,745.
Clothing	6,691.
Housing	33,748.
Medical Care	6,601.
Education	2,481.
Transportation	15,741.
Miscellaneous	14,536.
Total	102,767.

Family Economics Review 1987, No. 4

Children bring parents many joys. They also bring many expenses.

Economic Factors

The national **economy**—the way the country makes, buys, and sells material goods—can greatly affect a family's standard of living. **Inflation**—a continuous rise in prices—lessens a family's buying power. In most sections of the country, the last 10 years have seen a considerable rise in housing costs. Other major family expenses have increased too. Local economic events can also influence a family's lifestyle. The loss of a job by one of the family members who provide for its material needs can cause financial hardship. So can large medical bills or other unexpected large expenses. A family's living standards may also improve, for example when one of its members gets a big raise.

DISCUSS: What are the advantages and disadvantages of living in a mobile society? What are the advantages and disadvantages of living in an extended family?

See page T53 for answers.

For Review

1. What is the difference between a nuclear and a blended family?
2. How has inflation affected family life in the last few years?

Section 5.2

Family Members and You

As you read, think about:

■ how an adolescent's role within the family changes. (p. 102)

■ how you can promote understanding among members of your family. (p. 102)

At this stage of your life the role you play in your family is changing. When you were a child, you were completely dependent on your parents for all of your needs. As you take on additional responsibilities, your parents depend on you for certain things. Attitudes toward brothers and sisters may also change in the adolescent years. What can you do to promote better understanding among the members of your family?

Children in a Family

The role of a child in a family of several siblings depends on many factors. *Age span*, the number of years between children in a family, can affect how siblings relate to each other. Whatever the age

ENRICHMENT: Have students write about ways in which their attitudes toward a brother, sister, or other family member have changed during the years.

An older brother or sister can teach you many things.

span, the order in which siblings were born has the greatest influence on their role in the family.

The Eldest Sibling

The eldest child in a family often helps care for younger siblings and participates in family decisions more than they do. This tends to make him or her capable and responsible. Sometimes, however, the child feels that this added responsibility is unfair. If this is true in your case, discuss your concerns with your parents. Remind yourself of the pleasure you get from the admiration of your younger siblings. Remember, too, the satisfaction you feel when you teach one of them a new skill such as riding a bicycle.

The Middle Child

If you are a middle child you may sometimes feel that you have the best and worst of both worlds. Your elder brother or sister has more privileges than you. On the other hand, because your younger sibling is the "baby" of the family, less is expected of him or her. However, there are advantages, too. Parents tend to be more relaxed than they were with their firstborn. You may get to try things earlier than your elder sibling did. And you can share the skills and knowledge you have with your younger sibling. Sometimes you are the peacemaker between older and younger siblings. Middle children often grow up to be the kind of people who get along well with others.

REINFORCEMENT: Ask students what they would rather be— eldest, middle, or youngest? Why?

Sometimes differences in age don't matter a bit.

The Youngest Child

The youngest child has the advantage of following in the footsteps of older siblings and of getting help and affection from them. If you are the youngest, however, you may feel that everyone in the family "babies" you. You may have to speak up and point out that you are growing up and deserve more responsibility.

It can be difficult to follow an older sibling who has special talents that you do not possess. People may expect you to be like your elder brother and sister. You should remember that you have your own skills. It is important that both you and your family accept you for your own personality and abilities.

The Only Child

Only children have the advantage of their parents' full attention. If you are an only child, you don't have to share your things with siblings. Only children are often more socially mature than children from big families because they spend more time with adults. They sometimes feel a great deal of pressure, however, since all their parents' hopes are placed on them. It helps to talk over feelings of pressure with parents, trusted family members, or other concerned adults.

Being an only child may seem lonely, but friends can provide the companionship and affection others get from siblings.

Adopted Children

Some parents choose to adopt a child who is not born into their family. If you are adopted, you belong to the family just as much as if you were your parents' biological offspring. You were especially chosen to become an important member of your family.

Foster Children

If a child's family is having problems, that child may be taken into a foster family to become a part of that household. A foster family can create the mutual respect and support necessary for any warm and loving family relationship.

Disabled Children

Many families include a child with a physical or mental disability. In this situation, all family members, including the children, require great understanding and patience. If you have a handicapped brother or sister, you probably sometimes resent all the special attention your disabled sibling requires. Like all children, a handicapped child needs love and respect. It is also important that he or she learns to be as self-sufficient as possible. You can make this process easier by your help and encouragement.

Relationships with Siblings

In even the happiest families, brothers and sisters sometimes disagree. When problems arise, it is important to talk things over with your siblings. Regular family meetings are a good way to clarify misunderstandings, divide up household chores, and support each other. Cooperation and fair play are just as important to your relationship with your siblings as they are to team players.

Parents and Other Care Givers

The role of parent is one of the most responsible jobs there is. Parents are on the job 24 hours a day. The needs, safety, and well-being of their children rest on them.

We are so used to our parents taking care of us that we often take them for granted. We forget that they have other responsibilities and interests. Also, we may be more critical of our parents than we are of anyone else; we want them to be perfect. It requires maturity to accept parents as people and to appreciate that they have problems and changes of mood like everybody else.

Every family member has something to offer the others.

As you strive for independence, your parents' concern for your safety and success often causes stress.

Your parents set rules about your behavior and activities. It may take special effort on your part to see things from their point of view. Remember that they are still responsible for you. Talk over problems and be willing to compromise. Accept responsibility for your own behavior and for your part in making your home a happy place to be.

The Single Parent

A single parent bears total responsibility for his or her children and must make important decisions alone. A single parent

ENRICHMENT: Ask students to role-play a family meeting to discuss the following situation: father has been offered a great job; however, it is located 700 miles away.

REINFORCEMENT: Ask students to list five safety or health concerns that most parents have about their children.

Do you have something to share with older family members?

usually shoulders all the family's financial obligations as well as being responsible for running the household and caring for the children. If you are part of a single-parent family, you can help by understanding all of the stresses your parent faces. Do your share of the household chores and be available to supervise younger siblings.

Did You Know?

■ One out of six (about six million) children in the United States between the ages of six and sixteen lives in a single-parent family.

Older Family Members

There are probably a number of older members in your extended family. In addition to grandparents, you may have older aunts and uncles. Some of them may live busy, independent lives. Others may have problems such as loss of hearing, failing eyesight, and memory loss. They may live with you, nearby, or far away. They may live alone or with others.

Older people have a lot to give: love, experience, time, and skills. Include them in your life. They need respect, acceptance, and affection just as all of us do.

You can learn a lot about the past by having older people tell you about their early growing-up experiences. These may be very different from your own.

ENRICHMENT: Have students interview an older family member or neighbor about a political event that took place before the students or even their parents were born.

REINFORCEMENT: In class, have students write a letter to a grandparent or other older relative or friend who lives far away.

Sometimes older people are lonely. They may have recently lost their husbands or wives of many years. It is often difficult for them to go out to meet new friends.

You can show you care about older family members by giving some of your time to them. An older person who has trouble getting around will appreciate your running errands. He or she certainly could use help with some of the heavier household and yard chores. An older relative will appreciate sharing a hobby with you or hearing about your daily activities. He or she may have more time to listen than parents or siblings. An older person draws on a wealth of experience to help you understand many of the things that are bothering you.

If grandparents and other older family members live far away, they will welcome your occasional cards and letters.

Other Relatives

Your entire family is an invaluable resource. You will find it well worth your time to make the effort to keep in touch with your extended family. They provide you with both physical and emotional support in good times and in bad times. They help you realize who you are. They are a vital part of your individual family's roots and traditions.

Sharing responsibility and spending time with your extended family will provide warmth and security in your life. Set aside time for family get-togethers. Keep in touch by calling and writing to relatives who live some distance away.

See page T53 for answers.

For Review

1. How does your role in the family change as you move from childhood to adolescence?
2. Name three advantages of regular family meetings.
3. Name one way you can show you care about older family members.

Section 5.3

The Family Life Cycle

As you read, think about:

■ what kinds of changes and stages families go through. (p. 107)

■ how parents' lives change when their children have grown. (p. 109)

Families go through a series of changes just as individuals do. This pattern is called the *family life cycle.* Most often, it begins with marriage. It continues through childbearing to raising preschoolers, school-age children, and then teenagers. Next the family launches the children into further schooling or jobs. Finally the children are grown and move away from their parents' home. Then the parents focus again on their own interests and upon each other. Not all families go through the life cycle in exactly this way. A family can be involved in more than one stage at a time.

ENRICHMENT: Ask students to brainstorm a list of errands they could run or pleasant activities they could provide for an older family member. Then have each student write a paragraph explaining what such a list tells about older family members and their needs.

DISCUSS: What are some of the barriers that your students perceive to spending time with older family members? Focus the discussion on how students might overcome those difficulties.

When do you think is a good time in a marriage to adopt or to have a first child?

Marriage

Marriage marks the beginning of the family life cycle. Newlywed couples learn how to get along with each another and with their new in-laws. During this period, they adjust to their new partner's personality, standards, and goals. They usually settle into a new home and work out the best way to handle their combined income and expenses.

Childbearing

The next step in the family life cycle occurs when the first child is born or adopted. It is a big step for the couple to adjust to caring for a baby. The new parents must reschedule their time and resources to give their new child the loving care an infant needs. The couple's entire lifestyle changes.

They may have another baby while the first is still only a toddler. It takes great energy and concentration to care for a newborn together with a lively young child who needs constant supervision.

Families with Preschool Children

At the preschool stage, children learn and change rapidly. They become **socialized,** that is, they learn to relate to many different people, both adults and children their own age.

Families with School-age Children

By the time children begin school, they have learned to be independent in many ways. School-age children begin developing relationships on their own with people outside their families. They are still dependent on their parents for their physical needs—clothing, shelter, and food. However, they take on progressively more responsibility for their behavior and their relationships at school.

Families with Teenage Children

The teenage years are difficult for both the teenagers themselves and for their families. In adolescence, people begin to break away from their dependence on family. However, they still need the trust, acceptance, and guidance of their parents and other adults. At this

NOTE: Refer to Chapter 6 for additional information on the growth and development of a preschooler.

Have you ever felt happy and afraid at the same time?

stage families must work hard to keep communicating. They must also remember how much they mean to each other.

Families as Launching Centers

Following high school, young people often leave home to go on to further schooling or to begin work. A good family relationship at this stage is one in which parents and children can depend on each other. Leaving home for the first time can be scary. This stage, therefore, requires a great deal of encouragement and understanding from parents.

"Empty Nest" Families

The time comes when the last grown child moves away. At this stage, parents may feel lonely. They need to focus on their own activities and perhaps develop new interests and skills. Of course, parents care about their children's welfare throughout their lives, but the children no longer depend on them for physical support. Nor do they have the daily contact with their parents that they formerly had. At this stage, the children may have married and begun their own family life cycle. This brings their parents the pleasures of grandchildren without the major responsibility of caring for them.

One of the greatest advantages of retirement is all the leisure time that people have.

See page T53 for answers.

For Review

1. Define the family life cycle.
2. Name the various stages of the family life cycle.

Families with Older Members

In the later stages of the family life cycle, a couple may retire from their jobs. They may have less money to spend during the retirement years. What they *will* have is more time. This means they can enjoy the younger generation and pursue hobbies, part-time work, long-range projects, and leisure activities.

ENRICHMENT: Divide the class into six groups. Assign each group a stage of the family cycle, and have them create a collage of that stage. Use them as wall displays.

Section 5.4
Family Crises

As you read, think about:

■ how problems are part of family life.   (p. 11●

■ how you can learn to cope with major family crises.   (p. 111)

Part of family living is the stress of changing situations and day-to-day problems. The family moves, a parent begins a new job, a baby is born, a family member has a minor accident. A *family crisis* is different from these normal events. It has a serious and often lasting effect on the entire family.

Major Family Crises

You will cope better with a major family crisis that arises if you understand how it can affect you and the rest of the family.

Families whose members talk over their problems together and who lend each other support and encouragement can function well as a group. These families are often the best qualified to cope with a major crisis.

NOTE: The word *crisis* comes from the Latin word meaning "to separate." What can separate during a crisis?

Serious Illness

Coping with a serious illness is difficult for everyone in a family. A sick person in the home requires a great deal of attention, so parents have less time for their children. The patient may need quiet, causing children's play to be restricted. There may be long hospital trips. Most disruptive of all, everyone is worried.

In this situation, it is important that the entire family meet together. They should express their concerns and offer support to each other as well as to the patient. All family members should try to share their emotions rather than withdrawing.

Family members turn to one another for support in times of crisis.

Death

The death of a member of the family is among the most painful situations in life. Psychologists have found that almost everyone reacts to death in a similar way. The first stage is one of *disbelief and anger.* You feel it cannot be true that the person you loved is gone. The second step is *grief,* an overwhelming sadness. At this stage, you must express your sorrow. Don't bottle it up. You need to go through a mourning stage before you can accept the death. The third stage is *acceptance.* You are able to go forward without the person who has died.

It is difficult for very young children to understand death. They think it is like sleep. Older children may be afraid that they themselves are about to die. Some teenagers, on the other hand, may understand the death of another but feel that nothing can happen to them personally.

As people get older, they appreciate how fragile life can be.

It is best to explain a death in the family to children gently and in a simple way that they can understand. It is also important to be truthful and straightforward. If older family members explain to the children about death, they will be less frightened than if their imaginations take over.

Families can help one another greatly through mutual support and love. They can also gain comfort from uncles, aunts, and other extended family members. If you have a death in your family, you may find your friends don't know what to say to comfort you. They might not even mention the death at all. Most people are uncomfortable in this situation, but their silence does not mean that they are not concerned.

NOTE: The word *grief* comes from the Latin word meaning "heavy."

ENRICHMENT: Have students role-play the following situation: You, the parents, give your only child a puppy. After a week, the dog becomes very ill. You take the dog to the vet, who says that the dog must be put to sleep. What do you say as your child greets you at the door?

Health and Safety

Help for Children of Alcoholics

You already know that people who suffer from alcoholism have an illness and are not just "weak" or "bad." Now, researchers believe that the alcoholism of one family member is an illness that affects the whole family. Children of alcoholics (COAs) suffer emotional symptoms because of their parent's illness both when they are young and later as adults. However, the National Association for the Children of Alcoholics has also found that counseling can help COAs.

Approximately seven million American children under 18 have a parent who is an alcoholic. Because alcoholism makes the parent's behavior unpredictable, often neglectful, and sometimes abusive, these children suffer a great deal of anxiety. They often show physical symptoms such as sleeping problems and eating disorders. Many young COAs also have psychological symptoms. Some deny the problem, just as the alcoholic parent does, pretending that nothing is wrong. Often they cope by trying to make their home seem normal. They may become loners or troublemakers. Almost all COAs suffer undeserved guilt well into adulthood.

Of course, not all COAs have these problems, but help is available for those who do. Contact Al-Anon for information. Is there an Al-Anon group in your community?

ART: Have students identify their life expectancy according to this chart. Have them speculate on what life will be like during the last decade they would live if these life expectancy figures proved to be correct for them.

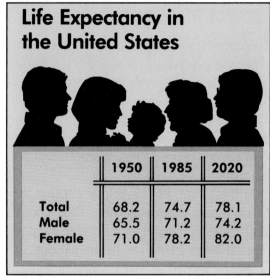

Life Expectancy in the United States

	1950	1985	2020
Total	68.2	74.7	78.1
Male	65.5	71.2	74.2
Female	71.0	78.2	82.0

People are living much longer now than they once did.

Alcohol or Drug Abuse

Everyone in a family is seriously affected if a member abuses drugs or alcohol.

Families often make the mistake of trying to ignore or cover up the situation. The biggest step in solving the problem is admitting it exists. The family and the person who is a serious drinker or drug abuser must recognize there is a real problem. Then they can begin to cope with it. Usually, however, outside help is needed.

As you learned in Chapter 3, there are many ways to get help—through school counselors, family doctors, members of the clergy, or social workers. They can put a family in touch with people especially trained to deal with problems of alcohol and drug abuse. There are also self-help groups such as AA (Alcoholics Anonymous), Al-Anon, and Alateen, which are organizations for families and friends of alcoholics. There are no membership fees

NOTE: Al-Anon publishes a book called *What's Drunk Mama?* It is a clear and simple explanation of alcoholism to a young child.

or dues required. To contact any of these groups, look up Alcoholics Anonymous in your local telephone book. This organization can refer you to the specific group you need in your area.

Separation or Divorce

When parents separate or divorce, the entire pattern of family life changes. *Divorce* is the legal ending of a marriage. When a marriage is legally ended, decisions about the distribution of property and income must be made. If there are children, the issue of **custody,** that is, who will take care of them, must be decided. Sometimes parents are given equal responsibility; this is called *joint custody.* Under joint custody, children divide their time between each parent. This can cause problems in their schooling and means they must form friendships in two places. Children in this situation do, however, have a chance to see each parent on a day-to-day basis for an extended period of time.

In many divorce or separation cases, one parent gets custody of the children. They then live with that parent all the time, while the other parent has visiting rights. This arrangement is called *sole custody.* In this situation the children benefit from the continuity of living in one place. However, they may not see the visiting parent as much as either the children or the absent parent would like.

When a couple with children separate or divorce, they should discuss the situation with their children in a simple, open way. Many children, even in the teenage years, feel guilty when their parents separate, imagining they are in some way

Remember that there are people to help you. Alateen helps alcoholics, their families, and their friends.

to blame. Parents need to reassure children that this is not the case. It is equally important that neither parent ask their children to take sides in arguments or to blame the other parent.

Family Violence

The use of physical force against another person is called *violence.* Some families experience violence against a spouse or a child. Parents or other family members who use violence are often suffering from extreme stress. They usually have low self-esteem. They feel that the only way they can be in charge in a family conflict is by the use of violence. Studies show that almost all people who abuse children were themselves abused as children.

Abuse can be verbal and emotional as well as physical. Any type of abuse can cause long-term personality changes.

DISCUSS: What would be the ideal living situation for a child whose divorced parents have joint custody and also live in the same town?

REINFORCEMENT: Have students list five reasons why a child would think he or she is to blame for a divorce.

Chapter 5/*The Family*   **113**

People who abuse their spouses or their children are in urgent need of counseling. Their families may avoid seeking help because they are afraid or embarrassed. Violence in a family is usually repeated, so if it occurs in your family, face the problem right away. If family discussions do no good, find outside help.

Financial Problems

Unemployment or other severe financial problems can cause a major family crisis. If a parent loses his or her job, or if a family faces heavy financial demands such as large medical expenses, family life changes. Children need to understand why their parents are so worried or why they can no longer afford to buy certain things. Parents should explain the situation to their children in a way that they can grasp. They need to explain that the family income has been reduced.

Getting Help

No matter what family crisis occurs, there are ways to get help. Families usually turn first to their extended family. Grandparents, uncles, aunts, or grown children can often provide the necessary emotional support, financial aid, or temporary shelter. Often, however, help from outside the family must be found.

Professional Help

You may feel your family needs help in a time of emotional crisis. If so, you can ask a teacher or guidance counselor at your school to recommend people who can give professional help. A minister, rabbi, priest, or other religious counselor can also provide emotional support in family crises. Troubled families can also be referred to other professionals who can help them work out problems.

When money is a problem, tempers can and often do rise.

Hotline Phone Numbers

If you are thinking about running away or have **run away,**

- Call **NATIONAL RUNAWAYS HOTLINE** 800-231-6946 (in Texas, 800-392-3352) They provide: counseling on resolving home problems, referrals to local social service agencies and to safe shelters. They will send help to your home in an emergency **abuse** situation or refer you to OPERATION HOME FREE for free transportation home.

- Call **NATIONAL HOTLINE FOR MISSING CHILDREN** 800-843-5678 They provide: counseling, referrals to local social service organizations, recommendations of local shelters.

- Call **NATIONAL RUNAWAY SWITCHBOARD** 800-621-4000 They provide: crisis intervention (for such problems as **drug abuse, child abuse,** and **sexual abuse**), referral to local service agencies and shelters, and transmittal of messages to parents without disclosing the runaway's location.

These hotline numbers offer confidentiality to callers.

If you are the victim of or have observed **child abuse,**

- Call **NATIONAL CHILD ABUSE HOTLINE** 800-422-4453 They provide: crisis intervention counseling and referrals to local services.

If you or someone you know has a **drug problem,**

- Call **COCAINE HELPLINE** 800-662-HELP (800-662-4357) or **800-COCAINE** (800-262-2463) They provide: counseling on drug problems, referrals to local support groups (such as **NARCOTICS ANONYMOUS** and **COCAINE ANONYMOUS**), to outpatient counseling programs, and to residential treatment centers.

If you have a **drinking problem,**

- Call **AA (ALCOHOLICS ANONYMOUS)** See your local telephone directory They provide: referral to their local support groups.

If you have a parent, friend, or relative with a **drinking problem,**

- Call **ALATEEN** See your local telephone directory under **AL-ANON** They provide: referral to local support groups of teenagers who have relatives or friends with drinking problems.

If you feel **depressed** or **suicidal,**

- Call a local **suicide prevention hotline.** Most telephone directories list these and other Crisis Numbers in the Community Services section at the front of the White Pages.

If you want information about AIDS,

- Call the **NATIONAL AIDS HOTLINE** 800-342-2437

If you had a big problem, where would you turn?

ART: Ask students to research one hotline in your community. What services does it provide? At what hours can a person call? Whom does it refer calls to? How many people does it serve?

You may be surprised at the number of people who can help.

Community agencies such as departments of health and welfare also make referrals. Social workers and social agencies, both public and private, can help families cope with financial crises and other disruptive situations. These include divorce, long-term illness, or cases of violence. Psychologists and psychiatrists can provide counseling in many crises.

Support groups are also very successful in working with addicts and their families. Other support groups exist for people with a variety of problems that affect them and their families. Most communities have self-help organizations for single parents, people recovering from specific illnesses, families of mental patients, and teenage children of abusive families. School guidance counselors, health services, and social service agencies can provide lists of such support groups.

Most large communities also have crisis centers where people can get immediate help in an emergency. Crisis centers provide services for victims of family violence, homeless families, runaway children, and people who are suicidal. There are also telephone "hotlines" for people who need someone to listen to their problems. Trained volunteers can refer callers to an agency for further help.

See page T53 for answers.

For Review

1. What kind of family is best able to cope with a major crisis?
2. Why do children often feel guilty when parents separate?
3. What kind of person is apt to use violence to solve family conflicts?

Learning to Manage

Keeping Active

Look back at the conversation between Mark and his mother on page 98. Now read how Mark and his family manage to improve the situation. Then answer the questions that follow.

Mark found his grandfather sitting alone in the living room when he came home from school the next day. He decided to try to talk to him.

"How's it going, Grandpa?"

"To tell the truth, Mark, I'm bored!"

"What would you like to be doing, Grandpa? We've all been trying to give you time and space to rest and get used to us, but maybe you've had enough!"

"Well, Mark, I'd like it if your mother would let me help her out with the laundry and cooking. You remember my famous chicken and dumplings, don't you?"

"I sure do. We all love it. Why don't you plan to cook it for us tomorrow night? Mom's going to the store tonight. Just give her a list of the ingredients."

Grandpa chuckled. "And reveal my cooking secrets? Never. I'd like to go with her and help her to shop."

Mark noticed that his grandfather was excited and happy about something for the first time since he had moved in two weeks ago. He decided that his hunch had been right—Grandpa needed to feel useful and busy. They had all been too busy themselves to notice.

That night they had a family talk. Grandpa explained how much he wanted to help out. They worked out a new schedule of home responsibilities so that Grandpa could share in the chores.

Mark's dad spoke up. "And how about helping me with my latest woodworking project, Dad? The bench I'm working on now could certainly use some of your finishing touches."

"Whoa! Slow down, everyone! You'll wear me out! Remember, I'm a retired man now." Grandpa laughed, then got more serious. "What I mean is, I'm retired from my *job,* but not from *life!* Thanks, family. We get to work tomorrow!"

Questions

1. Describe two ways in which the life of an older family member changes as a result of retiring and growing older.
2. How could you make a positive difference in the life of an elderly person who was living alone?
3. What resources are there in your community to help the elderly?

Chapter 5 Review

Summary

There are many different kinds of families, ranging from large, extended families to the two-person family. Families are always changing and adjusting to new situations. As well as dealing with a range of minor problems, families must also cope with some major crises. These include serious illness, death, divorce, and other extremely disruptive events.

Whatever kind of family you belong to, good communication, cooperation, and affection among all family members will contribute to making it a happy one.

Vocabulary

Complete each of the following sentences with the correct word from the vocabulary list below.

inflation (p. 102)   nuclear family (p. 99)
mobile (p. 101)   socialized (p. 108)
custody (p. 113)   economy (p. 102)
blended family (p. 100) rural (p. 100)
urban (p. 100)   siblings (p. 99)
family (p. 99)   extended family (p. 100)

1. Children become _____ when they learn to relate to a variety of other human beings.
2. A _____ society consists of people living on farms.
3. A _____ society is fluid or moving, with families moving to other parts of the country.
4. A _____ is a group of people who are related by blood or by marriage.
5. The national _____ is the way the country makes, buys, and sells material goods.
6. After a divorce, the parent who has _____ takes care of the children.
7. A _____ _____ is formed when two people who each have children get married and form a newly-created family.
8. In an _____ society most of the people live around big cities.
9. An _____ _____ includes the nuclear family plus other relatives.
10. A family consisting of a husband and wife and their children is called a _____ _____.
11. Brothers and sisters are called _____.
12. _____ occurs when prices rise continuously over a period of time.

Questions

• 1. Name at least three different kinds of families.
• 2. What is the difference between a rural society and an urban society?
•• 3. Why do many family members spend less time at home now than families did in the past?
•• 4. Why is it difficult for many extended families today to get together for a family reunion?
••• 5. How might inflation affect your family's decision to buy a new home?

The dots represent skill levels required to answer each question or complete each activity:

• requires recall and comprehension
•• requires application and analysis
••• requires synthesis and evaluation

6. Why is the eldest child in a family usually capable and responsible?

7. Name several advantages of being the middle child in a family. Think of a book or television character about whom this is true.

8. What can be difficult about having an elder sibling who has special skills in music or athletics?

9. How can you work toward improving relationships with siblings?

10. Why is the role of a single parent especially difficult?

11. Name two ways you can show you care about older family members.

12. Name the different stages of the family life cycle.

13. Why is it important for adolescents to be able to communicate well with their families?

14. How could you help out during a family crisis?

15. How should you explain the death of a family member to the children in that family?

Skill Activities

Many more activities are contained in the annotations within this chapter.

 1. Critical Thinking Select a family television show to watch with your entire family. After the show, share your opinions about it. How realistic was the family itself? Was the situation believable? Were the roles of the mother, father, and children similar to real life roles? Why or why not?

 2. Communication Speak to two older family members or other adults. Ask them to describe what their teenage years were like. What are their memories of school? What style of clothing did they wear? What family tasks did they share? Did they work after school? What did they like to do in their spare time? What are their fondest memories? What five things do they think are most different about teenage life today?

 3. Laboratory Contact a senior citizen center or a preschool near your school. Ask if you could prepare a special recipe for them. Make the food in class; then arrange a convenient time to deliver it as a class. When you go, visit with the residents or children for a while.

4. Decision Making Using a local telephone book, locate an agency or other resource that would help a family under stress. The family might face problems such as unemployment, housing, or financial difficulties. Record the agency's telephone number and share it with the class to create a "Family Stress Directory."

Using the directory you have put together, take turns role-playing family situations needing assistance. Choose a situation, look up the telephone number, and decide what questions you would ask to try to solve your problem.

Chapter 6
Child Development & Parenting

The dialogue below introduces "Being a Super Sitter," the Learning to Manage feature in this chapter. The case study is continued and the situation discussed further on page 141. See page T57 for teaching suggestions.

Vocabulary

"Bobby, let's do your robot puzzle."

"No, I don't want to. It's too easy for me."

"How about watching television?"

"I'm sick of television. Mike, don't you know any good things to do?"

"Why don't you think of something you want to do? You've certainly changed a lot since I babysat for you a few months ago!"

Section 6.1
Stages of Development

As you read, think about:

- the importance of proper diet and medical care for a pregnant woman. (p. 121)
- how children develop mentally and socially, as well as physically. (p. 123)
- the rapid growth that occurs in the first year of life. (p. 123)

At what time of life do the most dramatic and rapid changes occur? In the first five years we grow and change more than we do in all the remaining years of our lives. The most spectacular changes of all, however, take place during the nine months before we are born. During these months, all of our body parts and systems grow and develop.

The Prenatal Stage

The nine months that precede birth are referred to as the **prenatal stage** of development. During the first two months of development, the unborn baby is called an **embryo.** From the third month until birth, it is called a **fetus.**

The first three months of the prenatal stage are the most important. During this early period, vital organs such as the heart, the lungs, and the brain are formed. The digestive and nervous systems are formed then also. The embryo is particularly sensitive to the effects of viruses, radiation, and drugs at this early stage of development.

ENRICHMENT: Have students ask their mothers or other mothers they know if they are willing to discuss what they felt like when they were pregnant. Were they tired or active? Did their eating habits change, and if so, how?

What concern do you see here for the unborn baby?

Prenatal Care

It is important for any woman planning to have a baby to be in good health. Eating the right foods, having regular medical checkups, and avoiding harmful substances are some of the most important guidelines a pregnant woman should follow.

Diet

A developing fetus gets all its nutrients from what its mother eats. A nutritionally balanced diet is therefore essential for a pregnant woman. She should eat lots of green leafy vegetables, fresh fruit, milk, and whole-grain cereals. She should avoid empty calories in sugary and fatty foods.

REINFORCEMENT: Make the word *prenatal* less mysterious. Break it into syllables for pronunciation. Discuss the prefix *pre-* meaning "before," and explain that *natal* comes from the Latin for "birth."

121

Those first steps are big ones!

Medical Checkups

An expectant mother should be under medical supervision throughout her pregnancy. Her doctor will advise her concerning the diet and amount of exercise that is right for her. The doctor will also be on the alert for potential health problems of both mother and fetus.

Harmful Substances

A pregnant woman should take *no* drugs or medicines unless they are prescribed for her. *Everything* she takes into her body affects the fetus. Even aspirin and cold remedies can be dangerous. Some research indicates that the drug caffeine, found in colas, chocolate, tea, and coffee, can be harmful in large amounts.

Throughout pregnancy, a woman should not drink any alcohol. Cigarette smoking is also extremely harmful to the fetus. Tobacco contains poisons, among them nicotine and carbon monoxide, which are carried to the baby through the mother's bloodstream. Clearly, then, all controlled substances are potentially dangerous to the health of both the mother and the fetus.

For a Healthy Pregnancy

To help her baby get a good start in life, an expectant mother should follow these steps.

- Eat a balanced diet suggested by a nutritionist or doctor. Cut down on coffee, tea, cola drinks, chocolate, and sugary and fatty foods.
- Through proper diet and exercise, maintain the correct weight gain —neither too much nor too little.
- Follow a moderate exercise program recommended by her doctor. Avoid lifting heavy objects and activities that could cause physical strain or injury.
- Have regular checkups and carefully follow medical advice.
- Avoid all medicines and drugs, including simple home remedies such as aspirin.
- Consume no alcohol, tobacco, or other dangerous substances.

Types of Development

Children learn at different rates, but they learn new skills in the same order. First they learn to sit up, then they learn to

REINFORCEMENT: Have each student create a Healthy Pregnancy poster listing the six steps an expectant mother should follow. Have a contest to select the three best posters.

122   Unit 2/*Relationships*

stand. They understand pictures before they can read words. The activities that children learn as they grow are called **developmental tasks.** Children master these tasks partly by watching the people around them; they **pattern,** or model, their behavior on what they observe others doing. They also figure things out by experimenting.

Physical Development

Children's growth in size, proportion, and muscle coordination is referred to as their **physical development.** Babies grip objects and wave their arms, but they have little control over their movements. Toddlers have much greater control; for example, they can scribble with a crayon. However, children cannot form letters well until they are four or five.

Mental Development

The growing ability to learn, to reason, and to make judgments is called **mental development.** A large part of mental development involves children's ability to understand language. Most of our thoughts are formed in words. Children can understand words before they can speak them. Step-by-step, they understand and can use words, sentences, and then paragraphs.

Emotional Development

As children grow up, they learn to express their feelings in acceptable ways. They learn how their emotional expression af-

fects the people around them. At a later stage, they learn to understand other people's feelings. If you have a baby sister or brother, you probably remember the first time your younger sibling smiled back at you.

Social Development

As children develop, they become increasingly aware of other people. The way children learn to relate to the people around them is referred to as their **social development.** Children of a similar age react to people in a similar way. Toddlers, for example, do not share their toys with one another; this behavior is learned at a later stage of development.

The First Year of Life

Enormous changes and growth occur in the first year of life. Newborns cannot lift their heads or roll over, but by the end of the first year, many babies can move around by themselves. Most babies triple their birth weight by the end of their first year. Besides physical changes, babies also make great strides in mental and social development during their first year of life.

The First Three Months

A newborn baby is sometimes a strange-looking little person. New babies are often red and wrinkled, and their eyes do not focus. Their sight is not fully developed; they hear better than they see. Newborn infants are completely dependent; they

RETEACHING: Even though the words *growth* and *development* are sometimes used to mean the same thing, *growth* is measurable change in a child's size. *Development* means an increase in physical, emotional, social, and intellectual skills.

ENRICHMENT: Have students ask their parents to tell them when they first walked, talked, wrote their names, and so on. Have students make a time line showing some of the great events in their early development.

Lifting up the upper body is a big accomplishment at six months.

need constant care and a lot of affection. They can communicate only by crying. Their **reflexes** (automatic responses) are strong. They suck and grasp and cry whenever they are feeling uncomfortable or hungry.

When a baby cries, it is important to see what is the matter. The baby could be hungry, wet, hot, cold, or tired. The baby may also be in pain. Whatever the reason, he or she needs attention. Picking up and comforting a crying baby is not "spoiling" the infant. Experience will tell you which kind of cry indicates hunger and which means the baby is uncomfortable in some other way. Never leave an infant of this age to cry for any length of time. Doing so can affect later development, for it causes the baby to feel insecure.

Three to Nine Months

Between the third and ninth month of the first year, babies begin to respond more to people. Parents and other care givers, such as relatives or babysitters, should talk to the baby at this stage even though what they say is not understood. Usually, babies at this stage respond to a soft, friendly voice, especially the voices of their parents, with babbling and cooing sounds. Talking, singing, and reading to babies will help them use language at a later stage of development.

The first year brings great changes.

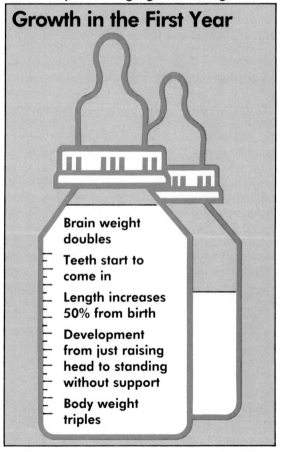

Growth in the First Year

Brain weight doubles

Teeth start to come in

Length increases 50% from birth

Development from just raising head to standing without support

Body weight triples

At age one, food doesn't always make its way to the mouth.

During these months most infants learn to sit without support. They become more active—kicking, rolling, wiggling, and trying to crawl. At this stage, some babies cut their first teeth.

Nine to Twelve Months

All babies develop at a different rate. During the last part of their first year, many babies crawl or stand up holding on to something. Some pull themselves along on their stomachs, others crawl on hands and knees. Either way is normal. Some babies walk alone by this time.

Within this period, some infants become shy with anyone outside their close family. This behavior does not last long, but it can be a problem when a baby is left with a sitter.

As babies approach their first birthday, they begin to understand when parents approve or disapprove of what they are doing. They know the meaning of the word *no*.

Many one-year-olds learn to feed themselves with their fingers, though they may also have fun dropping food on the floor. This stage is one of the messiest, and it requires a lot of patience from parents. Fortunately, by this time parents are probably getting more sleep. Most one-year-olds sleep through the night and still take short naps during the day.

PHOTO: Ask students to comment on why they think children are so fond of sandboxes.

Toddlers are experts at exploring the world.

Toddlers

Children between one year and three years old are often called *toddlers,* because they are learning to walk or toddle around. Children at this stage are extremely demanding. They are constantly exploring and are therefore apt to get into trouble. They must be watched all the time so that they will not hurt themselves falling or pulling down heavy objects.

Toddlers at this stage want to be independent but have little reasoning ability. They are easily frustrated or upset when they do not accomplish what they set out to do. They are eager to communicate long before they can form sentences that express their ideas. Children in these years often become fussy about food. They are very active and need a lot of exercise as well as a lot of rest. They can easily get overtired. They enjoy having people around them, including children, but they have not yet learned to cooperate with other children.

Preschoolers

Children's growth rate slows down after their fourth birthday, but their mental development advances rapidly. Their language abilities increase greatly. They ask endless questions, which can be tiresome for parents to answer. It is important to

RETEACHING: Stress that because of the enormous curiosity of toddlers, they have an uncanny capacity for overturning objects, breaking things, and hurting themselves. Toddlers must be watched constantly.

spend time talking and listening to children at this stage, even if you can't answer every question. It takes energy and patience to care for small children.

Most children are becoming more independent; they can dress, bathe, and brush their teeth themselves. They can be taught acceptable social behavior such as table manners. Parents should not expect too much at this stage, however. Children in this age group are often afraid of the dark and of being left alone. They are quite capable in many ways. They are, however, still too young to be left by themselves or with older children.

Children of all ages enjoy being read to. Preschoolers especially like to hear the same story over and over again; it gives them a feeling of security. They also enjoy repeating stories or making up their own. This use of imagination should be encouraged. It is extremely important to read to young children. It teaches them the joy of reading and prepares them for learning to read themselves.

At the preschool stage, children begin to relate directly to other children and to understand sharing and following a few simple rules.

Did You Know?

A child's sense of humor changes as the child develops. Children between 18 and 24 months think pretending that a shoe is a telephone is hilarious. At two and three, they have learned to use words to create similar "jokes" and may call a cat a cow just for the fun of getting it wrong on purpose. Between three and six, kids laugh at the unusual, such as a cat with wings or upside-down furniture. By six or seven, they can enjoy jokes based on double meanings and will roar at "Grandma says I've grown a foot—so I need an extra shoe!"

See page T58 for answers.
For Review
1. Name at least three important guidelines for a healthy pregnancy.
2. Give two examples of developmental tasks.
3. Name three dramatic changes that take place in the first year of life.

Section 6.2
Parenting—Caring for Children

As you read, think about:
■ the important roles and responsibilities parents have. (p. 128)
■ the emotional, physical, and mental needs of children. (p. 128)

One of life's greatest challenges is being a parent. It is a great responsibility to meet the physical, mental, and emotional needs of a child. And it's a 24-hour a day job. It means work, but it also means fun.

ENRICHMENT: Ask students to take a preschool age sibling, cousin, or neighbor for a walk around the neighborhood or for a quiet chat in the yard. Have students report to the class the type of questions the preschooler asked.

DISCUSS: What can you do to make a bedtime story more interesting to a young child?

Sometimes it's hard to tell whether the parent or the child is enjoying an activity more.

A Parent's Roles and Responsibilities

Raising a child is a long-range undertaking that demands time, energy, and money. Being a parent requires a great amount of unselfishness and maturity. It takes a responsible person who is able, when necessary, to put the child's needs before her or his own.

Some couples postpone having children or remain childless because they want to continue their education or concentrate on their careers. Others feel they cannot afford the expense of raising children.

Most married couples, however, choose to make the necessary sacrifices for the pleasures of having a family.

Economic Factors

Raising a child is a major expense for a family. Besides the initial cost of having the baby—hospital bills, basic baby equipment—expenses increase as the child grows up. More living space may be needed. Food, clothing, medical care, transportation, child care costs, and recreational expenses can add up to a large sum. Educating a child can also be very expensive particularly if the education includes college. Family income may decrease if a parent leaves a job in order to care for one or more children.

Meeting Children's Needs

As you learned in Chapter 1, everyone has basic physical and emotional needs. It is most important that these needs be met from birth. Children can then grow up to be healthy, productive adults. Children depend on their parents and other care givers to provide love, food, clothing, and shelter. Without these basics, children have difficulty moving from one stage of development to the next.

Emotional Needs

Children's emotional needs are not as obvious as their physical needs, but they are equally important. Most children tell

REINFORCEMENT: Write the word *parent* vertically on the blackboard. Have students think of words that begin with each letter to describe qualities or characteristics of a parent.

RETEACHING: Stress that students can help to build a child's sense of confidence and security by always having a positive attitude when talking to a child.

128   Unit 2/*Relationships*

others directly when they are tired, cold, or hungry. On the other hand, it is not easy for children to say "I need love" or "I need attention." They might throw blocks, whine and moan, or just sit and pout in an attempt to get attention.

Love and Acceptance From birth onward, children need to be shown a great deal of affection. They need to be comforted when they are hurt or upset. They need to know that their families accept them, trust them, and enjoy being with them. Children whose emotional needs are not met can develop both physical and mental problems. They may become withdrawn. They may lose their appetites and show a lack of energy. They may develop learning problems at school and have difficulty making friends. Children, like adults, need to feel secure.

Positive Self-Concept Parents have a great influence on the way their children view themselves. To develop a positive self-concept, children need to know that their families support them and take pride in their accomplishments. They need to know that their parents not only care about what they do and say but also enjoy their company. A child's self-concept is built on awareness of the acceptance and love offered by his or her family.

Discipline One of the most difficult and important aspects of parenting is learning how to discipline children effectively. **Discipline** (*DIS*–uh–plin) is the task of teaching children what is acceptable behavior and what is not.

PHOTO: Ask students what concern for the child's safety they see in this photograph.

Pride is a common emotion among parents.

Children must know that while parents may disapprove of their behavior, they never withdraw their love.

To be effective, discipline must be suited to the age and developmental stage of the child. You cannot teach children to behave in a way that is beyond their physical, mental, or emotional development. For example, there is no point in disciplining a two-year-old for eating in a messy way. The child is too young to avoid making a mess.

Discipline should never be an outlet for a parent's anger. Its only purpose should

DISCUSS: Four-year old Joshua takes his two-year-old sister's toy away. You explain carefully that he shouldn't do that. Joshua does it again. What do you do?

REINFORCEMENT: Have students list five ways to develop self-confidence in a child.

Chapter 6/*Child Development & Parenting* **129**

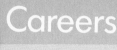

Parenting as a Career

Entertainer, supervisor, protector of the weak, role model for the young, care giver to the sick, counselor to the troubled, teacher, coach, one-on-one listener, group leader—which of these careers would you like to have? If you become a parent, you will have them all—and others, too. What's more, you will practice these varied careers day in and day out.

Parenting is often taken for granted, but it is very important. It's a career of commitment to others, but there are no prizes. It's a career of great rewards but no salaries. It's a career of sacrifices, some large, some small. They range from giving up sleep to comfort a crying baby to taking a second job to pay for college tuition. It's a career that you can't give up once you've begun it. It's a career based on love. Parents begin to communicate love and security by holding, talking to, and providing for their newborn baby. The growing child's use of language marks a big step. Parents are usually the primary teachers of this important skill. When a child can use words, the parents' communication role changes and expands. *Really* listening, negotiating compromises, and "being there no matter what" are some of the communication skills parents need. And these—like the rest of parenting skills—are in demand all the time. Can you think of a career more challenging than parenting?

be to teach a child to behave in an acceptable way. Discipline should be carried out calmly but with firmness. It should be consistent. If a specific behavior is sometimes punished and sometimes not, the child will be confused. Children must understand the reason they are being disciplined.

Physical Needs

Correct diet, clothing, and enough sleep and exercise are more important during childhood than at any other time of life. By being aware of their children's physical needs, parents can help them to lead the healthiest lives possible. Particular atten-

What are the advantages of eating a snack like this one?

NOTE: Before entering school, children must receive the following immunizations: diphtheria, tetanus, and pertussis; measles, mumps, and rubella; meningitis vaccine and tuberculin skin tests.

tion should be paid to medical checkups, nutrition, and safety.

Medical Checkups

All babies and young children should have regular medical checkups. During the infant's first year, parents should be in close contact with a doctor or health clinic. In this way they can make sure that their child is developing at the correct rate. Parents can also get advice concerning correct diet, clothing, and other physical needs.

It is also important that young children receive **immunization** against common childhood diseases such as diphtheria, polio, and measles. Immunization protects against these dangerous diseases.

Nutrition

What babies and young children eat in their first few years significantly affects their health for all their remaining years. They grow so fast that an improper diet for even a few months can prevent bones, muscles, and vital organs from developing correctly. A child's mental development can also be permanently damaged through insufficient nutrients during the first few years of life.

Young children should be encouraged to establish good eating habits. Family meals should include protein, green vegetables, yellow vegetables, fresh fruit, and whole-grain cereals. Candy, rich desserts, and fried foods such as french fries and potato

Could you add any information on body language?

How to Talk to a Child

Instead of saying: "You are so clumsy!"
Say: "We all have accidents. Help me wipe it up."

Instead of saying: "Come in the house, *now*!"
Say: "Let's go inside and have some juice."

Instead of saying: "What is *that*?"
Say: "Tell me about your picture. "

Instead of saying: "What a mess! Clean it up!"
Say: "Here are some boxes to put your toys in."

Instead of saying: "You're a bad girl!"
Say: "That's a bad thing to do."

Instead of saying: "Stay off the slide."
Say: "Let me push you on the swings."

ART: Ask students to add two more examples to this list.

ENRICHMENT: Ask students to speculate on why some mothers prefer formula. Have them make a chart comparing infant formula and mother's milk in terms of cost, ease of use, and nutritional value.

What would a child like most about this room?

chips should be kept to a minimum. Highly spiced and peppery food can upset a young child's digestion. Milk and fruit juice contain healthful nutrients. They do not contain the caffeine and other harmful ingredients found in sugary soft drinks.

Clothing Young children's clothing should protect them from the environment and should be comfortable. In cold weather, clothes should protect children from cold and damp. In hot weather and inside well-heated buildings, clothes should be light and loose. Clothing should never be so tight that it restricts movement nor so loose that a child can get tangled up in it.

It will help children to dress themselves if their clothes are easy to put on.

Exercise and Rest Children need to exercise in order for their bodies to grow.

Children require plenty of rest. In addition to a long night's sleep, they need naps during the day. Parents should schedule regular nap times and see that children have a quiet, comfortable place to rest.

DISCUSS: Many daycare centers and preschools do not allow children to bring candy, chocolate, gum, or soft drinks to school. Discuss reasons for that rule.

Shelter and Safety Children need comfortable, safe, and happy living space. Parents must provide close supervision

New parents often need and want a safety checklist.

Child Safety Checklist

Falls
- Keep crib sides up.
- Put gates across stairways.
- Tie kitchen chairs to table legs.
- Fasten high chair safety straps.

Poisons
- Keep medicines locked up.
- Lock up cleaning materials.
- Place cosmetics out of reach.

Water
- Never leave a child alone in a wading pool or bathtub.
- Keep children away from open or frozen bodies of water.

Dangerous Objects
- Remove pins and sharp objects.
- Remove sharp-edged furniture.
- Remove low-hanging tablecloths.
- Lock up dangerous tools and equipment.

Burns
- Lock up matches and cigarette lighters.
- Turn pot handles away from the front of the stove.
- Keep electrical cords out of reach.
- Place gates or screens in front of fireplaces and wood stoves.
- Put safety plugs in outlets.

NOTE: Research shows that moderate but regular exercise is more beneficial than long sessions of strenuous exercise.

Can you pick out the concerns for safety here?

and a safe environment. Young children must be protected from falls, burns, and dangerous toys. Rooms where young children play should be childproof. The chart on page 132 lists various ways to protect children.

Babies need to sleep in a crib or a bed with sides, so that they cannot roll off. If a crib is used, it should have properly spaced bars so that the baby's head will not get caught between the slats. Plastic covers and pillows should not be used. It is possible for a baby to smother if covered by thin plastic.

Parents should begin teaching children safety rules as soon as they can understand them. Young children should never be allowed to run into the street. When preschoolers walk with parents, they should be shown how to follow traffic lights and cross streets safely.

Mental Needs

Children learn through their senses: sight, hearing, smell, taste, and touch. From birth onward, children learn more quickly if their environment provides a variety of things for them to experience. Even a tiny baby will get bored without stimulation. Children's senses should be stimulated, too. Babies need to have a variety of shapes and colors to look at. They should hear people laughing, singing, and talking to them. Infants should be played with and talked to from birth.

When a child learns a new skill or even tries something new, parents should offer encouragement and praise.

Language The most important aspect of mental growth in young children is the

DISCUSS: Give examples of ways in which parents can childproof a home. List examples on the blackboard, and have students add to the list.

REINFORCEMENT: Have students brainstorm a list of places where they could take children to see new and colorful sights.

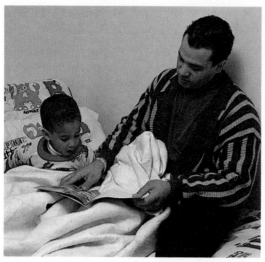

Can you think of an ending to each long, exciting day that would be any more cozy than this?

stage when they learn to understand and speak language. As you have learned, children should be talked to at all stages of development. They should also be listened to and encouraged to express ideas verbally. Adults can also help children develop their imaginations by playing with them, explaining things to them, and telling them stories.

Adults should help children understand words by pointing to and naming people and objects. Rather than using baby talk, parents and other care givers should speak in sentences, using regular conversational tones. Telling a child what you are doing as you do it also helps. The child can learn new words and begin to understand the way words are put together into sentences.

Reading to Children Research shows that reading to young children helps them later when they themselves learn to read.

Children should also have simple books of their own that they can look at. Even very young children like to look at illustrations.

Preschool children enjoy trips to the children's section of the library, where they can help select their own books. It is a good idea to schedule time every night to read to children before they go to sleep. Get them to participate by asking them questions about the illustrations and what they think will happen next in the story.

Television Parents should regulate how much television children watch and what programs they see. When possible, programs should be prescreened for suitability.

Television watching is a *passive* activity, that is, the viewer just watches rather than actively participating. Children need the stimulation of *active* play, where they join in and use their imaginations. They need to interact with adults and with other children. Parents should therefore set clear limits on television time.

Some television programs help children expand their knowledge about the world at large. However, there are many programs that can overexcite children and frighten them. Seeing violence and other unacceptable behavior on television may lead children to imitate that behavior.

Children with Special Needs Some children have learning disabilities. It takes them longer to learn certain skills such as walking and talking. These children need a great deal of loving care and patient teaching of simple tasks. They may require extra attention from people who are especially trained to help them. Like all children, they also need to see and hear a variety of things and to interact with other people.

Children who are unusually intelligent or who have a special talent also need special attention. They learn quickly and may become bored with games and books that interest other children of their age. Such children need toys, games, and other activities that challenge them to perform at their full capacity.

See page T59 for answers.

For Review

1. What are the three major responsibilities of a parent?
2. How is a child's self-concept built?
3. Name the three basic physical needs of a child.

Section 6.3

Successful Babysitting

As you read, think about:

- ■ the steps involved in being a successful babysitter. (p. 135)
- ■ the basic needs of children who are cared for by a babysitter. (p. 136)
- ■ how to deal with different kinds of children when babysitting. (p. 138)

Babysitting is a great way to learn about children. It gives you the satisfaction of being in control of a situation. Furthermore, you get paid for your work.

DISCUSS: If you were a parent of two young children, what qualifications would you be looking for in a babysitter to take care of them on Saturday nights? List qualifications on the board.

PHOTO: Ask students why it is often such a difficult moment for the babysitter when parents leave.

A babysitter's first priority is to follow the parents' instructions.

Babysitting, however, is not an easy job. It requires an alert, responsible attitude. What does a babysitter need to know in order to do the job well?

Getting the Information

When you take a babysitting job, you are accepting responsibility for the health and safety of someone else's children. Your babysitting job will run more smoothly if you plan it carefully. You'll find it helpful to keep a babysitting notebook with all the information you need written in it.

Accepting the Job

First you need your parents' permission to babysit. Find out what time you must be back home before you take on the job.

Establish what your duties will be and how much you will be paid. Babysitting

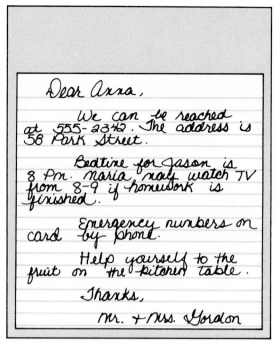

Dear Anna,

We can be reached at 555-2342. The address is 58 Park Street.

Bedtime for Jason is 8 PM. Maria may watch TV from 8-9 if homework is finished.

Emergency numbers on card by phone.

Help yourself to the fruit on the kitchen table.

Thanks,
Mr. + Mrs. Gordon

When you babysit, be sure parents give you the information you need.

jobs are usually paid by the hour. Agree on the span of time the job will cover.

Find out how many children you will be caring for and their ages.

Once you accept a job, write down the family's name, address, and telephone number and the exact time you are expected. It is most important to be on time. If you cannot keep the appointment, call at the earliest moment and explain why you must cancel or be late. The family is depending on you.

Interview the Parents

Be sure you get all the information you need before the parents leave you in charge. Bring your notebook and write down the children's names and ages.

ENRICHMENT: Ask students to make a chart comparing baby-sitting with other part-time jobs for rate of pay, flexibility, and levels of responsibility and reward.

Telephone Numbers Write down the address and telephone number where the parents will be. If they cannot be reached by telephone, get the number of a responsible adult you can call in an emergency. Take the number of the family's doctor and write down emergency numbers— police, fire department, poison control center, and hospital.

Schedules and Routines Take notes on the children's routines. Include the time they go to bed, what you should give them to eat, what they are allowed to watch on television, and any other special activities.

Ask for a brief tour of the house or apartment. You need to know where to find the children's clothing, first-aid supplies, fire extinguishers and fire exits, and a flashlight.

Find out if the children need special food or medicines and if they should take baths. It is better not to take the responsibility for bathing a small baby, since this job can be hazardous. Be sure you know how to change a diaper if that may be required.

Basic Care

Your most important duty is to keep the children in your care safe and take care of their basic needs. You should give the children your full attention. Even when they are asleep, you should check on them at least every half hour. Parents may suggest that you do housework in addition to watching the children. If they do, explain that you cannot do housework, since

REINFORCEMENT: Ask students to list common minor accidents that could happen to a young child in the home. Discuss ways to guard against these accidents.

you need to spend your time caring for the children.

Watch the Children If you have to answer the telephone or are preparing food, do not forget to see that the children are safe. Do not let them wander into another room. If the telephone rings, take a small, active child with you when you go to answer it. Don't get so busy cooking or talking that you become unaware of what the children are doing.

Your Own Behavior

Avoid making any unnecessary telephone calls. Do nothing that would intrude on the privacy of the family. Do not entertain friends. Let *no one* into the house unless you have specific instructions to do so. Do not open the door to strangers, and keep first floor windows locked. Do not give information over the telephone about where the family is or say that you are alone with the children. Keep the television, stereo, or radio low.

Safety

Pay close attention to what the children are doing and take care to see that their surroundings are safe. Most accidents can then be prevented. The safety chart on page 132 will prove helpful. In spite of your careful safety procedures, an emergency may occur. It is important to be prepared for possible emergencies.

Stay calm. Know what immediate steps are necessary. Don't be shy about getting immediate help, either by telephone or from a neighbor.

First Aid

Be prepared for possible injuries. See Chapter 3 for information about first aid and Chapter 11 for tips on home safety. If at all possible, take a first-aid course. Your school, local hospital, or health center can direct you to first-aid classes.

If a child gets a small scrape or bruise, you can handle the situation yourself. Apply cold water to the bruise. Bathe the small wound with soap and water and apply antiseptic. Stop minor bleeding with clean gauze or tissue.

If a child is more seriously injured, get adult help as quickly as possible. If you can't reach a neighbor or the parents quickly, call the emergency number,

Do you know where you can find the supplies and information that you'll need?

which is 911 in most areas. Give the address and describe the injury. Remember, you have other emergency numbers in your notebook. Call the parents and tell them what has happened.

In Case of Fire

In case of any fire, calmly get the children out of the building. Take them to a neighbor and call the fire department from there, or use a fire box. As you exit, feel each door to see if the next room is burning. If smoke is a problem, cover your own and the children's faces with a wet cloth and stay close to the floor. (Smoke rises, so stay as low as possible.) You should always know where fire exits and a flashlight are at the beginning of a babysitting job.

Care Plus

All babysitters try to fulfill their most important responsibility—keeping children safe. However, a babysitter who provides basic care is different from one who gives the children care *plus* special attention. There are some things you can do to be a super babysitter. Know how to calm a child who is upset. Be able to find the right stuffed animal at bedtime and provide special toys for children of different ages.

When Parents Leave

Young children often cry when their parents leave. Comfort them and explain that

Did You Know?

Supplies for many children's art projects can be found in the kitchen.

■ Children like to color on large grocery bags. The bags make excellent masks with string and tinfoil glued on for hair or decorations.
■ Using brown paper sandwich bags and crayons, children can make hand puppets.
■ Uncooked pasta of many different shapes can be glued onto construction paper to make interesting designs.

their parents will come back. Then draw their attention to something of interest. For example, you might draw a funny picture and ask them to guess what you are drawing. Do not expect them to quiet down right away.

Aggressive Children

If a child becomes aggressive and tries to hit or kick you, respond with calmness. Never hit back, but hold the child so that you are not hurt. Children who behave like this should be told firmly that this is not allowed. *Distract* the child, that is, get the child interested in something else—a game or another activity. Some children test babysitters by trying to get around rules and misbehaving. Be calm but firm. Be sure to tell parents about any problems you have with behavior like this.

Bedtime

Getting children to sleep can be a problem. Before parents leave, have them tell you in front of the children when they are to go to bed. Give children plenty of advance notice when bedtime approaches, so that they can finish their game or other activity. Be sure you know the child's special bedtime routine. Some children need a special blanket or stuffed animal to sleep with. Many children enjoy hearing a story read before they go to sleep.

Games for Children

A good babysitter of young children does not actually do much "sitting." Small children are active and need a lot of mental and physical activity. It is fun to play interactive games with them. You may want to use some of the suggestions given below. Just be sure that active games are not dangerous and do not damage anything in the house. Do not allow children to "rough house." Keep them active but under control. If they get overexcited, switch from an active game to a quiet one, or tell or read them a story. If parents permit, the children might watch a television program appropriate for their age.

Infants Babies up to one year old like a lot of attention balanced with quiet times. From around six months they like the games of "Pat-a-Cake" and "Peek-a-Boo." They like to be bounced gently and enjoy being sung to. They like nursery rhymes even though they may not understand them. As they learn to sit up, they

When the game is a good one, children will play it over and over.

can entertain themselves with blocks and toy animals. Be sure any toys and other objects are not small enough to swallow and have no sharp edges or have dangerous parts. For example, infants can choke on the eyes of toy animals.

Toddlers Children between one and three can play simple games, such as easy forms of hide-and-seek. They enjoy it if you roll a ball to them and they try to roll it back. They also enjoy simple dancing and singing games. Children of two or three enjoy building blocks and like to put objects into containers. They also like to scribble on paper and work with play dough.

Preschoolers Preschoolers are more coordinated than toddlers. They can throw and sometimes catch a large ball. They like games of "Follow the Leader"

Chapter 6/*Child Development & Parenting*   **139**

PHOTO: Have any of your students ever tried a very messy activity with children? What are some of the things care givers can do to minimize the mess?

How can you let children use their imaginations?

and enjoy dancing, singing, and skipping games. They like to march around to music and play "London Bridge." For quiet activities, they enjoy drawing, painting, and working with clay. (These activities require supervision and cleanup time afterward.) Children in this age group are very imaginative and enjoy role-playing, dressing up, and storytelling. They enjoy playing with toy cars and trucks and with dolls and hand puppets.

School Age Children between the ages of six and eight enjoy outdoor active games. They need careful supervision. Parents should give permission before children go to a playground, park, or anywhere else outside the house. Children of six and seven enjoy simple card games and board games. Older children can play more difficult games. They may

enjoy puzzles and word games, too. For example, they may like "Twenty Questions" or thinking of things that begin with each letter of the alphabet. They love general conversation and listening to, telling, and reading stories. They also like to dance and to sing children's songs, especially those with many verses such as "Old MacDonald Had a Farm."

See page T59 for answers.

For Review

1. Name at least three points you need to establish before you accept a babysitting job.
2. What are the major responsibilities of a babysitter?
3. How should you respond to an aggressive child?

DISCUSS: Talk about evening television programs that might be appropriate for children between the ages of six and eight.

ENRICHMENT: Have students make a babysitter's idea book of activities for various ages. They should write a title for it and decorate its cover.

See page T57 for teaching suggestions.

Learning to Manage

Being a Super Sitter

Look back at the conversation between Mike and Bobby on page 120. Now read how Mike tries to manage the situation. Then answer the questions that follow.

Somehow Mike got through the evening with Bobby, but neither of them was too happy about the way it went. Mike loved working with children and decided to try to get some good babysitting tips before he saw Bobby again. He was amazed at how much Bobby had changed in just a few months. Where could he get some good babysitting ideas?

On Monday, Mike passed the new Home Economics class bulletin board on his way to gym. He stopped to read. The Future Homemakers of America (FHA) group was holding a workshop that Wednesday to help make toys for a local hospital. EVERYONE WELCOME was written in large letters. Mike decided to go. He knew a lot of kids in FHA. Besides, he might learn about something to entertain Bobby.

The meeting was a great success. The Home Economics class had cut out patterns for hand puppets made from washable cloth.

They made play dough in the kitchens and sealed it into plastic storage bags. They combined 1 cup of flour, ½ cup salt, 2 teaspoons cream of tartar, 1 cup water with a few drops of food coloring, and 2 tablespoons of vegetable oil. They put this in a saucepan and cooked it until it formed a ball when stirred. Another great idea for Bobby!

The last project was Mike's favorite: a spaceship made from a large carton. They cut holes for a hatch door and windows and created a control panel using a tin pie plate as a wheel. Mike was beginning to feel like a four-year-old himself and couldn't wait for the chance to make a spaceship with Bobby.

When the meeting ended, Mrs. Chin, the Home Economics teacher, smiled at Mike and thanked him for coming.

"I should thank *you,* Mrs. Chin! With all of these great ideas for toys, my babysitting business will be booming!"

Questions

1. How can you find out more about taking care of children? Include any home, school, and community resources you have.
2. Write out a simple babysitting plan for spending a day with a preschooler.

See pages T59–61 for answers and suggestions.

Chapter 6 Review

Summary

Caring for babies and young children is a great responsibility, but it is a rewarding job. Understanding the role of parents and the way children grow and change will help you understand and relate to the needs of children.

Babysitters also need to understand what to expect of the children of various ages that they care for. Babysitting experience will help you if you become a parent later on. It could also lead to a future career working with children.

Vocabulary

Complete each of the following sentences with the correct word from the vocabulary list below.

immunization (p. 131)   reflexes (p. 124)
fetus (p. 121)   physical
embryo (p. 121)   development (p. 123)
mental   discipline (p. 129)
  development (p. 123)   social
prenatal   development (p. 123)
  stage (p. 121)   developmental
pattern (p. 123)   tasks (p. 123)

1. Automatic responses are called _____ _____.

2. When children learn tasks by observing the people around them, we say that they _____ their behavior.

3. The nine months that precede birth are called the _____ _____.

4. _____ prevents children from catching dangerous diseases, such as diphtheria, polio, and measles.

5. _____ _____ concerns children's growth in size and proportion as well as their muscle coordination.

6. _____ is the task of teaching children what is acceptable behavior and what is not.

7. A child's growing ability to learn, to reason, and to make judgments is called _____ _____.

8. During the first two months of prenatal development, the unborn child is called an _____.

9. _____ _____ is the way children learn to relate to the people around them.

10. _____ _____ are activities that children learn as they grow.

11. From three months until birth, the unborn child is referred to as the _____.

Questions

1. Why is a nutritionally balanced diet so important for a pregnant woman?
2. What effect does a pregnant woman's smoking have on the fetus?
3. Name two ways that young children learn developmental tasks.
4. How is language important to a child's development?
5. Why do newborn babies cry? Name at least three possibilities.

The dots represent skill levels required to answer each question or complete each activity:

• requires recall and comprehension
•• requires application and analysis
••• requires synthesis and evaluation

142

6. What do you think might be most frustrating about being a toddler? Explain your answer. What do you think is the most frustrating thing about taking care of a toddler?

7. Why do preschoolers ask so many questions?

8. Discuss the importance of reading stories to preschoolers. Explain which kinds of development are affected by this activity.

9. What do you think is the most important emotional need of a child? How is that different from what you think is the most important emotional need of an adolescent? Explain your answer.

10. Why is a proper diet so important for babies and young children?

11. Name three household items that can be dangerous to children. Describe ways to protect children from them.

12. In your opinion, what is the most important way to stimulate a baby's mental needs? Explain your answer.

13. What should you do if the telephone rings while you are taking care of a small child?

14. How would you comfort a child who is crying because his or her parents have just gone out?

15. What activities would you plan if you were asked to babysit for two children, aged three and six? Explain how the age differences influenced your answer.

Many more activities are contained in the annotations within this chapter.

Skill Activities

1. Laboratory With your lab partners, create cooked play-dough. Use the recipe on page 141. Divide the dough into four balls and add different colors of food coloring. Show a preschool child in your family or neighborhood the many things that can be made with it.

2. Decision Making You are babysitting for two preschoolers on a rainy day. In class, brainstorm a list of activities you can do with the children. Be sure to suit the activities to the ages of the children.

3. Communication Create a "Babysitter Information Sheet" to take with you on your next babysitting job. Include questions that cover all the information that you will need to have to take care of the children. What time do they go to bed? How can you reach the parents? What is the telephone number of their doctor? What snacks can the children have?

4. Laboratory Observe a child or a group of children at play. Take notes on their behavior and their abilities. What toys and activities do they enjoy? How do they respond to other children? Share your notes with your class.

Unit 3

Resource Management

Chapter 7
Careers

Vocabulary

The dialogue below introduces "Focus on the Future," the Learning to Manage feature in this chapter. The case study is continued and the situation discussed further on page 163. See page T63 for teaching suggestions.

"How do we find out what home economics jobs are really like, Mrs. Lopez? I'm working on that careers assignment you gave us. I've looked in the library and read job descriptions, but they don't tell the whole story."

"The best way is to talk to people working in a specific job, Tom. They can tell you the real advantages and disadvantages."

"Can we do that at school, Mrs. Lopez? What if we plan a "Career Day" and ask people in home economics jobs to come to talk to us? Even though we won't be choosing jobs for a while, it will give us great firsthand information."

Section 7.1
Decisions About Work

As you read, think about:

- why people need and want to work. (p. 147)
- ways to select the right career. (p. 148)
- how to get information about various fields of work. (p. 149)

As Tom's class is learning, one of the major decisions in life is choosing a career. What do you need to know to make this decision? You need to analyze your special interests, skills, and aptitudes. You must explore the requirements, training, and education for a wide variety of jobs. It is not too early to begin thinking about the world of work.

Will you find the career that's right for you? You should begin by thinking about the things you enjoy most.

Why Work?

Most adults must earn a living. People work to pay for their own needs and the needs of their families. There are, however, more reasons for having a job than just making money. Work satisfies the basic human desire to be useful and active. Doing a job well makes you feel satisfied with yourself. It gives you a sense of accomplishment and allows you to spend your time and effort constructively. Work gives life focus and dignity.

We Work for Money

A primary reason for working is to earn a living. People need money to pay for basic needs such as food, shelter, clothing, medical care, and transportation. Many people also want the luxuries that money can buy. These luxuries include travel, entertainment, meals in restaurants, expensive electronic equipment, and the like.

Work as Satisfaction

The amount of money people need and want varies with their values and goals. Some people feel that what they earn is the most important factor in a job. Others feel that the personal satisfaction is most important. Think about which of these applies to you. You may choose a career in social services that does not pay a high salary but gives you the satisfaction of helping people. Jobs in the arts often pay

NOTE: Research shows that more than 75% of all Americans eventually end up in careers for the wrong reasons: they find a job out of necessity that eventually becomes their career; parents persuade them to choose a certain career; or they end up in their careers by accident.

RETEACHING: Emphasize the importance of students finding the right careers, since so much of their lives will be spent in them.

147

PHOTOS: Ask students to name the careers that are shown here. Have them list some of the rewards and some of the difficulties presented by each career.

It's a great feeling to do a job that you're good at.

little, but many creative people want to spend their lives painting, writing, acting, or performing music. Working at high-paying jobs outside their field of interest would not satisfy them.

Work and the Community

The work each person does contributes to the good of his or her local community and to society as a whole. Your job gives you a place in your community; you help provide a service or a product. The money you earn makes it possible for you to buy local products and to pay for local services. The community and society also benefit from the taxes you pay from your earnings. Taxes pay for schools, libraries, streets, fire and police departments, and for many other government services.

DISCUSS: What are the most important issues in choosing a career: salaries? schedules? status? emotional rewards? projected market need for that particular job?

Our society survives because people support themselves and their families. The taxes people pay provide all the federal, state, and local services that make communities nice places to live.

Assessing Yourself

Once you finish school, you will probably spend most of your waking hours at work. Most Americans work for at least forty years. You can see how important it is to select the right career. To begin, take a look at your personal resources.

Your Interests

What do you like to do? Do you like to work with your hands? Are you good at organizing people? Perhaps you especially

ENRICHMENT: Ask each student to list five personal skills that could be translated into job skills.

like working with numbers or doing research. Caring for young children may appeal to you. Think about your special interests and how they might relate to a future career.

Your Skills

What skills do you have? Perhaps you are a whiz at computers. You may be an excellent cook or carpenter or be planning to develop these skills. Find out how your skills can be used in various careers.

Your Aptitudes

Your **aptitudes** are your special talents and abilities. You may have a natural ability to run machinery or a talent for singing or dancing. You may have an

Do your special talents and interests shine when you help others?

aptitude for managing and organizing projects, or for learning languages, or for working with animals. You can narrow your choices by investigating careers that relate to your particular aptitudes.

If you are not sure what your aptitudes are, ask your school counselor about taking an aptitude test to pinpoint areas in which you can excel.

Exploring Careers

Assessing your interests, skills, and aptitudes will give you some idea of what kind of career might be right for you. Next, you need to find out about those different fields of work.

Looking at Job Clusters

A **job cluster** is a group of jobs that require similar skills and knowledge. For example, there are many occupations that

Home Economics Teacher

Look at the table of contents of this book. It will give you an idea of how versatile a home economics teacher has to be. The subjects that are chapters or units of this text are all part of their courses. Home economics teachers may teach Child Development, Family Life, Consumer Education, Clothing Construction, Housing and Home Furnishings, and/or Food and Nutrition all in the same year. They may also manage, demonstrate, and "coach" in the foods lab, clothing lab, and a lab nursery school.

As you can imagine, it takes a good education to prepare for this. Home economics teachers hold at least a bachelor's degree, and they have studied much more than cooking and sewing. They need chemistry, too (to understand the makeup of foods and textiles). They must also understand psychology and sociology (to learn about family and other relationships) and economics (to develop consumer skills). They need to know nutrition, too (to understand different diets).

Their students produce real food and textile products and work with real children. Home economics teachers may also help others use the labs. A French class may prepare French cuisine or a hiking club may plan an outing. Like all teachers, they must communicate well and enjoy working with students.

Would this career interest you?

involve working with young children. These include day-care center workers, nursery school teachers, playground attendants, and doctors and nurses who care for young children. These jobs require quite different amounts of training and skills. However, people in these occupations all need to have certain abilities in common. They must be able to communicate well with young children and to remain calm under stress. They need to be patient and empathetic and to understand how children grow and develop.

Other job clusters include business, sales, construction work, agriculture, education, and medicine. Within each cluster there are entry level jobs, skilled jobs, and advanced level positions.

Entry Level Jobs

Entry level jobs require little or no special training or experience. Some require a high-school degree; others do not. The pay is low in entry level positions. They can, however, provide you with the experience and training you need to advance to a higher level. For example, an entry level job in the food service industry might be a dish washing job in a restaurant. A job like this can give you an opportunity to see at first hand if a particular field of work interests you.

Skilled Jobs

Skilled jobs require special training. There are several ways to get this training. Many high schools offer courses that teach special job skills ranging from auto

NOTE: Displaced homemakers entering the job market will often take entry level positions. Have students discuss the reasons for this and suggest alternatives.

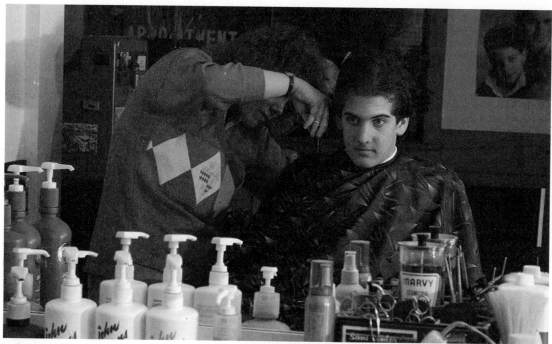

What skills, talent, and training are needed in this career?

repair to secretarial and word-processing skills. Vocational schools also have special programs in areas like food service or construction trades. Or you might want to consider a barber or beautician school after high-school graduation.

Many companies offer on-the-job training for employees who wish to move up from entry level positions. The advantage of this training is that it pays you while you learn.

Some well-paying trades also offer on-the-job training. This training is called an **apprenticeship.** An apprentice receives some pay for helping an experienced worker while learning the trade at the same time. Some states require would-be tradespeople such as plumbers, carpenters, and electricians to serve an apprenticeship in order to get a license.

Advanced Level Jobs

Advanced level jobs usually require a degree from a four-year college. Jobs that require specialized college degrees are often called **professions.** These include teaching, engineering, and archietecture.

Most of these professional jobs demand education beyond college. To become a doctor, lawyer, dentist, veterinarian, or university professor, you need one or more advanced degrees. Usually, you also need on-the-job experience before you become fully qualified.

Practical Career Planning

When choosing a career, you need to keep in mind the practical aspects of the job. Do not let your daydreams lure you into

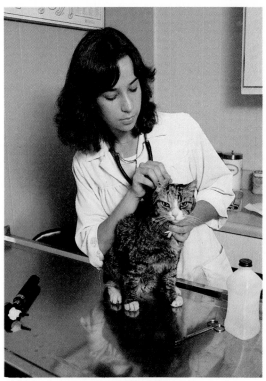

What can this girl learn as a part-time veterinary assistant?

planning for a career that does not fit your skills or financial possibilities. You may long to become an opera singer, but you have to be extremely talented to consider reaching this goal. You may have to accept the fact that your dream will not be realized. Still, there may be other ways in which you can make music an important part of your work or your personal life. You should also investigate less obvious, practical aspects of a career choice. Some careers demand constant travel or moving from one community to another. Suppose you have family ties that keep you close to home or you hate to fly. In those cases, careers requiring a lot of travel would not be good choices, however appealing their other aspects.

RETEACHING: Students should understand that career success involves applying the basic skills (reading, writing, and math) to their more specific education and training.

Trade-offs

When planning the path you will take toward a future career, it is necessary to make trade-offs. As you know, when you make a trade-off, you give up one thing in order to gain another. For example, some people choose to delay earning a full-time salary after four years of college. Instead they get a higher degree that will lead to a more satisfying career and higher earnings in the long term.

Career Trends

The job market today is shifting. Many industries that hired thousands of people a few years ago are closing down. New careers are opening up. It is a good idea to find out more about the kind of work you are planning to do. Perhaps the field is overcrowded or no longer profitable. You can check the *Occupational Outlook Quarterly,* published by the U.S. Department of Labor. The Labor Department also publishes the *Occupational Outlook*

Did You Know?

For centuries, apprenticeship was the way to learn a trade. In colonial America, apprentices also lived with their "masters." They instructed the boys in reading, writing, arithmetic, and religion as well as in their trade. Apprentices received no money but did get food, clothing, and lodging. In return, they worked hard —usually for seven years!

ENRICHMENT: Ask students to interview someone whose career interests them. Each student should ask what training was involved to enter that career, what the person likes and dislikes about the job, and what the future may hold for those in that career.

ART: On the board, list careers that your students are interested in and speculate with them on what the future outlook might be for such jobs.

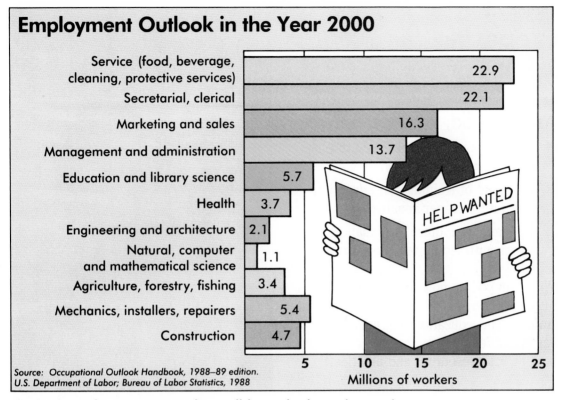

Employment Outlook in the Year 2000

Field	Millions of workers
Service (food, beverage, cleaning, protective services)	22.9
Secretarial, clerical	22.1
Marketing and sales	16.3
Management and administration	13.7
Education and library science	5.7
Health	3.7
Engineering and architecture	2.1
Natural, computer and mathematical science	1.1
Agriculture, forestry, fishing	3.4
Mechanics, installers, repairers	5.4
Construction	4.7

Source: Occupational Outlook Handbook, 1988–89 edition.
U.S. Department of Labor; Bureau of Labor Statistics, 1988

Think about future careers that will be in highest demand.

Handbook. This gives current information about careers in over 300 fields and lists which fields have the most jobs available. You can find these books in your local library or school guidance office.

Gathering Career Information

The publications mentioned above should be available at your public library. For other books and magazines that will help you plan your future career, look up "Careers" in your library catalog. If you have a specific career in mind, look under that title. For example, you might check under "Accounting" or "Child Care."

Your school guidance counselor can also provide you with information. When you meet someone working in a field that interests you, ask that person about opportunities in the field. A teacher may be able to help you arrange to interview someone whose work interests you.

See page T64 for answers.

For Review

1. Name at least three reasons for working besides making money.
2. How can learning more about your aptitudes help you to find the right career?
3. Name two government publications you can consult to find out what fields have the most jobs available.

DISCUSS: Brainstorm ways to find a part-time job in a career field that students ultimately want to pursue.

REINFORCEMENT: Ask students to think of jobs they could do in their fields of interest. For example, students could run errands for a lawyer or assist a chef on shopping trips.

Section 7.2

Preparing for Your Career

As you read, think about:

- what steps you can take now to plan your future career. (p. 154)
- what kind of training and education your future career requires. (p. 155)
- the planning required to balance a career with family responsibilities. (p. 157)

What can you do now to help decide on a future career? You can find out what training and education are needed for a variety of jobs. Then you can see which best fit your resources and abilities.

Start Now

Begin to plan your future career now. Part-time work provides helpful job experience in working toward the career of your choice.

Part-time Work

Working part-time after school and in the summer gives you more than spending money. Work experience of any kind helps you discover your skills and aptitudes. It helps you learn to work well with other people and to communicate with them. It teaches you how to follow directions and to organize your time. These skills are needed in any job. Part-time work also allows you to see if a particular field interests you.

What can a part-time job teach you about the career you want?

You may not be old enough now to begin working. When the time comes, though, you may be lucky enough to find a part-time job in your chosen field. For example, if you are considering a career in the fashion industry, look for a part-time job selling clothing.

In most states, if you are at least fourteen, you can work outside of school hours. However, the job must not be dangerous or hazardous to your health.

NOTE: Some companies offer unpaid internships to young people, who in turn can translate their job experience into some form of school credit.

ENRICHMENT: In a one-page paper, have students describe how a junior high or high school after-school activity could help them learn about or consider new careers.

Volunteer Work

If you cannot find paid part-time work in a field that interests you, you may be able to volunteer. Volunteers give their services without pay. In exchange for your help, you will have the opportunity to explore one or more fields of work. For example, if you are considering a career in health care, volunteer in a hospital or health clinic. Even a few hours a week can show you some of the skills required. You can also see if you like the work environment.

After-school Activities

Joining various after-school activities and clubs can also help you choose a career you will enjoy and do well in. Being a member of FHA/HERO will help you learn about a number of careers in home economics. Playing in the school band could lead to a career in music. Joining a drama group could be the first step in an acting career. Experience on a debating team could eventually lead to a political career.

Training and Education

You can prepare for some jobs in special high-school courses such as tailoring or word-processing classes. Some high schools have *co-op programs*. These allow a student to take courses in the morning and work in a related field in the afternoon. Or, you may choose to attend an area vocational-technical school. There, you will learn a trade while you are in high school. You can also take courses at the

Do you participate in after-school activities? They can open up many new career possibilities.

Are you prepared for years of study? Some careers demand them.

of interest as well as specialized courses. For example, a lab technician takes courses in various sciences as well as learning how to operate laboratory equipment and carry out experiments. An elementary, or grade-school, teacher must study English literature, history, and art as well as child development and methods of teaching reading and math.

Some careers require a master's degree, which usually takes two or more

post-secondary level, that is, following high school. These *vocational,* or job training, programs can vary in length from several months to several years. They are available at technical schools and community and junior colleges. They range from sales techniques to auto repair to various *clerical,* or office, skills.

Apprenticeships provide workers with a salary while they are learning a trade. Trade apprenticeships are available through labor unions, government programs, and employers. State and federal employment centers can give you information about them.

Many jobs require a two- or four-year college degree, which provides students with a general background in their fields

Did You Know?

Many surnames (also called last names or family names) come from the occupations people pursued during the Middle Ages. You can guess what the ancestors of people named Baker, Cook, Shepherd, Carpenter, and Taylor did for a living. But did you know that both Smith and Wright refer to "workers in" or "makers of" particular objects? Goldsmiths made jewelry, wheelwrights made wheels, and wainwrights made wagons. Millers ground grain at their mills, masons were builders in stone, and coopers made casks, tubs, and barrels. Check a genealogy reference in your library for the origin of your surname. Is your surname related to an occupation?

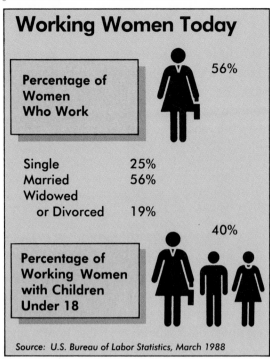

Working Women Today

Percentage of Women Who Work		
		56%

Single	25%
Married	56%
Widowed or Divorced	19%

Percentage of Working Women with Children Under 18		
		40%

Source: U.S. Bureau of Labor Statistics, March 1988

More and more women are entering the job market.

years of study following a bachelor's degree (awarded for four years of college work). A master's degree in business administration, an MBA, is one example.

Some highly skilled careers take years of study. To become a medical doctor, you must study four or more years beyond a first four-year degree. After this, doctors receive a degree from a medical school. Then they must spend still another year or more training in a hospital before they are fully qualified. Doctors who become specialists spend further time training.

Work Plus Family

Balancing work with family responsibilities requires thought, work, and planning. The years of education required to enter

some careers are very expensive. To go to college, many students borrow money that they must pay back when they start full-time work. Others work full-time in order to save money for their education. They may put off getting married and having children for a number of years because of education costs. Sometimes one spouse works while the other is in school, and both finish their education or training in stages.

Many other people work full-time and go to school at night in order to qualify for a better job. It can be difficult to combine all this with family responsibilities. This is another example of how adults are homemakers as well as wage-earners.

Whatever the arrangements, student and working parents make trade-offs to give both their children and their work the attention they need. They must divide their time among several roles: employee or student, parent, and homemaker. They have to find adequate and affordable child care. They also need to manage their time extremely carefully so that they can meet these various responsibilities. To do so requires careful planning and energy.

See page T64 for answers.

For Review

1. Name three advantages of doing part-time work after school or in the summer.
2. What are the requirements for becoming an elementary school teacher?
3. Name one trade-off that working parents make.

PHOTO: Suggest what newspapers might be best for your students to check for job openings and what day it is best to check them.

Before you answer an ad, study it. Know the questions you want to ask.

Section 7.3

Getting the Job You Want

As you read, think about:

- how to find out where there are job openings in your field of interest. (p. 158)
- the steps involved in the process of applying for a job. (p. 159)
- how to make the right start in a job. (p. 160)

How do you go about getting a job when the time comes? As with other goals, it helps to have a plan.

Finding Job Openings

The first step in looking for a job is to decide what kinds of jobs are right for you. Be realistic in choosing something that matches your skills. Do not, however, set your goals too low, even if you end up with your second or third choice. Make a list of the kind of jobs that interest you.

Newspaper Ads

Look under "Help Wanted" in the classified ads sections of some local newspapers. Sunday papers usually have the most ads for employment. First check every ad that seems a possibility. Consider which openings offer the best salary, hours, and location. Then review the checked ads and circle the top choices. Answer these ads right away.

Employment Agencies

Most states have employment agencies in cities and larger towns. These agencies set up job interviews with private businesses and offer information on government jobs. There is no charge for these services. There are also private agencies, some of which specialize in a particular field such as medical or editorial work. You should read their agreements very carefully. Some agencies charge large fees, to be deducted from your salary once you get the job. In some cases, however, the employer pays the fee.

Some communities have job banks for teenagers looking for part-time work. Many high schools and colleges offer job counseling or place students in jobs.

REINFORCEMENT: Have students bring the Help Wanted section of the Sunday newspaper to class. Have them study the jobs advertised. They should circle three jobs that would appeal to them if they were adults looking for employment. Have them note the qualifications required for each.

Do you have a social security card yet? You'll need one to get a job.

Personal Contacts

Friends and relatives often are a good source of information about jobs. Talk to teachers, local business people, and anyone else you know who might put you in touch with employers.

Canvassing

You may decide to canvas, or survey, local employers. Call businesses and institutions in the field you are interested in and talk to their personnel departments.

The Job Application

Applying for a job requires organization. You will need your social security number, a list of former employers, and details of your previous jobs. You may need your school record, too. Many employers ask for references. A **reference** is a recommendation from people you have worked for or have known for some time. These should be people who can assure the employer you will be a good employee. Get permission from the people whose names you want to use as references. Be sure you know their full names, job titles, addresses, and telephone numbers.

Sometimes job applications require a letter. Be sure your letter presents a good picture of you as the person that should be hired. You should write it in a formal style, using correct spelling, grammar, and punctuation. Tell the employer your education, training, and experience, and why you think you are right for the job.

Job Interview

Everyone is nervous when being interviewed for a job. After all, a great deal depends on the interviewer's impressions of the job applicant. Being prepared for an interview will make it less stressful. Here are some tips you can use to help make an interview a success.

- Allow plenty of time to get to the interview. Arrive at least five minutes

Neatness is important on a job application. Be sure to proofread.

Would you have a positive impression of this applicant?

early. Tell the receptionist your name and whom you are to see. Do not bring friends along with you.

- Bring your social security number, dates of employment, school background, and addresses and telephone numbers of your references. You will need this information if you are asked to fill out an application.
- Wear formal clothes. Boys should wear a jacket and tie, and girls should wear a businesslike dress or suit, neither too dressy nor too informal.
- Be prepared to talk specifically about why you would be a good person for the job. Think of a few examples in your school and work experience that show you are qualified and reliable. You can rehearse an interview by having an adult friend or family member play the role of the interviewer. Be prepared to answer the question, "Tell me about yourself." Your answer should focus on skills and experiences that show you would make a valuable employee.

- Find out in advance about the company or institution you are applying to. This shows interest and helps you discuss how your skills match the job.
- Ask questions during the interview. Find out what the job involves. Ask what opportunities there are for *promotion*, that is, advancement to a higher level. You should also find out about **fringe benefits**: paid sick days, holidays, vacations, and health and life insurance.
- Following the interview, write a brief thank-you note. State that you are interested in the job and feel that you would do it well.

Making It Work

You have been hired! Now you need to make the job work. You will enjoy your work if you concentrate on learning the job and doing it well. You will also improve your self-concept. Take care to be prompt, reliable, and dress correctly. Follow safety rules and job procedures carefully. Be sure you understand your employer's expectations and work your hardest to live up to them. Be willing to accept increasing responsibilities and to

Careers Related to Home Economics

Education or Training Needed	Child Development/ Family Relations	Foods and Nutrition	Clothing and Grooming	Housing
College degree or more	Home economist in public health Family counselor Social worker Teacher Librarian Psychologist Therapist Nurse	Home economist in textiles or fashion Fashion designer or buyer Fashion illustrator Costume designer	Home economist in food-related field Dietician Nutritionist Agricultural engineer Food health inspector	Home economy in housing field Designer Architect City planner Engineer
Training after high school	Medical assistant Health technician Nursery school teacher Dental assistant	Chef Butcher Food technician Nutrition assistant Restaurant manager	Tailor Sewing teacher Barber Cosmetologist Beautician Professional dress maker Weaving instructor	Realtor Builder Interior decorator Plumber Electrician Carpenter
High school diploma	Home companion Teacher aide Day care aide Nutrition aide	Chef trainee Caterer Baker	Sewing machine sales Dressmaker's or tailor's assistant Wedding consultant Fashion advisor	Painter Upholsterer Furniture refinisher Custodian Decorator's assistant
Possible high-school experience	Babysitter Day care volunteer Hospital volunteer	Grocery store clerk or stock room worker Waiter/waitress Volunteer at community kitchen or a meal delivery service	Sales clerk in fabric, or clothing store Seamstress aide Sewer Volunteer at a community clothing center	Sales clerk in home furnishings store Volunteer to help build or decorate public housing or shelters

Does any of these jobs match up with your talents and goals?

ART: Be sure students note the varying degrees of education and training needed for each job. Ask them to group the jobs by amount of training needed.

carry out your work with less supervision as you learn the job. It is important to listen carefully to instructions and, in turn, to give clear directions to other employees. Getting along with other workers is most important, although socializing on company time should be avoided. Remember, you are on the job, not at a social event.

The goal-setting procedures you learned in earlier chapters will help you move up in your work. Set long-term and short-term goals for career advancement. Then apply your management and communication skills to your job. You will be working each day to meet your long-term career goals.

Professional Home Economics Careers

The careers listed on the chart on page 161 all relate to the field of home economics. In addition to these, there are careers in teaching home economics at the elementary, high-school, and college levels. School-teachers need at least a bachelor's degree, and most college professors must have a doctoral degree.

Home economists are also hired by public and private agencies to educate the public and develop new uses for products. For example, a food manufacturer may hire home economists to develop recipes and cooking procedures that will help sell their product. And utilities, such as gas or electric companies, use them to promote their products. Less skilled positions are also available as assistants to home economists working in various fields.

Magazines and newspapers also hire home economists to write about nutrition, home improvements, family management, and other related subjects.

See page T64 for answers.

For Review

1. Name four good sources of job information.
2. How should you dress for a job interview?
3. List three ways to work toward succeeding at a job.

Learning to Manage

Look back at the conversation on page 146. Now read how Mrs. Lopez and the class manage to hold their "Career Day." Then answer the questions that follow.

The class got more excited about the idea of a "Career Day" as they talked. Mrs. Lopez asked for volunteers to help to set up a plan. They decided to invite local people working in different areas of the home economics field, including chefs, nutritionists, interior decorators, and day-care workers.

Several students in the Home Economics class had parents, relatives, or neighbors who worked in these areas. The students agreed to ask if these people could spare any time from work to talk to them. One committee was set up to write the letter of invitation to each possible speaker. The letter explained what kinds of information the class wanted to know about the person's job.

As the weeks passed, more volunteer speakers responded. Another committee of students wrote down individual questions to ask about specific jobs.

The response from community members grew as word spread about the "Career Day." A police officer, a visiting nurse, and the head librarian all called Mrs. Lopez to say they would enjoy participating. Even though their jobs were not home economics ones, their offers were accepted. By now the number of speakers had grown to the maximum. Each speaker had fifteen minutes to talk and answer questions, and the day was fully arranged. Mrs. Parks, the principal, asked the class if they would hold "Career Day" in the auditorium so that everyone could attend. Regular classes would be cancelled for that day.

The first annual "Career Day" at Johnston Junior High was a great success. The class were commended on all their organization and hard work. All the students learned a lot by talking to people who were actively involved in jobs and careers. In addition, the audiovisual department recorded the day's events for future students to see and hear.

Questions

1. Describe the general job or career area that you think you might enjoy. List the characteristics and strengths you possess that would help you to succeed in this field.
2. Discuss the possibility of holding a "Career Day" at your school. What types of information would you want to gain from each speaker?

Chapter 7 Review

Summary

There is a world of exciting and rewarding careers available. Now is the time to begin exploring your interests, skills and aptitudes and how they relate to your future career. Part-time and summer jobs can give you practical experience to help you decide on a particular career. Investigating a number of occupations will help you find one that matches your aptitudes and resources. Volunteering and joining after-school activity groups can help you to learn more about a field you may be considering. Begin now to set long-term goals for your work future.

The amount and cost of education and training you need will vary widely for specific jobs. Generally, you will need more expensive and longer training as you progress from entry level to skilled to professional jobs.

Vocabulary

Complete each of the following sentences with the correct word from the vocabulary list below.

fringe benefits (p. 160) professions (p. 151)
job cluster (p. 149) reference (p. 159)
entry level (p. 150) aptitudes (p. 149)
apprenticeship (p. 151)

1. A _____ is a recommendation to a potential employer from people for whom you have worked or who know you well.

2. _____ are special talents and abilities that a person possesses.

3. _____ _____ consist of paid sick days, holidays, vacations, and health and life insurance provided by an employer to a worker.

4. A _____ is a group of jobs that require similar skills and knowledge but not necessarily the same training.

5. _____ jobs require little or no special training or experience.

6. On-the-job training in a trade is called an _____.

7. Jobs that require specialized college degrees are often referred to as _____.

Questions

•• 1. Since jobs in the arts do not usually pay well, why does anyone work in such a field?

•• 2. What three factors should you take into consideration when you are deciding on a career?

••• 3. Name at least six jobs that are often referred to as professions.

•• 4. Is there any value in taking an entry level position? Explain your answer.

• 5. Name after-school clubs or groups that might help students who want to enter politics or may want a career in farming. Explain your answers.

The dots represent skill levels required to answer each question or complete each activity:
• requires recall and comprehension
•• requires application and analysis
••• requires synthesis and evaluation

6. What would be a good part-time job for someone who wants a career in the fashion industry?

7. Should you get permission to use someone's name as a reference? Explain how you would go about getting permission.

8. If a potential employer asks you about yourself during a job interview, what do you think you should focus on when you answer?

9. What very important part of a job interview takes place after the interview itself is over?

10. Name three kinds of jobs in the home economics field.

Skill Activities

Many more activities are contained in the annotations within this chapter.

1. Critical Thinking Think of all of your past and present experiences that could help you to get a part-time job. Make a list of all the skills and talents you have. If you have a part-time job now, list all the duties it includes. Include all of the responsibilities you have at home and at school. If you babysit at home or for others, list all of the responsibilities included in that job. Share your list with your classmates and discuss the many life skills you have already acquired.

2. Communication Interview a person who has a job you are interested in learning about. Discuss the job opportunities, educational requirements, personal qualities and talents needed, how the job was obtained, and the salary. You may choose to tape record the interview. Share your interview with the class.

3. Human Relations Stage a mock (pretend) job interview for an after-school or a summer job that you would be interested in. As a class, choose four or five realistic jobs for your age group. Choose an interviewer for each position. Take turns as the person seeking employment and as the interviewer. Record questions and answers of both the interviewer and the interviewee that you think are particularly good. Offer constructive criticism when you can.

4. Laboratory Choose a job cluster in the home economics field. Brainstorm all of the entry level, skilled, and professional jobs you can think of that would be included in this job cluster. Then select one of these jobs that you might enjoy and find out more about it. Find out how much education it requires and the salary range of the job. Combine the information you have found on a class bulletin board of "Jobs in Home Economics."

Chapter 8
Managing Your Money

The dialogue below introduces "You Can't Always Get What You Want," the Learning to Manage feature in this chapter. The case study is continued and the situation discussed further on page 185. See page T67 for teaching suggestions.

"But, Mom . . . Everyone has those great cowboy boots—and I need a pair of boots anyway."

"Billy, those boots are much too expensive. They just don't fit into the family budget right now. If you really want them, you'll have to earn half of the money yourself."

"OK, Mom. I'll start today."

Section 8.1

Money as a Resource

As you read, think about:

- the importance of using money in the wisest possible way. (p. 167)

- the various sources of money. (p. 167)

- How to set priorities when managing your money. (p. 168)

Like Billy, you'll find out that money is one of the major resources you need to meet your goals. Since its supply is limited, you must use it wisely. Good money management will stretch your dollars.

Sources of Income

Your parents provide most of the money for your basic needs of food, shelter, and clothing. You may also have a part-time job that pays for some of your expenses. You may get an allowance from your family that covers some of the costs of your transportation, books, and recreation. However, no matter how much money you have, you probably wish you had more. There may be ways for you to earn more money.

If you do not already have a part-time job, consider working after school and part of the weekend. There may be summer jobs available too. You might find a job in a local store or supermarket, or babysitting. Find out if your neighbors need help with some chores such as yard work, cleaning, or car washing. You can

What are your sources of income? Do you want to increase them?

advertise your services on bulletin boards in your neighborhood or in a community newspaper. Consider getting together with a few friends to do chores in your neighborhood together on a regular basis.

When you **barter,** you exchange something you have for something someone else has. For example, suppose a neighbor with a young child knits and sells beautiful sweaters. You would love to have one, but they cost more than you can afford. It might be possible for you to babysit a certain number of hours in exchange.

Making Money Choices

Whatever your resources, they will go further if you manage them carefully. To use your money effectively, apply the same decision-making skills you learned in Chapter 2 for managing your time.

1. *Identify the problem.* You want to buy a new pair of running shoes, but your money is limited.
2. *Consider your choices.* You find out the approximate prices of both a cheap pair and an expensive pair of shoes.
3. *Gather information.* You examine different brands and compare prices in various stores. You ask some experienced people you know which shoes they recommend and where to shop for the best value.
4. *Consider the outcome of each choice.* The more expensive shoes will probably last longer, but buying them will use up all your savings. The less expensive brands may not fit as well and will probably wear out more quickly.
5. *Make your decision.* You decide to buy medium-priced running shoes.
6. *Evaluate your decision.* You try out the shoes, and they are comfortable. You have not used all your savings. Your choice was a good one.

Sometimes your decisions are not so good. When you make a bad decision, do what you can to correct it. In any case, you will have learned something from the experience.

The Difference Between Needs and Wants

To manage your money effectively, you have to understand the difference between your economic needs and your economic wants. You *need* bus fare to and from school if you live too far away to walk. You may *want* a new pair of jeans very much, but you do not necessarily need them. They are not essential. The things you *want* are those things that make your life easier and happier. Records, concerts, and movies, for example, may be important to you, but you do not need them.

Setting Priorities

When you set priorities, you list items in the order of their importance. To manage money well, you must set priorities for spending it.

Did You Know?

Family garage sales are a great way to make extra money. Here are some tips to make your tag sale a success.

- Have a big selection—you then attract all types of buyers.
- Group similar items together for easy browsing.
- Clean things up—no one wants to buy something that's dirty.
- Be prepared to bargain—reasonably.
- Have a good, safe place to keep money.
- Be prepared to make change.
- Set aside lots of time for "minding the store."

DISCUSS: What are your students' future saleable talents or skills? Brainstorm a list on the board. Discuss the monetary worth of each talent or skill. Is it saleable?

DISCUSS: Put the following items on the board. Have students determine whether each item is a need or a want: school clothes, tapes, stereo, braces, allowance, lunch money, piano lessons, movie money, a television, and glasses.

Does every shop window attract you? Remember the priorities that you have set.

It takes maturity and experience to spend money according to a plan. Children usually spend whatever they have on the first thing they see that appeals to them. They can do this without causing major problems because their basic financial needs are taken care of by adults.

Now that you have reached adolescence, you are taking increasing responsibility for your life. This includes spending your own money. You have probably already found that impulse buying can prevent you from being able to afford things you really want. You may have many financial resources—your earnings, your allowance, an occasional gift of money. To benefit fully from them, you need to set priorities for how and when you spend your money. How will you set them?

First you should examine the standards and values which determine what you want to buy. Then you need to evaluate your financial resources. Finally, you can work out a plan for spending your money.

Setting Goals

To buy major items, you must set long-term goals based on saving money regularly over a period of time.

For example, you want to go to summer camp in July. Your parents agree to pay most of the cost if you will contribute $200. Your long-term goal is to have this amount by July 1, six months away.

You can reach your goal more easily if you use the management process described in Chapter 2.

What is this family's long-term goal?

Analyze your resources. You have to save a little less than $35 per month, or slightly less than $9 per week. How can you do this? Make a plan. If you need all of your present income, you will have to find a new source of earnings. You could try regular babysitting jobs.

Next, set a short-term goal. See if you can do enough babysitting in the next month to earn $35—about $9 a week. If you fall short of this goal, rethink your plan. Perhaps you also need to cut down on your usual expenses and add these savings to your going-to-camp funds.

In addition to a series of short-term goals, set a medium-term goal halfway through the six months. Your earnings will probably vary from week to week, but after three months you should have at least $100. Remember that you rounded off the short-term goal amounts. You may be pleasantly surprised to find you have exceeded your target. Keep going; you are halfway toward your final goal. Continue to work toward your short-term goals of $9 each week. If you fail to meet a weekly target, try to make up the amount quickly. Keep your long-range goal in mind: the fun you will have at camp.

Building toward a long-term financial goal enables you to have something you could not otherwise afford. It will also prove what a mature, responsible person you are.

For Review

1. Name the six steps you can use to help you manage money wisely.
2. What sources of income do you have?
3. Explain the difference between needs and wants.

Section 8.2

A Spending Plan

As you read, think about:

- how to organize a spending plan. (p. 172)
- how to estimate a budget. (p. 173)
- how to follow a budget. (p. 173)

Have you ever noticed how some people always have enough money while others are always broke? This does not necessarily mean that the people with enough money start out with more than the others. The difference between these people often lies in the way they organize their financial resources.

Look at Your Spending

You will find that it is well worth the trouble it takes to examine the way you spend your money. Financial problems cause stress, which you can avoid by following a carefully developed spending plan, or **budget.** A budget is a tool for managing your spending. In this section, you will learn about making and following a budget.

Record Your Expenses

The first step in budgeting is to keep a record of all your expenses. Write down everything you buy and how much the item cost, no matter how small the amount may be. At the end of several weeks, you will begin to see a pattern in your spending.

Fixed and Flexible Expenses The second step in figuring out a budget is evaluating how you spend your money. Divide your expenses into fixed and flexible costs. **Fixed expenses** are those that do not change over a period of time. Many of these fixed expenses are for needs rather than wants. Transportation

Do you know what your expenses are for one week?

Expenses for a Week

Transportation	2.50
Lunch	3.00
Snacks	1.00
Entertainment	3.50
Gift (Dad)	4.00
Expenses for Week	14.00

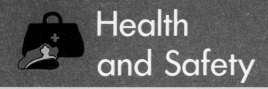

Health and Safety

Health-Care Costs

What costs Americans $50 billion a year and is going up at twice the rate of inflation? The answer is health care, and here is where the American health-care dollar goes:

- 39¢—hospital care
- 20¢—physicians' services
- 8¢—nursing home care
- 6¢—dentists' services
- 14¢—medicine/personal health care
- 13¢—research, administration, etc.

The $1800 per person per year the U.S. spends on health care is among the highest in the world. Typically, a complete check-up runs $200 to $300, and one day in intensive care can come to $2,000. The one-night stay in a regular hospital room, which was less than $200 in 1977, was more than $400 in 1985. While insurance "pays" some of the bills, the cost of premiums is rising rapidly too.

Overall, medical costs are expected to triple by the year 2000. One reason is that high-tech equipment, medicines, and training are all expensive. Today's informed patients often demand more tests and procedures. Some experts feel doctors now give more tests in order to protect themselves against malpractice charges. Also, the elderly population and health-care wages are increasing.

What efforts are being made nationwide to cut health-care costs?

to and from school is a fixed expense. As you take on more responsibility for supplying your basic needs, your fixed expenses will increase. Adults must pay many fixed expenses. These include rent or mortgage payments, utility bills for heat and light, insurance, taxes, and installment payments on automobiles and furniture.

Flexible expenses change from month to month. They are the variable amounts people spend on clothes, entertainment, grooming, meals in restaurants, travel, and so on.

List Expenses in Categories

After you have separated your fixed and flexible expenses into two lists, organize individual expenses into categories. For example, put all flexible transportation expenses together in one category. Similarly, combine all expenses for clothing in a second category. Your other categories should include food, entertainment, grooming, books, gifts, school supplies, and savings. (If you haven't been saving any money, now is the time to begin.) Put any leftover items under "Miscellaneous." Now add all the expenses in each category.

Your Spending Plan

Designing a budget can be satisfying and fun. If you plan wisely and can stick to the plan, you will be pleasantly surprised. You will find that you can buy some major items you thought you could not afford. You will also avoid uncertainty about whether you can meet your expenses.

DISCUSS: Determine whether the following items are fixed or flexible expenses: birthday presents for family members, club dues, after-school snacks, hair gel, magazines, and video rentals.

Estimating a Budget

Design your budget either by the week or by the month, depending on how often you receive your income. Add up the money you get for whichever period you choose and write the total under the heading "Income."

In a second column, headed "Expenses," list all of your expenses by category. For flexible expenses you will have to estimate, or predict, how much you will spend. An *estimate* is an educated guess. For example, to estimate your monthly entertainment costs, look over the expense account you have been keeping. Decide whether you spent an average amount or whether you spent more or less than usual. If you feel you spent too much on entertainment, budget less than you have been spending.

Remember to include an amount for savings for long-term goals and to allow for some unexpected miscellaneous expenses. Before you make a final copy of your predicted budget, you will almost certainly have to juggle some figures. Add up all your estimated expenses. Does the total match your income? It probably won't on the first try. If your expenses are higher than your income, you will have to find ways to reduce your flexible expenses. If your expenses turn out to be lower than your income, you can add the difference to your savings.

Follow Your Estimated Budget

Your estimated budget is now complete, and you are ready to see if your careful planning will work. Be sure to keep track

Does your budget include estimates for gifts?

of your expenses. Then you will know right away if you are spending too much in a particular category. At the end of your budget period, compare what you actually spent in each category with the amount you estimated. Adjust the differences and think about what caused them. Continue the process over the next budgeted time period. It takes practice. Don't be discouraged if it does not come out right at first. With experience you will find that your actual budget draws closer to your predicted budget.

ENRICHMENT: Have students determine their average weekly income based on allowance or part-time job money. Then they should review their list of weekly expenses and develop a budget plan. It should include money for weekly fixed expenses as well as flexible items.

ENRICHMENT: Ask students if they know an adult who will tell them about items that are fixed weekly expenses and flexible weekly expenses for a couple or a family. Students should write a one-page paper or make a chart describing what they learn.

Chapter 8/*Managing Your Money*   **173**

Adjust Your Budget

Evaluate your estimated budget whenever your income and expenses change. You should check it regularly to be sure it represents current income and expenses.

Changes in Spending Habits You may soon become aware that you are not spending your money as wisely as you would like. Try to recognize and change poor spending habits. If you find you cannot buy what you need, cut the amount you spend in a less important category.

Can you estimate what you spend on entertainment?

Advantages of a Budget

At first, focusing so much time on budgeting may seem too much trouble. However, try to get into the habit of noting expenses and keeping your budget up to date. The task will become easier, and you will discover the satisfaction that comes from managing your money effectively.

If you follow your budget over a period of time, you will have saved money for emergency spending. If your radio breaks or you need supplies unexpectedly, you should be able to meet these costs without borrowing money.

Avoid borrowing from friends. It is easy to run up a surprisingly large debt simply by borrowing a few dollars here and there. If you cannot pay back the money when your friend needs it, you may damage a good friendship. It is also unwise to borrow against your allowance. This throws your budget off balance, and you may not be able to get back on track. Include savings and emergency spending in your budget and make sure you do not overspend. In this way you will avoid the stress of being in debt. You will also show your family, friends, and above all yourself that you are a responsible person.

Sample Budgets

Everyone's budget is unique. However, all personal budgets are similar in many ways. You may find it helpful to study the design and categories of the two budgets on the next page. The first is that of a typical 14-year-old. Your own budget will probably include some of the same items.

ART: Have students read the budget for the 14-year-old. Ask: Is the allowance figure realistic? Are your fixed monthly expenses similar? What flexible expense items are not listed that you feel should be? How does your total monthly income compare?

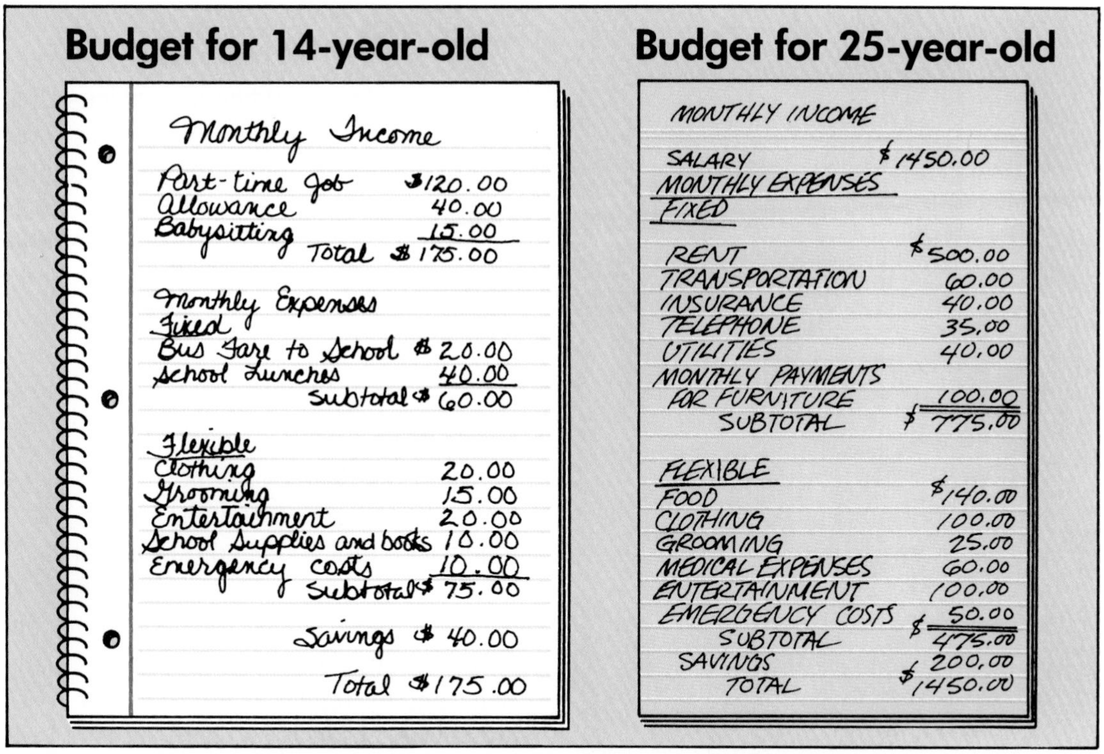

Budget for 14-year-old

Monthly Income

Part-time Job	$120.00
Allowance	40.00
Babysitting	15.00
Total	$175.00

Monthly Expenses
Fixed

Bus fare to School	$20.00
School Lunches	40.00
Subtotal	$60.00

Flexible

Clothing	20.00
Grooming	15.00
Entertainment	20.00
School Supplies and books	10.00
Emergency costs	10.00
Subtotal	$75.00
Savings	$40.00
Total	$175.00

Budget for 25-year-old

MONTHLY INCOME

SALARY	$1450.00

MONTHLY EXPENSES
FIXED

RENT	$500.00
TRANSPORTATION	60.00
INSURANCE	40.00
TELEPHONE	35.00
UTILITIES	40.00
MONTHLY PAYMENTS FOR FURNITURE	100.00
SUBTOTAL	$775.00

FLEXIBLE

FOOD	$140.00
CLOTHING	100.00
GROOMING	25.00
MEDICAL EXPENSES	60.00
ENTERTAINMENT	100.00
EMERGENCY COSTS	50.00
SUBTOTAL	$475.00
SAVINGS	200.00
TOTAL	$1450.00

Does your budget contain some of these items? How do your costs compare with those of the 14-year-old shown here?

The second example represents the budget of a 25-year-old, employed adult. It gives you some idea of the way you will be budgeting your money in the future. (Actual amounts are rounded off to the nearest dollar.)

See page T69 for answers.

For Review

1. Why is having a clear spending plan important?
2. Name two important advantages of following a budget.
3. What two important headings should you use when estimating a budget?

REINFORCEMENT: Brainstorm with your class a list of items that would fall into a teen's emergency spending category, such as an unexpected opportunity to go on an all-day outing.

Section 8.3

Money Management Services

As you read, think about:

■ the different kinds of checking and savings accounts available in banks. (p. 176)

■ ways of investing money. (p. 180)

■ the meaning and purpose of credit. (p. 181)

Fifty years ago, many people were paid in cash and paid their bills in cash. Today most bills are paid by check or by credit

ENRICHMENT: Ask students where money might come from in the 14-year-old's budget to pay for a large repair to a stereo. Discuss ways to solve this budget problem.

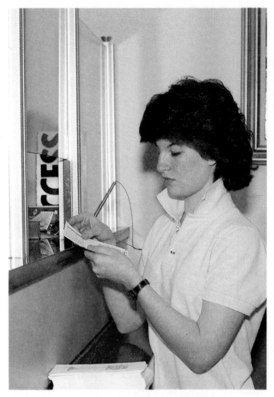

What banking services does your bank make available to you?

card, and almost everyone is paid by check. Many companies actually pay their employees by transferring the money directly into the employee's bank account. The trend today in money management is toward a *cashless society.* We may never reach the stage of using no cash at all, but we are heading in that direction.

If you work part-time, you may wish to open a savings or a checking account to manage your money more efficiently. When you begin working full-time, you will need to understand how banking services and *credit systems*—which extend money to you for future payments—help you control your money.

Banking

Banks provide a number of services that help people to manage money. First you need to know what kinds of bank accounts are available. Then you can decide which ones may be useful to you now and in the future.

Checking Accounts

Having a checking account is useful in several ways. You can deposit your paycheck and other income in it and keep the money safe until you need it. You can cash checks easily. Many banks will not cash a check for you if you do not have an account there. You can pay bills by mail. Cash sent by mail can be stolen or lost. You can, for a fee, stop payment on a lost or stolen check. Being able to pay for purchases by check means you can avoid the risk of carrying large amounts of cash. Your checks provide written proof that you have paid a bill. Your account records, together with the bank's statement of your checks and deposits, help you keep track of your spending.

How a Checking Account Works A checking account works like this. You first put money into the account, that is, you **deposit** cash or a check made out to you. You can then write a check to a person, a company, or yourself. The bank pays out the amount of the check to the person or company you name on the check. The amount of the check is subtracted from your **balance,** that is, the total amount in your account.

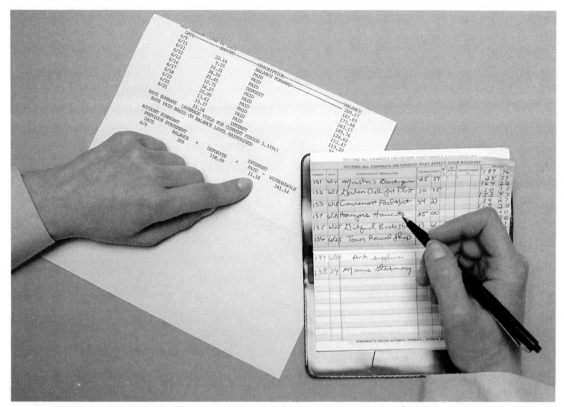

If you have a checkbook, you should keep a record of your
transactions to compare with the bank's record.

Choosing the Right Checking Account

There are several different types of
checking accounts, and the services each
type provides vary from bank to bank.
Regular accounts, NOW accounts, and
money market deposit accounts are
among the different types of checking
accounts. Some accounts pay interest and
others do not. **Interest** is money the
bank gives you in exchange for being able
to use your money for various banking
services. The rate of interest the bank
pays depends on the type of account. To
find the one that is best for you, compare
the checking services offered by a number of different banks.

Non-Interest-Bearing Accounts A
regular checking account does *not* pay
interest. When you open a regular checking account, some banks require you to
deposit a minimum amount. Some require
you to maintain a minimum balance. Others do not, but instead charge you for
every check you write.

Interest-Bearing Accounts A NOW
account pays interest providing certain
requirements are met. NOW (Negotiable

Order of Withdrawal) accounts require that a minimum balance be maintained before interest is paid. The rate of interest, however, is usually not as high as on special savings accounts.

There are other kinds of checking accounts that also offer interest, such as money market deposit accounts. A bank representative will explain the different kinds of accounts and what each provides. Money market deposit accounts, for example, often limit the number of checks you can write each month.

Savings Accounts

To save for long-term goals, you will find it helpful to make regular deposits into a savings account. Your money will be safe, and it will earn interest. The amount of money in a savings account is called the **principal.** Banks, savings and loan asso-

Did You Know?

Some banks charge you a fee if your savings account isn't big enough. While most savings accounts pay interest, some banks require a minimum balance of $100 or $500. Otherwise they subtract money from the account. Then you lose money by saving it! Shop around for a bank that pays interest on all accounts or makes an exception for depositors under 18.

ciations, and credit unions offer a variety of savings accounts. Interest rates vary from one kind of savings account to another and from one savings institution to another. Shop around to get the best interest rate. Remember to find out how often the interest is **compounded,** or added to your principal. Interest may be compounded daily, quarterly (every three months), or yearly. The more often interest is compounded, the more quickly your principal will increase. However, you must also consider which type of account offers the highest rate of interest overall.

Make sure that your money is insured by the federal government in case your savings institution runs into financial difficulty. Choose a bank insured by the Federal Deposit Insurance Corporation. A savings and loan company should be insured by the Federal Savings and Loan Insurance Corporation.

Savings Club Accounts Some savings institutions offer special short-term accounts in which you save a specific amount within a limited time. For example, you could deposit the same amount each week until you reach your goal of $100. You should check to see what, if any, interest such an account pays. As always, shop around before deciding.

Opening and Using Bank Accounts

To open either a savings or a checking account, you need to talk with a bank representative. He or she will tell you about the different kinds of accounts avail-

REINFORCEMENT: Make copies of blank savings account deposit and withdrawal slips. Show students how to fill them out.

DISCUSS: Talk about the types of savings clubs banks offer. Can students give examples of anyone they know who uses such a club and why that person chooses to save money in that way?

There are many pamphlets and brochures available to help you understand banking services.

able and how to use them. You will be asked for identification and perhaps also a reference from a responsible adult.

Once you have decided on the account you want, you will sign signature cards. The bank checks your signature on checks and withdrawal slips against these to be sure it is genuine. You must therefore always sign your name exactly the same way.

Next you deposit the opening balance in the form of cash or a check. If you are opening a checking account, checks will be ordered for you. You may also be issued with a special card to use at the bank's automatic teller machines. If you pay the opening deposit by check, the check must *clear* before you can withdraw money. A check is cleared when the bank has received the money from the account it was drawn on.

Endorsing checks In order to cash or deposit a check, you must **endorse** it. You do this by signing your name on the back of the check. When depositing a check to your own account, write above your signature, "Pay to the order of (*name of bank*), account number (*complete number of your account*)."

How to Write a Check Before you write a check, you record information about it in the *check register* or check stub in your checkbook. Write the check number, the date, the amount of the check, and the name of the *payee*. (The *payee* is the person or company to whom the check is made out.) Then subtract the amount from your balance. Now you can write the check, following these steps.

1. Be sure the check is numbered.
2. Write the date in the space provided.
3. Write the payee's name on the line after the words "Pay to the order of."
4. Write the amount in numbers in the space beside the dollar sign.
5. Write the amount in words below the name of the payee, starting close to the left-hand margin so that no one can add a word to change the amount.
6. Note the purpose of the check in the memo section if there is one.
7. Sign your name.

Your Bank Statement Your bank will send you a *statement* at regular intervals. This shows all the deposits and withdrawals that were made in your account within a period of time. The withdrawals include all the checks you wrote. Always check your statement immediately against your check register to be sure your figures agree with those of the bank.

Other Forms of Money Management

In addition to savings accounts, there are other ways people invest their money. When you **invest** money, you use it to make more money. In the future, you will

Many people like to buy government bonds, which enable them to save money and invest in their country at the same time.

work full-time and will be able to save larger amounts of money. At that stage, you will want to consider various ways to invest your savings.

Stocks

Businesses need money to operate. To get this money, they sell *shares* of *stock,* that is, small parts of the business. The people who buy these shares of stock are called **stockholders.** If a business does well, its stockholders share in the profits. If it does badly, the stockholders lose money. Investing money in stock may be profitable, but it involves risk.

Bonds

Both the government and private businesses sell bonds. When you buy a bond, you are lending your money. In return, you are paid interest on the loan. Most bonds cost $1,000 or more. The federal government, however, does issue bonds in smaller amounts.

Mutual Funds

Mutual funds are a collection of various stocks and bonds that are owned by one company. That company will sell you a share in these combined investments, on which you then either gain or lose.

Certificates of Deposit

CDs, or *certificates of deposit,* are accounts in which money is deposited for a specified amount of time. This can be

anywhere from one month to five years. At the end of the specified period, the account matures, and the deposited amount plus interest is paid.

What Is Credit?

You get **credit** when you borrow money or receive goods or services in exchange for a promise to pay at a future date. There are many forms of credit. A person receives credit when a telephone, gas, or electrical company provides service before billing someone for it. A store gives credit when a person charges an item by using a charge account or a credit card. It is possible under certain conditions to buy real estate or borrow money on credit.

Advantages and Disadvantages

There are advantages and disadvantages to using credit.

Buying on credit is convenient. It saves you from carrying large amounts of cash that can be lost or stolen. It helps you meet your needs and wants sooner. It allows you to take advantage of sales and discounts. It provides records of expenses. Credit can also provide an immediate source of funds to meet financial emergencies. In addition, if you pay credit debts promptly, you build up good credit references. This helps you to get additional credit more easily in the future.

Buying on credit also has disadvantages. It can lead to overspending. It requires you to pay out money at set times in the future when you may have less income. If

PHOTO: Ask students to research rates of interest currently paid on United States savings bonds.

ENRICHMENT: Have students make a chart comparing and contrasting stocks, bonds, mutual funds, and certificates of deposit as safe and profitable investments.

Is there a big purchase that you would like to make? You must consider what buying on credit will cost.

you cannot meet payments, you can suffer severe financial losses. Most credit buying also has a price.

Credit Costs

Buying on credit costs money. The store or business that gives you credit charges you a certain amount of money. This fee, or interest, pays for the time you use their services or their products in advance of payment. Some businesses, such as department stores, allow you a period of time before they actually bill you for credit costs. However, these businesses add the cost of giving credit to the price of their services or goods.

Finance Charges

Finance charges are all the charges you pay to get credit. They range from charges for processing a loan to insurance and annual service fees. The highest charge, however, is for the interest you pay.

Interest is calculated in different ways, and rates of interest vary. It can be difficult to figure out the total interest you are being charged. When you want to compare rates of interest on credit, look for the *annual percentage rate* (APR). The Consumer Credit Protection Act, known as the Truth-in-Lending Law, requires that the annual percentage rate be stated in all credit agreements.

If you make expensive purchases in the future using credit, be sure you understand the exact amount of the finance charges. In general, the longer you take to pay, the more interest you will be paying. There may be items that you will need, such as a refrigerator. If you did not have enough cash on hand, you would use credit. While you were paying the finance charges on this purchase, you would probably avoid using credit for luxury items. You will be making all of these decisions based on your personal budget.

Shopping for Credit

There are two kinds of credit: credit for specific purchases and *loan credit,* which is money loaned by banks and other institutions. Stores offer charge accounts and *installment plans* for expensive items. To buy on an installment plan, you agree to pay a fixed amount at regular intervals. This agreement may be handled by a finance company. You should compare the charges of such a finance plan with those offered by other companies. That way you can get the lowest interest rate.

Banks, savings and loan associations, and credit unions offer a wide variety of loans. Interest charges vary, as do the other terms of these loans.

Credit cards are issued by many banks and private companies. Most of them charge an annual fee as well as interest charges for late payments. Anyone choosing a credit card should make sure that the stores, restaurants, and hotels he or she uses accept it. Credit cards are especially convenient for travelers, who often cannot cash checks in places where they are not known.

Are the advantages of buying on credit always worth the cost?

Obtaining Credit

Before businesses or banks will give a person credit, they check that the applicant is responsible and able to pay. The applicant has to fill out forms that give information about general financial status and past records of paying debts. The lending institution then checks to be sure that the information is correct.

To get credit, a person must meet certain requirements. In most cases, these include being at least 18 years old, having a permanent address, and working full-time. A company giving credit may ask questions about an applicant's education, experience, and training. This is done to determine the person's future earnings potential. A new creditor will also check to see that an applicant has a checking and savings account in good order. In addition, a creditor will obtain a credit history by checking the person's credit rating.

Credit Rating

Credit rating reflects how much credit a person has received in the past and how promptly the debts have been paid. Banks, stores, and other creditors give information to a *credit bureau* about the people to whom they give credit. The credit bureau is connected to other bureaus nationwide that share credit information. From their records of all the credit given to an individual, they assign a credit rating. Ratings range from excellent through good, fair, and poor to one that indicates a person is a bad credit risk.

It is important that you establish a good credit rating as early as possible. Then you will be able to get the credit you need in the future. If you use credit wisely and pay bills on time, your credit rating will be good.

Know Your Rights You are entitled to know your credit rating and what information about you is in credit bureau files. If you feel you have been denied credit unfairly, you can ask to see your file. You can get the address of the credit bureau that has your file from your creditor. There could be a mistake in the records.

Before you sign a credit contract, read it carefully and clarify any points you do not understand. Do not sign any contract if there are blank spaces that have not been filled in. Do not be rushed into signing. Be sure you know what you are agreeing to and that you will be able to meet future payments.

See page T69 for answers.
For Review
1. Name at least five advantages of having a checking account.
2. List the seven steps you should take when writing a check.
3. What are mutual funds?
4. Name three advantages and three disadvantages of buying on credit.

RETEACHING: Explain that when people have bad credit ratings, they have difficulty obtaining a mortgage, a car loan, a credit card, and personal bank loans.

ENRICHMENT: Have students interview someone who has bought a car or a house. Have them find out what kinds of questions the bank asked and how it ran a credit check.

Learning to Manage

You Can't Always Get What You Want

Look back at the conversation on page 166. Billy wants something that his family can't afford right now. Now read how he tries to manage the situation. Then answer the questions that follow.

Billy tried to think of ways to earn extra money. He had to have those boots! He was disappointed that he couldn't go and buy them right away. Last year he would have been able to, but this year his father had been laid off from his job. Everything was different. They just didn't have extra money. Although he understood, those boots really meant a lot to him. Well, if he earned half of the cost . . .

Billy set to work doing extra chores for neighbors and saving more per week than usual from his paper route. This was hard, because some of his weekly pay was now being used for school lunches. His allowance had also been stopped. All of this turned saving for the boots into a much longer process.

Several weeks later, Billy had saved almost all of his share of the cost. That week everything else went wrong. Their washing machine broke down, and the car battery died. They bought a new car battery, but there wasn't enough money left to have the washing machine fixed. Billy noticed how tired and worried his parents seemed. As much as he wanted those boots, he realized this wasn't the time to get them. He knew what to do with the money he had been saving. At this point, the whole family needed a repaired washing machine a lot more than he needed cowboy boots. He could get what he wanted later.

He talked to his mother the next morning as she was packing up the laundry to take it to the laundromat.

"Mom, I was thinking . . . my old boots aren't in such bad shape. I tried them on last night and they still fit me."

"What about those new cowboy boots you wanted so badly?"

"They can wait. I want to give you the money I've earned to get the washing machine fixed instead."

His mother looked at him and smiled.

"Billy, you really are growing up to be a responsible young man. Thank you for your offer."

"It's OK, Mom. I'm learning that when it comes to money, I can't always get what I want."

Questions

1. Using what you have learned in this chapter, make a list of other family expenses that Billy's parents probably have to meet.
2. How can setting financial priorities now help you to budget in the future?

Chapter 8 Review

Summary

Your life can be more pleasant and less stressful if you manage your money well. If necessary, you may be able to find new sources of income. How wisely you spend your money is as important as how much you earn. You can develop and then follow a carefully planned and realistic budget. You will then be able to control your finances and avoid the stress that comes with overspending.

A savings account provides a safe way to save money and earn interest. A checking account is helpful when you begin to pay bills on a regular basis. It is important to understand the advantages and disadvantages of both credit buying and loans. By establishing a credit rating, you can obtain loans more easily. This will be useful when you are ready to buy a car, a house, or pay for future education.

Vocabulary

Complete each of the following sentences with the correct word from the vocabulary list below.

balance (p. 176)   deposit (p. 176)
credit (p. 181)   interest (p. 177)
invest (p. 180)   flexible expenses (p. 172)
barter (p. 167)   compounded (p. 178)
principal (p. 178)   endorse (p. 179)
stockholders (p. 181) fixed expenses (p. 171)
budget (p. 171)

1. The total amount of money in a checking account at a given time is called the _____.
2. _____ are expenses that do not change over a period of time.
3. When interest is _____, it is added to the principal.
4. People receive _____ when they borrow money or obtain goods or services in exchange for their promise to pay at a later date.
5. To exchange something you have for something someone else has is to _____.
6. To _____ money is to use it to make more money.
7. Putting cash or a check into an account is making a _____.
8. The _____ is the original amount in an account before interest is earned.
9. Expenses that change from month to month are called _____.
10. The money a bank gives you in exchange for being able to use your money to lend to other people is called _____.
11. People who buy shares of stock are called _____.
12. A carefully developed spending plan is called a _____.
13. When you sign your name on the back of a check in order to cash it or deposit it to an account, you _____ the check.

Questions

- 1. Why is it important to set priorities in managing money?
- 2. Name two important advantages of building toward a long-term financial goal by saving money regularly over a period of time.
- 3. What is the first step in budgeting your money?
- 4. Is it a good idea to keep your expenses lower than your income? Explain.
- 5. Do you think it is ever wise to borrow money from friends? Explain.
- 6. Give at least three reasons why most people have checking accounts.
- 7. What is a NOW account?
- 8. Why is it a good idea to shop around for a bank when you want to open a savings account?
- 9. Why is it important for you to be certain that the money you put in the bank is insured by the federal government?
- 10. What is the purpose of filling out a signature card?
- 11. When is a check cleared?
- 12. Why do companies offer stock for sale to the public?
- 13. Explain why buying something on credit sometimes costs more than paying cash.
- 14. Name one advantage of using credit.
- 15. Name three things a person must have in order to obtain credit.

The dots represent skill levels required to answer each question or complete each activity:

- requires recall and comprehension
- • requires application and analysis
- • • • requires synthesis and evaluation

Skill Activities

Many more activities are contained in the annotations within this chapter.

1. Decision Making Your aunt has just given you $100. You can spend this money on anything you want. Decide what you will do with it. Will you save all or part of it? Will you spend it all? If so, will you buy something you *want* or something you *need?* Make a written plan for your $100. Give reasons for your decision. List the advantages and disadvantages of your decision.

2. Critical Thinking Look through a fashion or sporting catalog and find one item that you would like to purchase. Make a plan for saving the money you will need to purchase that item. Look back at pages 169-170, which discuss how to save money to meet your goals. Consider the following questions while making your plan. Do you have money in a saving account? Will you need to find a job? Can you save from your allowance? Can you cut down on your expenses?

3. Laboratory Create a personal "Job Wanted" poster, showing ways you could use your talents to earn extra income. Use drawings and/or pictures you can find to illustrate what you can do. Look again at Skill Activity 1 in Chapter 7 to get ideas for your poster.

187

Chapter 9
You Are a Consumer

The dialogue below introduces "The Consumer Maze," the Learning to Manage feature in this chapter. The case study is continued and the situation discussed further on page 201. See page T73 for teaching suggestions.

"I don't believe this! My radio is broken already. I just bought it about a month ago, and I had to save for so long to buy it."

"Why don't you try to return it, Pete?"

"That's right! This radio did come with a warranty, and I saved the sales receipt, too. This is one consumer who plans to use the system to stand up for his rights!"

Section 9.1

Free Enterprise and Entrepreneurship

As you read, think about:

- how the wants and needs of consumers are met. (p. 189)
- the features of a free enterprise economic system. (p. 189)
- the characteristics that entrepreneurs have in common. (p. 191)

Do you want to start a business? In a free enterprise system, it's possible.

For hundreds of years, people have come to the United States from countries around the world in search of a dream. For some, it is to find political freedom. For others the dream is economic success through starting a business of their own.

In this country, the free enterprice system has made it possible for people to make these dreams come true. The freedom to produce goods and services for profit gives everyone the chance to own a business. Is this your dream too?

Free Enterprise

As a consumer, you have both wants and needs. These wants and needs include *goods,* or products. Goods are material items such as food, clothing, and appliances. People also want and need services. *Services* are actions performed for someone else for money such as a haircut. A **consumer** is a person who buys and uses good and services.

How are the wants and needs of consumers met? Countries have different *eco-nomic systems.* Every system of meeting wants and needs involves three main steps. These are production, distribution, and consumption. *Production* is making goods and providing services. *Distribution* is getting goods and services to the people. *Consumption* is selecting, buying, and using goods and services.

Although every economic system involves the steps of production, distribution, and consumption, not all economic systems are the same.

Features of Free Enterprise

The economic system in the United States is called **free enterprise.** Under this system people enjoy many freedoms and rights in carrying out economic activities. They have the freedom to choose

When businesses compete for your money, you have a greater choice of what you buy and where you buy it.

their own careers. They can choose what products and services to buy, and where to shop for their purchases. Free enterprise also gives every person the freedom to own private property, as well as the freedom to produce. That means people are allowed to start a business of their own to make a profit. The government's involvement in business is carefully controlled.

An important feature of a free enterprise system is **competition.** Competition is the effort similar businesses make to outdo one another in profits by produc-

ing the products consumers want most. Competition encourages businesses to produce high-quality goods and services and allows consumers greater freedom of choice. For example, when you shop for shampoo, you can choose from a variety of brands. The manufacturers of these brands are competing for your dollars.

All the choices you make as a consumer help to determine what businesses produce. This is the principle of supply and demand, another key feature of free enterprise. **Supply** refers to the amount and kinds of goods and services that are available for consumers to choose from. **Demand** is what consumers want. Consumer demand has a direct effect on supply. Each time you make a buying decision, you cast a vote for the product or service you purchase. Companies will not make products that consumers don't buy, because they can't make a profit on goods they don't sell. Consumers, therefore, have a powerful role in influencing what businesses produce.

What Is Entrepreneurship?

Do you have an idea for a product or a service that you think people may want or need? Like many other Americans who have started their own businesses, you too can become an entrepreneur. The ability to use your own resources and talents to develop an idea into goods or services is called **entrepreneurship.**

Characteristics of an Entrepreneur

What does it take to start a business? Successful entrepreneurs everywhere have a strong desire to make a profit, and to do it their own way! They also share these characteristics.

- *A creative imagination* One good idea is the basis of every business. Perhaps you have thought of a time-saving way to do your chores. Maybe you know how to solve a problem in your community. If so, you're on your way to success as an entrepreneur.

- *An awareness of people's needs and wants* To make a profit as an entrepreneur, you must provide a product or service that successfully meets people's wants and needs.

- *A willingness to take a risk* Starting a new business involves many risks. You must develop skills in planning and organizing your resources to minimize problems and maximize profits.

- *A readiness to accept responsibility* An entrepreneur must be able to accept financial loss as well as profit.

- *An ability to use resources skillfully* Knowing what resources you have and how you can use them are two key ingredients of business success. You and your friends may have resources and skills that could be helpful in starting a business in your community.

Did You Know?

At one time, you could "make change" or "break a dollar" by literally breaking a large coin into smaller pieces. The coins were large Spanish silver dollars called "pieces of eight." They were used in the American colonies along with other foreign coins. The pieces of eight could be broken into eight pie-shaped sections called "bits." Four bits equaled a half dollar, and so on. Some people still use the expression "two bits" to mean a quarter.

Leadership and Citizenship

Corporate Citizenship

Many businesses, large and small, contribute to good causes. Sometimes they contribute ideas as well as money. Here are two examples.

- In 1971, Stride Rite, a manufacturer of children's shoes, opened an affordable, high-quality day-care center for its employees' children. Having child care at the workplace helped parents to keep in touch with their preschoolers during the day, worry less, and work better. The center began to attract top people to work for the company. It also served as a good neighbor by admitting local children.

- A child is very sick and must go to a hospital far from home. To make it a little easier, McDonald's restaurants have sponsored homes-away-from-home for such children and their families. Since 1974, Ronald McDonald Houses have provided a homelike setting for children who can leave the hospital briefly. Families can visit them or stay there safely, inexpensively, and in a supportive atmosphere. Volunteer staffs run the Houses, but "guests" also serve as temporary volunteers, keeping things clean and orderly. Over 100 Houses have served one million families.

Do you know about any other companies that contribute?

Teen Entrepreneurs

Teenagers throughout the country are actively involved in entrepreneurship. Their success stories are proof that you can make profts if you are aware of people's wants and needs.

Look at the fundraising activities of some of the clubs in your school. Groups such as Future Homemakers of America demonstrate entrepreneurship whenever they make a profit on baked goods or child care services. Junior Achievement and the 4H organization also allow teens to develop skills as entrepreneurs. Clubs such as Future Business Leaders of America (FBLA), Vocational Industrial Clubs of America (VICA), and Distributive Education Clubs of America (DECA) encourage young entrepreneurs as well.

Experience as a teen entrepreneur can be very valuable. Choose a business that interests you. You can set your own hours so your work won't interfere with school. You can set your own pay rate, too. Working independently, you'll gain experience that will help you reach your long-term career goal. As your business grows, you can even help solve teen unemployment by hiring your friends.

See page T74 for answers.
For Review
1. What are goods and services?
2. Name five characteristics of a successful entrepreneur.
3. Name five ways in which experience as a teen entrepreneur can be valuable.

REINFORCEMENT: Have students think of services they could perform that could develop into business ventures. Discuss ideas in class to determine which ideas are realistic.

Section 9.2
Consumers in Action

As you read, think about:

- the rights you have as a consumer. (p. 193)
- the importance of exercising your responsibility as a consumer. (p. 193)
- the various laws that protect your rights and interests as a consumer. (p. 195)

You have learned that freedom of choice is the foundation of our economy. Consumers, businesses, and the government must be responsible to each other in order to protect that freedom.

You can help. Learning more about your consumer rights is the first step. Then, by exercising your rights and living up to your responsibilities, you can show your support for free enterprise.

Consumer Rights

As a consumer in the American economy, you have clout. That is, you have a great deal of power and influence. Your spending habits help decide what goods are produced. Your buying decisions also determine what services are provided. You have this power because you have rights.

- **The right to safety** Every consumer is protected from the sale of goods and services that are unsafe to use.
- **The right to choose** This means that you have the right to select from a variety of goods and services. When you shop for jeans, for example, you can choose from more than one brand.

NOTE: The right to consumer education arose in the 1970s. Consumer education focuses on being informed about our economy; the way in which goods and services are bought and sold; and the relationship of consumers and producers to one another as well as to the economy.

PHOTO: What choice is this boy making? In what ways is his making a choice like voting?

Do you select goods carefully? It's your right to do so.

- **The right to be informed** This right entitles you to all the information you need to make informed choices about products or services.
- **The right to be heard** This right gives you the power to speak out when you have a complaint about a product.
- **The right to redress** All consumers have the right to have their complaints heard and acted upon.
- **The right to consumer education** You are entitled to information about our economic system and your rights as a consumer.

Consumer Responsibilities

Each consumer right you have also carries responsibilities. You earn and protect your rights by meeting these obligations.

DISCUSS: What is your responsibility as a consumer if the products or services you choose turn out to be unsatisfactory?

Understanding your responsibilities is an important part of being a concerned consumer and a good citizen.

- **Use products safely.** Use products according to the manufacturer's directions and warnings. Be sure to read labels and booklets that accompany products.
- **Think about your choices.** Don't buy the first product you see. Learn about the many choices available to you.
- **Gather accurate information.** Find out all you can about a product before you buy it. Read labels and hangtags carefully. Ask questions if you need more information.
- **Make complaints when neccessary.** Speak out if you are not satisfied with a product or service.
- **Know your consumer rights.** Learn about our economic system and your rights as a consumer.

Remember to fill out and mail your warranty cards.

Consumer Protection

When you purchase a product, there are two different ways you can be certain your rights will be protected. If you buy a product with a warranty or if you sign a contract, you have a binding agreement. This guarantees your right to be satisfied with your purchase.

Warranties

"Can I see the warranty?" is one of the first questions a smart consumer asks when making a purchase. That's because a warranty protects your consumer rights. A **warranty** is a promise from the manufacturer or seller. It guarantees that the product you are buying can do what it is intended to do if you use it properly. Thus, a warranty ensures that an alarm clock must ring when set correctly.

If a product doesn't work properly, your money may be refunded or the product may be replaced. Sometimes this must be done within a specific time period, depending on the type of warranty.

Often, manufacturers require consumers to fill out a *warranty registration certificate*. This is usually a card that you will find in the box with your purchase. To receive service under the warranty, you have to fill in the card and mail it to the manufacturer. If you fail to do so, the warranty may not be valid.

Before you buy, it is your responsibility to read the warranty carefully. Remember, a warranty is effective only if the product doesn't do what it was made to do. You have no claim if you damage the product or use it incorrectly.

REINFORCEMENT: Brainstorm a list of purchases that a teenager might buy that would carry a warranty.

Proof of Purchase To receive the service promised in your warranty, it may be necessary to have *proof of purchase.* This means your sales receipt, a copy of the warranty, and the model number of the product. That's why it is extremely important to save all this information each time you make a purchase.

Contracts

When you hear the word "contract," do you think of a document that's impossible to read and understand? A **contract** is an agreement between two or more people to do something. Some contracts are complicated, but others are not. In fact, any type of exchange of money for the purchase of goods and services can be called a contract.

Before you sign any written contract, be sure you read it carefully and understand all of its terms.

Laws That Protect You

Dishonesty and consumer fraud are against the law. To protect you from unfair business practices, the government has made it illegal to mislead or deceive consumers. Many rules and regulations have been passed to protect your rights and interests.

- The Care Labeling Act is an important piece of consumer legislation. Enforced since 1972, it requires clothing manufacturers to attach care labels permanently to every garment they produce. These labels must show clearly how to care for the garment.

Do you want to return an item? You'll need your proof of purchase.

- To protect consumers from the manufacture and sale of unsafe goods, the Consumer Product Safety Act was passed in 1972. It established the Consumer Product Safety Commission (CPSC). The CPSC conducts safety tests on toys, tools, and household appliances. If a product is unsafe, the CPSC can order the manufacturer to stop selling it.
- The goal of the Truth-in-Advertising Act is to prevent false or misleading advertising. The act requires manufacturers to be able to prove that a product can do what is promised in the ad. This act also makes it illegal for sellers to advertise a low price for a product and then charge a higher price. Both the Federal Trade Commission (FTC) and the Federal Communications Commission (FCC) are active in enforcing the Truth-in-Advertising Act.

Can you be both firm and polite? That's the route to success here.

Making a Verbal Complaint

Once you determine that you have a complaint, it's time to take positive action. The following six steps will help you get results.

1. As soon as possible, take the product back to the store with the sales slip, contract, or warranty. Don't wait. The store may not be able to replace the product, or the warranty on it may run out.
2. If you bought a product that is damaged or defective, check to see whether this is covered under the warranty. In this way you will know what course of action you should take.
3. Take notes on what is wrong with the product or why you were dissatisfied with the service. Also decide how you would like the problem to be solved. Do you want to have the product replaced or repaired? Or do you want your money back?
4. Take the paperwork and the product to the department in the store where you made your purchase. If the salesperson is unable to help you, ask to see a department manager, store manager, or customer service representative.
5. Use your notes to explain the problem. Be brief, firm, and polite; anger will complicate the issue, not solve the problem. Propose your solution. If the store is not willing to meet your terms, find a compromise, that is, a mutually agreeable alternative.
6. If the store refuses to cooperate, you need a new strategy. It's time to put your complaint in a letter.

Writing a Complaint Letter

Using your letter-writing skills is an effective way to voice a complaint. Both you and the company at fault will have a record of the problem. A well-written complaint letter should contain the following five specific parts.

Personal Information In addition to your name and address, be sure to include your telephone number. The company may respond by phone or may need to call you for more information.

The Salutation "To Whom it May Concern" or "Dear Sir" are poor choices for a greeting when writing a complaint letter. If you want results, it's important to address the letter to the person in charge. Call the company and ask for the

ENRICHMENT: Role-play the following situation: The sporting goods store is having a going-out-of-business sale. You buy a basketball, and your receipt is stamped "Final sale." After playing with the ball for an hour, you realize it doesn't have nearly the bounce a new ball should.

196   Unit 3/*Resource Management*

ART: As reinforcement, go over each part of the letter of complaint. Show how the writer has a clear purpose and audience in mind. Also call attention to the format.

A Complaint Letter

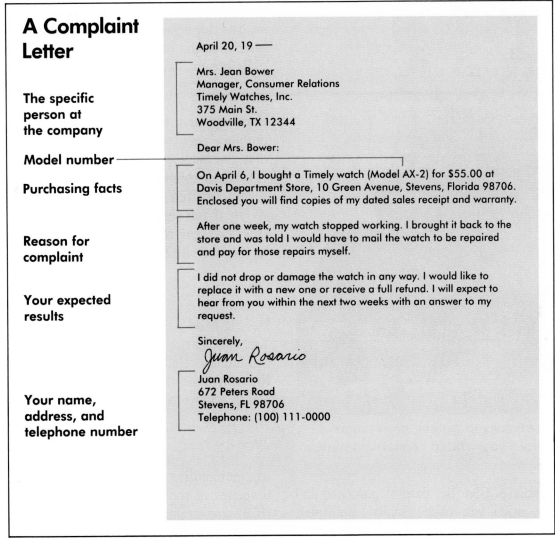

The specific person at the company

Model number

Purchasing facts

Reason for complaint

Your expected results

Your name, address, and telephone number

April 20, 19 ——

Mrs. Jean Bower
Manager, Consumer Relations
Timely Watches, Inc.
375 Main St.
Woodville, TX 12344

Dear Mrs. Bower:

On April 6, I bought a Timely watch (Model AX-2) for $55.00 at Davis Department Store, 10 Green Avenue, Stevens, Florida 98706. Enclosed you will find copies of my dated sales receipt and warranty.

After one week, my watch stopped working. I brought it back to the store and was told I would have to mail the watch to be repaired and pay for those repairs myself.

I did not drop or damage the watch in any way. I would like to replace it with a new one or receive a full refund. I will expect to hear from you within the next two weeks with an answer to my request.

Sincerely,

Juan Rosario

Juan Rosario
672 Peters Road
Stevens, FL 98706
Telephone: (100) 111-0000

Sometimes it's best to state your complaint in writing.

name and title of the manager, president, or customer service representative. If the company is not local, find out if they have a toll-free telephone number. If not, check the product carton for the manufacturer's address. Address the letter to the attention of the customer service department if you cannot get a specific person's name. *Standard & Poor's Register of Corpora-* *tions* lists the names and addresses of major companies throughout the country. You can find this publication at your local library.

The Facts Identify the name of the product or service and the style or model number if available. Write the name and address of the store where you made your

ENRICHMENT: Have students exercise their right to be heard by writing a letter of complaint to Ms. Jane Jones, President, Video Corporation, Willowtree, NJ 02731, regarding the purchase of two new $29.95 videos that are defective.

REINFORCEMENT: Is there a student in your class who has an actual problem to write a letter about? Write the letter as a class, using the board or the overhead projector.

Make calls to gather information before you write a complaint letter.

Your Expected Results Propose your solution and suggest a reasonable time, such as three weeks, for the manufacturer to resolve the problem.

Before mailing your written complaint, be sure to make a copy of the letter. Keep it in a file with the original copy of your warranty and sales slip. Then, if the problem isn't resolved, you have proof that you made a formal complaint.

Often a company works quickly to resolve a written complaint. But what can you do if you send one or two letters and still don't get results? Then it's time to turn to outside sources for help.

Where to Go for Help

Do you need help resolving a complaint? You can learn about resources in your community that provide this service. Knowing how they can help will enable you to achieve your rights as a consumer.

purchase. Give the date of purchase and the price you paid. Finally, you must mention whether or not you have a warranty, sales slip, or bills from the purchase. If so, include copies of these items (not the originals) with the letter.

The Reason for Your Complaint Give a simple, brief, and polite statement explaining why you are dissatisfied with the product or service. For example, say a garment's colors ran even though it was labeled colorfast and you followed washing instructions.

The Better Business Bureau

In communities throughout the country, branches of the Better Business Bureau (BBB) are an important resource for help and information. The BBB is a nonprofit organization sponsored by local businesses. Since 1916 it has actively promoted honest business practices and protected consumer interests. If you need help resolving a complaint, you can ask the Better Business Bureau to step in and help out. The Bureau will let you know if other consumers have complained the same store or service in your community. It will also tell you how the complaint was handled.

DISCUSS: Explain the role of the Better Business Bureau in helping people to resolve a complaint after a written complaint has had no effect in getting results.

The goal is to be satisfied with your purchase. If you're not, a consumer action line might help you.

Consumer Action Lines

In recent years, newspapers and television and radio stations have taken an active interest in consumer problems. They have created action lines that consumers can use to help resolve their complaints. When you contact one of these lines, your complaint gets media attention. The threat of community-wide publicity often causes a company to handle problems quickly in order to protect its reputation.

Government Agencies

In addition to supplying information, many federal agencies are directly involved in resolving consumer problems. If you have a complaint about an unsafe product or

Did You Know?

"Money talks" is a figure of speech that expresses the power of money—or financial resources—to get things done. But money also "talks" in the following expressions that people use every day. Can you translate these figures of speech? Can you think of others?

- They're a dime a dozen!
- He's a penny-pincher.
- I'll bet you dollars to doughnuts.
- Penny for your thoughts.

REINFORCEMENT: Have students find out the address and telephone number of the Better Business Bureau office nearest you.

ENRICHMENT: Ask students to research consumer action lines in your area. What types of consumer issues do they routinely help to resolve?

Federal Agencies for Consumers

FEDERAL AGENCY	RESPONSIBILITIES
Consumer Product Safety Commission	Sets standards of safety for household products
Federal Trade Commission	Monitors advertising procedures and selling practices; regulates competition among businesses
Food and Drug Administration	Inspects food and drug production plants; regulates the quality of food, drugs, and cosmetics
Department of Agriculture	Inspects and grades food
Federal Communications Commission	Sets standards for radio and television broadcasting and advertising
Interstate Commerce Commission	Sets standards and regulates rates for train and bus travel
Postal Service	Prevents mail fraud; regulates mail practices
Office of Consumer Affairs	Provides consumer education
Securities and Exchange Commission	Regulates the sale of stocks and bonds

Do you know where to go or whom to call for help? Many agencies exist to help you.

false advertising, you can contact the appropriate agencies for assistance. To find a local and state office of a federal agency, check the blue pages of your telephone book.

Obtaining Legal Help

The legal system in the United States also works to protect consumer rights. To resolve a complaint against a store or company in your community, you can go to *small claims court*. There you can informally present your own case to a judge. Because you don't need a lawyer, there are no expensive legal fees. The judge decides how the complaint should be settled. Then you and the business concerned must comply, that is, go along, with the court's decision.

For Review

1. Name four of your consumer rights.
2. Explain the responsibilities that go with those rights.
3. Name three laws that protect you as a consumer.
4. Name the five parts of a well-written complaint letter.

Learning to Manage

The Consumer Maze

Look back at the conversation on page 188. Now read how Pete tries to manage his consumer situation. Then answer the questions that follow.

Pete took his broken radio, sales receipt, and warranty information to the store where he had bought the radio. He was sure that he would walk out with a brand new radio a short time later.

A *long* time later, Pete got to the front of the "Returns" line. He told his story to the clerk and asked how he could get a replacement for his radio. The clerk pointed to the sign stating store policy: NO RETURNS ON MERCHANDISE AFTER 30 DAYS FROM THE DATE OF PURCHASE. Pete's heart sank. He had bought the radio six weeks ago. What now? He had the warranty. That still meant he could get a new radio, didn't it? The clerk asked him if he had read the warranty. Pete said that he hadn't, but he remembered that it was effective for 90 days.

As he read the warranty paper now, Pete realized it did not give the full coverage that he had assumed. In fact, only problems with the plastic casing of the radio were covered. The repairs that were needed to the inside of the radio were not. The address of the repair department was given in the warranty. The company would repair the radio—for a price. However, Pete would have to pay to ship it to them, along with the warranty and the sales slip. There were actually price listings in the warranty booklet for different repairs. How did he know which repair he needed? If he knew what was wrong, he could fix it himself. "Allow six to eight weeks for repairs." That was another piece of bad news. He really didn't like the idea of waiting all that time for his radio to come back. He couldn't, however, afford to buy a new one.

Pete vaguely remembered friends telling him that he should pay a little more for a better brand of radio. Now it looked as though he'd be paying the difference anyway—in repairs!

Questions

1. If you were Pete, what would you do next? Explain why, as a consumer, you would take this action.
2. Using what you have learned in this chapter, explain one error that you think Pete made.
3. Compare the warranties on any two similar small appliances in a store. Is one warranty better than the other? What are the terms of each?

Chapter 9 Review

Summary

In the United States the economic system is called free enterprise. Under this system, citizens have many freedoms in the marketplace. Competition among businesses protects freedom of choice and makes entrepreneurship a career opportunity for everyone.

As a consumer, you have many rights. Government agencies and nonprofit groups are at work protecting you. Warranties and contracts are documents that also protect you from possible fraud in the marketplace.

As a consumer, you have two important obligations. You must voice your opinion by making verbal or written complaints and seek help when you have been treated unfairly. Acting on your rights reinforces your power in the economy.

Vocabulary

Complete each of the following sentences with the correct word from the vocabulary list below.

demand (p. 191) warranty (p. 194)
contract (p. 195) consumer (p. 189)
supply (p. 190) free enterprise (p. 189)
competition (p. 190) entrepreneurship (p. 191)

1. _____ is the effort similar businesses make to outdo one another by producing better goods and services at lower prices.

2. A _____ is someone who buys and uses goods and services.

3. The ability to use your own resources and talents to develop an idea into profitable goods or services is called _____.

4. _____ is the amount and kinds of goods and services that are available for consumers to choose from.

5. A _____ is a promise from the manufacturer or seller that a product can do what it is intended to do if used properly.

6. _____ consists of the goods and services consumers want.

7. An agreement between two or more people to do something is called a _____.

8. Under the system of _____ people have many rights and freedoms to work, to buy and sell products, and to own property.

Questions

•• 1. Describe two characteristics of the free enterprise system.

• 2. Explain the difference between *goods* and *services*.

3. Explain the three steps in the system of meeting needs and wants.

••• 4. Government involvement in businesses in the United States is carefully controlled. Why is this important to our economic system?

The dots represent skill levels required to answer each question or complete each activity:
• requires recall and comprehension
•• requires application and analysis
••• requires synthesis and evaluation

5. How do you, as a consumer, benefit from competition between one business and another?

6. How does the principle of supply and demand work?

7. Study the characteristics of an entrepreneur on page 191. Now rank them in order of importance giving reasons for the order you have chosen.

8. Name four basic rights you have as a consumer.

9. Manufacturers must produce products that are safe for you to use. What is the consumer's responsibility regarding the safety of a product?

10. Should you complain about a product that does not meet safety standards? Explain your answer.

11. What should you do before you sign a written contract?

12. What is the Truth-in-Advertising Act?

13. List the six steps involved in making an effective verbal complaint.

14. Why do you address a letter of complaint to the person in charge?

15. What is the Better Business Bureau?

Skill Activities

Many more activities are contained in the annotations within this chapter.

 1. Laboratory As a class, set up a mock business to sell a product you could make in class. What will you make to sell? What are your costs? What will be the selling price? How will the profits be spent? Create an advertising campaign for the product.

 2. Communication Have you ever put on a brand new jacket only to find that the zipper does not work? Think about a product or service that you or someone in your family has purchased that was not satisfactory in quality or performance. Write a letter to the company or manufacturer involved. Include the information shown on page 197 in the sample complaint letter. Share your letter with the class. Make improvements in the letter based on the comments of your classmates.

 3. Decision Making Using a source like *Consumer Reports* magazine, research one product that you or your family is considering purchasing. Which brand best meets your needs and family budget?

 4. Communication Using the television show "People's Court" as your model, role-play the following complaint. You purchased a pair of jeans that shrank drastically after the first washing. You are claiming a refund of the purchase price. One student acts as the defendant, who claims that the plaintiff did not follow the instructions on the label. After the case is presented to the jury (class), decide whose claim is more valid.

Chapter 10
Skillful Shopping

The dialogue below introduces "A Clear Shopping Picture," the Learning to Manage feature in this chapter. The case study is continued and the situation discussed further on page 219. See page T79 for teaching suggestions.

"A new television! That's great, Dad. There's a special show on tonight. Now I can watch it without all of those fuzzy lines on it."

"Hold on a minute, Tina! We've decided to buy one, but it won't be bought today."

"Why not?"

"We have to find out all about brands, prices, and stores before we make a choice. Smart shoppers don't make a big purchase like this in one day."

Section 10.1
Planning Your Purchases

As you read, think about:

■ how to make a shopping plan. (p. 205)

■ how to get information about products and services before you make a purchase. (p. 205)

■ how to choose the best place to shop. (p. 206)

■ how advertising, peer and family influences, and sales affect your shopping decisions. (p. 208)

Shopping in today's marketplace is a risky business. With so many products and services to choose from, you have to know how to use your resources wisely. That way, every time you buy a product or service, you will get the best possible value for it.

Your Shopping Plan

First you need to develop an effective shopping plan. This is a six-step process. You define your needs; consider your alternatives; identify your specific requirements; review your budget; gather information; and, finally, organize your trip.

1. Define Needs You have many needs in your life. Your first step in planning is to decide which of them to satisfy.

2. Consider Alternatives Evaluate other possible ways to meet your needs before you make a purchase.

PHOTO: Ask students to think about the best purchase that they ever made. Then ask what was most important to them—where they bought it, the price they paid, or how much satisfaction they have gotten from the item.

A little bit of planning can go a long way in the marketplace.

3. Identify Requirements You must decide what special features you want or the type of model that you must have. Make a list before you shop.

4. Review Budget Because you are using a limited resource—money—you have to check that this purchase fits into your total spending plan. Have you set aside money for such a major purchase? If you make the purchase now, will you still be able to meet all your monthly expenses? Are you counting on help from your parents? If so, how will making this purchase affect your family budget?

5. Gather Information Begin by carefully examining the competing goods and services available in the marketplace. This is called **comparison shopping.**

DISCUSS: Talk about the characteristics of a good shopper. List some characteristics on the board and have students add to the list.

ENRICHMENT: Ask students to imagine that they have won a $1,000.00 shopping spree at their favorite store and that they will have one hour to make purchases. Students should list twenty items they want to purchase, estimate the cost of each, and add up the total. Then they should adjust their lists as needed.

Your community has several resources that can help you to get the information you need. The following are a few:

- **Personal recommendations** Talk to people who own a product or have used a service. Ask their opinions.
- **Mass media** Look in printed materials and listen to television and radio ads for facts about products and services.
- **Telephone** Call stores to locate items and to get prices if possible.
- **Other sources** Nonprofit organizations such as Consumers' Union are good sources. *Consumer Reports* is one of their publications. Federal, state, and local agencies and the Better Business Bureau also provide helpful consumer information.

You can see that the planning process we have discussed takes both time and energy. Is it necessary to go through it all each time you make a purchase? Not always. It doesn't pay to spend a lot of time comparison shopping for inexpensive items, such as a felt-tipped pen. But for all your major expenses—clothing, household goods, and even insurance and credit—you should use your comparison shopping skills. Only then can you feel confident that you have exercised your rights to be informed and to choose. In this way you can act responsibly by making a knowledgeable choice.

6. Organize the Shopping Trip You've compared prices and features of different products or services. Now it's time to write all the information you gathered into a form you can carry easily. This way you'll have all the facts at your fingertips when you shop.

Where to Shop

At one time you could walk to the general store and purchase everything from cornmeal and flour to boots and saddles. Today, you are faced not only with a large variety of goods and services but also with many different stores. Knowing more about the types of sellers in the marketplace can be a tremendous help in making your buying decisions. The chart on the next page shows various alternatives available and indicates their advantages and disadvantages.

How to Decide

How can consumers in today's marketplace decide where to buy their goods and services? Certainly, one important factor to consider is where you can get the best price. There are, however, five other questions you should ask yourself before you pick a place to shop.

- Is it convenient? Always weigh the time, energy, and money needed to travel to a discount store against the savings.
- Is quality merchandise available? A store may have the best prices in town, but you could end up paying good money for poor quality.
- Does the seller offer a good selection of products and services? If not, you can't comparison shop there.
- Does the seller have a good reputation? You should deal only with businesses that value and respect their customers and honor their return policies.
- Does the seller accept alternatives to cash? Find out if you can pay by check or credit card, if this is what you prefer.

Shopping Alternatives

Type of Shopping	Advantages	Disadvantages
1. Department Stores	• wide variety of goods and services • broad range of prices • competitive prices • various methods of payment, including store credit card • Liberal return policy	• some have slightly higher prices to pay for goods and service
2. Discount Stores	• low prices • various methods of payment, including store credit card	• no special services • labels often removed • plain surroundings • restricted return policies
3. Specialty Stores	• special items • wide selection of one kind of item • salespeople know product well • various methods of payment	• prices may be high • no store credit card
4. Factory Outlets	• low prices	• merchandise may be imperfect, out of style, • few services • labels often removed • limited methods of payment
5. Mail-order or Catalog Shopping	• variety of items • no store crowds • payment by check or credit card	• shipping and handling may be added • can't examine merchandise first • returning may be difficult
6. Door-to-door Selling	• convenient • can cancel order of over $25. within three days of sale	• may feel pressure to buy
7. Electronic Shopping	• convenient • range of products • low prices • can use credit card • purchase mailed	• some merchandise not good quality, out of date, discontinued • fosters impulse buying • can't examine merchandise first • limited comparison shopping

A department store isn't the only place to find exactly what you're looking for at the price you want to pay.

ART: Ask students which of these alternatives, other than the department store, they have taken and how the experience compared with shopping in a more traditional way.

DISCUSS: Ask students if they have ever done any comparison shopping. What did they shop for, and what factors determined their choice?

What do advertisers do to try to influence what you buy?

Influences on Buying

Certainly, you play a major role in deciding what goods and services will satisfy your needs and wants. But there are outside influences that affect your buying decisions, too. Understanding more about these influences will help you to make wiser choices in the marketplace.

Advertising

Advertising, the messages companies send out about their products and services, is all around you. You hear ads on the radio. You read ads in magazines, newspapers, and in your mail. You see ads on highway billboards, at stores, and even on the grocery cart.

With so much advertising in the marketplace, it seems that manufacturers are out to get you. They are. Advertisers spend billions of dollars each year trying to entice you to buy what they are selling. They appeal to consumers in many different ways. Some ads suggest that you will have more love in your life, more friends, and greater success if you use their product. **Emotional appeals,** as these ads are called, target consumers' feelings.

There are different kinds of emotional appeals. For example, a toothpaste advertisement that shows a man and a woman kissing uses a form of *sex appeal*. A magazine ad for acne medication shows a horrified teenager who has broken out just before a big date. This uses *fear appeal* to get your attention.

Did You Know?

Advertisers use many of the same devices poets and songwriters do. To attract your attention and be remembered, they use rhyme (the same sound h*eard* at the end of a w*ord*) and alliteration (the *s*ame *s*ound *s*ignaling the *s*tart of words). They also use rhythm, especially in jingles. See if you can find rhythm, rhyme, and alliteration in your favorite ads.

Other ads employ *rational appeals*. They satisfy your need to be practical by offering detailed information. For example, a breakfast cereal ad might claim that the brand has more vitamins and minerals than other leading brands.

Some ads also use humor or a combination of these appeals to stimulate your interest in a product or service.

Advertising Techniques Have you ever decided to buy one brand of soda because you saw your favorite television celebrity drinking it in an ad? You're not alone. Millions of people are influenced by what famous people eat, drink, drive, and wear. That's why advertisers frequently use celebrities to promote a product or service. This type of advertising technique is called an *endorsement*.

Advertisers sometimes use ordinary people to praise products, too. This technique is called a *testimonial*.

The Value of Advertising It may seem to you that advertising works only for the benefit of manufacturers. However, advertising helps consumers in many ways. It lets us know what products and services are currently available. It is also a way to introduce items in the marketplace. Many ads provide important information about sales, rebates, and discounts that you can use when you are comparison shopping.

Does advertising take advantage of consumers? It can—but that's up to you. You must look beyond the techniques used to sell a product to what the ads actually tell you about it.

ENRICHMENT: Have students give one example of a current ad for each of the following appeals: sex appeal, fear appeal, and rational appeal.

PHOTO: Ask students to talk about items that they have purchased as a result of seeing or hearing about what someone else purchased.

Why do we buy certain items? Is it because of what other people have?

Peer Influences

One of our most important psychological needs is to be a part of a group. Belonging gives us self-esteem and security.

To satisfy this need, however, consumers often make purchases based on what's "in" rather than on what's best. You may have seen this happen in your school. A whole group may start wearing white sneakers without shoelaces. Soon everybody in school has white sneakers and leaves the laces at home!

Some adults are influenced by their peers, too. Have you heard talk about people "keeping up with the Joneses"? This means making the same expensive purchases as one's peers just for show. These expensive purchases are called **status symbols** because they are intended to show off financial and social status.

ENRICHMENT: Ask students to interview three adults to find out what status symbols were popular or "in" when they were teenagers. If possible, they should interview someone who was a teen during the '50s, the '60s, and the '70s.

Technology

Cash Box to Computer

Have you ever "shopped" at a child's lemonade stand? If so, you paid cash, and the "shopkeeper" used cash to make change. All shopping used to be just as simple, and some still is. However, if you buy lemonade in a supermarket, paying for it probably involves electronic wizardry.

It all started with the cash register, invented by James Ritty in 1879. Ritty's first model was really a gear-operated adding machine. Later, automatic models *registered*, or recorded, cash sales and printed out slips. As time went on, more advanced cash registers showed the amount paid and how much change was owed. People still made their payments in cash, however.

In the 1950s, credit cards, which depended on computerized record keeping, became popular. Soon after, computers also revolutionized cash registers. The new models were faster than mechanical ones. They could check customer credit, bill charge accounts, issue itemized receipts, and keep the store's inventory. With some models, you just touch the screen with an electronic pointer, or scanners "read" codes on packages and "know" each price. These are becoming so popular that the next generation of lemonade stand operators may soon be ordering them!

What do you think of these changes?

Teenagers have their own status symbols. Wearing a football jersey may be a symbol of importance. "Designer" clothing can also be a status symbol.

Family Influences

Parents and other family members often influence our spending habits a great deal. Can you think of a time that you purchased something at the suggestion of a family member? Unlike advertisers who are out to make a profit, members of your family have your best interests in mind. They may have learned the value and quality of a product or service through comparison shopping. They may also have had either a positive or negative experience with a store or business in your community. Your family, therefore, can influence your buying habits by providing valuable information.

Sales

It's not often that you can walk into a store without seeing any sale signs. Many consumers buy sale merchandise because they think they are getting a good buy. But they may not be getting the best value, even though the product is marked down. Let's first consider the reasons stores put their merchandise on sale.

Why Hold a Sale? Why do sellers hold storewide sales? There are a few basic reasons. A store may advertise a sale to attract new customers and to bring regular customers back into the store.

Sales also help sellers to unload goods that have not sold well. Customers may buy these goods at reduced prices.

NOTE: Clothing stores generally work on a 100–150% markup. If a pair of jeans costs the store $30.00, it would retail for $60.00 to $75.00, depending on the rate of markup.

Lastly, sellers may advertise and promote a variety of sales to compete with similar stores. In this way they hope to win a greater share of the market.

Naturally, all retailers hope that, while you're visiting the store during the sale, you purchase some of their regular merchandise, too. Remember, sellers usually make a greater profit on these goods than they do on their sale merchandise.

Kinds of Sales Knowing how to shop at a sale is a special skill smart shoppers learn. Stores hold a variety of different sales at which you can find different kinds of merchandise. For example, at an *end-of-season* sale held in December, you can find some good buys on fall and winter clothes. Another example would be bathing suits on sale in September after the summer season. As stores make room for new merchandise, you can save money.

A sale on *seconds* may be common in your community. Some stores buy goods that are slightly flawed, or damaged, and sell them at lower prices. You may be able to get a good buy at these sales if you examine the merchandise carefully.

A *final sale* usually indicates that whatever you buy is not returnable. These products may be leftovers from a previous season. If you select final sale items, be certain you are satisfied with them before you buy.

Sales Versus Bargains Perhaps you once went to a sale at your favorite store and bought a great sweater. Then you realized afterwards that you had nothing to wear with it. You *did* get a great price on the sweater, but it was no bargain.

A sale can offer you great buys, but it can also be a consumer trap.

That's because the sweater has no value to you until you buy a coordinating pair of pants or a skirt. A *bargain* is a product or service you buy at a low price that also satisfies one of your needs.

There are several instances when you may think you're getting a bargain, but in reality, you're not. Suppose you buy a tape recorder on sale without a warranty. It's no bargain if you have to pay for costly repairs. If you need accessories to operate a sale product, you may end up paying the regular price of a fully equipped product. That's no bargain, either.

With all the "mumbo jumbo" in the marketplace, how can you be sure you get a bargain at a sale? Suppose you want to

PHOTO: Ask students to discuss their experience with marked-down items. Are sales always as attractive as they may at first seem?

Sure, it's a great price. But do you really need the item?

buy a portable room heater on sale at a local store. In making your decision, there are several questions to consider.

- Do you need the heater?
- Is it in usable condition?
- Is the sale price less than the regular price at other stores?
- Would you pay full price for the item?

If you can answer "yes" to each of these questions, you have definitely found a true bargain.

See page T80 for answers.

For Review

1. Name the six steps that are part of a shopping plan.
2. What five factors should you consider in deciding where to shop?
3. Besides advertising, name two factors that often influence your buying decisions.

NOTE: The term "Brand X" arose during the time when it was illegal for advertisers to use the names of competing products in their ads. Now that advertisers can refer to other products by their names (as long as what they say is true) this bit of advertising jargon may disappear from our language.

Section 10.2
Shopping Wisely

As you read, think about:

- how to adjust in your shopping plan. (p. 213)
- how to shop for quality merchandise. (p. 215)
- the importance of knowing store policies regarding returns and exchanges. (p. 219)

What is the best tactic for becoming a successful shopper? You have learned that you must analyze your needs, review your budget, and gather information before making your buying decision. You know you should compare prices and quality, organize your trip, and use outside influences to your advantage.

You have also seen that the foundation of all successful shopping trips is a good plan. Your football coach uses a game plan to help your team win on the field. You must use your plan, too, to be a winner when you shop.

Making Your Plan Work

As you may recall, part of the planning process is listing your specific requirements of a product or service. Suppose, for example, you are choosing a new typewriter. You may be considering full-line correction, a spelling memory, and different printing styles.

You go to a store that a relative recommends to you. He or she has shopped there and has found its prices competitive. The store carries a wide variety of typewriters. Using your plan, you com-

DISCUSS: Which of the following items require one to comparison shop for the best quality: ice cream, a college education, a raincoat, a video casette recorder, a music video, a car, health care, laundry detergent, and a sofa.

A big purchase requires careful planning. Make sure you're getting the best product for your money.

pare features and prices. You look at Model A, which has only some of the features you require but is priced within your budget. You also examine Model B, which has every feature you want but costs $50 more than you planned to spend. You carefully planned to buy a quality product in your price range with the features you need. But the plan doesn't seem to be working! Your problem may seem hopeless, but there are two steps that will help you.

1. *Set your priorities.* Before you shop, know which features you absolutely need and which features you would like to have. The full-line correction, for

example, is especially useful if you make a lot of mistakes when you type. The different printing styles are handy if you type a variety of materials, such as term papers and poetry. Listing which features are most important to you determines your priorities. If the product within your budget has the features at the top of the list, it will satisfy your needs.

2. *Adjust your plan.* You may decide that all of the features you listed are important to you. Then you must be flexible and adjust your plan.

When planning your purchase you reviewed your budget to see if you

What do you own that you've bought too quickly? Where is the item now?

would have enough left for all your financial responsibilities. To adjust your plan, review your budget again. Perhaps you can afford to pay an extra $50 for the typewriter that has all the features you require. If not, can you comparison shop in other stores to see if this particular model costs less elsewhere?

Remember that the plan you create is meant to guide you, not restrain you from buying what you need. By being flexible, you can still meet your needs by adjusting your plan to suit your individual priorities.

Buying on Impulse

Each time you walk into a store, you are surrounded by thousands of products. Some of them you need; others you just want. Because your resources are limited, you can't buy everything. That's the point of a shopping plan: to meet your needs, and to avoid spending money you just can't afford.

Unfortunately, sellers don't make it easy for you to limit yourself to planned spending. They tempt you with low-cost items attractively displayed in key locations—at the door and near the check-out counters. Some businesses, like television home shopping programs, depend entirely on consumers who make spur-of-the-moment purchases.

When you give in to such temptations, you are an **impulse buyer,** a consumer who makes an unplanned purchase. Buying something without enough thought can, in an instant, ruin your plan, and even your whole budget!

Usually, if you buy an inexpensive item on impulse, like chewing gum or a notebook, you can handle it. After all, you've probably allowed for unexpected expenses in your budget.

However, over a period of time, these small purchases can add up. Impulse buys also use money that you would otherwise save toward your long-term goals. What's the key to controlling impulse buying? Keep your plan in hand and stick to it!

Quality Counts

In every purchasing decision, it is important to look for the highest quality that you can afford. That way you will get the best value for your money. Do this in the store when you are comparison shopping.

Suppose you want to buy a telephone for your room. When you are comparing products, you find one model that costs $55 and another model for $75. Should

Do you look for quality? Ask salespeople to help you. Read the information that is available. Compare features.

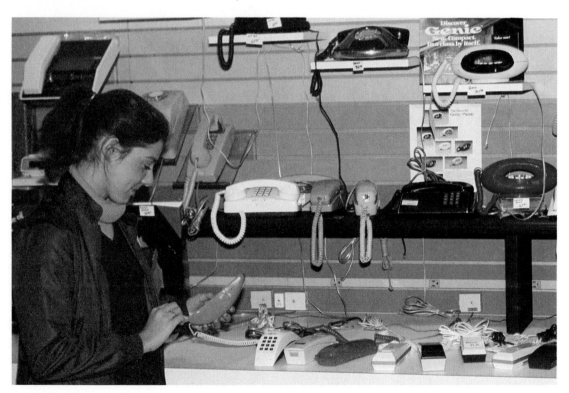

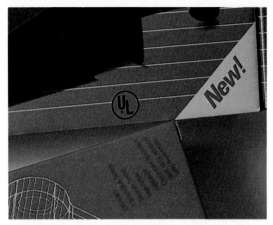

Is the product safe? This symbol tells you that it is.

you assume that the more expensive model is the better product? No. Higher prices are not always good indicators of quality. However, comparing the following factors will help you determine the quality of the products or services you are considering buying.

Safety

Any product or service that threatens your well-being is inferior. Some goods, such as electrical appliances, are hazardous if you don't use them correctly. But if you follow the instructions, you should not have to worry about injuries. Check to see that the products are well made. Also, look for seals of safety, for example, the Underwriter's Laboratory (UL) seal on electrical products.

Performance

Does the product do what it is supposed to do, and do it well? Does the shampoo really make your hair clean and shiny? You

can judge the quality of many products by whether or not the claims made about them hold true. You can often use a trial-size sample of a product to test its performance. For major purchases, ask the salesperson for a demonstration before you make a decision. Finally, check the *Consumer Index* to see if any of the leading consumer publications has tested this particular product.

Durability

Is the product made to last? Compare the construction features. Well-made goods won't wear out in a few weeks. Poor quality merchandise probably will wear out quickly.

Did You Know?

There are several ways to test a pair of sneakers to see if they'll be good for your feet.

■ Try to twist the sole. If it offers resistance, it will also give good side support.

■ Put the sneaker down "tippy-toe" and push. It should give at the widest part of the sole.

■ See if the heel cup is firm; if not, your heel may "slosh" around.

■ Be sure the seam at the back stands straight; and check that the sole is wide enough, especially at the heel.

Convenience

Is the product difficult to use or operate? If you have trouble zipping a suitcase or turning the key in a bicycle lock, chances are that the product is not right for you. When you are evaluating a product, try to test all the working parts before you decide to buy it.

Consumer Protection

You have learned how a warranty can protect you if you purchase a faulty product. Compare warranties to see which product offers you the best protection on your investment. You may find that it pays to spend a little more money for a product that offers a better warranty. This is especially true when you are making major purchases.

Manufacturer's Reputation

Many producers have earned a reputation for making quality goods. Find out who these manufacturers are to help you in your search for quality.

Care and Maintenance

Investigate the amount of care and up-keep needed to keep products functional and attractive. For example, a sweater that needs dry cleaning costs you more in terms of upkeep.

Try out products in the store. Be sure you like the way they work. Make certain they have the features you want.

PHOTO: Have students list some of the questions they should ask each time they purchase a product like the one shown above.

Take care of what you own. That's the last step in smart shopping.

Considering these factors when you comparison shop will ensure you find quality goods and services in the marketplace. Remember, however, that many items have even more features to look for to determine product and service quality. For example, experts have developed specific standards for consumers to use in judging the quality of food and clothing. You'll find this information in the appropriate chapters in this text.

Returns and Exchanges

With careful planning, you can purchase goods and services that meet your needs and use your resources efficiently. But even the most careful shoppers some-

times make a purchase with which they are not satisfied. For, example, you buy a backpack that rips the first time you use it. Or you choose a sweater for your brother's birthday that's the wrong size.

Check Store Policies

When you are dissatisfied with a purchase, you can take the merchandise back to the store where you bought it. Most stores allow you to exchange the merchandise for an identical item or another product of equal value. Some stores may even refund your money. Others issue a store credit in the amount of the returned item. You can then use it to make another purchase either then or later.

Some sellers in the marketplace refuse to take back any goods without price tags. This protects them against consumers who unfairly return goods that they originally purchased elsewhere.

As you learned in Chapter 9, it is essential to understand the store procedure for returning merchandise when you shop. Always look for signs in the store, or ask a salesperson before you buy.

See page T81 for answers.

For Review

1. How can you be flexible when using a shopping plan?
2. Name seven factors you should consider when judging the quality of a product.
3. What should you do to make sure that you will be able to return or exchange a purchase?

Learning to Manage

A Clear Shopping Picture

Look back at the conversation on page 204. Now read how Tina's family manages to buy a television. Then answer the questions that follow.

Of course, Tina's family all wanted the best quality they could get within their budget. But they all had different ideas. Tina's mother suggested that they buy one of the models that *Consumer Reports* recommended highly. She had looked up the television ratings in the latest issue at the library. Tina's brother, Jim, wanted the same model his friend's family had, because it had a very large screen. Tina's father wanted to look around for sales. Tina just wanted it *soon*. She voted for buying one at the warehouse nearby until her father told her some of their merchandise was damaged. After a week of discussions and checking the newspaper, they started shopping. "Sale" prices varied by as much as $50 from one store to the next. They found that the models rated most highly by *Consumer Reports* had more features than they really needed. This made them unnecessarily expensive. The oversized screens were also too costly. Finally, they agreed on one basic, brand-name model that had the features they needed and was in their price range. It also had a better warranty than most other brands. This was the one. Now they just had to compare prices and services.

The small local appliance store offered free delivery, but the price was too high there. The larger chain store in town did more business, so it had the lowest price —but no free delivery. They decided to pay less and bring the television home themselves. Tina's father paid cash because the interest rate on the installment plan was high. The final issue to be decided was whether or not to pay for a service contract. This would cover repairs for a year. When they compared it with the warranty coverage, they realized they didn't need the service contract. They made their purchase.

"I learned a lot about shopping, Dad," Tina said, as they were watching their new television. "I'm glad you slowed me down so we could get the best!"

Questions

1. If Tina's family had found the television they wanted for less money at a "going-out-of-business" sale, should they have bought it? Why or why not?
2. Think about the next major purchase either you or your family may make. Write out a plan for smart shopping. Include all the comparison shopping steps you would take.

Chapter 10 Review

Summary

Consumers are faced with many decisions in the marketplace. In order to make responsible decisions, you need to develop a range of skills. You can then use your resources efficiently to satisfy your wants and needs.

It is important to work out a plan for all your purchasing decisions. First you must master the skills you need to create and use a plan. Then you can go into the marketplace with confidence. You will obtain products and services of the best value and quality that your money can buy. And that, after all, is what being a smart shopper is all about.

Vocabulary

Complete each of the following sentences with the correct word from the vocabulary list below.

emotional appeals (p. 208)
status symbols (p. 209)
comparison shopping (p. 205)
impulse buyer (p. 215)

1. Possessions that people feel they must have in order to be part of a certain social class are called _____.

2. _____ is the process of comparing various prices and brands, as well as the quality of a product you wish to purchase.

3. Ads that target consumers' psychological needs and wants are called _____.

4. A consumer who makes an unplanned purchase without enough thought is an _____.

Questions

1. Name the six steps in a shopping plan.
2. Is it always practical to buy the least expensive item? Explain your answer.
3. Why do companies spend so much money on advertising?
4. Give an example of a television ad that uses rational appeal.
5. Compare these two advertising techniques: *endorsement* and *testimonial*.
6. Do you believe that advertising helps consumers or that it hinders them by trying to trick them into spending a great deal of money? Explain your answer.
7. Give two examples of products that are status symbols in today's society. Explain your answer.
8. Do you always get a bargain when you shop at a sale? Explain your answer.
9. Name at least four types of stores and give advantages and disadvantages of shopping at each one.
10. Does a high price always indicate a better product? Explain your answer.

The dots represent skill levels required to answer each question or complete each activity:

- requires recall and comprehension
- • requires application and analysis
- • • requires synthesis and evaluation

Skill Activities

Many more activities are contained in the annotations within this chapter.

 1. Laboratory Choose a pair of brand name sneakers to "shop" for. Look for this same pair of sneakers in a shopping catalog, a department store, and a discount store. Record the price of the sneakers from each of these sources. Use newspaper ads if you can't go to the stores. Decide which shopping source offers you the best value. Remember to include any reasons for paying a higher price if you decide to. For example, if the sneakers are advertised as "slightly irregular" in one place, you might decide to pay more somewhere else.

 2. Critical Thinking Find five ads in a magazine or select five television ads. Identify whether the advertisement uses an emotional appeal or a rational appeal. Which type of advertising do you find the most persuasive? Why?

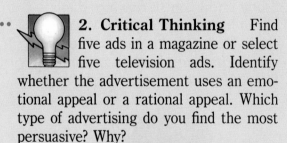 **3. Human Relations** Talk to your parents or other adults about their consumer experiences. Ask them if they ever paid for a product or service that did not meet their expectations. Have they ever returned products that did not meet the claims of an ad? Find out what happened. Did they get their money back? If they were not satisfied, did they pursue the matter further? Ask why or why not. Discuss your findings with the class.

4. Communication Create a written ad for a new product. Use your imagination to create a product that a teenager would want to buy. A shampoo, a soft drink, a skin medication, and a bicycle are a few possibilities. Use either rational appeals or emotional appeals that are described in this chapter to "sell" your product. Display your finished ads and discuss why some are more persuasive than others.

5. Decision Making Think of an item that you need to purchase. Perhaps you need a new raincoat or a new gym bag for school. Using what you have learned in this chapter, write a shopping plan for the item you have in mind. Be sure to include the six steps of the shopping plan outlined on pages 205-206. Share your plan with members of the class.

 6. Laboratory *Consumers' Research Magazine* and *Consumer Reports* test and compare different brands and models of many products. Choose a product (anything from toothpaste to toaster ovens to stereos) and research its ratings. Report on how products are tested and judged. Is the most expensive always the best?

Chapter 11
Housing and Home Furnishings

Vocabulary

The dialogue below introduces "Making Room," the Learning to Manage feature in this chapter. The case study is continued and the situation discussed further on page 245. See page T85 for teaching suggestions.

"Well, we'll have to rearrange everything first."

"Gee, Mom. I hope Judy and I get along. I'm glad you're marrying Tom, but I'm not so sure about getting an instant sister! I like her so far, but living in the same room is another thing."

"I know, Anna. We need to come up with a plan so that you can both have the privacy and the space you need—without spending a lot."

"Judy and I can sit down and talk about ideas for our room. We'll check it all out with you and see if we can put our plan into action before she moves in next month."

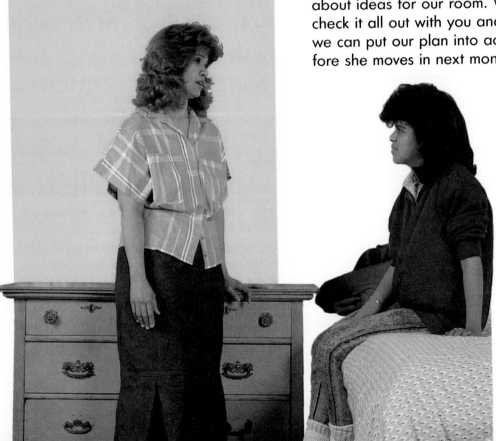

Section 11.1
Housing Decisions

As you read, think about:

■ how a home provides shelter and satisfies emotional needs. (p. 223)

■ how the kind of home people choose is influenced by economics, values, and availability. (p. 223)

■ the advantages and disadvantages of renting and buying housing. (p. 225)

Wherever you live, your space should feel like a home. A home can be a small apartment or a two-story house. It can be a mobile home or even a houseboat. People choose different kinds of homes because they have different needs and wants. Their choices are influenced by resources and availability.

Why do people say "home is where the heart is"?

What Is a Home?

Many factors will influence you when you choose your own home some day. Understanding more about these factors will help you to choose wisely.

Basic Needs

Shelter is one of our most basic needs. People need shelter from the elements —rain, snow, freezing temperatures, or the blazing sun—and somewhere to eat and sleep. People also need protection from danger. Windows and doors that can be locked help provide security.

A home also fills emotional needs. It is a place to relax and be with family and friends. A secure, comfortable home provides an environment in which people of all ages can continue to develop and grow. This kind of home makes it possible for people to express their own personalities and interests. Whether through conversation or music, woodworking or cooking, people find forms of self-expression in their own homes.

Influences

In choosing housing, people are influenced by a number of factors. The first is cost. Housing is more expensive in some areas than in others. Large houses usually cost more than smaller ones. Again, however, location is important. A large house in one

Green spaces are relaxing and good to look at. Are you willing to do the hours of work required to have such a pleasure?

area might be the same price as a small house somewhere else. A family with several children would probably find the larger house more comfortable but may have to consider other factors. The larger house might be too far from schools or day-care centers. So the family might decide to do without the extra space and choose the smaller house because the location is better.

This kind of trade-off occurs often. Imagine you are looking for a place to live. You enjoy gardening, so you are considering a small house with a yard. It is just outside town, and bus service is not available. You also find an apartment in town. You give up the yard if you take the apartment, but then you will be right beside a bus stop. What you finally decide depends on which factor you think is more important.

Housing Choices

The following are some of the choices you may have when you select housing.

Single-family houses may have one story, like ranch-style houses, or they may have several stories. Most single-family houses stand alone. Townhouses are also designed for single families, but they are attached to another house on either side.

A *duplex* houses two families. It may be divided vertically or horizontally. A building of this sort that houses three or more families is called a *multiplex*.

Apartments may be only one room or as large as a whole house. Some apartments have small gardens, patios, or balconies. A group of apartment buildings under the same management is called an apartment complex. Some complexes have special features, such as a swimming pool or tennis courts.

Mobile homes, also called manufactured homes, are made in a factory and moved by truck to a permanent site. Mobile homes have become increasingly popular. They are much less expensive than single-family homes. Some people find that they are more private than an apartment. In mobile home parks, laundry facilities and a swimming pool are sometimes available.

Renting Versus Buying

One of the first decisions to be made about housing is whether to rent the space or buy it. When people rent, they pay a monthly fee to the owner of the property. When they buy a home, most people pay only part of the cost in cash. They take out a long-term loan to pay for the rest. There are advantages and disadvantages to both renting and buying.

Renting Housing Most of the living space that is rented in the United States is found in apartment buildings. Apartments are rented for different periods of time, usually by the month or by the year. During that time, housing costs do not change very much. It is the property owners who are responsible for the building repairs and most of the upkeep. Many people like the convenience of apartment living, though some are bothered by noise. An apartment may have limited storage space. Some buildings do not allow children or pets. Families who live in apartments may have difficulty finding playgrounds for young children.

Buying Housing People who buy houses usually take out a loan to pay for the property. They pledge the house as

Do you dream of a house by the sea? Many people do. What are the good and bad features of this location?

What are the moods, emotions, and stresses that most people experience on moving day?

security if they do not pay the loan back. This pledge is called a **mortgage.** A financial institution such as a bank lends the money for a period of years. The buyer then pays back the money, plus interest, monthly. The interest is the money the bank charges in return for making the loan.

People who are able to buy may choose from several types of ownership. Besides single-family homes, condominiums and co-ops are available in some areas. A **condominium** is a unit, often an apartment, that can be bought rather than rented. Besides the cost of the unit, the owner pays a condominium fee, usually monthly. This covers building upkeep and any extras such as a swimming pool. A **co-op** is a building that is owned jointly by

many people. (The term *co-op* comes from the word *cooperative.*) Each owner may have living space and shares in building expenses. Condominiums and co-ops are often less expensive than single-family houses. They appeal to people who like the conveniences of apartment living but also wish to be home owners.

See page T86 for answers.

For Review

1. Name two important human needs that a home fulfills.
2. Why is the location of a new home important to a family?
3. Name three different types of housing available today.

Making a House a Home

As you read, think about:

- how design elements and principles can be used to decorate a home. (p. 227)
- the best way to organize the space in your home. (p. 231)

When you combine a sweater of a particular color with jeans and a belt, you are creating a design. You can do the same thing with rooms in your home. There may be spaces in your home that could be more comfortable and attractive. Whether working with large or small areas, you can use the elements of design to create a pleasing living space.

Elements of Design

The arrangement of lines, colors, textures, and patterns to create a desired effect is called **design.** You see the elements of design in almost everything you use. When you choose clothing or arrange furniture in a room, you use these elements to decide what you like.

Line

Look around you. There are lines everywhere. You can see lines in the outlines of doors, windows, and objects in a room. Lines make your eyes follow a certain direction. Objects with lines that go up and down (vertical lines) create an impression of height. Lines that go from side to side (horizontal lines) create a feeling of width. Diagonal lines, for example in a

What special touches make this design attractive?

REINFORCEMENT: Have students cut out pictures from home furnishing and decorating magazines of living spaces that are pleasing to them, and ask students to explain exactly what elements appeal to them.

ENRICHMENT: Using the pictures students have selected from the magazines, or using the photo above, have students list all the vertical and horizontal lines they can pick out.

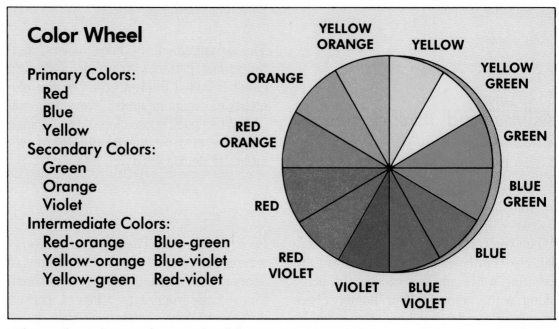

Color Wheel

Primary Colors:
- Red
- Blue
- Yellow

Secondary Colors:
- Green
- Orange
- Violet

Intermediate Colors:
Red-orange	Blue-green
Yellow-orange	Blue-violet
Yellow-green	Red-violet

What colors do you frequently choose? Do you prefer cool or warm colors? light or dark?

bold poster with zigzag patterns, can add excitement to a room.

The lines that stand out affect the atmosphere in a room. A large, tall chest, for example, calls attention to height. A long, low chest emphasizes width. Some people feel that a room with vertical lines is handsome and interesting. Other people like the restful feeling of a room with horizontal lines. Still others combine lines for variety and interest.

Shape

The shape of furniture and other objects also contributes to atmosphere. If the furniture is curved, the room has a softer feeling than if the shapes are angular. A combination of shapes often creates an informal feeling.

Texture

Texture is the way the surface of an object feels when you touch it. You can use shiny textures such as high-gloss wood and glass to give a room a formal look. A rough texture, such as a nubby fabric, helps create an informal feeling.

You can combine textures if you take care. A nubby couch might look fine with a glass coffee table. However, rough-textured dried flowers would look better set in a rough-textured basket than in a glossy plastic container.

Color

Color is one of the most important elements in design. Combinations of yellow, yellow-orange, orange, red-orange, and

What meal would you like to eat in this room? Does color help to determine your answer?

red give a feeling of warmth. These warm colors also make objects seem larger in size and closer in perspective. Green, blue, blue-green, blue-violet, and violet are cool, soothing colors. They make objects seem smaller and farther away.

The value of a color also affects how objects appear. **Value** is the lightness or darkness of a color. For example, the lightest value of red is pink and the darkest value is maroon. A room seems larger if the walls are light in color and smaller if they are dark. A dark color can also make a room feel cozy.

Like value, intensity affects the mood in a room. **Intensity** is the brightness or dullness of a color. A high-intensity red, for example, makes a room feel vibrant and exciting.

Color Schemes Colors can be combined to create a pleasing effect in a room. Look at the color wheel on page 228. Contrasting colors are opposite each other, while similar colors are grouped together. You can use the wheel to create an attractive color scheme for a room.

Using different values and intensities of one color creates a **monochromatic** (mon–oh–kro–*MAT*–ik) color scheme. A pale green rug and deep green slipcovers form a monochromatic color scheme. So do a brown rug and tan upholstery.

An **analogous** (a–*NAL*–*uh*–*gus)* color scheme uses colors that are closely related. On the color wheel, they are next to each other. A room decorated in orange, yellow-orange, and red-orange has an analogous color scheme.

Chapter 11/*Housing and Home Furnishings*   **229**

A color scheme formed by using colors that are direct contrasts is called **complementary** (kom–pleh–MEN–tar–ee). These colors are found opposite each other on the color wheel. A bedroom decorated with yellow walls and violet bedspreads uses complementary colors.

A color combined with the color on either side of its complement forms a **split-complementary** color scheme. Green is opposite red on the color wheel. Red-violet and red-orange are on either side of red. Green, red-violet, and red-orange, for example, form a split-complementary color scheme.

A **triadic** (try–AD–ik) color scheme uses three colors that are the same distance from one another on the color wheel. Red, yellow, and blue form a triadic color scheme.

A room has harmony when all the objects seem to belong together.

Design Principles

Achieving exactly the look and mood you want in a room is a complex task. You need to use design principles as well as combining line, shape, texture, and color. These principles are scale, balance, harmony, proportion, and emphasis.

Scale

Scale is the size of an object compared with another object. For example, if you were to place a toy car next to a real car, they would look out of scale. Similarly, a long couch may look fine in a large room but out of scale in a small room.

Balance

Imagine how lopsided a room would look if all the furniture were on one side. *Balance* gives a room a restful, even quality. A balanced design creates the sense that all elements are equal in weight. When a room has formal balance, objects on each side of the center are the same or the same size. In informal balance, objects around the center are arranged unevenly.

Harmony

When you group objects together in a room, they should seem to belong together, or to be in *harmony*. The objects do not all have to match each other. A sofa can be one color and chairs another. They should, however, have something in common, such as style or size.

Proportion

Proportion is the way parts of a design relate to one another and to the whole. Pictures grouped together, for example, should look right together. Most people consider objects to be in proportion if they are grouped slightly unevenly. Try arranging pictures in a rectangular shape. Put two pictures on the short side and three on the long side. This is more appealing than a simple square.

Emphasis

Emphasis is the center of interest in a design. It determines where your eye goes first. Emphasis in a room can be achieved by one large painting. Or a handsome desk or a fireplace might attract your attention first.

Organization of Space

The elements and principles of design can help you create beautiful living spaces. However, these spaces should also be right for you and your family. Different activities take place in each room in your home. These activities will be more enjoyable if space is well organized and adequate storage is available.

What is the center of interest, or *emphasis*, in this room?

PHOTO: How many different types of items can your students count here?

A Floor Plan

A good way to begin is to make a floor plan. By moving furniture around on paper, you can figure out the most efficient use of space. You will also save yourself a lot of time and frustration. Your floor plan should be drawn to scale. This means that the size of the cutouts representing the furniture should be in proportion to the real objects.

As you do this, consider how the room is used. What different things do you and other family members do in the room? Is there enough space for these activities? Keep in mind the *traffic patterns,* or how you move from place to place. Remember that paths from one area to another should not be blocked by furniture. Also keep in mind that space is needed to open doors and drawers or to pull out a chair from a table or desk.

Storage

Store things where you can get them when you need them. Put items you seldom use in a box under the bed or in the basement. Keep things you use daily in concealed spaces like closets, drawers, and cabinets. Other items might be stored on open shelves. A good way to build low shelves quickly and easily is to combine bricks and boards. You can acquire extra storage by using crates and baskets. Also consider using shoebags and towel racks for extra storage. They can hang on closet doors and can hold a variety of items.

Special Needs

When planning living space, consider the needs of all family members. In your home, there may be people who are elder-

How is the second floor plan an improvement over the first? Be sure to note traffic patterns as well as space.

Making a Floor Plan

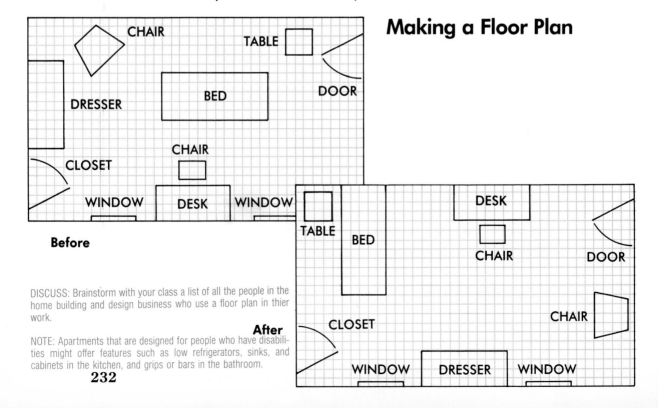

Before

After

DISCUSS: Brainstorm with your class a list of all the people in the home building and design business who use a floor plan in thier work.

NOTE: Apartments that are designed for people who have disabilities might offer features such as low refrigerators, sinks, and cabinets in the kitchen, and grips or bars in the bathroom.

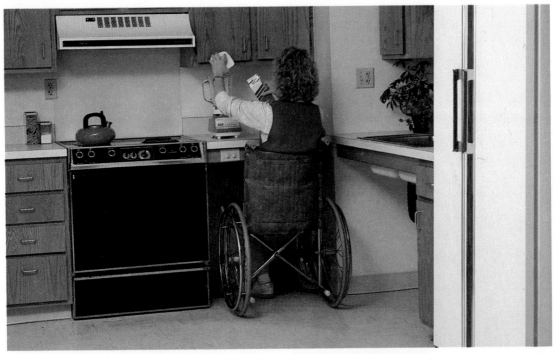

How many special features can you find here that make this room more usable and accessible for someone in a wheelchair?

ly or who have disabilities. Good use of space, along with special features, can help make it more comfortable and convenient for these people.

Traffic paths should allow people in wheelchairs to move around easily. There should also be space under tables and sinks for a wheelchair to roll up easily. For those who can use stairs, railings on both sides are a good idea. Ramps can be used to replace steps outside the house.

In the kitchen, open shelving, low counters, and faucets with long handles are helpful. Braille knobs and controls are available for the blind. The bathroom will be safer and more convenient if there are grab bars by the bathtub and toilet. Nonskid strips in the tub or shower are another good safety feature. Some people may find that a hand-held shower makes bathing easier.

Wood or vinyl floors are best for people in wheelchairs or those who have trouble walking. Any carpeting should be smooth and level and should not have padding. Scatter rugs can cause falls. Adequate lighting is important in any household and especially if people have poor vision.

See page T86 for answers.

For Review

1. Name the four elements of design.
2. Name three important principles of design that can be used in decorating a home.
3. Why is a floor plan important?

In what ways does your room feel right for you?

Section 11.3

Your Own Space

As you read, think about:

■ how to use your space better. (p. 234)

■ how you can add your personal decorating touch. (p. 234)

■ how to maintain personal space when you must share. (p. 235)

Everyone needs a special place to be alone or to be with others. This can be almost anywhere, but it is often a room in your home. Even if you share it with someone else, your own space can serve many different purposes.

Your Use of Space

Think about how you spend your time. Do you study, read, paint, or listen to music? Perhaps you like to work on special projects, such as building a model. Maybe you occasionally invite a friend over to play a game or just talk. Once you have figured out what you like to do, you can design your space accordingly.

This does not mean that you have to throw out everything or spend a lot of money. Just a few changes can make a big difference. If you like to paint, you might set up an easel near a window. If you like to relax and listen to music, you could put a radio on a table by your bed.

By rearranging your furniture, you can create definite areas for certain activities. Consider the things you will need in each area. For example, you may study in your room. A study area should have a writing surface, a comfortable chair, space for storing books, and a good light. Use a floor plan like the one described on page 232 to help you arrange different areas.

Your Own Touch

Along with making your room serve many purposes, you can also make it more a reflection of *you*. Use your favorite colors and textures to give your space the look you want. With a parent's permission, you might paint or wallpaper your walls. One of the best ways to personalize a room is to use accessories and displays.

Accessories Accessories are the extra touches in a room, such as pictures, pillows, and plants. Some accessories, like lamps, are functional as well as decorative. Such items can be changed easily. They are often inexpensive or cost nothing at all. They can also reflect your own special interests.

The elements and principles of design can help you select accessories that complement your furniture. For example, if your room is furnished casually, choose a lampshade in a rough texture rather than a satin one. In a more formal room, the satin shade may be more appropriate.

Displays   Displays can be anything from a collection of rocks to photographs you took during a trip. Record albums, pennants, and stamp albums all make interesting displays. Shells you found on a beach would also be attractive and decorative. You can even make a display by hanging hats on a pegboard. In this way you also create new storage space. Like accessories, displays tell other people about your interests. Walls, shelves, and windowsills are good places for displays.

Sharing Space

You may share your space with a brother or sister. You also share when a friend stays overnight with you. No matter who

What improvement do you think this girl is making? How much time and effort do you think it will cost?

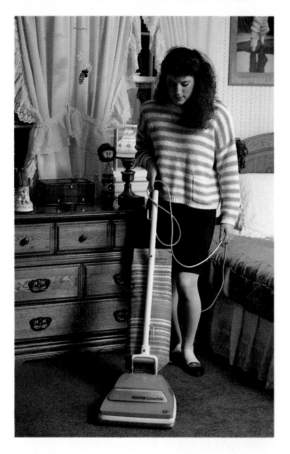

A simple way to improve the looks of your room is to clean it.

your roommate may be, respect and consideration for one another are extremely important. If you play music when someone is trying to sleep, you may disturb that person. Keep in mind that different people have different needs. By respecting those needs, you can experience the pleasures of sharing.

You can arrange your furniture to create private areas. For example, you can divide the room in half using bunk beds or a bookcase as a divider. Shelves of plants, roll-up blinds, and folding screens are other ways to divide your space.

REINFORCEMENT: Have students list five activities that they do in their bedrooms. Students can compare lists for the purpose of seeing how their classmates utilize the time spent in their room.

Cleaning Your Room

Your room will serve you best if you keep it clean and orderly. How you care for your space also affects other people. Your room is part of your family's home.

Your task will be much easier if you begin with an organized room. For example, clothes lying around look messy. Finding a sweater and putting it away will be easier if you have a drawer or shelf just for sweaters. You can save time by hanging things like slacks and shirts together in the closet. Small boxes can be used for items such as jewelry or makeup. Use the storage ideas on page 237 to help you start out right. Then get into the habit of putting things away.

The next step is to have a plan for caring for your space. Some things need to be done daily. If you make your bed in the morning, your room will be more pleasant to come home to. Hang up clothes when you take them off, and put dirty clothes in the laundry basket. Set aside a time once a week to vacuum or sweep and to dust. These tasks take only a few minutes when done regularly, and they make your space a much nicer place.

See page T87 for answers.

For Review

1. Name one way to improve your use of personal space.
2. What accessories or displays could make your room uniquely yours?
3. What are some ways you can share your room and still have your own space?

ENRICHMENT: Ask students to choose partners. All students should then make a list of everything they have used to decorate their rooms. Then have students exchange lists with their partners to see what one student can determine about the other student's personality based on the list.

Section 11.4

Home Care

As you read, think about:

■ how to care for your home by keeping it clean and organized. (p. 237)

■ how family cooperation helps to make home care easier. (p. 238)

■ how to conserve energy in your home. (p. 240)

You may have heard the expression, "A stitch in time saves nine." This means that making small repairs right away is easier than doing a large job later on. This may apply to your home as well as to clothing repair. Regular care and maintenance make a home more appealing and safer. They also make life much easier.

Home care is not just keeping the house clean and orderly, important as this is. Homes also need to be maintained, repaired, and insulated against the cold. All of these tasks can be done more efficiently if you and your family share the chores involved.

Controlling Clutter

Have you ever stumbled over toys, books, or even clothes? Clutter can be a hazard. Putting things away is important throughout your home, as well as in your personal space. For each room in your house, these guidelines are important.

• Put away items as soon as possible after you use them.
• Keep items where they are used.

• Store items you use often where they can be reached easily.

Here are some additional storage tips your family might consider.

• Store clothes you are not presently using in empty suitcases.
• Use cardboard suit boxes to store flat items or shoes under beds.
• Hang sporting equipment on walls.
• Build shelves under stairways to store canned goods.
• Hang a mesh bag in the shower for shampoo containers.
• Put a hook on the bathroom door for shower caps and robes.
• Use foam egg cartons or plastic margarine containers in desk or chest drawers for items like pins or coins.
• Put a small shelf above a bed for a clock or magazines.

How quickly and easily can you find your clothes and shoes? Could a closet organizer help you?

Cleaning the House

Housework may not be everyone's favorite task, but it can be a most satisfying experience. A clean home makes people feel good. Some homes are neater than others, because each family sets its own standards for cleanliness. For any family, however, using the proper tools and sharing responsibilities can make housework more efficient.

Cleaning Equipment

Having the correct cleaning equipment and products can save time and energy. The most basic equipment includes brooms, brushes, buckets, mops, sponges, dust cloths, and vacuum cleaners. When you select cleaning products, read labels to see how they can be used. Those that serve more than one purpose are the most economical.

A Cleaning Schedule

Some cleaning jobs need to be done daily; others can be done weekly, monthly, or seasonally. A cleaning schedule can help your family plan when jobs will be done and who will do them.

Many families have to juggle schedules as they work out home care plans, especially if there is no full-time homemaker. A spirit of cooperation can help make the plan work smoothly.

Garbage Control

Garbage should be disposed of each day, as it contains germs and can give off an unpleasant odor. Leftover food on dishes should be removed right away and put in a garbage disposal, small can with a lid, or garbage can. Ideally, all trashcans should be emptied daily into a central container with a secure lid.

What household tasks could your family do together?

PHOTO: Ask students to estimate how long this cleaning job would take if only one person were to do it. How does that compare with the amount of time that might be spent by this family?

DISCUSS: With your class, brainstorm a list of things people need to do regularly to maintain the outside and grounds of a home in your area.

Home Cleaning Schedule		Mom	Dad	Greta	Kevin
Daily	Make your bed.		✓	✓	✓
	Do laundry.				✓
	Put away clean clothes.			✓	
	Wash dishes. Put them away.				✓
	Take out garbage.			✓	
	Clean kitchen.	✓	✓		
Weekly	Clean and dust your room.	✓		✓	✓
	Dust and vacuum the rest of the house.			✓	
	Change linens.	✓		✓	✓
	Clean bathroom.		✓		
	Clean refrigerator.	✓			✓
Monthly	Clean out medicine cabinet.		✓		
	Polish furniture.				✓
	Clean throw rugs.	✓			
	Check smoke detectors.			✓	

When you put a job off, it has a way of growing. Doing things according to a schedule keeps tasks manageable.

Pests

Pests can threaten your house, your clothes, and even your health. Pests like cockroaches and mice carry germs that can make you ill. Some pests, like moths, eat clothing. Termites eat into wood and can destroy the structure of a house. Pests thrive on dirt and garbage, so a clean house is a good form of pest control. Commercial pest control products are available but should be used with care. For extreme problems, you may need a professional pest control service.

Maintenance

A good home maintenance plan includes making repairs and improvements as soon as they are needed. If paint begins to peel, it is time for a new paint job. Walls with cracks should be repaired by caulking.

Did You Know?

Baking soda cleans up—from kitchen, to bathroom, to garage.

- Put two tablespoons in two cups of warm water and you have a great cleanser for microwave ovens.
- Sprinkle some on a damp sponge to remove mildew from shower tiles.
- Dissolve baking soda in water to remove salt deposits from car bumpers.

What are the advantages of doing a task as a family?

or filling the cracks with plaster or other materials. Repairs like replacing a floorboard or attaching molding to a wall require some carpentry skills, as well as tools. Have on hand basic home care and repair tools. These should include a hammer, saw, screwdriver, wrench, pliers, nails, screws, and nuts and bolts.

Energy Conservation in the Home

There are several ways to conserve energy in the home. One of the best of these is to use *insulation,* materials put inside walls or ceilings. Insulation keeps the house at a comfortable temperature. Drafts can be prevented by *weatherstripping.* This means putting fiber, metal, or plastic strips around doors and windows to prevent air from leaking in. Storm windows, or even sheets of plastic tacked over windows, also keep out cool air. Window shades or drapes help keep out hot air.

These are some additional ways to conserve energy in your home.

- Take shorter showers to save hot water.
- Defrost the refrigerator regularly. This makes it work more efficiently.
- Do not leave the refrigerator door open.
- Turn off lights and appliances when they are not needed.
- Use fluorescent bulbs; they use less heat than incandescent ones.
- When using a washing machine, use warm or cold settings.
- Do not overload a clothes dryer.
- Do not use the dryer if line drying will do as well.
- When using a dishwasher, wash full loads only.
- Make sure your faucets do not drip.

See page T87 for answers.
For Review
1. Name three storage ideas you could use to keep clutter under control in your home.
2. What is the purpose of a cleaning schedule?
3. Name at least four ways to conserve energy in your home.

DISCUSS: Working adults are always looking for people to do housekeeping and maintenance for them. Discuss the advantages and disadvantages of earning money this way.

ENRICHMENT: Have students obtain a brochure on energy conservation from their local heating or electric company, or have them create one of their own.

Home Safety

As you read, think about:

- how you can prevent accidents in your home. (p. 241)
- how to keep your home secure. (p. 243)

Millions of home accidents occur in the United States every year. Perhaps your family has avoided such problems so far, but home accidents sneak up on you. The most innocent things, such as a child's doll or a small rug, can cause an accident. Falls, fires, poisoning, and electric shocks are all threats to your family. Safety precautions help prevent such accidents. Home safety also means having adequate security to protect your home from robberies and other crimes.

Preventing Falls

Keeping your home free of clutter is one of the best ways to prevent falls. Here are some additional ways.

- Wipe up spills right away. Be sure that greasy spills are wiped up completely.
- Use nonskid mats and rugs. Make sure carpets are firmly tacked down.
- Use stepstools to reach items on high shelves.
- Keep stairways clear, well lit, and in good repair.
- Arrange furniture so that it does not interfere with traffic paths.
- Do not run or climb where you are not supposed to.

NOTE: If a grease fire occurs, put baking soda on it. Never put water on a grease fire.

Fire Prevention

Kitchen grease fires, faulty wiring, and cigarettes are among the most common causes of home fires. Every home should be equipped with smoke detectors and a fire extinguisher. A monthly fire drill is also a good safety procedure.

You and your family should design an escape plan from every room in the house, especially bedrooms. Choose a meeting place outside. Keep fire extinguishers where you can easily reach them.

Follow these guidelines to prevent fires.

- Keep the area around the stove clean and free of grease.
- Do not let items like potholders or paper towels get too close to the stove.
- Keep electric cords in good repair. Do not put them under rugs.
- Make sure no one smokes in bed.

Did You Know?

Installing smoke detectors can cut your risk of dying in a home fire by 50 percent. The most important place for detectors is in the hallway near the bedrooms. There, detectors will sound an alarm to warn sleeping residents before smoke seeps into the bedrooms. A detector on each floor of the house ensures that small fires will be detected before they spread.

NOTE: See Chapter 14 for information on preventing kitchen burns and fires.

Health and Safety

Childproofing Your Home

Little children find ways to hurt themselves that bigger people would not think of. One way to prevent these accidents is to get down on your hands and knees. Look at your home from a toddler's viewpoint. What looks interesting? That electrical outlet? Maybe a finger would fit into it. . . .

Your toddler's-eye tour will reveal many potential hazards. Adapt them using these childproofing guidelines.

- Cover all unused electrical outlets. Repair frayed cords and appliances that could cause shocks. Keep cords out of reach, and put away appliances when not in use.
- Use safety gates at the top and bottom of stairs and near other danger zones, such as food preparation areas. Install guards on dangerous doors and windows. Put childproof locks on cabinets containing matches, medicine, vitamins, cleaning supplies, and cosmetics. Use child-resistant caps on all medicine.
- Remove unstable furniture and tie kitchen chairs down so that they can't be used to climb up to the stove. Always turn pot handles away from the edge of the stove so that they can't be pulled or knocked down.
- Remove sharp or pointed objects. Keep drapery cords out of reach.

Can you think of additional ways to childproof your home?

- Keep matches away from children. Make sure matches are cold and wet before throwing them away.
- Use screens in front of fireplaces, and keep them closed while the fireplace is being used.
- Do not let papers or trash accumulate.

Poisons

Things you use every day can be deadly to small children. Soap, shampoo, paint, and household cleaning products can all be poisonous if swallowed. Medicine can also be dangerous if too much is taken. A home with small children should be childproofed against such dangers. Particularly in the bathroom and kitchen, items should be stored on high shelves or in locked cabinets. Also make sure children do not put houseplants in their mouths, as some leaves and berries are poisonous.

If a poisoning accident does occur, call immediately for assistance. Keep the telephone numbers of poison control centers and of your local hospital emergency room by the telephone. Be prepared to give information about what and how much was swallowed and the victim's approximate age and weight.

Electricity

Electric shocks are usually caused by problems with electrical cords and outlets and by incorrect use of appliances. Follow these guidelines.
- Inspect cords and make sure they are in good repair.
- Keep all wires away from water. Do not plug in cords using wet hands.

REINFORCEMENT: On the blackboard, write the telephone number for the Poison Control Center nearest you. Have students copy the number and place it close to their telephones at home.

A new lock is often very easy to install. Can you think of anything better to do for your family?

- Cover outlets that young children may be able to reach.
- Do not use a hair dryer or telephone in the bathtub or when standing on a wet spot on the floor.

Security

Many crimes can be prevented if you use proper security precautions and a little common sense. The first step is to secure your home with good locks.

Windows and Doors

Hard as it may be to believe, about 50 percent of burglars enter through unlocked doors and windows. Deadbolt locks are better for doors than spring latch ones with the key in the knob. Make sure locks can't be reached by breaking glass or door panels. For glass doors, you can either use

Did You Know?

Every 11 seconds, someone is accidentally hurt in a very dangerous place—the home. More disabling injuries occur in the home than anywhere else. Falls happen most often at home, and they are the leading cause of death in the home.

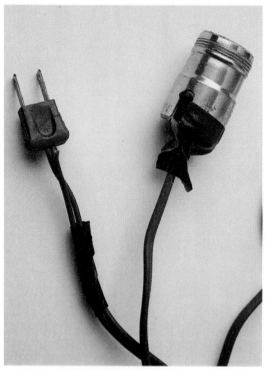

Don't wait! Replace frayed wires immediately.

commercial locks or secure them by putting a wooden dowel in the track.

Window locks are available at hardware stores. You can also use a nail to lock double-hung windows. Drill a hole at a downward angle in each corner of the inside sash and part way through the outside sash. Then slide a bolt or nail through the hole.

Answering the Door

Do not open the door to a stranger without first checking the person's identity. To see who is at the door, install a peephole or a wide-angle viewer. A short chain between the door and the door jamb is less reliable, as it can be easily broken.

NOTE: Often neighbors will invest in a joint burglar alarm system. If the alarm is triggered in one house, a buzzer will go off in every house that shares the system. That way, people can quickly notify the police of a possible break-in.

Answering the Telephone

You may receive different kinds of calls from people you do not know. If you receive a "wrong number" call, do not give information to the caller. Instead, ask what number was dialed and tell the caller politely that it is a wrong number.

Hang up at once if you receive threatening or annoying calls, and inform your parents. If the calls continue, inform the police and the telephone company.

Sometimes you may receive calls requesting information. The best policy is to offer to call the person back rather than to respond immediately. People who conduct surveys often ask questions about family habits. By pretending to take a survey, burglars can acquire information enabling them to enter your home while you are away. Before any questions are answered, your parents may wish to check the caller's references. If someone calls while you are alone, never say, "My parents are not home." Instead, say, "My mother (father) cannot come to the phone right now. May I take a message?" Be polite, but firm.

See page T87 for answers.
For Review

1. Describe three ways to prevent home falls.
2. Name at least three guidelines for preventing fires.
3. Name two ways of preventing electric shocks in your home.
4. What should you do if you receive a "wrong number" phone call?

ENRICHMENT: Have students role-play each of the following: You are home alone. 1) Someone calls several times claiming to have a wrong number. 2) Someone calls claiming to be conducting a survey. 3) A stranger calls who wants to drop something off now for one of your parents.

Learning to Manage

Making Room

Look back at the conversation between Anna and her mother on page 222. They are thinking about changes that will have to be made to Anna's room when her new stepsister moves in. Now read about the plan that Judy and Anna come up with. Then answer the questions that follow.

Anna called Judy and they decided to get together to talk about their room. Judy came over and they sat in the bedroom and looked around.

"I know this is tough for you, Anna, giving up your own room and all."

"Well, it's tough for you, too, Judy, but if we plan it out, it should work OK."

The girls read through old decorating magazines and a do-it-yourself book they found at the library. They decided that the closet was the first priority since they would have to fit so much more into it. They realized that there was a lot of wasted space. If they hung another bar a bit below the one already there, they could double the usable space. Skirts, shirts, and sweaters could hang up above, and pants and jeans below. Buying a few inexpensive storage boxes for extra sweaters and bulky sweatsuits would help, too. They could fit them under their beds. Judy said she had a bureau and a desk to bring. So the girls measured to see where the furniture would fit into the room. They saw a picture of a folding screen room divider. Judy suggested making one themselves.

Next, they discussed their schedules to find ways to allow each other some time alone in the room. This turned out to be easy. Judy worked in the afternoons, and Anna usually tried to get her homework done at that time and watched television after dinner.

Then Judy raised the issue of cleaning and maintenance. Anna confessed to being on the messy side. Judy groaned and explained that she was a "neatnik." They worked out a shared schedule for dusting and vacuuming. Judy said she would tidy up when things got bad. That was if Anna would iron some of her shirts —a job that Judy hated and Anna didn't mind. They smiled at each other.

"We can make it work."

Questions

1. What solutions would you propose if Judy and Anna needed their room at the same time?
2. Do you think that Judy and Anna's plan for their room is realistic and workable? Why or why not?
3. Think of one way you can reorganize your own living space to improve it.

Chapter 11 Review

Summary

People need homes for shelter and also to fill emotional needs. Housing choices are influenced by economics, values, and availability. Options include single-family homes, duplexes, apartments, and mobile homes. These spaces are either rented or purchased. Within homes, the elements and principles of design can be used to create and plan appealing living spaces.

A good home care plan includes a cleaning schedule and proper equipment. Regular maintenance and energy conservation are an important part of home care.

Accidents in the home can be prevented with proper safety precautions. Home safety also includes good security to prevent burglaries and other crimes.

Vocabulary

Complete each of the following sentences with the correct word from the vocabulary list below.

proportion (p. 231)   complementary (p. 230)
mortgage (p. 226)   value (p. 229)
monochromatic (p. 229)   co-op (p. 226)
triadic (p. 230)   analogous (p. 229)
condominium (p. 226)   design (p. 227)
(p. 230) split-complementary   intensity (p. 229)

1. An apartment that can be bought rather than rented is called a _____.

2. _____ is the lightness or darkness of a color.

3. A color scheme that is made up of different values and intensities of color is called _____.

4. A _____ color scheme combines a color with the color on either side of its complement.

5. _____ is the brightness or dullness of a color.

6. A _____ is a legal pledge of property given to a bank or savings and loan association as security in case a loan is not repaid.

7. A color scheme that uses colors that are closely related is called _____.

8. A _____ color scheme is one that uses colors that are direct contrasts of one another.

9. When a unit within a building or apartment complex is owned jointly by all its residents, that unit is called a _____.

10. A _____ color scheme is one that uses three different colors that are the same distance from one another on the color wheel.

11. _____ is the way parts of a design relate to one another and to the whole.

12. The arrangement of lines, colors, textures, and patterns to create a desired effect is called _____.

Questions

- 1. How does a person who has a mortgage repay the loan?
- 2. What is the difference between a condominium and a co-op?
- 3. How does the shape of furniture and other objects contribute to the atmosphere of a room?
- •• 4. If you were decorating a small room, how can you make it seem larger?
- 5. What do we mean when we say that something is out of scale?
- •• 6. How would you arrange furniture to achieve informal balance in a room? How does that differ from arranging for a formal balance?
- 7. What is one of the best ways to personalize a room?
- 8. What is the purpose of insulation in a home? Describe several insulating methods or materials.
- 9. Name the three most common causes of home fires.
- 10. What is the first thing you should do to make your home secure?

Skill Activities

Many more activities are contained in the annotations within this chapter.

•• **1. Human Relations** As a class, make a cleaning schedule for the Home Economics room. List the tasks and the rotation of duties. Keep track of how smoothly your cleaning system is running for one month. Do some tasks require a lot more time and work than others? Schedule a class meeting at the end of the month to talk about any problems that may have come up.

At home, talk to your family about how you share home maintenance chores. Decide how each family member can make the most efficient contribution. Make a list of your own cleaning responsibilities. As you did in school, meet after a month to work out any problems.

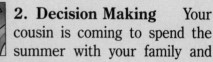 •• **2. Decision Making** Your cousin is coming to spend the summer with your family and will have to share your room with you. How can you arrange your room to create personal space for both of you? Use the ideas in this chapter and those you find in magazines and books to come up with your decisions. Sketch how it would look.

 • **3. Laboratory** Make a wall hanging, banner, or pillow to coordinate, personalize, and brighten up your room. Bring in scraps of fabric from old clothing or colorful sheets if you have them. Perhaps you can recover an old pillow or stretch colorful fabric onto a frame you already have. If you make a banner, decorate it with shapes made of felt or other fabric. These might be shapes of objects such as sports equipment or musical instruments that express your personality.

The dots represent skill levels required to answer each question or complete each activity:

- • requires recall and comprehension
- •• requires application and analysis
- ••• requires synthesis and evaluation

Unit 4

Foods and Nutrition

Chapter 12
Food and Health

Vocabulary

The dialogue below introduces "Snacking for Health," the Learning to Manage feature in this chapter. The case study is continued and the situation discussed further on page 275. See page T91 for teaching suggestions.

"*Healthy snacks are easy to make and will provide you with a lot more energy.*"

"*How do you know how healthy snacks taste, or how you'd feel if you ate them, unless you try them, Ron? We all need to think more about why we eat what we eat so that we can be healthier.*"

"But 'healthy' tastes boring, Mr. Torres. Besides, I seem to be doing fine, and I snack on soda and sweet stuff all the time."

Section 12.1

Why We Eat What We Eat

As you read, think about:

- how both your body and your mind need food. (p. 251)

- how your culture, religion, and family influence what you eat. (p. 252)

- how the availability of food affects what it costs. (p. 253)

Do you usually think about what you eat? For example, can you remember exactly what you ate the last time you had a snack? Why do you choose certain foods? Well, you probably choose them because you like them. There are other reasons, however, why you eat what you eat. Food satisfies both physical and emotional needs. When you make food choices, you are influenced by habits and customs established through many years. You are also influenced by the food that is available and by how much it costs. Understanding the factors that contribute to your eating habits can help you make wise choices. These choices are important. Food affects your health, your energy, and your looks. Therefore, it affects your whole life.

Physical Needs

Your body needs food. This need is *hunger*. Without food you would starve, because food supplies your body with essential **nutrients.** These are materials that

Do you want to look and feel good?

provide energy and help your body function, grow, and repair itself. Nutrients give you the energy you need for your daily activities.

Psychological Needs

Food is also related to emotional, or psychological, needs. Do you ever eat because you are nervous or bored? If so, you are not satisfying hunger, your body's need for food. Instead, you are eating to satisfy an *appetite,* the psychological need to eat.

Habit can trigger an appetite. If you always have popcorn at the movies, you may crave it whenever you are at a movie theater, just because you associate popcorn with movies. Smells can stimulate

DISCUSS: Ask students to list ten snack foods they eat regularly. Discuss the nutritional value of each food, and suggest healthy snacks that could be substituted for those snacks that are junk food.

REINFORCEMENT: Have students list the foods that they associate with enjoyable occasions. Ask: Is it the occasion that dictates their enjoyment of a particular food, or is it the food itself?

How does your family influence what you eat?

your appetite when you are not actually hungry. Why do you like the taste of certain foods? One reason may be that you associate them with a particular occasion you have enjoyed.

Social and Cultural Influences

Your family is one of the strongest influences on what you eat. You probably like chicken if your family eats it regularly. Perhaps certain foods are never served in your home. You may say you don't like these foods even if you have never actually tried them.

Your family's food customs may have begun as far back as your great-great-grandparents. When this country was first settled, people brought their food customs with them from other countries. Your favorite foods may originally have come from the country or region where your family had its roots. Many other foods came from Native Americans. This blend of customs and traditions created the rich mixture of foods we have today.

Along with family customs, your friends influence your food choices. Perhaps a very good friend eats yogurt as a snack and convinced you to try it. Maybe your friends like to have pizza on Saturday night, so you started to eat it, too. You are likely to form a habit of eating the same foods as other people in your group.

Religious customs also play a part in food choices. Some religions forbid the eating of certain foods, thereby limiting a person's food selections. Religious holidays often involve special foods, even for people who do not follow all the customs of a particular religion.

Advertising can be a powerful influence on food choices. You probably have seen mouth-watering commercials that make you want to rush out and buy a food. Young children often ask their parents for a particular food because they have seen it advertised on television. Some of these foods can be good choices, but others may not be.

In what ways does advertising affect your food choices?

Did You Know?

It would take you only a few days to "eat your way around the world" without leaving home. Start with a (French) croissant for breakfast, and have a (Middle Eastern) pita pocket sandwich for lunch. Then choose (Italian) pasta or (Indian) curry for dinner. Or you might prefer (English) muffins for breakfast, a Greek salad for lunch, and either (Chinese) stir-fried meat and vegetables or (Mexican) tacos for dinner. All of these foods are now "as American as apple pie." Can you think of other foreign dishes we've adopted?

Availability and Cost

Many food choices were developed because of location and climate. For example, people who lived near the water ate fish, while people in tropical climates had fresh fruit. Today there are many choices available at all seasons of the year, in all regions of this country. Due to advanced technology and transportation, food markets provide a variety of fresh, frozen, and packaged food.

When choosing among these foods, consider the cost of particular items. Fresh strawberries may be available out of season in your area, but they are likely to be expensive. You may like fresh berries

Chapter 12/*Food and Health*   **253**

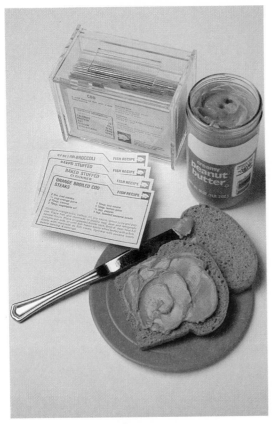

Not all sources of protein are expensive.

more than the less expensive frozen ones and decide to pay the higher price. On the other hand, the cost of the berries may not fit your budget.

See page T92 for answers.

For Review

1. What is the most important reason for eating?
2. Name three factors that influence your food choices.
3. Explain why a food grown locally may be less expensive than a food grown far away.

Nutrition and You

As you read, think about:

■ why your body needs the essential nutrients. (p. 254)

■ specific food sources of proteins, carbohydrates, fats, vitamins, minerals, and water. (p. 254)

Are there times when you feel low in energy and just want to flop on your bed? This could mean you have run out of fuel. Your body, just like a motorcycle or car, needs to be refueled regularly. Food is the body's source of fuel, but not just any kind of food will do. For your body to be in tiptop shape, you need food that contains specific nutrients. The essential nutrients that give your body energy are proteins, carbohydrates (kar–boh–*HY*–drayts), fats, vitamins, minerals, and water.

Proteins

You have protein in every cell in your body. Protein makes you grow; it builds and repairs body tissues. Without protein, broken bones would not mend and cuts would not heal.

Protein is made up of different amino (uh–*MEE*–noh) acids. We know of about twenty amino acids. Your body produces all but nine of them. The nine that the body cannot make on its own are called **essential amino acids.** You must get the essential amino acids from the food that you eat.

Most animal foods—such as meat, fish, poultry, eggs, and dairy products, including cheese—contain the essential amino acids. For this reason, these foods are called *complete* proteins. Amino acids are also found in some plant foods. No one plant, however, contains all the essential amino acids. These plant foods are therefore called *incomplete* proteins. Cereals, nuts, and some vegetables are sources of incomplete protein.

You can improve the quality of an incomplete protein by combining it with a complete protein. Some combinations people enjoy are macaroni and cheese, rice and fish, and peanut butter (a complete protein) and whole-grain bread. Rice and beans are an example of two incomplete proteins that can be combined to make a complete protein.

Carbohydrates

Your body's major source of energy is carbohydrates. When you do not have enough carbohydrates in your diet, you cannot use other nutrients properly. The three kinds of carbohydrates are starch, sugar, and fiber.

Rice, bread, pasta, potatoes, and corn are good sources of starch. Natural sources of sugar include fruit, sweet potatoes, peas, and milk. Sweet foods like candy and sugary soft drinks are often called "empty-calorie" foods. They supply carbohydrates, but they are fattening and have few other nutrients.

Fiber is not digested by the body. It therefore does not supply energy but is

These are the right kinds of carbohydrates to supply your body's needs. What are the wrong kinds?

REINFORCEMENT: Have each student develop a list of five food combinations that include both a complete and incomplete protein.

PHOTO: Which of these sources of carbohydrates are the favorites among your students?

Chapter 12/*Food and Health*   255

important because it helps the body get rid of waste. Some very good sources of fiber are fruits with peel, whole-grain breads and cereals, and vegetables.

Fats

Fats are the oily substances in some foods. They provide twice as much energy, or calories, as carbohydrates. For this reason, your body needs only a small amount of fat.

Fats carry certain vitamins into the body. These vitamins, called **fat-soluble vitamins,** are transported by fat rather than water. Without some fat, the body could not use these specific vitamins. Fats also help to promote normal growth and healthy skin.

Foods that contain fat fall into two groups. Animal fats are found in foods like meat, poultry, egg yolks, and dairy products. Vegetable fats are found in salad dressing, mayonnaise, cooking oils, avocados, and nuts.

While a small amount of fat is an important part of the diet, eating too much can cause weight problems. Medical researchers believe that some fats contribute to heart disease. **Saturated fats** are those that are solid at room temperature. They are found in meat, butter, and cheese. **Unsaturated fats** are liquid, like salad oil. Saturated fats are now considered to be unhealthful. They are high in **cholesterol** (kuh–*LESS*–tuh–rohl), a fatlike substance in the body cells. Too much cholesterol can clog the arteries in the body, causing heart attacks and strokes.

Some fats actually appear to lower cholesterol. They are called *polyunsaturated* (pol–ee–un–*SACH*–uh–ray–tid). You may have seen this term on oils made from corn, safflowers, sunflowers, and soybeans. Fish and soft margarine are also high in polyunsaturated fats.

What can you do to keep your cholesterol at an ideal level?

Cholesterol		
Total Cholesterol		**Ideal Amount in Blood**
		Less than 200 mg
HDL* Cholesterol Margarine, oil, fish		Women: greater than 55 mg Men: greater than 45 mg
LDL** Cholesterol Butter, Bacon, Cold Cuts		Less than 120 mg

*High-density lipoprotein: carries "good" cholesterol in blood.
**Low-density lipoprotein: carries "bad" cholesterol in blood.

ART: Review the spelling and pronunciation of the word *cholesterol* with your students. Break it into syllables on the board, and call attention to the things your students might confuse, such as the beginning *ch* and the ending that may sound like the word *all* but is spelled *ol.*

ENRICHMENT: Have students make a chart with two columns, *saturated* and *unsaturated*. Have them research five fats to place in each column.

Do you make sure that you eat a variety of foods every day?

Vitamins

While vitamins do not provide energy, your body could not function properly without them. Vitamins work with other nutrients to promote growth and maintain good health.

Fat-Soluble Vitamins

The fat-soluble vitamins—those that enter the body with fat—are vitamins A, D, E, and K. Your body can store an extra amount of these vitamins. You therefore

NOTE: Vitamins are not a source of energy; however, they do help the body use energy.

need to be careful about taking too many vitamin pills. Too much vitamin A, for example, can lead to headaches and skin problems. The best practice is to eat a variety of foods to get the vitamins you need. Your doctor can advise you if you think you may need additional vitamins.

Vitamin A helps your eyes adjust to darkness after exposure to bright areas. It also helps keep your skin, bones, and teeth healthy and promotes growth. Some good sources are liver, milk, cheese, eggs, deep yellow fruits and vegetables, and dark green vegetables.

REINFORCEMENT: Megadoses (large amounts) of vitamins can be harmful. Have students research why.

The Importance of Vitamins

Vitamin	Where You Get It	Why You Need It
Vitamin A	Whole milk, cream, butter, margarine, cheese, dark-green and deep yellow vegetables	Good skin and mucous membranes; growth; eye pigment
Vitamin B$_1$ (thiamin)	Enriched or whole-grain cereals, pork and other meats, poultry, fish, dried beans and peas	Health of nerves; digestive function; helps release energy from carbohydrates; promotes good appetite
Vitamin B$_2$ (riboflavin)	Milk, cheese, ice cream, whole-grain and enriched cereals, eggs, meat, liver, poultry, fish, dark-green vegetables	Smooth skin, good eye function; aids body in use of protein and energy foods
Vitamin B$_{12}$	Meats, organ meats, fish, poultry, eggs, milk	Red blood cell formation; nerve function
Folic Acid	Deep-green leafy vegetables, muscle meats, eggs, whole grains	Mature red blood cells
Niacin (part of B complex)	Enriched and whole-grain cereals and breads, milk, cheese, meat, fish, poultry, peanuts	Helps body use other nutrients; maintains good nerves and digestion
Vitamin C (ascorbic acid)	Oranges, lemons, limes, tomatoes, strawberries, cantaloupe, dark-green leafy vegetables,	Helps to firm cementing material of cells and strong blood vessel walls
Vitamin D	Vitamin-D milk, egg yolks, butter, margarine, fish-liver oils	Helps body use calcium and phosphorus for strong bones and teeth
Vitamin E (tocopherols)	Oil, shortening, dairy products, eggs, liver, green leafy vegetables	Protects vitamin A and salty acids against too much oxygen; aids in use of energy foods
Vitamin K	Dark-green leafy vegetables, cauliflower	Helps blood clot properly

Which of these foods do you eat regularly now? Which of these foods should you add to your diet?

ART: As an enrichment activity, have students keep track of their diet for three days and note each time they eat a food that is a source of one of these major vitamins.

Vitamin D helps the body build strong bones and teeth. This is called the "sunshine" vitamin, because your body makes it when your skin is exposed to sunlight. A good source of vitamin D is milk that has had this vitamin added to it.

Vitamin E protects vitamin A and fatty acids from damage caused by too much oxygen. It also helps form red blood cells, muscles, and other tissues. It is found in vegetable oils, whole-grain foods, liver, and leafy green vegetables.

Vitamin K helps blood to clot. It is manufactured by the body and is also found in some foods. These include leafy greens, cabbage, and cauliflower.

Water-Soluble Vitamins

The **water-soluble vitamins,** which mix only with water, are vitamin C and a group of vitamins called the B complex. These vitamins are not stored in the body, so you need them in your food each day. Those the body does not need are usually discarded with body waste.

Vitamin C helps maintain healthy bones, teeth, and blood vessels. In addition, it helps the body to form *collagen* (*KOL*–uh–jen), a substance that binds cells and tissues together. Too little vitamin C can cause bleeding gums, loose teeth, and dry skin. Good sources of vitamin C are citrus fruits like oranges and grapefruits, strawberries, cantaloupes, tomatoes, cabbage, turnip greens, and collards.

Because the vitamins in this group are similar, the B complex was once thought to be one vitamin. Each, however, has its own distinct tasks. The best-known B vitamins are B1, B2, and niacin.

Vitamin B1 (thiamin) helps the body use carbohydrates for energy. Some sources of B1 are whole-grain foods, pork, liver, pasta, and dried beans.

Vitamin B2 (riboflavin) helps the body use protein and energy foods and helps maintain smooth skin and healthy eyes. Vitamin B2 is found in dairy products, whole-grain foods, liver, milk, meat, fish, dark green vegetables, pasta, and dried peas and beans.

Niacin helps break down food to provide energy and maintain healthy nerves and digestion. Some of the best sources are liver, fish, poultry, whole-grain foods, eggs, peanuts, and dried peas and beans.

Minerals

Minerals, like vitamins, help the body function properly. Your body cannot make minerals, so you must get them from foods. The minerals you need most of are calcium, phosphorus, magnesium, sodium, potassium, and chlorine. Your body needs only tiny amounts of certain minerals. The most common of these *trace* minerals are iron, iodine, and zinc.

Calcium and phosphorus work together. They are extremely important for building healthy bones and teeth. In fact, your bones would be like rubber without these minerals. Calcium aids the functioning of the heart and nervous system. It also helps prevent a bone condition called *osteoporosis* (oss–tee–o–puh–*RO*–sis). In this condition bones become very fragile and break easily. As well as teaming up with calcium, phosphorus helps the body to produce energy and also to use other nutrients.

Milk is an especially good source of calcium and phosphorus, because it supplies the correct amount of each mineral. Many carbonated soft drinks are so high in phosphorus that they can interfere with the teamwork between these two minerals. For this reason, it is important to drink enough milk and to limit your intake of carbonated soft drinks. Along with dairy products, some of the best sources of phosphorus are meat, dried beans and peas, and poultry. Green vegetables like broccoli and mustard greens supply smaller amounts of calcium.

Magnesium is important for muscles, nerves, bones, and teeth. It is supplied by eating a balanced diet including whole-grain foods, leafy green vegetables, meat, milk, nuts, and beans.

Fish is a great source of potassium, iodine, and zinc.

Sodium, chlorine, and potassium work together to control the water balance in your body. Table salt is a major source of sodium and chlorine. (The chemical name for salt is sodium chloride.) Sodium is found in many prepared foods, including potato chips, pretzels, ketchup, pickles, sausages, and bacon. Research indicates that too much sodium in the body can cause high blood pressure. For this reason, many people are cutting down on sodium in their diets. Some good sources of potassium are citrus fruits, bananas, dried fruits, fish, and meat.

Iron is found in red blood cells. It carries oxygen throughout the body and turns food into energy. A lack of iron can cause *anemia* (uh–*NEE*–mee–uh), an illness resulting in tiredness, weakness, pale skin, and a poor appetite. Iron is supplied by liver, red meat, eggs, dried fruits, dried peas and beans, whole grains, and leafy greens. Ask your doctor before taking iron supplements. Too much iron can be harmful.

Iodine is important to the body's rate of growth. It helps the thyroid gland make the hormone that controls your body's growth. Although you need only a small amount of iodine, too little can cause goiter, a swelling of the thyroid gland. Seafood, saltwater fish, and iodized salt are good sources of iodine.

Zinc is needed for the body's growth and maintenance. Zinc helps in the body's use of carbohydrates, proteins, and fats. It helps heal wounds and protects against disease. Some of the best sources are meat, seafood, eggs, milk, and whole-grain foods.

ENRICHMENT: Ask students to plan a lunch menu that includes foods high in magnesium, phosphorus, iron, and zinc.

NOTE: The word *anemia* comes from the Greek prefix *an-*, meaning "without" and a root word meaning "blood."

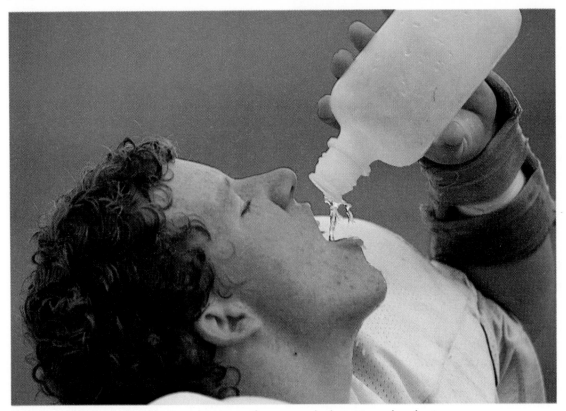

Do you drink at least six glasses of water daily? Your body is using water every minute of every day.

Water

You cannot live for very long without water. Even if you had no food for several weeks, you could survive as long as you had water. Without it, you could live for only three or four days.

Water makes up around 60 percent of your body weight. Water does many jobs in the body, among them aiding digestion, carrying nutrients throughout the body, and carrying away waste. Water also helps control your body temperature. When you perspire, water evaporates from your skin and your body cools off.

You need to drink at least six glasses of water a day. Besides drinking plain water, you also take water in when you have soups and sauces and when you eat some juicy fruits and vegetables.

See page T92 for answers.
For Review

1. Explain the difference between complete and incomplete proteins.
2. Why does your body need carbohydrates?
3. Name one food source for each of the essential nutrients.

Health and Safety

The Food and Drug Administration

What do you think about when you're buying food? You probably don't worry about whether wholewheat bread *really* contains the whole grain or if canned peaches can poison you. You are confident that your shampoo will not make your hair fall out. You believe your medicine is safe if you follow the directions. That's because the Food and Drug Administration (FDA) regulates the purity and safety of most foods, drugs, and cosmetics. Here's a sample of questions the FDA has already answered for you.

- How do I know what's *really* in this spaghetti sauce? The FDA requires all ingredients to be listed on the label.
- How can I tell if these chemicals I've never heard of are safe to eat? The FDA tests all food additives for safety.
- What will happen if this makeup gets in my eyes? The FDA tests all cosmetics for safety and for truthful labeling. Always read labels for special warnings.
- Could anything extra have gotten into this can of beans? The FDA regulates food processing plants for cleanliness.

  What question can you think of to ask the FDA about medicines?

Section 12.3
Using the Daily Food Guide

As you read, think about:

■ how following the Daily Food Guide can help you to have a balanced diet. (p. 263)
■ how following dietary guidelines can help you to be healthy. (p. 263)

You may have heard people say, "You are what you eat." This old saying actually has a lot of truth in it. Scientific evidence indicates that the food you eat affects the kind and quality of life you can lead. If you are not accomplishing some of the things

Does your diet include butter, cheese, and milk?

you would like to, it may be because of your eating habits.

A poor diet now can also cause problems in your adult life. Scientists have linked diet to health problems such as heart disease and cancer. Forming the right eating habits can help you to be more energetic and productive now and at any age. The key to this is learning to combine certain foods so that they work together for your good health.

Daily Food Needs

The Daily Food Guide can help you plan how to eat a balanced diet each day. This guide divides foods into five groups, according to the nutrients in each group. The five food groups are milk and cheese; meat, poultry, fish, and beans; fruits and vegetables; breads and cereals; and fats and sweets.

Look at the Daily Food Guide on page 477. As you will see, a certain number of servings is recommended for each of the first four food groups. Servings of fats and sweets are not recommended. These should be eaten only in small amounts.

The Milk-Cheese Group

Milk and milk products, such as cheese, yogurt, and ice cream, are some of the foods in the milk-cheese group. Foods with a high milk content, like dairy puddings or creamed soups, are also part of this group. Teenagers need four servings from this group each day. Examples include 1 cup of milk or yogurt, or 2 slices of hard cheese.

RETEACHING: List the five food groups on the board. Have students give examples of foods in each group.

PHOTO: Ask students to identify as many of these protein sources as they can. Stress that protein is available in sources other than meat.

Do you include selections from the meat-poultry-fish-bean group in your daily diet?

The milk-cheese group provides calcium and phosphorus, needed for strong bones and teeth. It also supplies vitamin D, which is added to milk, as well as riboflavin and protein.

The Meat-Poultry-Fish-Bean Group

This group includes meats, like liver, beef, pork, and lamb; poultry; and fish. It also includes nuts and legumes, such as peanuts and dried peas and beans. These foods supply complete or incomplete protein, used by the body to build and repair tissue. They are also a good source of iron, thiamin, and niacin.

ENRICHMENT: Divide the class into five groups. To each, assign one of the five food groups. Have students develop a collage of foods from that particular food group.

Chapter 12/*Food and Health* **263**

A snack from this group will give you energy, vitamins, and water.

Two servings daily from this group are recommended for everyone. Examples include 2 to 3 ounces of lean meat, fish, or poultry or one cup of legumes.

The Fruits-Vegetables Group

A rich variety of fruits and vegetables is included in this group. Some of the foods that provide vitamin C are citrus fruits, strawberries, and cantaloupes. Vitamin A is provided by dark green and deep yellow fruits and vegetables, such as broccoli, carrots, and apricots. Peels and seeds add fiber to your diet. Fruits and vegetables also add water.

At least four daily servings of fruits and vegetables are recommended. A serving could be one whole apple; 1 cup of raw

fruit or vegetables; or ½ cup of cooked fruit or vegetables.

The Bread-Cereal Group

Foods made of whole grains or enriched flour are in the bread-cereal group. In addition to cereals and breads themselves, this group includes pasta, rice, barley, muffins, waffles, and pancakes. Foods in this group are very good sources of carbohydrates, B vitamins, and some iron.

Everyone needs at least four servings from the bread-cereal group each day. A serving is 1 cup of ready-to-eat cereal; 1 cup of cooked cereal; grits; pasta; or rice; one slice of bread; or one biscuit, muffin, or roll.

The Fats-Sweets Group

The two foods in this group are sweets (candy, cookies, sugary soft drinks) and fats (butter, salad oil, mayonnaise). These foods provide more fats and carbohydrates than your body normally needs, and they are high in calories. It is therefore best to eat them only in small amounts. Also remember that if you fill up on fats and sweets, you won't be hungry for more nutritious foods.

Dietary Guidelines

North America has a rich choice of healthy foods. Nevertheless, many people select foods that are now linked to health problems such as heart disease and cancer. About 40 percent of the people in this country are overweight. Scientists believe

NOTE: Grape Nuts, the first ready-to-eat breakfast food, was introduced by Charles Post in 1897.

ENRICHMENT: Have students write a list of recommendations for reducing a typical junior high or middle school student's intake of fats and sweets.

that too much fat, sugar, sodium, and empty calories contribute to these health problems.

To encourage people to change their eating habits, the United States government has prepared dietary guidelines. These guidelines are based on moderation and variety. If you like potato chips and ice cream, for example, eat them only occasionally. Combine foods to meet your daily nutrition needs. The dietary guidelines can help you stay healthy now and in the future. (Chapter 13 contains information about the United States Recommended Daily Allowances.)

The following are Dietary Guidelines for Americans.
1. Eat a variety of foods. No one food has all the nutrients you need.
2. Maintain your ideal weight.
3. Avoid too much fat, saturated fat, and cholesterol. Eat lean foods and limit butter and eggs.
4. Eat foods with enough starch and fiber —whole grains, produce, and nuts.
5. Avoid too much sugar. Eat fresh fruits instead of candy and soft drinks.
6. Avoid too much sodium. Limit the salty foods you eat and cut salt use in cooking and at the table.

See page T92 for answers.
For Review
1. What is the importance of the Daily Food Guide?
2. What are the six dietary guidelines that can help you get the nutrients you need?

Comment on current ideas more strongly linking fats, rather than carbohydrates, to weight gain.

For most people, selecting from the bread-cereal group is no problem.

Section 12.4
Calories and Weight

As you read, think about:
■ how proper eating habits and regular exercise can help you maintain your ideal weight. (p. 267)
■ why fad diets are unhealthy. (p. 270)
■ why eating disorders should be treated as serious illnesses. (p. 273)

Weight is a sensitive issue for many people. Some people want to weigh more, others want to weigh less. It is important to realize that there are guidelines concerning what your ideal weight should be. You may feel that your weight should be different. If so, your doctor can help you design a program of diet and exercise to help you make some changes. To understand the subject of weight, you should know something about how your body uses food. This includes an understanding of how much food your body needs.

NOTE: The word *calorie* comes from the Latin word meaning "heat."

What Are Calories?

You may have seen advertisements stating that a particular food is low in calories. Such claims are often made, but exactly what is a calorie? It is not something you can see or touch. It does not supply you with nutrients. A **calorie** is the energy that food provides. As you go about your activities, your body burns energy, or calories. To keep going, you need a certain number of calories.

The food that you eat is *oxidized,* or burned, by the body. When this happens, your body gives off heat. This heat is measured in calories. When food is burned as energy, the value of the heat produced is a calorie.

You don't have to be running or jumping to burn calories.

Calories Burned Per Minute During Activities

	Body Weight				
	110	130	150	170	190
Walking, 3 MPH	3.9	4.5	5.1	5.7	6.3
Walking, 5 MPH	7.3	8.3	9.3	10.3	11.3
Bicycling, 10 MPH	5.4	6.2	7.0	7.8	8.6
Running, 6 MPH	8.8	9.9	11.0	12.0	13.0
Cleaning	3.1	3.7	4.2	4.8	5.3
Cooking	1.7	2.0	2.3	2.6	2.9

Vitamins and minerals do not have any calorie content. Fats, carbohydrates, and proteins are the nutrients that do. As most foods contain several nutrients, you usually do not consume pure fat, carbohydrate, or protein. However, the following information gives you an idea of how many calories are in these nutrients.

1 ounce (28 g) of pure fat = 252 calories

1 ounce (28 g) of pure carbohydrate = 112 calories

1 ounce (28 g) of pure protein = 112 calories

You can see that high-fat foods are also highest in calories. For example, 3 ounces (85 g) of lean ground beef has 190 calories. The same amount of regular ground beef has 270 calories.

Calorie content is also affected by the way a food is prepared. Notice how the calorie content in these foods differs.

1 medium baked potato = 90 calories

1 cup mashed potatoes with butter and milk = 200 calories

1 cup potato salad = 250 calories

1 ear corn = 70 calories

1 cup cream-style corn = 210 calories

1 raw apple = 80 calories

1 cup sweetened applesauce = 230 calories

1 slice two-crust apple pie = 400 calories

How Many Do You Need?

The exact number of calories you need depends on several factors. These include your age, size, weight, lifestyle, and basal metabolism. Your **basal metabolism** (meh–*TAB*–uh–liz–um) is the rate at which your body burns calories for normal body functions. These include breathing, heartbeat, blood circulation, tissue repair, and elimination (getting rid of waste).

Your age is an important factor in determining how many calories you need. Growing children and teenagers need more energy than older people. The rate at which you are growing is also a consideration. Tissues and large bones need energy in order to develop. The period of most rapid growth usually takes place around age 12 for most girls and age 14 for most boys.

Your height and body type are additional factors that affect your energy needs. If you are short, you probably need fewer calories than a taller person. If you have more muscle than fat, you need more calories than someone with more fat and less muscle.

You burn calories when you exercise. Therefore, your level of activity is important in determining your calorie needs. Playing basketball, for example, requires more energy than walking a few steps. A simple formula can give you a rough idea of your daily calorie needs. Suppose you weigh 118 pounds and are fairly active. In order to stay at your present weight, you need about 20 calories per pound. This means you should have 2,260 calories a day. If your activities are light, you need only 15 calories per pound. Your calorie needs drop to 1,770. If you are involved in practically no activity, you need about 12 calories per pound, or 1,416. As you can see, each person has his or her own specific calorie needs.

After exercise, answer those thirst and hunger signals from your body.

Weight Control

What is an ideal weight? The answer to this varies, literally all over the world. In some cultures, what we think is overweight is considered beautiful. In this country, advertisements depict thin as the ideal way to be. A truly ideal weight, however, is what is best for your height, build, and overall health.

What Is Your Ideal Weight?

Height-weight tables giving average weights are available. Most, however, are intended for adults. Do not use such a chart unless it is designed for your age group. Even then, a chart might not show the right weight for you. A better plan is

Do you have a favorite exercise? It can help you burn calories.

to consult your family doctor or health clinic. By using special techniques, doctors can determine your ideal weight. They can then tell you how many calories you should have each day to reach or maintain it. You can plan your diet according to this information.

You can do a simple test yourself to get a rough idea if you are underweight, overweight, or just right. The *pinch test* measures the fat stored under the skin. To do this test, pinch your skin at the back of the upper arm, halfway between the elbow and shoulder. The thickness should be ½ to 1 inch (12 to 24 mm). If you have more, you could be overweight. If you have less, you could be underweight. Keep in mind that the pinch test is not

completely reliable. Some people may be the right weight but have unusually heavy or thin upper arms.

Exercise

Exercise is at least as important for your health as diet. If you are eating less to lose weight, your body will think it is starving. Your basal metabolism rate will slow down as soon as you lower your calorie intake. Your body will then begin to use fewer calories for all of its functions. Thus you often lose weight during the first two weeks of a diet but lose very little after that. Your body has adjusted to having fewer calories. So your weight loss has slowed down.

Exercise can speed up your basal metabolism rate, causing the body to burn more calories. This is why exercise is essential. Exercise also keeps your body from becoming flabby while you are trying to lose weight.

A daily exercise program is one of the best ways to burn calories. There are other advantages to regular exercise. Your body will burn calories at a higher metabolic rate up to 15 hours after vigorous exercise. So if you exercise in the morning, your body will burn calories during the day. By exercising again in the afternoon, you will burn calories even while you sleep.

Exercise is not just for people who wish to lose weight; it has many benefits. These include firming up the body, keeping the heart healthy, lifting the spirits, and simply making you feel good. These benefits apply to all people, whether they wish to lose, gain, or maintain weight.

ENRICHMENT: Using a "Calories Used For Activities Chart," show students how to calculate the number of calories they burn doing various activities throughout the day. Ask them to compare that total against the number of calories they can consume daily.

RETEACHING: Emphasize that people are always using up calories. Exercise increases the *rate* at which we use them.

Forming New Eating Habits

People sometimes go on crash diets to lose weight. After losing a few pounds, they abandon the diet because it is so limiting. They then regain the weight, and so they start dieting again. This is called *seesaw dieting.* It is a dangerous practice, as the body must keep adjusting to weight losses and gains. Seesaw dieting can cause health problems such as thyroid disorders, heart disease, and depression.

The secret to losing weight is not crash dieting but developing new eating habits. A good way to change your eating habits is to keep track of what you eat.

For one week, write down everything you eat and drink. This may seem too much trouble at times, but the effort will be worth it. Keeping a record has helped many people change their eating habits.

After you have evaluated what you eat, you can make a new food plan to help you reach your goal. If you want to lose weight, you do not have to give up all of the foods you like best. Rather, cut down on high-calorie foods and eat smaller portions. You can still have your favorite desserts if you don't have them as often.

Counting calories can help you get started on a food plan to lose weight. In time, however, you will develop a sense of which foods are high in calories and you won't have to count. High-calorie foods tend to be oily (fried chicken), thick (milk shakes), sweet or sticky (cake or candy), and concentrated (jam). Low-calorie foods have distinct qualities, too. They tend to be watery and crisp (carrots), juicy (oranges), coarse (whole-grain breads), and airy or puffed (cereals).

Did You Know?

One of the hottest new health-food ingredients in America has been a staple in the Orient for centuries. The Chinese first "discovered" tofu 2,000 years ago. It is made from soybean curd in a process similar to cheese making. Tofu has many advantages besides the fact that it is inexpensive. It is high in calcium; low in calories, fat, and sodium; contains no cholesterol; and supplies B vitamins and iron. Perhaps most important in today's American market, it can be "disguised" in hamburgers, stews, and soups. It can also be sprinkled over casseroles, stuffed into pastas, or used as a base for dressings, sauces, and "ice cream."

Making a Diet Work

If you are trying to lose weight, you may start out all right but have trouble sticking to your food plan. People who have lost weight successfully have passed on tips you might find helpful.

- Do not skip a meal, as you are likely to snack or to overeat at the next meal.
- Eat slowly. Your brain will let your stomach know when you are full, but this process takes about 20 minutes. Eating more slowly gives your brain

time to send a signal before you have a second helping.
- Eat smaller than average portions. Also, use a small plate.
- Sit down to eat. If you eat while wandering around, you can lose track of how much you are eating.
- When at home, eat in only one place. You will then cut down on the number of places you associate with food.
- Drink a glass of water before meals. Water does not add calories and can help you feel full.
- Prepare low-calorie snacks ahead of time. For example, cut up fresh fruits and vegetables and store them in plastic bags so that they are just as convenient as high-calorie snacks.

There are many books about diets, but not all of them make sense.

- If you snack while watching television or listening to music, find something to do with your hands. Sew on a button, sort your record collection, or file your nails. By keeping your hands occupied, you will be less likely to snack.
- Ask relatives and friends not to offer you more food, nor to urge you to have second helpings.
- Keep food out of sight. Don't leave things like cookies or potato chips where they can tempt you.
- Plan ahead. Before going to a party, eat only low-calorie foods so that you can have a few extra calories later.
- Burn calories through a regular exercise program. Look for ways to get more exercise, such as climbing stairs or riding a bike rather than taking a bus.

Fad Diets

"Follow our fabulous diet plan! Eat all you want, and still lose pounds in just one week!" Have you seen ads making such claims? Fad diets promise quick and easy weight loss. Some people follow them for a while, lured by the promise of miracles. One serious problem with fad diets is that they can damage your health. Another is that they don't work.

Although you may lose some weight on fad diets, you will not develop new eating habits. Instead, dieting usually falls into a seesaw pattern. Weight that is lost quickly is regained quickly.

High Protein and Carbohydrate Diets Many fad diets are based on the myth that carbohydrates are fattening and

REINFORCEMENT: Have students develop a daily menu of foods that are high in nutrients and low in calories.

should be avoided. These diets are built around high-protein and low-carbohydrate foods. Such diets claim you can lose weight by eating mainly meat, poultry, and fish. You are often steered away from foods like milk, grains, and some fruits and vegetables. Some people lose a little weight for a short time. However, these diets do not supply enough carbohydrates. They can cause headaches and make you feel weak. They are also high in fat. If followed over a period of time, they can lead to health problems like heart or kidney disease. Diets like this may appear under many different names, but they are all essentially the same.

"One Food Only"

One-food diets are based on eating the same food, such as grapefruit or yogurt, over and over. These diets do not provide enough nutrients. Also, they are boring. Most people do not follow them for very long.

Diet Pills

Diet pills are supposed to reduce your appetite. They do not change your eating habits after you stop using them, nor maybe even while you're taking them. Serious health problems have been reported among people taking diet pills. These include high blood pressure, shakiness, rapid heartbeat, and kidney failure. There have also been reports of such pills leading to drug abuse.

Liquid Protein

Liquid protein diets have sometimes been used to help people lose weight. These diets should be followed only under a doctor's supervision. A number of deaths have been linked to liquid protein diets.

Diet Candy

Diet candies may lower your appetite temporarily, but they do not change your eating habits. Most diet candies contain sugar.

Fasting

Fasting is abstaining from food altogether. Some diets recommend fasting for a few days, claiming that your stomach will shrink. This is not what happens. When you lose weight by fasting, you are losing mainly water. You start gaining again as soon as you start eating again. Fasting to lose weight can cause depression or even sudden death.

In addition to everything else, fad diets can be expensive. A well-planned diet that includes nutritious foods and exercise is safer and less expensive. Be guided by your doctor or other health professional when you plan a diet. With a plan that really works, you will end up looking and feeling better.

Do you believe these claims? Does your doctor?

Diet Product Claims

Want to be thin????

After one week on our liquid protein diet, you can lose as much as **20 pounds !!!**

Just drink three glasses of DELISHNUTE a day, and nothing else, and watch those pounds melt away.

NOTE: The word *fad* means something that people do very enthusiastically and very briefly. Can your students think of any silly fads they know of from the past?

ENRICHMENT: Have students find an ad for a currently popular diet that makes big claims about how easy or how successful it is. Discuss with students how these claims can be dangerous.

PHOTO: Ask your students what they think is the difference in their own eating habits when they eat alone in contrast to when they eat with other family members.

What can you do to make meal times more pleasant in your house? Conversation and good manners will go a long way.

Eating Habits

"I get up too late for breakfast."

"A snack is all I need."

"Our family is too busy for us to eat meals together."

Have you heard any of these statements? Eating habits are influenced by lifestyle. Family members often have different activities scheduled on a given day. Your own schedule might include not only school but also basketball practice or a club meeting. Different activities and schedules often make it hard for families to relax and enjoy meals together.

Your eating habits are also influenced by the atmosphere around you. If the school cafeteria is hectic, you may decide to have a soft drink and potato chips instead of lunch. This might not be harmful if done very occasionally. If you develop unhealthy eating patterns, however, you run the risk of gaining too much weight or becoming ill.

Healthy Eating Patterns

Your body needs a regular supply of energy. This is why you should have three meals a day, regularly spaced.

REINFORCEMENT: Ask students to describe what being either very busy or very bored does to their eating habits. If these things have a negative effect, have students suggest one thing they could do to change this pattern.

Breakfast is especially important. Without it, your body is not refueled for up to 12 hours. You may feel you don't have time for breakfast. You could, however, get up a little earlier or making some preparations the night before. For example, put out the breakfast dishes. You could even make a peanut butter sandwich and have it ready in the refrigerator.

There are many interesting foods you can have for breakfast if you are tired of what you usually have. For example, you might have fish, a bagel and cream cheese, pizza, or a tortilla with cheese. Yogurt with nuts and raisins is tasty and also nutritious.

Your lunch should supply a third or more of your nutrients for the day. Prepared lunches are available in most schools. If your school participates in the National School Lunch Program, a balanced meal will be planned for you. If you pack your own lunch, remember to include foods from the first four food groups. For example, you could have tuna on whole-grain bread, carrot or celery sticks, fruit, and milk. Containers that keep food hot or cold are very convenient for packed lunches. You can use them for foods like salads, desserts, or for any of your favorite soups.

Although the evening meal has traditionally been the largest in many families, some health professionals suggest making it the lightest. This is because there are only a few hours left to burn off calories. However, the evening meal is important for families. This is the time to relax and share events of the day. Even if your family cannot always eat together, try to enjoy the times when they do.

If you like snacks, get into the habit of choosing those that provide nutrients. Some good choices are nuts, unbuttered popcorn, raw fruits and vegetables, peanut butter on wheat crackers, and cheese. You can make your own fruit pops by freezing juices in ice cube trays.

Whatever you eat, your eating habits affect your digestion. Eating in a hurry or swallowing food before it is chewed can cause digestive upsets. Have you ever gulped down food when you were angry about something? Anger can cause the churning motion of the stomach to increase. Food is pushed along to the small intestine too fast and you get indigestion. Other emotions—resentment, sadness, fear—can also affect your digestion.

As often as possible, try to relax in a calm environment when you are eating. This might be difficult at times; some places—like the school cafeteria—are not always the best eating environments. Eating slowly and chewing food thoroughly will help you avoid digestive problems.

Eating Disorders

Some eating patterns fall into the category of eating disorders. Two illnesses can occur when people take extreme measures to lose weight.

Those suffering from **anorexia nervosa** (an–uh–*REX*–ee–uh ner–*VOH*–suh) are obsessed with thinness and usually have severe psychological problems. Victims may start by wanting to lose a few pounds, but then they cannot stop dieting. They starve themselves, even when they are skin and bones. The results can be serious illness or death.

How can you tell that this athlete is preparing for an event?

Victims of **bulimia** (buh–*LIM*–ee–uh) eat compulsively for a short period of time. After this "binge" eating, they induce vomiting or use laxatives to rid the body of food. This can cause serious medical problems. The victim can even starve to death as the disorder becomes more serious.

Both anorexia and bulimia are very dangerous. They require medical attention immediately. Consult health care professionals if you or anyone you know has either of these problems.

Food for Athletes

Some people believe that athletes need a different diet from people who are not athletic. Actually, athletes need the same balanced diet as anyone else. They may, however, need a little more food to give them more energy. You may participate in team sports, or you may sometimes jog or bicycle. Whatever your athletic involvement, these guidelines can be helpful.

- Drink plain water to replace the salt lost in sweating. Salt tablets are not needed and can even be dangerous. Normal seasonings in food, plus adequate water, will keep the body from becoming *dehydrated,* or starved for water.
- Eat nutritious carbohydrates for extra energy. Good choices include breads, potatoes, rice, pasta, and fruits. There is no evidence that a high-protein diet improves athletic ability. Red meat does not provide strength or build muscle. There is also no evidence that vitamin and mineral supplements are helpful. Before an athletic event, you should eat food high in carbohydrates and low in fats and protein.
- Eat three or four hours before an athletic event to allow food to be digested.

For Review

1. Name the factors that influence your ideal weight.
2. Describe the dangers of diet pills and fasting.
3. What are eating disorders? Describe two.

Learning to Manage

Snacking for Health

Look back at the classroom conversation on page 250. Now read how Mr. Torres and the class work out a plan to answer the snacking question. Then answer the questions that follow.

"Be honest, who else thinks that 'healthy' tastes boring?" Mr. Torres asked.

As several hands were raised, Mr. Torres smiled. "I see I have my work cut out for me, but I bet you'll change your minds soon!"

"Not me, Mr. Torres. I will *never* give up my TWINKLE cupcakes," Ron said dramatically, as the class laughed.

"We'll see, my friend," Mr. Torres replied. "First, let's use this class time to brainstorm ideas for healthy snacks."

"That's easy enough. Carrots and celery," Marty said.

"I think you have diet food in mind rather than nutritious snacks," said Mr. Torres. "You people are so active, you can afford to eat higher-calorie snacks than plain celery and carrots. I have some simple snack recipes that will make you enjoy both fruit and raw vegetables more. We'll start making them in class, and you can sample them to find your favorites."

The next day, the "great snack experiment," as Ron called it, began. Each of the four lab groups made a snack to share with the rest of the class. The first group made a large pot of popcorn and tossed it with grated cheddar cheese while it was still warm. Another group made a fruit snack with melon balls and apple slices dipped in lemon juice. To go with this, they made a dip combining sour cream and whipped cream. The next group made a snack of mini-pizzas. They spread spaghetti sauce on melba crackers and added a slice of pepperoni and a sprinkling of grated mozzarella cheese. They put this under the broiler until the cheese melted. Finally, Ron's group made what they called "Peanut Butter Delights" by combining peanut butter, chopped apple, and raisins. They spread this on crackers.

"Well, what do you think, class? Is there life beyond junk food? Does 'healthy' really have to be boring?"

"I'm not bored," Ron said. "My taste buds are calling for more."

Questions

1. List the ingredients in your favorite snack. Beside each ingredient, name the food group it belongs in.
2. Create a recipe for one new snack, using a fruit or a vegetable and at least one other ingredient.
3. Have your snacking choices changed because of what you have learned about nutrition? Why or why not?

Chapter 12 Review

Summary

The essential nutrients needed by the body are proteins, carbohydrates, fats, vitamins, minerals, and water. In a balanced diet, these nutrients are provided by foods from four major groups. These groups are milk-cheese, meat-poultry-fish-beans, fruits-vegetables, and breads-cereals. There is a fifth group, fats-sweets, which provides a smaller amount of essential nutrients.

An ideal weight is influenced by basal metabolism and factors like age and lifestyle. Weight control is affected by both calorie intake and exercise. The key to losing, gaining, or maintaining weight is to form the proper eating habits. Fad diets should be avoided. Healthy eating patterns include regular meals and eating slowly in a relaxed environment. Some unhealthy eating patterns can develop into eating disorders.

Vocabulary

Complete each of the following sentences with the correct word from the vocabulary list below. (p. 256)

essential
  amino acids (p. 254)
bulimia (p. 274)
basal metabolism (p. 267)
saturated fats (p. 256)
calorie (p. 266)
unsaturated fats (p. 256)

fat-soluble vitamins
cholesterol (p. 256)
water-
  soluble vitamins (p. 259)
nutrients (p. 251)
anorexia
nervosa (p. 273)

1. _____ are materials that provide energy and help your body function, grow, and repair itself.
2. Individuals obsessed with thinness are victims of _____.
3. The nine amino acids that the body cannot make are called _____.
4. Vitamins transported by fat instead of water are called _____.
5. _____ are those that are solid at room temperature.
6. _____ are liquid, like salad oil.
7. A fatlike substance in the body cells is called _____.
8. Vitamins which mix only with water, like vitamin C and B-complex vitamins, are called _____.
9. A _____ is the energy that food provides the body.
10. The rate at which your body burns calories for normal body functions is called _____.
11. Victims of _____ eat compulsively for a short period of time. Then they induce vomiting or use laxatives to rid the body of food.

Questions

•• 1. What is the difference between *hunger* and *appetite?*

• 2. What are the functions of protein in the body?

• 3. Name several foods that are complete proteins.

The dots represent skill levels required to answer each question or complete each activity:

  • requires recall and comprehension
  •• requires application and analysis
  ••• requires synthesis and evaluation

4. Name four sources of dietary fiber.

5. Should you avoid all fat in your diet? Explain your answer.

6. Is it necessary to take vitamin pills? Explain your answer.

7. Name the vitamin that helps the body form collagen.

8. What two minerals are essential for building healthy bones and teeth?

9. Name the five food groups from which you need to eat each day in order to have a balanced diet.

10. How many servings of fruits and vegetables are recommended each day for a balanced diet?

11. Explain how age, height, and body type affect a person's energy needs.

12. Name at least four important benefits you can derive from a regular exercise program.

13. Name all six of the Dietary Guidelines for Americans.

14. Should a person who is trying to gain weight eat large amounts of fatty foods? Explain your answer.

15. What can result from a diet low in carbohydrates and high in protein?

Skill Activities

Many more activities are contained in the annotations within this chapter.

1. Decision Making In small groups, decide what would be a balanced diet for one day for the following kinds of people: 1) a soccer player; 2) an overweight person; 3) an inactive person. Share your balanced diet plans with the class. Explain why you selected certain food items from the four major food groups.

2. Critical Thinking Working in small groups, brainstorm how your emotions influence what you eat, when you eat, and how much you eat. Discuss how satisfying your emotional needs by eating may lead to psychological and physical problems.

3. Laboratory List all foods, including beverages and snacks, that you have eaten in the last 24 hours. Compare what you have eaten with the recommended amounts for each food group in the Daily Food Guide. Did the foods you ate include all the food groups? If not, which ones were not included? Did you eat enough servings in each food group? Did you eat more than the recommended amount for any one food group?

4. Communication Role-play and then discuss some situations about food and nutrition. For example, one situation could involve a mother trying to get a teenager to eat breakfast. Another situation might involve urging a young child to try new foods. Think of other food-related situations to role-play and discuss.

Chapter 13
Meal Planning

Vocabulary

The dialogue below introduces "Caught Short," the Learning to Manage feature in this chapter. The case study is continued and the situation discussed further on page 301. See page T96 for teaching suggestions.

"Karen, Jane is in charge while Dad and I are away, but I'm giving you the food shopping duties."

"OK, Mom. What do I do?"

"Well, Bob will take you shopping. I've made out a list and left the money on your bureau."

"Is that all I have to do—shop?"

"You'll put the food away when you get it home, too."

"No problem. Don't worry, Mom. I'll take care of everything."

Section 13.1

Making Your Meal Choices

As you read, think about:

■ your nutrition needs. (p. 279)

■ the relationship between your schedule and the time you need for meal planning. (p. 280)

■ how to plan appealing meals on a budget. (p. 281)

Taking care of everything related to food shopping and storage is a big job. A delicious, nutritious meal is no accident. The key to well-balanced, appealing meals is *planning*. This means choosing foods carefully and taking into account both the food budget and the time available. Good shopping skills and an efficient food storage system are also important.

Planning makes everything about mealtimes more interesting. Have you ever thought about the way food looks on a plate? Giving some attention to such details results in more appetizing meals.

What Are Your Nutrition Needs?

Use what you learned about the Daily Food Guide in Chapter 12 to begin your planning. (The chart on page 477 is a handy reference.) Use the guide for each meal to make sure you are including essential nutrients. Plan a meal with the whole day's eating in mind. Read food labels and take care in selecting products. Evaluate the nutrition claims made about

PHOTO: Have students explain what foods they think look appetizing here and why.

What makes a meal irresistible?

particular foods. Also keep in mind the individual needs of each family member.

Individual Needs

If you or other family members are on a special diet, you need to consider this fact when planning meals. Those who are losing weight need to have low-fat foods like fish and lean meat. If someone in your family is on a low-sodium diet, foods can be seasoned with spices other than salt. Family customs and preferences also play a part in meal planning. As you know, many families celebrate special religious and personal occasions with particular foods. On an everyday basis, families have certain preferences. Some families like bread at every meal, for example, while other families seldom eat bread.

ENRICHMENT: Have students find two cereals at the supermarket with labels that suggest nutritional value such as "no salt added" or "no artificial sweeteners." Have students bring the list of ingredients to class for discussion of the cereal's nutritional merit.

REINFORCEMENT: Have students list two examples of dinners they would like to serve their families. Critique the meals for color and nutritional appeal.

How Much Time Do You Have?

Your schedule is an important consideration in meal planning. If you have a paper route before school, the time you can spend preparing breakfast or making lunch is limited. Sports or other after-school activities can make your supper preparations rushed. If someone helps, your job will be easier. Read recipes carefully to see how much time they require, including time to cook or chill a food. Also add time needed for chopping or mixing. If these things take too long, you may need to select a different recipe.

After you have considered your daily schedule, block out the time you have to prepare meals. Remember to plan time to make breakfast, even if you're rushed in

Sometimes you have to do two things at once to make time for breakfast.

PHOTO: Ask your class to brainstorm a list of five things that could be prepared in less than ten minutes for a nutritious breakfast.

Did You Know?

Forty guests will consume approximately

- 2 gallons of soup
- 2 quarts of gravy or sauce
- Lemonade made from 2 dozen lemons, 2 pounds of sugar, and 2 gallons of water
- 1 peck (8 quarts) of potatoes
- 20 pounds of chicken or turkey, dressed
- 2 gallons of ice cream

the morning. If you are responsible for planning a family meal, think about ways to save time. For example, you could use spare time in the afternoon to make a casserole ahead of time and freeze it. Baked chicken pieces can be prepared in advance and refrigerated. Having the ingredients on hand for quick last-minute dishes, such as stir-fried vegetables, is another good planning idea.

If you have time-saving kitchen equipment, learn how to use it. Chapter 14 has information about using specific kitchen equipment.

Plan Appealing Meals

How a meal looks may be more important than you realize. Variety in color, shape, and texture improves a meal's chances of success. Look at the menu below and think about how to make it look more appealing.

DISCUSS: Ask students what kinds of foods they or their parents prepare ahead of time. Ask for ideas on how food preparation time could be saved in their families.

Fish

Mashed Potatoes   Creamed Cauliflower

Roll   Butter

Vanilla Pudding

Milk

Although the foods are nutritious, they are all soft, similar in color and shape, and fairly bland. The next menu looks a lot more interesting.

Fish

Baked Potato   Broccoli

Cornbread   Butter

Fresh Fruit Cup

Milk

To plan meals that are varied and appetizing, keep these guidelines in mind.

- Vary the flavors in a meal. If you make sweet and sour meatballs and carrots glazed with sugar and butter, the overall taste could be a bit *too* sweet. Crisp green beans would be a better choice of vegetable. Spaghetti with tomato sauce is a good combination because the spicy tomato taste blends well with the bland spaghetti.
- Use foods of different colors. Breaded chicken, carrots, and sweet potatoes are similar in color. If you substitute green peas and french fried potatoes, your meal will be more appealing to the eye.
- Include different textures to add interest to a meal. A crisp salad with crunchy cucumbers and celery contrasts well with a soft food like sweet potatoes.
- Serve foods of different shapes. Hamburger patties, boiled potatoes, and

What attention to variety and nutrition do you see here?

peas are all round. If you substitute carrots cut lengthwise for one of the vegetables, your meal will look much more interesting.

Consider Food Costs

If you are doing the family food shopping, first look carefully at exactly how much money you have to spend. Your family may budget food by the week or by the month. Then plan ahead to stay within your budget. Look for specials on canned and frozen foods that you can store for future use. If meat is on sale, you might buy more than you need and freeze some of it. You can save money *and* time by creating your own convenience foods. Suppose that

ART: Have students compare the rates of increase, especially between 1890 and 1980. As an enrichment activity, ask students to calculate percentages of increase.

Food Costs Today and Yesterday

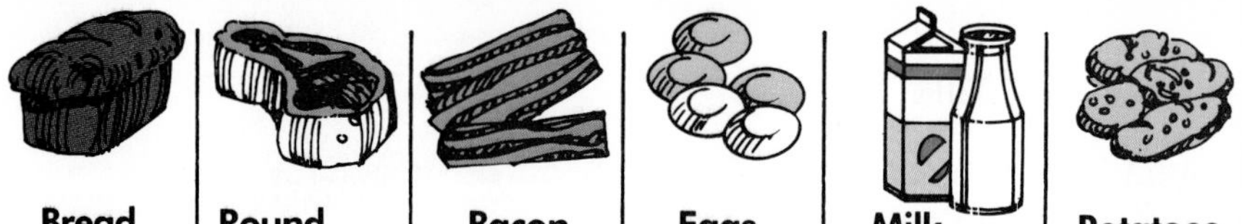

Year	Bread (loaf)	Round Steak (lb.)	Bacon (lb.)	Eggs (doz.)	Milk ($\frac{1}{2}$ gal.)	Potatoes (10 lbs.)
1980s	1.39	2.89	2.69	.95	1.09	1.59
1970s	.24	1.30	.95	.61	.66	.90
1950s	.18	.88	.57	.60	.48	.68
1930s	.09	.43	.43	.45	.28	.36
1890s	.03	.12	.13	.21	.14	.16

What are some of the factors that account for the increase in food costs during the time period shown above?

stewing beef is on sale. You might cook double the amount of stew and freeze half of it.

See page T97 for answers.

For Review

1. How can you season food for someone who is on a low-sodium diet?
2. Give one example of a way to save time preparing meals.
3. Why is it important to serve foods of different colors at a meal?

ENRICHMENT: Have students compare the cost of a prepared food that their family eats frequently with the cost of preparing that same item from scratch.

Section 13.2

Shopping for Food

As you read, think about:

- the various kinds of food stores. (p. 283)
- the importance of smart shopping. (p. 285)
- what food labels tell you. (p. 288)
- how to store various kinds of food. (p. 290)

The next time you are in a grocery store, stop for a minute to appreciate the colors, textures, and aromas. Food shopping can

ENRICHMENT: As a homework assignment, have students ask parents or other adults about what they think can be done to make food shopping more time- and cost-efficient.

be a truly enjoyable experience. Mounds of colorful fruits or fragrant smells from a bakery are reminders of the rich variety of foods available.

Making Shopping Choices

There is more to shopping, however, than appreciating the abundance of food. Efficient food shopping is a skill. As you learn more about it, you will be able to shop more efficiently for nutritious foods.

Where You Shop

You can buy food in many different kinds of stores. You will be choosing where you shop depending on the factors that are important to you. Prices, distance from the stores, and the quality of the food are three important factors to consider. Services may vary, but you should expect cleanliness no matter which type of store you choose.

Supermarkets Most communities of any size have supermarkets. Some may be fairly limited, while others carry thousands of items. Supermarkets sell fresh produce, meat, poultry, fish, frozen and canned items, dairy products, baked goods, and household supplies. Most also stock health and beauty items. They may even have a pharmacy. Some supermarkets are open 24 hours a day. Supermarkets are the most popular kind of food store in this country, as they have the widest selection of foods.

What are some of the products and specialty items available in a large supermarket?

DISCUSS: Do you most often do your shopping in a supermarket? Why or why not?

PHOTO: Ask students to survey three people on their favorite places to shop for food. Why do these people prefer these places?

Technology

Super-Marketing

In the 1930s, when shoppers were accustomed to small, specialty food stores, the idea of a supermarket was revolutionary. The supermarket made possible one-stop shopping for well-known brands, prepackaged meats, fish, and baked goods of predictable quality. Customers did not have to wait to be waited on. However, stores were designed so that shoppers passed through every aisle even if they wanted only a few items. Particular products were "pushed" by being placed prominently, at eye level, or at checkouts to promote impulse buying.

According to current market research, today's busy consumers want speed and convenience. On the other hand, they miss the wide selection of fresh goods and personal service found in old-fashioned specialty stores. New, larger *superstores* resemble a "town" of small businesses, banks, appliance or clothing "shops," bakeries, fresh meat and fish markets, and gourmet take-outs. Some even have fast-food outlets or cafés for in-store snacks. Superstores speed shopping for prepackaged goods by putting all foods designed for microwave cooking together, and by grouping ingredients for a particular meal, such as an Italian dinner. More parking and faster checkouts complete the ins and outs of superstores.

What kinds of food stores are there near you?

Food Warehouses "No frills" stores, called food warehouses, focus on keeping prices low. This usually means there are fewer services. For example, you may have to supply your own boxes or bags and fill them yourself. There may also be fewer products or brands than in regular supermarkets. Some food warehouses keep prices low by selling food in large quantities.

Convenience Stores Small neighborhood convenience stores are often open 24 hours a day. They carry fewer items than supermarkets and usually charge higher prices.

Farmers' Markets Farmers sell fruit and vegetables they have grown at a farmers' market. The produce is fresh, and prices are usually low. You can stroll from stand to stand, much as you would at a food fair, and select what you need.

Produce Stands During growing season, people set up small roadside stands to sell produce. This kind of stand can be found in the city as well as in the country.

Co-ops Food co-ops are nonprofit associations of families and groups who buy food in large quantities at low prices. Co-op members divide up the food and share in the savings. A well-managed co-op is an economical way to buy food, but the selection may be limited. Food is delivered regularly to a central place. Members go to pick up the food and often serve themselves or take turns dividing the food into separate orders.

ENRICHMENT: Give students a list of ten common food items. Have them research prices of each food in both the supermarket and a convenience store.

Specialty Stores Stores that sell one type of food or a range of special foods are called specialty stores. Specialty stores include bakeries, meat markets, cheese shops, and ethnic food stores such as Chinese or Italian groceries. A variety of unusual foods is sold in gourmet shops. Delicatessens sell cold cuts and prepared foods like potato salad and cole slaw. Prices can be high in these specialty stores. However, they usually offer a much better variety of a particular kind of food. And, people often say that the quality of the food is better. Specialty stores reflect the eating tastes of a particular area. Another advantage of specialty store shopping is the personal service that you receive.

Smart Food Shopping

Planning ahead can help you save as much as 20 percent of each dollar you spend for food. Smart shoppers begin by reading store flyers and newspapers to see what is on sale. Next they check the refrigerator to see if any foods should be used before they spoil. They then decide what they will serve for the next week. Next they make out a shopping list, including paper products and other nonfood items needed. A list not only helps avoid return trips to the store but also keeps shoppers from buying a lot of extras. Before going shopping, smart shoppers make one final check to see if they already have any of the items on their list.

A farmers' market can offer extremely fresh produce and unusual items at very affordable prices.

Are brand names always worth what they cost?

Coupons and Rebates

Coupons can be a good way to save money. Some stores give double or even triple value on certain items. Coupons can save money if they are used for necessary items. Buying items that are not needed just because a coupon is available will only add to the food bill. Before shopping, match coupons to your list. Then compare prices when you get to the store.

Rebates, or product refunds, can also save you money. Manufacturers sometimes offer rebates or coupons if you buy one of their products. You may have to fill out a special form. You then mail it, together with proof of purchase (usually a label and a sales slip), to the manufacturer. This takes time, but you can save quite a lot of money by taking advantage of rebates.

Comparison Shopping

One of the best ways to save money is to compare items for price and quality. *Name brand* products are usually the most expensive. Nationally advertised, these products represent a particular manufacturer. *Store brand* products carry the name of the store, or chain, that sells them. They are often produced at the same plants as brand name products. Since the stores save on advertising and distribution, store brands cost less than national name brands. Products with plain labels and no manufacturer's name are called **generic** (jeh–*NEHR*–ik) **brands.** They usually cost less than either brand names or store brands. The lower prices reflect slightly lower quality, inexpensive packaging, and little advertising.

Check the labels on all brands for nutritional value. If you find that the nutrients on different brands are alike, try out several to compare taste. You may find that you prefer some more expensive brands. If you like the lower-priced items just as well, you can save money by buying them.

When you are doing comparison shopping, keep in mind that a food's packaging can add to its cost.

Did You Know?

An envelope makes a great organizer for grocery shopping. You can write your list on the outside and put coupons and receipts on the inside.

Is the fanciest looking can the most expensive one? Not always. Check the unit price before you select your items.

Unit Pricing

Once you have selected a brand, you need to decide what size to buy. Unit prices, which most stores display below the products on their shelves, can help you do this. The **unit price** is the cost per ounce (gram) or other unit of measure. Suppose you are trying to decide between a large box of cereal and a small box. Check to see what the price per ounce is for each size. Although larger sizes usually cost less per ounce, you might be surprised. Before deciding, consider how much storage space you have and whether you would use the larger box before it became stale.

Convenience Foods

Foods that are partially or completely prepared are called **convenience foods.** Mixes for both cakes and pancakes are convenience foods, as are frozen, canned, or freeze-dried items. Convenience foods can save you time, and they involve little waste. In some cases they cost more than cooking the same recipe starting from

scratch. In other cases they may cost the same or even less. It is more difficult to control the nutritional value of convenience foods. Check labels on items like canned fruits and vegetables. You will usually get more nutritional value from comparable fresh foods if they are available. Also check labels for fat and sodium content. If you use a lot of convenience foods, you could be eating more fat and sodium than you should.

With convenience foods, you often save time. What might you be losing?

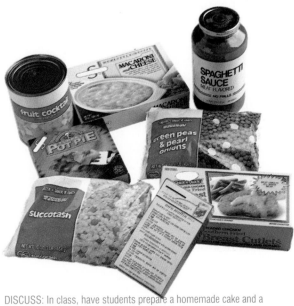

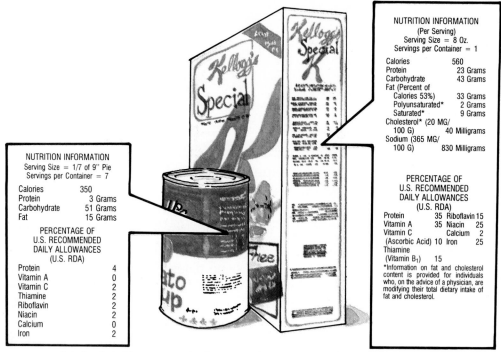

NUTRITION INFORMATION
(Per Serving)
Serving Size = 8 Oz.
Servings per Container = 1

Calories	560
Protein	23 Grams
Carbohydrate	43 Grams
Fat (Percent of Calories 53%)	33 Grams
Polyunsaturated*	2 Grams
Saturated*	9 Grams
Cholesterol* (20 MG/ 100 G)	40 Milligrams
Sodium (365 MG/ 100 G)	830 Milligrams

PERCENTAGE OF U.S. RECOMMENDED DAILY ALLOWANCES (U.S. RDA)

Protein	35	Riboflavin	15
Vitamin A	35	Niacin	25
Vitamin C (Ascorbic Acid)	10	Calcium	2
		Iron	25
Thiamine (Vitamin B$_1$)	15		

*Information on fat and cholesterol content is provided for individuals who, on the advice of a physician, are modifying their total dietary intake of fat and cholesterol.

NUTRITION INFORMATION
Serving Size = 1/7 of 9" Pie
Servings per Container = 7

Calories	350
Protein	3 Grams
Carbohydrate	51 Grams
Fat	15 Grams

PERCENTAGE OF U.S. RECOMMENDED DAILY ALLOWANCES (U.S. RDA)

Protein	4
Vitamin A	0
Vitamin C	2
Thiamine	2
Riboflavin	2
Niacin	2
Calcium	0
Iron	2

Do you read labels? They can help you determine whether you are getting the right amounts of nutrients.

Reading Food Labels

Federal law requires that labels give the following information:

- The name of the product.

- The name and address of the company that manufactures, distributes, or packs the product.

- A description of the product.

- A list of ingredients, in order of quantity. The list must begin with the largest amount and include flavorings, preservatives, and artificial colorings.

- Nutrition labeling when a nutrient has been added or on foods that make a nutritional claim, such as "low-fat" or "low-calorie."

United States Recommended Daily Allowances

Food labels list the **U.S. Recommended Daily Allowances** (U.S. RDA). These are percentages of the daily requirements of nutrients in that food product. These percentages are based on the Recommended Dietary Allowances (RDA). The RDA charts in the Appendix list amounts of nutrients that should be eaten daily. The food that you eat in one day should add up to 100 percent of the U.S. RDA. The information is based on one serving. The label gives the number of calories and the amounts of protein, carbohydrates, and fat contained in a serving.

Some labels also give information about the food when it is combined with another ingredient. For example, a serving of oatmeal might provide 6 percent of the U.S. RDA for protein. Adding ½ cup (120 mL) of 2 percent low-fat milk will provide 20 percent of your daily protein needs. In addition, some labels give information about the amount of sodium and cholesterol in a serving.

Open Dating

Dates on food packages indicate how fresh products are and until when you can use them safely or successfully. This system is called **open dating.** Open dating is not required by law, so you will not find a date on all products.

There are several kinds of dates. A *sell by* or *pull* date is found on items that lose their freshness quickly, such as bakery or dairy products. This is the last date on which the store should sell the product. The date allows for some storage time at home, however.

A *use by* date gives the last day you can expect top quality and freshness from a product. Packaged cold cuts and refrigerated doughs often have this kind of dating.

The *pack date* is usually found on products that can be stored a long time, such as canned goods. This gives the date the food was packaged.

The *expiration date* is often found on baby foods and yeast. This date is the last day the food can be used safely.

Food Additives

Unless you grow all of your own food, most of what you eat has been treated in some way. An **additive** is a substance added to food for a specific reason. Additives are often discussed today as people become increasingly conscious of exactly what they are eating. There is nothing new about additives, however. Spices have been added to foods for centuries. Some additives have names like sodium nitrite; additives with more familiar names are sugar, salt, and corn syrup.

Additives are used in foods to add nutrients, to prevent spoilage, and to add color or flavor. The use of additives helps preserve the world's food supply. Still, there is debate over some additives. For example, sodium nitrite can produce

Be sure to check dates on the foods you buy. Dates can sometimes be hidden by price stamps and stickers.

ENRICHMENT: Ask students to go to a store to find "sell by" and "use by" dates for the following items: milk, yogurt, fresh fish, canned peas, crackers, and cereal. Then ask students to put these items in order of what must be used first, second, and so on.

ENRICHMENT: Have students research what the following additives are used for in food: monosodium glutamate, sodium nitrate, sorbic acid, sodium propionate, carrageenan, and guar gum.

How ripe should it be? Think about when you will use it.

chemicals that cause cancer. To reduce the formation of harmful substances, vitamin A, ascorbic (uh–*SKOR*–bik) acid, is added to meats treated with sodium nitrite. Scientists are constantly researching food additives to see how they affect the body. As you learned in Chapter 12, government agencies regulate the way food is prepared, packaged, and labeled. This constant watch over food products helps protect your health.

Shopping Tips

The following tips provide some valuable advice for the smart food shopper.
- Buy only what you can use. If only one person in your family drinks tomato juice, buying a lot of it is wasteful.
- Buy only what you can store easily. Large packages of frozen vegetables are usually a good buy and can be stored in your freezer. You can avoid waste by scooping out just the amount you need.
- Organize your shopping list to save time. List items according to the way the store is arranged. Put food in the first aisle at the top of the list. Group similar foods together.
- Avoid buying items simply because they look tempting. Stick to your list, except when you see a chance to stock up on good buys.
- Don't go shopping when you are hungry. An empty stomach can encourage impulse buying. You may also be tempted to buy junk foods to munch on.
- Buy fresh fruits and vegetables that are in season. They are a good buy and are nutritious foods.

Storing Foods

Perishable foods (those that spoil easily) can cause illness if they are not refrigerated at once. Fish and meat are examples of such foods.

A refrigerator meat keeper will keep meat fresher because it is colder than other parts of the refrigerator. A crisper or vegetable bin helps keep vegetables and fruit moist. Shelves on the inside of the refrigerator door are a good place for foods like pickles and ketchup.

Make sure you do not overload refrigerator shelves. For the refrigerator to stay at the correct temperature, air needs to circulate. Save space by storing foods in the smallest containers possible. Look at the chart on page 291 for tips on storing food correctly.

NOTE: The Food and Drug Administration publishes a list of food additives called the GRAS (Generally Recognized as Safe) list. Food manufacturers wanting to use additives not on the GRAS list must get permission from the FDA.

RETEACHING: Stress that a shopping list is helpful because it prevents people from buying food items they may not use. It also helps them save time and energy when shopping.

Food Storage

Milk and Cheese

Store milk in a tightly covered container near the cooling unit in the refrigerator. Cheese should be tightly wrapped and stored in the refrigerator.

Meat

Most cuts of meat should not be stored in the refrigerator for more than three days. Ground meat can be refrigerated for one day. When it is stored in the refrigerator, meat should be wrapped loosely in foil or plastic wrap to allow air to circulate. When putting meat in the freezer, wrap it tightly in freezer paper, foil or plastic.

Poultry

Poultry should be stored in the refrigerator for no more than two days. Before putting it in the refrigerator poultry should be wrapped loosely in wax paper. To freeze poultry, wrap tightly in freezer paper or foil.

Eggs

Eggs should be stored in their original container with the blunt end up. Do not wash eggs before storing them. Eggs will keep in the refrigerator for up to five weeks.

Fish

Fish should be cooked the same day it is bought. If not used in one or two days, fish develops a stale odor and slime on the skin. When storing fish for a short period of time, wrap it tightly in plastic wrap and put it in the refrigerator.

Fruits

Unripe fruit may be stored uncovered at room temperature until it ripens. Store ripe fruit in the crisper section of your refrigerator. Cut fruit should be wrapped tightly and refrigerated. Do not wash berries before storing them as this causes spoilage.

Vegetables

Most fresh vegetables should be covered with moisture proof wrap and stored in the crisper section of the refrigerator. Frozen vegetables can be stored in the freezer for 8 to 12 months. Canned vegetables and fresh vegetables such as turnips, potatoes and onions should be stored in a cool, dark, dry place.

Grains, Breads and Cereals

Store flour and grains in tightly closed containers in a cool, dry place. Opened cereal containers should be reclosed tightly. Store bread in tightly sealed plastic bags.

Fats and Oils

Cover fats and oils tightly so that they will not absorb other flavors. To store butter, margarine, and lard, cover and refrigerate.

Do you know how long foods will stay fresh? Refer to the chart above.

See page T98 for answers.

For Review

1. Name seven different kinds of food stores.
2. What is the purpose of planning ahead for food shopping?
3. Name the five kinds of information that must by law be included on food labels.
4. How should meat be wrapped for storage?

Section 13.3

Buying High Quality Food

As you read, think about:

■ the various kinds of food products. (p. 292)

■ ways to determine the freshness of food when you are shopping. (p. 292)

■ how to shop for high quality food. (p. 292)

Shopping for food can be confusing. How can you choose tender pieces of meat? How is poultry graded? Why does a flour package have the word "enriched" on it? Understanding the way food is processed, graded, and packaged can help you answer such questions.

Buying Dairy Products

Do you know how many varieties of dairy products there are? It is important to know what the different milk and cheese products are in order to make smart buying decisions.

REINFORCEMENT: Have students think about milk products that can be main course foods, beverages, snacks, and desserts. Develop a list on the board.

Milk and Milk Products

Many people consider milk a nearly perfect food because it contains so many essential nutrients. In addition to milk itself, a wide variety of milk products is also available.

Most milk today is treated to make it safer and easier to use. Have you seen the term **pasteurized** (*PASS*–chu–ryzd) on milk cartons? This means that the raw milk has been heated to a temperature below boiling to destroy harmful bacteria. This does not affect the flavor of the milk or its nutritional value. The term **homogenized** (huh–*MAHJ*–uh–nyzd) also appears on many milk cartons. When milk is homogenized, fat particles are broken up so that they remain distributed throughout the milk. The cream therefore does not rise to the top. There are several kinds of milk. Whole, low-fat, and skim milk are the most common. Nonfat dry milk, a powdered form of milk, keeps well and is a good buy. To learn about the many choices of milk and milk products, look at the chart on page 293.

Cheese Products

Cheese is made by treating milk to make it curdle, or thicken and separate. Then the *whey*, the liquid part, is drained away from the *curd*, the solid part. Most cheeses are made from cow's milk. However, cheese can be made from the milk of goats, sheep, camels, or reindeer.

There are over 400 kinds of cheese. The texture and flavor depend on how the cheese is processed and the kind of milk

ENRICHMENT: Ask students to look up the word *fortified* and to research Vitamin D. Then have them explain why milk is fortified with Vitamin D.

Milk and Milk Products

Whole milk	Usually homogenized; has at least 3.24% milk fat
Low fat milk	Has from 1% to 2.5% milk fat
Skim milk	Has the least amount of milk fat; 0.5% or less
Nonfat dry milk	Skim milk without the water; is usually fortified with vitamins A and D
Buttermilk	Made from pasteurized skim milk that has been treated with lactic acid bacteria; has tart flavor and thick consistency
Yogurt	Can be made from whole, low-fat, or skim milk; has a custard like consistency; made by fermenting milk with special acid forming bacteria
Cream	Can have fat content that is between 18% (light cream) and 36% (heavy cream)
Sour Cream	A cream that has been soured by lactic acid bacteria; contains at least 18% milk fat
Evaporated milk	Milk from which 60% of the water has been removed
Condensed milk	Concentrated milk that has at least 40% sugar added

There are many different ways to fill your daily requirements from the milk group.

used. Some cheeses develop holes during ripening. Some become hard and crumbly, while others become very soft.

Process cheeses are made from a blend of different cheeses. They have a mild taste and keep well. Since they are soft in texture, they tend to blend well with other ingredients.

Cheese is usually priced by the pound. Imported cheese is likely to be more expensive than domestic varieties. Prices are also usually higher when the cheese has been grated, sliced, or cubed. You can save money by doing these things yourself at home.

Shopping for Eggs

Most eggs are sold according to grade and size. The grade tells you how fresh the eggs are. Standards for grading are set by the U.S. Department of Agriculture. Eggs are graded AA, A, and B.

The color of the eggshell gives no indication of the egg's quality. Eggs that are both a higher grade and a larger size are usually more expensive. However, prices vary according to the supply of eggs in a particular size.

When you choose eggs, make sure they are in cold storage and not cracked.

Prime beef is the highest quality and the most expensive.

Shopping for Meat

Meat can be an expensive food item. The smart shopper therefore considers carefully which grades, cuts, and forms of meat will best serve specific needs.

Kinds of Meat

Beef, veal, pork, lamb, mutton, and liver are among the kinds of meat found in food markets. Variety meats are from animal organs such as the kidney and tongue. These have good nutritional value. Cured meats such as bacon have been treated with salt, sugar, chemicals, and often wood smoke.

Inspection and Grading

To protect consumers, federal laws ensure that all meat sold is from healthy animals slaughtered under sanitary conditions. Have you ever noticed a purple stamp on some meat? This is an inspection stamp. You won't find it on all cuts, as large sections of meat are stamped before being cut into smaller portions. The stamp is made of a safe vegetable dye, so you don't have to cut it off.

Meat is also graded for quality. Grading is not required by law, but most meat packers do it. Standards for the different grades are set by the U.S. Department of Agriculture.

The quality of meat is determined by several factors. These include the proportion of meat to bone, the amount and location of fat, and the meat's texture and color. The highest quality beef is *prime.* *Choice* beef is the next best grade, followed by *good.* Choice and good are the grades sold in most food markets. The lower quality meats are graded *standard, commercial,* and *utility.* Veal and pork have similar grades. The grade *cull* is the lowest for both veal and pork.

Tenderness

Some meats are generally classified as tender. Pork is one of these. Lamb is another, except for the neck and shoulder. The rib and loin sections of beef are considered tender, but other sections are less tender. Veal has a great deal of connective tissue, which holds muscle fibers together, and very little fat. These characteristics make it less tender.

When shopping for beef in particular, learn to recognize signs of tenderness. You should look out for:

- The amount of marbling, or deposits of fat scattered through the muscle. (This does not include the fat around the edges of meat or between the muscle.) Meats with more marbling are generally more tender.
- The location on the animal of the meat cut. The less muscles are exercised, the more tender the cut. Back, loin, and rib muscles receive very little exercise. These muscles therefore make the most tender steaks, such as sirloin, T-bone, porterhouse, and club. They also make the most tender roasts, like rib and standing rib. Less tender steaks and roasts, such as round and chuck, are from the leg and shoulder, which receive more exercise.
- The shape of bones. The rib, T-bone, and wedge bone are other clues to tenderness. In all meat except beef, the round bone indicates a tender cut. In all animals, the blade bone indicates the least tender cut.

How Cuts Are Labeled

Most meat packages are labeled with the name of the cut. The labels usually show the kind of meat, such as beef or lamb, then the name of the large cut. For beef this might be rib, round, or chuck. Follow-

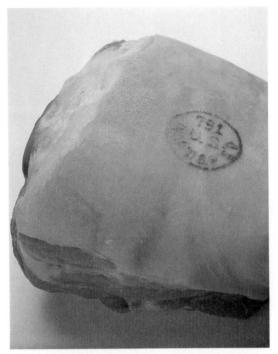

The inspection stamp tells you that federal standards have been met.

ing this is the commonly used retail name, for example, "steak" or "roast." A label might read "Beef Porterhouse Steak" or "Beef Chuck Roast." Learn to match different cuts of meat to specific meals. For example, a less tender cut like chuck roast is suitable for pot roast and costs less than a rib roast.

"Meatless" Meat

"Meatless" meat looks very much like actual meat. It is made from textured soy products. After the oil is removed from soybeans, the protein is formed into fiber and used in meatlike products. Its nutritional value is similar to that of real meat. Textured soy products can be added to ground meat to create more servings.

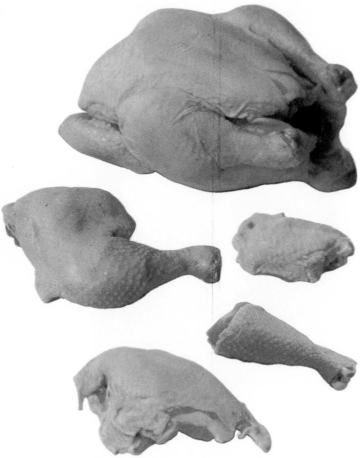

Do you want part of a chicken or all of it? Many parts are available.

Shopping for Poultry

Chicken and turkey are the most common poultry items. Duck, geese, Cornish hen, squab, and pigeons are less available and usually more expensive.

Fresh poultry is sold whole or cut up in various ways. You can, for example, buy a package of chicken breasts or legs. When you buy a whole bird, you will find the giblets inside the body cavity. Giblets are the liver, heart, and gizzard. Some people like to use giblets in gravy. You might also

find cooked birds in some stores, for example, barbecued chicken.

Chicken, turkey, Cornish hens, and ducks are among the frozen birds available. The frozen food section of a store might also have items such as chicken nuggets that are ready to cook, or fried chicken that just needs to be heated in the oven on a cookie sheet.

Canned poultry items include chicken, turkey, and special foods such as chicken chow mein. Poultry is usually boned before it is canned.

Inspection and Grading

Poultry is inspected to ensure that it comes from healthy birds and has been processed under sanitary conditions. If it passes federal inspection for wholesomeness, poultry may be graded for quality. You may have seen an inspection mark on a tag attached to a bird. The highest grade is Grade A. This indicates that the poultry is full-fleshed and meaty. Grade B poultry is still good quality but is slightly less meaty. Grade C poultry has less fat and less flesh. Usually, you will find only Grade A poultry in food markets.

For poultry farmers, as for students, the highest grade is Grade A.

Clues to Quality

High quality poultry has certain characteristics. Look for the following:

- meaty breasts and legs
- fat that is well distributed
- skin with few pinfeathers or blemishes

Keep in mind that a bird does not have to be large in order to have these characteristics. A small bird can be good quality and also desirable in some cases. For example, some people prefer small pieces when frying chicken.

When selecting poultry, you may decide that some brand names are of a higher quality than others. Most shoppers try more than one brand to find out which they prefer. Pale, dry, frosty areas are signs of freezer burn and can indicate improper storage. Wrappers should not be broken or stained. Make sure that labels state whether frozen or canned poultry passed inspection before processing. You should also remember to look for open dating on the package.

Shopping for Fish

Fish is available fresh, frozen, and canned. You can also find cured fish; this has been salted, smoked, or pickled. Salted cod and kippered herring are types of cured fish.

Fresh fish can be bought whole, just the way it came from the water, or dressed and ready for cooking. *Fish steaks* are slices cut across the body of the fish. *Fillets* (fih–*LAYS*) are sides of the fish, cut away from the backbone; they are usually boneless. Fish prices vary greatly,

NOTE: It is perfectly correct to spell the word *fillet* with one *l (filet)* or two.

PHOTO: Many people purchase fish at fish stores or the pier in order to get it very fresh. Is this either possible or common in your area?

Fresh fish is a great choice for its nutritional value. Whole fish is usually a better buy than fish that has been cut, shelled, or filleted.

depending on the supply of fresh fish. Both season and location affect how much you have to pay. You are likely to pay more if you do not live near the water.

Frozen fish is available all year round and often has a very fresh taste. Freezing techniques have improved over the years. Most frozen fish is sold as steaks or fillets. Some items, like fish sticks, are breaded and partially cooked before they are frozen. Some frozen fish is completely cooked and needs only to be heated.

Check both fresh and frozen fish to make sure it smells fresh. Don't buy fish that has an unpleasant odor. If you have

NOTE: Fish that are low in fat and high in protein are tuna, halibut, cod, flounder, haddock, ocean perch, and carp. Fish that are slightly higher in fat are salmon, mackerel, herring, and lake trout.

With fish, freshness means flavor. To be sold fresh, fish must be moved very quickly to the markets.

any doubt, do not buy it.

Salmon, tuna, and sardines are popular canned fish. Canned shellfish, such as oysters, clams, crabs, and shrimp, is also widely available.

Inspection and Grading

The inspection of fish is voluntary. However, the U.S. Department of Interior provides an inspection program for the fish industry. If fish is inspected, it will have an inspection stamp. The grading standards are U.S. Grade A, U.S. Grade B, and Substandard. When grades are available, they can help you to buy high quality fish.

REINFORCEMENT: Bring a variety of canned fish to class to show examples of what is available.

Shopping for Fruits and Vegetables

Fruits and vegetables are usually available in several forms. Fresh, frozen, and canned are the most common. Some fruits and vegetables can be bought dried.

The most important clues to good quality in fresh fruits and vegetables are their color and firmness. They should be ripe but not overly ripe, and neither bruised nor wilted. Look for grading on canned products. Grade A indicates the highest quality. Avoid buying frozen products that are stained or not completely frozen.

Advances in transportation have made fresh produce more widely available throughout the year.

Shopping for Grain Products and Bread

Do you eat corn flakes, rice, macaroni, or bread? If so, you are eating grain products. Today, grains are prepared in many different ways. However, people have been eating grains for over 7,000 years.

Grain Products

Grains are the edible seeds or fruits of cereal grasses. Wheat, corn, oats, rice, rye, barley, and buckwheat are all grains. Grain products include cereals, pasta or macaroni, rice, and flour. Wheat is the major grain used in the United States. Corn, often used as a vegetable, is second to wheat. Foods such as grits and hominy are made from corn.

Cereals Many cereals are considered breakfast food, although they can of course be eaten at any time. Ready-to-eat cereals, such as corn flakes or rice puffs, require no cooking. These cereals are made from wheat, corn, rice, and oats.

Popular hot cereals include oatmeal and cream of wheat. They are cooked in water or other liquid, usually milk. Many of these cereals have been processed to cook quickly. Package labels indicate whether a cereal is quick-cooking or instant. Quick-cooking cereals are ready in just a few minutes. You need only add boiling water to instant cereals.

Pasta Pasta or macaroni products are available in all shapes and sizes. Along with popular versions like spaghetti, you can buy tubes, shells, spirals, and many other kinds. Macaroni products can be used for a main dish, like macaroni and cheese, or to accompany other foods.

Rice White rice is the kind of rice that is found most often in grocery stores. It is enriched to replace nutrients lost in processing. *Converted,* or *parboiled,* rice has been partly cooked so that it retains more of its original nutrients. *Precooked* rice cooks very quickly but costs more. Brown rice has more nutrients than white rice but takes longer to cook; it has a chewy texture and nutlike flavor.

Flour White flour is the most common kind of flour, although wheat flour is also

Grain has always been abundant on our continent.

PHOTO: As our world changes, more and more students may be unaware of how grains grow, are harvested, and are processed.

Bread comes in a great variety of shapes, flavors, and sizes.

The nutritious wheat germ that has been removed from white flour can be bought separately. It tastes good on cereals and can be added to meats and desserts.

There are several kinds of white flour. Among the most common are all-purpose flour, self-rising flour, and cake flour. Self-rising flour contains baking powder or baking soda and salt in the right amounts for baking. Cake flour, is made from soft wheat and is especially suitable for baking.

Bread

You can buy bread completely prepared, partially prepared, frozen, or in mix form. When selecting any kind of bread, keep these guidelines in mind.

- Check dates on loaves and packages for freshness.
- Compare the nutrition content of different types of breads, as well as that of similar kinds.
- Check how many types of additives or preservatives are used. Although some are probably needed, you may wish to avoid too many.

available. When buying white flour, make sure it has been enriched to replace nutrients lost in processing. Wheat contains bran, the hard outer coating, and a part of the seed called the *germ*. Although these elements are extremely nutritious, they are removed during the process of making flour. If they were not, the flour would be coarse in texture and would spoil more easily. However, the bran and germ contain most of the B vitamins, iron, and roughage. For this reason, flour is enriched to restore these lost nutrients.

Wholewheat flour still contains the bran and the germ. It is coarser in texture than white flour and has a nutlike flavor.

For Review
1. Explain the difference between skim milk and nonfat dry milk.
2. Name three ways to tell if beef is tender.
3. What are three clues to quality when buying poultry?

Learning to Manage

Caught Short

Look back at the conversation between Karen and her mother on page 278. Karen is in charge of buying and storing food while her parents are away. Now read how she tries to manage the situation. Then answer the questions that follow.

"Don't worry, Mom. I'll take care of everything." Karen thought about her final words before her mother left and felt slightly ill. The week was almost over and the food supply was not holding out; neither was the money. She tried to figure out what had gone wrong.

On Monday night, she had arrived at the supermarket just as it was closing. As a result, she had shopped at the small corner grocery store instead. She had bought all the items on her list but had used almost all of the food money. She had forgotten to look through her mother's coupon holder. There weren't any store brands to buy. Karen had had to buy the brand name items even though she realized they cost more. She had been really hungry when she shopped and had bought snack items that weren't on her shopping list.

She had bought a large package of hamburger at the beginning of the week. She should have divided it into thirds before freezing it, because it was enough for three meals—hamburgers, meatloaf, and meatballs. But they had had to eat it for three nights in a row!

The lettuce looked and felt as if it had been left out in the rain for a week. Somehow, it hadn't made it into the vegetable drawer. And the *smell!* She had put the fish into the refrigerator in its paper wrapper. Jane had chosen to cook chicken, then steak, then hot dogs. Now the fish would have to be thrown out. Even the butter tasted like fish. She hated to think how much all this wasted food had cost. Worse than that, what would they eat for the next two nights? She did have enough money to buy eggs and pasta . . . . Karen sighed. There was a lot more to this food business than she had ever imagined.

Questions

1. Using what you have learned in this chapter, explain three of the mistakes that Karen made.
2. Plan a meal for one night for your own family. List items you would need and write down what you think each item would cost. What would you do with any leftovers?
3. After visiting your local food store, list the real price of each item on your menu in question 2. How did your estimated costs compare?

Chapter 13 Review

Summary

Meal planning involves the consideration of nutrition requirements, costs, and schedules. Efficient food shopping requires a knowledge of different kinds of food stores, an organized shopping list, and pricing information. Sales, coupons, and rebates can save money. However, you need to use them wisely to really save. Labels provide valuable information about nutrition, freshness, and additives. Here too, it's up to you to use the information available. Storing foods properly is essential for good nutrition and efficiency. Foods have different storage needs.

Shoppers need to know what foods are available and to understand how food is processed, graded, and inspected. By reading labels carefully and looking for clues to tenderness and freshness, shoppers can become skilled at purchasing high quality foods.

1. The _____ are percentages of the daily requirements of nutrients in a food product.

2. _____ _____ have plain labels, no brand names, and usually cost less than brand names or store brands.

3. Milk that has been _____ has been heated to a certain temperature in order to destroy harmful bacteria.

4. An _____ is a substance added to a food for a specific reason.

5. _____ _____ is the cost per ounce (gram) or other unit of measure.

6. The date on a food package that indicates how fresh a product is or how long you can use it safely or successfully is called _____ _____.

7. Foods that are partially or completely prepared are called _____ _____.

8. Milk in which fat particles have been broken up so that cream does not rise to the top has been _____.

Vocabulary

Complete each of the following sentences with the correct word from the vocabulary list below.

convenience foods (p. 287)

open dating (p. 289)

unit price (p. 287)

homogenized (p. 292)

generic brands (p. 286)

U.S. Recommended Daily Allowances (p. 288)

pasteurized (p. 292)

additive (p. 289)

··Questions

1. What do we mean when we say that using various textures adds interest to a meal?

··2. If you were asked to do the family food shopping, would it be best to shop in a supermarket or a convenience store? Explain your answer.

The dots represent skill levels required to answer each question or complete each activity:

- • requires recall and comprehension
- •• requires application and analysis
- ••• requires synthesis and evaluation

3. What is the difference between a supermarket and a food warehouse? How are they alike?

4. Why do you think produce in a farmer's market is usually fresher and less expensive than the same produce in a supermarket?

5. If you clip coupons for shopping, should you use every coupon that is available? Explain your answer.

6. Here is what is on a label for ingredients in a cereal: corn, sugar, salt, flavoring. Which ingredient does the cereal contain the largest amount of? How can you tell?

7. Explain the *sell by* date that appears on some food packages.

8. Why is it important to check the *expiration date* on baby food?

9. Some people feel that sodium nitrite is a dangerous food additive. Do you agree or disagree? Give reasons for your answer.

10. Give two examples of foods that spoil quickly.

11. Why is it best not to go food shopping when you are hungry?

12. When shopping for beef, how can you tell if a particular piece of meat will be tender?

13. What is a "meatless" meat?

14. What is a fillet of fish?

15. Explain the difference between white rice and brown rice.

Skill Activities

1. Laboratory With your lab partners, prepare and compare a "convenience" pizza from a mix, a frozen one, and a homemade one. Compare the prices, preparation time, taste and appearance of the three pizzas. Which one tasted the best? Which took the least amount of time to prepare? Which was the least expensive to prepare?

2. Communication Be creative! Draw a label for a new cereal that you have created. Make sure you include all of the information required by federal law as described in the chapter. Use a cereal box that you have at home to help you. Share your drawing with the class.

3. Critical Thinking Plan a luncheon menu with your lab partners that could be served in the school cafeteria. Be sure it includes one food from each of the four basic food groups. Present your menu to the cafeteria manager for his or her comments.

4. Laboratory Pick three food items and compare their prices at two different types of food stores. For example, compare prices of items at a convenience store with those at a supermarket. Share your results.

Chapter 14
Basic Kitchen Skills

Vocabulary

sanitation
bacteria
toxins
hygiene
cookware
bakeware
recipe

The dialogue below introduces ''Organizing the Kitchen,'' the Learning to Manage feature in this chapter. The case study is continued and the situation discussed further on page 325. See page T102 for teaching suggestions.

''Thanks, Mom. That was a great dinner. While I'm cleaning up, I have an assignment to do for school.''

''What's the assignment?''

''My Home Economics teacher wants us to check out our kitchens. She wants us to list anything we could do to make our kitchens more efficient.''

''That sounds good for me, too, Dan. I'm in here so much I don't even think about how the kitchen is organized. I just cook.''

''And I just come here to eat when I smell something good cooking. Well, I'd better get going. After tonight, we'll have a plan for a new and improved kitchen!''

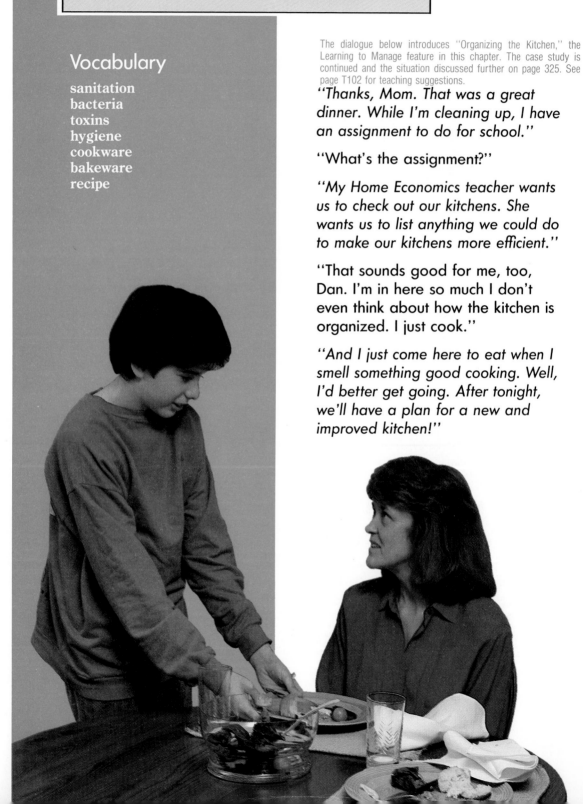

Section 14.1

The Organized Kitchen

As you read, think about:

■ how a kitchen is divided into several work areas. (p. 305)

■ what each work area needs in terms of tools, equipment, and space. (p. 305)

Think about the kitchen in your home. It is really like a carpenter's workshop or a scientist's laboratory. In order to prepare and cook food you need both tools and work space. An efficient kitchen also has convenient storage space for food and equipment. How is your kitchen organized? Sometimes just a few changes can make a kitchen not only more efficient but also a more enjoyable place.

Today's Kitchen

Not all homes have the large "dream kitchens" shown in magazines. A lot goes on, however, even in very small kitchens. Of course, the kitchen is where food is prepared, but families often eat there, too.

The kitchen may also be a place where children play or guests relax and visit. With careful organization and a little imagination, you can make the best use of space in your kitchen.

Consider the different activities that go on in your kitchen. What do you need for preparing and cooking food? for cleaning up? For example, you need a bowl for mixing batter. You need a sink for wash-

Is your kitchen a place to gather and discuss the day?

ing lettuce. In each area of the kitchen, you carry out tasks that require special tools or equipment.

Preparation Area

For preparing food, you need adequate counter space that is convenient to other work areas. This area should also include storage space for staples such as flour or pasta, as well as for bowls and utensils. Small appliances that are used often may be kept on the counter if there is enough room.

Keep the preparation area clean, washing countertops and other surfaces often. Thorough cleaning after preparing meals and snacks helps prevent food-related illness. Wipe up all crumbs and particles of food to avoid attracting insects.

NOTE: In colonial times, the kitchen was the center of all family activity. Ask what activities other than meal preparation take place in today's modern kitchens.

ENRICHMENT: If your students or their parents could make only one improvement to their kitchens, what would it be? Ask students to write a paragraph describing the change.

How many times do you think a cook uses a sink while preparing a meal?

Sink/Cleanup Area

The sink area in a kitchen provides the water supply. It is also used for washing dishes and utensils and for cleaning foods. You need storage space here for cleaning supplies and for utensils used to clean fruits and vegetables. Use cabinets in this area to store items after they are washed. You need counter space for stacking dishes and for preparing foods that require water, such as rice or pasta.

You may have an automatic dishwasher in your sink area. Depending on the space available, it may be built-in and front-loading or small and portable.

Refrigerator Area

Most kitchens contain a refrigerator-freezer with counter space near it for unpacking groceries. Counter space is also useful for preparing some foods as they are removed from the refrigerator.

The majority of refrigerator-freezers have the freezer above the refrigerator. Side-by-side models have two doors, with the freezer next to the refrigerator.

Care for your refrigerator-freezer by wiping up spills at once. Wash the refrigerator with mild detergent and water or with baking soda and water. Do not use scouring powder or pads, as they can damage the appliance.

Range Area

The area where the cooking is done usually has either an electric or a gas range. There might also be a microwave oven. Pots, pans, and pot holders should be

The refrigerator area is often the center of kitchen activity.

PHOTO: Note that refrigerators are designed to store large quantities of food as efficiently as possible.

What advantages do you see to working in a space that is set up just like this one?

The work triangle links the range, refrigerator, and sink areas.

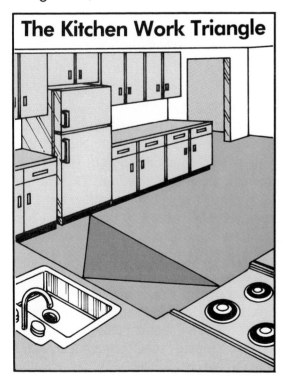

The Kitchen Work Triangle

stored nearby. Small kitchen tools, called utensils, should be within easy reach. Spoons and spatulas are examples of utensils you use often in the range area. Counter space near the range gives you somewhere to put the cooked food before serving. In some kitchens, the range and oven are built into the counters.

All parts of a range should be kept clean. Some parts can be removed and washed in warm, soapy water. Spills should be wiped up with a mild detergent and water as soon as the range is cool.

Eating Area

The eating area in your kitchen may be a table and chairs or part of the counter. If you have a table, you need enough space to pull out the chairs. You can use stools at counters with space underneath. Push them under the counter when not in use.

Chapter 14/*Basic Kitchen Skills*   **307**

Keep the eating area, like the rest of the kitchen, clean and free of spills. It is especially important to keep the kitchen floor clean and dry. Traffic is likely to be heavy in this area, and damp floors can cause accidents.

See page T103 for answers.

For Review

1. Name the five major work areas found in most kitchens.
2. Describe the cookware and utensils usually found in the range area.
3. What tools and equipment should be kept near the preparation area?

What concern do you see here for keeping the kitchen clean?

PHOTO: Have students identify the two different activities occurring here. What other tasks would be done in the sink area?

Section 14.2
Safety First

As you read, think about:

◾ why sanitation is extremely important in the kitchen. (p. 308)

◾ ways to protect foods from spoilage. (p. 309)

◾ how to maintain a safe kitchen and handle kitchen emergencies. (p. 311)

Did you realize that many more accidents occur in the kitchen than in any other room in the home? People cut themselves, fall, and burn themselves in kitchens. Some people become ill from food poisoning. By following certain guidelines, you can make both your home and school kitchens safer.

Keeping Everything Clean

In order to enjoy the food you prepare in your kitchen, you need to follow rules of cleanliness and sanitation. **Sanitation** (san–i–*TAY*–shun) is keeping your environment clean and healthful. This means keeping it as free of bacteria and dirt as possible. **Bacteria** are tiny one-celled creatures that give off waste products called **toxins.** Many of these toxins are poisonous. If eaten, they can cause illness or even death. Practicing proper sanitation in the kitchen can prevent illness caused by food containing bacteria. This means keeping food, equipment, and yourself clean.

RETEACHING: Review the words *bacteria, toxins,* and *sanitation.* Restate their meanings for your students.

PHOTO: Stress that bacteria multiply quickly in a kitchen. Odors also arise easily wherever there is moisture.

Personal Hygiene

Personal **hygiene** (*HY*–jeen), or cleanliness, is where sanitation begins. Wash your hands with soap and hot water before handling food and after handling raw fish, meat, poultry, or eggs. Also wash them after sneezing, coughing, touching a pet, or going to the toilet. If you touch your face or hair while working, wash your hands again. Use plastic gloves if you have an open sore or cut your hands.

Make sure your clothes are clean. (An apron will help protect them.) Avoid loose clothing that might touch food, and roll up your sleeves if they are long. If you have long hair, tie it back to keep it from getting into food.

Kitchen Cleanliness

Cooking can be a messy business. But if you clean up as you work, you will avoid a major job when you are finished. Before you prepare food, wash all countertops and cutting surfaces in the work area. Keep the surfaces clean by wiping up spills right away. After using utensils and a cutting board, use hot, soapy water to scrub them thoroughly. This is especially important when handling raw foods. Wash any tools used for raw foods before you use them for cooked foods.

Wash pots and other containers as soon after use as possible. If you cannot wash them right away, rinse them to remove any food. Dirty pots can attract bacteria.

If you practice good work habits in the kitchen, your kitchen will be more sanitary. Change your kitchen towels often, and use separate towels for drying hands

Cleaning up as you go along can save time and effort later.

and wiping dishes. Most cooks taste food while cooking. If you do this, use the spoon only once. Using the same spoon for tasting and stirring spreads germs.

By keeping yourself and your kitchen clean, you can prevent illness.

Keeping Food Safe

If you have an upset stomach, chills, or a fever, you could have the flu. You might, however, have food poisoning. This illness results from food spoilage. Spoilage occurs when bacteria growing in the food make it unsafe for eating. There is often no way to tell if food is spoiled. A food might smell or taste just as it usually does. To guard against food poisoning, make sure hot foods are hot and cold foods are cold.

RETEACHING: Emphasize the importance of keeping a first-aid kit and a small fire extinguisher in the kitchen at all times. Fire extinguishers can be purchased from a hardware store or from the local fire department.

REINFORCEMENT: Have students make a list of ten things they could do at home to help keep their own kitchens cleaner and more organized.

Temperature of Food for Control of Bacteria

°C	°F	
121	250	Canning temperatures for low-acid vegetables, meat, and poultry in pressure canner.
116	240	Canning temperatures for fruits, tomatoes, and pickles in water-bath canner.
100	212	Cooking temperatures destroy most bacteria. Time required to kill bacterial decreases as temperature is increased.
74	165	Warming temperatures prevent growth but allow survival of some bacteria.
60	140	Some bacterial growth may occur. Many bacteria survive.
52	120	DANGER ZONE. Temperatures in this zone allow rapid growth of bacterial and production of toxins by some bacteria. (Foods in this temperature zone should not be held for more than 2 or 3 hours.
16	60	Some growth of food poisoning bacteria may occur.
4	40	Cold temperatures permit slow growth of some bacteria that cause spoilage. (Raw meats should be used within 5 days, ground meat, poultry, and fish within 2 days.)
0	32	
−18	0	Freezing temperatures stop growth of bacteria, but may allow bacteria to survive.

What can you do to keep harmful bacteria from multiplying?

REINFORCEMENT: Ask students to survey their parents or other adults to find out what things they routinely do to prevent food spoilage.

Hot Foods

Even when a food contains harmful bacteria, the bacteria can be killed by proper cooking. However, the temperature and cooking time required vary from food to food. Fresh fish can be cooked in only a few minutes, while roast pork may need two or three hours. Pork may occasionally contain tiny worms that cause *trichinosis* (trik-un-*NO*-siss), a serious illness. If the pork is cooked thoroughly, these organisms are killed. To be on the safe side, cook pork until its internal temperature is 170°F (75°C).

Salmonella (sal-muh-*NELL*-uh) *poisoning* is caused by bacteria that can grow quickly at room temperature. These bacteria can be easily killed by thoroughly heating foods at the correct temperature.

Botulism (BOCH-ul-liz-um) is the most deadly form of food poisoning. Toxins in improperly canned foods are the most common source of botulism. If cans are leaking or bulging, do not buy or use them. Further, if any foods you are preparing do not smell or look right to you, throw them away.

Serve food while it is still hot, above 140°F (60°C). If food is left at room temperature for more than two hours, bacteria can grow. Refrigerate leftovers as soon as possible. Thaw frozen foods in the refrigerator, not on the counter.

Cold Foods

Keeping foods cold, below 40°F (5°C), can keep harmful bacteria from multiplying. Therefore, storing foods in the refrigerator can keep them safe, but only for a

NOTE: Botulism and salmonella are very serious forms of food poisoning. More than half the cases of botulism are fatal. The least dangerous form of food poisoning is called staph poisoning.

limited amount of time. Store foods such as fish, poultry, meat, milk, and eggs in the refrigerator or freezer. Meringue pies, custards, and cakes with rich fillings should be allowed to cool slightly before they are refrigerated.

Dry Storage

Many unopened cans, jars, or boxes can be kept in dry storage. This means a cool, dark, dry place, such as a pantry or basement. Dry storage is also suitable for dried beans and peas, onions, potatoes, and unripe fruit. Do not store foods near the range, refrigerator, sink, or radiator. Warmth and moisture can lower eating quality or even cause spoilage.

Before storing foods, check labels for any special instructions. Also check cans for bulges before you open them. If you notice a bulge, throw the can away.

Safety in the Kitchen

Most kitchen accidents can be prevented if you use common sense and organize your kitchen well. The guidelines below can help you keep your kitchen safe.

Storing Kitchen Items

- Keep household cleaners where children cannot reach them.
- Keep cabinets and drawers closed. Lock all cabinets that are within reach of young children.
- Place items on shelves so that they will not fall out when doors are opened.
- Store knives away from other items.
- Keep cabinets free of pests.

ENRICHMENT: Have students make kitchen safety charts listing the five most important things they think should be done in every kitchen.

Are these items stored properly?

Preventing Burns and Fires

- Turn pan handles toward the back of the stove. This prevents pans from being knocked off.
- Lift the lid of a pan away from you so that you will not be burned by steam.
- Lift utensils with dry pot holders. Wet pot holders can cause steam burns.
- Do not use dish towels or paper towels near the stove. They can catch fire.
- If grease catches fire, put baking soda on the fire or use a fire extinguisher. Do NOT put water on a grease fire.

Preventing Cuts

- Make sure knives are sharp. Dull knives are not as safe as sharp ones.
- Hold a knife by the handle. Cut by moving the blade away from you.

REINFORCEMENT: Do a lesson on kitchen safety. Demonstrate turning pot handles toward the back of the stove, lifting lids off pans, properly holding and washing a knife, and wiping up spills.

It only takes a few seconds to turn handles safely inward.

- Disconnect an appliance by pulling out the plug rather than jerking the cord. Worn cords can cause an electric shock. Repair or throw away frayed cords.
- Make sure your hands are dry before touching electrical equipment.
- Do not connect electrical equipment if you are standing on a wet surface.
- Do not put any part of an appliance in water unless it is marked "immersible."
- Unplug a cord from the outlet before you remove it from the appliance.
- Do not stick metal objects such as forks into an appliance.
- Do not plug more than two small appliances into an outlet at the same time. Overloading circuits can cause fires.

- Wash knives separately. Do not put them in the sink to soak.
- Avoid sharp edges when opening cans.
- Sweep up broken glass at once. Throw away cracked or chipped dishes.

Preventing Falls

- Use a stepstool when reaching for items on high shelves.
- Wipe up spills from the floor at once.
- Do not leave objects on the floor where people can trip over them.
- Use only rugs with nonskid backing.

Safe Use of Appliances

- Follow instruction booklets for correct use of appliances.
- Do <u>NOT</u> turn on a gas stove if you can smell gas.

In Case of Emergency

Even when you are as careful as possible, accidents can still happen. When they do, don't hesitate to call for help. Put emergency numbers near the telephone, and teach any children in your home to use them. Also make sure children know how to give their own telephone number and address to rescue workers.

If kitchen accidents occur, you should know what to do while waiting for help.

Fires and Burns

When grease fires occur, do one of the following:
- Put a lid on the pot or close the oven.
- Pour salt or baking soda on the fire.
- Use a fire extinguisher if the fire is a very small one.

If a fire occurs, turn off the heat source first. Then get what you need to put the fire out.

- If the fire is spreading, leave the building and then call the fire department.
- Treat minor burns with cold water or ice packs. Then add bandages. Do not use butter. If burns are large, keep the person warm and lying down until professional help arrives.

Electric Shock

Do not touch someone who is in contact with electricity. The electric current will pass through you, too. Pull out the plug or remove the fuse to turn off the current. Break the connection between the electric current and the victim. You can do this by using wood, cloth, rope, or other materials that will not conduct electricity. Begin rescue breathing if needed until help arrives. (The chart on page 65 of Chapter 3 shows the basics of rescue breathing. If you have had instructions from a medical expert, you would use this technique.)

Food Poisoning

When symptoms of food poisoning occur, call a doctor or hospital emergency room immediately. Although some types of food poisoning cause only minor discomfort, others can be very dangerous. It is best to see a medical professional.

Choking

First ask the person if he or she is choking. If the person is unable to breathe, cough, or speak, use the *Heimlich Maneuver* to dislodge the food or object. As described in Chapter 3, follow these steps.
1. Stand behind the person.
2. Wrap your arms around the victim's waist.
3. Make a fist with one hand. Place your fist thumbside against the stomach just above the navel, well below the ribs.
4. Grasp your fist with your other hand.
5. Press into the person's stomach with a quick inward and upward thrust. Repeat the thrust if necessary.

See page T103 for answers.

For Review

1. What are some examples of personal hygiene that you should follow when handling food?
2. What is a good rule to observe regarding hot and cold foods to prevent food poisoning?
3. Name three ways to prevent fires and burns in the kitchen.

Section 14.3

Kitchen Tools and Equipment

As you read, think about:

- what basic kitchen tools are required for cooking and baking. (p. 314)
- the difference between cookware and bakeware. (p. 317)
- how to select different kinds of small appliances. (p. 318)

Using the correct kitchen tools and caring for them properly can help you prepare a variety of tasty foods more easily.

Kitchen Tools

You can find a large selection of kitchen tools available today. The most basic kitchen tools are listed below. These are used for cutting, stirring or moving, measuring, separating, mixing, and baking.

Cutting

- Utility knife for cutting, slicing, dicing, and paring
- Butcher knife for cutting large items
- Grater for shredding cheese, vegetables, and other items
- Carving knife for carving and slicing meat and poultry
- Bread knife for slicing bread or cake
- Paring knife for peeling and cutting fruits and vegetables.
- Cutting surface for protecting countertops and tables

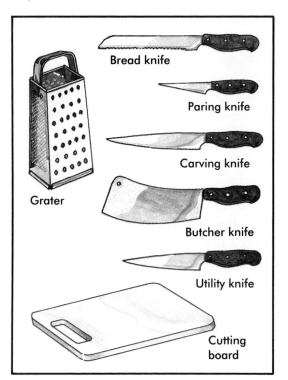

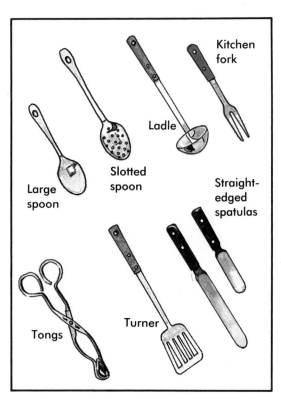

RETEACHING: Display and identify the following equipment: a utility knife, a butcher knife, a grater, a large spoon, a slotted spoon, a spatula, and a ladle.

ENRICHMENT: Have students visit the home appliance section of a hardware or department store to price the following equipment: a utility knife, butcher knife, grater, large spoon, slotted spoon, spatula, and ladle. You can then stress the expense of setting up a kitchen.

314   Unit 4/*Foods and Nutrition*

Stirring/Moving

- Large spoon for stirring
- Slotted spoon for removing foods cooked in liquids
- Turner, or spatula, for foods such as hamburgers and pancakes
- Ladle for serving soups and stews
- Kitchen fork for turning and lifting large cuts of meat
- Tongs for lifting and turning food without piercing it.

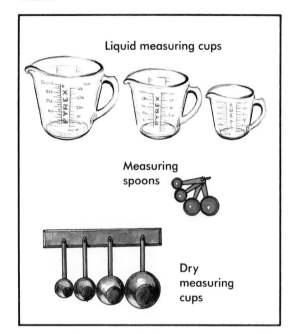

Liquid measuring cups

Measuring spoons

Dry measuring cups

Measuring

Some of these measuring tools are marked for both standard and metric measures.

- Measuring spoons for small amounts of liquid and dry ingredients
  standard: ¼ teaspoon, ½ teaspoon, 1 teaspoon, 1 tablespoon
  metric: 1 mL, 2 mL, 15 mL, 25 mL
- Measuring cups for liquids
  standard: 1 cup, 2 cups, 4 cups
  metric: 250 mL, 500 mL, 1 L
- Measuring cups for dry ingredients
  standard: ¼ cup, ⅓ cup, ½ cup, 1 cup
  metric: 50 mL, 125 mL, 250 mL

Separating/Mixing

- Sifter for dry ingredients like flour
- Wire whisk for beating egg whites and blending sauces
- Strainers for draining liquids from foods
- Colander for draining foods such as vegetables and pasta
- Pastry blender for cutting shortening into dry ingredients

Colander

Wire whisk

Pastry blender

Sifter

Strainers

ART: Mention to students how versatile a rubber scraper is. It can be used for removing items from cans, scraping mixing bowls, and folding in egg whites and other ingredients.

Baking

- Small, medium, and large mixing bowls
- Rolling pin and pastry cloth
- Cutters for biscuits and cookies
- Mixing spoons
- Wooden spoons
- Rubber scraper

General Tools

- Can opener
- Bottle opener
- Pot holders

Cleaning Tools

- Brush for washing vegetables
- Scouring pads for cleaning pots
- Dish drainer
- Dishpan
- Sponge

Wooden spoons

Mixing bowls

Rubber scraper

Cutters

Spoon

Rolling pin and cover

Pastry cloth

Dishpan

Vegetable brush

Dish drainer

Scouring pad

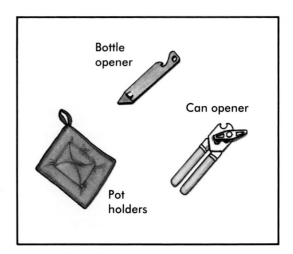

Bottle opener

Can opener

Pot holders

DISCUSS: Which of the items on these two pages would every kitchen have to contain? Which items are not as crucial?

ENRICHMENT: Display all cookware and bakeware in the classroom. Write the name of each piece on a card, and place all cards in a hat. Randomly select students to pull a card from the hat and place it in front of the appropriate piece of cookware or bakeware.

Pots and Pans

The dishes and pans that you use in the oven are **bakeware.** The pots and pans you use on the top of the range are **cookware.** The following list describes the bakeware and cookware you will need most often.

Bakeware

- Roasting pan and rack
- Broiling pan
- Casseroles in different sizes, with lids
- Square, round, and oblong cake pans
- Loaf pan (for baking breads or meatloaf)
- Pie pans in different sizes
- Muffin tins
- Cookie sheet

Cookware

- Pans in different sizes, with lids (for cooking foods in liquids)
- Skillets or frying pans in different sizes, some with lids
- Large pot (for cooking foods such as soup or pasta)

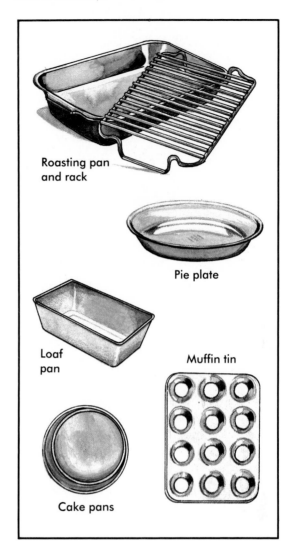

Roasting pan and rack

Pie plate

Loaf pan

Muffin tin

Cake pans

Saucepans

Skillets

Chapter 14/*Basic Kitchen Skills*   **317**

Kitchens Are Our Business

Managing your kitchen efficiently, safely, and with delicious results takes knowledge, skill, and organization. So does managing the test kitchens of a large food company. In addition, the business home economists who run test kitchens must be able to supervise a staff. They must also be good at communicating within their company and with the public. This job requires at least a bachelor's degree in home economics or a closely related field.

Business home economists in this job develop and evaluate recipes for their company's products. They provide the directions, recipes, and other serving suggestions on labels and in advertisements. They also organize displays and demonstrations in stores and malls. Answering consumer questions is part of their job, too. They suggest new products based on what consumers say they want.

In the test kitchens, these home economists train company executives and sales staff in different product preparations. They also test new recipes. First they see if the ingredients meet their nutritional standards. Then they prepare the recipe and have it taste-tested and evaluated for quality, value, and convenience.

Have you ever thought of a way to improve a canned soup or boxed cake recipe?

General Care

To clean your cookware and bakeware, use detergent in hot water. If needed, allow time for soaking. In addition, follow the guidelines below for items made of particular materials.

Material	Care
aluminum	Do not put in dishwasher.
cast iron	Do not scour. Before using, "season" with oil and heat to prevent rust.
glass	Do not scour.
glass ceramic	Scour if needed.
nonstick finish	Do not scour with metal pads or harsh powders.
enamel	Do not scour.
stainless steel	Scour if needed.
copper	Do not scour. Use a special copper cleaner.

Small Appliances

Many small appliances save time and are enjoyable to use. Others, however, are just gimmicky gadgets that you won't use often. When you consider buying a small appliance, think first about its use. Will you need it often enough to make it a worthwhile investment? Do you have a convenient place to put it? Also check the safety features, energy use, and warranty before you make a purchase. These are some of the most popular small appliances in homes today.

- *Toasters* brown bread. They usually hold from two to four slices. Some toasters can be used for thick breads such as muffins as well as for frozen items such as waffles.

NOTE: The proper way to clean a cast-iron pan after use is to sprinkle it with salt, pour oil on a paper towel, and use the paper towel to wipe the pan clean. Never clean it with detergent.

- *Toaster ovens* can warm and bake small amounts of food in addition to toasting. Some can be used for broiling foods.
- *Mixers* are available in different sizes and designs. Portable, hand-held mixers are good for jobs like mashing potatoes. Stand mixers have bowls that fit on the stand and rotate as food is whipped or beaten. Heavy-duty mixers are best for heavy doughs or bread batters.
- *Blenders* liquify, mix, grate, chop, crumb, and perform other tasks. They work best with foods containing liquids.
- *Food processors* have different blades and discs for chopping, grating, grinding, shredding, and mixing. They can quickly slice vegetables, grate cheese, make peanut butter, and perform many other tasks.
- *Electric frying pans* fry, bake, simmer, roast, and pan-broil. A thermostat control keeps the temperature even.

When using any small appliance, be sure to follow the safety guidelines on page 312. Also check the owner's manual for proper care. The manual will tell you which parts of the appliance may be immersed in water or put in the dishwasher. Be sure to clean it after each use.

See page T104 for answers.
For Review
1. Name the six basic types of kitchen tools.
2. What is the difference between cookware and bakeware?
3. Name three different functions of a food processor.

ENRICHMENT: Have students make an inventory of all the small appliances in their kitchens at home. Which ones are most frequently used?

Section 14.4
Using Recipes

As you read, think about:
- ▣ how to evaluate and select a recipe. (p. 319)
- ▣ what a clear recipe should include. (p. 319)
- ▣ the four different recipe formats. (p. 320)

A **recipe** is a set of directions for preparing a food. It is a kind of plan, or blueprint, to guide you. Recipes tell you what ingredients to use and how to put them together.

Choosing a Recipe

When you choose a recipe, ask yourself if it will appeal to family or guests as well as to you. Check to see if you have the ingredients you need. If you have to buy ingredients, stay within your budget.

Also keep in mind the time and skill needed. Choose recipes that you can follow easily in the time you have available.

Components of Recipes

A clearly written recipe should include the following information.

- The ingredients you will be using
- The amount of each ingredient required
- Step-by-step instructions for preparing the food
- What kind and size of pan or dish to use
- The cooking time and temperature, and other instructions, such as "chill"
- The number of servings the recipe will yield

REINFORCEMENT: Does a food processor save time? Select two students and give each student the same amount of vegetables to be sliced. Have one student slice vegetables manually and have the other student use a food processor. Then have each clean up. Which was faster?

STANDARD FORMAT

Peanut Butter Balls.
 1 cup (250 mL) peanut butter
 3/4 cup (180 mL) honey
 1 cup (250 mL) coconut
 4 cups (0.95L) dry cereal
 1. Mix peanut butter, honey and coconut.
 2. Add 2 cups (500 mL) cereal and stir.
 3. Form mixture into balls.
 4. Spread remaining cereal on cookie sheet.
 5. Roll balls in cereal.
 6. Serve immediately.
            Serves 10-15.

DESCRIPTIVE

Peanut Butter Balls.
 peanut butter   1 cup (250 mL)
 honey   3/4 cup (180mL)
 coconut   1 cup (250mL)
 dry cereal   4 cups (0.95L)
    Mix peanut butter, honey and
 coconut. Add 2 cups cereal (500 mL)
 and stir. Form mixture into balls.
 Spread remaining cereal on cookie
 sheet. Roll balls in cereal.
 Serve immediately.
            Serves 10-15.

ACTION FORMAT

Peanut Butter Balls.
 Mix   peanut butter, honey and coconut.
       1 cup (250mL) peanut butter
       3/4 cup (180 mL) honey
       1 cup (250 mL) coconut
 Add   dry cereal and stir.
       2 cups (500mL) cereal
 Form mixture into balls.
 Spread dry cereal on cookie sheet.
       2 cups (500mL) cereal
 Roll balls into cereal.
 Serve immediately.   Serves 10-15

NARRATIVE FORMAT

Peanut Butter Balls.
 Mix 1 cup (250mL) peanut butter,
 3/4 cup (180 mL) honey, and
 1 cup (250 mL) coconut. Add 2 cups
 (500 mL) dry cereal. Form
 mixture into balls. Spread 2 cups
 (500 mL) dry cereal on cookie sheet.
 Roll balls in mixture.
 Serve immediately.

 Serves 10-15.

Four paths lead to the same result.

Can you tell what format was used?

Formats of Recipes

Recipes appear in a number of styles, or formats. The four formats most commonly used are standard, descriptive, action, and narrative.

In a *standard format,* the ingredients and amounts are listed first. The directions follow in a numbered list or in a paragraph.

Three columns are used in a *descriptive format.* The ingredients are listed in the first column and the amounts in the second column. The directions are in the third column.

The *action format* presents step-by-step directions. The ingredients and amounts are right below each direction.

In the *narrative format,* the ingredients, amounts, and directions are included in a paragraph. This format can be difficult to follow unless the recipe is short.

On the left is a recipe for Peanut Butter Balls shown in all four formats.

Before you begin, have all the ingredients ready. That way, you won't discover you're missing something at a bad moment.

What Ingredients Do

When you change the ingredients in a recipe, you are likely to change the final product. This is because of the way different foods affect each other during the cooking process.

Flour provides the structure for baked foods and is used to thicken liquids.

Milk adds flavor and helps preserve foods. It moistens other ingredients so that they can be blended.

Eggs add lightness, color, and flavor to breads and cakes. They thicken foods like custards and hold together foods like meatloaf. Eggs can also coat fried foods so that grease will not sink in.

Sugar sweetens and adds texture to foods. It also aids browning.

Fats add tenderness, flavor, and texture. They help fresh foods to brown.

Spices add flavor and help to keep foods fresh.

These basic foods often appear in recipes because of the way they interact in the cooking process. You will learn more about this in Chapter 15.

See page T104 for answers.

For Review

1. What two questions should you ask before trying a new recipe?
2. Name six components of a clearly written recipe.
3. Name the four standard formats for writing recipes.

REINFORCEMENT: Every ingredient plays an important role in the end product of any recipe. Discuss how salt adds flavor, how eggs add color, and how baking powder and baking soda help the food rise.

ENRICHMENT: Select a recipe that includes flour, milk, eggs, sugar, and fat. Divide the class into five cooking groups. Have each group make the recipe after you have eliminated one of the ingredients mentioned. Analyze differences in taste and appearance of the final product.

Measuring

Systems of Measurement

As you read, think about:

■ the standard and metric systems of measurement used in recipes. (p. 322)

■ different ways to measure dry ingredients, liquid ingredients, and shortening accurately. (p. 323)

What do you think might happen if you put too much hot pepper in a sauce? or too much baking powder in biscuits? You might have a sauce that's *too* tangy and very large biscuits. You can avoid such problems by measuring carefully.

Two systems of measurement are used in the United States today. The more common system of measurement is called the standard system. It employs measures such as cups, tablespoons, and teaspoons. The metric system, which is used worldwide, is also used in this country. This system uses measures such as liters and grams. Many recipes use standard measures. However, more and more recipes are using metric measurements. As this happens, use metric measuring equipment to make sure your recipe turns out successfully.

For handy reference, keep a chart like this one in your kitchen or favorite cookbook.

Equivalent Measures

Standard Measure	Standard Equivalent Measures	Approximate Metric Measure
1 gallon	4 quarts	3.8 liters
1 quart	4 cups, 2 pints	946 milliliters or 0.95 liter
1 pint	2 cups	500 milliliters or 0.47 liter
1 cup	½ pint, 16 tablespoons	250 milliliters
¾ cup	12 tablespoons	180 milliliters
⅔ cup	10⅔ tablespoons	160 milliliters
½ cup	8 tablespoons	120 milliliters
⅓ cup	5⅓ tablespoons	80 milliliters
¼ cup	4 tablespoons	60 milliliters
⅛ cup	2 tablespoons	30 milliliters
1 tablespoon	3 teaspoons	15 milliliters
1 teaspoon		5 milliliters
½ teaspoon		2.5 milliliters
¼ teaspoon		0.5 milliliters
⅛ teaspoon		450 grams or 0.45 kilogram
1 pound	16 ounces	225 grams or 0.23 kilogram
½ pound	8 ounces	28 grams
	1 ounce	

RETEACHING: Review liquid and dry measuring techniques in class.

REINFORCEMENT: Ask students what ingredients they think are typically added in amounts as small as 1/4 and 1/8 teaspoon.

Abbreviations

Most recipes use a set of abbreviations, or shortened forms of words, for measurements. Below are abbreviations for some measurements in both the standard and the metric systems.

Standard	*Metric*
c=cup	mL=milliliter
pt=pint	L=liter
qt=quart	g=gram
gal=gallon	kg=kilogram
tsp=teaspoon	C=degrees Celsius
Tbs=tablespoon	
oz=ounce	
lb=pound	
F.=degrees Fahrenheit	

Measuring Dry Ingredients

Flour, sugar, salt, and baking powder are among the dry ingredients used most often. To measure dry ingredients, fill a measuring cup or spoon marked for dry measures with the correct amount. Then use the straight edge of a spatula to level off the ingredient.

If ingredients such as baking powder or spices have lumps, stir them before you measure. Fill a measuring spoon to overflowing and then level it.

Measuring Flour

If a recipe calls for sifted flour, sift the flour before you put it into a measuring cup. First, fill the cup to overflowing.

Then level it, using a utensil with a straight edge. Do not pack the flour down in the cup. If flour rather than sifted flour is called for, simply spoon the flour into a measuring cup and level it.

Sifting flour onto waxed paper.

Leveling dry ingredients with a straight edge.

You do not have to sift whole-grain flour or meals such as cornmeal. Stir them before you spoon them into the measuring cup. Then level them off.

Measuring Sugar

Measure white sugar exactly the way you measure unsifted flour. Confectioner's sugar, however, may be lumpy and require sifting before measuring. It can then be spooned into a measuring cup and leveled. If brown sugar is lumpy, use a rolling pin to crush the lumps. Then pack the sugar firmly into a measuring cup. It will hold the cup's shape when turned out.

Packing down brown sugar into a measuring cup.

White sugar is measured as sifted flour is.

Measuring Liquids

Use a measuring cup marked for liquid measures for liquids used in large amounts, such as milk or water. The cups are clear, so you can see when the liquid is at the correct level. Place the cup on a flat surface and check the measurement at eye level. For small amounts of liquids, simply fill the correct measuring spoon.

Measuring liquid at eye level, on flat surface.

Pouring liquids into measuring spoons.

Beating eggs before placing them into a measuring cup.

Beating eggs before measuring them

Measuring Shortening

When measuring liquid shortenings such as salad oil, pour the correct amount into a liquid-measuring cup. Measure solid shortenings in a measuring cup for dry ingredients. Pack the shortening firmly into the cup and level off.

You can also use the water displacement method for measuring solid shortening. In this method, you first subtract the

amount of shortening needed from the amount the cup will hold. If your recipe calls for ¼ cup of shortening and you have a 1-cup measure, subtract ¼ from 1 cup. You now have ¾ cup. Fill the measuring cup with cold water to the ¾-cup mark. Then spoon in the shortening, a little at a time. When the water rises to the 1-cup level, you will have ¼ cup of shortening.

Packing solid shortening into a measuring spoon.

Using liquid displacement to measure shortening.

Packaged sticks of butter and margarine are usually marked in measured amounts. This allows you to cut off the amount you need.

Weighing small amounts of food on waxed paper, or larger amounts in a container, on a kitchen scale.

See page T104 for answers.
For Review

1. What are the two systems of measurement in use in the world today?
2. Name two methods for measuring dry ingredients accurately.

REINFORCEMENT: Measure a cup of white vegetable shortening into a measuring cup and demonstrate the ease of removing it from the cup with a spatula instead of a spoon.

ENRICHMENT: Ask a student to demonstrate the water displacement method of measurement to the class.

Learning to Manage

Organizing the Kitchen

Look back at the conversation between Dan and his mother on page 304. Now read about Dan's plan and what he discovered. Then answer the questions that follow.

Dan cleared the table and washed up the dishes and pans. He decided to begin his assignment while the dishes were drying in the rack.

First, he sketched a quick floor plan of the kitchen, including the cabinets. Dan labeled the large and small appliances on the sketch. He then wrote down what each cabinet contained.

Dan searched for organization problems, looking at his sketch and at the room. He noticed that the cabinet containing the bakeware was across from the stove and all of the baking ingredients. Moving the bakeware next to the stove would make baking those great chocolate chip cookies easier!

As he started to put the dry dishes away, Dan realized how far he was from the cabinet. "Why don't we store these dishes closer to the sink?" he thought. The same was true of the silverware they used every day. That could easily be switched closer to the sink, too.

When he'd finished drying and storing the dishes, Dan realized that they had no rack or hook for dish towels. The paper towel rack was also too far from the sink. So water dripped onto the counters as you reached for a paper towel.

"How does Mom figure out which spice she needs?" Dan wondered. The spices needed to be organized and moved away from the heat and moisture of the stove.

The cooking utensils were all bunched together in a large drawer. This made it hard to find the right one. Maybe he could put up an inexpensive rack to hold utensils like slotted spoons and spatulas that they used often. The same was true of the cabinet where all the pots and pans were stored. It was so jammed that it was hard to find the right ones. Also, it was a dark, corner cabinet that his mother often referred to as the "black hole." It was the only cabinet large enough to hold the pots and pans, so moving them was not possible. They could be reorganized, though. Hanging a magnetic flashlight would help.

Who would have thought there would be so many improvements to be made? This was one homework assignment that really would help their *home work!*

Questions

1. List ways to make your home kitchen more efficient.
2. What resources are needed to make your kitchen improvements? Which changes will not cost any money?

Chapter 14 Review

Summary

Successful cooking begins with an organized kitchen. Special tools and equipment are needed in the preparation area, clean-up area, refrigerator area, range area, and eating area. In all these areas, safety is important. Proper sanitation can help prevent illness caused by spoiled food. Good safety practices can prevent falls, cuts, burns, and other accidents.

Choosing and following a good recipe is the key to good results in cooking. When selecting a recipe, consider tastes, time, ingredients, budget, and skill needed. Recipes come in different formats. In all recipes, careful measuring is essential. Use equipment for liquid and dry measuring correctly. Understanding abbreviations and equivalent measures helps.

Vocabulary

Choose the correct vocabulary words to complete the paragraphs below.

cookware (p. 317) hygiene (p. 309)
toxins (p. 308) recipe (p. 319)
sanitation (p. 308) bacteria (p. 308)
bakeware (p. 317)

Proper ___(1)___, that is, keeping your kitchen clean and free from ___(2)___, helps to reduce illness or death from contaminated food. The poisonous substances produced by bacteria are

___(3)___. Obviously, personal ___(4)___, or cleanliness, is also very important.

You should keep all kitchen tools clean. These include the pans you use on the top of the range, called ___(5)___, and the pans you use in the oven, called ___(6)___. Maintaining a clean kitchen and carefully following the directions of your ___(7)___ will produce safe, delicious meals.

Questions

- 1. Where is the best place to store pots and pans?
- 2. What happens to a person who eats foods containing toxins?
- ●● 3. Why is it important to practice personal hygiene when handling food?
- ●● 4. Should a cook use the same spoon for both tasting and stirring? Explain your answer.
- ● 5. What causes food poisoning?
- ● 6. What is *trichinosis*?
- ● 7. How can you tell whether or not canned food is spoiled?
- ●● 8. Explain the best way to disconnect an electric appliance.
- ● 9. Name at least one way to put out a grease fire.
- ●● 10. Choose a cookware or bakeware item of a particular material from the list on page 317. Describe how it should be cleaned.

The dots represent skill levels required to answer each question or complete each activity:

- ● requires recall and comprehension
- ●● requires application and analysis
- ●●● requires synthesis and evaluation

326

11. What do you think is the most useful small appliance available today? Explain your answer.

12. What is your favorite recipe format? Explain your answer.

13. Why is it important to follow a recipe carefully? When might you need to adjust the ingredients in a recipe?

14. Why is flour used in baked foods?

15. Why is it important to know metric measurements?

Skill Activities

Many more activities are contained in the annotations within this chapter.

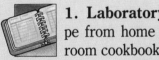

1. Laboratory Choose a recipe from home or from a classroom cookbook. Write the same recipe in the four different types of formats: standard, descriptive, action, and narrative. As a class, discuss which recipe formats were easier to write. Give reasons for your choices. Which ones do you prefer to use? Explain your answer.

2. Laboratory Using a dry measuring cup, measure out one cup of unsifted flour. Use a small food scale to weigh the flour. Now measure a cup of sifted flour and weigh it. What is the difference between the two? How do you think using unsifted flour would affect the outcome of a recipe calling for sifted flour?

3. Decision Making If you could design your own kitchen, what would it look like? Before you work on a plan of your own, find some magazines that have photographs and floor plans of kitchens. Look at them to see if they include the five work areas described in this chapter. Now, using what you know about organizing kitchen space, decide on and draw a kitchen floor plan. Try to design your kitchen so that it is as efficient as possible.

Exchange finished plans with a classmate. Look for ways to improve them.

4. Laboratory Bring a favorite family recipe to class. Use all of your recipes to create a class recipe booklet. Print the recipes neatly into a notebook for everyone to use as a cooking reference.

5. Critical Thinking What should every person know about safety in the kitchen? Write a safety checklist to find out if a kitchen is safe. Be sure to include information about storage, cleanliness, and cooking procedures that will make a kitchen safer. Now use your safety checklist to rate your school and home kitchens. Are there improvements that should be made? List any changes that will make the kitchens safer and plan to make those changes.

Chapter 15
Food Preparation

The dialogue below introduces "Bakers' Blues," the Learning to Manage feature in this chapter. The case study is continued and the situation discussed further on page 357. See page T108 for teaching suggestions.

"Before today, I thought baking a cake would be so easy! Just look at this. It looks as flat as a board!"

"Well, Joanne, this one doesn't look as though it will bring in much at the FHA bake sale. Before your group makes another one, let's figure out what went wrong."

"You told us baking was a combination of chemistry and art, Mrs. Thomas. Now I believe it!"

Section 15.1

Working in the Kitchen

As you read, think about:

■ the importance of having a plan for working in the kitchen. (p. 329)

■ how to prepare work plans for both school and home. (p. 329)

Achieving success in the kitchen requires a strategy, or plan. This is true for experienced cooks as well as for beginners. To serve a well-prepared meal on time, you need to think carefully about the steps involved in cooking it.

First, consider your skill level and the time available. Then think about which recipes would be appealing to you and the other people eating with you. After making your selections, check to see whether you have all the ingredients. If you need to go shopping, make out a grocery list. Assemble all the ingredients and equipment you will need.

A Work Plan

Once you have decided which recipe you are going to use, you need to make out a work plan. A **work plan** is a step-by-step guide for preparing food. Your plan should list the jobs to be done, the steps to follow, and the time required for each task.

If you are preparing a whole meal, begin with the foods that take the longest to cook. For example, spaghetti sauce

REINFORCEMENT: Show students a video or TV program on food preparation featuring a well-known chef such as Julia Child. Note how the equipment and ingredients are all assembled beforehand.

PHOTO: Remind students that it is important as well as courteous to leave the foods lab clean and organized for the next group of students coming in.

In what ways does a work plan help you in the kitchen?

might take 15 minutes to combine and another two hours to cook. You can make an apple pie and chop up a salad while the sauce is simmering.

At School

When you cook in a school foods lab, there will be several people available to do different jobs. However, your time will also be limited, so each person needs to know exactly what to do. One advantage of working with a group is that several jobs can be done at once. One person can chop while another is sifting. Still another person can be greasing the pan. By cooperating and using a work plan, you can prepare delicious food with time left over to enjoy it. The two-day lab plan on page 330 shows how jobs can be assigned to prepare a meal.

RETEACHING: Working together in a food lab is a team effort. Stress the importance of knowing one's job and cooperating with other group members.

Two-Day Lab Plan

MENU BROCCOLI SOUP
TOSSED SALAD
ITALIAN BREAD
ICED TEA

DAY ONE	JOB	TIME
ALL	GET READY TO WORK	11:00 - 11:05
STUDENT 1	PICK UP SUPPLIES	11:05 - 11:10
STUDENT 2	ASSEMBLE EQUIPMENT	11:05 - 11:10
STUDENT 3	WASH COUNTERS	
	ASSEMBLE CLEAN-UP EQUIPMENT	11:05 - 11:10
STUDENT 1	PREPARE BASE FOR SOUP	11:10 - 11:25
STUDENT 2	CHOP AND COOK BROCCOLI FOR SOUP	11:10 - 11:25
STUDENT 3	PREPARE CHEESE GARNISH FOR SOUP AND STORE	11:10 - 11:30
	MAKE SALAD DRESSING AND STORE	
STUDENT 4	PREPARE SALAD AND STORE	11:10 - 11:30
STUDENT 1	COMBINE BROCCOLI WITH SOUP BASE AND STORE	11:25 - 11:30
ALL	CLEAN UP	11:30 - 11:40

DAY TWO	JOB	TIME
ALL	GET READY TO WORK	11:00 - 11:05
STUDENT 1	PICK UP SUPPLIES	11:05 - 11:10
STUDENT 2	ASSEMBLE EQUIPMENT	11:05 - 11:10
STUDENT 3	WASH COUNTERS	11:05 - 11:10
	ASSEMBLE CLEAN-UP EQUIPMENT	
STUDENT 4	SLICE AND SERVE BREAD	11:10 - 11:15
	SERVE CHEESE GARNISH	
STUDENT 1	HEAT AND SERVE SOUP	11:10 - 11:15
STUDENT 2	ADD SALAD DRESSING AND SERVE SALAD	11:10 - 11:15
STUDENT 3	SET TABLE	11:10 - 11:15
	PREPARE ICED TEA	
ALL	EAT	11:15 - 11:30
ALL	CLEAN-UP	11:30 - 11:40

The work plan you see here is probably a lot like the one you will use at school.

Home Work Plan

Menu: Baked fish, mashed potatoes, green peas, melon	
Job:	Time
Assemble ingredients and equipment.	5:30-5:35
Preheat oven to 400°	5:30-5:35
Peel potatoes and put on to boil	5:35-5:40
Melt butter and wash fish	5:40-5:45
Coat fish in bread crumbs and put in baking dish; drizzle butter on. Put fish in oven and bake 12 minutes.	5:45-5:54
Put frozen peas on to cook	5:54-5:57
Prepare mashed potatoes	5:57-6:00
Drain peas	6:00-6:01
Remove fish from oven	6:01-6:02
Slice melon when ready to serve	6:02-6:05

Take the time you need to write a plan. It could save you hours.

At Home

When you cook at home, your time is often more flexible than it is in a school lab. However, you may be doing all the jobs yourself. The work plan above shows how one person can prepare a meal for a whole family in less than 45 minutes.

For Review

1. What should be included in a work plan for preparing food?
2. Name one advantage of working in a group when preparing a meal.

Section 15.2
Using a Recipe

As you read, think about:

- how knowledge of certain cooking terms can help you develop your cooking skills. (p. 331)
- the principles involved in making changes to a recipe. (p. 333)

Cooking has a language of its own. Recipe terms describe many different techniques. Understanding exactly what recipe terms mean will give you better results.

Recipe Terms

Directions in recipes include special terms that describe how to prepare, cut, mix, and cook foods. For the best results, it is important to understand these terms and follow the directions. The following terms are used in most recipes.

Preparation Terms

- **bread:** to cover a food with a coating of bread, cereal, or cracker crumbs. The food is often dipped in a liquid such as milk or egg before coating.
- **dredge:** to cover a food with a dry ingredient, such as flour or sugar. The food may be rolled in, sprinkled with, or shaken in a bag with the dry ingredient.
- **marinate:** to soak food in a sauce to make it tender and more flavorful
- **brush:** to cover a food lightly with another food, such as melted butter

- **grease:** to rub with oil or solid fats
- **season:** to add salt, herbs, and other seasonings to a food
- **dot:** to put tiny pieces of food, such as butter, on the surface of another food

Bread

Dredge

Cutting Terms

- **chop:** to cut into small pieces
- **cube:** to cut into small squares
- **mince:** to cut into very small pieces
- **julienne:** to cut into long, thin strips
- **pare:** to cut a thin layer of skin from fruits and vegetables
- **grate:** to rub food, such as cheese, against a grater, making it into fine particles
- **score:** to make thin, straight cuts through the outer edge of fat on meat to prevent the meat from curling during cooking

Dice

Julienne

Mince

Score

Mixing Terms

- **beat:** to mix ingredients with an over-and-under motion, using a spoon, whisk beater, or electric mixer
- **blend:** to combine two or more ingredients thoroughly
- **cream:** to blend ingredients until soft and smooth, using a spoon, whisk, or electric mixer
- **cut in:** to combine shortening and dry ingredients with a pastry blender, two knives, or a fork

Cream

Cut in

- **mix:** to combine two or more ingredients by stirring or beating
- **whip:** to beat rapidly, introducing air
- **fold in:** to combine ingredients by bringing a rubber spatula down through the center of the mixture, turning the spatula at the bottom, and bringing the underneath mixture up
- **knead:** to press and fold dough to make it smooth and elastic

Cooking Terms

- **bake:** to cook with dry heat, usually in an oven
- **baste:** to brush or pour liquid over food as it cooks, in order to add flavor and prevent dryness
- **boil:** to cook in a hot bubbling liquid
- **braise:** to cook meat slowly, covered in a small amount of liquid or steam
- **broil:** to cook by direct heat, as over a grill, under an electric coil, or under a gas flame
- **fry:** to cook in fat
- **poach:** to cook gently in a hot liquid below the boiling point
- **sauté:** to cook in a small amount of fat
- **simmer:** to cook in liquid that is just below boiling point
- **steam:** to cook over boiling water
- **stew:** to simmer at low heat
- **stir-fry:** to cook quickly in a small amount of fat

Poach

Stew

Steam

Braise

Substitutions Chart

Ingredient	Substitution
1 c (250 mL) whole milk	$\frac{1}{2}$ c (125 mL) of evaporated milk plus $\frac{1}{2}$ c (125 mL) of water or 1 c (250 mL) reconstituted nonfat dry milk, plus 2 tsp (10 mL) butter
2 Tbs (30 mL) flour for thickening	1 Tbs (15 mL) of cornstarch or 2 tsp (10 mL) quick-cooking tapioca
1 c (250 mL) butter or margarine	7/8 c (210 mL) lard plus $\frac{1}{2}$ tsp (2.5 mL) salt
1 square (1 oz or 28 g) unsweetened chocolate	3 Tbs (45 mL) cocoa plus 1 Tbs (15 mL) of solid shortening
1 c (250 mL) heavy cream	3/4 c (180 mL) milk plus 1/3 c (80 mL) butter

Are you missing an ingredient? Is there something you can substitute?

Changing a Recipe

Experimenting with food is part of the fun. As you become a more experienced cook, you may want to try out different combinations and seasonings. For example, you might decide to add Chinese noodles to a casserole or wheat germ to your meatloaf. The more you learn about food, the more you will be able to adjust recipes to your own tastes. There may also be times when you will need to make substitutions because you're missing an ingredient. The chart above shows some useful substitutions.

Chapter 15/*Food Preparation*   **333**

Ready to go? The foods lab is your chance to use everything you've learned.

Increasing or Decreasing

Imagine that four guests are joining your family for dinner. With three family members besides you, there will be eight in all. You are helping to prepare a recipe for a tuna and cheese casserole that serves only four. What do you do? You double the recipe. Another time you may have the opposite problem. If the recipe serves too many, you will need to cut it in half.

You can double or halve a recipe by using a little math and the Equivalent Table on page 322. Always write down the new measurements before you begin

your preparations. If you double a recipe, you will need to use a larger pan and allow more cooking or baking time. Some foods, such as breads, may need double the *number* of pans, instead of a pan double the *size*.

For Review

1. Name the three kinds of terms you will find in a recipe.
2. Why is it sometimes necessary to change a recipe?

Section 15.3

Principles of Cookery

As you read, think about:

- how different foods react when they are combined in recipes. (p. 335)
- the different cooking techniques used to prepare food. (p. 335)
- the difference between dry-heat and moist-heat cooking methods. (p. 343)

Why can't you roast an egg in the shell in the oven? The egg would explode, that's why. You can, of course, roast chicken or beef without such drastic results. Different foods react in different ways when they are cooked. Food chemistry is an important part of cooking.

Milk, cheese, eggs, fats, and sugar serve important functions in cooking. That is why you will find some or all of these ingredients in most recipes. If you want particular foods to turn out successfully, you must use certain techniques in cooking them. These techniques are based on the chemical qualities in foods. It is importnat to know how cooking methods affect meat, poultry, and vegetables.

Cooking with Milk and Cheese

Milk and cheese are used in many recipes. They improve the flavor, texture, and nutritional value of a food. They also affect the appearance of foods. The addition of milk or cheese helps give baked foods that nice golden-brown look. There are, however, basic rules to follow when cooking with milk and cheese.

There's a lot of planning, organizing, and studying to do before you can reach this point.

REINFORCEMENT: Brainstorm with your class three lists of foods; those that are prepared by boiling, those prepared by baking, and those prepared by cooking on a range.

PHOTO: Show your class a double boiler. Demonstrate how deep to fill the bottom, and stress that the water can boil away if left unattended.

Heating milk can be tricky. Use low heat or a double boiler.

Heating Milk

When preparing some foods, such as cocoa or cream sauces, you need to heat milk. It is important not to let a film, or skin, develop when heating milk. This film is caused primarily by the protein in the milk. The film forms as liquid evaporates from the surface of heated milk. If you simply remove it, another one will form.

One of the easiest ways to prevent the formation of scum is to cover the pan. You can also stir the milk or beat it with a rotary beater. If you use a beater, foam will form on the surface of the milk. Hot cocoa is sometimes prepared in this way.

Milk can *scorch*, or burn, very easily if you do not use a low heat. This is because the proteins are sensitive to high temperatures. Proteins can collect around the sides and bottom of the pan, which are often the hottest parts. To prevent scorching, heat the milk using a very low

heat or over hot water in a double boiler.

Also heat milk slowly when a recipe calls for scalded milk, that is, milk heated to just below the boiling point.

Curdling (*CURD*–ling) is an additional problem that can occur if milk is cooked at too high a temperature. When milk curdles, it separates into liquid and small lumps. To prevent curdling, use low temperatures when cooking foods that include milk. Scalloped potatoes, for example, will be less likely to curdle if cooked at a low temperature.

Milk can also curdle when combined with acids like lemon juice or tomato soup or hot foods like gravy. To prevent these kinds of curdling, pour some of the acid or hot mixture into the milk and stir constantly. Then *slowly* add the milk to the rest of the mixture and continue to stir.

Another way to prevent curdling is to thicken either the milk or the food that will be added. To do this, use some kind of starch. For example, you can thicken milk with flour and then add tomato soup; or you can thicken the soup and then add the milk.

A basic guideline to prevent curdling is to use fresh milk. If milk is stored improperly or too long, it will curdle more easily. Preventing curdling is the best practice, but if it does happen, beat the mixture vigorously to remove the lumps.

Milk in a Microwave Oven

If you are heating milk by itself in a microwave oven, use a low power setting. Milk is delicate and can easily overcook or curdle. Use a large container and fill it about two-thirds full to prevent the milk

REINFORCEMENT: Demonstrate the difference between scalding, scorching, and curdling milk on a conventional range and in a microwave oven.

ENRICHMENT: Prepare two quiche recipes in class. In one recipe, add cold milk, and in the second recipe, scald the milk before adding it to the egg mixture. Observe the differences in firmness, texture, and appearance of the finished products.

from boiling over. Watch carefully, and turn the power off if you see signs of foaming. If you are heating milk together with other ingredients, you can use a slightly higher setting.

Cooking with Cheese

Cheese increases both the flavor and the nutritional value of a dish. However, it has a high protein content. This means it can become lumpy or tough and rubbery if overcooked. Cook cheese for a short time only at a low or moderate temperature to keep it soft and tender. When adding cheese to other ingredients, cut it into small pieces or shred it. It will then melt and blend easily with the other foods. Ripened or aged cheeses blend better than unripened varieties. Cheddar, Monterey Jack, and Colby are examples of cheeses that work well in recipes that require heating.

Cooking with Eggs

Eggs are an important ingredient in many recipes. They can be used to thicken foods like custards and in batters for frying foods like chicken and chops. Dipping fish in egg and breadcrumbs before baking helps to keep it moist. Eggs can also be used as a *leavening* (*LEH*–ven–ing) *agent.* This means they help some foods, such as popovers, to rise. In addition, eggs are an emulsifying agent. An **emulsion** is a combination of oil and another liquid, beaten so that the ingredients do not separate. Egg yolks are the emulsifying agent in mayonnaise.

For some foods, such as sauces and custards, eggs are beaten and then added to a hot liquid. Do not add eggs to a hot mixture all at once, as they can curdle. Instead, stir a little of the hot mixture into the eggs. Then slowly add the rest of the hot mixture, stirring constantly.

Beaten egg whites are used in some foods, such as puffy omelets, soufflés, and meringues. To separate the whites from the yolks, hold the egg over a small bowl and crack the shell in the middle. Pour the yolk from one half of the shell to the other half, allowing the egg white to drain down into the bowl. Be careful not to let any yolk get into the bowl. If any does, its presence will interfere with the beating of the whites. The fat in the egg yolk prevents the whites from being beaten to the fluffy or stiff stage.

You can use the beaters to check egg whites for stiffness.

Egg whites can be beaten more quickly if they are at room temperature. Use a bowl with a small rounded bottom and sides that slope out to a wider top. Make sure both bowl and beater are free of grease, which will also interfere with the beating of the whites.

As you beat the whites, a foam will form. Some recipes call for whites beaten to a *soft peak*. The eggs are beaten enough when the peak just bends over as the beater is lifted out of the foam. In recipes calling for whites beaten to a *stiff peak,* the peak should hold when the beater is lifted out.

Cooking with Fats

Fats add flavor and tenderness to foods and help baked products to brown. Liquid fats, called oils, are extracted from vegetables, fruits, and nuts. Vegetable oils come from the seeds of plants like sunflowers, soybeans, and corn. Coconut and

Can you taste the flavors of different fats used in cooking?

olive oil come from fruits. Peanut, hickory, and walnut oil are extracted from nuts.

Butter, margarine, and shortening are solid fats. Butter, which is made from cream, gives baked foods a sweet, rich taste. Margarine is usually made from vegetable oils and milk. When used in place of butter, it produces a similar taste. Margarine usually costs less than butter. Shortening is made from different kinds of oils, such as corn, peanut, and soybean. It produces a soft, delicate texture in baked goods. It is less expensive than butter and margarine and can be substituted when a recipe calls for butter. Lard, or animal fat, can be used when a recipe calls for shortening. Some cooks use it for pastry, as it gives crusts a flaky texture. It contains cholesterol; margarine does not.

Do not use a liquid fat in place of a solid one, as this will affect the final product.

Most fats, solid or liquid, can be used successfully for frying. When deep-fat frying, keep the heat at a fairly high temperature. This will seal the food outside and keep moisture and nutrients inside. If the temperature is too low, the food will soak up the fat. If it is too high, however, the fat will begin to smoke. The temperature at which fat smokes is called the *smoking point.* Different kinds of fat have different smoking points, so watch the temperature carefully. When fried foods are done, drain them on a paper towel to remove excess fat.

Cooking with Sugar

When cooking with sugar, be sure to use the kind called for in the recipe. Different kinds of sugar have different textures and

NOTE: Margarine is a blend of hydrogenated vegetable oils, mixed with emulsifiers, coloring, vitamins, and other ingredients. Originally called "oleomargarine," the patent on it was issued in 1871.

Sugar always makes food sweet. Different types of sugars and varying amounts control just how sweet something is.

sweetening capacities. The kind you use will affect the final product.

White table sugar, or *granulated* sugar, is the most common kind used in cooking. Use it when a recipe simply specifies "sugar." Granulated sugar is made from sugarcane or sugar beets. It is used for cakes, pies, custards, and to flavor many other foods. It is also used for canning, since sugar acts as a preservative for foods like canned fruits.

Powdered, or *confectioner's,* sugar is made by grinding granulated sugar to a fine powder. A small amount of cornstarch is often added to confectioner's

sugar to prevent caking and hardening. Many frosting recipes call for confectioner's sugar.

Brown sugar is granulated sugar with molasses added for flavor and color. You can buy dark or light brown sugar. The dark brown variety has the stronger flavor. Brown sugar is sometimes specified in recipes for baked goods. It is also used in barbecue sauces and ham glazes.

Remember to use low to medium heat when cooking with sugar. High heat causes sugar to caramelize, or turn to liquid and develop a brown color. Using heavy pans will also help prevent overcooking.

NOTE: A *confection* is a sweet preparation such as a candy or preserve. A *confectioner* is a person who makes or sells such items.

REINFORCEMENT: Show students the difference between granulated and confectioner's sugar. Give examples of their different uses.

Technology

Food from Space Lands Safely

Do you ever have trouble keeping food fresh, preparing it quickly, and serving it when it's "just right"? So did the astronauts—until NASA developed new food processing, packaging, and preparation technologies. NASA created tasty nutritious, lightweight meals that could be stored easily, and prepared quickly and simply. Many of these technologies now appear in "spinoff" products often used by hikers, campers, and elderly or handicapped people.

- **Freeze-Dried Foods** In freeze-drying, water is removed from freshly cooked foods at very low temperatures. Sealed pouches keep out moisture and oxygen, the major causes of food deterioration. Freeze-dried food does not need refrigeration, and adding hot or cold water makes it ready to eat.
- **Retort-Pouch Foods** The retort pouch combines the advantages of boil-in-the-bag foods and metal cans. These products can be stored without refrigeration and are lightweight enough to be transported easily and heated in their pouches.

Can you think of other uses for this new food technology?

Cooking Fruits and Vegetables

Proper preparation of fruits and vegetables is important to ensure that you will benefit from their vital nutrients. Many of these nutrients are in the peel or skin. An important guideline, then, is to prepare fruits and vegetables in their skins as often as possible.

Fruits

Some fresh fruits, such as apples, pears, and bananas, have a low acid content. This causes them to turn dark soon after they are cut. To prevent discoloration, sprinkle the fruit with an acid juice, such as lemon or orange. Even better, cut the fruit just before serving, as this also prevents the loss of vitamins that occurs when cut fruit is exposed to air. Vitamin C in particular can be destroyed by exposure to air.

Fruit retains more nutrients when eaten raw. If you do cook fruits, use as little water as possible to preserve vitamins and minerals. Vitamin C can dissolve in water and is easily destroyed by heat. You can cook berries with no water; apples and peaches require only a tiny amount. Serve the liquid along with the cooked fruit, as it contains vitamins and minerals.

Vegetables

The most common methods for cooking vegetables include boiling, steaming, baking, stir-frying, and cooking in a microwave oven. No matter what method you

For the best nutritional value, eat fruits raw.

use, it is important to control the cooking time and the amount of water used. Vegetables should be cooked so that their colors, tastes, textures, and nutritional values are not lost.

Boiling One common way to cook fresh vegetables is to boil them. The disadvantage of this method is that some of the nutrients seep out when vegetables are cooked in water. Therefore, use as little water as possible. Put the vegetables into boiling water and turn the heat down to simmer. Do not put vegetables into cold water and then bring the water to the boil. Cover the pan, since air destroys vitamins. Heat does also, so avoid overcooking. Vegetables will retain the most nutrients if they are cooked until just tender, and no longer.

Steaming When vegetables are steamed, they retain most of their color and texture. Steaming is a nutritious way to prepare vegetables, since they are not actually immersed in water. All you need is a pan with boiling water and a steamer basket to hold the vegetables. Place the basket in the pan over the boiling water.

Stir-frying As you learned earlier in this chapter, stir-frying is cooking food quickly in a small amount of fat. This method is a very convenient and tasty way to cook vegetables. Stir-fried vegetables are usually served slightly crisp. Use a fork to test for doneness.

Baking Baking is one of the easiest ways to prepare vegetables with skins. Potatoes and squash, for instance, need only to be washed before baking. When baking potatoes or cooking them in a microwave, first pierce them with a fork so that steam can escape. Otherwise, they might burst.

Frozen and Canned Vegetables Preparing frozen and canned vegetables is easy and quick, since the vegetables have been partially or completely cooked.

Frozen vegetables should be placed in boiling water without thawing. Package labels tell you how much water to use. Because vegetables are scalded before freezing, they cook more quickly than fresh vegetables. Some frozen vegetables are good steamed.

Canned vegetables are already cooked and you need only heat them. The liquid in the can contains nutrients, but these are often lost when the food is served. If you evaporate some of the liquid, you will

Do you like vegetables to be flavorful and just a little crunchy? Try stir-frying them.

end up with the right amount for serving. First, drain the liquid from the vegetables and heat it in an uncovered pan. When about two-thirds of the liquid has evaporated, add the vegetables and heat. Serve the liquid along with the vegetables.

The Microwave Method A microwave oven is excellent for preparing vegetables, because little or no water is needed for cooking. Vegetables keep their shape, color, and nutritional value and require very little cooking time.

The final section in this chapter will give you more information about cooking vegetables in a microwave oven.

Cooking Eggs

Eggs are both nutritious and versatile. They can be served as a main dish, like scrambled agges or an omelet. As you read earlier in this chapter, they can b' used as a thickener or as a leavening agent in foods.

Cooking Eggs in the Shell

You may soft-cook or hard-cook eggs in the shell. Begin by placing the eggs in cold water. Bring the water to boiling point. There will be bubbles at the edge of the pan but not in the middle. Turn the heat down to simmer and cover the pan. Simmer the eggs in the pan three to five minutes if you want them soft-cooked. For hard-cooked eggs, allow 20 minutes. After cooking, remove the eggs from the water immediately and cool them with cold water. This makes the shells easier to remove and prevents overcooking. (A greenish ring around the yolk is a sign of overcooking.) Eggs taken directly from the refrigerator can take a little longer to cook than eggs at room temperature.

Eggs in a Microwave Oven

Never cook an egg in the shell in a microwave oven. The egg may explode, since the yolk cooks faster than the white because of its high fat content. When cooking an egg by itself, crack it into a custard cup. Pierce the yolk with a toothpick and cover the egg tightly. Eggs are delicate and should therefore be cooked at a low setting. When using them as an ingredient in a casserole or other dish, you can cook them at a higher setting.

An omelet is a tasty main dish.

Cooking Meat

Meat is cooked to impart flavor, tenderness, and color. Cooking also destroys harmful bacteria that might be in the meat. The principles of cooking meat are influenced by its high protein content. When meat is cooked, the protein of the muscle, or lean meat, becomes firmer. The protein of connective tissue is softened. The cooking method that is best is determined by the particular cut of meat. Therefore, lean meat, such as sirloin steak, does not need much cooking time. Meat with a lot of connective tissue, such as a chuck roast, needs longer cooking to ensure tenderness.

Dry-heat Methods

Some meats are cooked with dry, that is, direct heat, uncovered, and with no added water. Roasting, broiling, and pan-broiling are dry-heat methods. You can cook tender cuts of meat with dry heat.

Large cuts, such as rib roast, should be roasted. Place the meat fat side up on a rack in the pan. This allows fat to drip down. Set the oven temperature around 300° to 350° F (150° to 180° C). Cookbooks provide timetables to help you estimate the cooking time. After meat is removed from the oven, it will continue cooking for a time.

Smaller cuts like steak can be broiled. With this method, you cook the meat above or below the direct source of heat. Place the meat in a broiler pan or on a barbecue, usually about 3 to 6 inches (7.5 to 15 cm) from the heat.

REINFORCEMENT: Brainstorm a variety of dessert foods in which eggs are a major ingredient.

DISCUSS: Have students list five ways in which meat can be cooked. Discuss the methods they prefer most and why.

A tender cut like this one can be cooked with dry heat.

You can also cook small cuts in a skillet. *Pan-broiling* is cooking meat without adding fat. When this method is used, pour off the fat as the meat cooks. Use low heat to allow the meat to cook slowly until it browns on one side. Then turn the meat and cook the other side.

Moist-heat Methods

Less tender cuts of meat are cooked by moist heat, or heat and some amount of liquid. You may cook the meat on the range top, in the oven, or in a special pressure cooker. Braising, simmering, and stewing are all moist-heat methods of cooking.

REINFORCEMENT: What degree of doneness do your students prefer when they order a steak or hamburger? How do they think the amount of cooking affects the flavor and texture?

Braising is cooking meat using a small amount of liquid in a covered container. You can use a little water, stock, or vegetable juice. The meat itself releases juices that provide moisture. You can braise meat on the range top or in the oven at around 300° to 325° F (150° to 160° C). Some cuts suitable for braising are beef steak (round or blade) and beef blade chuck roast.

Simmering and stewing are ways of cooking meats in liquid. When large cuts of meat are covered with liquid, they are *simmered.* Smaller cuts that are almost covered are *stewed.* For both methods, heat must be low so that the liquid simmers rather than boils. Beef brisket and stew beef are among the cuts suitable for cooking in liquid.

Slow cooking with moist heat blends flavors and makes meat tender.

NOTE: The word *stew* comes from the Old French word meaning "to bathe in hot water." Ask students how this relates to the cooking term.

Frying Methods

You can cook thin pieces of meat in fat on a range top. Pan-frying and deep-fat frying are two methods of cooking in fat.

Cooking in a small amount of fat is *pan-frying,* or sautéing. Cook the meat in an uncovered skillet at a moderate temperature. Turn it occasionally, but do not pour off the fat. Some cuts suitable for pan-frying are T-bone steaks, beef patties, and pork chops.

In *deep-fat frying,* the fat covers the food. This method is best for meats that have been breaded, such as croquettes. The cooking temperature should be fairly high so that the food will not absorb too much fat.

REINFORCEMENT: Give a matching quiz on the following cooking methods: pan-broiling, braising, simmering, stewing, pan-frying, and deep-fat frying.

PHOTO: Explain to your students that a meat thermometer is not an expensive purchase and that it takes only a moment to use.

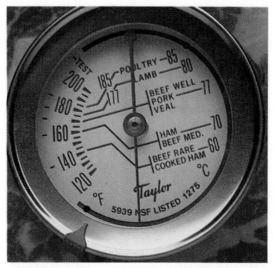

Why guess? A meat thermometer is easy to use and read.

Testing for Doneness

Some meats can be cooked to different degrees to suit individual tastes. Beef, lamb, and veal can be rare, medium, or well done. Pork should *always* be well done in order to avoid the risk of trichinosis (trik–uh–*NO*–siss). This is a disease caused by a small worm that can live in pork. If pork is still pink inside, it needs further cooking.

Use a meat thermometer to test for doneness in roasts. Insert the thermometer into the thickest part of the meat. Do not let it touch the bone. The meat is done when the correct temperature is shown on the thermometer. For meats cooked by other methods, such as pan-frying, use a sharp fork to test for doneness. The meat is well done when the juices are clear and not bloody. If you are cooking a steak, the juices will be red for rare or medium meat.

REINFORCEMENT: Distribute copies of a drawing of a meat thermometer without a dial. Have students work in pairs to practice reading the various settings on a meat thermometer. To do so, they should take turns drawing the dial in at different positions and determining the indicated reading.

Chapter 15/*Food Preparation*   **345**

Cooking Poultry

Poultry should be cooked at low to medium temperatures. Because of the high protein content in poultry, high oven temperatures cause it to shrink or toughen. Fats used for frying should not be too hot, and liquids should be kept at the simmering level.

The age of the bird determines the best cooking method. Both dry-heat and moist-heat methods can be used.

Dry-heat Methods

You can roast tender birds—chickens, turkeys, and ducks—in a 325° F (160° C) oven. Put the bird, uncovered, on a rack in a shallow pan. Do not add water. If the bird browns enough before it is cooked through, cover it with a loose tent of aluminum foil.

Barbecuing is a fun and flavorful way to cook poultry.

Broiler-fryers are suitable for broiling. The chickens are usually quartered or split in half. To broil chicken, place it on a broiler rack skin side down. Cook it 4 to 5 inches (10 to 12.5 cm) from the source of heat for around 15 minutes. Turn the chicken when browned and cook it for 15 minutes more.

Tender chicken pieces can be fried. To prepare the chicken, roll it in flour or egg and bread crumbs; or dip it in a batter. Use about ½ inch (1.2 cm) of heated fat. Turn the chicken as it browns. Continue to cook it slowly over low heat in a skillet or in the oven.

Moist-heat Methods

Mature poultry is more tender when cooked by the moist-heat method. Hens or whole chickens can be braised or stewed. They can also be steamed in a pressure cooker.

To braise chicken pieces, first brown them in fat. Then add 2 to 3 tablespoons (30 to 45 mL) water. Cover the pan and continue cooking over low heat on the range top or in the oven at 325° F (160° C). Cook about 45 minutes to an hour. During the last 10 minutes, remove the cover so that the skin will be crisp.

To stew poultry, use a large pot. Cover the poultry with water or other liquids called for in the recipe. Simmer until the meat can be easily removed from the bones. Make sure the liquid does not boil. The cooked poultry can be used in a variety of dishes, such as salads, casseroles, sandwiches, and soups. The liquid broth remaining can be flavored and used for soup.

ENRICHMENT: Have students survey their classmates to see how often students ate poultry during the last week. Ask about the various ways in which it was prepared.

For variety and great taste, try cooking fish over a campfire. Fish can be cooked in pieces or whole.

Cooking Fish

Fish has very little connective tissue, so it requires only a short cooking time. In fact, some people eat fish raw. Fish can be broiled, baked, poached, or fried. It can also be cooked in a chowder with liquid and vegetables.

Broiling is a good method for cooking fatty fish. Place the fish in an oiled pan and brush it with butter. Cook it several inches from the heat source. If the fish is thick, you may need to turn it.

To bake a whole fish, brush it with butter and put it into an oiled baking dish. Cook the fish uncovered in a 350° F (180°

C) oven. The cooking time will depend on the size of the fish. One rule of thumb is to cook fish 10 minutes for every inch of thickness. When cooking small pieces of fish, such as fillets, use a temperature around 400° F (200° C).

Poached fish is simmered in liquid in a covered pan. The liquid may be seasoned water or stock. Tying the fish in cheesecloth will keep it from falling apart. Fish that is to be fried can be dipped in flour, cornmeal, or a batter before cooking.

With any cooking method, be careful not to overcook fish, since this can cause dryness. The fish is done when it flakes easily. Use a fork for testing.

PHOTO: Ask students to describe why the addition of fruit makes this breakfast both more appealing and more nutritious.

Cereals get a nutritional boost from adding fruit or nuts.

Cooking Cereals, Grains, and Breads

Although some grain products are ready-to-eat, many require cooking. Proper cooking is essential if grain products are to have a desirable texture and flavor.

Cereals and Grains

Hot breakfast cereals, similar cereals and grains, pasta, and rice are cooked in water or other liquid. Because nutrients escape into the water, it is important to use as little water as possible. Check to see exactly how much water is required.

When cooking breakfast cereals, you may find that lumps form. One way to avoid this is to add the cereal slowly to rapidly boiling water, stirring constantly. Check package labels for instructions. Mix fine-grain cereals like cream of wheat with a little cold water before putting them into boiling water.

DISCUSS: Ask students what hot cereals they think are most popular now and what it is about them that makes them big sellers.

When rice, pasta, and other cereals are cooking, they expand to three times their original volume. Keep this in mind when choosing a pan. Water must be drained from pasta. Rice will absorb it all.

When you cook pasta, add it slowly to boiling water. This will keep the water boiling and will help keep the pieces of pasta from sticking together. You can also add one or two drops of oil to the water to keep the pasta apart.

Some people rinse rice and pasta before or after cooking. Although this can prevent stickiness, it is not a good practice. Water tends to rinse away some of the nutrients.

Breads

There are two categories of bread: quick breads and yeast breads. Quick breads are those that leaven, or rise, quickly. Either baking soda or baking powder is the usual leavening agent in these breads. Muffins, biscuits, and pancakes are some popular quick breads. Yeast breads include white or wholewheat bread, rolls, and hamburger buns. In this group, the leavening agent is yeast. These breads take longer to prepare than quick breads. This is because the dough has to rise before the bread can be baked.

Quick Breads The basic ingredients in quick breads are flour, liquid, a leavening agent, salt, sugar, fat, and eggs. Other ingredients vary. Two methods are used to mix quick breads. These are the muffin method and the biscuit method.

In the muffin method, you mix the dry ingredients and the liquid ingredients separately and then combine them. The way

NOTE: It takes about the same amount of time to cook pasta and rice in a microwave oven as it does to cook them the conventional way.

you mix the liquid and dry ingredients is extremely important. You should stir the mixture just enough to moisten the dry ingredients, and no more. It is normal for the batter to be lumpy. Overmixing can make muffins tough.

The biscuit method is used for baking powder biscuits. After mixing the dry ingredients, you add shortening (solid fat). Use two knives or a pastry blender to cut the shortening into the dry mixture. This process breaks up the shortening into pea-sized pieces. Then mix in the liquid.

Next, knead the dough, that is, press and fold it with your hands. (See the kneading instructions on page 350.) You should knead biscuits about 10 times. This will make them flaky and fine-textured. Too much kneading can cause toughness. If you do not knead, the biscuits will be tender but small and of a coarser texture.

Yeast Breads Yeast breads need different amounts of time to rise, depending on the recipe. Some rise at room temperature, while others can be put in the refrigerator and left for several hours. When making yeast breads, read the recipe carefully to see how much time is needed. Also make sure you understand each step in the recipe. Usually, dry

There are many methods for making bread and a large variety of delicious results.

ART: Demonstrate the process of kneading by making a yeast bread in class. Give each student the opportunity to knead the bread.

The Kneading Process

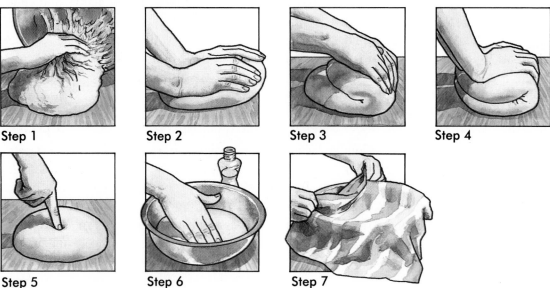

Step 1 Step 2 Step 3 Step 4

Step 5 Step 6 Step 7

Some people find kneading relaxing and enjoyable. What do you think you would enjoy in the process of making bread?

ingredients and wet ingredients are mixed separately and then combined.

The kneading process spreads the yeast throughout the dough. These are the steps in kneading yeast dough.

1. Turn the dough out onto a floured board. Then flour your hands.
2. Flatten the ball of dough by pressing it away from you with the heels of your hands.
3. Lift the far end of the dough and pull it toward you. Fold the dough over.
4. Move the dough one-quarter turn.
5. Continue pressing away and folding over for as long as the recipe directs. Test to see if the dough is kneaded enough by poking it with a finger. If the dough springs back, it is ready.
6. Put the dough in a bowl large enough for it to rise. Rub the dough with

butter or oil and cover the bowl with plastic wrap or a towel.

7. Put the dough in a warm, dry place to rise. Check the recipe for rising time. When you think the dough is ready, poke your finger in again. If your finger leaves a mark, the dough is risen.

See page T109 for answers.

For Review

1. Name five ingredients that are often found in recipes.
2. What is the difference between the dry-heat and the moist-heat method of cooking?
3. Give three examples of cooking meat or poultry with moist heat.
4. Name four ways to cook fresh vegetables.

ENRICHMENT: Using the quick method of preparation, have students prepare yeast bread in the foods laboratory.

ENRICHMENT: Prepare baking powder biscuits in class. Give half of the class a recipe using the muffin method of preparation and the other half the biscuit method of preparation. Compare preparation times and results.

Section 15.4
Convection and Microwave Cooking

As you read, think about:

- the difference between convection ovens and microwave ovens. (p. 351)
- the principles of cooking in a microwave oven. (p. 353)
- the importance of proper care and safe use of microwave ovens. (p. 356)

The conventional way to cook food is to place it on a hot burner or in a hot oven. Many kitchens today, however, include special kinds of ovens. The most popular of these are convection ovens and microwave ovens.

Convection Ovens

Convection ovens are like conventional ovens in most ways. The primary difference is that convection ovens have fans that circulate the air at a high speed. The heated air hits the food from all sides, cooking it more evenly and quickly. Meats, for example, brown more evenly and are therefore juicier. Also, low temperatures can be used in convection ovens. You can use the same kind of cookware in both kinds of ovens.

Microwave Ovens

Microwave ovens cook food about four times faster than conventional ovens do. Some foods cook in only a few seconds.

For speed and convenience, it's hard to beat a microwave.

For example, a cup of liquid can be heated in about a minute and boiled in about two minutes. Microwave ovens are different from conventional ovens in many ways. To use them successfully, you need to know how they work and to understand the special requirements of microwave cooking.

How Microwave Ovens Work

Microwave ovens do not get hot as conventional ovens do. Instead, they give off tiny waves of energy called **microwaves.** These are similar to radio waves. They are produced by a magnetron tube within the oven. A fan or stirrer distributes the microwaves throughout the oven. They bounce off the oven walls and hit the food from all sides. This causes the food molecules to rub against each other, which produces friction. The friction creates the heat that cooks the food. If you rub your hands together rapidly, they will become

REINFORCEMENT: Have students interview a parent or neighbor who has a microwave oven to discuss reasons why the person enjoys cooking with a microwave. What prompted that person to buy one?

REINFORCEMENT: Demonstrate use of the microwave oven in your foods lab. Explain the setting and timer.

 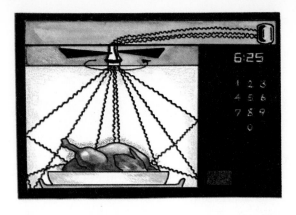

Convection ovens use fans to circulate heated air. Microwave ovens cause food to vibrate, thus creating heat.

warm. This is an example of heat produced by friction.

Microwave ovens today have special features that earlier models did not have. Several power settings are available, and computerized controls allow you to select different processes. Some ovens have a temperature probe. This senses the internal temperature of food and turns off the power when it is done. Some microwave ovens also have a sensor to measure the level of moisture given off by cooking food. In some ovens, microwaves enter from both sides, allowing you to cook several foods at the same time.

Containers and Utensils

To cook food in a microwave oven, you need special cookware that transfers the microwaves. You cannot use metal, which reflects the microwaves and prevents them from reaching the food.

You can use glass, paper, and some plastics, as well as china or pottery with-

out gold, silver, or other metal trim. It is best to test ceramic containers before cooking in them, since the glaze might contain metals. To do this, put the container in the microwave oven. Place a cup of cold water next to it. Turn on the power to high for 1 minute and 15 seconds. If the dish is hot and the water is warm, do not use the dish. If the dish is cool and the water in the cup is hot, you can use the dish.

Paper towels or napkins help retain heat and absorb extra moisture. Use white paper towels. You do not need to use those especially for microwave ovens. Waxed paper also retains heat and allows some moisture to evaporate.

Cooking bags and freezer bags are good for holding in steam and moisture. You should pierce them with a knife, however, to allow some steam to escape. If the ties that come with plastic bags contain metal, do not use them. Cut a strip of plastic from the end of the bag and tie it loosely.

Plastic wrap can act as a lid. Make sure the wrap you use is safe for the microwave, because some brands can melt. Make slits in the wrap for steam to escape. Foam cups and plates are useful for thawing foods in a microwave oven.

If you check your kitchen, you may find that you already have enough cookware suitable for a microwave oven. Items like glass pie dishes and casseroles are especially useful. If you do need to buy microwave cookware, keep these guidelines in mind.

- Look for labels indicating that the item is approved for microwave cooking.
- Look for containers that are round and deep. Food can overcook in the corners of square or rectangular containers.
- Select containers that are made of durable materials.
- Select containers that you can use for several kinds of food.
- Select containers with handles so that you can move food around easily.
- Select containers that can also be used for freezing.

Principles of Microwave Cookery

There are advantages and disadvantages to microwave cooking. As well as saving time and energy, microwave ovens are easy to clean and do not heat up a room. Because foods do not require water for cooking, they retain more nutrients. On the minus side, not all foods can be cooked in less time. A large item like a turkey can actually take longer. Some foods, such as yeast breads, look and taste better if cooked in a conventional oven. You will learn through experience which method of cooking is better for certain foods and types of cooking. In addition, some people are concerned about the possibility of radiation from microwave ovens.

Before using a microwave oven, become familiar with the way it works. Read the owner's manual and study microwave recipes. Do not begin to cook, however, until you are familiar with the basic principles of microwave cookery.

Be sure to select safe, durable cookware that can be used for a variety of purposes.

Read the cooking instructions first. Then select your settings.

Uses of a Microwave

Microwave ovens are used for cooking, heating, and defrosting foods. When cooking, you are likely to have the best results with foods that normally cook quickly. If a long cooking period is needed, you may have difficulty controlling the rate of cooking. This can affect the quality of the final product. For some slow-cooking foods such as turkey or roast beef, you may wish to use a conventional stove.

Microwave ovens usually heat foods satisfactorily. Foods like breads and pastries heat quickly. Some foods, such as casseroles, may need to be stirred or allowed to stand for a few minutes after reheating. This permits the heat to move from the outside to the center of the food without overcooking the edges.

Most microwave ovens have low power settings for defrosting. Foods like breads and cakes thaw quickly; meats and casseroles take longer. Large cuts of meat need to stand for a little while after being removed from the oven. This gives the center of the meat time to thaw without letting the outer part cook. Smaller portions of meat will defrost quickly and remain juicy. One pound (.45 kg) of hamburger takes only about five minutes to defrost.

Cooking Time

Several factors affect the cooking time in a microwave oven. Keep these guidelines in mind.

- The colder the food, the longer it will take to heat.
- The larger the size or amount of food, the longer the cooking, heating, or defrosting time will be.
- Dense foods like meat need longer than porous foods like bread.
- Foods with a high moisture content require more cooking time than foods low in moisture.
- Foods low in fat or sugar take longer than foods that are high in fat or sugar.
- Thin, flat foods heat more quickly than chunky, thick foods.

Cooking Techniques

You need to use certain techniques to be successful in microwave cooking. The following are some of the most important.

- Stir or rearrange food to distribute the heat evenly. This moves the warmer

What happens when people forget to stir food that is cooking?

food inward to the center and the colder food outward from the center. Casseroles and puddings are the kinds of foods you should stir. Whole vegetables and cupcakes are examples of foods that should be rearranged.

- Turn foods to redistribute the heat within the food. Turn meat or poultry over. Reposition cakes or soufflés by moving them a quarter or half turn.
- You should cover some foods to speed cooking or to prevent drying out. Use a lid, an inverted plate, or a plastic wrap to provide a tight cover. (Plastic covers should not touch hot foods.) Paper towels and napkins provide a loose cover.
- Allow some foods to stand after they are removed from the oven. This enables the heat from the outside of the food to reach the center without overcooking the outer edges. Dense foods such as large cuts of meat benefit most from standing time.

Adapting Recipes

There are many microwave recipes available, but you can also adapt some of your conventional recipes. In general, foods can be cooked in a microwave oven in about one-quarter of the time required for conventional cooking. After you have figured out how much time is needed, subtract a little more time. This will prevent overcooking. You can always cook the food a little more if needed.

When adapting a recipe, keep in mind the factors that affect cooking time and the special techniques of microwave cooking. In addition, the following tips may be helpful.

- Precook vegetables that are part of a recipe. Foods like onions, potatoes, carrots, and a number of other vegetables,

Many recipes can be easily adapted for the microwave oven.

Chapter 15/*Food Preparation*   **355**

A microwave oven is easy to clean. Spills don't bake on.

will not cook thoroughly if used raw.
- Reduce liquids in the recipe by about one-quarter. Moisture does not evaporate as easily in a microwave oven.
- Reduce seasonings slightly. Taste at the end of the cooking time and add more seasonings if needed.
- Use a large container so that food has room to boil up.

Care of a Microwave Oven

The owner's manual will include instructions for caring for a microwave. In general, care is easy. Spattered foods do not bake into the oven since it is not heated. You can clean surfaces with mild detergent and water. Do not use abrasive cleaning products. Remove the drip tray at the oven bottom and wash it in warm water and detergent. Put it back correctly before you use the oven again.

Safety and Microwave Ovens

Keep these safety precautions in mind when you use a microwave oven.

- Pierce the skins of whole fruits and vegetables to allow steam to escape during cooking.
- Stir or pour liquids immediately before heating to allow air to mix in.
- Use only popcorn designed for microwave ovens.
- Do not use containers that have small openings, such as ketchup bottles or baby food jars.
- Do not use metal objects or objects with metal decorations.
- Do not use a microwave oven for canning foods.
- Do not use recycled paper products, as they may contain small pieces of metal, which could cause the paper to catch fire. Also, do not use newspapers or paper towels that contain nylon.
- Do not cook eggs in the shell.
- If a fire occurs in the oven, push the stop button and leave the door closed until the fire is out.

For Review

1. What is the difference between a conventional oven and a convection oven?
2. What causes food to cook in a microwave oven?
3. Why shouldn't you use metal cookware in a microwave oven?
4. Name two advantages and two disadvantages of microwave cooking.

Learning to Manage

Bakers' Blues

Look back at the conversation on page 328. Now read below how the class manages to solve its cooking crises. Then answer the questions that follow.

As Joanne's kitchen group gathered to figure out where it had gone wrong, John's group and Dionne's group called out that they too had dessert disasters.

"Make that four out of four, Mrs. Thomas!" Kate moaned. Our cake grew and oozed all over the place!"

"Well, class, luckily we have one more class before the FHA bake sale on Saturday. Let's go over the entire recipe and baking process before we start over."

Each group sat down and talked about what it had done and looked at the recipe again. They all thought they had been careful. As they looked over the directions and ingredients, however, each group discovered where mistakes had been made.

Kate's group had made two errors that had caused the batter to overflow. First, Pete realized that he had put in twice the amount of baking powder called for in the recipe. This had made the cake rise too much. Also, Jean had greased and floured a pan that was slightly smaller than the one the recipe called for. As a result, the cake had overflowed.

The members of Joanne's group talked over their procedure. They discovered that they hadn't added any baking powder at all, so the cake hadn't risen.

Dionne's group went through each step of the recipe. They had used regular flour instead of cake flour; that had made the cake too heavy. They also realized that they had set their oven temperature at 325° F instead of 350° F.

John's group had used all the correct ingredients, the right pans, and had baked at 350° F. Nobody had set the timer, however, and the cake had been taken out too soon. The group also forgot to test for doneness, so the cake had sunk.

Mrs. Thomas asked all the groups to write a short report on their results.

"I'll see you all Friday when we'll bake those perfect cakes for the sale," she said.

"And this time we'll follow *all* of the directions!" Joanne exclaimed.

Questions

1. Choose a basic cake recipe from a cookbook. Be sure it calls for simple ingredients you have at home. Make the cake and write a brief report on the results.
2. Make a plan for a bake sale. Choose recipes and estimate your costs for ingredients. Plan to make everything from scratch rather than using mixes. What would you have to charge for each cake to make a 10 percent profit?

Chapter 15 Review

Summary

Success in the kitchen requires a work plan and an understanding of standard recipe terms. Successful cooking also requires an understanding of how to prepare different kinds of food. Milk and cheese should be cooked by low heat to avoid problems like curdling and toughness. Vegetables and fruits should be cooked in small amounts of water to retain nutrients. Special techniques are used for cooking eggs in the shell and for adding eggs to other foods.

Meat and poultry can be cooked by dry heat, by moist heat, and with fat. Fish can be broiled, baked, poached, or fried. Proper preparation of grain products helps ensure texture, flavor, and nutritional value. Different forms of fats and sugar affect foods in different ways.

Microwave cooking requires special methods, equipment, and techniques. Safety precautions should be observed when microwave ovens are used.

Vocabulary

Complete each of the following sentences with the correct word from the vocabulary list below.

emulsion (p. 337) work plan (p. 329)
microwaves (p. 351) curdling (p. 336)

1. An _____ consists of oil and another liquid mixed together and beaten so that the ingredients do not separate.
2. A step-by-step guide for organizing food preparation activities and tasks is called a _____ _____.
3. _____ are tiny waves of energy that can be used for cooking.
4. _____ occurs when milk separates into liquid and small lumps.

Questions

•• 1. What is the purpose of a work plan in food preparation?
•• 2. How would you adapt a recipe for two people so that there would be enough food for four?
• 3. What would happen if you roasted an egg in its shell in the oven?
•• 4. Why is it advisable to prepare fruits and vegetables in their skins?
• 5. What happens to cut fruit when it is exposed to air?
•• 6. Why is steaming a good way to prepare vegetables?
• 7. What do we mean when we say that eggs are an emulsifying agent?
•• 8. Name a cut of meat that does not need much cooking time. Explain your choice.
• 9. Explain the following methods of cooking as they apply to meat: frying, braising, roasting and broiling.

The dots represent skill levels required to answer each question or complete each activity:

• requires recall and comprehension
•• requires application and analysis
••• requires synthesis and evaluation

10. What kind of meat should always be well done?

11. Why does fish require only a short time to cook?

12. Should you rinse rice before or after cooking? Explain your answer.

13. What is brown sugar?

14. Why can you use a glass container for cooking in a microwave oven?

15. Why should food cooked in a microwave be stirred or rearranged?

Skill Activities

Many more activities are contained in the annotations within this chapter.

 1. Decision Making Decide on a menu for a chicken dinner to be served to four people. First, choose a chicken recipe that matches your skill, time and budget requirements. Decide what side dishes you will serve with the chicken. Make sure you select foods with a variety of color and texture. Make a list of all the ingredients you will need to prepare the meal. Think about the kind of chicken you will have to buy to suit your recipe. Make out a work plan for your meal. Share your information with members of the class.

2. Communication Make a poster showing the proper use and care of the microwave oven. Be sure to include safety guidelines that are common to most oven models. The guidelines should indicate what foods, cookware, and other materials should not be heated in a microwave oven. Your poster could also show a list of foods that are most successfully prepared by microwave cooking. Display your completed poster next to the microwave oven at home or at school.

 3. Laboratory Select a vegetable to prepare in two different ways. Boil one portion of the vegetable on top of a gas or electric stove. Cook the other portion in a microwave oven. Compare the two cooked portions for color, texture and flavor. Which cooking method do you prefer? Which preparation method is better for retaining the vegetable's nutritional value?

4. Laboratory Prepare individual menus for people on special diets. Do the research necessary to prepare a written menu for a balanced dinner for each person. Uncle Bob is on a salt-free diet. Your cousin Carol is on a low-sugar diet. Your grandfather is on a low-cholesterol diet.

Each person will be coming for dinner on a separate occasion. Write out a separate menu for each dinner. Try to make each special-diet dinner well-balanced, appealing, and delicious. Bring your menus to class. Share your ideas.

Chapter 16
Meals and Manners

Vocabulary

The dialogue below introduces ''Party Planning,'' the Learning to Manage feature in this chapter. The case study is continued and the situation discussed further on page 381. See page T113 for teaching suggestions.

''We want this to be the best surprise dinner party ever.''

''Mrs. White will be so impressed that we did it all ourselves.''

''We'd better decide on committees now. She retires in a month and we have 20 teachers to entertain!''

''We have a lot of planning to do to make sure it's a great meal.''

Section 16.1
Breakfast

As you read, think about:

■ the importance of eating a good breakfast. (p. 361)

■ the variety of good breakfast foods. (p. 361)

■ how to make some good breakfast foods. (p. 362)

Great meals, including breakfast, always need planning. The word breakfast means to "break the fast." After sleeping through the night, you have not eaten for 10 or 12 hours. Your body needs fuel for the day ahead. Eating breakfast can help your performance at school by supplying you with necessary nutrients.

Have you ever tried making a quick, tasty breakfast in a blender?

Quick Breakfast Ideas

If breakfast is so important, why do people skip it? One reason is time. Some people are in too much of a hurry in the mornings to fix breakfast. People also get bored with the usual breakfast foods and decide not to eat at all. By using quick breakfast ideas and a variety of foods, you can make breakfast enjoyable.

Some people like a traditional breakfast of juice, cereal, toast, and maybe eggs. However, if you aren't one of those people, eat what appeals to you. Have some fruit, a sandwich, or a cheeseburger. Remember to avoid too many sweets. Otherwise, any food can be breakfast food.

Leftovers can provide a good breakfast. Perhaps you had fried beans and tortillas

for supper the night before. Add juice and a glass of milk, and you have a meal that is both nutritious and quick to prepare. Pizza can be popped into the oven and heated while you are dressing for school. With fruit and milk, your meal is balanced. Another quick way to fix breakfast is to make a meal in a blender.

Eggs for Breakfast

Eggs are a traditional breakfast food. Most medical experts do not recommend eating eggs every day due to their cholesterol content. Many people, however, like to have them a few times each week. Scrambled eggs are especially popular and only take a few minutes to prepare.

RETEACHING: It is important to include one food from each of the four main food groups in every meal. Have students give an example of a breakfast that would include all four.

REINFORCEMENT: Ask students to plan a breakfast menu that includes two traditional breakfast foods.

SCRAMBLED EGGS

3 eggs
2 Tbs. (30 mL) milk or water
½ tsp. (2.5 mL) salt (optional)
pepper
1 Tbs. (15 mL) butter or margarine

1. Crack eggs into a mixing bowl. Add milk or water and seasonings. Beat with a fork until mixture is blended.
2. Heat butter or margarine in a skillet until it is bubbly or golden brown.

3. Pour egg mixture into skillet and cook slowly. Use a spoon or spatula to move eggs about gently turning if necessary and allowing mixture to thicken in large portions.
4. When eggs have thickened but are still soft, remove them to a serving platter.
5. Garnish with parsley.

Yield: 2 servings.

Scrambled eggs are a snap and a good source of protein.

This recipe for scrambled eggs makes two generous servings.

Omelets are also a popular food. They are good for breakfast and other meals as well. A plain omelet has the same ingredients as scrambled eggs. However, it is cooked in the form of a thick, light pancake. A plain omelet is cooked in a skillet and folded in half when done. A filling, such as shredded cheese or a sauce, can be added just before the omelet is folded. A fluffy omelet is made by separating the eggs and beating the whites. The egg whites are then folded into the yolks. A fluffy omelet is baked in an oven.

Making Quick Breads

There is nothing like the taste of bread fresh from the oven to help you start off the day. Quick breads offer a tasty variety of breakfast foods. These include waffles, pancakes, muffins, tortillas, biscuits, and corn bread. Quick breads also include some loaf breads, such as banana bread, and coffee cakes. Although they are all good freshly baked, loaf breads and muffins can be even better when reheated.

Using the Muffin Method

The *muffin method* is used to prepare muffins, pancakes, and other batters that you pour or drop. The basic ingredients

Muffins are especially tempting when they're fresh from the oven.

BANANA BREAD

1 c. (250 mL) flour
1 tsp. (5 mL) baking powder
½ tsp. (2.5 mL) baking soda
1 egg
½ c. (125 mL) sugar
¼ c. (60 mL) margarine (softened)
⅓ c. (80 mL) milk plus 1½ tsp.
  (7.5 mL) white vinegar
2 mashed bananas

1. Preheat oven to 350°

2. Sift flour, baking powder and baking soda together.
3. Cream margarine and sugar. until light and fluffy.
4. Add egg and milk mixture. Beat well.
5. Add flour mixture alternately with bananas, a small amount at a time. Beat after each addition until smooth.
6. Pour into a well-greased loaf pan and bake for 45 minutes. Yield: 1 loaf

For flavor and nutrition, try this recipe for a quick banana bread. It's easy and delicious.

are usually flour, baking powder or baking soda, salt, sugar, milk, eggs, and oil. These are the basic steps for making quick breads by the muffin method.

1. Measure and sift the dry ingredients together in a bowl. When using whole-grain flour, mix dry ingredients by stirring rather than sifting.
2. Mix the liquid ingredients together in a separate bowl.
3. Pour the liquid ingredients all at once into the dry ingredients. Stir *only* until the dry ingredients are just moistened. Overmixing can cause toughness in the baked product. The batter should be lumpy.
4. When making muffins and bread, grease the muffin tins or loaf pan and dust with flour. Then spoon in the batter. Muffin tins should be no more than two-thirds full. Fill them evenly so they will cook evenly.
5. Bake muffins and bread according to the recipe. To test for doneness, insert a wooden toothpick in the center. When the toothpick comes out clean, it means that the bread or muffins are done.

Additional ingredients give a particular bread its distinctive flavor and texture. For example, a recipe for oatmeal muffins would include oatmeal and perhaps raisins or nuts. The muffins might also be sprinkled with a topping, such as cinnamon and sugar or chopped nuts.

Pancakes and Waffles When making pancakes or waffles by the muffin method, pour small amounts of batter onto a hot, greased skillet or waffle iron. Pancakes should be turned when the bubbles on top start to break. They are done when the underside is golden.

See page T114 for answers.

For Review

1. Explain why breakfast is such an important meal.
2. What foods are included in a traditional American breakfast?
3. Name five kinds of quick breads.
4. Describe the muffin method.

Do you wrap your lunch foods to keep them fresh?

Section 16.2
Lunch and Snacks

As you read, think about:

■ how to pack a healthy lunch.   (p. 364)

■ how to plan for special lunches. (p. 365)

■ how to plan nutritious snacks.   (p. 366)

For some people, lunch is the biggest meal of the day, and supper is lighter. This is actually a good idea. It allows plenty of time during the active hours for the body to digest food and burn calories. Snacks between meals supply additional energy if needed.

Packing a Good Lunch

Whether your own lunch is light or heavy, it should include foods from the four major food groups. If you are not watching

your weight, you may also wish to add something you like from the fats and sweets group.

The prepared lunches served in schools are planned to be nutritious. If you prepare your own lunch, however, it is up to you to select wisely.

When packing a lunch, remember that hot foods must be kept hot and cold foods cold. Some foods, such as meat, milk, and eggs, spoil quickly at room temperature. That means they may taste all right but can still make you sick. Here are some suggestions for keeping lunch foods fresh and appetizing.

• Use vacuum bottles and containers for keeping foods hot or cold. They are especially good for soups, salads, milk, and juice. They are also a good way to pack some leftovers, such as casseroles. Just heat up the food before you leave for school and put it in the vacuum

Did You Know?

Instant soup is older than the United States! An interesting eighteenth-century version of instant soup was called "pocket soup," because it could be carried in a pouch or "pocket." A 1753 recipe for veal pocket soup involved boiling a leg of veal until the liquid thickened. After being strained and gelled, the concentrated jelly became soup again with the addition of hot water and salt.

REINFORCEMENT: Ask students to plan lunch meals for one week that a preschooler could take to school or day care in a lunchbox. Meals should be appealing and nutritious.

ENRICHMENT: Ask students to exchange the lunch menus that were planned for the preschooler. Each student should evaluate every lunch to see if it includes a food from the four main food groups. Have students add foods for any of the four food groups that were missed.

364   Unit 4/*Foods and Nutrition*

SOMETHING DIFFERENT LUNCH

10. Crackers
10 cheese wedges
3 oz. (848g) peanuts
3 oz. (848g) raisins
melon slice
cucumber slices
radish garnish
8 oz. (224g) milk

1. Arrange each food in a creative and attractive way on a luncheon plate. Garnish with radish.
2. Pour milk into a drinking glass.

Yield: 1 lunch

How often do you try something different for lunch?

container. You can then enjoy hot food as part of your lunch.

- Add a frozen item to your lunch to keep everything cool. For example, you might freeze juice in a plastic container with a tight lid. (Leave room for the liquid to expand as it freezes.) It will turn into a cold drink by lunchtime and keep the rest of your lunch fresh. Another way to keep foods cool is to buy a sealed container of freezable gel. You can reuse this many times. Keep it in the freezer until you are ready to use it.
- Wrap foods with materials that will help to keep them fresh. Some good choices are plastic wrap and bags, aluminum foil, waxed paper, and plastic containers with lids.

- Pack certain items separately and combine them at lunchtime. For example, a salad tastes best if the dressing is added just before you eat it. You can put the dressing in a separate small container. Your lettuce will stay crisp in a small plastic bag. Even some sandwiches will taste better if you pack the filling separate from the bread.

Lunch Recipes

During a busy day filled with school and other activities, you may not have much time for lunch. Sometimes it is nice to plan a special lunch on a weekend or holiday when you have more time. You might, for example, plan a picnic. Or, you could invite several friends to your home for lunch. Perhaps you would like to prepare lunch for one good friend. The "something different" lunch recipe on this page is one idea.

Look in cookbooks for others. Soups and salads make great lunches if you are

Did You Know?

You can make your own healthy orange drink refresher. Mix orange juice and carbonated water (seltzer or club soda), using either equal amounts or slightly more juice than water. You'll get nutritious juice and bubbly refreshment, with none of the sweeteners or additives of commercial sodas.

tired of the usual sandwich. You can add variety by combining foods in different ways. For example, you might combine fresh fruit and plain yogurt. Another combination might be leftover rice, vegetables, and meat. Use your imagination, and you can have lunches that are both nutritious and interesting.

Snacks

Like other meals, snacks should be planned carefully. Many popular snack foods, such as potato chips and candy bars, are high in calories but low in nutrients. Look for snacks that are both nutritious and tasty.

Snacks at Home

Foods like fresh fruits, fresh vegetables, and nuts have a nice crisp texture and are easy to store at home. Popcorn is a nutritious snack that can be prepared in minutes. If you like rich foods, try cheese, bananas, or avocados. Fruit juices or whole fruits like apples and papayas can satisfy a sweet tooth. For example, you can spear fruits to make a fruit kabob.

Do you vary your snacks? Are there some possibilities for new textures and flavors that you're overlooking?

Snacks to Go

You can usually find snacks when you are away from home. Even if there is no store nearby, snacks are often available in machines. However, many of these are likely to be sugary soft drinks or candy. Plan to take snacks with you so that you can choose nutritious foods. Fruit is easy to carry. If you want something a little more filling, take along a peanut butter sandwich. When you go to a baseball game, you can take your own peanuts or popcorn. If you like to snack during the school day, take some healthy snacks with you.

Fast-food Snack Choices

People often stop at a fast-food restaurant for snacks such as fries, little fruit pies, shakes, or soft drinks. However, such foods are high in sodium, fat, or sugar. Fast-food restaurants now offer more choices. You can often get a salad in a small container, or there might even be a salad bar. Rather than choosing the usual snacks all the time, try a salad for a change. A nice cold carton of milk is also refreshing and nutritious.

See page T115 for answers.

For Review

1. When packing a lunch, why is it important to keep hot foods hot and cold foods cold?
2. How can you keep lettuce crisp when you want to include it in your school lunch?
3. Name three nutritious snacks that you can prepare easily.

NOTE: A snack-to-go that has recently become popular is juice in a box. These boxes need no refrigeration and are a nutritious alternative to soda.

PHOTO: Discuss with students what kinds of things make a dinner with their families particularly enjoyable for them.

Dinner is often a time for families to relax and discuss the day.

Section 16.3
Dinner

As you read, think about:

■ the importance of eating a healthy dinner every day. (p. 368)

■ how to prepare nutritious and enjoyable dinners for one person. (p. 369)

In this country, dinner is traditionally the largest meal of the day. Many people think of evening as dinnertime, but dinner is served at noon in some areas. Customs differ in other parts of the world. In Europe, for example, people who live outside cities often eat dinner in the afternoon. Many families in this country serve dinner in the afternoon on Sundays and holidays. In this case, the lighter evening meal is called supper. Whatever customs your own family follows, dinner is an important meal.

ENRICHMENT: Have students interview a member of three different families to compare dinner times, customs the family follows, and types of foods they typically eat.

ENCHILADAS

12 Corn tortillas
½ lb. (225g) ground beef
½ lb. (225g) Monteray Jack cheese
1 large onion, chopped coarsely
1 clove garlic, chopped fine
1 16 oz. (450g) tomato sauce
½ Tsp. (2.5 mL) sugar
1 tsp. (5 mL) ground cumin
1 c. (250 mL) water

1. Preheat oven to 350°

2. Brown beef, onion and garlic in a saucepan.
3. Add tomato sauce, sugar, cumin and water and stir. Allow mixture to simmer on very low heat for an hour.
4. Divide cheese into 12 slices.
5. Soften tortillas by gently placing them in the sauce and turning once. Place softened tortillas into a lightly greased, shallow baking pan.
6. Spoon sauce and one slice of cheese into each tortilla and roll up. Pour remaining sauce over tortillas, cover with foil and bake for 40 minutes.
7. Serve with shredded lettuce and refried beans.

How does this recipe satisfy your nutritional requirements?

A Nutritious Dinner

Several elements work together to make dinner a healthy meal. One is the kind and amount of food you eat. Another is the atmosphere, or mood of the setting, in which you eat it.

Dinner should include foods from the four food groups. A well-planned meal will provide needed protein, vitamins, and minerals. The main dish at dinner is usually meat, poultry, fish, or occasionally a cheese or egg dish. Along with these protein dishes, other foods are chosen to complement the main dish. These other foods often include a vegetable; rice, pasta, or bread; a salad; and milk or another beverage. Dinner may also include a dessert. Fruits, custards, and milk puddings are good choices, as they help fill your nutrient needs. Sometimes an *appetizer* (AP–peh–ty–zer) is served before the main part of the meal. An appetizer should be something light, such as a clear soup, fruit, or fruit juice.

How Much Dinner?

Dinner does not need to be a large meal in order to be nutritious. In fact, many health professionals recommend a light dinner, especially if you are eating late in the evening. Your body needs time to burn calories and digest the food before you go to bed. To judge the amount of dinner you need, consider what you have already eaten during the day. Perhaps you had a large meal at lunch and maybe a snack as well. Then you might want only a salad, bread, and milk for dinner. Just keep the Daily Food Guide in mind and make sure to have any foods you are still lacking.

Time for Family Dinner

Dinner is an important time for families to relax together and talk about the day's events. However, varied schedules often make it hard, or even impossible, for the entire family to gather at dinnertime. If this is the case in your family, try to have dinner with at least one other family member. No matter how many or how few people eat together, try to make dinner a time that is unrushed. This will make the dinner atmosphere more enjoyable.

Dinner for One

Many single people must frequently eat alone. People in families sometimes also eat alone, because of different schedules. If you find yourself alone for dinner, you may be tempted to skip it or have a snack instead. Fixing dinner may seem too much trouble. However, there are some efficient ways to prepare dinner for one.

Tips for Preparing Food

You may find the following tips helpful.

- Buy bags of frozen vegetables so that you can cook small portions and reseal the bag for later use. This saves money and avoids waste.
- Buy small amounts of fresh fruits and vegetables that you can enjoy while they are still at the peak of freshness.
- Buy larger packages of foods like poultry and meat. Freeze unused portions in individual packages for later use. Mark each package with the name of the food and the date.

Don't skip dinner! Set aside time to eat it, rather than eating on the run. Try to sit in pleasant surroundings while you eat. Plan as attractive and nutritious a meal as you would if you were having company.

ENRICHMENT: Ask students to make a list of things to consider while shopping if they are preparing dinner for one.

PHOTO: Explain to your students that stir-frying is a method of preparing vegetables that requires very little cooking time.

Eating alone gives you the chance to prepare exactly what you want.

Dinner Recipes for One

Homemade pizza and egg dishes make easy, nutritious meals for someone eating alone. So does a chef's salad, Waldorf salad, or a seafood salad. Stir-frying small amounts of vegetables and meats also makes a quick, healthy meal for one.

See page T115 for answers.
For Review
1. What kinds of foods should be included in a well-planned dinner?
2. Why do many health professionals recommend a light dinner?
3. Name three helpful tips for preparing dinner for one person.

NOTE: Pizza is a popular one-dish meal. *Pizza* is an Italian word meaning "a sort of cake." Pizza was made popular centuries ago by the king of Naples.

Leadership and Citizenship

Serving the Elderly

You know that a nutritious diet is necessary for a healthy life. Unfortunately, many elderly people living alone are unable to enjoy the healthy pleasures of good meals. They need some help from government or privately sponsored programs.

Many older people are eager to preserve their independence and live on their own. Some, however, are unable to travel to the market. For them, shopping assistance programs—in the form of van pickups or individual "chauffeuring"—can make a tremendous difference. For those who also have difficulty preparing meals, there are several kinds of food delivery services. Meals on Wheels and similar programs deliver hot, nutritious meals daily. Other programs bring well-balanced, packaged meals that require only heating or adding water.

For many elderly people who live alone, companionship at mealtimes is almost as important as the meals themselves. Some food delivery personnel will stay and keep the recipient company. But some older people, if they are physically able, prefer to go to senior centers or other group meal programs. There they find low-cost, nutritious meals and the friendship that can make mealtime the best time of day.

Are there any of these programs or centers for the elderly in your area?

Section 16.4

Table Settings and Etiquette

As you read, think about:

- the variety of ways in which meals can be served. (p. 370)
- the correct way to set a table. (p. 373)
- the value of table manners, both at home and elsewhere. (p. 376)
- the importance of knowing and observing the basic rules of restaurant etiquette. (p. 376)

People follow many customs at mealtime. Certain customs have developed over a period of time. They have come to be accepted as the correct way to act in certain situations. Such customs are called **etiquette** (*ET*–ih–ket). When you know the rules of etiquette, you do not have to wonder what to do or what to expect. You can relax and enjoy yourself.

These many customs include a variety of ways to set a table and to serve food. The rules of etiquette include manners, too. Good table manners are appropriate at all times, whether you are at home, visiting friends, or eating in a restaurant.

Serving Food

Families have their own customs concerning the way a meal is served. Your family may serve food one way on an everyday basis and another way on special occasions. There are certain ways food is served at formal events, such as teas or

REINFORCEMENT: Ask students to list two examples of table manners that their parents insist on at meal time.

Family-style serving is often informal. People serve their own portions from plates that everyone passes.

receptions. The way food is served depends on the kind of occasion, the type of food, and the time and space available. The number of people being served and the number helping with preparations must also be considered.

Family-style Service

Family style is a simple and popular way to serve food. The table is set with plates and *flatware,* or eating utensils, at each person's place. The food is put in serving dishes with serving utensils beside them. Dishes are passed around and people serve themselves. To avoid confusion, food should be passed in one direction.

DISCUSS: What flatware is required at a meal of spaghetti, meatballs, salad, and bread with butter?

Plate Service

Plate service means that food is brought to the table on individual plates from the kitchen. The plates might be served by one person or by each family member. This kind of service saves on cleanup time, as there are no serving dishes to wash. It also helps to control portions. Plate service is used in restaurants as well as in homes.

Formal Service

This type of service is rarely used in homes, as it requires one or more people to serve the food. Formal service may be

REINFORCEMENT: Seat six students at a dining room table and have them demonstrate to the rest of the class the correct way to pass serving dishes and condiments.

used in restaurants for banquets and on other formal occasions.

The table setting in formal service is elegant and elaborate, and there are usually several courses. There might be three pieces of flatware on each side of the plate, as different flatware is used for each course. After the first course, which might be soup or an appetizer, the plates are removed by the people who are serving. The next course is then served on its own plate.

Head-of-the-table service is a form of formal service. It is sometimes used for special occasions in homes. The person sitting at the head of the table serves the food and passes it to others. Plates and serving dishes are at the end of the table near the server. Sometimes one person serves the main dish. A second person then serves the vegetables, or the rest of

Have you ever attended a buffet? What kinds of foods were served?

the food is served family style. Salad might be served by a person at the table or might be placed beside each person. Foods like bread and butter are passed.

Serving Tips

These are some serving guidelines that can be helpful.

- Pass all of the serving dishes around the table in the same direction (usually clockwise).
- If you are waiting on table, always offer food from the person's left. Use your left hand.
- When clearing the table while people are still seated, remove serving dishes first. Remove each person's dishes and flatware from the person's left. Use your left hand and change the plates to your right hand.
- Remove any flatware not needed for dessert. Check to make sure each person has flatware for dessert.

Buffet Service

Buffet service works well for a group of people. Buffets can be very informal or very elegant. The food is put on a table or buffet and guests help themselves. Plates, flatware, and napkins are also on the table. After serving themselves, guests take their plates and find a comfortable place to sit. Snack trays or card tables are useful at buffets. It is best to serve easy-to-eat foods like casseroles.

A convenient way to arrange a buffet is to stack the plates on the table where guests are to begin. Place the main dish

On what occasions does your family use head-of-the-table service? Who does the serving?

next, followed by vegetables, salad, and rolls. Flatware, rolled up in napkins, can come last.

Buffets are suitable for outdoors as well as indoors. Paper plates can be used for informal buffets.

Teas and Receptions

Teas and receptions are held on special occasions, such as a graduation or wedding anniversary. They are also used for club parties or almost any large gathering. Guests usually come for a while, then leave to make room for others.

The food is served buffet style. Coffee is usually served at one end of a long table and tea at the other. Fruit punch might also be provided. Small sandwiches, fancy cookies, candies, and nuts are attractively arranged on serving plates and trays.

ENRICHMENT: Have students plan a tea and invite the school principal, vice-principal, and each department head. They should plan a menu that includes punch, tea, sandwiches, and cookies.

For large groups, different plates of the same food can be placed on each side of the table. This allows people to move in two lines rather than one.

Setting the Table

The place where one person sits at the table is the place setting, or **cover.** The cover includes all of the dishes, flatware, glasses, and napkin the person will use. It is best to allow 20 to 24 inches (50 to 60 cm) for each cover.

Guidelines

Follow the guidelines on the next page for setting a table. As you read them, refer to the photograph of a table setting shown on the following page.

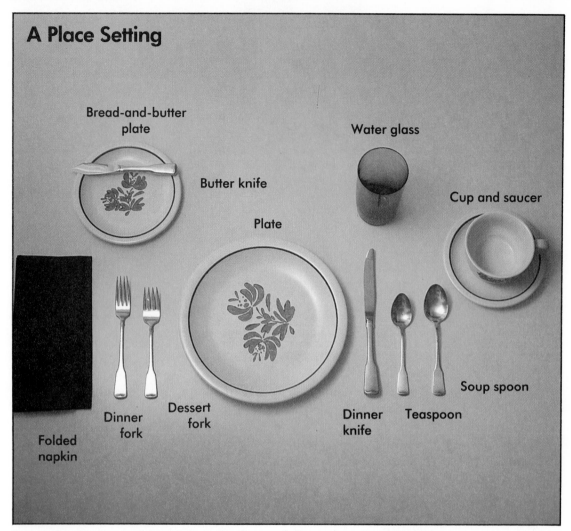

A Place Setting

Bread-and-butter plate

Water glass

Butter knife

Cup and saucer

Plate

Dinner fork

Dessert fork

Dinner knife

Teaspoon

Soup spoon

Folded napkin

Does this look confusing? It isn't if you follow the simple steps provided on these pages.

1. Place the plate in the center of the cover, or leave space for a plate.
2. Place the flatware on either side of the plate according to its order of use. The flatware to be used first is on the outside. The flatware to be used last is next to the plate. Flatware should be placed approximately 1 inch (2.5 cm) from the edge of the table.
3. Put the forks to the left of the plate, with the tines, or prongs, facing up. When using more than one fork, arrange them in the order in which they will be used. If the salad will be eaten before the main course, the salad fork should be on the outside. If it will be eaten with the meal, place the salad fork to the right of the dinner fork. A dessert fork, if used, should be placed next to the plate.

4. If no knife will be used, place the dinner fork to the right of the plate.

5. Put the dinner knife to the right of the plate. The cutting edge should be next to the plate. If a butter knife is used, place it across the butter plate with the handle to the right. You can also put it vertically, along the right side of the butter plate.

6. Place the spoons, bowls up, to the right of the dinner knife. Put the teaspoon to the right of the knife. Soup is usually eaten first; the soup spoon should therefore be placed to the right of the teaspoon.

7. Put the folded napkin to the left of the fork. The open edges should be next to the left side of the fork. Napkins may also be placed on the dinner plate or in the space where it will go.

8. Put the water glass at the tip of the knife. Any other glass should be placed to the right of the water glass.

9. If a bread-and-butter plate is used, place it above the fork. If a salad plate is to be used at the same time, place it above the napkin. If a bread-and-butter plate is not used, the salad plate goes above the fork.

10. If a cup and saucer are used, place them to the right of the spoons. Arrange the cup handle so that it is parallel with the table edge.

When setting a table, be sure to handle flatware, dishes, and glasses carefully so that they will remain clean. Avoid touching the areas that will touch food. Hold flatware and cups by the handles and plates by the edges. Avoid touching the insides of glasses or bowls.

Centerpieces

Centerpieces are not necessary on a table, but they add an attractive touch. You could use a bowl of fresh flowers or a small potted plant. Your home probably includes other items that would make good centerpieces. Here are some ideas.

- fresh fruit in a basket
- fresh vegetables or gourds in a basket
- an arrangement of candles in candleholders
- a single large candle surrounded by greenery
- a craft object, such as a figurine, on a place mat

Whatever centerpiece you use, make sure it is not too tall. People have trouble talking across the table if they have to peer around a tall arrangement.

Add a splash of color and beauty to your table with some flowers.

Table Manners

Your table manners are both a reflection of you and a way to be considerate of others. The general rules that follow are basic to all meals.

- Before you enter the dining area, make sure that you are well groomed and appropriately dressed. You show consideration for the hosts when you arrive for a meal a few minutes before the scheduled time. Be sure to let your hosts know if you will be late.
- You should not go to the table until the meal is announced. Sit down from the left side of your chair. When the chair is properly placed, you do not need to move it to seat yourself.
- Place your napkin on your lap after you are seated. Use it throughout the meal to wipe your fingers and blot your lips.
- Sit straight with your shoulders back, your arms close to your sides, and your feet flat on the floor. Keep your hands in your lap when you are not eating. Keep your free hand in your lap as you eat your meal.
- Take cues from others at the table as to mealtime procedure. Remember not to put too much food in your mouth at once. Chew with your mouth closed, and do not talk with food in your mouth.
- Take your turn with conversation at the table. Keep it pleasant, and include topics of general interest to the group.
- Assist with passing food, but do not help yourself first unless asked to do so. Foods are generally passed to the right.
- When the meal has ended, place your napkin at the left of your plate.
- Thank the cook. Ask to be excused if

REINFORCEMENT: Have students role-play arriving at a restaurant, waiting to be seated, and sitting down.

Did You Know?

If you are invited to tea in England, you will probably be served a whole meal. English afternoon tea usually includes light sandwiches, breads, and pastry along with the beverage itself. If you are invited for tea in Japan, you will remove your shoes at the door. You will then kneel on the floor for a formal and beautiful ceremony that has remained unchanged for centuries.

you wish to leave the table while others are still seated.

Dining Out

People in this country are fond of eating out. Sometimes the reason is simple convenience. The person who does the cooking gets a break. At other times people go to a restaurant to celebrate a special occasion, such as a birthday. Whatever your reason for dining out, you have a wide choice, ranging from fast-food chains to elegant, formal restaurants. Along with different types of restaurants, there is also a range of prices.

Fast-food Restaurants

Fast-food chains became popular during the early 1960s. These chains are made up of identical restaurants in different

ENRICHMENT: Divide the class into groups and seat each group at a table. Explain to the groups that every student is responsible for maintaining three minutes of table conversation that will include everyone at the table. Give students a few minutes to prepare.

locations. They used to specialize in only one kind of food, such as hamburgers or fried chicken. Now, however, many fast-food chains are offering a larger selection of foods, such as breakfast or a salad bar.

The food is partially prepared before it is brought to fast-food restaurants. It is then usually cooked in batches and kept warm. People go to a counter and order. The food arrives quickly, and customers take their own trays to a free table. Containers for waste are usually provided to encourage customers to clear their places after eating.

These restaurants are inexpensive, convenient, and fast compared to other restaurants. They can, however, be very busy. The atmosphere is not always restful for eating. Also, the food choices are often high in fat and sodium.

Informal Restaurants

There are more informal restaurants than any other kind. This group includes cafeterias, diners, lunch counters, steak houses, and family restaurants. Some informal restaurants feature one kind of food, such as fish or ethnic dishes.

Dress can be informal. You have to wear a shirt and shoes, but neither a jacket nor a tie is required for men. As always, your clothes should be appropriate for the occasion.

In most informal restaurants, someone takes your order and serves the food. In cafeterias, you select the food and carry it on a tray to a table. Much of the food is prepared right in the restaurant kitchen. Some items, like breads or pie, may be brought in.

Good manners are also needed when paying the bill. How do you think the people at this table should be acting now?

DISCUSS: Talk about "favorite restaurants" and why students enjoy eating there. Is there one restaurant that they go to with their families for special occasions?

PHOTO: Emphasize that it is not impolite to check the bill for its correctness or to point out politely that it may be incorrect.

People act more formally in traditional restaurants. Knowing how to act can make you feel more secure.

Informal restaurants come in many price ranges. Most are more expensive than fast-food restaurants. The atmosphere can also vary. Some of the more informal restaurants are cramped and noisy, while others are comfortable and attractively decorated.

Formal Restaurants

Formal restaurants are the most traditional kind. They are also usually the most expensive, as they offer very special food and services. Some restaurants even feature strolling musicians and flaming desserts! The overall atmosphere might be quietly tasteful or very elegant.

Customers are expected to dress more formally than in some other kinds of restaurants. Appropriate dress for women includes dresses, suits, and dress slacks. Men are usually required to wear jackets and ties.

Going to a Restaurant

You may need to make a reservation before going to some restaurants. Making a **reservation** means calling in advance for a table. Not all restaurants accept or require reservations, but those that do usually cannot seat you without one. Even if a reservation is not required, you should make one when the restaurant is likely to be crowded.

To make the reservation, call the restaurant on the telephone. Give your name, the date and time you wish to eat, and the number of people who will be eating. You may also wish to ask about the menu, the general price range, and appropriate dress.

After arriving at the restaurant, you will usually be greeted by someone who will seat you. After giving your name, follow the person to your table. He or she may pull out a chair. One person in your group should sit down as long as the choice of table is agreeable to all.

In less formal restaurants, you may be expected to choose a table and seat yourself. Look for a sign directing you to do this. If you are unsure of what to do, ask before seating yourself.

Ordering from a Menu

The menu listing the food may be one page or several pages. Different courses are grouped together. For example, all of the desserts will be listed in one place. A number of courses are listed on menus in more formal restaurants. These include appetizers, soups, entrées, salads, vegetables, and desserts. The appetizer, or first course, might be tomato juice or a shrimp cocktail. Some people skip the appetizer and go on to the **entrée** (*AHN*–tray), or main course. This might be meat or fish.

You may be able to order a complete meal for one price, or you might have to order each item separately. A complete meal served for a set price is called **table d'hôte** (tah–bul *DOTE*). Another name for this is **prix fixe** (pree *FEEX*), which means fixed price. When you order a complete meal, you get several courses.

You are ordering **à la carte** (ah–la–*CART*) when you order each item separately. In this case, each item is separately priced on the menu.

In some restaurants, you can order either *à la carte* or *table d'hôte*.

After you have studied the menu, the person waiting on your table will ask if you are ready to order. This raises the question of who should order first. The waiter or waitress might direct the question to a specific person. If not, the important thing is for someone to go ahead and order. If you order first, the person on your left should order next, and so on. Also, ordering your courses in sequence will be less confusing for the person serving you.

Restaurant Behavior

These guidelines can help make dining out a pleasant experience for you and other people.

- Avoid noisy conversation that can disturb others.
- If you wish to sample someone else's food, do not reach over and spear it. Instead, ask your companion to put some food on your fork or the corner of your plate.
- If you need to get the attention of your waiter or waitress, wave your hand gently. If necessary, quietly say, "Waiter" or "Waitress." If the person isn't nearby, ask another waiter or waitress to get the person serving you.
- If you do not understand something on the menu, ask for an explanation.
- If flatware or napkins are missing, ask your waiter or waitress to replace them.
- Ask your waiter or waitress for help if something is spilled.

RETEACHING: Write the words and phrases *entrée, table d'hôte, prix fixe,* and *à la carte* on the board. Ask students to write a definition for each.

REINFORCEMENT: Read each of the guidelines on restaurant behavior, and call on students to explain or demonstrate each one.

Can't finish everything? Ask for a doggie bag.

- If you have a complaint about the food, quietly explain your problem to the waiter or waitress. You have a right to exactly what you ordered, cooked the way you specified. Remember, however, to remain courteous when you discuss the problem.
- It is perfectly all right to take home leftovers if you can't eat all of your food. Just ask the person serving you for a doggie bag.
- It is NOT all right to take home "souvenirs" from a restaurant. Taking utensils or other items is petty theft, and the restaurant management could take legal action against you.

Paying the Bill and Tipping

The most graceful way to pay the bill is to determine ahead of time how you will do it. If you are going to the restaurant with a group, discuss how you will split the bill.

This will prevent confusion at the restaurant. If there are only two of you, you may wish to pay for the other person. You might also decide before going out to each pay your share. Either way, make sure you both know who is paying. When someone invites you out and you're unsure how the bill will be paid, don't hesitate to ask. If you have no opportunity to find out in advance, take your own money to be on the safe side.

Before paying a bill, check to make sure it is accurate. Remember that a sales tax is added in some states.

Sometimes the person serving you takes your bill to the cashier and brings you change. If a check says "Pay the Cashier," you pay on the way out.

In restaurants with sit-down service, tipping is customary. A *tip* is extra money you leave for the person who served you.

A tip is a way to express appreciation for good service. The usual amount is 15 percent of the total bill. If your service was especially good, you may want to add a little more. Remember that the tip is for service, not food. Even if the food was bad, leave a tip if the service was good.

For Review

1. Explain *head-of-the-table service.*
2. Where should the dinner knife and the butter knife be placed when setting a table?
3. According to good manners, what should you do at the end of a meal?
4. What is the purpose of a tip in a restaurant?

See page T113 for teaching suggestions.

Learning to Manage

Party Planning

Look back at the conversation on page 360. Now read how Mrs. White's Home Economics class manages the surprise retirement party for her. Then answer the questions that follow.

The class worked with their student teacher to form five committees to plan Mrs. White's party. These committees' responsibilities were: meal planning and shopping; cooking; table setting; decorations; and cleanup.

The meal planning and shopping committee decided on a lasagna dinner with tossed salad and warm garlic bread. They voted to have apple pie and ice cream for dessert, since they knew this was Mrs. White's favorite. They made a list and chose a shopping date. The pies and lasagna could be made ahead of time and frozen, so the cooking committee wanted to get going.

They brought their list to the principal, who approved it. He told them that there was enough money in the fund collected from the teachers to pay for all the food. The remainder of the money would be used for a gift for Mrs. White. The principal thanked the class for volunteering to put on the meal as their gift to their teacher.

The cooking progressed and the food was stored in home freezers, but there was one problem. The decorating committee had no funds. They used their imaginations to come up with ideas. They made a colorful felt banner and borrowed ribbon from the classroom to use as streamers. Then they blew up balloons and strung them.

On the evening of the party, the table setting committee set up the two long tables in the cafeteria. Then they put vases of fresh flowers on them. They used candles to make the scene more formal.

They would never forget the look of happiness and surprise on Mrs. White's face as they welcomed her. It made all the work and planning worthwhile. In his speech, the principal said Mrs. White was one of the best home economics teachers he had ever known. Her class had proven it that night.

Questions

1. Imagine that you are going to have a dinner party for 10 people. Write down the menu you would like to have and list the planning steps you would have to take.
2. Draw one place setting for your party and an idea for a table centerpiece.

Chapter 16 Review

Summary

Breakfast, lunch, and dinner can include a variety of easily-prepared foods. Eating regular meals that include foods from the four food groups is the best guideline to follow. Planning to eat in a relaxed atmosphere is also important. Snacks should be nutritious and not too high in sugar and fat content.

Mealtime etiquette includes ways of serving food, the correct way to set the table, and table manners. Correct behavior is important in restaurants as well as in homes. Restaurants range from informal to very formal. An understanding of menu style and customs such as tipping can help to make dining out a pleasant experience.

Vocabulary

Complete each of the following sentences with the correct word from the vocabulary list below.

entrée (p. 379)   reservation (p. 378)
à la carte (p. 379)   table d'hôte (p. 379)
etiquette (p. 370)   cover (p. 373)
prix fixe (p. 379)

1. Making a _____ means calling in advance for a table in a restaurant.
2. The two terms that are used to refer to a complete meal served at a set price are _____ _____ and _____ _____.
3. To order meal items separately is to order _____.
4. The main course of a meal is called the _____.
5. A place setting is also called a _____.
6. Customs considered by society to be the correct way to act in certain situations are called _____.

Questions

•• 1. Are there only certain kinds of food that are appropriate for breakfast? Explain your answer.
• 2. Why should you not be careful not to overmix the batter when using the muffin method?
• 3. Name two ways to keep a packed lunch cool.
• 4. What is a nutritious snack for a person who likes rich foods?
•• 5. Why is it a good idea to avoid buying snacks from machines?
• 6. Name five different kinds of food that could be used for the main dish at dinner.
• 7. What is an appetizer?
• 8. How can dinner together be an important family time?
• 9. What type of dishes are best for a buffet service?
• 10. Where do you place the salad fork at a meal when the salad will be eaten before the main course?

The dots represent skill levels required to answer each question or complete each activity:

- • requires recall and comprehension
- •• requires application and analysis
- ••• requires synthesis and evaluation

11. Name five kinds of centerpieces you could use to decorate a table.
12. From the list of table manners on page 376, choose the one that you think is most important. Explain your answer.
13. Name three kinds of restaurants.
14. What information should you give when making a reservation?
15. What should you do if you have a complaint about the food you have been served in a restaurant?

Skill Activities

Many more activities are contained in the annotations within this chapter.

1. Laboratory Think up a breakfast–on–the–go recipe and prepare it with your lab partner. Try to create a recipe with ingredients that can be mixed in a blender or combined in a sandwich. Be sure your breakfast invention is a balanced meal. Share the food and the recipe with other students in the class. You may want to combine the recipes in a booklet of "on-the-go" ideas.

2. Decision Making Visit a fast-food restaurant and copy the menu selection. Write the menu on the chalkboard in your classroom. Use the menu to select a nutritious meal. Try to choose a low-fat, low-calorie dinner that includes one food from each of the major food groups. Compare your choices with other students in the class. How many different low-fat, low-calorie meal combinations were you and your classmates able to make?

3. Communication With a group of classmates, prepare a skit to demonstrate incorrect behavior at a restaurant. Choose one of your classmates to be the waiter or waitress, while the rest of the group play the customers. Before you begin, review the rules of restaurant behavior on page 379. Choose one particular aspect of dining out—ordering food, making a complaint, paying the bill—to focus on in your skit. Share your scene with the rest of the class. Ask the class to point out all the mistakes made by the restaurant customers. Then repeat the scene showing the correct behavior.

4. Laboratory Set a table for four to six people in your Home Economics classroom. Make sure you use the correct placement of dinnerware, glassware, and flatware as shown on pages 374–375. With a group of your classmates, demonstrate the correct way to serve, pass, and clear dishes. Also, practice the table manners described on page 376. Using some of the suggestions mentioned in this chapter, you may want to create a simple centerpiece.

Unit 5

Clothing and Textiles

Chapter 17
Your Clothes

Vocabulary

The dialogue below introduces "Making Smart Style Choices," the Learning to Manage feature in this chapter. The case study is continued and the situation discussed further on page 413. See page T118 for teaching suggestions.

"How do you like this gray blazer on me, Ann?"

"What about a brighter color?"

"But this soft gray will go with so many outfits I already have. I can add color with blouses and less expensive items like scarves."

"Well . . . it's OK, Marie, but wouldn't you rather have a jacket in the latest style?"

"I really need clothes that will last for a few seasons, Ann. Those new styles are too extreme. Besides, they don't look right on me."

Section 17.1
Clothing Choices

As you read, think about:

- the three main functions of clothing. (p. 387)
- how your clothes affect the impression you make on others. (p. 388)
- how fashion and your peers influence the clothes you choose to wear. (p. 389)

Is this your idea of a modest and comfortable bathing suit?

Like Marie, you may have asked yourself, "Does this look right on me?" You are not alone in asking yourself this question when choosing clothes. Appearance, however, is not the only reason for selecting a particular garment. You choose clothes for many reasons, depending on your own needs and resources. Your choices are important, as clothes are one way to express your personality and tastes. Like good grooming, the right clothes add to the immediate overall impression you make on other people.

Why You Dress

Have you ever thought about why you dress as you do? Maybe you think style is the only influence on you. However, your clothing also needs to be comfortable and appropriate for different activities. That sounds simple enough, but several factors influence your choices. Society's standards, climate, and customs within groups all play a part in determining how you dress. They all affect the three main functions of clothing: modesty, protection, and image.

Modesty

Throughout history, people have worn clothes that reflect the standards of the times. In the 1800s, for example, it was considered appropriate for women to expose their shoulders, but they had to conceal their ankles. Society sets these standards for *modesty,* or what is considered proper, in regard to behavior as well as clothing. Parents teach these standards to their children.

In your own community, certain rules, or customs, may be written down. For example, you may have a dress code at school. In some areas, laws state that customers may not enter stores without shoes or shirts. Most clothing customs, however, are unwritten. It would no doubt be considered improper to wear casual clothing and sneakers to a formal wedding. A baseball uniform is correct dress if you're playing baseball but not for a job or for a family gathering.

Clothing keeps these children warm. What else does it do?

Protection

The weather is another reason people choose particular clothes. During a Michigan winter, heavy coats and boots are needed as protection against the cold. In a moderate climate such as California's, people dress in lighter clothing. Loose clothing and light colors are most comfortable in hot climates. Loose clothing allows air to move over your body, while light colors reflect the sun's rays away from it.

Special clothing provides protection in certain kinds of jobs, such as firefighting and construction work. It also protects players in sporting events, such as football and hockey.

Image Through Clothes

Your clothes help create your image, or the way others see you. Dressing like other people in a group may be important to you. If your friends wear jeans and sweaters, you may be most comfortable doing the same. Even so, you can still give your clothes an individual touch, for example, with an unusual belt or scarf. Or, you may want to dress differently from those around you.

Sometimes your clothing reflects not only your own image but also that of a special group. If you belong to a school band, club, or team, you might wear a uniform. This identifies you as a member of that group.

Did You Know?

Many now-classic styles for both men and women were inspired by military uniforms.

- The *trench coat* gets its style and name from the weather-proof coat first worn by Allied soldiers in the trenches during World War I.
- The original *blazer* was worn by British sailors aboard the ship *HMS Blazer* during the 1860s, while the *pea coat* comes from U.S. Navy garb.
- Leather *bomber jackets* with sheepskin linings, *parachute pants,* and *aviator glasses* are all copied from pilots' apparel.

People also choose clothes to achieve status or to impress others. "Designer" jeans and expensive, name-brand running shoes are examples of "status clothes." They are often more expensive than similar items without a well-known designer's label. Sometimes they also go out of style before too long.

Fashion Influences

A **style** is a design that is clearly recognizable. The T-shirt is an example of a clothing style that is easy to recognize. T-shirts and jeans are two styles that have lasted many years. This is not true, however, of all styles.

Fashion Changes

Fashion is the style of clothing that is popular at a given time. Fashionable pants legs may be narrow at the ankle for a while, then bell-shaped for a season or two. One year, skirts might be worn down to the ankles. The next year, mini-skirts could be "in." A style that lasts for a long time is called a **classic.** Blazers and cardigan sweaters have become classics. Fashions that last only a short period of time are called **fads.** Brightly colored shoelaces and legwarmers are examples of recent fads. Jeans were a fad that became a classic.

Why do fashions change? One reason is that people like change. Another is that the fashion industry wants people to keep buying new clothes; changing styles encourage them to do this to stay "in style." You might also get bored with your

Usually, fashion changes quickly. Why do some styles stay the same?

clothes and feel that the new fashions are more interesting. However, fashions also change because the world changes. *Technology* is the use of science and inventions to make new products to meet our needs. The fashion industry uses technology to produce clothes more quickly and less expensively. Technology has also made new easy-care fabrics possible. At one time, only the wealthy could afford to own and care for fabrics such as silk. Now, however, clothes in silklike fabrics are available at a reasonable price. In addition, many of these new fabrics do not require dry cleaning or hand washing and ironing. This means that recent technology has saved everyone time and money.

PHOTO: Ask for spontaneous responses to this teen's clothing. What kind of image do these clothes project?

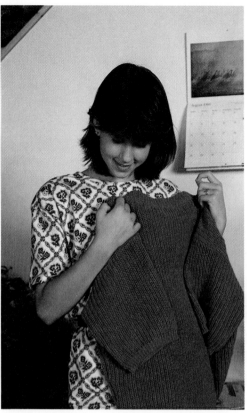

How could these items of clothing serve as parts of other outfits?

Sources of Styles

Clothing designers create styles using their own ideas and observing the world around them. They draw from events past and present, newspapers, movies, and many other sources. A new fashion might begin with a popular television show. If a leading character always wears baggy overalls, designers might incorporate this style in their clothing designs.

A style, however, can start with almost anyone. Before jeans became fashionable, workers had worn them for years. Then young people began to wear jeans. Now people of all ages wear them.

NOTE: Before television, film celebrities were often sources of new fashion trends. Can your students name styles popularized by TV and film stars?

Putting Fashion in Its Place

Changing fashions can be interesting and fun. However, comfort and a sense of your own style are more important considerations in choosing clothes.

Think first about the things you do and the clothes you need for each activity. Then choose items that you can use for several occasions. For example, select a shirt that you could wear to school and also to a party.

Learn to mix and match your clothing. When you mix and match, the many clothing combinations you create make your wardrobe appear larger. You may have a sweater and pants outfit that is one color. Try mixing and matching them with other clothes. Experiment to see which combinations look best. When buying clothes, choose a sweater that goes with pants or skirts you already have. Or try to find a jacket that goes with several outfits.

Casual clothes are the most practical. A shirt decorated with sequins is less useful than a simple white shirt. You will want some fads in your wardrobe. Most of the time, however, be guided by your needs as well as by what appeals to you.

See page T120 for answers.

For Review

1. Name the three main functions of clothing.
2. How does your clothing affect your image?
3. Why do fashions change from year to year?

DISCUSS: Mention companies that design and manufacture jeans. What brand names do your students prefer and why? What look in jeans is most popular now? What is the price range?

Do these clothes flatter the girls who wear them? Look at the colors, textures, and lines.

Section 17.2
Design Elements

As you read, think about:

- the elements of clothing design. (p. 391)
- ways to choose clothes that are flattering to you. (p. 391)

Have you ever wished you were taller? Or thinner? Or shorter? Most people would like to change something about their appearance. Growth will take care of many things that bother you now. In the meantime, you can create an illusion through your clothes. An *illusion* is something that fools the eye. You can appear shorter or taller, thinner or heavier, by choosing your clothes carefully.

Clothing Design

As you know, design is the arrangement of lines, patterns, textures, and colors to create a desired effect. The way these elements work together helps determine how a garment will look on you. These are the same elements of design you learned about in Chapter 11. There you learned how they applied to decorating your home. Now, by applying the elements of design to clothing, you can emphasize your most attractive features and play down problem areas.

Choosing Lines

Clothing lines can be seen not only in the overall shape of a garment. They can be found in the way it is sewn together and in

Is this shirt a good color for this boy's hair, eyes, and skin tone?

the pattern of the fabric, including the trim. All of these things affect the way other people see you.

Horizontal lines go from side to side. They tend to make you appear shorter and heavier. Horizontal lines appear in belts and in stripes and seams that go across.

Vertical lines go up and down and make you appear taller and thinner. Pleats, stripes, and seams running from the shoulder to the hem form vertical lines.

Curved lines may be all or part of a circle. They create the appearance of softness and fullness. A jacket with a curved seam across the chest and a blouse with a draped neckline are both examples of curved lines.

Diagonal lines are slanted. They create

different effects, depending on the length and angle of the line. For example, a short diagonal line going from the left shoulder to the right hip creates the impression of width. A longer diagonal line, from the shoulder to the hemline, gives a narrower appearance. Some diagonal lines, such as zigzags, can also add excitement.

Proportion

The lines in clothing make your eye follow their direction. This helps achieve *proportion,* or the relationship of one part to another. You can observe proportion in the length of a jacket in relation to the length of a pair of pants. When you select clothing, keep in mind that it can make a difference to your own proportions, too. If you feel your legs are too short, you can make them appear longer by choosing a short jacket rather than a long one.

Choosing Colors

Some days you might wear a bright color because it makes you feel more cheerful. Other days you may choose a cool green because it makes you feel more relaxed. Colors can influence your moods, perhaps without your being aware of it. Colors, like lines, can also affect how you appear to other people.

You will look best wearing colors that complement your hair, eyes, and skin tone. Professionals are available to analyze your coloring and tell you which colors do the most for you. You can do your own color analysis, however, with a mirror and a good light. Hold up different

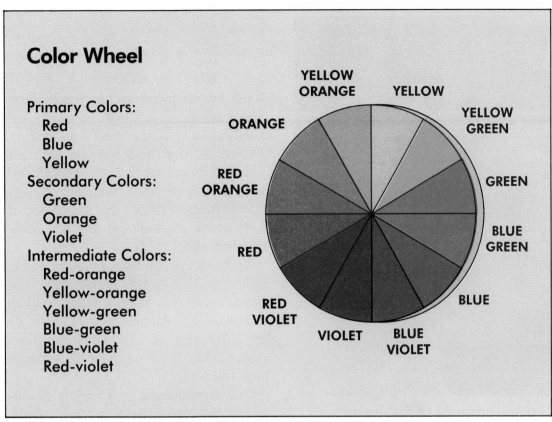

Color Wheel

Primary Colors:
   Red
   Blue
   Yellow
Secondary Colors:
   Green
   Orange
   Violet
Intermediate Colors:
   Red-orange
   Yellow-orange
   Yellow-green
   Blue-green
   Blue-violet
   Red-violet

Which colors look best on you? Experiment with a color wheel to find the best combinations for your complexion.

colors to your face to see which are most flattering. Try out different color values (light or dark shades of a color). Also try out different color intensities (variations in dullness and brightness). Experiment a little, and you will find the colors that are right for you.

The colors you select to wear can make you seem larger or smaller. Light, bright, warm colors, such as red or yellow, tend to make you appear larger. Dark, cool colors, such as deep blue or green, help to make you look smaller. Wearing all one color can make you look larger, while dressing in contrasting colors will make you appear shorter.

REINFORCEMENT: Ask students to recommend colors for the following body types: short, tall, thin, and overweight.

Putting Colors Together

When you put together an outfit, you use various colors to make a color scheme. Refer to the color wheel above as you read about color schemes. In Chapter 11, you learned how these color schemes apply to decorating. Here you can use them to choose clothing colors.

A *monochromatic* color scheme is built around variations of the same color. The combination of a light blue shirt and dark blue slacks is an example of a monochromatic color scheme.

A *complementary* color scheme uses colors that are direct opposites. These

REINFORCEMENT: Using fashion magazines, have students find examples of monochromatic, complementary, and analogous color schemes.

Can you name all of the design elements shown here?

colors can be found opposite each other on the color wheel. A sweater with green and red stripes or a yellow and violet design has complementary colors.

An *analogous* color scheme is based on colors that are closely related to each other. They can be found close to each other on the color wheel. Blue slacks, a blue-violet shirt, and a blue-green sweater make up an analogous color scheme.

You probably have clothes in your closet that fit together in an attractive color scheme. Try new color combinations of clothes you already own. As you add new items to your wardrobe, keep in mind both colors that flatter you and colors that go together.

ENRICHMENT: Ask each student to develop a color scheme for a particular season or holiday. Then have each student create a fashion collage of their particular seasonal color scheme.

Choosing Textures and Patterns

Some fabrics invite you to touch them. The texture of a fabric refers to the smoothness or coarseness of its surface. Texture is something you can both see and feel. Some fabrics are smooth and silky. Others are bulky and nubby. Jackets may be made of fabrics that are quilted or furry. Some sweaters are soft, while others are rough.

Textures that are fuzzy or shiny tend to make you look larger. A dull fabric like denim makes you seem smaller. Smooth fabrics, such as flannel and wool jersey, do not affect apparent size. All fabrics, however, tend to accent weight if the garment hugs the body.

Fabrics also come in a variety of patterns. You can choose among stripes, plaids, dots, prints, and many others. A pattern's size, color, and arrangement all affect how it will look on you.

In general, the size of a pattern should be in proportion to the size of your body. If you are small to average size, you probably look best in patterns with a fairly small design. Very large, bold designs are more suitable for taller people. Heavy people, however, should avoid large, splashy patterns that will make them appear even heavier. If you feel you are too thin, you can combine pattern and texture to create an impression of added size. For example, wear a bulky sweater with a bright, geometric design.

All of the design elements—line, color, texture, and pattern—can help you choose clothes that are becoming to you.

REINFORCEMENT: Discuss fabrics that have texture. Ask students to point out examples of clothing they are wearing that have texture. Show examples from magazines of clothes with a variety of textures.

Study these aspects of a garment carefully before you buy it but, most important, always try it on.

See page T120 for answers.

For Review

1. What are the four elements of clothing design?
2. How do horizontal lines in clothing affect the way a person looks?
3. What kind of patterns are best on people of small to average size?

Section 17.3

Planning Your Wardrobe

As you read, think about:

■ how to take a complete inventory of your clothes. (p. 395)

■ how to buy clothes that fit well and look good on you. (p. 397)

■ how to save money on clothes. (p. 398)

Suppose you are going to a party. You want to look your best, so you get out your favorite blue shirt. As you are putting it on, you discover that a button is missing. All is not lost, however, as you have a yellow shirt in perfect condition. It goes well with your gray slacks—but you've grown, and they are too short.

Sound familiar? Problems like this can be avoided. A wardrobe plan can help you make sure you have what you need when you need it.

REINFORCEMENT: Develop an inventory sheet on which students can list clothes they wear, clothes they have outgrown, and clothes they need to repair.

PHOTO: Suggest charitable organizations in your town to which students might send old clothes. Suggest consignment stores as well.

Begin your wardrobe planning by taking an inventory of what you own.

Taking a Clothing Inventory

Taking inventory of your own clothes is much like the process that the owner of a clothing store goes through. The store owner counts every single item of clothing to see what is there and what stock should be added. You can do the same thing with your own clothes. This is the first step in shaping up your wardrobe.

Sorting and Listing

Begin by writing down your different activities across the top of a piece of paper. You might, for example, list school, work, sports, and special social occasions.

ENRICHMENT: Have students examine their "clothes inventory list" and then categorize items as school clothes, sports clothes, work clothes, and special occasion clothes.

What does the sash do for this outfit? What else could it be worn with?

Then take all of your clothes out of your closets and drawers. Sort them into three piles, or categories.

- clothes you like and wear
- clothes you like but which need repair
- clothes you have outgrown or don't like and feel sure you will not wear again

Most of the clothes in the first two piles will be useful wardrobe items. As you sort, list each of these under an activity. For example, put a bathing suit under sports. Include a brief description, such as "green bathing suit." Some items might be listed more than once. A sweater, for example, might be worn for both "school" and "work." Jeans might be used for

"school," "work," and "sports." Be sure to include any items that are at the dry cleaner's or in the laundry or are being stored elsewhere because they are out of season. Also, don't forget accessories, such as shoes and belts. Make separate lists for undergarments and sleepwear.

Repairing and Sharing

The clothes in your second pile can become active again as soon as they are repaired. You can sew on a button or replace a hem while you are listening to music or watching television. If some items are not worth repairing , put them in the third pile or save them for household use. For example, any soft clothing that is beyond repair can be used as cleaning cloths.

The clothes in your third pile can be given to a relative, neighbor, or charitable organization. You might also consider trading with someone, if your parents agree to this idea. You may have a friend who always admired your green sweater. Perhaps you admire the yellow windbreaker your friend never wears anymore. By making a swap, you each end up with a garment you like.

Study your clothing inventory. Are there ways to make new outfits by combining clothes differently? Do you have too few clothes for some activities? Careful planning can help you fill the gaps.

Have a Buying Plan

After you have finished your clothing inventory, you will have a clearer idea of what you need. Now you can come up with a buying plan. A buying plan can help you to acquire useful clothing within your budget. These guidelines may be helpful:

- Make a list of what you need. Avoid buying clothes that are not on your list.
- Buy versatile (*VER*–suh–tul) clothes, that is, clothes that can be used in different ways. Select items you can use for several kinds of activities. Include some all-season fabrics, such as denim or poplin.
- Invest in some classic items. Limit fad purchases to small things, such as belts, scarves, and hats.
- Read newspaper ads and look for sales. Shop around and make comparisons before you buy.
- Decide how much you can spend, and stay within your budget.

Shopping for Clothes

Sometimes a garment will look wonderful on the rack but quite different when you put it on. Always try on clothes to see if they fit and look good on you. Lift your arms, sit down, and walk to make sure a garment does not pull, tear, or wrinkle. Remember to be gentle. The garment belongs to the store until you buy it.

Checking for Quality

Even when a garment fits well, do not purchase it until you have checked it for quality. These are some signs of quality.

- Stitching is straight and even, and the color of the thread matches the fabric.
- Seams do not show signs of puckering or raveling.

Does the designer's name ensure that the garment is well made?

- Hems are even, and stitches do not show through.
- Closings do not pucker or wrinkle. Zippers work smoothly. Hooks and eyes are sewn in securely. Buttonholes are reinforced with extra stitching at the ends.
- Facings such as extra fabric at the neckline lie flat.
- Fabrics such as plaids or stripes are matched at the seams.

Reading Labels

Federal law requires garments to have labels providing instructions for their care. Check these labels carefully. Your decision to buy or not to buy could be determined by what this care label says.

Consider whether sewing or buying an item is more expensive.

You may not want a light-colored garment that has to be washed by hand, for example. If the garment must be dry-cleaned, you may be unable to afford this expense.

Some clothing labels feature a designer's name and are regarded as status symbols because the designer is well-known. Remember, however, that such a label is not a guarantee of quality. Evaluate a "designer" garment as you would any other clothing. Use the guidelines on page 397. Let your own sense of style and taste guide you, not the label.

Some "designer" items are made in the same factories and with the same materials as less expensive clothing. Also be aware that sometimes the designer's label is an outright counterfeit.

Return Policies

Be sure to find out about a store's return or exchange policy. Some stores allow you to return a garment and get your money back, often within a certain number of days. Other stores have an "exchange only" policy. This means you cannot get your money back, but you can exchange the garment for another one. Save your sales slip, as you will probably need it if you return an item. Some stores, particularly during special sales, do not allow any exchanges or returns. Store policies vary, so check before you buy.

Saving Money on Clothing

Building a wardrobe can be enjoyable, but it's not easy. Even when you plan carefully, you may find that your wardrobe gaps are bigger than your budget. There are several ways, however, to stretch your money. You can even add to your wardrobe without spending any money at all.

Sales

Sale items are available in stores year round. There are also special sales at the end of a season and on some holidays. When you shop at sales, check items for quality and flaws. Buy an item only if you really like it and can use it, no matter how much the price has been reduced. If you buy clothing at the end of a season, keep in mind that your size could change. A coat purchased in February, for example, could be too short by the following winter.

Sewing

If you have time, skill, and a sewing machine, you may decide to make your own clothing. Sewing your own clothing can give you a sense of pride and satisfaction. Sewing allows you to choose a fabric and style you especially like. You can give a garment your own personal touch by your choice of buttons or trim.

Although sewing can be a big money saver, there are times when it can actually cost more. If you select an expensive fabric for a sewing project you might spend more than you would for something ready-made. If your intention is to save money, compare costs carefully before you make a garment.

If you shop wisely, your wardrobe will cost you less.

Sharing

Along with trading clothes, you can stretch your wardrobe by sharing. With your parents' permission, you might share clothes with a relative or friend. This can be especially useful for occasions like formal dances or weddings. If you buy a dressy garment, you might wear it only once. Sharing can add variety to your wardrobe at no cost.

Consignment Stores

People take clothing items they no longer want to a consignment store. They receive part of the money from any sales. Consignment stores are a good place to look for expensive, dressy clothes you may wear only once or outfits you will probably soon outgrow.

REINFORCEMENT: Ask students to compare the cost of making a skirt or other simple item with buying one at a retail store. Be sure they include the price of the pattern, fabric, thread, button or snap, zipper, and interfacing. Do they find a significant savings in making the item?

ENRICHMENT: Have students develop a list of guidelines for fair and considerate sharing of clothing with friends and siblings. Remind them that parental permission is always necessary.

Outlet Stores

Outlet stores sell clothes made by a particular company. The prices are reduced for various reasons. Some of these stores sell **factory surplus** items, which the manufacturer could not sell to regular retail stores. If you see any clothing marked as a *second* or an *irregular,* look it over carefully. You may find minor flaws, such as a pull in the fabric or slightly uneven color. You may also find serious flaws, such as tears, irregular shapes, or noticeable splotches of dye. It is a good idea to ask a store manager how that store defines *seconds* and *irregulars.*

These clothing items can be a good buy if they have only minor flaws. If problems are more serious, you will have to consider the cost of repairs or the skill and time needed to do them yourself. Be sure to find out about the store's return policy. Some factory outlet stores do not allow you to return merchandise.

You may not be able to try on clothes, or the space may be crowded and lack privacy. Some outlets require you to pay cash. Although checks may be accepted, credit cards usually are not.

See page T120 for answers.
For Review

1. What three categories would you use if you were taking a clothing inventory?
2. Name five guidelines that can help you work out a successful clothes buying plan.
3. Name at least three ways to save money on clothing.

REINFORCEMENT: Can students name outlet stores in your area? Do students shop there, and, if so, which ones do they feel have the best selection and price?

Section 17.4
Fibers and Fabrics

As you read, think about:

■ how different fibers are used in the fabrics you wear. (p. 400)

■ how fabrics are made. (p. 402)

■ how finishes are added to improve the fabrics you wear. (p. 406)

Have you ever looked carefully at a piece of yarn? If you were to untwist it, you would find that it is made up of tiny, hairlike strands. These strands may be so small that you can barely see them; yet they are the basic elements in fabric.

All About Fibers

The fine strands used to make fabric are called *fibers.* Until about 100 years ago, nature provided all of the fibers used for clothing. Then people began to make other fibers. Today there are three main kinds of fibers.

Natural Fibers

Natural fibers are those that come from plants and animals. The most common plant fiber is cotton. Linen is made from the stalk of the flax plant. Ramie (*RA*–mee) is made from the fiber in the stem of the ramie plant. Wool is made from sheep's hair and also from the hair of goats, rabbits, camels, and alpacas. Silk fibers are spun by a small insect, the silkworm.

REINFORCEMENT: Bring several skeins or balls of yarn to class so that students can see that it is composed of many tiny fibers.

Natural Fibers in the Clothes You Wear

Fiber name and source	Clothing uses	Clothing Characteristics
Cotton (cotton plant)	blouses shirts skirts underwear jeans dresses	is very durable is comfortable in warm weather wrinkles easily without special finish washes easily if colorfast needs to be ironed at high temperature burns readily
flax (linen) (flax plant)	blouses dresses skirts suits	is very durable is comfortable in warm weather wrinkles easily without special finish washes easily if colorfast needs to be ironed at high temperature burns readily
ramie (ramie plant)	sweaters blouses skirts suits (when blended with other fabrics)	is very durable withstands wear has a silk-like luster
wool (sheep)	sweaters skirts coats slacks suits gloves	is warmer than other natural fibers resists wrinkles is durable needs careful handling when washed needs protection against moths
silk (cocoon of silkworm)	skirts blouses dresses neckties scarves	is smooth, lustrous and strong needs ironing at low temperature setting shows water spots unless it has a special finish needs to be hand washed or dry cleaned

Which of these natural fibers do you like to wear?

ART: As an enrichment activity, have students identify one thing they own that is made of each of these fibers. Have them list, in their own words, characteristics of each garment and then compare those characteristics against this chart.

Cotton is a soft, white fiber attached to the seeds of the cotton plant.

Natural fibers have both advantages and disadvantages. Because cotton and linen absorb moisture, they are comfortable in warm weather. However, they can wrinkle and shrink unless they have been specially treated. Wool is absorbent and resists wrinkling, but it shrinks if washed in hot water. Silk is a strong fabric that absorbs moisture. It feels soft and comfortable against the skin. It is expensive, however, because the supply is limited. It is also expensive to care for if you dry-clean it. Silk garments that can be hand-washed are difficult to iron.

Manufactured Fibers

Manufactured fibers are made from chemicals. Polyester, rayon, and acrylic are examples of manufactured, or syn-

NOTE: Some words related to fabrics and weaves are named for their places of origin. For example, *madras* is named after Madras, India; *denim* is named after Nîmes, France since it comes *de* (from) Nîmes; and *worsted* is named after Worthstede, England.

thetic fibers. Synthetics are easy to care for. They do not shrink easily and they dry quickly. However, some, like nylon, do not absorb moisture well and are uncomfortable in hot weather.

Blends

Blends combine natural fibers and manufactured fibers and take advantage of the best qualities of each. For example, a fabric may be 65% polyester and 35% cotton. The polyester provides easy care and wrinkle resistance. The cotton makes the garment absorbent and cool.

How Fibers Become Fabrics

Fibers are twisted, or spun, into yarn. The yarn is then used to make fabrics. Weaving, knitting, and bonding are the most common ways of making fabrics.

Woven Fabrics

Fabrics are woven on a loom. The yarn that runs crosswise is the *warp*. Yarn that runs lengthwise is the *filling*. There are four main kinds of weaves.

In a *plain weave,* each strand of filling yarn passes over and under each warp yarn. Muslin and broadcloth are plain weaves. Sheets and shirts are made from plain weave fabrics.

In a *twill weave,* at least two strands of warp yarn pass over and then under two filling yarns. The rows shift to the right or left to create a diagonal ridge. Durable fabrics like denim are twill weaves.

Manufactured Fibers in the Clothes You Wear

Fiber	Clothing Uses	Clothing Characteristics
acetate (generic name) **Chromspun, Estron** (trademark names)	underwear shirts dresses blouses sportswear	drapes well does not shrink resists fading from sunlight and perspiration
acrylic (generic name) **Acrilan Creslan** (trademark names)	sportswear knitted garments ski wear	soft, warm, lightweight resists wrinkles, damage from sunlight, chemicals and oil builds up static electricity
nylon (generic name) **Antron Crepset Cantrece** (trademark names)	sportswear swimwear hosiery underwear	strong, durable resists mildew absorbs oily stains is damaged by strong sunlight washes easily
rayon (generic name) **Avril Coloray Zantrel** (trademark names)	sportswear blouses shirts neckties	comfortable in warm weather wrinkles easily without special finish burns readily damaged by sunlight and acid solutions
polyester (generic name) **Dacron Kodel Fortrel** (trademark names)	sportswear suits blouses dresses shirts neckties	washes easily, dries quickly resists wrinkling absorbs oily stains melts if ironed at high temperature

How many of these fibers can you find listed on the contents labels of the garments you own?

ART: Note that in addition to nylon, other synthetic fibers that do not absorb moisture well are polyester, triacetate, spandex, and acrylic.

Technology

Jacquard loom

A machine "programmed" by punch cards to do complex tasks automatically—is it a computer? Yes, but it's also a loom invented almost 200 years ago! Joseph-Marie Jacquard, a Frenchman, built such a loom in 1801. Today both the loom and the type of fabric it produces—tapestry, brocade, and damask—bear Jacquard's name.

The Jacquard loom weaves complex patterns directly into the cloth. Jacquard fabrics have both lustrous and dull areas, and they sometimes have raised outlines around the designs. In order to create Jacquards, each warp yarn must be controlled separately. To do this, a pattern of holes is punched in a series of cards. As the cards rotate they allow only certain needles to pass through the holes.

The loom saved both time and money. Because it also saved labor, the loom was opposed by French silk weavers who feared losing their jobs. They attacked both the looms and Jacquard himself. By the 1820s, however, the spread of Jacquard looms had started a technological revolution in the textile industry.

Jacquard's use of hole-punched cards was also adopted by other industries and became the basic method of feeding information into computers.

What would the textile and computer industries be like without Jacquard's invention?

A *satin weave* has yarns that float on the surface, giving the fabric a shiny look. Either the warp or the filling yarns pass over four or more yarns at a time. Satin fabrics are used for blouses and dressy evening clothes.

A *pile weave* is made with three sets of yarn. The back of the fabric is a plain, twill, or satin weave. On the surface, extra yarns form a pile. Corduroy and velvet are pile weaves.

Knitted Fabrics

Knitted fabrics can be made by machine or by hand. One or more yarns are used to form interlocking loops. Knitted fabric requires very little care. T-shirts, sports shirts, and many other items are knitted. The fabric is comfortable, stretches easily, and is widely available in several textures and weights.

Single knits are lightweight and are often used for summer clothes. They are smooth on the right side and have horizontal loops on the wrong side. These knits, also called jersey, are good for sportswear and dresses with simple lines.

Double knits are made with two layers of fabric that are knitted together. These sturdy knits do not ravel and are wrinkle resistant. They are good for pants and jackets. Double knits are available in both natural and manufactured fibers.

Tricot (TREE–coh) knits are made with vertical ribs on the front and crosswise ribs on the back. The big advantage of these knits is that they will not run or ravel, and they resist snags. Dresses, shirts, swimwear, and underwear are among the items made from tricot knits.

REINFORCEMENT: Bring a small, conventional loom to class for examination and demonstration.

Basic Weaves and Their Uses

PLAIN WEAVE

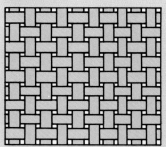

DESCRIPTION AND USES

Plain weaves vary from sheer and fragile to heavy and sturdy.

Plain weaves are used in many shirts, blouses, skirts, and other sportswear.

FABRIC NAMES

Some plain weave fabrics are seersucker, gingham, oxford cloth, duck cloth, and percale.

TWILL WEAVE

DESCRIPTION AND USES

Twill weaves have a diagonal surface design. They tend to be very strong and durable.

Twill weaves are used for general sportswear including jeans and jackets.

FABRIC NAMES

Some twill weave fabrics are denim, garbardine, ticking, and serge.

SATIN WEAVE

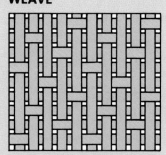

DESCRIPTION AND USES

Satin weaves are smooth and may have a shiny appearance. They are not as durable as plain and twill weaves. Their threads snag easily.

Satin weaves are used for gowns and dressy clothing items.

FABRIC NAMES

Some satin weave fabrics are sateen and satin.

Looms are used to make woven fabrics. A twill pattern is used to create one of the most durable weaves.

Nonwoven and Bonded Fabrics

Not all fabrics are knitted or woven. Nonwoven fabrics are made from fibers that interlock (lock together) as heat, moisture, and pressure are applied. Felt, used for clothes like hats and vests, is a nonwoven fabric. In bonded fabrics, fibers are joined together by chemicals, machines, or heat. Items like disposable hospital gowns and cloth diapers are made from bonded fabrics.

ENRICHMENT: Distribute ¼″ x 12″ strips of construction paper in two colors. Work with students to create plain, satin, and twill weave samples.

Adding Color and Design to Fabrics

Dyes are added to fabrics to give them color and patterns. In *solution dyeing,* the dye is added to fibers before they are spun into yarn. In *yarn dyeing,* it is added to the yarn. Fabrics that are plaid or striped are usually dyed this way. In *piece dyeing,* the dye is added after the fabric has been made. This is the most common method.

REINFORCEMENT: Give examples of nonwoven materials used in home furnishings, such as carpeting and floor coverings.

At one time, dyes came only from natural sources like black walnuts and berries.

Printing is another way to apply color. In roller printing, designs are etched into rollers, and a cylinder is used for each color. Patterns such as flowers and polka dots can be applied like this. In screen printing, dye is forced through the holes of screens onto the fabric, creating the desired pattern.

Fabric Finishes

Along with color and design, special finishes are added to many fabrics. These finishes improve the fabric in various ways. Check labels to see what kind of finish a garment has. If you are buying an all-weather coat, for example, look to see if it is water-repellent. These are some of the finishes used most often.

- Durable press and permanent press finishes condition fabrics so that they require little or no ironing.

- Flame-retardant finishes keep fabrics from burning easily.
- Antistatic finishes reduce static electricity and help prevent clinging.
- Wash-and-wear finishes help fabrics dry smoothly, without wrinkling.
- Waterproof finishes shed water.
- Water-repellent finishes help fabrics resist water but do not waterproof them.
- Stain-and-spot resistant finishes help to protect fabrics from stains and spots.
- Soil-resistant finishes help keep dirt from settling on fabrics.

See page T121 for answers.

For Review

1. Describe the three main kinds of fibers used in making fabrics.
2. Describe the most common ways fabrics are made.
3. How do finishes improve the fabrics you wear?

Section 17.5
Clothing Care and Storage

As you read, think about:

- how to launder your clothes according to care labels. (p. 407)

- how repairing and storing your clothes properly will keep them in good condition. (p. 410)

Have you ever had your day ruined by a spaghetti stain? When the garment you planned to wear has a spot on it, you have to search around for something else. Another time, you may find that a zipper is

Did You Know?

It was the invention of the buttonhole that made buttons popular as fasteners for clothing. Buttons existed as long ago as prehistoric times, and the ancient Greeks and Romans used them as both decorations and fasteners. But in early medieval times, people in Europe used buttons only for decoration. They fastened their clothes with strings, pins, or belts. The buttonhole was developed in the 1200s. It made "buttoning up" the most practical way to close clothes for hundreds of years to come.

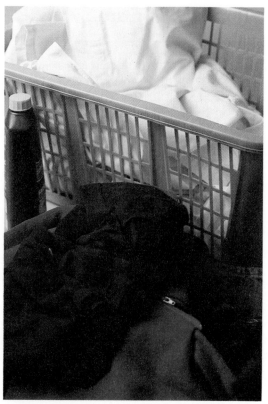

Successful laundering begins with careful sorting.

broken. On yet another occasion, you might not even be able to find your favorite garment. To keep your wardrobe in shape, care for your clothing regularly and have a good storage system.

Laundry

Keeping clothes clean is basic to good clothing care. Always check the care label in a garment. While many clothes can be put in the washer and dryer, hand washing or dry cleaning is recommended for some. Care labels also give other special instructions and information, such as "line dry" or "dry flat."

International Care Symbols

🔲 60°	**WASHING SYMBOL** gives washing instructions: 60°C (140°F) means you may safely wash in hot water; 30°C (86°F) indicates special care is necessary.
▭	**DRYING SYMBOL** indicates the garment may be tumble dried.
△	**TRIANGLE** instructions pertain to chlorine bleaching.
🏷	**IRON** gives ironing instructions: one dot indicates cool iron; two dots tell you to use a medium iron; three dots mean you may safely use a hot iron.
◯	**CIRCLE** gives dry-cleaning instructions: A indicates all normal dry-cleaning methods; P specifies perchlorethlyene cleaning; F indicates the "Solvent F" process.
✕	**X through symbol** means DO NOT wash, tumble dry, bleach, iron, or dry clean.

Have you seen these symbols on the care labels of your clothes?

Automatic Washing and Drying

Many people use automatic washers and dryers, either at home or in places that have coin-operated machines. When using a washer and dryer, follow these basic guidelines.

- Read the care labels as you sort the clothes. Make separate piles for clothes that need different temperatures and washing cycles. Separate light-colored clothes from dark ones.
- Check pockets for pens and other items.
- Check for stains that need pretreating, or special attention, before washing.

- Choose the correct water temperature. Generally speaking, hot water is good for light-colored cotton and white fabrics. Warm water is usually best for brightly colored and dark clothes and for synthetic fabrics.
- Do not overload the washer.
- Use the correct amount of laundry detergent. If you add other products, such as bleach, follow the instructions on the label. Be sure that the bleach is mixed with water before adding clothes. Bleach can damage or even make a hole in a fabric. Some care labels advise against using bleach.
- When drying clothes, choose the correct temperature if your machine has different settings. Shaking out clothes before you put them in the dryer helps to dry them sooner and more evenly.
- When clothes are dry, remove them right away to prevent extra wrinkling.
- Clean out the lint filter in the dryer after each use. A large accumulation of lint could cause a fire.

Ironing and Pressing

Many clothes will be ready to wear when you remove them from the dryer. Others, however, may need a final touch. Ironing and pressing are two procedures for removing wrinkles. *Ironing* is sliding the iron back and forth across the fabric to remove wrinkles. *Pressing* is lifting and lowering the iron onto the fabric. Pressing is recommended for fabrics such as knits and wools, as it does not stretch the fabric. Steam irons, which use a combination of moisture and heat, are especially useful for pressing.

Stain Treatment Guide

Stain	Washable Fabric	Dry-Cleanable Fabric
grease and oil	Rub in detergent to loosen stain. Wash in water as hot as possible using plenty of detergent. Stain may not come out of certain fabrics.	Send to dry cleaner.
ink (ballpoint pen)	May be difficult or impossible to remove. Sponge stain with rubbing alcohol, or spray with hair spray until wet. Rub in detergent. Then wash, following usual procedure. Repeat if necessary.	May be difficult or impossible to remove. Try dry-cleaning powder on rough-textured fabric. Or, send to dry cleaner.
catsup	Scrape off with knife. Soak in cold water about 30 minutes. Rub in detergent and wash using chlorine bleach if recommended.	Send to dry cleaner.
carbonated drinks	Sponge or soak in cold water immediately. Rub in detergent and wash using chlorine bleach if recommended. Stain may be difficult to remove after it dries.	Send to dry cleaner while stain is fresh. Sponge with water if no risk of leaving ring.

For best results, treat stains immediately.

Both efficiency and safety are important when you are ironing or pressing. These guidelines can be helpful.

- Check the care label for instructions. If you are uncertain what temperature to use, test the temperature on a hidden area, such as a seam. Generally, use higher settings for cotton and linen and lower settings for synthetics.
- Press or iron small areas, such as collars, first.
- To prevent shine, press dark fabrics and wool on the wrong side, or use a lint-free cloth.

- Use a well-padded ironing surface and, if possible, a heat-resistant cover.
- When the iron is not in use, keep it in an upright position.
- Do not allow your hands or face to come too close to the steam.
- Make sure the cord is positioned so that the iron cannot accidentally be pulled off the ironing board.
- After using the iron, turn it off and unplug it. Empty water from steam irons immediately after use.
- Do not store the iron until it is cool.
- Clean the iron whenever necessary.

Chapter 17/*Your Clothes*   **409**

Chemicals are used to dry clean clothes.

Dry Cleaning

Some fabrics should be dry-cleaned rather than washed. In dry cleaning, water and detergents are not used. Instead, clothes are cleaned with chemicals. After a garment has been cleaned, it is put on a body-shaped form. Steam is then blown through the fabric to remove any wrinkles. Creases and other special touches can be added by using steam irons and presses.

Two types of dry cleaning are available: professional and coin-operated machines. Professional dry cleaners usually do a good job of removing spots and stains, but they are more expensive. Coin-operated machines cost less, but you have to treat spots and stains yourself.

Routine Care

Routine, or everyday, care is one of the best ways to make sure your wardrobe is in tiptop shape. Daily care of your clothes can become just as much of a habit as putting on your shoes and socks.

Whether you are putting on or taking off clothing, remember to open all zippers and fasteners. This helps prevent tears. Allow clothes to air on a chair or on a hanger outside the closet. Be sure the clothes hang straight on hangers, with buttons and zippers closed. If clothes are wet, do not throw them in a pile. This can cause mildew, a fungus that grows on damp clothes. Check all of your clothes for tears and stains. Make simple repairs and remove spots as soon as possible.

How to Sew on a Button

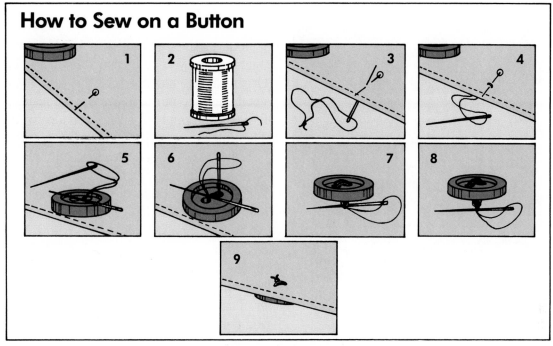

When a button is missing, a garment can't look its best.

Sewing on Buttons

A missing button can be a most annoying problem, but one that is easily solved. All you need is a button, scissors, needle, thread in a matching color, and a pin. For sew-through buttons, you need to use a shank, or stem. This keeps the button loose enough to go through the button-hole. Follow these steps.

1. Use a pin to mark where the button will go.
2. Thread a needle and double the thread. Knot the thread at the end.
3. Begin at the wrong side of the garment and push the needle up to the right side.
4. Take a small stitch. Make sure the knot is secure and then remove the pin.

5. Put the button in place and bring the needle up through it. Then place a toothpick or pin on top of the button to serve as a thread shank. Some buttons already have shanks.
6. Make several stitches up through one hole and down through the other. The thread should always go smoothly over the toothpick or pin.
7. Remove the toothpick or pin.
8. Bring the needle and thread out between the fabric and the button. Wind the thread firmly around the thread underneath the button. This forms a thread shank.
9. Bring the needle back to the wrong side and make three or four stitches. Your button is now in place and you can clip the threads.

A patch is often the easiest solution to your repair problem.

Repairing Rips and Tears

There are several ways to make simple repairs. If you have a ripped seam, you can repair it on the sewing machine or by hand. Match the thread color to the fabric. The new stitches should be made a little beyond the ripped area. Mending tape and patches may be helpful when repairing heavier, more durable fabrics.

Iron-on mending tape is an easy way to repair tears. The tape color should match the fabric. All you have to do is iron the tape onto the inside of the garment. Instructions will be on the package.

Patches are another good way to repair tears. You can stitch the patch to either side of a garment by machine or by hand. In most cases you will want the patch to match the fabric as closely as possible. However, you might also consider decorative, contrasting patches.

Storage

If your clothes get all in a jumble, you might think you have run out of space. Organization, however, is the key to a good clothes storage system. Consider first the amount of space you do have. Then make use of every inch.

For a good closet arrangement, place rods at different heights. You can then hang different kinds of clothes, such as long garments, skirts, and slacks, more efficiently. Shelves above or below the rods can hold shoes or sweaters. A hook on the closet door is a handy place for bags or belts. Store similar items together. That way, you will be able to find what you need.

You can buy closet organizers or use boxes to make them. Boxes can also increase your total storage space. For example, store clothes you wear only occasionally under the bed in boxes. Use inexpensive crates for extra storage.

If you store some clothes at the end of a season, make sure they are clean and repaired. Garment bags are good for hanging these clothes. Sweaters or loose knits should lie flat. Store clothes in a cool, dry place, away from sunlight.

For Review

1. Explain why care labels on your clothes are important.
2. Describe five of the important steps to remember when using a washer and dryer.
3. Give three examples of routine care for clothes.

See page T118 for teaching suggestions.

Learning to Manage

Making Smart Style Choices

Look back at the conversation between Marie and Ann on page 386. The girls are shopping for clothes for Marie, Ann's older sister. Now read about the rest of their shopping trip. Then answer the questions that follow.

As Marie and Ann continued to shop, Ann remarked, "Your taste in clothes has really changed, Marie! I remember when you *had* to have that bright orange coat with the big sleeves, for one thing."

Marie smiled. "I remember that coat —and so does anyone else who ever saw it! I also remember that it didn't last more than one year, and it didn't even look right on me. But I was so happy to be wearing what my friends were that I didn't realize it. What's "in" at school this year?"

"*Everyone* has ZAP sneakers, for one thing. You know, I saved to buy them, and they wore out twice as fast as my old, cheaper brand."

"Sometimes the name means nothing, Ann. I remember that the zipper on my KELVEN jeans broke after one washing! Well, let's get going. I have to buy an outfit to wear to job interviews. These navy blue suits are nice."

"BORING," Ann said, making a face.

"Do you know how many outfits I can make using this skirt and jacket with other clothes I have? It's expensive, but it's a classic style that will last for a while. And it will be great for interviews."

"Just don't hand it down to *me*!"

"You just may want it someday, Ann. You're buying some of your own clothes now. So you can appreciate how expensive it was for Mom and Dad to dress Paul and you and me."

"I understand that *now*. Let's get to the fun stuff! I want to buy one of the latest pocketbooks and some crazy jewelry!"

"OK, Ann. I just might buy a little crazy jewelry myself!"

"YOU?? I thought everything you bought had to be practical!"

"Well, I like to buy a few fad items, too, as long as they aren't too expensive. I think I'll buy a chunky bead necklace and earrings to go with my blue sweater."

"Now you're talking, Marie. Let's go!"

Questions

1. How is Marie managing clothing decisions that meet both her situation and her resources?
2. Do you think that Ann is learning about wise clothing decisions? Why or why not?
3. What is more important to you— wearing what looks good on you or wearing what your friends are wearing? Explain your answer.

Chapter 17 Review

Summary

People choose clothing for modesty, for protection, and to create an image. Clothing styles change according to current fashions and can also be affected by technology, which provides many new fabrics and processes.

When choosing clothes, comfort and a personal sense of style should be more important than following fashion. By using the elements of design, you can decide what looks best on you.

Wardrobe planning begins with a clothing inventory to determine what you have and what you need. Having a buying plan that includes versatile clothing within your budget also helps. Before buying, check clothes for quality, read care labels, and investigate a store's return policy.

Correct care and storage of clothing will help your clothing to last. Following the instructions on care labels and making simple repairs as soon as possible are two important procedures to follow.

Vocabulary

Complete each of the following sentences with the correct word from the vocabulary list below.

fads (p. 389)
natural fibers (p. 400)
style (p. 389)
manufactured fibers (p. 402)
blends (p. 402)
fashion (p. 389)
classic (p. 389)
factory surplus (p. 400)

1. A type of clothing with a design that is clearly recognizable is a _____.
2. A style of clothing that lasts for a long period of time is called a _____.
3. Items of clothing that a manufacturer could not sell to regular retail stores may be sold as _____.
4. Fibers that come from plants and animals are called _____.
5. The style of clothing that is popular for a given time is _____.
6. Combining natural fibers and synthetic fibers creates _____.
7. Fashions that last only a short period of time are called _____.
8. Fibers that are made from chemicals are called _____.

Questions

•• 1. Explain how unwritten dress codes apply to what is considered proper dress for a guest at a wedding.
•• 2. Is it preferable to wear light or dark colors during hot weather? Explain your answer.
• 3. How can you dress as an individual while wearing the same kind of clothing that your friends wear?
•• 4. What are "status clothes"?
•• 5. Should you dress according to fads or in a classic style? Give reasons for your answer.
• 6. What kind of lines in clothing make you look taller and thinner?

The dots represent skill levels required to answer each question or complete each activity:

• requires recall and comprehension
•• requires application and analysis
••• requires synthesis and evaluation

414

7. What length jacket would you choose to make your legs look shorter than they are?

8. How can you tell what colors look best on you?

9. Give an example of an outfit with a complementary color scheme.

10. What kind of texture might a small person choose to wear in order to appear larger?

11. Name six signs of quality to look for in clothing.

12. Why do most stores require that you present a sales slip when you wish to return an article of clothing?

13. What fibers are most comfortable in warm weather? Which are least comfortable? Explain your answers.

14. What is the meaning of the word *warp* as applied to weaving?

15. Is it ever practical to buy clothes that need to be dry-cleaned? Give reasons for your answer.

Skill Activities

Many more activities are contained in the annotations within this chapter.

 1. Critical Thinking With a small group of classmates, brainstorm a list of factors that affect personal appearance. Discuss how each one affects your own appearance. Which factors do you feel influence personal appearance the most? the least? Share your group's results with the rest of the class.

 2. Communication Write a paragraph entitled "Clothing and Me", in which you explain why you choose the clothing you do. What affects your choice of clothing? Do you feel you dress to look like others or to please yourself? Share your paragraph with a friend.

 3. Laboratory Bring several pairs of jeans or slacks to class. Compare the stitching on each of these garments to see how well they are made. Check zippers and other sewing details. Are brand name garments sewn better? Write a brief report stating your conclusions.

 4. Human Relations At home, help out by sorting the laundry according to the fabric care labels. Separate clothing into piles for cold water wash, permanent press wash, hand wash, and dry cleaning. If you are unsure, ask an adult at home to check your sorting.

5. Laboratory With a classmate, choose colors that look best on you by holding construction paper or pieces of fabric in different colors under your face. Cut 1-inch squares of the colors that best suit you. Mount them on index cards to take with you when you are shopping for clothing.

Chapter 18
Getting Ready to Sew

Vocabulary

The dialogue below introduces "Not Sew Easy," the Learning to Manage feature in this chapter. The case study is continued and the situation discussed further on page 429. See page T124 for teaching suggestions.

"Pam, I like this fabric best. It's so dressy and delicate. It will make a great choir skirt."

"It's pretty, Chris, but don't you remember what we learned in Home Ec? I think this type of fabric is hard to work with."

"You get what you want, Pam. I like this fabric, so I'm going to buy it. I think I'll use the pattern with the ruffles and bow on it. I'm sure I can figure it out in the sewing lab."

Section 18.1

In the Sewing Laboratory

As you read, think about:

- the importance of following safety rules in the sewing laboratory. (p. 417)
- how you can work smoothly and productively by cooperating with other people in your class. (p. 418)
- how to plan your time and organize your materials for successful sewing projects. (p. 418)

Attention to quality and attention to safety are both important.

When you begin to learn the basic skills and techniques of sewing, you will work in a sewing laboratory. This lab is different from the classrooms you are used to. You will work with tools and equipment that may not be familiar to you. Learning some simple rules and procedures will make the sewing lab a safe and productive place to work. At home or at school, working carefully and in an organized way is very important.

Working Safely

In a sewing lab many people take turns using equipment such as sewing machines and hot irons. These items can be dangerous if used carelessly. You need to be especially careful of what the people around you are doing. Take care not to bump into them. Move slowly. Look where you are going. A combination of good manners and safety rules can prevent serious accidents.

Sewing Safely

A sewing machine can be dangerous if not used correctly. Sew at an even speed and always pay close attention to what you are sewing. Be very careful that your fingers do not get near the needle. Whether you are working at home or at school, be sure you follow basic safety rules. Place all electric cords as close to an outlet as possible. Never run a cord along a space where people can fall over it. For the same reason, avoid using extension cords.

Ironing Safely

You will use an iron to press the seams and other parts of your garment at each stage of your sewing project. Always be

REINFORCEMENT: Display small sewing equipment and discuss specific safety procedures with students.

NOTE: Operating a sewing machine at an excessive speed can cause the needle to snap and break in two.

417

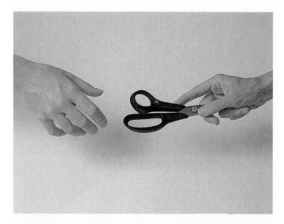

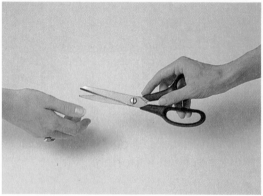

The top photo shows the correct way to pass scissors.

very careful that you do not burn your fingers. If you step away from an ironing board, even for a moment, be sure the iron is off and resting. Then it cannot fall over and burn something.

Other Safety Measures

Store scissors and shears in a safe place. Keep the blades closed when they are not in use. When you hand scissors to someone, hold them by the closed blades and present the handle to the other person. While you are working, keep scissors apart from your fabric, so that they cannot fall when you move the fabric.

REINFORCEMENT: Demonstrate the proper way to carry scissors as well as the proper way to hand scissors to another person.

Put pins and needles where they cannot get lost. Keep them in a pin cushion or felt patch while you are working. Never hold pins or needles in your mouth. Be particularly careful to keep pins and needles off chairs and floors, especially at home, where people may be barefoot.

Working with Others

Your project will go more smoothly if you cooperate with the other students in your class. You should be willing to wait your turn for sewing machines and ironing boards, and to get the teacher's help. Allow time for delays; you can study directions for the next step while you wait.

Always clean up at the end of a sewing lab. Be sure the sewing machine is down or covered and that the floor and other surfaces are free of scraps. Check that equipment is turned off. Return any borrowed equipment to its assigned place.

Organize Yourself

Planning your time and organizing your materials will make your sewing projects run more smoothly. Do not rush to finish

Did You Know?

A magnet is good cleanup tool. After working with pins and needles, use the magnet to pick up any strays. That way, you won't have anyone "sitting on pins and needles"!

REINFORCEMENT: Stress that it is important to put projects and equipment away after each sewing lab. Remind students to remove their thread and bobbins from the sewing machine.

a project. If you do, chances are you will have to rip out stitching or cut a new piece of fabric. Take the time to arrange your work space and to gather your materials. You will learn how to plan a project properly later in this chapter.

Schedule Your Time

Schedule your sewing project. Estimate the time it will take to complete it and how much of the work you can do in class. Revise your schedule as you go along. Allow extra time for steps you will need help with. You may need your teacher's help when attaching a collar, sleeves, or a zipper. You will need a friend's help to measure hems.

Mark Personal Equipment

Label all your personal equipment with your name to avoid mixups. The night before a class, check that you have all the materials you need. Keep your materials together in a box or sewing basket, and store it in a safe place.

See page T126 for answers.

For Review

1. Name three important safety rules you should follow when using a sewing machine.
2. Name two ways you can cooperate with the other students in your sewing laboratory.
3. Name two ways that you can organize yourself to make your sewing project more efficient.

DISCUSS: Could a person apply the six steps of the management process (see Chapter 2) to a sewing project? Why or why not?

PHOTO: Stress that many steps are involved between conceiving and completing a project. Planning and organization are fundamental to success.

To save time, buy all your notions when you buy your fabric.

Section 18.2

Choosing Your Project, Pattern, and Fabric

As you read, think about:

- the importance of choosing a sewing project that is suitable for you. (p. 420)
- how to choose and read a pattern envelope. (p. 421)
- how to take your measurements. (p. 422)
- how to select the correct fabric and notions for your sewing project. (p. 426)

Knowing how to sew can be helpful to you in many ways. If you can make a vest or tote bag, you can choose just the fabric,

DISCUSS: Brainstorm with the class a list of reasons why people should know how to sew. Discuss the ways in which time and money can be saved. Also emphasize the personal satisfaction involved.

Secondhand Business Is First Rate

Operating a consignment shop is a good way to become an entrepreneur. And you don't need much money to invest.

A consignment store "recycles" secondhand goods. Clothing consignment stores range from thrift shops to stores with only upscale, "designer" fashions. Or, they may be boutiques that specialize in vintage or period clothing.

Here is how it works. The consignor, that is, the original owner of the garment, leaves the item to be sold. The store owner sets the price and splits the amount with the consignor, usually 50-50, when the garment is sold. Thus the store owner doesn't invest any money in merchandise. Instead, shop space, a few fixtures, racks, and a small advertising budget are all that is needed.

A good business sense, fashion flair, and the willingness to give customers personal attention are also essential. The owner must know what to accept and how to price it. He or she must understand how to refuse unsuitable items tactfully and how to develop a following among customers. Finally, the owner must give the shop a "personality" to suit the neighborhood or a particular clientele. You can see that owning a consignment store takes planning and imagination.

Are there any consignment stores in your neighborhood?

color, and style you want. Sewing allows you to become, in effect, a designer. You are the one who will select the trim or other details that give an item an individual look.

Before you start to sew, you need to think carefully about the kind of project that is best for you. The success of your project will depend on choosing the right pattern and selecting a suitable fabric.

Deciding on a Project

Sewing your own clothes can be satisfying and fun, but you have to do some planning ahead of time. Before you start a sewing project, think about your resources. These include your experience and skills, time, and money. Keep these guidelines in mind.

- Choose something you will enjoy making and will really use. A good way to get ideas is to look in a pattern catalog.
- If you have done very little sewing, choose a simple project. If you already have some sewing skills, choose something more challenging.
- Consider the amount of time you have. You should not feel rushed when you are sewing. You need time to correct mistakes. If you allow yourself plenty of time, you will be more satisfied with the final product.
- Consider the amount of money you have to spend. Some materials, such as silk, are beautiful but very expensive (and difficult to work with). Also consider the type and number of notions required for the item. Be sure to choose a project within your budget.

REINFORCEMENT: Have students select three or four patterns from a catalog. Review their choices with them. Have they selected something fun, simple, and usable? Are the projects within their budgets?

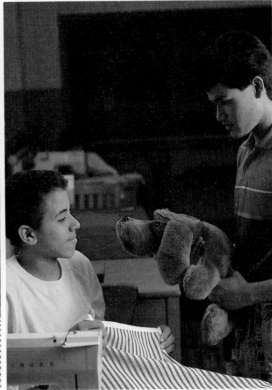

Part of the fun of finishing a project is showing off your results. It's also a time to share all you've learned.

If you are just beginning to sew, your teacher may select a project for you. A simple project in class usually includes all of the basic sewing skills.

Choosing a Pattern

Once you have decided what to sew, you need to know how to sew it. A **pattern** is a model and a set of instructions for you to use to carry out your project. A pattern shows you what your garment will look like when it is finished. It also includes step-by-step directions for completing the project. Along with choosing a style you

like, you need to select the right type and size of pattern. Patterns are grouped according to figure types, such as *Girls, Misses, Boys,* and *Men.*

In order to select the right pattern for your figure type and size, you need to know your body measurements. Pattern books are divided into different sections according to these figure types. For example, a section might be labeled "Juniors." Within each pattern type, there are patterns for different sizes and styles. There is also a section in catalogs for crafts and accessories. If you are making something like a pillow cover, you should look in this section.

NOTE: Fabric stores will sometimes offer discount cards to students in the local school system. Discounts can range from 10–20% off fabric, notions, and patterns.

REINFORCEMENT: Explain how to read a pattern envelope for size, amount of fabric, suggested fabrics, and notions.

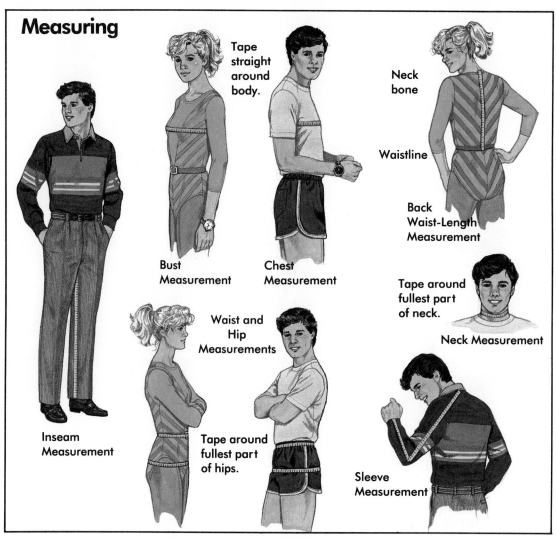

Measuring

Tape straight around body.

Neck bone

Waistline

Back Waist-Length Measurement

Bust Measurement

Chest Measurement

Tape around fullest part of neck.

Neck Measurement

Waist and Hip Measurements

Inseam Measurement

Tape around fullest part of hips.

Sleeve Measurement

Accurate measurement affects every stage of your project.

Taking Measurements

It is difficult to take your own measurements accurately, so ask a friend to help you. Measurements are most accurate if you have them taken over smooth-fitting garments such as leotards or underwear. Do not measure over bulky, heavy sweaters or jackets. Write each measurement as it is taken. Double-check by taking each measurement a second time.

As you are taking measurements, hold the tape measure so that it is neither too tight nor too loose. When someone is measuring you, stand straight and look directly in front of you.

Your Type and Size

To determine your figure type, find the size chart in a pattern catalog. Read the descriptions of different figure types and

ART: Stress that it is not always easy to find your measurements on a size chart. There is nothing unusual or embarrassing about not fitting exactly into one of the categories below.

Finding Out Your Size

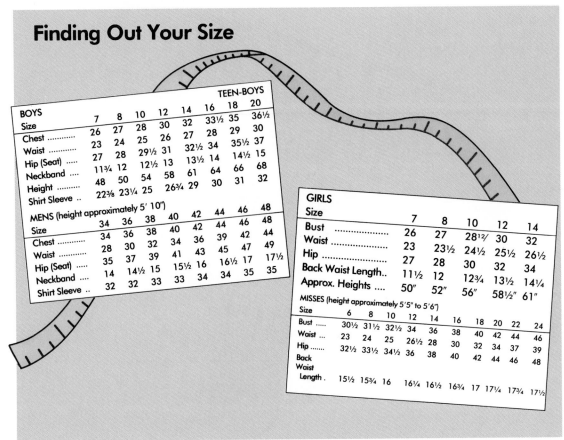

BOYS Size	7	8	10	12	14	16 (TEEN-BOYS)	18	20
Chest	26	27	28	30	32	33½	35	36½
Waist	23	24	25	26	27	28	29	30
Hip (Seat)	27	28	29½	31	32½	34	35½	37
Neckband	11¾	12	12½	13	13½	14	14½	15
Height	48	50	54	58	61	64	66	68
Shirt Sleeve	22⅜	23¼	25	26¾	29	30	31	32

MENS (height approximately 5′ 10″)

Size	34	36	38	40	42	44	46	48
Chest	34	36	38	40	42	44	46	48
Waist	28	30	32	34	36	39	42	44
Hip (Seat)	35	37	39	41	43	45	47	49
Neckband	14	14½	15	15½	16	16½	17	17½
Shirt Sleeve	32	32	33	33	34	34	35	35

GIRLS Size	7	8	10	12	14
Bust	26	27	2812/	30	32
Waist	23	23½	24½	25½	26½
Hip	27	28	30	32	34
Back Waist Length	11½	12	12¾	13½	14¼
Approx. Heights	50″	52″	56″	58½″	61″

MISSES (height approximately 5′5″ to 5′6″)

Size	6	8	10	12	14	16	18	20	22	24
Bust	30½	31½	32½	34	36	38	40	42	44	46
Waist	23	24	25	26½	28	30	32	34	37	39
Hip	32½	33½	34½	36	38	40	42	44	46	48
Back Waist Length	15½	15¾	16	16¼	16½	16¾	17	17¼	17¾	17½

First, identify your figure type. Then find your size.

find your own. Once you know your type, find your size by comparing your measurements to those on the chart.

You may not find your exact measurements on the chart. If not, choose the pattern size that comes closest to them. Girls should use the bust measurement for clothes like blouses, dresses, and suits. For pants, skirts, and shorts, the hip measurement should be used. Boys should use the neck measurement for shirts and the chest measurement for coats and jackets. For slacks, boys should use either the waist or hip measurement, whichever is larger.

REINFORCEMENT: Once students have completed their measurements, explain how to read the size chart in the pattern catalog.

Do not be surprised if you find that your pattern size is different from your size in ready-made clothes. Patterns are sized differently from ready-made clothes.

The Pattern Catalog

Pattern catalogs show pictures of the clothes or crafts you can make from different patterns. Catalogs also give practical information, such as the amount of fabric you will need for a particular item. In addition, they often provide clues to a pattern's difficulty. For example, you might see phrases like "very easy" or

RETEACHING: Emphasize the importance of buying the correct size pattern. Buying the incorrect size requires altering the pattern to your size.

pattern number → **3412** Medium

Body Build and/or Pattern Size

Pattern Company Name → *quick stitch*

Learn-to-Sew Pattern ← **Type of Pattern**

$3.95 ← **Pattern Price**

Style View → A

B ← **Style View**

Will you look as good in this garment as the model does? Choose a pattern based on what looks good on you.

"learn-to-sew." The patterns in the catalog have numbers so that you can find a particular pattern easily.

The Pattern Envelope

Your pattern will come in an envelope. The pattern envelope contains the paper pieces needed to cut out the fabric and an instruction sheet. The envelope itself also provides valuable information.

The front of the envelope shows drawings or photographs of clothes made from the pattern. These pictures are shown in various fabrics to give you an idea of the different looks one pattern can have. Variations in details may also be shown. You may see a dress with both long and short

The Back of a Pattern Envelope

3412 8 Pieces	TEEN BOYS' or GIRLS' SHORTS: Pull on shorts in two lengths, with side seam pockets; has drawstring in waistline casing.			
FABRICS—Cotton, cotton blends, seersucker, lightweight denim	**NOTIONS**—Thread; 1 3/4 yds. of 1/8" Cable Cord			
STANDARD BODY MEASUREMENTS Hip	**x-small** 32 1/2–33 1/2 in.	**Small** 34 1/2–36 1/2 in.	**Medium** 37–40 in.	**Large** 41–44 in.
FABRIC REQUIRED				
VIEW A SHORTS				
44/45"	1 1/2 yds.	1 1/2 yds.	1 1/2 yds.	1 1/2 yds.
58/60"	1 yd.	1 1/8 yds.	1 1/8 yds.	1 1/2 yds.
VIEW B SHORTS				
44/45"	1 yd.	1 yd.	1 1/8 yds.	1 1/8 yds.
58/60"	7/8 yd.	7/8 yd.	7/8 yd.	1 1/8 yds.
FINISHED GARMENT MEASUREMENT AT HIPLINE	39 in.	41 1/2/ in.	45 1/2 in.	49 1/2 in.

VIEW A   VIEW B

Estimate your costs. Can you afford all the fabric, supplies, and interfacing that you will need?

sleeves or several different kinds of collars. The pattern number, size, and, sometimes, figure type will also appear on the front of the envelope.

These important details are given on the back of the pattern envelope:

- the number of pattern pieces in the envelope
- back views of the garment
- a description of the garment telling more about style and details
- suggestions for fabrics that will work well with the pattern, along with a list of fabrics that should *not* be used
- a chart showing how much fabric you will need depending on the view you are making, your size, and the width of your fabric
- a chart showing body measurements and sizes
- a list of notions you will need to complete the garment. **Notions** are small sewing items like thread, buttons, zippers, and trim. (You will learn more about notions on page 428.)

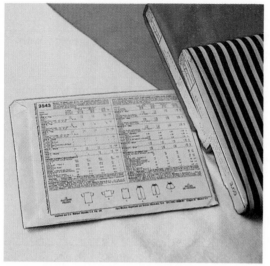

The pattern envelope provides advice on suitable fabrics.

Selecting Your Fabric

One enjoyable part of a sewing project is selecting a fabric from the wide variety of colors and textures available. Set aside the time you need for going to a fabric shop. Choose a fabric you really like. You will be working with it for a while and wearing the garment even longer. Along with satisfying your personal taste, there are several other things to consider when you select fabric.

What Kind of Fabric?

Some fabrics are more suited to a certain kind of project than others. For example, a delicate, sheer fabric is not appropriate for a tote bag; a sturdy fabric like denim is. In addition, the pattern itself can limit your choice of fabrics. If you are making a loose-fitting garment, you will want fabric that is soft and flowing. A bulky fabric

could create a heavy look. The fibers, weight, weave, and design of a fabric all help determine if it is suitable.

The pattern envelope can guide your selection. Remember to take it with you when you shop. If you are not using a commercial pattern, your teacher will advise you about fabrics.

How Much Fabric?

The amount of fabric you need depends on several factors. One of these is the width of your fabric. You will usually find fabric widths of 36 inches, 45 inches, and 60 inches (90 cm, 115 cm, and 250 cm). The size and kind of item you are making are also considerations. If you are using stripes or plaids, they have to be matched at the seams. This means you will need extra fabric.

The chart on the pattern envelope can guide you in buying the right amount of fabric. Make sure you know the view, size, and fabric width you are using. You can practice determining fabric amounts using the illustration on page 425.

Care Needs and Care Labeling

Be sure to find out how you will need to care for your fabric. Information about fabric content and special finishes is listed on the end of a bolt of fabric. Care labels are sometimes available for sewing into your garment. Ask a salesperson about labels when you purchase fabric.

Make sure the care needed for the fabric is appropriate to the use of an item. If a garment will get a lot of hard wear,

 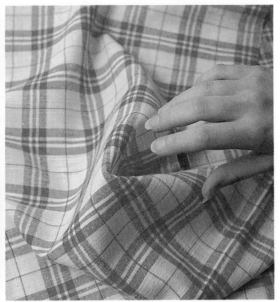

Will the fabric you're buying wrinkle? It's easy enough to find out before you purchase it.

avoid a fabric that has to be hand-washed or ironed. A machine washable fabric with a permanent press finish would be more practical.

Find out if the fabric needs special care to protect its color. The ability of a fabric's dye to keep its exact color is its **colorfastness.** It is important to know if frequent washing will affect the colorfastness of a fabric. Sunlight, perspiration, and chemicals used in dry cleaning may also change the color of a fabric.

Quality and Cost

The fabric you choose should be good enough to last and wear well. However, it should not be more expensive than necessary. Nor should it cost more than your family can afford. Before you buy fabric, think about using pieces of clothing that

you know you won't wear again. See Chapter 20 for more ideas for recycling clothes. These guidelines can help you get the best quality for your money.

- Check for imperfections such as snags, spots, and faded colors.
- Do the wrinkle test. Gather some fabric in your hand and crinkle it for about 30 seconds. Then release the fabric. If it is wrinkle-resistant, it will return to its original shape. If it stays wrinkled, it will do the same thing when you wear it.
- Do the stretch test when selecting a knit. First, check the fabric against the knit gauge on the pattern envelope. This will tell you if the fabric is right for the garment. While you are doing this, notice if the fabric returns to its original shape after stretching. If it does not, it may also stretch out of shape when you wear the garment.

Notions are usually little items of great importance. Select them to match your fabric and your taste.

Fabrics for a First Project

If you are a beginning sewer, your choice of fabric is especially important. A loosely-woven fabric can be hard to work with, as it ravels easily. It is best to stick to a firm, uniform weave. Slippery fabrics can also be difficult to handle. Plaids, stripes, and corduroy require special layouts and extra attention. If you use fabric that has imperfections, you will have to avoid those areas. Make sure your fabric has even coloring and no white spots. Your teacher can suggest some fabrics that are easy for a beginner to handle.

Notions

Notions, the small items you need for sewing a pattern, will be listed on the pattern envelope. Notions include thread, buttons, zippers, trim (like ribbon or rick-rack), elastic, hooks and eyes, snaps, and hem tape. You should buy your notions when you buy your fabric. One reason for this is that notions should match or co-ordinate with your fabric. Second, you need to have them on hand so that you won't be held up during your project. You will waste time if you find you're missing a zipper or other item.

Shopping for notions is fun, and you will have a wide choice. If you cannot exactly match items like thread or zippers, a color that is slightly darker than the fabric will look better than one that is lighter.

See page T126 for answers.

For Review

1. List four guidelines to follow when deciding on a sewing project.
2. What six kinds of information can you find on the back of a pattern envelope?
3. Explain how the fabric you choose affects your sewing results.

REINFORCEMENT: Bring in samples of denim, chino, broadcloth, and duck as examples of fabrics to use when learning how to sew.

REINFORCEMENT: Familiarize students with notions like hem tape, bias tape, rick-rack, types of elastic, hooks and eyes, snaps, and zipper types.

Learning to Manage

Not "Sew" Easy

Look back at the conversation on page 416. Now read how Chris and Pam manage to make their choir skirts. Then answer the questions that follow.

Chris and Pam made their purchases and hurried to Pam's house to cut out their skirt pieces. As they unfolded their patterns, Chris saw that she had many more pieces than Pam did. She finally sorted out all the pieces for the ruffles and bow. Carefully, both girls followed the pattern directions for layout. Then they pinned the pattern pieces to the fabric and cut into the material.

Pam had chosen a medium-weight polished cotton. It wasn't as fancy as the crepe Chris had bought, but it wasn't as expensive either. It also had a "permanent press" sticker on the bolt of fabric. Although they were making full-length choir skirts, Pam hoped to shorten her skirt later to wear with her black-and-white turtleneck. Her material was cutting smoothly.

Chris was having some trouble because her fabric kept slipping as she tried to cut it out. Also, the cutting wasn't even with the pattern edges. "Mrs. Tully will be proud of us for getting a head start," Chris said, as she packed up the skirt pieces. "I can't wait to sew it together on Monday after school."

Mrs. Tully, however, had wanted the students to wait. She wanted to check their layout and pinning before they cut out their pattern pieces. She knew how enthusiastic Pam and Chris were, but she also saw immediately that Chris had made an expensive error. As soon as Chris began to sew on the machine, she had trouble keeping her sheer material from puckering. Even when she changed the tension, she was still struggling with bunched-up fabric. Meanwhile, Pam was almost finished with the side seams.

"I'm afraid your fabric is more suitable for an evening skirt, Chris," Mrs. Tully said gently. "It's also very difficult for a beginner to work with. Your pattern is complicated, too."

"I should have paid more attention in class, and to Pam."

"Well, let's see what we can do with it. But, before you buy material for another project, let's talk more about choosing patterns and fabrics that you can handle. Ruffles and bows can wait for a while!"

Questions

1. Using what you have learned in this chapter, choose a sewing project for a beginner. List all of the steps needed to complete the project.
2. Explain three smart sewing choices that Pam made.

Chapter 18 Review

Summary

When working in the sewing lab, remember to cooperate with other students and to use care in using equipment. Safety procedures are of vital importance both at school and at home.

The success of a sewing project depends on careful decision making about the kind of project to be undertaken. It is important to select the correct size and type of pattern, and to choose an appropriate fabric.

Organization is important, also. Take the time to plan and understand each step of your project before you begin work on it.

Vocabulary

Complete each of the following sentences with the correct word from the vocabulary list below.

notions (p. 425)
pattern (p. 421)
colorfastness (p. 427)

1. A _____ consists of a model and a set of instructions that explain how to sew a particular garment.
2. _____ are items such as thread, buttons, zippers, and trim that are needed for making a garment.
3. The ability of a fabric's dye to keep its true color throughout the life of a garment is its _____.

Questions

• 1. Why should you not use an extension cord with a sewing machine?
• 2. Why should you turn off the iron and leave it in a resting position when you leave the ironing board?
• 3. How can you spend your time profitably while waiting to use a sewing machine in the sewing laboratory?
• 4. Name three factors to take into consideration when you schedule a sewing project.
• 5. How can you avoid getting your personal equipment mixed up with someone else's?
• 6. Where can you look to get ideas for a sewing project?
•• 7. Why is it important to take each measurement twice when you are preparing to make a garment?
• 8. What size pattern should you buy if you cannot find one with measurements that are exactly the same as your measurements?
•• 9. How can the pattern envelope help you to choose a fabric for the garment you are making?
• 10. What four factors should you think about when selecting a fabric?
•• 11. How might a pattern limit your choice of fabrics?
• 12. How do you know how much fabric to buy when you make a garment from a pattern?

The dots represent skill levels required to answer each question or complete each activity:

• requires recall and comprehension
•• requires application and analysis
••• requires synthesis and evaluation

13. If you were making a shirt for casual, everyday wear, would silk be a good choice? Explain your answer.

14. Name three guidelines to follow regarding quality and cost when you are shopping for fabric.

15. What can you do if you cannot find a zipper that exactly matches the fabric you are using?

Skill Activities

Many more activities are contained in the annotations within this chapter.

1. Decision Making Select a pattern for a sewing project to be made in class. Think about the fabric that would work best for your project. After reading the back of the pattern envelope, create a shopping list for the supplies you will need. Be sure your list includes notions and fabric.

2. Communication Using pictures from a pattern book, create a bulletin board of project ideas that would appeal to both boys and girls. Arrange the pictures to show categories such as "Sports" (sweatbands, sweatpants, tote bags) and "Room Accessories" (shoe bags, pillows).

3. Decision Making Collect a variety of fabric samples from your home or your classroom. Examine the fabric for weave, uniformity of color, texture, and pattern. Separate the fabric that would be easy to work with from fabric that presents some kind of special sewing challenge. Attach each fabric sample to a piece of paper. Write a description of the fabric underneath it. Explain why the fabric would be a good choice for a sewing project or why it would be difficult to work with. Also describe how easy or hard it is to mantain.

4. Laboratory Ask a classmate to help you take your measurements. Use the information on page 422 to make sure you measure accurately. Once you know your measurements, use the back of a pattern envelope to find your size and type. Write all this information in a notebook so that you will choose the correct pattern size for all your sewing projects.

5. Communication Make a set of safety posters for your sewing laboratory. Review the safety guidelines on pages 417–418. Be sure to include any additional rules that apply to your particular laboratory. Post the safety rules in specific areas of your classroom. For example, place ironing safety reminders in the ironing area and hand sewing safety rules near the sewing machines. Use illustrations and large clear lettering to make your posters eye-catching and easy to read.

Chapter 19
Equipment and Preparation

Vocabulary

The dialogue below introduces "Fabric Fumbles," the Learning to Manage feature in this chapter. The case study is continued and the situation discussed further on page 455. See page T129 for teaching suggestions.

"I'm ready to get started laying out my pattern!"

"Me too, Tony. Right now I need a good pair of scissors and some straight pins to tack the pattern pieces down."

"I think we'd better gather all of the equipment we'll need before we get started. Where are those pins?"

Section 19.1

Equipment for Sewing

As you read, think about:

■ the importance of having the proper small equipment for sewing. (p. 433)

■ the importance of proper use and care of a sewing machine. (p. 436)

■ how serger sewing can help you to sew well and save time. (p. 443)

Trying to sew without the proper equipment is like trying to play softball without a bat and ball. Along with a sewing machine, which is your most important piece of equipment, you need a number of smaller items. Even if you could struggle along without some of them, you would waste time and might spoil your project.

Small Equipment

As you work on a sewing project, you will do some measuring, cutting, and marking of fabric. For each of these jobs there are pieces of equipment that help to get the work done efficiently.

Measuring Tools

Often, the first job in any sewing project is measuring. The more accurately you perform this task, the easier your whole project will be. The following equipment will help you with your measuring tasks.

• A *sewing gauge* is a 6-inch (15-cm) ruler with a slide marker. It is used to mea-

Measuring Tools

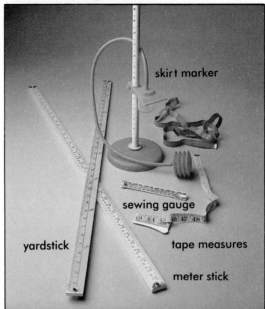

Can you identify each of these important measuring tools?

sure small areas, such as seams or hems.

• A *yardstick,* or *meter stick,* is used to measure the pattern and fabric, to check grain lines, and to mark hems.

• A *tape measure* is used to take body measurements.

• A *skirt marker* is used for marking skirt lengths with pins or chalk.

Cutting Tools

Several tools are designed for cutting fabric. It is best to use the right type of cutting tool for each job. Obviously, the sharper you keep your tools, the better they will work.

This is the equipment you will need.

• *Scissors* are used to trim fabric and to clip threads. Both small cutting scissors

REINFORCEMENT: Distribute a list of the sewing equipment that will be used in class. Display each piece of equipment and explain its use.

DISCUSS: Which of the measuring tools discussed above do your students think they use most frequently? Have them give examples of what they use them for.

433

and those with larger blades are available. The rings (for inserting the fingers) on the handles of scissors are usually small and of equal size.

- *Shears* have long blades and are used to cut fabric. If you get shears with bent handles, it is easier to keep the fabric flat as you cut. Shears have a small ring for the thumb and a larger ring for the other four fingers. You can buy either left-handed or right-handed shears.
- *Pinking shears* cut fabrics in a zigzag pattern. They can be used to finish the edge of firmly woven fabrics to prevent the fabric from raveling easily.
- A *seam ripper* is a penlike object with a small blade that removes stitches. To

You may be surprised at how often you'll use a seam ripper.

Cutting Tools

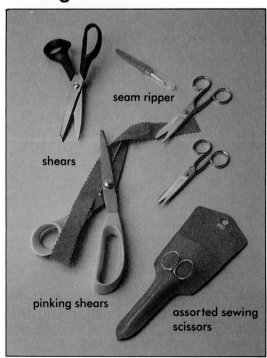

seam ripper

shears

pinking shears

assorted sewing scissors

NOTE: Pinking shears may not be used to cut out a pattern either by itself or when it is on the fabric. Explain reasons why.

use a seam ripper, cut a stitch every inch (2.5 cm). Then pull at the thread from the bottom of the fabric.

Marking Tools

The following equipment is used to mark the location of items like pockets, buttonholes, and darts.

- A *tracing wheel* and carbon paper are used to transfer pattern markings to the fabric. Wheels with needle-toothed edges can be used for heavy fabrics. Don't use carbon paper on sheer fabrics. Those with saw-toothed edges are used for lightweight to medium-weight fabrics. There is also a toothless wheel, which is best for delicate fabrics.
- The *carbon paper,* or *tracing paper,* used with a wheel comes in several colors. Use a color that is close to the fabric color but still visible. Lay carbon paper on the wrong side of the fabric.
- *Tailor's chalk,* used to mark fabric, comes as a pencil or a small square of wax or chalk. Use wax for wool. You can mark all other fabrics with chalk.

Other Small Equipment

There are other pieces of small equipment that you will need as you sew. Items like pins, needles, and an iron are needed at various stages in sewing.

- *Straight pins* hold the pattern to the fabric while you cut. They also hold pieces of fabric together. Use sharp pins for woven fabrics and ball point pins for knits. Pins with plastic heads are the easiest to use.

REINFORCEMENT: Demonstrate how to open a seam using a seam ripper.

Marking Tools

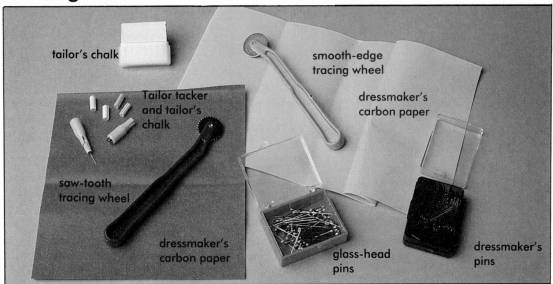

tailor's chalk

smooth-edge tracing wheel

Tailor tacker and tailor's chalk

dressmaker's carbon paper

saw-tooth tracing wheel

dressmaker's carbon paper

glass-head pins

dressmaker's pins

Use a small box to store all these little things. This way, you're less likely to misplace a few.

- *Needles* for hand sewing are available in sizes 1 to 12, with size 1 being the largest. Sizes 7 and 8 are good for general sewing. Ball point needles have a rounded point, which makes them useful for knitted fabrics.
- A *thimble* protects your finger when you push a needle through fabric. You wear it on the middle finger of the hand holding the needle. A thimble should fit your finger snugly.
- A *pin cushion* holds needles and pins when you are not using them. An *emery bag* is attached to many pin cushions. This strawberry-shaped bag will clean rusty or sticky needles. To do this, just push them into the bag a few times.
- A *magnet* helps to clean up loose pins and needles.

NOTE: When pinning a pattern to the fabric, pins should be placed perpendicular to the cutting line. This keeps the pattern from moving or slipping.

Small Equipment for Sewing

sewing needles

glass-head pins

wrist pincushion

thimbles

darning needles

dressmaker's pins

pincushion and emery pack

NOTE: Pins and needles can be a serious hazard where young children crawl. Accidents can also occur when people go barefoot, exercise, or get down on their hands and knees. Be sure to clean up thoroughly after you use them.

Health and Safety

Danger: Children at Work!

Throughout the 1800s and into this century, young children were often expected to work. Many were the only wage earners because their parents were unemployed. Child workers were exploited: they could be paid less than adults and were less likely to complain about working conditions. These conditions were so terrible that reformers battled to make child labor illegal and to improve conditions.

Many children worked in textile mills, spinning yarn and weaving cloth. New machines made the work "so easy even a child could do it." That meant it didn't require training or strength, and children's small hands often did better than adults'. But the machines did require speed. Those who could not keep up were often whipped or lost their jobs—or worse. The machines never stopped to rest. Neither did the children, even though the factories were poorly lit, dirty, and either too hot or too cold.

The workday at the mills began at 6am. Children arrived on time—they would be locked out and lose their pay otherwise. They had 15 minutes for breakfast and 30 minutes for lunch. The rest of the time, until 5pm, they stood at the machines. Mill children worked six days a week.

What laws in your state protect children in the workplace?

Ironing and Pressing Tools

Pressing is a task performed both as you sew and after your project is completed. Pressing as you sew gives your finished product a professional look. These are items you will find helpful.

- An *electric iron,* preferably a steam iron, with a range of temperature settings is essential.
- An *ironing board* is necessary for pressing straight seams and flat areas of a garment. The board should have a clean cover and padding.
- A *press cloth* is placed between the fabric and the iron. It prevents shiny marks caused by the heat of the iron.
- A *tailor's ham* is a firm, ham-shaped cushion. It is used for pressing curved seams and darts.
- A *sleeve board,* or small ironing board, allows you to press sleeves or other small areas.
- A *press mitt* is a small tailor's ham that fits over your hand or a sleeve board. It is used to press hard-to-reach areas.
- A *steam roll* is a long, firm, tube-shaped cushion. It is used to press long seams and small curved areas.
- A *point presser* has a narrow wooden surface with a pointed end that is used to press collar points. Other edges on this item can be used for pressing straight edges or curves.

The Sewing Machine

The sewing machine automatically stitches fabric together by causing two threads to interlock. Many different types of sew-

NOTE: Press cloths can be purchased. They can also be made from cheesecloth or lightweight muslin.

ART: Ask students to identify each of the items shown here and explain its purpose.

ing machines are available. Today some computerized models require only the touch of a button to do each job, such as decorative stitching. A basic sewing machine allows you to do straight stitching and sometimes zigzag stitching. You can also get attachments, such as a buttonholer, for basic machines. Between the basic and deluxe models is a range of machines with different features. Whichever type of machine you are using, read the instruction manual that comes with it. This will help ensure that you use the machine correctly. Page 438 shows the basic parts of a sewing machine. The location of some parts may vary with different equipment.

Threading the Machine

Many sewing machine problems are the result of improper threading. The instruction manual that comes with your machine will tell you exactly how to thread it. However, the order for threading a machine is generally the same. Look at the

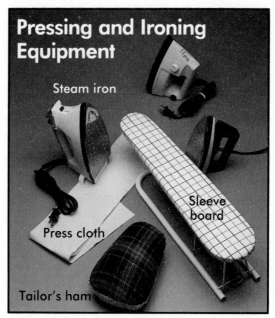

Pressing and Ironing Equipment

Steam iron

Sleeve board

Press cloth

Tailor's ham

Many tools are available to help you press carefully and exactly.

threaded sewing machine on page 438 to make this process clearer. The thread moves from the spool, through the upper tension discs and thread take-up lever, down to the hole in the needle. There are thread guides to hold the thread in place. The needle will be easier to thread if you cut the thread at an angle.

The bobbin must also be threaded. A self-winding bobbin is put into the bobbin case and then filled with thread. A conventional bobbin is threaded before it is put into the case. Again, check your instruction manual.

Using the Sewing Machine

If you are a beginning sewer, you may find it helpful to practice stitching with an unthreaded machine. Use lined paper, and guide the machine along the lines. Work

Did You Know?

Clear plastic pill bottles make great containers for sewing needles. For needles with thread attached, add an adhesive bandage. Wrap the bandage around the bottle, and stick the needle through the padded part. The extra thread can be wrapped around the bottle.

NOTE: The first electric sewing machine was manufactured by the Singer Company in 1889.

REINFORCEMENT: Have each student choose a partner. Each should practice threading the machine needle and winding the bobbin, calling on the other for help as necessary.

The Sewing Machine

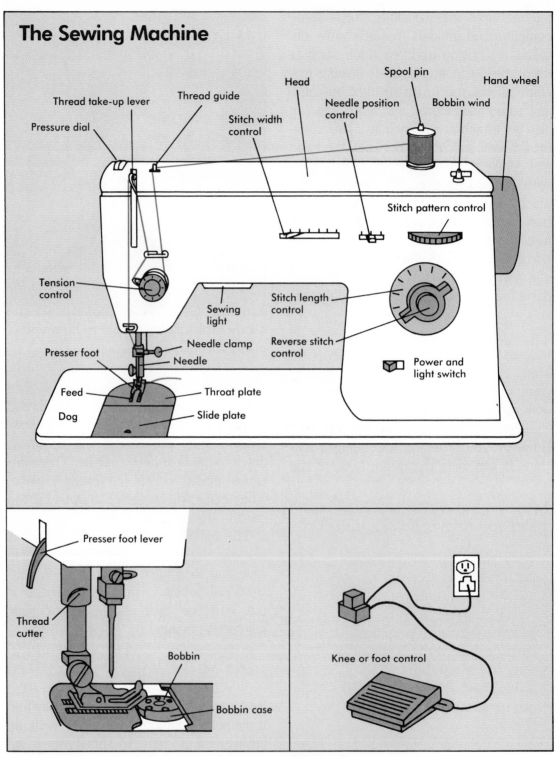

Knowing the parts helps you solve any problems that arise.

ART: Reinforce students' understanding of the machine parts by demonstrating what each machine part does and/or how it works.

NOTE: The bobbin thread should be the same as the spool thread. When the thread types differ, the machine has a tendency to stitch improperly.

Parts of the Sewing Machine

- The **head** is the main part of the sewing machine. It contains most of the sewing parts.
- The **handwheel** or **balance wheel** controls the movement of the needle and the thread take-up lever.
- The **thread take-up lever** feeds thread from the spool to the needle.
- The **bobbin** is a small spool that holds the lower thread. This lower thread forms the under half of a stitch.
- The **bobbin case** holds the bobbin and regulates the tension for the bobbin thread.
- The **bobbin winding spindle** is used to wind thread onto a bobbin.
- The **slide plate** covers the bobbin case.
- The **needle** is the thin metal shaft that carries the thread through the fabric.
- The **throat plate** or **needle plate** is the metal plate directly under the needle.
- The **feed** or **feed dog** moves the fabric toward the back of the machine as you stitch.
- The **tension control** regulates the looseness or tightness of the upper thread.
- The **presser foot** holds the fabric in place as you stitch.
- The **presser foot lever** raises and lowers the presser foot.
- The **stitch length control** regulates the length of stitches.
- The **stitch width control** regulates the width of stitches.
- The **stitch pattern control** is used to make different decorative stitches.

slowly at first, and increase your speed as you become more comfortable with the machine. Then follow these guidelines using a threaded machine.

- Before you begin to stitch, raise the take-up lever and needle to the highest point. This will keep the thread from pulling out of the needle.
- Make sure the upper thread and the bobbin thread are pulled back behind the presser foot. This will keep them from getting tangled in the bobbin case.
- Place the fabric under the presser foot, with the bulk of the fabric to the left of the machine. Smooth out the fabric so you can feed it beneath the needle.
- Place the point of the needle on the stitching line.
- Lower the needle onto the fabric by turning the handwheel. Lower the presser foot. Then use the knee or foot control to stitch at a slow, even speed.
- When you finish stitching, turn the handwheel to raise the take-up lever and needle to the highest position. Do not pull the fabric toward you, as this could bend the needle. Instead, slide the fabric toward the back of the machine. Then clip the threads.

Don't be discouraged if your first efforts at learning to stitch are not successful. The explanations that follow can help you perfect your stitching techniques.

Straight Stitching To make rows of straight stitches, use the guideline markings on the needle plate or throat plate. If your machine does not have markings, use a piece of tape. Place the tape on the throat plate ⅝ inch (1.6 cm) from the

REINFORCEMENT: Encourage students to develop the habit of tuning the machine hand wheel toward them. This helps to keep the machine gears in good working order.

ENRICHMENT: Divide students into groups of four. One person should point to machine parts; a second person should identify them; a third should tell what they are for; and a fourth should check the text for corrections. Roles can be exchanged.

Don't forget . . .

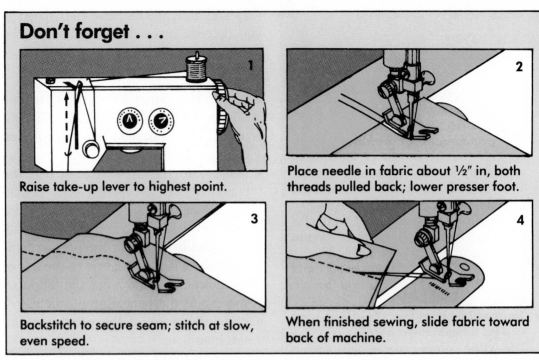

1 Raise take-up lever to highest point.

2 Place needle in fabric about ½" in, both threads pulled back; lower presser foot.

3 Backstitch to secure seam; stitch at slow, even speed.

4 When finished sewing, slide fabric toward back of machine.

Once you learn them, the steps for using a sewing machine are simple and quickly become routine.

needle. Line up your fabric with the guidelines, and keep your eyes on the fabric while you sew. Learn to use your hands to guide the fabric. Place one hand in front and one hand behind the presser foot. Be careful that you do not pull or push the fabric.

Stitching curves and turning corners take a little more practice. Try drawing curved lines on a piece of paper. Then practice stitching until you feel confident you can do it smoothly. When you need to turn a corner in the middle of a seam, stitch to within ⅝ inch (1.6 cm) of the corner. Stop stitching with the needle down in the fabric. Then lift the presser foot and pivot (turn) the fabric on the needle. Lower the presser foot and begin stitching again in the new direction.

Securing Stitches At the end of a seam, you need to secure the stitches so that they will not come out. You can use *backstitching* to do this. If your machine has a reverse stitching position, use it to backstitch. Begin on the seam line, ½ inch (1.3 cm) from the edge of the fabric. Stitch backwards to the edge of the fabric. Then stitch forward over the stitch you made. Finally, backstitch four or five more stitches.

If your machine does not have a reverse stitch position, you can secure the stitch another way. Making sure the needle is in the fabric, lift the presser foot and turn the fabric around. Lower the presser foot and then stitch back over the seam.

Another way you can secure stitches is to lockstitch. The lockstitch is the basic stitch used in sewing. To use it to secure stitches, first raise the presser foot slightly. Then take two or three regular stitches in the same place. You can also just turn the stitch length to zero before you begin to sew.

You can secure stitches by hand as well. Cut the thread ends so they are long enough for tying. Then remove the fabric from the machine. Bring the thread to the wrong side of the fabric and tie a knot.

Making Adjustments You will need to adjust stitch length and tension to fit the fabric you are using. Do this before you begin to sew, by checking stitches on a scrap of your fabric. For most fabrics, 10 to 12 stitches per inch (2 to 2.5 cm) is recommended. A shorter stitch should be used for lighter fabrics.

The **tension,** that is, the looseness or tightness of the stitches, is regulated by the tension control. You can tell if the

Always check the tension before you begin to sew.

Slow and steady sewing results in exact and even stitches.

tension is properly balanced by examining stitches on each side of the fabric. The stitches should be flat and smooth and look the same on both sides. If they don't, check your instruction manual and adjust the tension.

Care of Your Machine

Your sewing machine needs to be cleaned regularly if it is to work properly. A soft sewing machine brush is good for keeping a machine clean and free of dust. The feed and bobbin in particular should be kept free of lint. Machines should also be oiled occasionally with sewing machine oil. Be sure to wipe away any excess oil so that you won't spot your fabric. Check your instruction manual for details on cleaning and oiling.

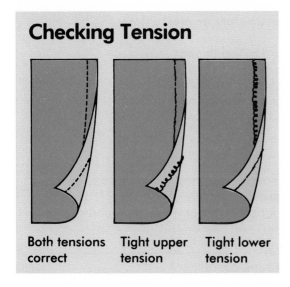

Checking Tension

| Both tensions correct | Tight upper tension | Tight lower tension |

ENRICHMENT: Divide students into groups. Distribute several swatches of material with poor stitching to each student. Have them speculate on how the tension should have been adjusted to avoid these problems.

REINFORCEMENT: Tell students that after they clean and oil a sewing machine, they should always run a scrap piece of fabric back and forth over the feed dog to absorb any excess oil.

Sewing Machine Problems

Problem	Possible Causes
Needle breaks	• Needle inserted incorrectly • Needle hitting pins • Pulling on fabric when sewing • Presser foot not tight enough • Too many layers of fabric or fabric too thick • Tension too tight
Thread breaks	• Wrong size or kind of needle • Wrong size thread • Thread knotted or uneven • Machine threaded incorrectly • Bobbin threaded incorrectly • Tension too tight
Skipped stitches	• Wrong size or kind of needle • Needle inserted incorrectly • Dull or bent needle • Machine threaded incorrectly • Wrong kind of thread • Tension too tight
Puckered seams	• Tension too tight • Needle dull or bent • Thread too coarse • Stitch length too long • Too much pressure on presser foot
Machine jams	• Matted or knotted thread • Bobbin threaded incorrectly • Thread caught in bobbin case • Needle position incorrect • Machine threaded incorrectly
Machine does not work ON OFF	• On/off switch or electrical cord not working • Hand wheel knob loose • Knee or foot control not working properly

Many sewing machine problems are easily remedied.

ART: As a matter of procedure, students should learn always to check machine threading and the correct insertion of the needle as a first step whenever a sewing machine problem develops.

RETEACHING: Go over the chart carefully. Then have students close their books. Name prlblems, and have students come up with possible causes.

Common Problems

Many sewing machine problems can be traced back to the needle. Always check the needle first. The chart on the opposite page shows several common problems and their possible causes.

Serger Sewing

There is a new, very fast sewing machine available today called the **serger.** This machine can stitch, trim, and finish off seams all at the same time. The garment industry has used the serger since the early 1900s. Industrial sergers can make 6,000 stitches per minute. Sergers developed for home use can sew 1,700 stitches per minute, twice the speed of a regular sewing machine. Swift as it is, however, the serger does not replace the conventional sewing machine. There are many tasks for which the serger is not suited. Used along with a regular sewing machine, it adds speed and efficiency. Still, these advantages must be weighed against the expense of buying a serger.

How the Serger Sews

A serger makes stitches by means of a knitting process. Each stitch is knitted over a metal prong, called a *stitch finger.* Sergers stitch using from two to four spools of thread at a time. They sew with fine, smooth thread especially designed for high-speed sewing. Heavier, decorative threads made just for serger use are sometimes used.

A serger will sew straight, curved, or cornered seams, and the fabric does not

Is the cost of a serger worth what you will do with it?

have to be pinned or basted. Serger-sewn edges do not unravel like fabric sewn on a regular machine.

How Sergers Are Different

The picture above shows the parts that are common to all sergers. There are several differences between the design and function of a serger and that of a conventional sewing machine.

- Sergers have knife blades, called cutters. These trim the seam allowance before it is stitched.
- Sergers do not have bobbins. Loopers are used instead.
- The serger can use more than one spool of thread at a time. There are two-, three-, and four-spool sergers.
- The serger cannot sew a straight lockstitch, the basic stitch in conventional

NOTE: In the garment industry, the serger machine is known as the overlock machine.

ENRICHMENT: Have students make a chart comparing and contrasting the features of conventional and serger sewing machines.

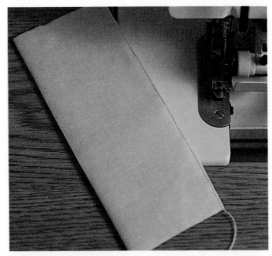

How can you tell that these seams were sewn with a serger?

sewing. However, some sergers can sew a chainstitch. This is a two-thread stitch that is a little bulkier than a lockstitch.

- Sergers can feed two layers of fabric smoothly. Stripes can be matched without basting as long as they start out matched.
- You do not have to lift the presser foot when starting to sew unless the fabric is thick. This is because the feed dogs on sergers are longer than those on a conventional machine. Serger feed dogs catch the fabric as it is placed under the toe of the presser foot.

See page T131 for answers.

For Review

1. Name four kinds of measuring equipment you can use.
2. Name six guidelines to follow when using a sewing machine.
3. What does a serger do that a regular sewing machine cannot do?

ENRICHMENT: Have students write a one-page paper describing why they think a serger machine is important in mass-producing garments.

Section 19.2

Preparing, Cutting, and Marking Fabric

As you read, think about:

- how to prepare a fabric for stitching. (p. 444)
- how to lay out a pattern and cut the fabric properly. (p. 449)
- how to mark your fabric properly. (p. 451)

There are certain very important steps leading up to the actual stitching of your project. You must first prepare the fabric so that the finished product will not shrink or change shape. Next you lay out the pattern and cut your fabric properly. You then need to mark on the fabric the location of pattern details such as buttonholes and trim.

Fabric Preparation

Before you begin to sew a piece of fabric, you should preshrink and straighten it. This is called *preparing* the fabric. If you omit the preparation tasks, the garment will not fit properly. To understand how problems can occur, think first about the fabric itself.

Preshrinking

Before you proceed with straightening the fabric, you should preshrink it. Otherwise it is likely to shrink later on, when the finished item is used and laundered. You may find information about preshrinking when you buy the fabric. A label on the

NOTE: Often, even after fabrics have been preshrunk, there still remains a small amount of shrinkage. This is called residual shrinkage.

bolt might state that the fabric is *Sanforized*. This means it has been preshrunk. The fabric will shrink only 2 percent or less when it is washed.

If the fabric has not been Sanforized and can be machine washed and dried, use an automatic machine to preshrink it. If you are using hand-washable fabric, fold it and put it in hot water for 30 minutes. Dry-clean wool or other fabrics that cannot be washed. Woven zippers, trims, tapes, interfacings, and linings should also be preshrunk. (Do not, however, preshrink bias tape.) Place tapes and trim, still wrapped in their cardboard, in hot water for 30 minutes. Bend the cardboard slightly to allow for some shrinkage.

Finding the Grain

You have learned that woven fabrics are made from two sets of yarn. The yarn running crosswise is the warp, and the yarn running lengthwise is the filling. These two sets are interlaced at right angles to each other. On the lengthwise edges of fabric, there are narrow finished borders called **selvages** (*SEL*–vej–ez). Usually, the selvage is stiffer than the rest of the fabric. When you lay out your pattern, use only fabric inside the selvage.

The **fabric grain** is the sewing term for the direction in which yarns run. The yarn running lengthwise (the filling) is called the *lengthwise grain*. The yarn running crosswise (the warp) is the *crosswise grain*. The lengthwise grain, which runs in the same direction as the selvage, is usually stronger. For this reason most garments are cut with the lengthwise grain running up and down. This increas-

Fabric Grain

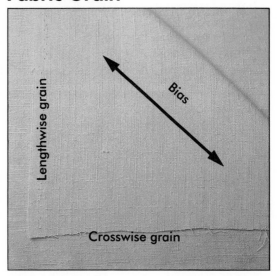

You must find the grain to lay out the pattern.

es a garment's strength and durability. When pattern instructions refer to "straight grain" or "grain line," this means the lengthwise grain. The crosswise grain runs from one selvage to the other. In most fabrics, the crosswise grain has a little stretch or give.

Bias grain runs diagonally across the fabric in any direction other than lengthwise or crosswise grain. In order to find the **true bias** (*BY*–as), where the fabric has the most stretch, pick up a corner of the fabric. Fold it so that the crosswise grain is parallel to the selvage. True bias is the diagonal edge formed when the fabric is folded.

Straightening Fabric

Sewing should be done on straightened fabric or the finished product will not hold its shape. **On-grain** fabric has crosswise

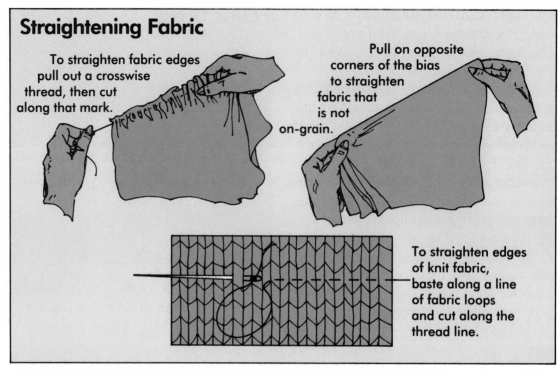

Straightening Fabric

To straighten fabric edges pull out a crosswise thread, then cut along that mark.

Pull on opposite corners of the bias to straighten fabric that is not on-grain.

To straighten edges of knit fabric, baste along a line of fabric loops and cut along the thread line.

First, straighten the fabric. Then press the fabric to keep it exactly on-grain.

and lengthwise yarns that are at right angles. To find out if your fabric is straight, or on-grain, first check the ends, or edges, of the material. Sometimes when fabric is cut off the bolt in the store, it is crooked. If you can clearly see crosswise yarns, cut along a yarn from selvage to selvage. If you cannot, use one of the methods described below.

You can straighten the edges of firmly woven fabric by tearing it. First, clip through the selvage. Then grasp each of the cut pieces and tear firmly. Do this *carefully*. You could pull the fabric off-grain, or the fabric might split along the lengthwise grain.

For fabrics that are soft, stretchy, or loosely woven, you can straighten the edges by pulling a thread. Clip the selvage. Then grasp a crosswise yarn and pull it. Use the other hand to push the fabric back gently. The yarn you pull out will leave a mark you can cut along. If the yarn breaks midway, cut up to the broken point. Then find the end of the broken yarn and continue pulling.

Some woven fabrics have a stripe, plaid, or check to guide you in straightening. Find a line near the selvage and cut the fabric crosswise.

Straightening the Fabric Grain

Once you have preshrunk your fabric, you can straighten the grain. Check your fabric carefully to see if it is on-grain. Fold

NOTE: Woven fabrics have their best drape in a bias direction. However, one problem that can result is that a garment cut on the bias may increase in length. A dress hem, for example, could then become uneven or irregular.

DISCUSS: Talk about problems that may show up in the finished product if the fabric grain is not straightened properly.

the fabric in half lengthwise and put the selvages together. Make sure the fabric is smooth. If the selvages and crosswise edges are perfectly even, the fabric is straight. If they are not even, you have to straighten the fabric. You can do this by pulling the fabric on the bias. Unfold the fabric. Use both hands, and pull the two opposite corners that are too short. Check to see if you have pulled enough by refolding the fabric. Once the fabric is straight, press it with steam to set it in position.

Pattern Guide Sheet

Once your fabric is straight and has been preshrunk, you can prepare to lay out your pattern. Begin by going over the items in the pattern envelope. You will find a **pattern guide sheet.** This gives information for laying out the pattern and for cutting, marking, and sewing the fabric. General information and layouts for cutting are on the front side of the sheet. Directions for sewing are on the back. Study the guide sheet and find the layout for the style, size, and fabric width you have selected. Circle the layout you are using so that you can refer to it easily. Then find the pattern pieces you will need. Put any unneeded pieces back in the pattern envelope.

Fitting Your Pattern

If you are making a garment, you need to find out how well your pattern fits you. Very few people have the exact same measurements as those listed for a particular pattern size. If your pattern does

need some adjustments, you must make them before you cut the fabric.

To check your pattern fit, use your list of body measurements. Compare your measurements with those on the pattern envelope and write down where adjustments need to be made. However, the pattern envelope does not list some measurements. For these, measure the actual pattern pieces. Measure only from seamline to seamline. Do not include the seam allowances on the pattern pieces or any darts, pleats, or tucks. Remember that a garment should be a little larger than your body measurements. You need *ease* allowance, or room to move around easily in your clothes.

Altering Your Pattern If your pattern is too long or too wide, simply pin tucks in the pattern pieces to adjust them.

Careless pinning or cutting can result in a size difference.

Pattern Guide Sheet

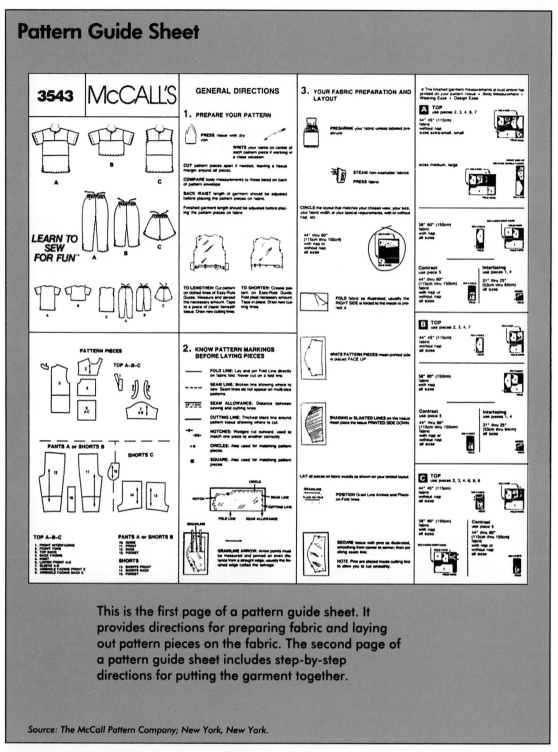

This is the first page of a pattern guide sheet. It provides directions for preparing fabric and laying out pattern pieces on the fabric. The second page of a pattern guide sheet includes step-by-step directions for putting the garment together.

Source: The McCall Pattern Company; New York, New York.

Keep your pattern guide sheet handy at all times.

ART: Explain to students that pattern guide sheets are prepared very carefully to ensure clarity and exactness. Therefore, even if an instruction does not seem logical, it should be followed.

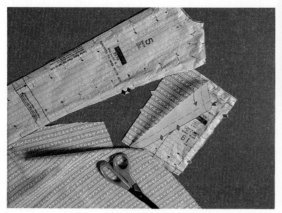

The success or failure of a project can sometimes be traced back to how it was cut. Don't rush to get it done!

If the pattern is too short or too narrow, insert paper strips and tape them in place. You may need to redraw details such as darts after you make adjustments. Also, redraw the cutting line.

Cutting Layout

The diagram that shows how to place pattern pieces on fabric is called the **cutting layout.** This diagram is usually found on the pattern guide sheet.

It is important that you follow the cutting layout exactly. If you do not, you may end up with too little fabric or two

left arms. It is also important that you lay out all of the pattern pieces before you begin cutting.

If your pattern pieces are printed on one large sheet of tissue paper, cut them apart. You do not need to trim away extra tissue paper from around the pieces. This will be cut off when you cut the fabric.

There will be several markings on the cutting layout and on the pattern pieces. Look for a heavy solid line with arrows at both ends. This is the *grain line.* You will find a grain line on all pattern pieces except those cut on a fold. When you position pattern pieces on your fabric, make sure they are placed exactly on the proper grain line. The *cutting line* is a heavy line outlining the pattern pieces. There may be a scissors symbol printed on the line to tell you the correct direction for cutting. The *stitching line* is a broken line inside the cutting line. There might be arrows or a symbol of a sewing machine presser foot to show which direction to stitch. There will also be special markings for details. These include notches, darts, buttonholes, and folded lines like the hemline or a cuff.

The cutting layout will show you how to fold your fabric. Fabric is usually folded with the right side in and the pattern pieces placed on the wrong side. Plaids, stripes, and prints should be folded with the right side out. This makes it easier to match the fabric design. When laying out your pattern, begin with the pieces that are located on the fold. Most pattern pieces should be placed with the printed side up. However, check the layout for pattern pieces that are shaded. Any shaded pieces should be placed on the fabric with the printed side down. Also, be sure to check the layout for pattern pieces that have to be cut twice.

Pinning

First, pin pattern pieces in place on the fold. Pins should be 3 to 4 inches (8 to 10 cm) apart. They should be at right angles to the cutting edge, with the points toward the edge. Make sure the points do not go past the cutting line. After pinning along the fold, smooth the pattern away from the fold. Then place pins diagonally in the corners. The remaining pattern

pieces should be pinned according to the grain line arrow. Position the pattern so that the grain line looks straight to you. Place a pin at the end of each grain line arrow. Then measure from each pinned end to the edge of the fabric. If the measurements are not exactly equal, remove the pins and shift the pattern until they are. Once you are sure the grain line is straight, pin the pattern in place. Then finish pinning the edges of the pattern to the fabric. Remember to check the pattern pieces against the layout guide to make sure you have not forgotten any pieces. It is also a good idea to have someone else check your pattern layout.

Cutting

You are now ready to cut your fabric. Use sharp, bent-handled shears. They are the most accurate, as they allow you to keep the fabric flat. Hold the fabric in place with one hand as you cut with the other. Cut with long even strokes and do not close the blades completely. Be careful to cut with the grain line. Follow the direction symbols printed on the pattern. If your pattern does not have symbols, cut

Did You Know?

A pair of scissors "loose" in a sewing basket can turn into a weapon. So that you won't stab yourself when reaching in, stick the points of the scissors in a piece of cork.

REINFORCEMENT: Demonstrate how a pattern is "placed on the fold" and pinned and "placed on the straight of the grain" and pinned.

RETEACHING: Stress that when your students cut fabric, they must keep the fabric flat on the table. If they put their hands underneath the cloth or lift it in any way, they risk inaccurate cutting.

Pattern Symbols for Marking Fabric

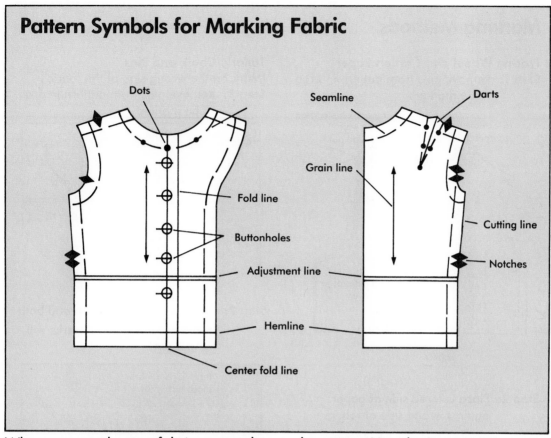

When you mark your fabric, remember to be exact. You don't want the markings to show in the finished product.

from the widest point to the narrowest point. Cut around notches with the tips of the shears. Cut outward, away from the pattern. Double and triple notches should be cut as though they were one big notch. These notches will help you join pattern pieces accurately when you are ready to sew. Put the pieces neatly aside as you cut them.

If you are inexperienced at cutting fabric, practice before you cut into your layout. Use some fabric scraps and experiment with straight lines, curves, corners, and notches.

NOTE: In the garment industry, a piece of equipment called a notcher is used to mark the darts, seam allowances, fold lines, center front, and center back lines. It resembles a hole puncher for paper.

Do not unpin your pattern pieces from your fabric. You will need them for marking your fabric.

Marking Fabric

The lines, dots, and other symbols on your pattern pieces will guide you in putting together your project. You should transfer these markings to your fabric before you unpin the pattern. You must be able to see the markings while you are sewing. However, they should not show on the outside of the finished item.

DISCUSS: Tracing wheels and carbon paper should not be used on sheer, heavily napped, or loosely woven fabric. Discuss reasons why tailor's chalk or tailor's tacks are better.

Marking Methods

Tracing Wheel and Carbon Paper

Step 1: Remove pins from pattern in area to be marked.

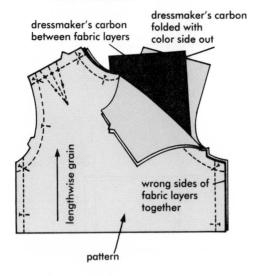

dressmaker's carbon between fabric layers

dressmaker's carbon folded with color side out

lengthwise grain

wrong sides of fabric layers together

pattern

Step 2: Place colored side of paper against *wrong* side of fabric.

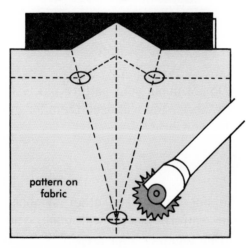

pattern on fabric

Step 3: Run tracing wheel along pattern marking lines.

Tailor's Chalk and Pins

(Mark on the wrong side of the fabric.)

Step 1: Remove pins from pattern in area to be marked.

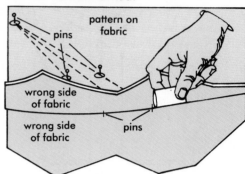

pattern on fabric

pins

wrong side of fabric

wrong side of fabric

pins

Step 2: Put pins through pattern and both layers of fabric where marks will be needed.

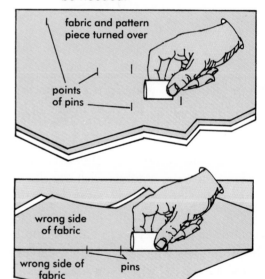

fabric and pattern piece turned over

points of pins

wrong side of fabric

wrong side of fabric

pins

Step 3: Lift up pattern piece and top layer of fabric. Mark site of each pin. Mark both layers of fabric.

When you mark your fabric, follow directions carefully. Concentrate on doing one step at a time.

ART: Discuss the reasons for using the tracing wheel and the tailor's chalk so that marks are made on the wrong side of the fabric.

Tailor's Tacks

Step 1: Do not unpin pattern.

Step 2: Thread a needle with regular sewing thread in a double thickness.

Step 3: Take a loose stitch through pattern and both layers of fabric at the place you want to mark.

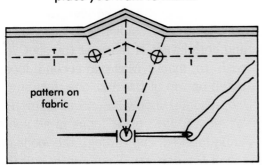

Step 4: Make a second loose stitch on top of first one to form a loop 1 in. (2.5 cm) in diameter.

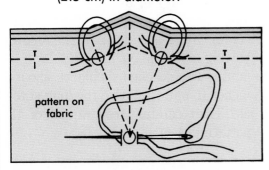

Step 5: Clip through loops on top of pattern.

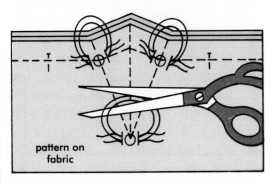

Step 6: Gently pull fabric pieces apart and clip threads between fabric layers.

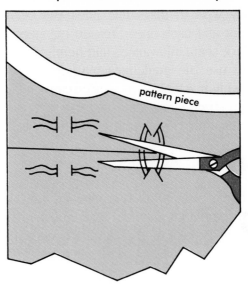

Basting

Step 1: Make uneven basting stitches on single layer of fabric. Make stitches 2 in. (5 cm) long.

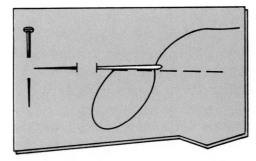

Step 2: Clip long stitches and carefully remove pattern.

ART: Emphasize that just the right amount of pressure is needed with a tracing wheel. If the pressure is too light, the image may not transfer to the bottom piece of fabric. If pressure is too heavy, pattern pieces may tear.

What to Mark

Darts, pleats, tucks, and dots for matching pattern pieces should be marked. Also mark the placement of buttonholes, buttons, pockets, and trim. In addition, you may wish to mark fold lines and center front and back lines. You do not need to mark seam allowances and hemlines. You can use the guidelines marked on your sewing machine to measure seam lines as you stitch. You can measure and turn hems after completing everything else.

Marking Methods

These are some of the marking methods you can use. As you read about these methods, look at the chart on pages 452 and 453 to see how they are done.

- *Tracing wheel and carbon paper.* A fast and easy way to mark fabric is to use a tracing wheel and carbon paper. This method can be used on most lightweight and washable fabrics. However, do not use this method for marking fabrics that are light-colored, sheer, heavily napped, or loosely woven. First, remove a few pins from the pattern in the area to be marked. Place the colored side of the paper against the *wrong* side of the fabric. Then run the tracing wheel along the pattern marking lines. The color from the carbon paper will be transferred to the fabric.
- *Tailor's chalk and pins.* When you work with thick fabrics like corduroy, you should use tailor's chalk and pins for marking. This method is more difficult than using a tracing wheel and carbon paper and requires practice. Be sure to mark on the wrong side of the fabric. Remove pins from the area you will be marking. Put pins through the pattern and both layers of fabric where marks will be needed. Then use the chalk to mark the indicated spots on the top layer of the fabric.
- *Tailor's tacks.* These can be used to mark sheer, loosely woven, or bulky fabric. Do not unpin the pattern. Take a loose stitch through the pattern piece and both layers of fabric at the spot you wish to mark. Make a second loose stitch on top of the first one, forming a loop about 1 inch (2.5 cm) in diameter. When you have made loops in all spots to be marked, clip through the loops on top of the pattern. Then gently pull the fabric pieces apart and clip the threads between fabric layers.
- *Basting.* You can use basting to mark long lines, such as placement lines and center front and back. Make uneven basting stitches on a single layer of fabric. The stitches should be about 2 inches (5 cm) long. Clip the long stitches. Then carefully remove all of the pattern pieces.

See page T131 for answers.

For Review

1. What are the two basic steps in preparing fabric for sewing?
2. Name three different purposes for the markings on pattern pieces.
3. Where do you find general information and layouts for cutting fabric?
4. Name four kinds of marking methods you can use on fabric.

REINFORCEMENT: Demonstrate the following marking methods in class: tracing wheel and paper, tailor's chalk and pins, tailor's tacks and basting. Show how to remove the pattern carefully when using the tailor's tacks and basting methods.

ENRICHMENT: Divide students into four groups. Have each group become "experts" on one of the marking methods and then demonstrate it to the class.

Learning to Manage

Fabric Fumbles

Look back at the conversation on page 432. Now read how Tony and Harry manage to prepare their pattern pieces. Then answer the questions that follow.

"My dad will really like this carpenter's apron I'm making for him. Let's see . . . there aren't too many pieces. . . ."

"Harry, do you remember all of the things we are supposed to do before we cut out our patterns? I don't want to ruin this!"

"I took notes in class, Tony. They're right here. I don't want to ruin my duffel bag either."

The boys proceeded to lay out their fabric and place the pattern pieces down carefully. They checked against their cutting layouts often to be sure they were correct. They didn't have to worry about size, since neither of their projects needed to be a particular size. They pinned the pattern pieces onto the fabric and then checked each other's layouts to see if they looked correct. So far, so good.

They decided they were ready to cut out their pattern pieces. Tony reminded Harry about cutting around the notches on the pattern and they started to cut. The carpenter's apron had more pieces, so Harry finished first. They carefully removed all of the pins, folded their fabric and pattern pieces, and put their equipment away.

The next day they brought their fabric pieces to class. Suddenly they both realized that they had forgotten to mark the fabric where tucks, pockets, and trim would be going. This meant spending a lot of time pinning the pattern pieces back onto the correct fabric pieces. After they had marked where it was necessary, they again prepared to sew. Now they were sure that everything was fine and they proceeded to the sewing machines.

Tony and Harry worked carefully on the sewing machines. They stitched as evenly as they could and were fairly happy with their projects when they had finished. Two weeks later, however, they were comparing disaster stories after they had laundered their projects. Harry's duffel bag now looked like a pocketbook, and Tony's carpenter apron would only fit his younger sister. What had gone wrong?

Questions

1. What important steps of fabric preparation did both boys forget?
2. Based on what you have learned in this chapter, list all of the steps used to prepare fabric and lay out a pattern.

Chapter 19 Review

Summary

The small equipment needed for sewing includes items for measuring, cutting, marking, pinning, hand sewing, and ironing. It is important to understand the function of each part of a sewing machine. You should also know how to thread the machine properly and how to care for it. You can soon develop skills in backstitching and in sewing straight lines, corners, and curves. As well as conventional sewing machines, sergers are now available for home use. While these machines are very fast, their uses are limited.

Before fabric is stitched, it must be prepared, laid out, cut properly, and marked. Preparation includes straightening the fabric and preshrinking it. The pattern guide sheet must be carefully followed for placing pattern pieces, pinning, and cutting. Marking methods include a tracing wheel and carbon paper, chalk and pins, tailor's tacks, and basting.

Vocabulary

Complete each of the following sentences with the correct word from the vocabulary list below.

on-grain (p. 445) cutting layout (p. 449)
serger (p. 443) tension (p. 441)
pattern guide sheet (p. 447) true bias (p. 445)
fabric grain (p. 445) selvages (p. 445)

1. A _____ gives information for laying out the pattern and for cutting, marking, and sewing the fabric.
2. _____ is the looseness or tightness of the stitches.
3. _____ is the part of the bias where the fabric has the most stretch.
4. The diagram that shows how to place pattern pieces in fabric is called the _____.
5. Narrow finished borders on the lengthwise edges of fabric are called _____.
6. _____ fabric has crosswise and lengthwise yarns at right angles.
7. The _____ is the sewing term for the directions in which yarns run.
8. A sewing machine that can stitch, trim, and finish off seams at the same time is called a _____.

Questions

- 1. What kind of measuring equipment would you use to measure small areas, such as seams or hems?
- 2. What is the difference between scissors and shears?
- 3. What equipment is useful for pressing curved seams and darts?
- 4. Name a good way to practice stitching curves and turning corners.
- •• 5. Explain how to care for both the feed and the bobbin case on a sewing machine. Why is this important?

The dots represent skill levels required to answer each question or complete each activity:

- • requires recall and comprehension
- •• requires application and analysis
- ••• requires synthesis and evaluation

6. Name the most common cause of sewing machine problems.
7. By what process are stitches made on a serger?
8. Name three advantages of using a serger.
9. What is used instead of a bobbin on a serger?
10. Why is it necessary to prepare fabric before stitching it?
11. What processes are involved in preparing fabric?
12. How can you straighten the edges of fabrics that are loosely woven?
13. Why should a garment be a little larger than your body measurements?
14. How should shaded pieces of a pattern be placed on the fabric?
15. What marking method is best for lightweight and washable fabrics?

Skill Activities

Many more activities are contained in the annotations within this chapter.

 1. Laboratory Practice making machine stitches accurately. Draw a large cartoon figure on a piece of unlined 8½″ × 11″ paper. Make sure your drawing is an outline or silhouette, not a detailed drawing. Have several copies of the drawing made. Using an unthreaded sewing machine, stitch on the lines you have drawn. Try to turn and guide the paper smoothly so that the stitches stay on the lines. Review the suggestions for stitching straight or curved lines and turning corners on pages 439–440. Look at your finished product. Circle your mistakes with a colored marker. Try stitching another copy of your drawing to see if you can improve your accuracy.

 2. Laboratory Work with a classmate to learn the names of sewing machine parts. Use the actual sewing machine or an unmarked diagram. One partner looks at the diagram on page 438. Reverse roles and let the partner who has been testing try to identify the sewing machine parts. Next work with your classmate in the same way to identify the purpose of the sewing machine parts. Use the information on page 439.

3. Critical Thinking Select a piece of clothing from your wardrobe and think about how it was made. Look carefully at the garment and try to answer the following questions. How many pattern pieces were used to make the garment? How many pattern pieces were cut on the fold line? What pattern markings were used on the pattern pieces? Was the pattern laid on-grain correctly? Write answers to these questions on a piece of paper. Try to draw the pattern pieces for your garment. Compare your results with those of another student.

Chapter 20
Construction Techniques

Vocabulary

The dialogue below introduces "New Styles and Old Lace," the Learning to Manage feature in this chapter. The case study is continued and the situation discussed further on page 473. See page T134 for teaching suggestions.

"That's just the dress I want for the spring dance. I've been coming here to look at it almost every day. But it's much too expensive."

"The color is great, Pat, and I love the lace. It would look really super on you."

"I wish I had a sewing machine— and more time before the dance. I could sew on the lace by hand."

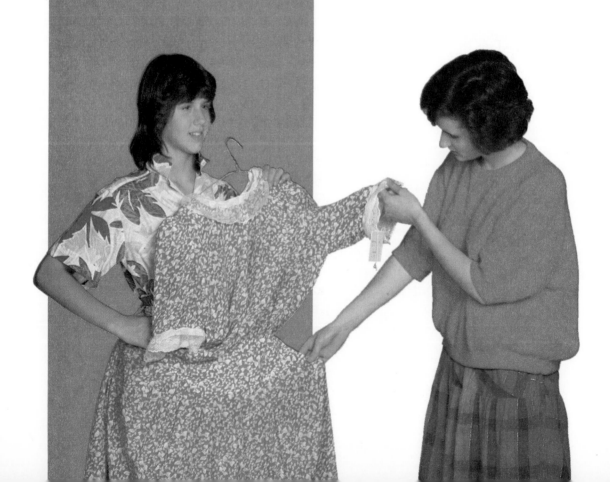

Section 20.1
Hand Sewing

As you read, think about:
- how to thread a needle properly. (p. 459)
- how to do temporary hand sewing. (p. 460)
- how to do permanent hand sewing. (p. 461)

There are a number of sewing procedures that are done by hand, using a needle and thread. Sometimes hand sewing is a temporary measure that precedes permanent sewing, either by hand or by machine. Other sewing tasks, such as hemming and making buttonholes, are often done completely by hand.

Threading a Needle

To thread a needle, unwind a length of thread no more than two feet long. If the thread is longer than your arm's length, it will tangle as you sew. Using scissors, cut the thread at an angle, so that it will slip through the *eye,* or hole, in the needle. (Breaking the thread causes it to fray or have a ragged end. This makes it difficult to get it through the needle's eye.) Hold the needle against a background that contrasts with the color of the thread. Pull the thread through the eye so that one length is at least twice as long as the other. Tie a knot at the end of the longer length of thread if you are sewing with a single thread. Some sewing requires a double thread, for example, sewing on a button. In this case hold the two lengths of thread together, match their ends, and then tie the knot.

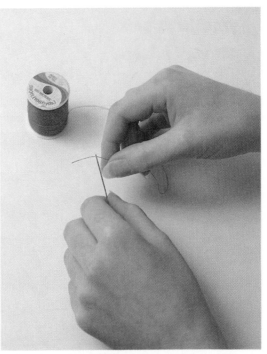

If you cut the thread with scissors, this job is much easier.

Using a Thimble

Always use a thimble when you are sewing by hand. Wear it on your middle finger. A thimble has small indentations to keep the needle from slipping. A thimble also protects your finger when you push a needle through heavy fabric. Buy a thimble that fits comfortably on your middle finger. It will seem awkward at first, but you will soon get used to it.

Tying a Knot

Tie a knot at the end of the thread this way. Hold the end between your thumb and index (first) finger. Wrap the thread around your fingertip one-and-a-half times. Roll the thread off your finger so

459

Tying Knots

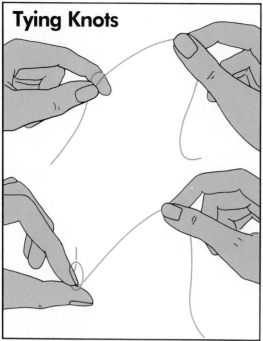

Do you want your stitches to stay in place? You need to knot your thread securely.

that the thread is twisted. The thread will form a loop. Hold the loop between your thumb and middle finger. Pull on the length of thread with your other hand until the loop closes and a knot is made.

Things to Remember

Use a needle and thread of the correct size and type for the fabric you are using. Use a ball point needle for knitted fabrics and a regular needle for most other materials. Your thread should match the color of your fabric. If you can't find an exact match, choose a slightly lighter shade. It should also be the right size and type for the fabric's weight and fiber. For example, medium-weight wool should be sewn with mercerized cotton thread, size A or 50.

460   Unit 5/*Clothing and Textiles*

Temporary Hand Sewing

It is often necessary to do some temporary hand sewing before the final sewing is done. Basting, easing, and gathering are three common sewing procedures.

Basting

Hand sewing two layers of material together temporarily to be sure they are correctly matched is called **basting.** You will find hand basting more accurate than either machine basting or pinning. Follow these steps to baste by hand.

1. If you are right-handed, sew from right to left. If you are left-handed, work from left to right.
2. Hold the fabric so that the area you are sewing is at the top. Work your needle in and out of the fabric in even stitches about ¼ inch long. Make longer stitches if fabric is heavy. This kind of stitch is called a *running stitch.*
3. To save time, take several stitches before you pull the thread through.
4. After you have permanently sewn the pieces, remove the basting.

Basting is often quick and easy.

Running Stitch

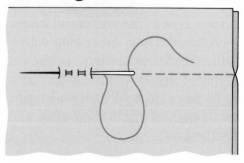

Easing and Gathering

The methods of easing and gathering are used to join two pieces of material of different lengths. **Easing** is done when one piece of fabric is only slightly larger than the other. Use this method for waistbands and for set-in sleeves, so that the material is not pulled when the body moves. Use **gathering** to form soft folds of material when making puffed sleeves, ruffles, and full, unpleated curtains.

To ease or gather, use a running stitch as you learned for basting. Make even stitches from ⅛ to ¼ inch long. Rather than making a knot in the thread, leave a length of several inches at either end. Then pull the thread to gather the fabric to the fullness you want. Generally, use hand-sewn easing and gathering only for small areas; you can do large areas on a sewing machine. Once you have done the permanent stitching, remove the temporary stitches.

Permanent Hand Sewing

You can do some sewing tasks better and more easily by hand. Depending on the task, there are several different stitches used in permanent hand sewing.

Overcast Stitch

Use the *overcast stitch* to finish raw edges and so prevent raveling. You can work in either direction. Space stitches evenly and at the same depth. They should be about ¼ inch deep for lightweight fabrics. Make

deeper stitches for heavy fabrics and fabrics that ravel (pull apart) easily. Avoid making your stitches so tight that the fabric curls.

Overcast Stitch

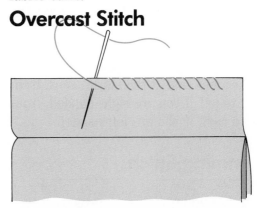

Overcast stitches should be loose.

Backstitch

The strongest of all hand-sewn stitches is the *backstitch*. Use it to make or mend seams, to sew in zippers, and to fasten thread ends. You can also use it in places that are hard to reach on a machine.

First make several running stitches about ⅛ inch long. Then insert the needle back at the beginning. Bring it out one stitch length in front of the previous stitch. Repeat the process. The stitches on the underside will be twice as long as those on top.

Backstitches are good for mending.

Backstitch

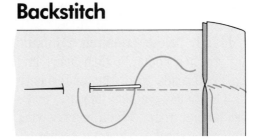

ENRICHMENT: Distribute two muslin swatches, one longer than the other, to each student. Ask students to run two rows of basting stitches across the top of the longer muslin piece and to hand-sew the easing on the other. Then have them practice easing and gathering.

ART: Stress that the slip stitch is used when the fabric is doubled over or folded.

Hemming Stitch

To hem a garment, first baste the hem. Then use a hemming stitch through the folded edge of the fabric. A *hemming stitch* is made with stitches spaced evenly about ¼ inch apart. The stitches should be slanted, and they should barely show on the right side of the fabric. Work from right to left if you are right-handed, from left to right if you are left-handed.

Hemming Stitch

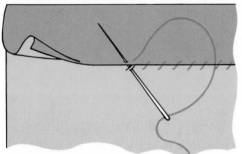

Hemming stitches are slanted.

Slip Stitch

The *slip stitch* is used to attach a folded edge to another piece of fabric. It is strong and almost invisible. Use it for hems, linings, and patch pockets.

Anchor the thread on the wrong side of the fabric by taking a small stitch through the hem edge. Then slip the needle through the fold of the upper fabric. Make a small stitch in the garment, picking up one or two threads of the underneath fabric directly below the stitch. Continue making stitches about ¼ inch apart and picking up threads from the underneath fabric. On heavy-weight fabrics, make stitches farther apart. When hand-sewing facings, make stitches closer together.

REINFORCEMENT: To provide practice in hemming, invite each student to bring to class a garment from home that needs to be hemmed.

Slipstitch

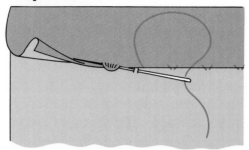

Slip stitches are durable.

Buttonhole Stitch

Use heavy-weight or double thread to make buttonholes. Work from right to left if you are right-handed and from left to right if you are left-handed. Stitches should be the same depth and evenly spaced. For lightweight fabrics, they should be about ¼ inch deep. Fabrics that are heavy or ravel easily require deeper stitches.

Put the needle through the buttonhole from the wrong side and bring it through the fabric. Loop the thread through the previous stitch and pull it up to form a knot. Repeat the process as you work around the buttonhole.

These are buttonhole stitches.

Button Hole Stitch

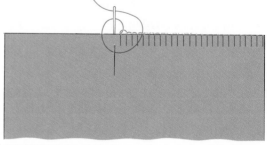

ENRICHMENT: Provide basting practice by having students sew a hand puppet for someone younger. Give each student two pieces of felt and a puppet pattern. Students should cut out the puppet and baste it using the running stitch. Colored felt can be glued on for eyes, nose, and mouth.

Running Stitch

You learned how to make a *running stitch* in the previous section on basting. The running stitch can also be used for permanent sewing. Use it in places where there will be little strain on the area and for easing, tucking, and quilting. Make stitches ¼ to ¹⁄₁₆ inch long. Remember to work from right to left if you are right-handed and from left to right if you are left-handed.

See page T134 for answers.

For Review

1. Why is it important, when threading a needle, not to unwind more than two feet of thread?
2. List four steps to follow when basting by hand.
3. What is the difference between easing and gathering?
4. Name the strongest king of hand-sewn stitch.

Section 20.2

Machine Construction

As you read, think about:

- how to construct a garment using the various sewing machine stitches. (p. 463)
- how to finish seams, and sew facings, fasteners, and hems. (p. 467)
- the various ways to recycle clothing. (p. 472)

You have chosen your pattern and fabric, cut out the pieces, and pinned them together. Now you are ready to construct

REINFORCEMENT: Have students list the six stitches they have just studied and give an example of how and where they would use each one.

PHOTO: Review for your students the things that this student must have already done to have reached this stage in his project.

Machine-sewn garments often look neater than hand-sewn ones.

the garment you are making on your sewing machine. You can use a variety of assembly techniques and stitches.

Construction

There are several methods of putting a garment together. One method is called **unit construction.** In this method, you complete each section separately and then sew them together. For example, to make a shirt, you first complete the back, the front, and the sleeves. Then you attach all the pieces. Another method is called the **assembly-line method.** To make a garment using this method, you

REINFORCEMENT: Refer to Chapter 2 on time management. Ask students to develop a time plan for completing their projects. They should first decide on unit construction or the assembly-line method and then list the steps in the order in which they will be completed.

"Constructing" a Difference

Do you ever wonder how you can make a difference in the world? So many problems seem too big to be taken on at your age. Although you have skills you're proud of, are they enough to "make a dent" where it counts? The answer is yes. Future Homemakers of America (FHA) have used their clothing construction skills to help people near and far.

Needy local families and African refugees received free clothing thanks to FHA projects. A Sullivan High, Indiana, chapter constructed clothes for Project Mercy. This relief organization supplies the donated fabric and patterns and then distributes the finished garments to refugees in need. At Bramwell High, West Virginia, FHA members opened a Community Clothes Closet to provide free clothing to people in need. They sorted, washed, mended, and pressed donated garments and housed the Closet in their school.

An FHA chapter in Nicholasville, Kentucky, also did some mending and alterations—in this case for nursing home residents. Students and seniors enjoyed getting to know each other, too. At Fort Defiance High, Virginia, the alteration project involved remodeling fashionable clothing to suit the needs of the handicapped.

How could you use your skills to make a difference to those in need?

complete each type of work on each piece. For example, you complete all the seams at one time on all the separate sections. This method is an efficient way for experienced sewers to work, but it requires more planning than the first method. However, even a beginning sewer can use it for a simple project, such as making several pillow covers at once.

Assembly Directional Stitching

Be sure that you always sew *with* the grain of the fabric. This *directional stitching* helps to prevent the fabric from stretching. To determine the direction of the grain, run your finger along the raw edge of the fabric. If the threads are smooth, you are going in the direction of the grain. If the threads are rough, you are going against the grain.

You should also stitch from the wide part of the piece you are sewing to the narrow part.

Stay Stitching

A line of machine stitching sewn in the direction of the grain on a single layer of fabric is called *stay stitching*. Stay stitching prevents the fabric edges from stretching. It should be done as soon as you cut a piece of fabric. Stay stitch about ½ inch from the raw edge. The stitches should not show on the right side. Seams on necklines, armholes, and waistlines should be stay stitched. Curved edges and fabric cut on the bias are especially likely to stretch and should therefore always be stay stitched.

ENRICHMENT: Ask students to cut muslins from copies of reduced patterns that contain curves. Instruct students to stay stitch all curved edges, stitching in the direction of the grain. Grade students on accuracy and neatness.

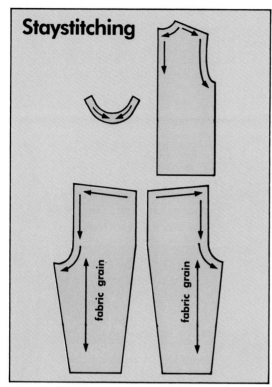

Follow the arrows on the pattern pieces when you stay stitch.

Darts

A **dart** is a small triangular fold that helps a garment fit smoothly over curved parts of the body. Darts are used at the waistline, the neckline, and under the sleeves. They vary in width and length and can be straight or curved. A *single-pointed* dart is shaped in a triangle. A *double-pointed dart* is the shape of two triangles placed base to base.

To stitch a dart, transfer the pattern markings for dart lines to the fabric. To stitch single-pointed darts, fold the fabric on the fold line, placing the right sides of the fabric together. Pin on the stitching line with the pins pointed toward the wide

part of the dart. Then baste along the stitching line toward the point of the dart and remove the pins. Place the wide end under the presser foot of the machine and stitch slowly toward the point. Tie a knot in the long length of thread. Stitch the dart and knot the thread. Then press the dart open or to one side depeding on the instructions in your pattern guide.

Seams

A **seam** is one or more lines of stitching that joins two pieces of fabric. Most seams are ⅝ inch wide. Unless your instructions direct you otherwise, sew a *plain seam,* that is, one made from one line of stitches. Put the right side of the two pieces of fabric together. Match the notches and seam edges. Place pins across the seam line at the notches and ends. Then baste the length of the seam and remove the pins. Start about ¼ inch from the top edge. Stitch backwards, then go forward. Stitch slowly, making sure the seam is neither so loose that it comes apart nor so tight that the thread pulls. When the seam is stitched, press it open.

To fit a curve, make a dart.

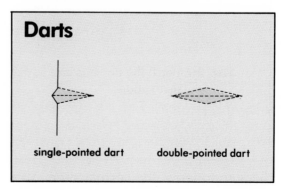

Sewing a Plain Seam

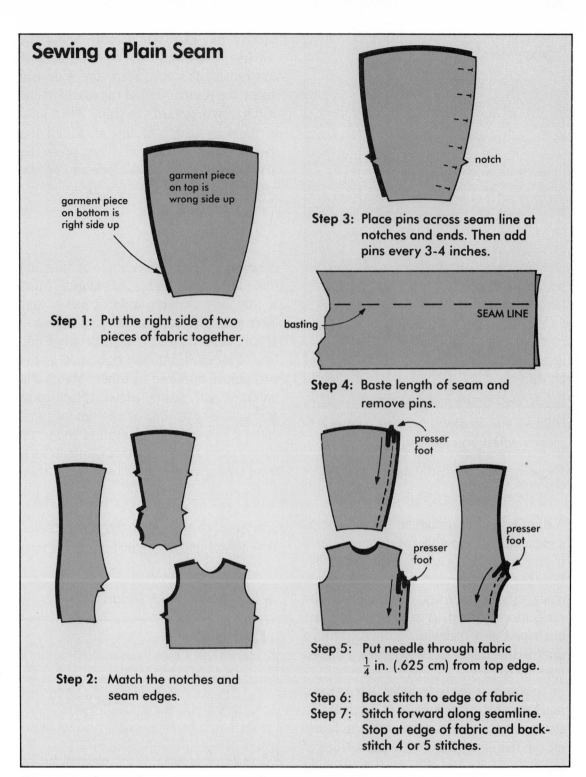

garment piece on top is wrong side up

garment piece on bottom is right side up

Step 1: Put the right side of two pieces of fabric together.

notch

Step 3: Place pins across seam line at notches and ends. Then add pins every 3-4 inches.

basting

SEAM LINE

Step 4: Baste length of seam and remove pins.

presser foot

presser foot

presser foot

Step 2: Match the notches and seam edges.

Step 5: Put needle through fabric $\frac{1}{4}$ in. (.625 cm) from top edge.

Step 6: Back stitch to edge of fabric

Step 7: Stitch forward along seamline. Stop at edge of fabric and back-stitch 4 or 5 stitches.

Be sure to leave the correct seam allowances.

ART: Stress that when students sew a seam on a machine, they should always be sure that the pins are facing up. If the pins are placed on the underside of the fabric, they can get caught in the feed dog.

Fitting

You should try on your garment several times as you make it to be sure it will fit. It is worth taking the time to make minor adjustments as you go along. In this way you will avoid a major adjustment in the finished product. Baste the seams together and then try on your garment. Do this before you add a collar, sleeves, or other details. Be sure to try on your garment again when the facings, collar, sleeves, and waistband are in place. Also pin the hemline and make sure it hangs evenly before you complete the hem.

Be sure to check all details at each fitting. See that darts taper correctly, seams are straight, and the garment hangs well and is not too tight. Make sure the sleeves begin at your shoulder and the collar lies smoothly. Sleeves, waistband, and hem should be the right length, and fasteners should be correctly placed. Pants legs should just brush the top of the shoe.

Pressing

It is most important to press at each major stage of sewing. You should never cross one line of stitching with another until you press the first line. Press the stitches flat, first on one side of the fabric, then on the other. Seams and darts should be pressed open or to one side, depending on the instructions in your pattern guide. Be sure to use a pressing cloth and a steam iron. It is helpful, but not necessary, to use a tailor's ham—a cushion shaped like a ham. A sleeve board—two

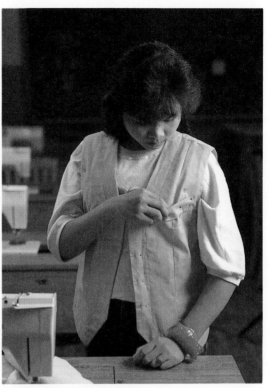

Will the garment fit exactly the way you want it to? Adjust it now.

small, connected ironing boards—is a useful attachment. It is helpful for pressing small areas that will not fit over a regular ironing board.

Seam Finishing

You may sometimes sew a fabric that ravels so that the edges have loose threads. In this case you should finish the seams of the fabric. Zigzag stitching is a method you can use to finish seams. Set the zigzag setting on your sewing machine for medium width and length and stitch along the edge of the seam. For heavy or loosely woven fabrics, use a wide stitch width.

DISCUSS: Go over the settings on a steam iron with your students. Be sure that they are familiar with all the features of the type of iron that is used in your sewing lab.

REINFORCEMENT: Demonstrate pinked, zigzag-stitched, and edge-stitched seam finishes. Ask students to do samples of pinked, pinked and stitched, zigzag, overcast and turned, and edge-stitched seam finishes. Check them for accuracy and have students place them in their notebooks for reference.

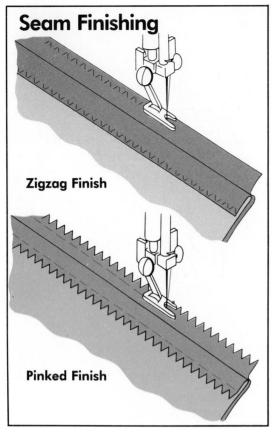

Seam Finishing

Zigzag Finish

Pinked Finish

Zigzag stitching can be done by machine. Pinking is done by hand.

On firmly woven fabrics that do not ravel much, you can use pinking shears— scissors that cut in a zigzag pattern. Simply trim the edges of the seams with these shears. This is called **pinking.**

If your machine does not zigzag, you can stitch ¼ inch from each edge and then use pinking shears. You can also hand sew overcast stitches over the edges of the seams. This is time-consuming but useful for very delicate fabrics.

You can also use a clean or turned and stitched finish. Turn the edges under to a depth of ¼ inch and press them. Then machine stitch close to the edge.

Facings and Interfacings

A piece of fabric that finishes a raw garment edge when applied or turned under or back is called a **facing.** There are three types of facings. *Shaped facing,* the most common type, is the shape of the area it covers. You stitch it and then turn it to the inside of the garment. *Extended facing* is cut at the same time as the garment and then folded inside. Use it for openings. *Bias facing* is a strip of fabric cut on the bias. It is stitched to the garment and then turned inside.

To attach facings, stay stitch and attach them to the garment as the pattern directs. Trim seams to ¼ inch and finish the unnotched outer edges. Press. Then place the right side of the facing against the garment, matching notches and seams.

Use stay stitching to attach these.

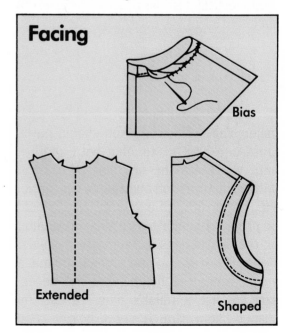

Facing

Bias

Extended

Shaped

Pin in place. Stitch the facing and then clip edges to reduce bulk. Press the facing away from the garment. Understitch the facing by stitching the facing side close to the seam line. Attach it by tacking it to the seam allowance or darts. Do not sew the entire facing edge to the garment, or it will pull.

Interfacing is a layer of fabric laid between a facing and a garment piece. Its purpose is to reinforce, hold a shape, or prevent the garment face from stretching. It is applied before facing is attached. It gives support to the fabric. Some interfacing is *fusible*. It has adhesive on one side, and, when pressed, becomes attached to the fabric by the heat of the iron. Other interfacing must be stitched on. Follow pattern instructions to find out the kind of interfacing required and how to apply it.

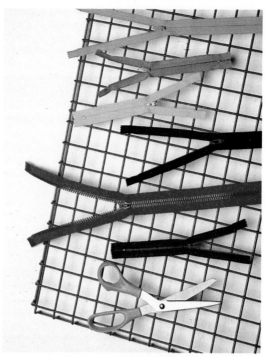

Most zippers are sewn in by machine. Be sure to use a zipper foot.

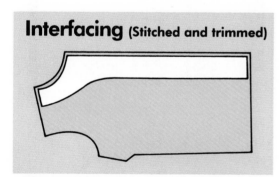

Interfacing gives a garment stiffness and shape.

Fasteners and Closures

Snaps are sewn by hand. Use small snaps for lightweight fabric and larger snaps for heavier material. Sew the ball section of the snap to the inside of the top flap of the opening. Take several stitches through one hole, then take a stitch under the snap and proceed to the next hole. Follow this procedure for all four holes. Rub chalk on the ball and close the opening so that the chalk marks the covering flap on the inside. This shows you where to place the other half of the snap. Sew it to the fabric following the same procedure used for the ball section.

Hooks and eyes are also attached by hand. First sew the hook ⅛ inch from the inside edge of the opening. Make several stitches through each loop and then stitch several times around the end of the hook. Chalk the hook and close the other flap of material to mark where the eye should be placed. Attach the eye using the same method as for the hook.

REINFORCEMENT: Mention that one way to finish the outer edge of a facing and put in interfacing at the same time is to place the facing and interfacing right sides together and stitch the outer edge of the facing ¼″. Notch the curved edge, press open the seam, and turn the interfacing to the inside.

NOTE: Iron-on or fusible interfacing is good for wash-and-wear fabrics, but it has a tendency to pull away from fabrics that are dry cleaned. Stress that nonfusible interfacing may be the best choice for students who are working with fabrics that must be dry cleaned.

Turning up a Hem

Step 1. Have someone mark the bottom of the hem.

Step 2. Fold and pin hem.

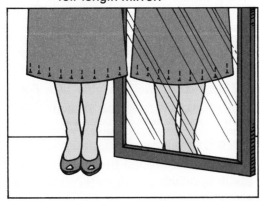

Step 3. Check length and evenness in full-length mirror.

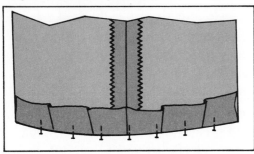

Step 4. Trim hem to desired depth.

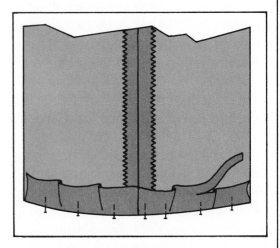

Step 5. Baste and finish edge.

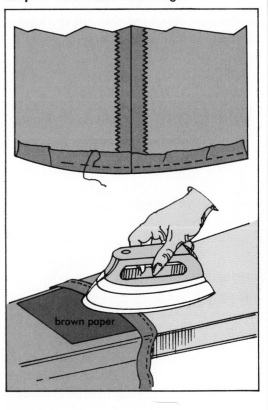

brown paper

Careful pressing is a must to insure a perfect hem.

470   Unit 5/*Clothing and Textiles*

PHOTO: Reassure students that many people find zippers to be confusing and difficult to sew, but that practice makes the process much easier.

Zippers can be tricky to attach. Read the instructions in your pattern guide and in the zipper package. Be sure the zipper you purchase is the correct size. You can attach a zipper with two rows of stitching, one on each side of the zipper. This is the *centered method.* Some zippers are attached on only one side. Ask an experienced person to show you how to sew in your zipper using a sewing machine.

Buttonholes can also present difficulties to the beginning sewer. Follow pattern directions carefully and get some help from an experienced sewer. The pattern will indicate the location and length of each buttonhole. Mark these locations and baste through all layers of fabric. Your sewing machine may have a special attachment to stitch buttonholes. If not, use a zigzag stitch. Your sewing machine instructions will tell you what the machine is equipped to do.

Putting in a zipper is a challenge and a great accomplishment.

Hems

The *hem,* or bottom, of a garment is made by folding the bottom edge of the fabric inward. It is then stitched either by hand or by machine. The inner edge is usually either turned under and then stitched down. Or, a facing may be added before it is stitched.

First you must be sure the hem hangs evenly and is the right length. Try on the garment. Wear the shoes or boots you will be wearing with the garment. Have another person mark the bottom of the hem with pins or chalk while you are standing up straight. The person should measure from the floor to the hem with a yardstick,

working completely around the hem. Next, fold the hem along the pin or chalk markings and pin it. Place the pins near the top of the inner edge. Check the new length in a full-length mirror to make sure it is correct and even.

Trim the hem to the desired depth, from 1 to 3 inches. If you are still growing, make the hem wide enough to let down later. You can add finishing tape to the edge to prevent the material from raveling. If the fabric is not too thick, you can turn the raw edge under to a depth of ¼ inch. Then stitch it in place. Finally, baste the hem and press it.

You can stitch the hem by hand as you learned earlier in this chapter. You can also stitch it on the machine. Your pattern guide will tell you if machine stitching is advisable, and if it is, how to do it.

ENRICHMENT: Give each student a 5″ or 7″ zipper and a piece of plain, firmly woven cotton fabric. Demonstrate a centered zipper application, and ask students to do a sample centered zipper in class.

DISCUSS: Talk about garments that do well with a machine-stitched hem and those that require a hand-sewn hem. Coach students to think about hems on their own clothing to use as examples.

Recycling Clothing

When you *recycle* something, you turn it into something you can use again. In many cases, clothing can be recycled even when it has gone out of style. You can make many garments reusable with a few simple changes, using your sewing skills.

Simple Alterations

Clothing alterations are changes made to a garment in order to improve its appearance or fit.

Hemlines can be lowered if there is enough material in the hem to do this. Hemlines can be shortened by cutting them evenly, then following the directions for hemming found earlier in this chapter. Pants or jeans that have worn knees can become shorts.

Altering sleeve lengths and necklines also gives a garment a new look. Adding or changing buttons, or dyeing a whole garment, are other easy, inexpensive alteration methods.

ENRICHMENT: Invite students to bring to class something from their wardrobes that needs a simple alteration. Set aside one class day for alterations. Work with each student individually. Also explain each alteration to the entire class so they can view and learn from the variety.

Gather Fashion Ideas

Look through fashion magazines for ideas or come up with your own. If there are new styles you like, you may be able to create a similar look by adding a few accessories. You may be able to change the color scheme of an outfit this way. Or, buying a belt or scarf and rolling up pant cuffs may be all you need to change an outfit you already own. Think about ways you can make small alterations and additions instead of making major clothing purchases.

Projects from the Scrap Pile

Once you know a garment cannot be repaired or altered, you can still cut the material up into useful scraps. These scraps can then be used for school or home sewing and alteration projects. Simple book bags, pillow covers, and laundry bags are examples of items that can be made from recycled scrap materials. You might make a tote bag out of old jeans. Pieces of shirts or skirts could be used to make patchwork pillows.

See page T134 for answers.

For Review

1. What is the difference between unit construction and the assembly-line method of machine sewing?
2. What is the purpose of directional stitching?
3. Name the three types of facings.
4. How can you recycle jeans that are worn at the knees?

ENRICHMENT: Work with your students to gather scraps of fabric over a period of several months. As a group project, construct a patchwork quilt either by hand or by machine. When the quilt is completed, sell raffle tickets for the quilt and use the money to have a class picnic.

See page T134 for teaching suggestions.

Learning to Manage

New Styles and Old Lace

Look back at the conversation on page 458. Now read how Pat managed to get the dress she wanted. Then answer the questions that follow.

As the girls walked home that afternoon, they discussed the dress with the lace that Pat liked so much.

"You know, Pat, I saw a dress in that same style at Juno's the other day for half the price of that fancy one. It didn't have any lace, but the rest of it looked just the same."

"But it's the lace that makes it so special, Kim."

"Have you ever been in the thrift shop downtown? They have lots of secondhand clothes. You might find something there with a lace collar and sleeves!"

"So?"

"So . . . you could buy the other dress and fix it up if you could find some old lace pieces to sew on!"

"That just might work! Let's stop at the thrift store and see what they have."

The girls went to the thrift store and found some old dresses trimmed with beautiful lace. They were inexpensive, and the lace could be cleaned.

Pat's mother was doubtful about the idea, but she agreed to look at both dresses the next day. The dress at Juno's was very plain, but well made. The back zipper lay flat, and the seams were reinforced. It fit well, and Pat could just picture the lace collar and sleeves on it. Her mother agreed that it could be done

and was a good idea after all. Pat could also wear the dress later without the lace if she wanted. They made the purchases.

The project was not as easy as Pat had thought it would be. She had to baste and sew the collar on carefully to get it to lie flat. The results were well worth the extra effort, though. The dress looked great and she *knew* no one else would be wearing one exactly like it. With some simple hand sewing and a great idea, she had created her own "designer original"!

Questions

1. How can you be creative and resourceful with your own clothing? Do you have any garments you could upgrade or alter?
2. If you needed an alteration in a garment that you couldn't do yourself, would you pay to have it done? Explain your answer.
3. Are there places in your community where you can donate good used clothing to charitable causes?

Chapter 20 Review

Summary

Your sewing projects can be both fun and successful if you prepare and organize each step carefully. You must know the various stitches and other procedures involved. Some stitching is easier or stronger when done by hand, but machine sewing is much faster. By learning both hand and machine sewing, you can soon master a variety of skills. These include basting, hemming, easing and gathering, and making darts and buttonholes. For sewing success, refer to the directions on the pattern guide sheet at every step. Be sure that you complete each step in the correct sequence, and remember to press your garment after completing each step. As you construct a garment, try it on several times during the sewing process to be sure it fits.

Consider using your sewing skills to recycle or alter old garments rather than throwing them away.

Vocabulary

Complete each of the following sentences with the correct word from the vocabulary list below.

unit construction (p. 463)   dart (p. 465) (p. 463)
interfacing (p. 469)   assembly-line method
seam (p. 465)   easing (p. 461)
pinking (p. 468)   gathering (p. 461)
basting (p. 460)   facing (p. 468)

1. _____ is used to join together two pieces of material of slightly different lengths to make waistbands of pants and skirts and set-in sleeves.
2. Hand sewing two layers of material together temporarily in order to be sure that they are correctly matched is called _____.
3. When you use the method of _____ you complete each section separately before sewing them together.
4. _____ is a layer of fabric laid between a facing and a garment piece to reinforce, hold a shape, or prevent stretching of the garment face.
5. When you use the _____ you complete each type of work on each piece.
6. _____ is used to join together two pieces of material of different lengths to form the soft folds in ruffles, and full, unpleated curtains.
7. The method of finishing that uses special shears to trim the edges of the seams is called _____.
8. _____ is a piece of fabric that is applied, or turned under or back to finish a raw garment edge.
9. A _____ is one or more lines of stitching that join two or more pieces of fabric together.
10. A _____ is small triangular fold that helps a garment fit smoothly over curved parts of the body.

The dots represent skill levels required to answer each question or complete each activity:

• requires recall and comprehension
•• requires application and analysis
••• requires synthesis and evaluation

474

Questions

1. Are all needles suitable for every kind of hand sewing? Explain.
2. Name three kinds of temporary hand sewing.
3. What is the purpose of a slip stitch?
4. When is a backstitch used?
5. Describe how you would make a shirt by the unit construction method.
6. Why do you do directional stitching?
7. What is the purpose of stay stitching?
8. In making a garment, what are three places you might need darts?
9. If you were in a rush to finish a garment, would it save time to eliminate fitting the garment until you were finished? Explain your answer.
10. What are pinking shears?
11. What is bias facing?
12. What is fusible interfacing?
13. Are buttonholes made by hand or by machine?
14. Name at least three ways to alter a garment so that it can be worn again.
15. How can fashion magazines help you to alter an outfit?

Skill Activities

Many more activities are contained in the annotations within this chapter.

1. Decision Making Choose a pattern for a project you would like to make. Read your pattern guide sheet and list the sewing procedures necessary to complete your project. These might include procedures such as sewing in darts or zippers, pressing, applying a facing, or hemming. Use this list to write out a schedule for your project. Leave space on your schedule so that you can make notes on your progress. Revise your schedule when necessary.

2. Human Relations Ask people in your community about possible uses of clothing you have outgrown or will never use again. Find out about agencies that may need good used clothing for either local or national purposes. Contact organizations such as the Red Cross. Find out if they collect or receive donations of used clothing and what use they have for them. Perhaps your local church or synagogue has clothing drives at certain times of the year. If you find an organization that needs used clothing, ask your teacher if you can arrange a collection at school.

3. Laboratory Make a quilt with other members of your class. Cut 6-inch squares of fabric and join them together with a $\frac{5}{8}$-inch seam. With right sides together, sew the joined squares to a large piece of fabric or a sheet. Turn the right side out to form the quilt. Finish stitching the outside borders of the quilt. You may want to donate the completed quilt to the nurse's office in your school.

Appendix

Daily Food Guide

VEGETABLE-FRUIT GROUP

Recommended minimum servings per day:
all ages   4 servings

Examples of one serving:
½ c (125 mL) cooked vegetable or fruit
½ c (125 ml) fruit or vegetable juice
1 c (250 mL) raw fruit or vegetable
1 whole medium-sized fruit or vegetable

Major nutrient contributions:
vitamin A and vitamin C
variety of minerals
carbohydrates (including fiber)
Note: Include 1 serving per day of a food high in vitamin C. Choose 1 serving 3 or 4 times a week of a food which provides vitamin A.

BREAD-CEREAL GROUP

Recommended minimum servings per day:
all ages   4 servings

Examples of one serving:
1 oz (30 g) slice of bread
1 oz (30 g) roll, muffin, or biscuit
½ bagel, hamburg or hotdog roll
½ c (125 mL) cooked cereal or rice
⅔ c (160 mL) cooked pasta
1 oz (30 g) ready-to-eat cereal
6 saltines
1 pancake, 4" (10 cm) in diameter

Major nutrient contributions:
carbohydrates (including fiber)
incomplete protein
B-complex vitamins
iron

FAT-SWEETS GROUP

Recommended servings per day:
No recommendations. A balanced diet includes some fats and sugars. Additional amounts are not necessary.

Major nutrient contributions: None

MILK-CHEESE GROUP

Recommended minimum servings per day:
children   3 servings
adolescents   4 servings
adults   2 servings

One serving = 1c (250 mL) milk or its equivalent

Equivalents:
1 c (250 mL) plain yogurt	= 1c (250 mL) milk
1 oz (30 g) hard cheese	= ¾ c (185 mL) milk
1 oz (30 g) process cheese	= ½ c (125 mL) milk
½ c (125 mL) ice cream	= ⅓ c (80 mL) milk
½ c (125 mL) cottage cheese	= ¼ c (60 mL) milk

Major nutrient contributions:
calcium and phosphorus
complete protein
riboflavin (a B-complex vitamin)
vitamins A and D (if fortified)

MEAT-FISH-POULTRY-BEANS GROUP

Recommended minimum servings per day:
all ages   2 servings

Examples of one serving:
2–3 oz (60–90 g) cooked meat, fish poultry (without bone)
3 oz (90 g) processed meats
2 eggs
4 Tbsp (60 mL) peanut butter
1c (250 mL) cooked dried beans or peas

Major nutrient contributions:
complete protein and incomplete protein B-complex vitamins and other B vitamins iron and phosphorus

Note: Include milk, cheese, egg, or small amounts of meat, fish, or poultry with meals based on dried beans, peas, or nuts

Recommended Daily Dietary Allowances (RDA), Revised 1980

Designed for the maintenance of good nutrition of practically all healthy people in the U.S.A.

	Age (years)	Weight (kg)	(lbs)	Height (cm)	(in.)	Protein (g)	Vitamin A (mg R.E.)[b]	Vitamin D (mg)[c]	Vitamin E (mgαT.E.)[d]	Vitamin C (mg)	Thiamin (mg)	Riboflavin (mg)
Infants	0.0–0.5	6	13	60	24	kg × 2.2	420	10	3	35	0.3	0.4
	0.5–1.0	9	20	71	28	kg × 2.0	400	10	4	35	0.5	0.6
Children	1–3	13	29	90	35	23	400	10	5	45	0.7	0.8
	4–6	20	44	112	44	30	500	10	6	45	0.9	1.0
	7–10	28	62	132	52	34	700	10	7	45	1.2	1.4
Males	11–14	45	99	157	62	45	1000	10	8	50	1.4	1.6
	15–18	66	145	176	69	56	1000	10	10	60	1.4	1.7
	19–22	70	154	178	70	56	1000	7.5	10	60	1.5	.7
	23–50	70	154	178	70	56	1000	5	10	60	1.4	1.6
	51+	70	154	178	70	56	1000	5	10	60	1.2	1.4
Females	11–14	46	101	157	62	46	800	10	8	50	1.1	1.3
	15–18	55	120	163	64	46	800	10	8	60	1.1	1.3
	19–22	55	120	163	64	44	800	7.5	8	60	1.1	1.3
	23–50	55	120	163	64	44	800	5	8	60	1.0	1.2
	51+	55	120	163	64	44	800	5	8	60	1.0	1.2
Pregnant						+30	+200	+5	+2	+20	+0.4	+0.3
Lactating						+20	+400	+5	+3	+40	+0.5	+0.5

a The allowances are intended to provide for individual variations among most normal persons as they live in the United States under usual environmental stresses. Diets should be based on a variety of common foods in order to provide other nutrients for which human requirements have been less well defined.

b Retinol equivalents. 1 Retinol equivalent = 1 mg retinol or 6 mg carotene.

c As cholecalciferol. 10 mg cholecalciferol = 400 I.U. vitamin D.

d α tocopherol equivalents. 1 mg d-α-tocopherol = 1 α T.E.

e 1 NE (niacin equivalent) is equal to 1 mg of niacin or 60 mg of dietary tryptophan.

Estimated Safe and Adequate Daily Dietary Intakes of Additional Selected Vitamins and Minerals[a]

	Age (years)	Vitamins			Trace Elements[b]		
		Vitamin K (mg)	Biotin (mg)	Pantothenic Acid (mg)	Copper (mg)	Manganese (mg)	Fluoride (mg)
Infants	0–0.5	12	35	2	0.5–0.7	0.5–0.7	0.1–0.5
	0.5–1	10–20	50	3	0.7–1.0	0.7-1.0	0.2–1.0
Children and Adolescents	1–3	15–30	65	3	1.0–1.5	1.0–1.5	0.5–1.5
	4–6	20–40	85	3–4	1.5–2.0	1.5–2.0	1.0–2.5
	7–10	30–60	120	4–5	2.0–2.5	2.0–3.0	1.5–2.5
	11+	50–100	100–200	4–7	2.0–3.0	2.5–5.0	1.5–2.5
Adults		70–140	100–200	4–7	2.0–3.0	2.5–5.0	1.5–4.0

a Because there is less information on which to base allowances, these figures are not given in the main table of the RDA and are provided here in the form of ranges of recommended intakes.

Reproduced from: Recommended Dietary Allowances, Ninth Edition, 1980, with the permission of the National Academy of Sciences, Food and Nutrition Board, Washington, D.C.

RDA (continued)

	Water-Soluble Vitamins					Minerals				
	Niacin (mg N.E.)e	Vitamin B6(mg)	Folacinf (mg)	Vitamin B12 (mg)	Calcium (mg)	Phosphorus (mg)	Magnesium (mg)	Iron (mg)	Zinc (mg)	Iodine (mg)
Infants	6	0.3	30	0.5g	360	240	50	10	3	40
	8	0.6	45	1.5	540	360	70	15	5	50
Children	9	0.9	100	2.0	800	800	150	15	10	70
	11	1.3	200	2.5	800	800	200	10	10	90
	16	1.6	300	3.0	800	800	250	10	10	120
Males	18	1.8	400	3.0	1200	1200	350	18	15	150
	18	2.0	400	3.0	1200	1200	400	18	15	150
	19	2.2	400	3.0	800	800	350	10	15	150
	18	2.2	400	3.0	800	800	350	10	15	150
	16	2.2	400	3.0	800	800	350	10	15	150
Females	15	1.8	400	3.0	1200	1200	300	18	15	150
	14	2.0	400	3.0	1200	1200	300	18	15	150
	14	2.0	400	3.0	800	800	300	18	15	150
	13	2.0	400	3.0	800	800	300	18	15	150
	13	2.0	400	3.0	800	800	300	10	15	150
Pregnant	+2	+0.6	+400	+1.0	+400	+400	+150	h	+5	+25
Lactating	+5	+0.5	+100	+1.0	+400	+400	+150	h	+10	+50

f The folacin allowances refer to dietary sources as determined by *Lactobacillus gaset* assay after treatment with enzymes ("conjugases") to make polyglutanyl forms of the vitamin available to the test organism.

g The RDA for vitamin B12 in infants is based on average concentration of the vitamin in human milk. The allowances after weaning are based on energy intake (as recommended by the American Academy of Pediatrics) and consideration of other factors such as intestinal absorption.

h The increased requirement during pregnancy cannot be met by the iron content of habitual American diets nor by the existing iron stores of many women; therefore the use of 30–60 mg of supplemental iron is recommended. Iron needs during lactation are not substantially different from those of nonpregnant women, but continued supplementation of the mother for 2–3 months after parturition is advisable in order to replenish stores depleted by pregnancy.

Estimated Safe and Adequate Daily Dietary Intakes of Additional Selected Vitamins and Minerals (continued)

	Age (years)	Electroytes					
		Chrominum (mg)	Selenium (mg)	Molybdenum (mg)	Sodium (mg)	Potassium (mg)	Chloride (mg)
Infants	0–0.5	0.01–0.04	0.01–0.04	0.03–0.06	115–350	350–925	275–700
	0.5–1	0.02–0.06	0.02–0.06	0.04–0.08	250–750	425–1275	400–1200
Children and Adolescents	1–3	0.02–0.08	0.02–0.08	0.05–0.1	325–975	550–1650	500–1500
	4–6	0.03–0.12	0.03–0.12	0.06–0.15	450–1350	775–2325	700–2100
	7–10	0.05–0.2	0.05–0.2	0.1–0.3	600–1800	1000–3000	925–2775
	11+	0.05–0.2	0.05–0.2	0.15–0.5	900–2700	1525–4575	1400–4200
Adults		0.05–0.2	0.05–0.2	0.15–0.5	1100–3300	1875–5625	1700–5100

b Since the toxic levels for many trace elements may be only several times usual intakes, the upper levels for the trace elements given in this table should not be habitually exceeded.

Calories, Fats, and Proteins in Common Foods

Food	Approx. Measure	Calories (Food Energy)	Fat (grams)	Protein (grams)
Milk, cow (whole)	1 cup	159	8.5	8.5
Milk (low-fat) (1%)	1 cup	100	3.0	8.0
American cheese	1 oz.	105	8.5	6.6
Ice cream (hard)	1 cup	257	14.1	6.0
Ice milk	1 cup	199	6.7	6.3
Instant pudding (whole milk)	1 cup	325	7.0	8.0
Cola	12 oz.	144	—	—
Chocolate Shake	10.6 oz.	355	8.0	9.0
Apple juice	1 cup	120	—	—
Apple (raw)	1 medium	125	1.0	—
Chocolate Chip cookies (home recipe)	4 (40 g.)	205	12.0	2.0
Graham crackers	4 (28 g.)	110	2.0	2.0
Carrotts (raw)	72 g.	30	—	1.0
Celery (raw)	40 g. (lg. stalk)	5	—	—
Potato chips	10 chips (20 g.)	115	8.0	1.0
Peanut butter	1 T	95	8.0	4.0
Pizza, cheese	1/8 of 12" diameter pie	145	4.0	6.0
Popcorn, plain	1 cup	25	—	1.0
Popcorn, popped in oil, salted	1 cup	41	2.0	0.9
French fries	10 strips (3–4" long)	214	10.3	3.4
Baked potato	1 med.	145	0.2	4.0
Chicken noodle soup (canned)	1 cup	130	3.9	6.9
Frankfurter	1.5 oz.	124	10.7	5.5
Hamburger	4 oz.	202	11.3	23.4
Turkey, light and dark meat	3 oz.	162	5.2	26.8
Scrambled egg	1 large	111	8.3	7.2
Tuna, canned in oil	6 oz.	333	13.9	48.7
Tuna, canned in water	7 oz.	251	1.6	55.4

Glossary

A

addiction The habitual and uncontrollable use of something; the body's physical or mental dependency on a substance.

additive A substance added to a food to increase nutrients, prevent spoilage, or improve color or flavor.

adolescence Youth; the period of life that begins with the early teenage years and ends at maturity.

à la carte A method of ordering in a restaurant which consists of a diner selecting items that are separately priced on the menu.

alcoholism A disease that involves the habitual, excessive use of alcohol.

analogous Similar in certain ways; a color scheme that uses closely related colors.

Anorexia nervosa A disease whose victims are obsessed with thinness and run the risk of starving themselves to death because they cannot stop dieting.

apprenticeship On-the-job training at low pay provided by certain trades to those interested in entering the trades.

aptitudes Natural abilities; special talents.

assembly line method A method of sewing a garment together where each type of work is completed on each piece and the various pieces are eventually sewn together.

B

bacteria Tiny, one-celled creatures that are invisible to the naked eye and give off waste products called toxins.

bakeware The dishes and pans that are used in the oven to cook food.

balance Whatever is left over; the total amount available in a bank account at any point in time.

barter To exchange a product or an ability that one person has for a product or an ability that someone else has.

basal metabolism The rate at which the human body burns calories to perform normal body functions.

basting Temporarily sewing two layers of material together to be sure that they are correctly matched.

blended family A combined family that is formed when people with children marry and bring the children together into a newly created unit.

blends Fibers that are made by combining natural fibers and manufactured fibers, providing the advantages of each.

body language The gestures, bodily movements, and facial expressions that communicate nonverbally.

budget A spending plan that indicates what monies are available for the purchase of goods and services over a specific period of time.

bulimia A disease whose victims cannot resist eating heavily for short periods of time but who then induce vomiting or use laxatives to rid the body of food.

C

calorie The energy from food that is burned by the body as an individual goes about daily tasks.

cholesterol A fatlike substance in the cells of the body that can clog arteries and cause heart attacks and strokes.

classic A model of a particular type or kind; a style of clothing that lasts for a long time.

colorfastness The ability of a dye in a fabric to keep its exact color after frequent washings.

communication A giving or exchanging of information; the exchange of information between people by sending and receiving messages.

comparison shopping The careful examination of competing goods and services that are available in the marketplace before a decision to purchase is made.

competition The effort that similar businesses make to outdo one another and gain greater profits by producing products that people want to buy.

complementary Making up what is lacking; a color scheme that uses colors that are direct contrasts.

compounded interest Interest computed on the original sum deposited plus interest already earned, and added to a depositor's savings account, daily, every three months, or once each year.

condominium A housing unit, often an apartment, that can be purchased rather than rented.

consumer Someone who buys and uses goods or services to meet needs.

contract An agreement between two or more people to do something.

convenience foods Foods that are partially or completely prepared before purchase.

cookware The pots and pans that are used on the top of a range to cook food.

co-op A building that is owned jointly by many people who have living space there and who share in the operating and maintenance expenses.

cover The place setting at a table where one person sits, including the dishes, flatware, glasses, and napkin that the person will use.

credit A willingness to lend money to an individual in exchange for a promise to repay.

curdling The separation of milk into liquid and small lumps when it is cooked at a temperature that is too high.

custody A caring for; an arrangement that determines which parent will provide for the primary care of children in the event of divorce.

cutting layout A diagram that shows how to place pattern pieces of fabric.

D

dart a small triangular fold that helps a garment fit smoothly over curved parts of the body.

demand The kinds of goods and services that consumers want.

deposit To put money into an account at a bank.

depression Low spirits; dejection; the state of feeling sad, anxious, and alone, usually accompanied by decreased activity.

design A plan; the arrangement of lines, colors, textures, and patterns to create a desired result or effect.

developmental tasks The activities that children learn as they grow and mature.

discipline The task of teaching children the difference between acceptable and unacceptable behavior.

drug Any substance that is used as a medicine; a habit-forming narcotic.

E

easing Joining two pieces of material of different lengths when one piece is only slightly larger than the other.

economy The management of the income and expenditures of a household, a business, a community, or an entire country; the way in which a country buys and sells material goods.

embryo The term used to refer to an unborn baby during the first two months of development.

emotional appeals Advertisements that focus on the psychological needs and wants of consumers.

empathy The ability to view a situation from another's point of view.

emulsion A combination of oil and another liquid, beaten so that the ingredients do not separate.

endorse To sign one's name on the back of a check in order to cash it or deposit it into a bank account.

entrée The main course of a meal; usually either meat or fish.

entrepreneurship The ability and desire to use one's resources and talents to develop an idea into profitable goods and services.

entry level Jobs that require no special training or experience.

environment Surroundings; all of the people, beliefs, and experiences that influence a person.

ethics An individual's moral beliefs about what is good or bad, right or wrong.

extended family A nuclear family and all other relatives, including grandparents, aunts, uncles, cousins, and grandchildren.

etiquette Customs that have developed over a period of time and have come to be accepted as appropriate behavior.

F

fabric grain The direction in which yarn runs.

facing A piece of fabric that finishes a raw garment edge when it is applied or turned under or back.

factory surplus The output of a manufacturer that could not be sold to retail stores.

fads Fashions popular for only a short time.

family A group of people who are related by blood or marriage; the parents and the children that they raise.

fashion The style of clothing that is popular at a given time.

fat-soluble vitamins Vitamins that are transported through the body by fat rather than water.

feedback The answer or response that the receiver of a message gives to a sender.

fetus The term used to refer to an unborn baby from the third month of its development until birth.

fixed expenses Expenses that are set and do not change over a period of time, many of which are for basic needs rather than wants.

flexible expenses Expenses that change from time to time; the cost of such things as clothing, travel, and entertainment.

free enterprise The system under which individuals enjoy certain rights and freedoms in carrying out economic activities.

fringe benefits Benefits that an employee receives over and above salary, such as paid sick days, holidays, and health and life insurance.

G

gathering Joining two pieces of material to form soft folds when making such things as puffed sleeves, ruffles, and full, unpleated curtains.

generic brands Food products that appear in containers with plain labels and without a manufacturer's name.

goals Aims; the things that one hopes to accomplish in life.

H

heredity All of the characteristics and traits that parents pass on to their children.

homogenized milk Milk in which the fat particles are broken up so that they remain distributed throughout, thereby preventing the cream from rising to the top.

human resources The knowledge, skills, abilities, and talents that people possess.

hygiene The science of health and its maintenance; the proper grooming of the body, including the maintenance of the skin, hair, and nails.

I

immunization A means of protection against certain diseases.

impulse A sudden desire to act; a sudden choice that is influenced by a person's mood at a given moment.

impulse buyer A purchaser who makes a spur-of-the-moment decision to buy without any prior thought.

inflation A continuous rise in prices, which lessens the buying power of consumers.

intensity The strength of something; the brightness or dullness of a color.

interest The money that a bank gives to a depositor in exchange for the right to use the depositor's money for some banking purpose.

interfacing A layer of fabric laid between a facing and a garment piece to reinforce, hold a shape, or prevent the garment face from stretching.

invest To use money to produce more money by depositing it into a savings account or by purchasing stocks, bonds, mutual funds, or certificates of deposit.

J

job cluster A group of jobs that require similar skills, knowledge, and abilities.

L

long-term goal An aim or desire that is not expected to be met or satisfied in the near future.

M

management The organization, direction, or control of something; the direction of one's life in a responsible way.

manufactured fibers Fibers that are made from chemicals, such as polyester and rayon.

mental development Growth in the ability to reason, learn, and make judgments.

message Information that is sent from one person to another.

microwaves Tiny waves of energy similar to radio waves, produced by a magnetron within an oven.

mobile Able to move easily or effortlessly.

monochromatic A color scheme that is made up of different values and intensities of the same color.

mortage A loan taken out to purchase a house, under the terms of which the house is pledged as security and the loan is paid back with interest each month over a period of years.

N

natural fibers Fibers that come from plants or animals, such as cotton or linen.

nonhuman resources Material, nonliving things, such as money, time, and physical surroundings, that people use.

nonverbal communication The sending of messages through gesture, facial expression, and other bodily movements.

notions Small items that are used in sewing, such as thread, buttons, zippers, and trim.

nuclear family A husband and wife and their children.

nutrients Anything that is nutritious; essential materials that the body needs to function, grow, and renew itself.

nutrition Anything that nourishes; the science or study of a proper diet which maintains health and promotes growth.

O

on-grain Fabric that has crosswise and lengthwise yarns that are at right angles to each other.

open dating Dates on food packages that indicate a product's freshness and state until when the product may be used safely or successfully.

P

parliamentary procedure A set of rules designed to keep order during a formal meeting.

pasteurized milk Raw milk heated to a temperature below boiling in order to destroy harmful bacteria.

pattern To model one's behavior on the observed behavior of others.

pattern guide sheet A sheet that provides information about laying out a pattern and about cutting, marking, and sewing the fabric to make a garment.

patterns Models and sets of instructions that show a person what a garment will look like when finished.

peers People of the same rank; people of the same age group who influence the behavior of others in that age group.

personality The quality of being a particular person; all of the physical and emotional qualities that make someone a unique individual.

physical development The growth of children in size, proportion, and muscular coordination.

pinking A method of finishing seams with zigzag stitching, used to prevent the edges of a fabric with loose threads from unraveling.

prejudice A judgment or opinion formed before the facts are known; prejudging people unfairly without knowing them.

prenatal stage The nine months of development before the birth of a baby.

principal The amount of money that a depositor has in a savings account.

prix fixe A complete meal served by a restaurant for a fixed or set price, also called *table d'hôte*.

process A continuing development that includes many changes; a series of actions and thoughts that lead to a particular result.

professions Jobs that require specialized college-level training.

proportion The comparative relationship between parts; the way the parts of a design relate to one another and to the whole design.

R

receiver The person who receives a message.

recipe A list of ingredients that must be used to prepare a particular food, together with a set of instructions that explain how those ingredients are to be combined and cooked.

reference A recommendation from someone who is familiar with an individual's work habits or general background and abilities.

reflexes Automatic and involuntary physical responses.

reservation An arrangement by which space is set aside, for example by calling a restaurant in advance so that immediate seating is available upon arrival.

rural Characteristic of the country or of country life; referring to a society in which most people live on farms.

S

sanitation The practice of maintaining a clean environment.

saturated fats Fats found in meat, butter, and cheese that are solid at room temperature.

seam One or more lines of stitching that join two pieces of fabric.

self-concept A person's assessment of himself or herself, including an evaluation of worth and abilities.

selvages The narrow finished borders on the lengthwise edges of fabric.

sender The person who sends a message.

serger A modern and very fast sewing machine that can stitch, trim, and finish off seams all at the same time.

short-term goal An aim or desire that is expected to be met or satisfied in the near future.

siblings Those who have one parent in common; brothers or sisters.

social development Growth in the ability to relate to other people.

socialized Made fit for social or group living; able to relate to a number of different people.

split-complementary A color scheme in which a color is matched with the color on either side of its complement.

standards Measures of attainment; guidelines that a person uses to measure values and behavior.

status symbols Things that are believed to demonstrate financial and social success.

stereotype A fixed image or idea about a person or group; an incomplete and oversimplified expectation of what someone believes a person or group will be like.

stockholders People who own shares of stock in a business and who share in its profits or suffer from its losses.

stress A straining force; the body's response to physical or mental tension.

substance abuse The misuse or overuse of any substance, such as tobacco, alcohol, and other drugs, to the point where it threatens the user's health.

supply The number and types of goods that are available for consumers to choose from.

T

table d'hôte A complete meal served by a restaurant for a fixed or set price, also called *prix fixe.*

tension The looseness or tightness of stitches that are sewn into a garment

toxins Waste products given off by bacteria, many of which are poisonous.

trade-off A giving up of one benefit to gain another.

triadic A color scheme using three colors that are the same distance from one another on the color wheel.

true bias The diagonal edge that is formed when a fabric is folded so that the crosswise grain is parallel to the selvage; the area where a fabric has the most stretch.

U

unit construction A method of putting a garment together in which each section is completed separately and then sewn together.

unit price The cost per ounce or other unit of volume or measure.

unsaturated fats Fats that are liquid and high in cholesterol.

urban Characteristic of the city as opposed to the country; referring to a society in which most people live in or near large cities.

U.S. Recommended Daily Allowances (U.S. RDA) Recommendations of the amounts of certain nutrients that should be eaten each day.

V

value The lightness, darkness, and shade of a color.

values The principles accepted by an individual; the beliefs, ideas, and convictions that an individual accepts or holds.

verbal communication The expression of ideas and emotions through the use of words.

W

warranty A guarantee or an assurance; a promise from a manufacturer or seller that a product will do what it is intended to do if used properly.

water-soluble vitamins Vitamins that mix only with water, are not stored in the body, and must therefore be taken in food every day.

wellness A feeling of complete well-being; a state of physical and mental good health.

work plan A step-by-step guide for preparing food.

Index

c indicates a chart or table
r indicates a recipe

Acknowledgments

PHOTO CREDITS

COVER/Unit Openers: Larry Lawfer/ Photosynthesis

David Dempster: **Chapter Openers/Learning to Manage Features for Chapters One, Four, Five, Six, Seven, Nine, Fourteen, Nineteen; Interior Photos on Pages 6, 8, 10, 12, 15, 17, 29, 39, 45, 58, 61, 62, 81 104, 105, 111, 113, 114, 134, 137, 158, 159, 167, 169, 173, 179, 180, 183, 193, 194, 195, 196, 198, 209, 211, 212, 214, 216, 217, 218, 233, 236, 237, 253, 255, 257, 262, 263, 264, 265, 280, 281, 286, 287, 289, 294, 295, 296, 298, 300, 306, 308, 312, 321, 325, 329, 334, 336, 337, 339, 341, 346, 364, 366, 372, 374, 375, 389, 390, 391, 396, 399, 407, 410, 412, 417, 419, 421, 426, 427, 428, 437, 441, 443, 444, 445, 447, 449, 459, 463, 467, 469, 471.**

Ted Cordingley: **Chapter Openers/Learning to Manage Features for Chapters Two, Three, Eight, Ten, Eleven, Twelve, Thirteen, Fifteen, Sixteen, Seventeen, Eighteen, Twenty; Interior Photos on Pages 9, 13, 18, 53, 55, 64, 82, 85, 87, 106, 116, 125, 132, 133, 135, 139, 151, 156, 174, 176, 177, 182, 199, 208, 227, 230, 234, 240, 305, 306, 335, 348, 377, 418.**

3 D. Hatch/The Picture Cube; **4L** R. Morsch/ The Stock Market; **4R** R. Daemmrich; **5** Boy Scouts of America; **7** Boy Scouts of America; **11** M. Heron; **14** R. Schleipman; **19** D. Sautzer/ Click, Chicago; **25** V. Holbrooke/The Stock Market; **31** R. Schleipman; **33** J. Curtis; **34** B. Kirk/The Stock Market; **35** E. Herwig/The Picture Cube; **36** D. Strickler/The Picture Cube; **37** R. Friedman; The Picture Cube; **38** E.V. Smith; **46** L. Long/The Stock Market; **47** R. Schleipman; **48** D. Smetzer/Click, Chicago; **50** L. Weber/O.P.C.; **51** S. Murphy; **52** Comstock; **57** B. Barnes; **59** R. 66 Custom Medical Stock; **74** B. Barnes; **75** R. Daemmrich; **76** D. Schaefer/The Picture Cube; **78** J. Curtis; **79** B. Barnes; **83** J. Persons/New England Stock; **84** D.D. Bryant; **86** R. Daemmrich; **88** B. Kirk/The Stock Market; **89** T. Gibbons/New England Stock; **91** P. Bailey/The Picture Cube; **92** D. Strickler/The Picture Cube; **93** R. Daemmrich; **100** B. Barnes; **103** R. Daemmrich; **108** J. Riley/Click/Chicago; **109** Constock; **110** S. Murphy/Click, Chicago; **121** A. Chaumat/P.R.I.; **122** C. Paris/The Stock Market; **124** T. Stack; **126** Learson/The Stock Market; **128** Hay/The Stock Market; **129** Thomason/Click, Chicago; **130** Kirk/The Stock Market; **140** B. Barnes; **147** E. Roth/The Picture Cube; **148R** A. Goldsmith/The Stock Market; **148L** W. Meyer/ Third Coast Stock; **149** R. Daemmrich; **152** E. Herwig/The Picture Cube; **153** N. Sheehan/The Picture Cube; **155** R. Daemmrich; **160** R. Daemmrich; **170** M. Heron; **187** C. Hammell/ The Stock Market; **190** K. Straiton/The Stock Market; **205** D. Strickler; **213** P. Chapman; **215** R. McElroy/Woodfin Camp & Associates; **223L** B. Barnes; **223R** J. Coletti/The Picture Cube; **224** J. Simons/The Picture Cube; **226** C. Palmer/The Picture Cube; **229** D. Frazier; **231** G. Peet; **235** R. Schleipman; **238** R. Daemmrich; **243** R. Daemmrich; **244** J. Curtis; **251** R. Daemmrich; **252** M. Yamashita/Woodfin Camp & Assoc.; **254** R. Schleipman; **260** R. Schleipman; **261** R. Daemmrich; **267** R. Daemmrich; **268** L. Lawfer; **270** R. Schleipman; **272** E. Herwig/The Picture Cube; **274** P. Chapman; **279** R. Marcialis/P.R.I.; **282** C. Jones/The Stock Market; **283** M. Ferri/The Stock Market; **285** R. Schleipman; **290** J. Curtis; **296** J. Curtis; **297** J. Perkell/The Stock Market; **299** Grant Heilman; **307** C. Hammell/The Stock Market; **309** S. Lapides; **311** P. Chapman; **320** J. Curtis; **338** J. Curtis; **341** J. Curtis; **342** R. Morsch/The Stock Market; **343** J. Brown/The Stock Market; **344** J. Curtis; **345** J. Curtis; Leeson/P.R.I.; **349**

J. Curtis; **351** P. Chapman; **353** P. Chapman; **354** P. Chapman; **355** P. Chapman; **356** P. Chapman; **361** J. Curtis; **362** J. Curtis; **361** R. Daemmrich; **369** F. Bodin; **371** L. Rorke/The Image Works; **372** McIntyre/P.R.I.; **378** R. Daemmrich; **380** R. Daemmrich; **387** Bettmann Archive; **388** C. Bonington/Woodfin Camp & Assoc.; **392** S. Lapides; **394** J. Curtis; **395** R. Daemmrich; **397** J. Curtis; **398** L. Lawfer; **402** Werner/Comstock; **406** J. Curtis; **433** L. Lawfer; **434** L. Lawfer; **435** L. Lawfer.

Styling done by Photosynthesis (Laurel Anderson/Barbara Bowman).

Technical Art Credits

Terry Presnall: pages 20, 26, 30, 32, 38, 56, 75, 93, 102, 112, 124, 131, 132, 136, 157, 171, 175, 256, 258, 282, 291, 307, 320, 330, 331, 362, 363, 365, 368, 409, 424, 438–439, 440, 446, 451, 452–453, 466, 468, 469, 470;
Publication Services: pages 8, 27, 82, 115, 153, 161, 197, 200, 207, 228, 232, 239, 266, 271, 293, 322, 333, 393, 401, 403, 405, 408, 423, 425, 442, 448, 477–480.

Susan Avishai: pages 287, 288, 314–317, 352.

Susan Banta: pages 323–324, 332–333, 350.

Lane Gregory: page 313

Grateful acknowledgment is made to the following:
Future Homemakers of America for the use of information and their FHA/HERO logo on page 94.
Newton-Wellesley Hospital/Cardiovascular Health Center for the use of their information on cholesterol.
Noromco, Inc. for the use of recipes from *Kids Kitchen Encyclopedia* found on pages 362, 363, 365, and 368.
Lynn Eastern Junior High School, Middle School East/Salem, Middle School West/Salem, and Wellesley Middle School for their cooperation and gracious hospitality.